The New Rhetoric
A Treatise on Argumentation

The New Rhetoric

A Treatise on Argumentation

CH. PERELMAN
and
L. OLBRECHTS-TYTECA

Translated by

JOHN WILKINSON AND PURCELL WEAVER
Center for the Study of Democratic Institutions

UNIVERSITY OF NOTRE DAME PRESS
NOTRE DAME   LONDON

Originally published as
La Nouvelle Rhétorique: Traité de l'Argumentation
Presses Universitaires de France, 1958

Library of Congress Catalog Card Number: 68-20440

Printed in the United States of America by
NAPCO Graphic Arts, Inc., Milwaukee, Wisconsin

FOREWORD

On the occasion of the publication of the American edition of *The New Rhetoric*, I would like to extend my warmest thanks to those in the United States who have helped me make my ideas known here or who have facilitated the appearance of this book.

I am grateful to Professor Richard P. McKeon of the University of Chicago, who in 1951 recommended to *Ethics* our first article to appear in America, "Act and Person in Argument." Mr. Henry W. Johnstone, Jr., was the first person to draw the attention of the American public to our work through his critical article published in *Philosophy and Phenomenological Research* in 1954. It was through him and Professor Robert T. Oliver, past president of the American Speech Association, that I received a joint invitation from the Departments of Philosophy and Speech at Pennsylvania State University, where I gave a seminar on "The Philosophical Foundation of Argumentation." Thanks to Professor Oliver, I was able to present my ideas at an annual meeting of the American Speech Association at Denver in 1963. These efforts at collaboration between philosophers and specialists in the techniques of speech and communication were continued in 1964 through a colloquium at Pennsylvania State University on the theme "Philosophy and Rhetoric," and have culminated in the appearance of a new review, *Philosophy and Rhetoric*, in 1968, under the editorship of Henry W. Johnstone, Carroll C. Arnold, and Thomas Olbricht.

I also wish to thank those colleagues who have been kind enough to invite me to present my ideas at the University of Chicago, Cornell University, Harvard University, and the University of Pennsylvania.

The invitation which I received from Carl J. Friedrich, head of the Department of Political Science at Harvard, was preceded by a generous review which he had published in 1962 in the *Natural Law Forum*. It was through him that I first met the editor of this review,

Professor John T. Noonan, Jr., presently at Berkeley, who published certain of my articles and recommended my work to the University of Notre Dame Press. I wish to thank the director of that press, Miss Emily Schossberger, for taking the risks involved in bringing out a work which is compactly written and demands close study from the very outset.

Finally, my sincere thanks go to the Center for the Study of Democratic Institutions at Santa Barbara. Mr. John Wilkinson, who is its director of studies on the theme "The Civilization of Dialogue," has enthusiastically propagated my ideas and has also translated part of the present treatise. But I know that without President Robert M. Hutchins, who supported my efforts and granted a generous subvention for translation, this volume would not have seen the light of day. I wish to thank him sincerely for his support and help.

Ch. P.

CONTENTS

INTRODUCTION

I

The publication of a treatise devoted to argumentation and this subject's connection with the ancient tradition of Greek rhetoric and dialectic constitutes a *break with a concept of reason and reasoning due to Descartes* which has set its mark on Western philosophy for the last three centuries.[1]

Although it would scarcely occur to anyone to deny that the power of deliberation and argumentation is a distinctive sign of a reasonable being, the study of the methods of proof used to secure *adherence* has been completely neglected by logicians and epistemologists for the last three centuries. This state of affairs is due to the noncompulsive element in the arguments adduced in support of a thesis. The very nature of deliberation and argumentation is opposed to necessity and self-evidence, since no one deliberates where the solution is necessary or argues against what is self-evident. The domain of argumentation is that of the credible, the plausible, the probable, to the degree that the latter eludes the certainty of calculations. Now Descartes' concept, clearly expressed in the first part of *The Discourse on the Method*, was to "take well nigh for false everything which was only plausible." It was this philosopher who made the self-evident the mark of reason, and considered rational only those demonstrations which, starting from clear and distinct ideas, extended, by means of apodictic proofs, the self-evidence of the axioms to the derived theorems.

Reasoning *more geometrico* was the model proposed to philosophers desirous of constructing a system of thought which might attain

---

[1] Cf. Perelman, "Raison éternelle, raison historique," *L'homme et l'histoire, Actes du VIᵉ Congrès des Sociétés de Philosophie de langue française*, pp. 347-354.

1

to the dignity of a science. A rational science cannot indeed be content with more or less probable opinions; it must elaborate a system of necessary propositions which will impose itself on every rational being, concerning which agreement is inevitable. This means that disagreement is a sign of error. "Whenever two men come to opposite decisions about the same matter," says Descartes, "one of them at least must certainly be in the wrong, and apparently there is not even one of them who knows; for if the reasoning of one was sound and clear he would be able so to lay it before the other as finally to succeed in convincing *his* understanding also."[2]

What is important to the partisans of the experimental and inductive sciences is not so much the necessity of propositions as their truth, *their conformity with facts*. The empiricist considers as evidence not "that which the mind does or must yield to, but that which it *ought to* yield to, namely, that, by yielding to which, its belief is kept conformable to fact."[3] The evidence which the empiricist recognizes is not that of rational but of sensible intuition, the method he advocates is not that of the deductive but of the experimental sciences, but he is nonetheless convinced that the only valid proofs are those recognized by the natural sciences.

What conforms to scientific method is rational, in the broader sense of the word. Works on logic devoted to the study of the methods of proof, essentially limited to the study of deduction, usually supplemented by some remarks on inductive reasoning which merely consider the means not of constructing, but of verifying hypotheses, seldom venture to examine the proofs used in human sciences. The logician is indeed inspired by the Cartesian ideal and feels at ease only in studying those proofs which Aristotle styled analytic, since all other methods do not manifest the same characteristic of necessity. This tendency has been strongly reinforced during the last century, a period in which, under the influence of mathematical logicians, logic has been limited to formal logic, that is to the study of the methods of proof used in the mathematical sciences. The result is that reasonings extraneous to the domain of the purely formal elude logic altogether, and, as a consequence, they also elude reason. This reason, which Descartes hoped would, at least in principle, solve all problems set to man the solution of which is already possessed by the divine mind, has become more and more limited in its jurisdiction, to the point that whatever

---

[2] Descartes, *Rules for the Direction of the Mind*, GBWW, vol. 31, p. 2.
[3] Mill, *A System of Logic*, bk. III, chap. XXI, § 1, p. 370.

eludes reduction to the formal presents it with unsurmountable difficulties.

Must we draw from this evolution of logic, and from the very real advances it has made, the conclusion that reason is entirely incompetent in those areas which elude calculation and that, where neither experiment nor logical deduction is in a position to furnish the solution of a problem, we can but abandon ourselves to irrational forces, instincts, suggestion, or even violence?

Pascal made an attempt to provide for the shortcomings of the geometrical method resulting from the fact that fallen man is no longer uniquely a rational being by opposing the will to the understanding, the "esprit de finesse" to the "esprit de géométrie," the heart to the head, and the art of persuading to the art of convincing.

The Kantian opposition of faith and science and the Bergsonian antithesis of intuition and reason have a similar purpose. But, whether we consider rationalist or so-called "antirationalist" philosophers, they all carry on the Cartesian tradition by the limitation they impose on the concept of reason.

We feel, on the contrary, that just here lies *a perfectly unjustified and unwarranted limitation of the domain of action of our faculty of reasoning and proving.* Whereas already Aristotle had analyzed dialectical proofs together with analytic proofs, those which concern the probable together with those which are necessary, those which are used in deliberation and argumentation together with those which are used in demonstration, the post-Cartesian concept of reason obliges us to make certain irrational elements intervene every time the object of knowledge is not self-evident. Whether these elements consist of obstacles to be surmounted—such as imagination, passion, or suggestion—or of suprarational sources of certitude such as the heart, grace, "Einfuehlung," or Bergsonian intuition, this conception introduces a dichotomy, a differentiation between human faculties, which is completely artificial and contrary to the real processes of our thought.

It is the *idea of self-evidence* as characteristic of reason, which we must assail, if we are to make place for a theory of argumentation that will acknowledge the use of reason in directing our own actions and influencing those of others. Self-evidence is conceived both as a force to which every normal mind must yield and as a sign of the truth of that which imposes itself because it is self-evident.[4] The self-evident would connect the psychological with

---

[4] Perelman, "De la preuve en philosophie," in Perelman and Olbrechts-Tyteca, *Rhétorique et philosophie*, pp. 123 et seq.

the logical and allow passage back and forth between these two levels. All proof would be reduction to the self-evident, and what is self-evident would have no need of proof: such is the immediate application by Pascal of the Cartesian theory of self-evidence.[5]

Leibniz rebelled against the limitation imposed in this way on logic. It was his wish "that means be shown or given to demonstrate all axioms which are not primitive; without distinction of whatever opinions men have of them, or being concerned with whether they yield assent to them or not."[6]

Now the logical theory of demonstration developed following Leibniz and not Pascal; it has never allowed that what was self-evident had no need of proof. In the same way, the theory of argumentation cannot be developed if every proof is conceived of as a reduction to the self-evident. Indeed, the object of the theory of argumentation is the study of the discursive techniques allowing us *to induce or to increase the mind's adherence to the theses presented for its assent.* What is characteristic of the adherence of minds is its variable intensity: nothing constrains us to limit our study to a particular degree of adherence characterized by self-evidence, and nothing permits us to consider *a priori* the degrees of adherence to a thesis as proportional to its probability and to identify self-evidence with truth. It is good practice not to confuse, at the beginning, the aspects of reasoning relative to truth and those relative to adherence, but to study them separately, even though we might have to examine later their possible interference or correspondence. Only on this condition is it possible to develop a theory of argumentation with any philosophical scope.

II

Although during the last three centuries ecclesiastics have published works on problems of faith and preaching[7] and though the 20th century has even been described as the century of advertising and propaganda, and a large number of works have been devoted to that subject,[8] logicians and modern philosophers have become

---

[5] Pascal, *On Geometrical Demonstration*, Section II: *Concerning the Art of Persuasion*, GBWW, vol. 33, p. 443.

[6] Leibniz, *Die Philosophischen Schriften*, vol. V, *Nouveaux essais sur l'entendement*, p. 67.

[7] Cf. Whately's *Elements of Rhetoric*, first published in 1828; and Cardinal Newman's *Grammar of Assent*, which appeared in 1870.

[8] See Lasswell, Casey, and Smith, *Propaganda and Promotional Activities,*

totally disinterested in our subject. It is for this reason that the present book is mostly related to the concerns of the Renaissance and, beyond that, to those of certain Greek and Latin authors, who studied the art of persuading and of convincing, the technique of deliberation and of discussion. Our work, therefore, is presented as a *new rhetoric*.

Our analysis concerns the proofs which Aristotle termed "dialectical," which he examines in his *Topics*, and the utilization of which he indicates in his *Rhetoric*. This appeal to Aristotle's terminology would justify the "rapprochement" of the theory of argumentation with dialectic, conceived by Aristotle himself as the art of reasoning from generally accepted opinions (εὔλογος).[9] However, a number of reasons have led us to prefer a "rapprochement" with rhetoric.

The first of these reasons is the confusion which a return to Aristotle's terminology might produce. Although the term *dialectic* served for centuries to designate logic itself, since the time of Hegel and under the influence of doctrines inspired by him, it has acquired a meaning which is very remote from its original one and which has become generally accepted in contemporary philosophy. The same cannot be said for the term *rhetoric*, which has fallen into such desuetude that it is not even mentioned, for example, in A. Lalande's philosophical lexicon: we hope that our attempts will contribute to the revival of an ancient and glorious tradition.

A second reason, which we consider much more important, has motivated our choice: the very spirit in which Antiquity was concerned with dialectic and rhetoric. Dialectical reasoning is considered as running parallel with analytic reasoning, but treating of that which is probable instead of dealing with propositions which are necessary. The very notion that dialectic concerns opinions, i.e., theses which are adhered to with variable intensity, is not exploited. One might think that the status of that which is subject to opinion is impersonal and that opinions are not relative to the minds which adhere to them. On the contrary, this idea of adherence and of the minds to which a discourse is addressed is essential in all the ancient theories of rhetoric. Our "rapprochement" with the latter aims at emphasizing the fact that *it is in terms of an audience that an argumentation develops*; the study of the opinionable, as described in the *Topics*, will have a place in this framework.

An Annotated Bibliography; and Smith, Lasswell, and Casey, *Propaganda, Communication, and Public Opinion. A Comprehensive Reference Guide.*
[9] Aristotle, *Topics*, I, 1, 100a.

It is clear, however, that our treatise on argumentation will, in certain respects, go far beyond the bounds of the ancient rhetoric and at the same time neglect certain aspects of the matter which drew the attention of the ancient masters of the art.

Their object was primarily the art of public speaking in a persuasive way: it was therefore concerned with the use of the spoken word, with discourse to a crowd gathered in a public square, with a view to securing its adherence to the thesis presented. It is evident that the aim of oratory, the adherence of the minds addressed, is that of all argumentation. We see, however, no reason to limit our study to the presentation of an argument by means of the spoken word and to restrict the kind of audience addressed to a crowd gathered in a square.

The rejection of the first limitation is due to the fact that our interests are much more those of logicians desirous of understanding the mechanism of thought than those of masters of eloquence desirous of making people practice their teaching. It is sufficient to cite the *Rhetoric* of Aristotle to show that our way of looking at rhetoric can take pride in illustrious examples. Our study, which is mainly concerned with the structure of argumentation, will not therefore insist on the way in which communication with the audience takes place.

If it is true that the technique of public speaking differs from that of written argumentation, our concern being to analyze argumentation, we cannot be limited to the examination of spoken discourse. Indeed, in view of the importance of and the role played by the modern printing press, our analyses will primarily be concerned with printed texts.

On the other hand, we shall completely neglect mnemonics and the study of delivery or oratorical effect. Such problems are the province of conservatories and schools of dramatic art, and we can dispense with examining them.

The result of our emphasis on written texts, since these latter occur in the most varied forms, is that our study is conceived with complete generality; it will not be confined to discourses considered as an entity of more or less conventionally admitted structure and length. In our opinion discussion with a single interlocutor, or even with oneself, falls under a general theory of argumentation, so that it is clear that our concept of the object of our study goes far beyond that of classical rhetoric.

What we preserve of the traditional rhetoric is the idea of the *audience*, an idea immediately evoked by the mere thought of a speech. Every speech is addressed to an audience and it is frequently forgotten that this applies to everything written as well. Whereas a speech is conceived in terms of the audience, the physical absence of his readers can lead a writer to believe that he is alone in the world, though his text is always conditioned, whether consciously or unconsciously, by those persons he wishes to address.

Thus, for reasons of technical convenience, and in order not to lose sight of the essential role played by the audience, when we use the terms "discourse," "speaker," and "audience," we shall understand by them, respectively, the argumentation, the one who presents the argument, and those to whom it is addressed. We shall not dwell on whether or not the presentation is spoken or written, or distinguish between formal discourse and the fragmentary expression of thought.

Among the ancients, rhetoric appeared as the study of a technique for use by the common man impatient to arrive rapidly at conclusions, or to form an opinion, without first of all taking the trouble of a preliminary serious investigation,[10] but we have no wish to limit the study of argumentation to one adapted to a public of ignoramuses. It is that aspect of rhetoric which explains why Plato opposed it so fiercely in his *Gorgias*[11] and which was propitious to its decline in the estimation of philosophers.

The orator indeed is obliged to adapt himself to his audience if he wishes to have any effect on it and we can easily understand that the discourse which is most efficacious on an incompetent audience is not necessarily that which would win the assent of a philosopher. But why not allow that argumentations can be addressed to every kind of audience? When Plato dreams, in his *Phaedrus*,[12] of a rhetoric which would be worthy of a philosopher, what he recommends is a technique capable of convincing the gods themselves. A change in audience means a change in the appearance of the argumentation and, if the aim of argumentation is always to act effectively on minds, in order to make a judgment of its value we must not lose sight of the quality of the minds which the argument has succeeded in convincing.

This justifies the particular importance accorded by us to philosophical arguments, which are traditionally considered to be the most "rational," for the reason that they are supposed to be addressed to readers upon whom suggestion, pressure, or self-interest have little effect. We shall show that the same techniques of argumenta-

[10] Cf. Aristotle, *Rhetoric*, I, 2, 1357a.
[11] Plato, *Gorgias*, notably 455, 457a, 463, and 471d.
[12] Plato, *Phaedrus*, 273e.

tion can be encountered at every level, at that of discussion around the family table as well as at that of debate in a highly specialized environment. If the quality of the minds which adhere to certain arguments, in highly speculative domains, is a guarantee of the value of these arguments, the community of structure between these arguments and those used in daily discussions explains why and how we succeed in understanding them.

Our treatise will consider only the *discursive means* of obtaining the adherence of minds: in the sequel, only the technique which uses language to persuade and convince will be examined.

This limitation, in our opinion, by no means implies that the technique in question is the most efficacious way of affecting minds. The contrary is the case—we are firmly convinced that the most solid beliefs are those which are not only admitted without proof, but very often not even made explicit. And, when it is a matter of securing adherence, nothing is more reliable than external or internal experience and calculation conforming to previously admitted rules. But, recourse to argumentation is unavoidable whenever these proofs are questioned by one of the parties, when there is no agreement on their scope or interpretation, on their value or on their relation to the problems debated.

Further, any action designed to obtain adherence falls outside the range of argumentation to the degree that the use of language is lacking in its support or interpretation: those who set an example for other people without saying anything, or those who make use of a stick or a carrot, can obtain appreciable results. We are interested in such procedures only when they are emphasized by way of language, for example, by resort to promises or threats. There are yet other cases—for example, blessing and cursing—in which language is utilized as a direct, magical means of action and not as a means of communication. Again, we shall not treat of such cases unless this action is integrated into the framework of an argumentation.

One of the essential factors of propaganda as it has developed above all in the 20th century, but the use of which was well known to Antiquity, and which the Roman Catholic Church has put to profitable use with incomparable art, is the conditioning of the audience by means of numerous and varied techniques that utilize anything capable of influencing behavior. These techniques have an undeniable effect in preparing the audience, in rendering it more accessible to the arguments presented to it. Our analysis will also neglect them: we shall treat of the conditioning of the audience by the discourse alone, which will result in certain considerations on the order in which arguments must be presented to exercise their maximum effect.

Finally, what Aristotle termed "extra-technical proofs"[13] meaning those proofs which are not related to rhetorical technique—will enter into our study only when there is disagreement concerning the conclusions that can be drawn from them. For we are less interested in the complete development of a discussion than in the *argumentative schemes* coming into play. The term "extra-technical proofs" is well designed to remind us that whereas our civilization, characterized by a great ingenuity in the techniques intended to act on things, has completely forgotten the theory of argumentation, of action on minds by means of discourse, it was this theory which, under the name of rhetoric, was considered by the Greeks the τέχνη "par excellence."

III

The theory of argumentation which, with the aid of discourse, aims at securing an efficient action on minds might have been treated as a branch of psychology. Indeed, if arguments are not compulsive, if they are not to be necessarily convincing but only possessed of a certain force, which may moreover vary with the audience, is it not by their effect that we can judge of this force? This would make the study of argumentation one of the objects of experimental psychology, where varied arguments would be tested on varied audiences which are sufficiently well known for it to be possible to draw fairly general conclusions from these experiments. A number of American psychologists have become involved in such studies, the interest of which is incontestable.[14]

We shall however proceed differently. We seek, first of all, to characterize the different argumentative structures, the analysis of which must precede all experimental tests of their effectiveness. And, on the other hand, we do not think that laboratory methods can determine the value of argumentations used in the human sciences, law, and philosophy; and this for the reason that the methodology of psychologists is itself an object of controversy and lies within the scope of our study.

[13] Aristotle, *Rhetoric*, I, 2, 1355b.
[14] Cf. Hollingworth, *The Psychology of the Audience*; Hovland, "Effects of the Mass Media of Communication," *Handbook of Social Psychology*, pp. 1062-1103.

Our procedure will differ radically from that adopted by those philosophers who endeavor to reduce reasoning in social, political, and philosophical matters by taking their cue from the models provided by the deductive or experimental sciences, and who reject as worthless everything which does not conform to the schemes which were previously imposed. Quite the opposite: we will draw our inspiration from the logicians, but only to imitate the methods which they have used so successfully for the last century or so.

We must not indeed lose sight of the fact that logic, in the first half of the 19th century, enjoyed no prestige either in scientific circles or with the public at large. Whately[15] could write in 1828 that, if rhetoric no longer enjoyed the esteem of the public, logic was some degrees lower in popular estimation.

Logic underwent a brilliant development during the last century when, abandoning the old formulas, it set out to analyze the methods of proof effectively used by mathematicians. Modern formal logic became, in this way, the study of the methods of demonstration used in the mathematical sciences. One result of this development is to limit its domain, since everything ignored by mathematicians is foreign to it. Logicians owe it to themselves to complete the theory of demonstration obtained in this way by a theory of argumentation. We seek here to construct such a theory by analyzing the methods of proof used in the human sciences, law, and philosophy. We shall examine arguments put forward by advertisers in newspapers, politicians in speeches, lawyers in pleadings, judges in decisions, and philosophers in treatises.

Our field of study is immense and it has lain fallow for centuries. We hope that our first results will incite other researchers to complete and perfect them.

---

[15] Whately, Preface to *Elements of Rhetoric* (1893) p. III.

PART ONE

The Framework of Argumentation

§ 1. *Demonstration and Argumentation*

The special characteristics of argumentation and the problems inherent to its study cannot be better conveyed than by contrasting argumentation with the classical concept of demonstration and, more particularly, with formal logic which is limited to the examination of demonstrative methods of proof.

In modern logic, the product of reflection on mathematical reasoning, the formal systems are no longer related to any rational evidence whatever. The logician is free to elaborate as he pleases the artificial language of the system he is building, free to fix the symbols and combinations of symbols that may be used. It is for him to decide which are the axioms, that is, the expressions considered without proof as valid in his system, and to say which are the rules of transformation he introduces which will make it possible to deduce, from the valid expressions, other expressions of equal validity in the system. The only obligation resting on the builder of formal axiomatic systems, the one which gives the demonstrations their compelling force, is that of choosing symbols and rules in such a way as to avoid doubt and ambiguity. It must be possible, without hesitation, even mechanically, to establish whether a sequence of symbols is admitted in the system, whether it is of the same form as another sequence of symbols, whether it is considered valid, because it is an axiom or an expression deducible from the axioms, in a manner consistent with the rules of deduction. Any consideration that has to do with the origin of the axioms or the rules of deduction, with the role that the axiomatic system is deemed to play in the elaboration of thought, is foreign to logic conceived in this manner, in the sense that it goes beyond the framework of the formalism in question. The search for unquestionable univocity has even led the formalistic logicians to construct systems in which no attention is paid to the meaning of the expressions: they are satisfied if the symbols introduced and the transformations concerning them are beyond discussion. They leave the interpretation of the elements of the axiomatic system to those who will apply it and who will have to concern themselves with its adequacy for the end pursued.

When the demonstration of a proposition is in question, it is sufficient to indicate the processes by means of which the proposition can be obtained as the final expression of a deductive series, which had its first elements provided by the constructor of the axiomatic system within which the demonstration is accomplished. Where these elements come from, whether they are impersonal truths, divine thoughts, results of experiment, or postulates particular to the author, these are questions which the logician considers foreign to his discipline. But when it is a question of arguing, of using discourse to influence the intensity of an audience's adherence to certain theses, it is no longer possible to neglect completely, as irrelevancies, the psychological and social conditions in the absence of which argumentation would be pointless and without result. For *all argumentation aims at gaining the adherence of minds, and, by this very fact, assumes the existence of an intellectual contact.*

For argumentation to exist, an effective community of minds must be realized at a given moment. There must first of all be agreement, in principle, on the formation of this intellectual community, and, after that, on the fact of debating a specific question together: now this does not come about automatically.

Even in the realm of inward deliberation, certain conditions are required for argumentation: in particular, a person must conceive of himself as divided into at least two interlocutors, two parties engaging in deliberation. And there is no warrant for regarding this division as necessary. It appears to be constructed on the model of deliberation with others. Hence, we must expect to find carried over to this inner deliberation most of the problems associated with the conditions necessary for discussion with others. Many expressions bear witness to this, but two examples may suffice. The first, relating to preliminary conditions as they affect persons, is such a saying as "Don't listen to your evil genius." The other, having to do with preliminary conditions as they affect the object of argumentation, is a saying like "Don't bring that up any more."

§ 2. *The Contact of Minds*

A whole set of conditions is required for the formation of an effective community of minds.

The indispensable minimum for argumentation appears to be the existence of a common language, of a technique allowing communication to take place.

But the minimum is not enough. No one shows this better than the author of *Alice in Wonderland*. The beings inhabiting that country understand Alice's language, more or less, but her problem is to make contact and open a discussion, as in Wonderland there is no reason why discussions should begin. The inhabitants know no reason for speaking to one another. On some occasions Alice takes the initiative, as where she plainly addresses the mouse with the vocative, "O, Mouse."[1] And she considers it a success to have managed the exchange of a few rather pointless remarks with the Duchess.[2] However, in her earlier attempt at conversation with the caterpillar, a deadlock is reached immediately: "I think you ought to tell me who you are, first," she says. "Why?" says the caterpillar.[3] In our well-ordered world, with its hierarchies, there are generally rules prescribing how conversation may be begun; there is a preliminary agreement arising from the norms set by social life. Between Alice and the inhabitants of Wonderland, no hierarchy, precedence, or functions requires one to answer rather than another. Even those conversations which do begin are apt to break off suddenly. The lory, for instance, prides himself on his age:

> This Alice would not allow without knowing how old he was, and as the lory positively refused to tell its age, there was no more to be said.[4]

The only preliminary condition fulfilled here is Alice's wish to enter into conversation with the beings of this new universe.

The set of those a speaker wishes to address may vary considerably. For any particular speaker it falls far short of all human beings. In the case of a child, however, to whom the adult world is in varying measure closed, the universe he wants to address is correspondingly extended by the inclusion of animals and all the inanimate objects he regards as his natural interlocutors.[5]

There are beings with whom any contact may seem superfluous or undesirable. There are some one cannot be bothered to talk to. There are others with whom one does not wish to discuss things, but to whom one merely gives orders.

[1] Carroll, *Alice's Adventures in Wonderland*, p. 41.
[2] *Ibid.*, p. 82.
[3] *Ibid.*, p. 65.
[4] *Ibid.*, p. 44.
[5] Cassirer, "Le langage et la construction du monde des objets," *Journal de Psychologie*, XXX (1933), 39.

To engage in argument, a person must attach some importance to gaining the adherence of his interlocutor, to securing his assent, his mental cooperation. It is, accordingly, sometimes a valued honor to be a person with whom another will enter into discussion. Because of the rationalism and humanism of the last few centuries, it seems a strange notion that the mere fact of being someone whose opinion is taken into account should constitute a quality; but in many societies a person will no more talk to just anybody than, in the past, a man would fight a duel with just anybody. It is also to be observed that wanting to convince someone always implies a certain modesty on the part of the initiator of the argument; what he says is not "Gospel truth," he does not possess that authority which would place his words beyond question so that they would carry immediate conviction. He acknowledges that he must use persuasion, think of arguments capable of acting on his interlocutor, show some concern for him, and be interested in his state of mind.

A person — whether an adult or a child — who wants to "count" with others, wishes that they would stop giving him orders and would, instead, reason with him and concern themselves with his reactions. He wants to be regarded as a member of a more-or-less equalitarian society. A man who does not cultivate this kind of contact with his fellows will be thought a proud, unattractive creature as compared with one who, however important his functions, takes pains to address the public in a manner which makes clear the value he attaches to its appreciation.

But, as has been said many times, it is not always commendable to wish to persuade someone: the conditions under which contact between minds takes place may, indeed, appear to be rather dishonorable. The reader will recall the story of Aristippus, who, when he was reproached for having abjectly prostrated himself at the feet of Dionysius the tyrant in order to be heard by him, defended himself by saying that the fault was not his, but that of Dionysius who had his ears in his feet. Is the position of the ears, then, a matter of indifference?[6]

The danger seen by Aristotle in carrying on discussion with some people is that the speaker may thereby destroy the quality of his argumentation:

> A man should not enter into discussion with everybody or practice dialectics with the first comer as reasoning always becomes embittered where some people are concerned. Indeed, when an adversary tries by every possible means to wriggle out of a corner,

---

[6] Bacon, *Advancement of Learning*, GBWW, vol. 30, p. 11.

it is legitimate to strive, by every possible means, to reach the conclusion; but this procedure lacks elegance.[7]

It is not enough for a man to speak or write; he must also be listened to or read. It is no mean thing to have a person's attention, to have a wide audience, to be allowed to speak under certain circumstances, in certain gatherings, in certain circles. We must not forget that by listening to someone we display a willingness to eventually accept his point of view. There is great significance in the attitude of a Churchill forbidding British diplomats even to listen to any peace proposals German emissaries might try to convey or in the attitude of a political party when it makes known its willingness to hear any proposals of a politician engaged in forming a ministry, because they prevent the establishment or recognize the existence of the conditions preliminary to possible argumentation.

Achievement of the conditions preliminary to the contact of minds is facilitated by such factors as membership in the same social class, exchange of visits and other social relations. Frivolous discussions that are lacking in apparent interest are not always entirely unimportant, inasmuch as they contribute to the smooth working of an indispensable social mechanism.

§ 3. *The Speaker and His Audience*

The authors of scientific reports and similar papers often think that if they merely report certain experiments, mention certain facts, or enunciate a certain number of truths, this is enough of itself to automatically arouse the interest of their hearers or readers. This attitude rests on the illusion, widespread in certain rationalistic and scientific circles, that facts speak for themselves and make such an indelible imprint on any human mind that the latter is forced to give its adherence regardless of its inclination. An editor of a psychological journal, Katherine F. Bruner, likens such authors, who do not worry very much about their audience, to discourteous visitors:

> They slouch into a chair, staring glumly
> at their shoes, and abruptly announce, to
> themselves or not, we never know, "It has
> been shown by such and such ... that the
> female of the white rat responds negatively
> to electric shock."

[7] Aristotle, *Topics*, VIII, 14, 164b.

"All right, sir," I say. "So what? Tell
me first why I should care; then I will
listen."[8]

It is true that these authors when addressing a learned society,
or publishing an article in a specialized journal, can afford to neglect
the means of entering into contact with their public, for the indispensable link between speaker and audience is provided by a scientific institution, the society, or the journal. In such a case, then, the
author has merely to maintain, between himself and the public, the
contact already established by the scientific institution.

But not everyone is in such a privileged position. For argumentation to develop, there must be some attention paid to it by those
to whom it is directed. The prime concern of publicity and propaganda
is to draw the attention of an indifferent public, this being the indispensable condition for carrying on any sort of argumentation.
It is true that in a large number of fields—such as those of education,
politics, science, the administration of justice—any society possesses
institutions which facilitate and organize this contact of minds. But
the importance of this preliminary problem must not be underrated
on that account.

Under normal circumstances, some quality is necessary in order
to speak and be listened to. In our civilization, where the printed
word has become a commodity and utilizes economic organization
to draw attention to itself, this preliminary condition is seen clearly
only in cases where contact between the speaker and his audience
cannot be brought about by the techniques of distribution. It is accordingly best seen where argumentation is developed by a speaker
who is orally addressing a specific audience, rather than where it is
contained in a book on sale in a bookstore. This quality in a speaker,
without which he will not be listened to, or even, in many cases, allowed to speak, will vary with the circumstances. Sometimes it will
be enough for the speaker to appear as a human being with a decent
suit of clothes, sometimes he is required to be an adult, sometimes
he must be a rank and file member of a particular group, sometimes
the spokesman of this group. Under certain circumstances or before
certain audiences the only admissible authority for speaking is the
exercise of particular functions. There are fields where these matters
of qualification to speak are regulated in very great detail.

This contact between the speaker and his audience is not confined
to the conditions preliminary to argumentation: it is equally neces-

---

[8] Bruner, "Of Psychological Writing," *Journal of Abnormal and Social Psychology*,
37 (1942), 62.

sary if argumentation is to develop. For since argumentation aims at securing the adherence of those to whom it is addressed, it is, in its entirety, relative to the audience to be influenced.

How may such an audience be defined? Is it just the person whom the speaker addresses by name? Not always : thus, a member of Parliament in England must address himself to the Speaker, but he may try to persuade those listening to him in the chamber, and beyond that, public opinion throughout the country. Again, can such an audience be defined as the group of persons the speaker sees before him when he speaks? Not necessarily. He may perfectly well disregard a portion of them: a government spokesman in Parliament may give up any hope of convincing the opposition, even before he begins to speak, and may be satisfied with getting the adherence of his majority. And, on the other hand, a person granting an interview to a journalist considers his audience to be not the journalist himself but the readers of the paper he represents. The secrecy of deliberations, by modifying the speaker's opinion of his audience, may change the content of his speech. It is at once apparent from these few examples how difficult it is to determine by purely material criteria what constitutes a speaker's audience. The difficulty is even greater in the case of a writer's audience, as in most cases it is impossible to identify his readers with certainty.

For this reason we consider it preferable to define an audience, for the purposes of rhetoric, as *the ensemble of those whom the speaker wishes to influence by his argumentation*. Every speaker thinks, more or less consciously, of those he is seeking to persuade; these people form the audience to whom his speech is addressed.

§ 4. *The Audience as a Construction of the Speaker*

The audience, as visualized by one undertaking to argue, is always a more or less systematized construction. Efforts have been made to establish its psychological[9] or sociological[10] origins. The essential consideration for the speaker who has set himself the task of persuading concrete individuals is that his construction of the audience should be adequate to the occasion.

---

[9] Sullivan, *The Interpersonal Theory of Psychiatry*.

[10] Millioud, "La propagation des idées," *Revue philosophique*, 69 (1910), 580-600; 70 (1910), 168-191.

This does not hold for someone engaged in mere essay-making, without concern for real life. Rhetoric, which has then become an academic exercise, is addressed to conventional audiences, of which such rhetoric can afford to have stereotyped conceptions. However, it is this limited view of the audience, as much as artificiality of subject-matter, which is responsible for the degeneration of rhetoric.[11]

In real argumentation, care must be taken to form a concept of the anticipated audience as close as possible to reality. An inadequate picture of the audience, resulting from either ignorance or an unforeseen set of circumstances, can have very unfortunate results. Argumentation which an orator considers persuasive may well cause opposition in an audience for which "reasons for" are actually "reasons against." Thus, if one argues for a certain measure that it is likely to reduce social tension, such argument will set against the measure all those who would like to see disturbances.

Accordingly, knowledge of those one wishes to win over is a condition preliminary to all effectual argumentation.

Concern with the audience transforms certain chapters in the classical treatises on rhetoric into veritable studies in psychology. For instance, in the passage in the *Rhetoric* dealing with the factors of age and fortune in audiences, Aristotle includes many shrewd descriptions of a differential-psychological nature that are still valid today.[12] Cicero shows the necessity of speaking differently to the class of men which is "coarse and ignorant, always preferring immediate advantage to what is honorable," and to "that other, enlightened and cultivated, which puts moral dignity above all else."[13] Later, Quintilian dwells on character differences, which are important to the orator.[14]

The study of audiences could also be a study for sociology, since a man's opinions depend not so much on his own character, as on his social environment, on the people he associates with and lives among. As M. Millioud has said: "If you want an uncultivated man to change his views, transplant him."[15] Every social circle or milieu is distinguishable in terms of its dominant opinions and unquestioned beliefs, of the premises that it takes for granted without hesitation: these views form an integral part of its culture, and an orator wishing to persuade a particular audience must of necessity adapt himself to

---

[11] Marrou, *Histoire de l'éducation dans l'Antiquité*, p. 278.

[12] Aristotle, *Rhetoric*, II, 12-17, 1388b-1391b. See also De Coster, "L'idéalisme des jeunes," *Morale et enseignement*, 1951-52, nos. 2, 3.

[13] Cicero, *Partitiones Oratoriae*, § 90.

[14] Quintilian, III, VIII, 38 et seq.

[15] Millioud, "La propagation des idées," *Revue philosophique*, 70 (1910), 173.

it. Thus the particular culture of a given audience shows so strongly through the speeches addressed to it that we feel we can rely on them to a considerable extent for our knowledge of the character of past civilizations.

Among the sociological considerations of possible use to an orator are those bearing on a very definite matter: the social functions exercised by his listeners. It is quite common for members of an audience to adopt attitudes connected with the role they play in certain social institutions. This fact has been stressed by the originator of the psychology of form:

> One can sometimes observe marvelous changes in individuals, as when some passionately biased person becomes a member of a jury, or arbitrator, or judge, and when his actions then show the fine transition from bias to an honest effort to deal with the problems at issue in a just and objective fashion.[16]

The same observation can be made of the mentality of a politician whose point of view changes when, after years spent in the opposition, he becomes a responsible member of the government.

The listener, then, in his new functions, assumes a new personality which the orator cannot afford to disregard. And what is true of the individual listener holds equally true of whole audiences, so much so that the theoreticians of rhetoric have found it possible to classify oratory on the basis of the role performed by the audience addressed. The writers of antiquity recognized three types of oratory, the deliberative, the forensic, and the epidictic, which in their view corresponded respectively to an audience engaged in deliberating, an audience engaged in judging, and an audience that is merely enjoying the unfolding of the orator's argument without having to reach a conclusion on the matter in question.[17]

We are presented here with a distinction of a purely practical order, whose defects and inadequacies are apparent. Particularly unsatisfactory is its characterization of the epidictic type of oratory, of which we shall have more to say later.[18] Though this classification cannot be accepted as such for the study of argumentation, it has nevertheless the merit of underlining the importance which a speaker must give to the functions of his audience.

It often happens that an orator must persuade a composite audience, embracing people differing in character, loyalties, and functions. To

---

[16] Wertheimer, *Productive Thinking*, pp. 135-136.

[17] Aristotle, *Rhetoric*, I, 3, 1358b, 2-7; Cicero, *Orator*, § 37; *Partitiones Oratoriae*, § 10; Quintilian, III, ɪv.

[18] Cf. § 11, infra: The Epidictic Genre.

win over the different elements in his audience, the orator will have to use a multiplicity of arguments. A great orator is one who possesses the art of taking into consideration, in his argumentation, the composite nature of his audience. Examples of this art may be found on close reading of speeches made before parliamentary assemblies, a type of composite audience whose constituent elements are readily discernible.

However, an orator does not have to be confronted with several organized factions to think of the composite nature of his audience. He is justified in visualizing each one of his listeners as simultaneously belonging to a number of disparate groups. Even when an orator stands before only a few auditors, or indeed, before a single auditor, it is possible that he will not be quite sure what arguments will appear most convincing to his audience. In such a case, he will, by a kind of fiction, insert his audience into a series of different audiences. In *Tristram Shandy*—since argumentation is one of the main themes of this book, we shall often refer to it—Tristram describes an argument between his parents, in which his father wants to persuade his mother to have a midwife:

> He ... placed his arguments in all lights; argued the matter with her like a Christian, like a heathen, like a husband, like a father, like a patriot, like a man. My mother answered everything only like a woman, which was a little hard upon her, for, as she could not assume and fight it out behind such a variety of characters, 'twas no fair match: 'twas seven to one.[19]

Notice that it is not only the orator who so changes his mask: it is even more so his audience—his poor wife in this case—which his fancy transforms, as he seeks its most vulnerable points. However, as it is the speaker who takes the initiative in this "breaking down" of the audience, it is to him that the terms "like a Christian," "like a heathen," and so on, are applied.

When a speaker stands before his audience, he can try to locate it in its social setting. He may ask himself if all the members fall within a single social group, or if he must spread his listeners over a number of different—perhaps even opposed—groups. If division is necessary, several ways of proceeding are always possible: he may divide his audience ideally in terms of the social groups—political, occupational, religious, for example—to which the individual members belong, or in terms of the values to which certain members of the audience adhere. These ideal divisions are not mutually independent; they can, however, lead to the formation of very different partial audiences.

[19] Sterne, *The Life and Opinions of Tristram Shandy*, bk. I, chap. 18, p. 42.

The breaking down of a gathering into sub-groups will also depend on the speaker's own position. If he holds extremist views on a question, there is nothing to restrain him from considering all his interlocutors as forming a single audience. On the other hand, if he holds a moderate view, he will see them as forming at least two distinct audiences.[20]

Knowledge of an audience cannot be conceived independently of the knowledge of how to influence it. The problem of the nature of an audience is indeed intimately connected with that of its conditioning. This term implies, at first sight, factors extrinsic to the audience. And all study of this conditioning assumes that this conditioning is considered as applying to an entity which would be the audience itself. But, on a closer view, knowledge of an audience is also knowledge of how to bring about its conditioning, as well as of the amount of conditioning achieved at any given moment of the discourse.

Various conditioning agents are available to increase one's influence on an audience: music, lighting, crowd effects, scenery, and various devices of stage management. These means have always been known and have been used in the past by primitive peoples, as well as by the Greeks, Romans, and men of the Middle Ages. In our own day, technical improvements have fostered the development of these conditioners to the point that they are regarded by some as the essential element in acting on minds.

Besides conditioning of this kind, which is beyond the scope of this work, there is the conditioning by the speech itself, which results in the audience no longer being exactly the same at the end of the speech as it was at the beginning. This form of conditioning can be brought about only if there is a continuous adaptation of the speaker to his audience.

§ 5. *Adaptation of the Speaker to the Audience*

Vico wrote, "the end sought by eloquence always depends on the speaker's audience, and he must govern his speech in accordance with their opinions."[21] In argumentation, the important thing is not knowing what the speaker regards as true or important, but knowing the

---

[20] Cf. the observations of L. Festinger on the lesser tendency toward communication found in those who hold moderate viewpoints: "Informal Social Communication," *Psychological Review*, vol. 57, no. 5, Sept. 1950, p. 275.

[21] Vico, *Opere*, ed. Ferrari, vol. II, *De Nostri Temporis Studiorum Ratione*, p. 10.

views of those he is addressing. To borrow Gracian's simile, speech is "like a feast, at which the dishes are made to please the guests, and not the cooks."[22]

The great orator, the one with a hold on his listeners, seems animated by the very mind of his audience. This is not the case for the ardent enthusiast whose sole concern is with what he himself considers important. A speaker of this kind may have some effect on suggestible persons, but generally speaking his speech will strike his audience as unreasonable. According to M. Pradines, the enthusiast's speech, even if capable of some effect, does not yield a "true" sound, the emotional reality "bursts through the mask of logic," for, he says, "passion and reasons are not commensurable."[23] The apparent explanation for this viewpoint is that the man swayed by passion argues without taking sufficiently into account the audience he is addressing: carried away by his enthusiasm, he imagines his audience to be susceptible to the same arguments that persuaded him. Thus, passion, in causing the audience to be forgotten, creates less an absence than a poor choice of reasons.

Because they adopted the techniques of the clever orator, Plato reproached the leaders of the Athenian democracy with "flattering" the populace when they should have led them. But no orator, not even the religious orator, can afford to neglect this effort of adaptation to his audience. "The making of a preacher," wrote Bossuet, "rests with his audience."[24] In his struggle against the demagogues at Athens, Demosthenes calls on the people to improve themselves so as to improve the performance of the orators:

> Your orators never make you either bad men or good, but you make them whichever you choose; for it is not you that aim at what they wish for, but they who aim at whatever they think you desire. You therefore must start with a noble ambition and all will be well, for then no orator will give you base counsel, or else he will gain nothing by it, having no one to take him at his word.[25]

It is indeed the audience which has the major role in determining the quality of argument and the behavior of orators.[26]

Although orators, in their relationship to the listeners, have been compared to cooks, and even to parasites who "almost always speak a language contrary to their sentiments in order to be invited to fine

---

[22] Gracian, L'homme de Cour, p. 85.

[23] Pradines, Traité de psychologie générale, vol. II, pp. 324-325.

[24] Bossuet, Sermons, vol. II, Sur la parole de Dieu, p. 153.

[25] Demosthenes, On Organization, § 36.

[26] Cf. § 2, supra: The Contact of Minds.

meals,"[27] it must not be overlooked that the orator is nearly always at liberty to give up persuading an audience when he cannot persuade it effectively except by the use of methods that are repugnant to him. It should not be thought, where argument is concerned, that it is always honorable to succeed in persuasion, or even to have such an intention. The problem of harmonizing the scruples of the man of honor with submission to the audience received special attention from Quintilian.[28] To him rhetoric as *scientia bene dicendi*[29] implies that the accomplished orator not only is good at persuading, but also says what is good. If, then, one allows the existence of audiences of corrupt persons, whom one nonetheless does not want to give up convincing, and, at the same time, if one looks at the matter from the standpoint of the moral quality of the speaker, one finds oneself led, in order to solve the difficulty, to make distinctions and dissociations that do not come as a matter of course.

The coupling of obligation on the orator to adapt himself to his audience, with limitation of the audience to an incompetent mob, incapable of understanding sustained reasoning, or of maintaining attention if in the least distracted, has had two unfortunate results. It has discredited rhetoric, and has introduced into the theory of speech general rules which actually seem only to be valid in particular cases. We do not see, for instance, why, as a matter of principle, use of technical argumentation should lead away from rhetoric and dialectic.[30]

There is only one rule in this matter: adaptation of the speech to the audience, whatever its nature. Arguments that in substance and form are appropriate to certain circumstances may appear ridiculous in others.[31]

If the same event is described in a work that claims to be scientific and in a historical novel, the same method of proving its reality need not be adopted in the two cases. A reader who would have found Jules Romains' proofs of the voluntary suspension of the action of the heart ridiculous, had they appeared in a medical journal, might consider them an interesting hypothesis when developed in a novel.[32]

---

[27] Saint-Évremond, vol. IX, p. 19, referring to Petronius, *The Satyricon*, chap. III, p. 3.
[28] Quintilian, III, viii; XII, i.
[29] Quintilian, II, xv, 34.
[30] Aristotle, *Rhetoric*, I, 2, 1357a, 1358a.
[31] Whately, *Elements of Rhetoric* (Harper), pt. III, chap. I, § 2, pp. 179 et seq.
[32] Reyes, *El Deslinde*, p. 40. Romains, *Les hommes de bonne volonté*, vol. XII: *Les créateurs*, chap I-VII. Cf. Belaval, *Les philosophes et leur langage*, p. 138.

The procedures to be adopted in arguing are to some extent con-ditioned by the size of the audience, independently of considerations relating to the area of agreement taken as a basis for the argument, which vary from audience to audience. In discussing style as affected by the occasion of the speech, J. Marouzeau has drawn attention to

> a kind of deference and self-consciousness imposed by numbers,... as intimacy decreases, qualms increase, qualms about gaining the esteem of the listeners, about winning their applause or, at least, their approbation as expressed in looks and attitudes.[33]

Many other observations might pertinently be made on character-istics of audiences that influence a speaker's behavior and mode of argument. In our view, the value of our study depends on consider-ation being given to the many distinct aspects of particular audiences in as concrete a manner as possible. However, we wish to stress in the following four sections the characteristics of certain audiences se-lected for their unquestionable importance to all concerned with ar-gumentation, and particularly to philosophers.

§ 6. *Persuading and Convincing*

We have said enough to show that audiences are almost infinite in their variety, and that, in the effort to adapt to their particular char-acteristics, a speaker faces innumerable problems. This is one reason, perhaps, why there is such tremendous interest in a technique of argumentation that would apply to all kinds of audiences, or at least to those composed of competent or rational people. Corresponding to this ideal, to this desire to transcend historical or local particularities so that theses defended may win universal acceptance, is the quest for objectivity, whatever the nature of this may be. In this endeavor, as Husserl says in a moving speech in which he defends the efforts of western rational thought, "we are, in our philosophical work, the *public servants of mankind.*"[34] In the same spirit, J. Benda accuses clerks of treason when they turn from concern with what is eternal and universal to defense of temporal and local values.[35] Here is re-sumed that age-old debate between those who stand for truth and those who stand for opinion, between philosophers seeking the ab-solute and rhetors involved in action. It is out of this debate that

---

[33] Marouzeau, *Précis de stylistique française*, p. 208.
[34] Husserl, *Die Krisis der europäischen Wissenschaften* in *Gesammelte Werke*, vol. VI, p. 15.
[35] Benda, *La trahison des clercs*.

the distinction between *persuading* and *convincing* seems to arise. We wish to reconsider this distinction in the context of a theory of argumentation and of the role played by certain audiences.[36]

To the person concerned with results, persuading surpasses convincing, since conviction is merely the first stage in progression toward action.[37] Rousseau considered it useless to convince a child "if you cannot also persuade him."[38]

On the other hand, to someone concerned with the rational character of adherence to an argument, convincing is more crucial than persuading. Furthermore, this rational character of conviction depends sometimes on the means used and sometimes on the faculties one addresses. In Pascal's view, persuasion is something applied to the automation—by which he means the body, imagination, and feeling, all, in fact, that is not reason.[39] Often persuasion is considered to be an unwarranted transposition of demonstration. Thus, according to Dumas, "in being persuaded, a person is satisfied with affective and personal reasons," and persuasion is often "sophistic."[40] But he does not specify in what respect this affective proof differs technically from objective proof.

The criteria relied on to distinguish between conviction and persuasion are always based on a decision requiring isolation from a totality, totality of procedures, totality of faculties, of certain elements conceived as rational. This process of isolation, it must be emphasized, is sometimes applied to the actual lines of reasoning. It may be shown, for instance, that a certain syllogism, while inducing conviction, will not induce persuasion: however, this way of speaking of a syllogism involves isolating it from an entire context, it supposes that the premises of the syllogism exist in the mind independently of the remainder, it transforms these premises into intangible and unshakable truths. We may be told, for example, that a certain person, although convinced of the dangers of too rapid mastication, will not on that account cease the practice.[41] Such a statement involves isolation, from the complete picture, of the reasoning which forms the basis of the conviction. It is overlooked, for instance, that this con-

---

[36] Cf. Perelman and Olbrechts-Tyteca, "Logique et rhétorique," *Rhétorique et philosophie*, pp. 3 et seq.

[37] Whately, *Elements of Rhetoric* (Harper), pt. II, chap. I, § 1. Cf. Stevenson, *Ethics and Language* (Yale), pp. 139-140.

[38] Rousseau, *Émile* (Dent, Dutton), bk. III, p. 146.

[39] Pascal, *Pensées*, GBWW, vol. 33, p. 219, no. 252.

[40] Dumas, *Traité de psychologie*, vol. II, p. 740.

[41] Scott, *Influencing Men in Business. The Psychology of Argument and Suggestion* (1920), p. 31.

viction may run up against another conviction affirming that time is gained by eating more quickly. It is apparent, then, that the concept of what constitutes conviction, though seemingly based on a singling out of the means of proof used or faculties called into play, often also involves the isolation of particular data from a far more complex totality.

However, even if one refuses, as we do, to adopt these distinctions in actual thought, one must recognize that our language makes use of two notions, convincing and persuading, and that there is a slight and perceptible difference in the meaning of the two terms.

We are going to apply the term *persuasive* to argumentation that only claims validity for a particular audience, and the term *convincing* to argumentation that presumes to gain the adherence of every rational being. The nuance involved is a delicate one and depends, essentially, on the idea the speaker has formed on the incarnation of reason. Every person believes in a set of facts, of truths, which he thinks must be accepted by every "normal" person, because they are valid for every rational being. But is this really the case? Does not this claim to an absolute validity for any audience composed of rational beings go too far? On this point, even the most conscientious writer can do no more than submit to the test of facts, to his readers' judgment.[42] In any case he will have done all he can to *convince*, if he thinks he is validly addressing such an audience.

Despite the similarity in their consequences, we prefer our criterion to that, quite different in principle, put forward by Kant in his *Critique of Pure Reason.* According to him, conviction and persuasion are two different kinds of belief:

> If a judgment is valid for every rational being, then its ground is objectively sufficient, and it is termed a *conviction.* If, on the other hand, it has its ground in the particular character of the subject, it is termed a *persuasion.* Persuasion is a mere illusion, the ground of the judgment, which lies solely in the subject, being regarded as objective. Hence a judgment of this kind has only private validity—is only valid for the individual who judges, and the holding of a thing to be true in this way cannot be communicated. ... Persuasion, accordingly, cannot be *subjectively* distinguished from conviction, that is, so long as the subject views its judgment simply as a phenomenon of its own mind. But if we inquire whether the grounds of our judgment, which are valid for us, produce the same effect on the reason of others as on our own, we have then the means, though only subjective means, not, indeed, of producing conviction, but of detecting the merely private validity of the judgment; in other words, of discovering that there

---

[42] Cf. Kant, *Critique of Pure Reason*, preface to the first edition, GBWW, vol. 42, p. 3.

is in it the element of mere persuasion. ... Persuasion I may keep for myself, if it is agreeable to me; but I cannot, and ought not, to attempt to impose it as binding upon others.[43]

The Kantian view, though rather close to ours in its consequences, differs from it in making the opposition of *subjective* and *objective* its criterion for distinguishing between persuasion and conviction. If conviction is based on the truth of its object, and is thereby valid for every rational being, then conviction alone can be proved, and persuasion has no more than individual significance. From this it is clear that Kant accepts only purely logical proof, and excludes from philosophy all argument that does not absolutely compel acceptance. Kant's conception is defensible only if it is conceded that what is not necessary is not communicable, and this would exclude all argumentation directed to particular audiences: but argumentation of the latter kind is the chosen sphere of rhetoric. And from the moment one admits the existence of other means of proof than necessary proof, argumentation addressed to particular audiences assumes a significance beyond mere subjective belief.

The distinction that we propose between persuasion and conviction expresses indirectly the connection that is frequently established, though in a confused way, between persuasion and action, on the one hand, and, on the other, between conviction and intelligence. Indeed, the timeless character of certain audiences explains why arguments addressed to them make no call for immediate action.

At first sight, this distinction, based on the characteristics of the audience addressed, does not seem to explain the difference between conviction and persuasion as it is experienced by the hearer himself. But it will readily be seen that the same criterion can nevertheless apply, if one bears in mind that the hearer imagines the transfer to other audiences of the arguments presented to him and that he concerns himself with the reception they would obtain.

Our viewpoint has the advantage of showing that the difference between the terms *convincing* and *persuading* is always unprecise and in practice must remain so. For whereas the frontier between intelligence and will, between reason and the irrational, can be clearly drawn, the making of distinctions between different audiences is a far less certain matter, particularly as the representation the speaker makes of an audience is the result of an effort that can always be abandoned and replaced.

The distinction we make between persuading and convincing has many features in common with the distinctions made by writers in the past,[44] even though we have not adopted their criteria. It also explains the use some writers make, out of modesty, of the word persuasion as opposed to conviction. For instance, Claparède, in the preface to one of his books, tells us that his decision to let the manuscript see the light of day was in accession "to the request of Madame Antipoff, who persuaded (but did not convince) me that the publication of these investigations was desirable."[45] In so writing, the author has no thought of making a theoretical distinction between the two terms, but he makes use of the difference between them to express both the slight guaranteed objective value and the power of the reasons given by his collaborator. The difference in shades of meaning conveyed by Claparède may correspond to the Kantian concept, but seems to fit in even better with the fact that he was confronted with reasons that were convincing to him, but which he thought might not be convincing to everybody.

Thus the nature of the audience to which arguments can be successfully presented will determine to a great extent both the direction the arguments will take and the character, the significance that will be attributed to them. What formulation can we make of audiences, which have come to play a normative role, enabling us to judge on the convincing character of an argument? Three kinds of audiences are apparently regarded as enjoying special prerogatives as regards this function, both in current practice and in the view of philosophers. The first such audience consists of the whole of mankind, or at least, of all normal, adult persons; we shall refer to it as the *universal audience*. The second consists of the single *interlocutor* whom a speaker addresses in a dialogue. The third is the *subject himself* when he deliberates or gives himself reasons for his actions. We hasten to add that it is only when the interlocutor in a dialogue and the man debating with himself are regarded as an incarnation of the universal audience, that they can enjoy the philosophic privilege conferred to reason, by virtue of which argumentation addressed to them has often been assimilated to logical discourse. Each speaker's universal audience can, indeed, from an external viewpoint, be regarded as a particular audience, but it none the less remains true that, for each speaker at each moment, there exists an audience transcending all others, which cannot easily be forced within the bounds of a particular audience. On the other hand, the interlocutor in a

[44] Cf., in particular, Fénelon, "Dialogues sur l'éloquence," *Oeuvres*, vol. XXI, p. 43.
[45] Claparède, "La genèse de l'hypothèse," *Archives de Psychologie*, vol. XXIV, introduction.

dialogue or the person engaged in deliberation can be considered as a particular audience, with reactions that are known to us, or at least with characteristics we can study. Hence the primordial importance of the universal audience, as providing a norm for objective argumentation, since the other party to a dialogue and the person deliberating with himself can never amount to more than floating incarnations of this universal audience.

§ 7. *The Universal Audience*

Argumentation aimed exclusively at a particular audience has the drawback that the speaker, by the very fact of adapting to the views of his listeners, might rely on arguments that are foreign or even directly opposed to what is acceptable to persons other than those he is presently addressing. This danger is apparent in the case of a composite audience, which the speaker has to resolve into its constituent parts for the purposes of his argumentation. For a composite audience, such as a parliamentary assembly, will have to be regrouped as a single entity to make a decision, and it is extremely easy for the opponent of an incautious speaker to turn against him all the arguments he directed to the different parts of the audience, either by setting the arguments against each other so as to show their incompatibility or by presenting them to those they were not meant for. This explains the relative weakness of arguments that are accepted only by particular audiences and the value attached to opinions that enjoy unanimous approval, particularly approval by persons or groups who agree on very few matters.

Naturally, the value of this unanimity depends on the number and quality of those expressing it. Its highest point is reached when there is *agreement of the universal audience*. This refers of course, in this case, not to an experimentally proven fact, but to a universality and unanimity imagined by the speaker, to the agreement of an audience which should be universal, since, for legitimate reasons, we need not take into consideration those which are not part of it.

Philosophers always claim to be addressing such an audience, not because they hope to obtain the effective assent of all men—they know very well that only a small minority will ever read their works—but because they think that all who understand the reasons they give will have to accept their conclusions. *The agreement of a universal audience is thus a matter, not of fact, but of right.* The basis for relying on the adherence of those who submit to the data of experience or to the light shed by reason is the speaker's affirmation of that which corresponds to an objective fact, of that which constitutes a true and even necessary assertion.

Argumentation addressed to a universal audience must convince the reader that the reasons adduced are of a compelling character, that they are self-evident, and possess an absolute and timeless validity, independent of local or historical contingencies. "Truth," according to Kant, "depends upon agreement with the object, and consequently, with respect to this object, the judgments of all understandings must be in agreement." Every objective belief can be communicated, because it is "valid for the reason of every man." It is only such an assertion that can be *affirmed*, that is, be expressed "as necessarily valid for everyone."[46]

In fact, a judgment of this sort is deemed to be binding on everybody, because the speaker himself is convinced that it does not admit of any question. This Cartesian certitude has been described very expressively by Dumas:

> Certitude is that complete belief, which entirely excludes doubt; it is necessary, universal affirmation; in other words, the man who is certain does not conceive the possibility of preferring the contrary affirmation, but imagines his affirmation as necessarily commanding the acceptance of everybody in the same circumstances. In short, it is the state in which we are conscious of thinking the truth, which is precisely this universal constraint, this mental obligation; subjectivity disappears, and man thinks as intelligence, as a man and no longer as an individual. The state of certitude has often been described with the help of such metaphors as light and luminosity; but the illumination brought by rational certitude carries its own explanation. It means rest and relaxation, even if the certitude is a painful one, as it puts an end to the tension and the worry of search and indecision. With it comes a feeling of power, but also of annihilation; one feels that prejudice, passion, and individual caprice have disappeared. ... In rational belief the truth becomes ours and we become the truth.[47]

It is to be observed that where rational self-evidence comes into play, the adherence of the mind seems to be suspended to a compelling truth, and no role is played by the processes of argumentation. The individual, with his freedom of deliberation and of choice, defers to the constraining force of reason, which takes from him all possibility of doubt. Thus, maximally efficacious rhetoric, in the case of a universal audience, is rhetoric employing nothing but logical proof.

Rationalism, with its claim to completely eliminate rhetoric from philosophy, announced a very ambitious program which would bring

---

[46] Kant, *Critique of Pure Reason*, GBWW, vol. 42, p. 240.
[47] Dumas, *Traité de psychologie*, vol. II, pp. 197-198, 200.

about the agreement of minds through universal yielding to rational self-evidence. But the exigencies of the Cartesian method had hardly been stated when Descartes, in the name of these exigencies, made some very questionable assertions. How, indeed, does one distinguish between true and false self-evidence? Does a person suppose that there is really objective validity in what convinces a universal audience, of which he considers himself the ideal representative? Pareto has made the penetrating observation that the universal consensus invoked is often merely the unwarranted generalization of an individual intuition.[48] For this reason it is always hazardous for a writer or speaker to identify with logic the argumentation intended for the universal audience, as he himself has conceived it. The concepts that men have formed, in the course of history, of "objective facts" and "obvious truths" have sufficiently varied for us to be wary in this matter. Instead of believing in a universal audience, analogous to the divine mind which can assent only to the "truth," we might, with greater justification, characterize each speaker by the image he himself holds of the universal audience that he is trying to win over to his view.

Everyone constitutes the universal audience from what he knows of his fellow men, in such a way as to transcend the few oppositions he is aware of. Each individual, each culture, has thus its own conception of the universal audience. The study of these variations would be very instructive, as we would learn from it what men, at different times in history, have regarded as *real, true,* and *objectively valid.*

If argumentation addressed to the universal audience and calculated to convince does not convince everybody, one can always resort to *disqualifying the recalcitrant* by classifying him as stupid or abnormal. This approach, common among thinkers in the Middle Ages, is also used by some modern writers.[49] There can only be adherence to this idea of excluding individuals from the human community if the number and intellectual value of those banned are not so high as to make such a procedure ridiculous. If this danger exists, recourse must be had to another line of argumentation, and the universal audience must be set against an elite audience, endowed with exceptional and infallible means of knowledge. Those who pride themselves on possession of a supernatural revelation or mystical knowledge, as well as those who appeal to the virtuous, to believers, or to men endowed with grace, show their preference for an elite audience; this elite audience may even be confused with the perfect Being.

[48] Pareto, *The Mind and Society*, vol. I, §§ 589, 599, pp. 354, 361.
[49] E.g. Lefebvre, *A la lumière du matérialisme dialectique*, I, *Logique formelle, logique dialectique*, p. 29.

The elite audience is by no means always regarded as similar to the universal audience. Indeed, the elite audience often wishes to remain distinct from the common run of men: if this is so, the elite is characterized by its hierarchic position. But often also the elite audience is regarded as a model to which men should conform in order to be worthy of the name: in other words, the elite audience sets the norm for everybody. In this case, the elite is the vanguard all will follow and conform to. Its opinion is the only one that matters, for, in final analysis, it is the determining one.

The elite audience embodies the universal audience only for those who acknowledge this role of vanguard and model. For the rest it will be no more than a particular audience. The status of an audience varies with the concepts one has of it.

Certain specialized audiences are readily assimilated to the universal audience, such as the audience of the scientist addressing his fellow scientists. The scientist addresses himself to certain particularly qualified men, who accept the data of a well-defined system consisting of the science in which they are specialists. Yet, this very limited audience is generally considered by the scientist to be really the universal audience, and not just a particular audience. He supposes that everyone with the same training, qualifications, and information would reach the same conclusions.

The same holds good when we are dealing with morals. We expect our judgments to be confirmed by the reactions of others. However, the "others" to whom we appeal are not just any "others." We make our appeal solely to those who have duly "reflected" on the conduct we approve or disapprove. As Findlay says :

> We make our appeal above the unreflecting heads of present company, to the great company of reflecting persons, wherever they may be situated in space or time.[50]

This sort of appeal is criticized by J.-P. Sartre in his remarkable lectures on the audience of a writer :

> We have said that the writer addresses himself, in principle, to all men. But, immediately afterward, we observed that he is only read by some of them. From this gap between ideal public and real public originates the idea of abstract universality. In other words, the author postulates a perpetual repetition over an indefinite future of the handful of readers he has in the present ... recourse to infinity in time tries to compensate for the failure in space (return to the infinite of the reasonable man of the seven-

---

[50] Findlay, "Morality by Convention," *Mind*, LIII, new series, 1944, p. 160. Cf. Prior, *Logic and the Basis of Ethics*, p. 84.

teenth century writer, extension to infinity of the writers' club
and of the public of specialists for the nineteenth century writer). ...
By concrete universality, on the other hand, is meant the totality
of men living in a given society.[51]

Sartre upbraids writers for neglecting the concrete universality to
which they could, and should, address themselves, in favor of an illusory abstract universality. But is it not Sartre's universal audience
which will have to judge the merits of this criticism and decide whether
or not the writer has been harboring up to now a voluntary or involuntary illusion, whether up to now he has failed in his self-appointed
"mission"? And it is Sartre's universal audience he himself addresses
when he wants to explain his views on this question of abstract and
concrete universality.

We believe, then, that audiences are not independent of one another,
that particular concrete audiences are capable of validating a concept
of the universal audience which characterizes them. On the other
hand, it is the undefined universal audience that is invoked to pass
judgment on what is the concept of the universal audience appropriate to such a concrete audience, to examine, simultaneously, the
manner in which it was composed, which are the individuals who
comprise it, according to the adopted criterion, and whether this
criterion is legitimate. It can be said that audiences pass judgment
on one another.

§ 8. *Argumentation Before a Single Hearer*

All those who, in antiquity, proclaimed the primacy of dialectic
over rhetoric, recognized the philosophic significance of argumentation addressed to a single hearer, and granted its superiority over
that addressed to a vast audience. Rhetoric confined itself to the
technique of the long, sustained speech. But this kind of speech, with
all the oratorical action involved in it, would be both ridiculous and
ineffective before a single hearer.[52] It is normal to take his reactions,
denials, and hesitations into account, and when he notices them the
speaker does not think of evading them. He has to prove the contested
point, apprise himself of the reasons for his interlocutor's resistance,
and thoroughly understand his objections. Discourse, of necessity,
degenerates into dialogue. That is why, according to Quintilian, dia-

[51] Sartre, *Situations*, vol. II, pp. 192-193.
[52] Quintilian, I, II, 29; cf. also, Carnegie, *Public Speaking*, and the distinction
between "one-way communication" and "two-way communication" made by
Riezler, in "Political decisions in modern society," *Ethics*, LXIV (1954), 45-46.

lectic, as a technique of dialogue, was compared by Zeno to a closed fist, because of its more concise style of argumentation, whereas rhetoric was more like an open hand.[53] There is indeed no doubt that the single hearer, having the opportunity to ask questions and raise objections, gets the impression that the arguments he eventually accepts are more solidly supported than the conclusions of a speaker who unfolds his arguments in sustained discourse. In Plato's view, the dialectician concerned with gaining the agreement of his interlocutor at each step in his reasoning is more certain of remaining on the path of truth. This opinion is clearly expressed in this little speech Socrates makes to Callicles:

> Well then, we have settled one thing; every time we are agreed on a point, that point will be considered to be sufficiently tested by both of us and will not need to be submitted to any further examination. For you could not have granted it to me from lack of knowledge or excess of timidity, nor yet from a wish to deceive me, for you are my friend, as you tell me yourself. Therefore our agreement will really prove that we have attained the truth.[54]

As Pareto points out,[55] this way of turning the adherence of a single person into an index of truth would be ridiculous if Socrates' interlocutor were expressing a purely personal point of view. It would perhaps be an exaggeration to say, as Goblot does, that "Plato seems confident that every interlocutor would have to make the same answer as the person who is speaking to him,"[56] but it is at any rate certain that each of Socrates' interlocutors is the spokesman—supposedly the most effective one—of partisans of a particular viewpoint and that their objections must first be disposed of in order to facilitate public adherence to the proposed theses.

The importance of dialogue as a philosophic genre, and of dialectic as conceived by Plato, does not lie in the actual adherence of the particular interlocutor involved—who is simply one particular audience among an infinity of others—but in the adherence of an individual, no matter who he is, who cannot but be yielding to the evidence of truth because his conviction follows from a close confrontation of his thought with that of the speaker. The relationship between dialogue and truth is such that Eugène Dupréel is inclined to think that Gorgias did not practice dialogue of his own accord: partiality for the dia-

---

[53] Quintilian, II, xx, 7.
[54] Plato, *Gorgias*, 487 d-e.
[55] Pareto, *The Mind and Society*, vol. I, § 612, pp. 368-369.
[56] Goblot, *La logique des jugements de valeur*, p. 17.

logue method, he believes, stems from Hippias of Elis, an opponent of rhetoric and a believer in the primacy of the only truth.[57]

Written dialogue, even more than spoken dialogue, assumes that the single hearer incarnates the universal audience. This conception seems justified, especially when, like Plato, one assumes that man is subject to the constraint of inner principles that guide the development of his thought.[58]

Argumentation in a dialogue of this nature has no philosophic significance unless it claims to be valid for all. It is easy to see how dialectic, just like argumentation directed to the universal audience, could come to be identified with logic. This was the view held by the Stoics and the medieval thinkers.[59] We think of it as merely an illusion, or a method, which admittedly has played an important role in the development of absolutist philosophy, striving by every means to go from adherence to truth. The philosophic significance of the interlocutor's adherence in dialogue is that the interlocutor is regarded as an incarnation of the universal audience. The hearer is assumed to have the same reasoning power at his disposal as the other members of the universal audience, the appreciation factors pertaining to purely technical competence being provided by the speaker or presumed to be abundantly at the hearer's disposal because of his social position.

The adherence of the interlocutor should not, however, be gained solely on the strength of the speaker's dialectical superiority. The one who gives in should not be beaten in an eristic contest but is supposed to yield to the self-evidence of truth. Dialogue, as we consider it, is not supposed to be a *debate*, in which the partisans of opposed settled convictions defend their respective views, but rather a *discussion*, in which the interlocutors search honestly and without bias for the best solution to a controversial problem. Certain contemporary writers who stress this heuristic viewpoint, as against the eristic one, hold that discussion is the ideal instrument for reaching objectively valid conclusions.[60] The assumption is that in discussion the interlocutors are concerned only with putting forward and testing all the arguments, for and against, bearing on the various matters in question. When successfully carried out, discussion should lead to an inevitable and unanimously accepted conclusion, if the arguments, which are pre-

---

[57] Dupréel, *Les Sophistes. Protagoras, Gorgias, Prodicus, Hippias*, pp. 76, 77, 260, 263.

[58] Cf. Perelman, *The Idea of Justice and the Problem of Argument*, pp. 161-167.

[59] Cf. Dürr, "Die Entwicklung der Dialektik von Platon bis Hegel," *Dialectica*, I, 1, 1947; McKeon, "Dialectic and Political Thought and Action," *Ethics*, LXV (1954), 1-33.

[60] Cf. Baird, *Argumentation, Discussion, and Debate*, p. 307.

sumed to weigh equally with everyone, have, as it were, been distribut-
ed in the pans of a balance. In a debate, on the other hand, each interlocutor advances only arguments favorable to his own thesis, and
his sole concern with arguments unfavorable to him is for the purpose of refuting them or limiting their impact. The man with a settled
position is thus one-sided, and because of his bias and the consequent
restriction of his effort to those pertinent arguments which are favorable to him, the others remain frozen, as it were, and only appear
in the debate if his opponent puts them forward. And as the latter
is presumed to adopt the same attitude, one sees how discussion came
to be considered as a sincere quest for the truth, whereas the protagonists of a debate are chiefly concerned with the triumph of their
own viewpoint.

Theoretically, this distinction may be useful. However, it is a very
rash generalization to consider the participants in a disinterested
discussion as spokesmen of the universal audience, and it is only through
a rather schematic view of reality that the determination of the weight
of arguments can be compared with the weighing of ingots. On the
other hand, the defender of a particular point of view is very often
convinced that he is sustaining what is objectively the best thesis
and that its triumph will be that of the best cause.

In practice, there are many occasions on which this distinction
between discussion and debate seems hard to draw with any exactitude.
In most cases, it is based on the intention which we, rightly or wrongly,
ascribe to the participants in the dialogue, and this intention may
vary in the course of the dialogue. It is only in those special cases
where the attitude of the participants is governed by the institutional
setting that we can know beforehand what will be the speakers' intentions. In a judicial settlement, for example, we know that the
lawyer for each party will tend to develop arguments in favor of a
thesis rather than to shed light on some question. The law, by determining the issues to be discussed, favors this one-sided attitude
and the adoption of a definite standpoint by the advocate, who then
has merely to press this point steadfastly against his opponent. In
many other cases, the intervention of institutions is more subtle, but
nevertheless effective: a member-elect defending a thesis against the
criticisms of the examining committee, or a member of Parliament
defending his party's program. Finally, this attitude may result from
the speaker's commitments: if he has promised someone he will support his candidacy before a selection committee, the dialogue he will
maintain with the members of the committee will, in fact, be more
a pleading than a search for the truth—in this case the determination
of the best candidate.

Except, then, where we know for what reason—institutional or other—the participants adopt the attitude of pleaders and consequently wish to embarrass their opponents, it is hard to maintain a clear distinction between a dialogue directed toward discovery of the truth and one that consists of a series of pleadings. Such a distinction can be maintained only where there is a clear preliminary distinction between truth and error, and this is something which, in the absence of bad faith, the very existence of the discussion makes it hard to establish.

The heuristic dialogue, in which the interlocutor is an incarnation of the universal audience, and the eristic dialogue, which aims at overpowering the opponent, are both merely exceptional cases. In ordinary dialogue the participants are simply trying to persuade their audience so as to bring about some immediate or future action; most of our arguments in daily life develop at this practical level. It is a curious and noteworthy fact that this everyday activity of persuasive discussion has received very scant attention from the theoreticians. Most authors of treatises on rhetoric have regarded it as foreign to their discipline. And the philosophers who have examined dialogue have mainly considered it under the very special aspect in which the interlocutor incarnates the universal audience or else under the more psychological, but at the same time more scholastic, aspect of eristic dialogue, where the dominant concern is with what Schopenhauer[61] calls "Rechthaberei." Alfonso Reyes has rightly pointed out[62] that private discourse is a field contiguous to that of ancient rhetoric; it is indeed in the course of daily conversation that the opportunity to engage in argumentation most commonly presents itself.

Even when the single hearer, whether he be taking an active part in the dialogue or merely silently listening to the speaker, is regarded as the incarnation of an audience, the audience he embodies is not always the universal audience. He can also be—and very often is—the incarnation of a particular audience.

This is obviously the case when the single hearer represents a group of which he is the delegate or spokesman, and in whose name he can make decisions. But it is also true when the auditor is regarded as a specimen of a whole category of listeners. A teacher, for example, may choose to address the student who seems to him the dumbest, the most intelligent student, or the student sitting where he is least able to hear him.

---

[61] Schopenhauer, "Eristische Dialektik," *Sämtliche Werke* (Piper), vol. 6, p. 394.
[62] Reyes, *El Deslinde*, p. 203.

The choice of the single hearer who will incarnate the audience depends on the aims the speaker sets himself, but also on his idea of the way in which a group should be characterized. The choice of the person who will incarnate a particular audience will often influence the methods used in the argumentation. Bentham approved of the custom of addressing the Speaker in the House of Commons, because he thought it secured courtesy in debate.[63] In this instance, the single hearer is chosen for his functions, not for his qualities; this is the choice which least commits the speaker and reveals least what opinion he has of his audience.

In other cases, the choice of the hearer is much more revealing. From the choice of the person to incarnate a particular audience, we can learn both the speaker's conception of his audience and the ends he hopes to attain. When Ronsard addresses Hélène, he sees her as the incarnation of all young people who should heed the advice: "Gather the roses of life this very day."[64] But, addressed to Hélène, this advice is bereft of didactic claims and merely reflects an emotion, an understanding, perhaps even a hope. We shall encounter this technique throughout the history of literature and politics. It is very rare indeed that the individual to whom a published speech is addressed should not be regarded as the incarnation of a definite particular audience.

§ 9. *Self-Deliberating*

The deliberating subject is often regarded as an incarnation of the universal audience.

It does indeed seem that a man endowed with reason who seeks to convince himself is bound to be contemptuous of procedures aimed at winning over other people. It is believed that he cannot avoid being sincere with himself and is in a better position than anyone else to test the value of his own arguments. To Pascal the best criterion of the truth is "your own assent to yourself, and the constant voice of your own reason."[65] This is also the criterion Descartes adopts, in his *Meditations,* for proceeding from the reasons that convinced him to the affirmation that he has "reached a certain and evident knowledge of the truth."[66] In contradistinction to dialectic—the

[63] Bentham, "Essay on Political Tactics," *Works* (Tait), vol. II, pp. 362-363.
[64] Ronsard, "Sonnets pour Hélène," II, xliii, *Oeuvres complètes*, vol. I, p. 260.
[65] Pascal, *Pensées*, GBWW, vol. 33, p. 220, no. 260.
[66] Descartes, "Preface to the Reader," *Meditations on the First Philosophy*, GBWW, vol. 31, p. 72.

technique of controversy with another person—and to rhetoric—
the technique of speech addressed to a large number of people— logic
is identified, both by Schopenhauer[67] and by J. S. Mill,[68] with the
rules applied in the conduct of one's own thought. And this because when
a person is thinking, his mind would not be concerned with pleading
or with seeking only those arguments that support a particular point
of view, but would strive to assemble all arguments that seem to it
to have some value, without suppressing any, and then, after weighing
the pros and cons, would decide on what, to the best of its knowledge
and belief, appears to be the most satisfactory solution. Just as one
attaches more importance to arguments presented in closed session
than to those presented at a public meeting, the secrecy of self-deliberation seems to guarantee its value and sincerity. Thus we find
Chaignet, in the last work in French to consider rhetoric as a technique of persuasion, contrasting persuasion and conviction in these
terms: "When we are convinced, we are overcome only by ourselves,
by our own ideas. When we are persuaded, it is always by another."[69]

Some authors have conferred a preeminent position to the methods
of conducting our own thought and regard this question as the only
one worthy of a philosopher's interest. Speech addressed to another
is in their view simply appearance and illusion. This individualistic
outlook has done much to discredit, not only rhetoric, but, in general,
any theory of argumentation. We feel, on the contrary, that it is
highly desirable to consider self-deliberation as a particular kind of
argumentation. We do not overlook the fact that self-deliberation
has its own special characteristics, but we think there is much to gain
by heeding Isocrates' opinion:

> The arguments by which we convince others when we speak
> to them are the same as those we use when we engage in reflection.
> We call those able to speak to the multitude orators, and we re-
> gard as persons of sagacity those who are able to talk things over
> within themselves with discernment.[70]

It also very often happens that discussion with someone else is
simply a means we use to see things more clearly ourselves. Agreement with oneself is merely a particular case of agreement with others.
Accordingly, from our point of view, it is by analyzing argumentation
addressed to others that we can best understand self-deliberation,
and not vice versa.

[67] Schopenhauer, *Sämtliche Werke* (Brockhaus), vol. III: *Die Welt als Wille
und Vorstellung*, Band II, chap. IX, p. 112.
[68] Mill, *System of Logic*, vol. I, Introduction, § 3, pp. 2, 3.
[69] Chaignet, *La rhétorique et son histoire*, p. 93.
[70] Isocrates, *Nicocles*, § 8.

In self-deliberation, can we not indeed discern reflections corresponding to a discussion and others that are merely a search for arguments in support of a previously adopted position? Can we wholly rely on the sincerity of the deliberating subject to find out whether he is in quest of the best line of conduct or is pleading a case within himself? Depth psychology has taught us to distrust even that which seems unquestionable to our own consciousness. However, the distinctions it makes between reasons and rationalizations cannot be understood unless deliberation is treated as a particular case of argumentation. The psychologist will say that the motives given by the subject in explanation of his conduct are rationalizations if they differ from the real motives which caused him to act and of which the subject is unaware. We shall give a wider meaning to the term rationalization, regarding it as immaterial whether or not the subject is unaware of the real motives for his conduct. At first sight, it may seem ridiculous that a well-balanced person, who has acted for very "reasonable" reasons, should try so hard, deep down inside, to give quite different reasons for his acts—reasons that are less plausible, but do place him in a more favorable light.[71] This kind of rationalization is perfectly explained if we regard it as a pleading that is thought out in advance for the benefit of others, and can even be adapted to each particular anticipated audience. This rationalization does not mean, as Schopenhauer claims, that our "intellect" merely disguises the real motives for our acts, themselves completely irrational.[72] Actions might have been performed after careful consideration, but yet have other motives than those one tries to make one's conscience admit to afterwards. Those who do not see, or will not allow, the importance of argumentation cannot account for rationalization: for them it would be merely the shadow of a shadow.

The significance of our view may become clearer by considering the situation described by J. S. Mill in the following passage:

> Almost every one knows Lord Mansfield's advice to a man of sound common sense, who, being appointed governor of a colony, had to preside in its courts of justice without previous judicial practice or legal education. The advice was to give his decision boldly, for it would probably be right, but never to venture on assigning reasons, for they would almost infallibly be wrong.[73]

If Lord Mansfield's advice here was good, this is because, after the governor had given his decision based on his sense of equity, his

---

[71] Crawshay-Williams, *The Comforts of Unreason*, pp. 74 et seq.
[72] Schopenhauer, *Sämtliche Werke* (Brockhaus), vol. VI: *Parerga und Paralipomena*, Band II, chap. VIII, "Zur Ethik," § 118, p. 249.
[73] Mill, *System of Logic*, bk. II, chap. III, § 3, p. 124.

legally trained assistants could "rationalize" the decision by adducing reasons which did not occur to the governor and were more in accord with the controlling law than the reasons he would have given in support of his decision. It is a common, and not necessarily regrettable, occurrence even for a magistrate who knows the law to formulate his judgment in two steps: the conclusions are first inspired by what conforms most closely with his sense of justice, the technical motivation being added on later. Must we conclude in this case that the decision was made without any preceding deliberation? Not at all, as the pros and cons may have been weighed with the greatest care, though not within the frame of considerations based on legal technicalities. Strictly legal reasons are adduced only for the purpose of justifying the decision to another audience. They are not adduced, as Mill suggests in his example, for the purpose of making an expert formulation of the general maxims of which the governor had only a vague idea. Mill's scientism makes him think of everything in terms of a single audience, the universal audience, and prevents him from providing an adequate explanation for the phenomenon.

Fresh arguments, brought in after the decision, may consist of the insertion of the conclusion into a technical framework, as in the instance just cited. But such arguments can also be of a nontechnical character, as illustrated in the story by Antoine de La Salle[74] in which a feudal lord and his wife discuss a grave matter during the night. The lord must choose between sacrificing the town and sacrificing his son. The decision is never in doubt, but Antoine de La Salle nonetheless attaches great importance to the wife's words, which he relates with a wealth of detail. Her words transform the way in which the decision is faced: she gives her husband a sense of pride in himself, poise, confidence, and consolation. She puts order into his ideas, gives the decision its setting, and, in so doing, reinforces it. She is like the theologian who provides the rational proofs for a dogma in which all members of the church already believe.

In political life too, one finds situations in which the reasons justifying a decision are awaited with impatience, as the adherence of public opinion depends on such justification. For instance, when the African king Seretse[75] was exiled, the press announced that the British government, though not altering its decision, would make a concession to public opinion by giving more detailed and more satisfactory

[74] Analyzed by Auerbach in *Mimesis, Dargestellte Wirklichkeit in der abendländischen Literatur*, pp. 234, 235. Text in "Le réconfort de Madame du Fresne," in Nève, *Antoine de La Salle*, pp. 109-140.
[75] Translator's note: Chief-designate of the Bamangwato tribe, in Bechuanaland.

reasons in justification of what it had done. In other words, the government sought to give a justification which would be acceptable to the audience it was addressing.

This preference for certain arguments may be due to the hearer's wish to have at his disposal arguments that would be valid for another audience, perhaps even the universal audience, and are thus capable of transfer to a modified situation.

As appears from all we have just said about audiences, the rhetorical value of a statement is not, from our point of view, destroyed because the statement is predicated on argumentation thought to have been elaborated after the inner decision had been made nor because it involves argumentation based on premises that the speaker does not himself accept. In these two cases, which, although distinct, are in some way connected, the charge of insincerity or hypocrisy might be made by an observer or adversary. However, such an objection is significant only when made from a quite different standpoint than ours. Usually, moreover, the objector's perspective in such a case will be based on a well-defined conception of reality or personality.

Our thesis is, on the one hand, that a belief, once established, can always be intensified, and, on the other hand, that argumentation is a function of the audience being addressed. Consequently, it is legitimate that the person who has acquired a certain conviction should be at pains to strengthen it for himself and, more especially, against possible attack from without. And he will naturally consider all arguments capable of reinforcing that conviction. These new reasons may intensify his conviction, protect it against certain lines of attack he had not thought of originally, make its significance clearer.

Moreover, it is only when a speaker is addressing an audience to which he is supposed to belong— which, of course, would be the case for the universal audience—that he can be reproached with any conflict there may be between the arguments he puts forward and those that convinced him. But even in this particular case, one cannot exclude the possibility that the speaker's inner conviction is based on elements peculiar to himself—an incommunicable intuition, for instance— and that he is obliged to resort to argumentation in order to share the belief these elements engendered.

To conclude, we would say that, while the study of argumentation enables us to understand the reasons that have led so many writers to assign a privileged status to inner deliberation, this same study gives us also the means of distinguishing between the different kinds of deliberation and of understanding both what is well founded in the opposition between *reasons* and *rationalizations* and the real interest, from the standpoint of argumentation, of these over-despised rationalizations.

§ 10. *The Effects of Argumentation*

The goal of all argumentation, as we have said before, is to create or increase the adherence of minds to the theses presented for their assent. An efficacious argument is one which succeeds in increasing this intensity of adherence among those who hear it in such a way as to set in motion the intended action (a positive action or an abstention from action) or at least in creating in the hearers a willingness to act which will appear at the right moment.

Practical eloquence, including judicial and deliberative genres, was the traditionally favored field of confrontation of litigants and politicians who defended, by argumentation, opposed and sometimes even contradictory theses. In such oratorical contests, the adversaries would seek to win the adherence of their audience on certain debated subjects, in which the pros and cons would often have equally able and apparently equally honorable defenders.

Such a state of affairs was deplored by the detractors of rhetoric, for whom there was but a single truth in every matter. According to them, the protagonists of such discussions were conducting their divergent arguments by means of reasonings which could only have illusory value in producing conviction. Plato tells us in the *Phaedrus* that the rhetoric worthy of philosophy, that which could convince the gods themselves, ought to put itself under the sign of truth. And, twenty centuries later, Leibniz, who realized that human knowledge is limited and often incapable of furnishing sufficient proof of the truth of all assertions, desired that the degree of assent given to any thesis should at least be proportional to the indications of the calculus of probabilities or of presumptions.[76]

The attacks made by philosophers on the theory of reasoned persuasion, which was developed in works on rhetoric, appeared to be all the more justified in that argumentation was limited, as far as the theoreticians were concerned, to questions reducible to problems of conjecture and of qualification. Problems of conjecture are concerned with facts, facts in the past for judicial proceedings, facts in the future for political debates : "Did X do what he is charged with?" "Will such-and-such an act entail such-and-such a consequence?"

[76] Leibniz, *Die philosophischen Schriften*, vol. V, *Nouveaux essais sur l'entendement*, pp. 445-448.

This is the type of question we will describe as conjectural. In problems of qualification, we ask if such-and-such a fact can be qualified in such-and-such a way. In both cases it was unthinkable that more than one point of view could honestly be defended. And it was up to the philosophers, who carried out an impartial study of general problems, to provide and justify this point of view. The practical conclusions to be drawn from a study of the facts would impose themselves automatically on any reasonable mind.

Now from such a standpoint argumentation, as we understand it, has no purpose. The facts, the truths, or at least the probabilities, subject to the calculus of probabilities, triumph of themselves. The speaker plays no essential role, since his demonstrations are timeless, and there is no cause to distinguish among audiences, since all men are supposed to yield to what is objectively valid.

And it is unquestionably true, in the domain of purely formal sciences (such as symbolic logic or mathematics), as well as in the purely experimental domain, that this fiction which separates from the knowing subject the fact, the truth, or the probability has certain undeniable advantages. And, because this "objective" technique is successful in science, some are convinced that its use in other areas is equally legitimate. However, where no agreement exists, even among experts, can this affirmation that the advocated theses are the manifestation of a reality or of a truth before which unprejudiced minds must bow be anything but a device to be exorcised?

It seems to us, quite on the contrary, that there is less danger of oversimplifying and distorting the situation in which argumentation takes place by taking as a special, though very important, case that in which proof of the truth or of the probability of a thesis can be adduced within a domain which is formally, scientifically, or technically, circumscribed, with one accord, by all the interlocutors. Only then is the possibility of proving the *pro* and the *contra* the token of a contradiction which must be eliminated. In the other cases, the possibility of arguing in such a way as to reach opposite conclusions actually implies that we are not in this special case with which the sciences have made us familiar. This will always be the case when the argumentation aims at bringing about an action which is the result of a deliberate choice among several possibilities, without previous agreement on a criterion by which to evaluate the solutions.

Those philosophers who were indignant over the fact that one might not behave in accordance with the conclusion that appeared to be the only reasonable one, have been obliged to supplement their view of human nature by endowing man with passions and interests capable of opposing the teachings of reason. Returning to Pascal's distinction, to action on the mind we must add the means of acting on the will. In this perspective, whereas the task of the philosopher, inasmuch as he is addressing a particular audience, will be to silence this audience's particular passions in order to facilitate the "objective" consideration of the problems under discussion, the speaker aiming at a particular action, to be carried out at an opportune time, will, on the contrary, have to excite his audience so as to produce a sufficiently strong adherence, capable of overcoming both the unavoidable apathy and the forces acting in a direction divergent from that which is desired.

One might ask if the existence of two treatises on argumentation by Aristotle, *Topics* and *Rhetoric*, the first devoted to the theoretical discussion of theses, the second taking the particularities of audiences into account, has not favored this traditional distinction between action on the mind and action on the will. As for us, we believe that this distinction, which presents the first kind of action as completely impersonal and timeless and the second as completely irrational, is based on an error and leads to an impasse. The error is that of conceiving man as made up of a set of completely independent faculties. The impasse consists in removing all rational justification from action based on choice, and thus making the exercise of human freedom absurd. Argumentation alone (of which deliberation constitutes a special case) allows us to understand our decisions. This is why we will consider argumentation above all in its practical effects: oriented toward the future, it sets out to bring about some action or to prepare for it by acting, by discursive methods, on the minds of the hearers. This way of looking at it allows us to understand some of its special features, in particular the significance for it of the oratorical genre which the ancients called *epidictic*.

§ 11. *The Epidictic Genre*

Aristotle and all theoreticians inspired by him make room in their treatises on *Rhetoric*, alongside the deliberative and the legal types of oratory, for the epidictic genre.

The latter had, unquestionably, asserted itself vigorously. Most of the masterpieces of academic eloquence, the eulogies and panegyrics of a Gorgias or an Isocrates, show-pieces famous throughout Greece, were speeches of the epidictic kind. Unlike *political* and *legal* debates, real contests in which two opponents sought to gain the adherence on debated topics of an audience that would decide on the issue of a trial or on a course of action to be followed, epidictic speeches had nothing to do with all that. A single orator, who often did not even appear in public, but merely circulated his written composition, made a speech, which no one opposed, on topics which were apparently uncontroversial and without practical consequences. Whether it be a funeral eulogy, the eulogy of a city for the benefit of its inhabitants, or a speech on some subject devoid of current interest, such as the praise of a virtue or of a god, the audience, according to the theoreticians, merely played the part of spectators. After listening to the speaker, they merely applauded and went away. These speeches were a central attraction at festivals attended periodically by the inhabitants of a city or of a group of cities, and their most visible result was to shed luster on their authors. Such a show-piece was assessed as a work of artistic virtuosity, but this flattering appraisal was considered as an end, not as the consequence of the speaker's having reached a particular goal. The speech was regarded in the same light as a dramatic spectacle or an athletic contest, the purpose of which seemed to be the displaying of the performers. Because of these special characteristics, the Roman rhetoricians abandoned its study to the grammarians, while they trained their pupils in the two other kinds of oratory which were deemed relevant to practical eloquence.[77] To the theoreticians, it was a degenerate kind of eloquence with no other aim than to please and to enhance, by embellishing them, facts that were certain or, at least, uncontested.[78] It is not that the ancients saw no other purpose to epidictic discourse. According to Aristotle, the speaker sets himself different goals depending on the kind of speech he is making: in deliberative oratory, to counsel what is expedient, that is, the best; in legal oratory to establish what is just; and in epidictic oratory, which is concerned with praise and blame, his sole concern is with what is beautiful or ugly. It is a question, then, of recognizing values. But in the absence of the concept of value-judgment, and of that of intensity of adherence, the theoreticians of speech, from Aristotle on, readily confused the concept of the beautiful, as the object of the speech (which was, besides, equivalent to the concept of "good") with the aesthetic value of the speech itself.[79]

The epidictic genre of oratory thus seemed to have more connection with literature than with argumentation. One result is that the division into oratorical genres helped to bring about the later disinte-

---

[77] Quintilian, II, 1, 1, 2, 8, 9. Cf. Chaignet, *La rhétorique et son histoire*, p. 235.

[78] Cf. Gwynn, *Roman Education from Cicero to Quintilian*, pp. 98-99.

[79] Cf. Aristotle, *Rhetoric*, I, 3, 1358b 2-7, and 1358b 20-29. See also, discussion of the hearer as spectator in § 4, supra: The Audience as a Construction of the Speaker.

gration of rhetoric, as the first two genres were appropriated by philosophy and dialectics, while the third was included in literary prose. Whately, writing in the nineteenth century, will criticize Aristotle for having paid too much attention to epidictic rhetoric.[80]

Our own view is that epidictic oratory forms a central part of the art of persuasion, and the lack of understanding shown toward it results from a false conception of the effects of argumentation.

The effectiveness of an exposition designed to secure a proper degree of adherence of an audience to the arguments presented to it can be assessed only in terms of the actual aim the speaker has set himself. The intensity of the adherence sought is not limited to obtaining purely intellectual results, to a declaration that a certain thesis seems more probable than another, but will very often be reinforced until the desired action is actually performed. Demosthenes, considered to be one of the models of classical eloquence, spent most of his efforts not just in getting the Athenians to make decisions in conformity with his wishes, but in urging them, by every means at his command, to carry out the decisions once they were made. He wanted the Athenians to wage against Philip, not just "a war of decrees and letters, but a war of action."[81] He had constantly to remind his fellow-citizens that:

> ... a decree is worthless in itself, unless you add to it the willingness to carry out resolutely what you have decreed, [for] if decrees could either compel you to do what has to be done or accomplish themselves what they prescribe, you would not, after voting so many decrees, have achieved so little, or rather, nothing. ...[82]

The taking of a decision stands halfway, so to speak, between a disposition to take action and the action itself, between pure speculation and effective action.

The intensity of adherence, aiming at effective action, cannot be measured by the degree of probability attributed to the accepted argument, but rather by the obstacles overcome by the action and the sacrifices and choices it leads to and which can be justified by the adherence. The existence of an interval, whether long or short, between the time of adherence and the time of the action it was designed to stimulate[83] explains the intervention into the debate, after

---

[80] Whately, *Elements of Rhetoric* (Harper), pt. III, chap. I, § 6.

[81] Demosthenes, *First Philippic*, § 30.

[82] Demosthenes, *Third Olynthiac*, § 14.

[83] Passage of time generally, but not always, diminishes the effect of a speech. American psychologists were surprised to find a deferred or "sleeper" effect under some circumstances. Cf. Hovland, Lumsdaine, and Sheffield, *Experiments on*

it has supposedly ended, of values that had been overlooked or played down, or maybe of new elements that arose after the decision was made. This intervention, the likelihood of which is increased if in the meanwhile there has been a change in the situation, has a two-fold result: on the one hand it is hazardous to evaluate the effectiveness of a speech, and, secondly, the adherence gained by a speech can always advantageously be reinforced. It is in this perspective that epidictic oratory has significance and importance for argumentation, because it strengthens the disposition toward action by increasing adherence to the values it lauds. It is because the speaker's reputation is not the exclusive end of epidictic discourse, but at most a consequence, that a funeral eulogy can be pronounced without lack of decency, beside an open grave, or a Lenten sermon can have a purpose other than the renown of the preacher.

Efforts have been made to show that the funeral oration of the Greeks was transformed by Christianity into a means of edification.[84] In fact, the type of speech remains the same, but it is concerned with different values. These new values are incompatible with a striving for earthly glory. So great is the fear that sacred discourse may be regarded as a spectacle, that Bossuet in his *Sermon on the Word of God* develops a lengthy analogy between the pulpit and the altar in order to reach this conclusion:

> ... You should now be convinced that preachers of the Gospel do not ascend into pulpits to utter empty speeches to be listened to for amusement.[85]

And this is not a mere oratorical precaution, which might be just a pretense or the anticipation of an imaginary danger. There is no doubt that speeches—particularly those of the epidictic kind—are often considered as spectacles. La Bruyère writes derisively:

> ... They are so deeply moved and touched by *Theodorus'* sermon that they resolve in their hearts that it is even more beautiful than the last one he preached.[86]

Mass Communication, pp. 71, 182, 188-200. As to the interpretation of this phenomenon, see Hovland and Weiss, "The Influence of Source Credibility on Communication Effectiveness," *Public Opinion Quarterly*, 15 (1952), 635-650; Kelman and Hovland, "'Reinstatement' of the Communicator in Delayed Measurement of Opinion Change," *Journal of Abnormal and Social Psychology*, 48 (1953), 327-335; Weiss, "A 'Sleeper Effect' in Opinion Change," *Journal of Abnormal and Social Psychology*, 48 (1953), 173-180.

[84] Saulnier, "L'oraison funèbre au xvie siècle," *Bibliothèque d'Humanisme et Renaissance*, vol. X, pp. 126, 127.

[85] Bossuet, *Sur la Parole de Dieu, Sermons*, vol. II, pp. 148-149.

[86] La Bruyère, "Les caractères. De la chaire," 11, *Œuvres complètes*, p. 460.

Unlike the demonstration of a geometrical theorem, which establishes once and for all a logical connection between speculative truths, the argumentation in epidictic discourse sets out to increase the intensity of adherence to certain values, which might not be contested when considered on their own but may nevertheless not prevail against other values that might come into conflict with them. The speaker tries to establish a sense of communion centered around particular values recognized by the audience, and to this end he uses the whole range of means available to the rhetorician for purposes of amplification and enhancement.

In epidictic oratory every device of literary art is appropriate, for it is a matter of combining all the factors that can promote this communion of the audience. It is the only kind of oratory which immediately evokes literature, the only one that might be compared to the libretto of a cantata,[87] the one which is most in danger of turning into declamation, of becoming rhetoric in the usual and pejorative sense of the word.

The very concept of this kind of oratory—which, in Tarde's phrase, is more reminiscent of a procession than of a struggle[87a]—results in its being practised by those who, in a society, defend the traditional and accepted values, those which are the object of education, not the new and revolutionary values which stir up controversy and polemics. There is an optimistic, a lenient tendency in epidictic discourse which has not escaped certain discerning observers.[88] Being in no fear of contradiction, the speaker readily converts into universal values, if not eternal truths, that which has acquired a certain standing through social unanimity. Epidictic speeches are most prone to appeal to a universal order, to a nature, or a god that would vouch for the unquestioned, and supposedly unquestionable, values. In epidictic oratory, the speaker turns educator.

§ 12. *Education and Propaganda*

Study of the epidictic form of oratory, of its object and of the role of the orator in it, casts some light on the controversial question of the distinction between education and propaganda, a question to which so many theoreticians are currently paying attention. In a recent well-documented book, J. Driencourt[89] examines and rejects

[87] Boulanger, *Aelius Aristide*, p. 94.
[87a] Tarde, *La logique sociale*, pp. 439.
[88] Timon, *Livre des orateurs*, pp. 152-172.
[89] Driencourt, *La propagande, Nouvelle force politique*.

numerous attempts to distinguish between education and propaganda and reaches no satisfactory conclusion, through failure to set his study in the framework of a general theory of argumentation. The American specialist on these questions, Harold D. Lasswell, believes that the essential difference between the propagandist and the educator is that the latter deals with topics which are not an object of controversy to his audience.[90] The Catholic priest teaching the precepts of the Catholic religion to the children of his parish is doing the work of an educator, but he becomes a propagandist when, with the same object, he addresses the adult members of another religious group. But, in our view, there is more to it than that. Whereas the propagandist must, as a preliminary, gain the goodwill of his audience, the educator has been commissioned by a community to be the spokesman for the values it recognizes, and, as such, enjoys the prestige attaching to his office.

Now, a moment's reflection enables one to see that, in this respect, the speaker engaged in epidictic discourse is very close to being an educator. Since what he is going to say does not arouse controversy, since no immediate practical interest is ever involved, and there is no question of attacking or defending, but simply of promoting values that are shared in the community, the speaker, though he is assured in advance of the goodwill of his audience, must nevertheless have a high reputation. In the epidictic, more than in any other kind of oratory, the speaker must have qualifications for speaking on his subject and must also be skillful in its presentation, if he is not to appear ridiculous. For it is not his own cause or viewpoint that he is defending, but that of his entire audience. He is, so to speak, the educator of his audience, and if it is necessary that he should enjoy a certain prestige before he speaks, it is to enable him, through his own authority, to promote the values that he is upholding.

The values eulogized by the speaker must be ones deemed worthy of guiding our action for otherwise, as Isocrates wittily remarks:

> Is it right to compose speeches such that they will do the most good if they succeed in convincing no one among those who hear them?[91]

The purpose of an epidictic speech is to increase the intensity of adherence to values held in common by the audience and the speaker. The epidictic speech has an important part to play, for without such common values upon what foundation could deliberative and legal

[90] Lasswell, "The Study and Practice of Propaganda," in Lasswell, Casey, and Smith, *Propaganda and Promotional Activities, An Annotated Bibliography*, p. 3.
[91] Isocrates, *Busiris*, § 47.

speeches rest? Whereas these two kinds of speeches make use of dispositions already present in the audience, and values are for them means that make it possible to induce action, in epidictic speech, on the other hand, the sharing of values is an end pursued independently of the precise circumstances in which this communion will be put to the test.

Simone Weil, examining the means that the French in London might have used during World War II to rouse their countrymen in France, included among them

> ... expression, either officially or under official sanction, of some of the thoughts which, before ever being publicly expressed, were already in the hearts of the people, or in the hearts of certain active elements in the nation. ... If one hears this thought expressed publicly by some other person, and especially by some one whose words are listened to with respect, its force is increased a hundredfold and can sometimes bring about an inner transformation.[92]

What she brings out so clearly is precisely the role of epidictic speeches: appeal to common values, undisputed though not formulated, made by one who is qualified to do so, with the consequent strengthening of adherence to those values with a view to possible later action. Seen in this light, what was called propaganda from London was a good deal closer to education than to propaganda.

It is because epidictic discourse is intended to promote values on which there is agreement that one has an impression of misuse when in a speech of this kind someone takes up a position on a controversial question, turns the argument toward disputed values and introduces a discordant note on an occasion that is liable to promote communion, a funeral ceremony for instance. The same abuse exists when an educator turns propagandist.

In education, whatever its object, it is assumed that if the speaker's discourse does not always express truths, that is, theses accepted by everyone, it will at least defend values that are not a matter of controversy in the group which commissioned him. He is supposed to enjoy such a large measure of confidence that, unlike any other speaker, he need not adapt himself to his hearers and begin with propositions that they accept, but can make use of arguments of the kind called "didactic" by Aristotle[93] that his hearers adopt because "the Master said so." While a speaker engaged in popularizing ideas must become a propagandist for the speciality he is concerned with and must fit it into a framework of a common knowledge, when a

---

[92] Weil, *The Need for Roots*, pp. 190-191.
[93] Aristotle, *On Sophistical Refutations*, chap. 2, 165b.

teacher sets out to introduce a particular discipline he will begin by stating the principles particular to the discipline involved.[94] Similarly, when he is made responsible for instilling the values of a given society into really young children, the educator must proceed by means of affirmations, without entering into a discussion in which the pros and cons are freely debated. To do so would be contrary to the very spirit of primary education, as all discussion presupposes adherence at the outset to certain theses, failing which no argument is possible.[95]

Educational discourse, like the epidictic one, is not designed to promote the speaker, but for the creation of a certain disposition in those who hear it. Unlike deliberative and legal speeches, which aim at obtaining a decision to act, the educational and epidictic speeches create a mere disposition toward action, which makes them comparable to philosophical thought. This distinction between kinds of oratory, though not always easy to apply, offers the advantage, from our viewpoint, of providing a single, uniform framework for the study of argumentation: seen in this way, all argumentation is conceived only in terms of the action for which it paves the way or which it actually brings about. This is an additional reason for which we prefer to connect the theory of argumentation with rhetoric rather than with the ancients' dialectic; for the latter was confined to mere speculation, whereas rhetoric gave first place to the influence which a speech has on the entire personality of the hearers.

Epidictic discourse, as well as all education, is less directed toward changing beliefs than to strengthening the adherence to what is already accepted. Propaganda, on the other hand, profits from the spectacular aspect of the visible changes it seeks to, and sometimes does, bring about. Nevertheless, to the extent that education increases resistance to adverse propaganda, the two activities may advantageously be regarded as forces working in opposite directions. Moreover, as we shall see later, all argumentation can be considered as a substitute for the physical force which would aim at obtaining the same kind of results by compulsion.

§ 13. *Argumentation and Violence*

Argumentation is an action which always tends to modify a pre-existing state of affairs. This is true even of epidictic speech: this is why it is argumentative. But while the person who takes the in-

[94] Cf. § 26, infra: Agreements of Certain Special Audiences.

[95] Cf. Perelman, "Éducation et rhétorique," *Revue belge de psychologie et de pédagogie,* XIV (1952), 129-138.

itiative in a debate is comparable to an aggressor, the one who by speaking wishes to strengthen established values may be likened to the guardian of dikes under constant assault by the ocean.

Any society prizing its own values is therefore bound to promote opportunities for epidictic speeches to be delivered at regular intervals: ceremonies commemorating past events of national concern, religious services, eulogies of the dead, and similar manifestations fostering a communion of minds. The more the leaders of the group seek to increase their hold over its members' thought, the more numerous will be the meetings of an educational character, and some will go as far as to use threats or compulsion to make recalcitrants expose themselves to speeches that will impregnate them with the values held by the community. On the other hand, the group leaders will regard any attack on the officially recognized values as a revolutionary act, and, by the use of such measures as censorship, an index, and control over all means of communicating ideas, they will try to make it difficult, if not impossible, for their opponents to achieve the conditions preliminary to any argumentation. Their opponents, if they wish to continue the struggle, will have to resort to force.

One can indeed try to obtain a particular result either by the use of violence or by speech aimed at securing the adherence of minds. It is in terms of this alternative that the opposition between spiritual freedom and constraint is most clearly seen. The use of argumentation implies that one has renounced resorting to force alone, that value is attached to gaining the adherence of one's interlocutor by means of reasoned persuasion, and that one is not regarding him as an object, but appealing to his free judgment. Recourse to argumentation assumes the establishment of a community of minds, which, while it lasts, excludes the use of violence.[96] To agree to discussion means readiness to see things from the viewpoint of the interlocutor, to restrict oneself to what he admits, and to give effect to one's own beliefs only to the extent that the person one is trying to persuade is willing to give his assent to them. "Every justification," writes E. Dupréel, "is essentially a moderating act, a step toward greater communion of heart and mind."[97]

There are those who claim that resort to argumentation is sometimes, or even always, a pretense. According to them, there is only the semblance of argumentative debate, either because the speaker

<hr/>

[96] Cf. Weil, *Logique de la philosophie*, p. 24.
[97] "Fragments pour la théorie de la connaissance de M. E. Dupréel," *Dialectica*, 5 (1947), 76. As to rhetoric as the triumph of persuasion over brute force, see Toffanin, *Storia dell' umanesimo*, pp. 173-175.

imposes on his audience the obligation to listen to him or because the audience is content to make a show of hearing what he has to say. In either case, argumentation is simply a delusion, and the agreement reached is, in the first alternative, a disguised form of coercion and, in the second, a symbol of good will. This opinion as to the nature of argumentative discussion cannot be turned down *a priori*: yet it is difficult to give a satisfactory explanation of the resort to the mechanism of argument if, at least in some cases, there is no real persuasion. In fact, any community, whether national or international, makes provision for legal, political, or diplomatic institutions that will enable certain disputes to be settled without the need for resort to violence. However, it is an illusion to imagine that the conditions for this communion of minds occur naturally. Since they cannot refer to nature, the defenders of critical philosophy, such as Guido Calogero, see in the willingness to understand others, in the very principle of dialogue, the absolute basis for a liberal ethic.[98] Calogero's conception of the duty of dialogue is

> freedom to express our belief and to try and convert others to it, with the obligation to let others do the same with us, and to listen to them with the same willingness to understand their truths and make them ours that we demand of them for our own.[99]

This "duty of dialogue" put forward by Calogero as a compromise between the absolutism of Plato and the scepticism of Protagoras is certainly not a necessary truth, or even a statement that no one would contest. It is actually an ideal pursued by a very small number of people, those who attach more importance to thought than to action, and, even among them, this principle would be valid only for the nonabsolutist philosophers.

There are very few people who would allow that all questions should be submitted to discussion. Aristotle's view was that:

> Not every problem, not every thesis, should be examined, but only one which might puzzle one of those who need argument, not punishment or perception. For people who are puzzled to know whether one ought to honour the gods and love one's parents need punishment, while those who are puzzled to know whether snow is white or not need perception.[100]

---

[98] Calogero, "Why Do We Ask Why?" *Actes du XIe Congrès international de philosophie* (North-Holland) vol. XIV, p. 260.

[99] Calogero, "Vérité et liberté," *Actes du Xe Congrès international de philosophie* (North-Holland) p. 97. Published also in Italian, as an appendix to *Logo e Dialogo*, p. 195.

[100] Aristotle, *Topics*, I, 11, 105a.

He goes even further, and advises his readers not to uphold any proposition that is improbable or contrary to conscience: such as "everything is in motion" or "nothing is in motion," "pleasure is the good," or "to do injustice is better than to suffer it."[101] It is true that this is just advice addressed to dialecticians, but it reflects the common-sense attitude. Common sense admits the existence of unquestioned and unquestionable truths; it admits that certain rules are "beyond discussion," and that certain suggestions "do not deserve discussion." An established fact, a self-evident truth, an absolute rule, carry in themselves the affirmation of their unquestionable character, excluding the possibility of pro and con argumentation. Unanimous agreement on particular propositions can make it very difficult to question them. Remember the oriental tale in which only an innocent and artless child dared to declare, contrary to everyone else, that the king was naked and so broke the unanimity born out of fear to tell the truth.[102]

To hold an opinion deviating from that held by everyone else is to impair a social communion considered—and more often than not rightly considered—to be based on data of an objective character. Eighteenth century France and Germany furnish us with the example of an effort— utopian, but none the less impressive—to establish a catholicity of minds on the basis of a dogmatic rationalism, which would guarantee a stable social foundation to a humanity infused with rational principles. This attempt to solve, thanks to reason, all the problems set by action, though it did help to spread education, unfortunately failed because it quickly came to be realized that unanimity was fleeting, illusory, or even unthinkable.

Nevertheless, all societies are anxious to secure this unanimity, for they are aware of its value and force.[103] Thus opposition to an accepted value may lead a person to prison or a mental institution.

On occasion, the mere questioning of a decision may be severely punished. Demosthenes, in the *First Olynthiac*, alludes to the Athenian decree which made it a capital offense merely to propose legislation

---

[101] Aristotle, *ibid.*, VIII, 9, 160b.

[102] Cf. § 71, infra: Techniques of Severance and Restraint Opposed to the Act-Person Interaction.

[103] As to the tendency toward unanimity, see Festinger, "Informal Social Communication," *Psychological Review*, 57 (1950), 271-282, and the experiments reported by Festinger and Thibaut, "Interpersonal Communication in Small Groups," *Journal of Abnormal and Social Psychology*, 46 (1951), 92-99, and by Back, "Influence Through Social Communication," *Journal of Abnormal and Social Psychology*, 46 (1951), 9-23.

that would alter the law on the utilization of the surplus revenue of Athens.[104]

Even when discussion is allowed in principle, there are times when it is cut short because of the necessity for action. Regulation of debate may cover not only such preliminary matters as the competence of speakers and hearers, and limitation of subject matter, but may extend to the duration and order of speeches, to the way in which the discussion is to be terminated, and to the conditions under which it may be resumed. This last point is very important. Life in society requires indeed that the binding force of the decision be recognized. But there may be a renewal of discussion, and this is indeed often planned, so that there is no need to wait for a private decision depending on the initiative of an individual: the bicameral system is a good example.

Institutionalization is not always complete, and there are countless slight variations in practice. But, generally speaking, the reexamination of the question does not have to wait for a particular decision: further debate is often provided for and expected; its organization corresponds to a deep social necessity. Even where some initiating act is needed to resume debate, this is very often regulated; the institution itself invites one to take the initiative: the judicial system, with its courts of appeal and cassation, provides the most typical example of this.

We may observe that cases in which reexamination of a question is forbidden are not confined to the legal system. The principle of *res judicata* may be invoked even outside courts of law: thus, long before the impossibility of squaring the circle was demonstrated, any attempt to do so was regarded by the Paris Academy of Sciences as a matter that might no longer be discussed.

We must also add that in social life there is rarely a clear line of demarcation to indicate when resumption of debate is allowable and when forbidden. There is a large intermediate zone between absolute prohibition of renewed discussion and its unconditional allowance: this zone is mostly governed by extremely complex traditions and customs. This is a non-negligible aspect of the life of a community.

Prohibition of the resumption of a given debate may be just as much a sign of intolerance as prohibition to question certain problems. There is, however, one major difference: any final verdict, as long as it is conceived as such, will not be entirely detached from everything that preceded it. From the moment the decision is taken, the

---

[104] Demosthenes, *First Olynthiac*, § 19; for a full explanation of the allusion, see *Demosthenes* (Loeb), vol. 2, note to pp. 16, 17.

social life of the community carries with it not merely the decision itself, but also the arguments that preceded it.

This is tied in with a rather important theoretical problem: since the purpose of argumentation is to obtain an assent, it might be said that argumentation tends to destroy the conditions preliminary to future argumentation. But rhetorical proof is never compelling, the imposed silence is not to be regarded as definitive, if, in other respects, the conditions permitting argumentation are fulfilled.

The institutions that regulate discussion are important because there is a close connection between argumentative thought and the action it paves the way for or brings about. It is because of its relationship with action, because it never develops in a vacuum, but in a situation that is socially and psychologically determined, that argumentation involves the practical commitment of those who take part in it. The final section of this first part of the book will be devoted to the problems connected with this commitment.

§ 14. *Argumentation and Commitment*

The impossibility of regarding argumentation as an intellectual exercise entirely divorced from all preoccupations of a practical nature compels us to transpose certain concepts pertaining to knowledge that have been developed in a quite different philosophical perspective, such as the opposition between objective and subjective. Objectivity, as it relates to argumentation, must be reconsidered and reinterpreted if it is to have meaning in a conception that does not allow the separation of an assertion from the person who makes it.

Very often, when there is a debate in which parties considered to have an axe to grind uphold contrary theses, one hears people asking that appeal be made to third parties who will settle the debate by resorting to objective criteria. But has one merely to be entirely unconnected with the interests involved to have at one's disposal an objective criterion which everyone would have to recognize? If this were the case, would it not be simpler to gather in a volume all these objectively valid rules which would make it as simple to solve conflicts as problems of arithmetic? There are, in fact, such works: the various treatises on law and morality, the rules recognized in a great variety of fields. But, as we know, these treatises and rules do not enjoy universal validity, nor are they perfectly univocal. If differences can arise in good faith, in spite of the rules, it is either because at least one of the parties does not recognize the validity of some rule or because the accepted rules are susceptible to different interpretations. The difficulties are even greater when no rule governs the matter; when it is a question of choosing the best candidate for a responsible position and there is no agreement on the criteria that will make it possible to grade the available candidates; when the problem is to make the best political decision but the decision is not covered by any existing rule. Is it good enough to say that one has merely to adopt the viewpoint of someone on Sirius, and be perfectly disinterested, in order to be able to provide an objectively valid opinion? The inevitable reaction of the parties to the controversy in the face of such an intrusion would be surprise, if not indignation, that a stranger to the debate should dare to interfere in something that is none of his business. Indeed, since these discussions must lead to a decision, bring about an action, the fact of being a disinterested spectator does not give the right to participate in the discussion and influence the outcome. Contrary to what happens in science, where all that is necessary for the solution of a problem is knowledge of the techniques that enable the solution to be reached, interference in a controversy whose outcome will affect a specific group may be made only by one who is a member of, or closely bound up with, the group in question. Where an opinion influences action, objectivity is no longer sufficient, unless one means by objectivity the viewpoint of a wider group embracing both the opponents and the "neutral." The latter is qualified to judge not because he is neutral—anyone can reproach him with this neutrality in the name of common principles of right or justice—but because he is impartial: being *impartial* is not being *objective*, it consists of belonging to the same group as those one is judging, without having previously decided in favor of any one of them. In many disputes, the problem of knowing who is qualified to interfere, indeed to judge, is a painful and delicate one, because many will have taken sides, and others will not be members of the group. When it was a question of judging the attitude of the French officers who put their loyalty as soldiers above continuance of the war against the Germans in 1940, Frenchmen were in a bad position to judge because they were biased, and so were foreigners, particularly neutrals, because they did not belong to the group involved.

Impartiality, if it is conceived as the impartiality of a spectator, may appear to be the absence of any attraction, an inquiry entirely divorced from participation in the discussion, an attitude transcending the dispute. But if the impartiality is that of an actor in events, then it stands for a balance of forces, maximum attention to the interests at issue, but with this attention equally divided among the different points of view.[105]

---

[105] Cf. Garlan, *Legal Realism and Justice*, p. 78.

Accordingly, in spheres where thought and action are closely mingled, impartiality stands between the objectivity which fails to qualify the third party for interference and the partisan spirit which positively disqualifies him.

Under the sway of an abstract objectivism, there has too often been a failure to appreciate the fact that thought which leads to action has a different status than the statements integrated in a scientific system. On the other hand, it is essential to foresee the possibility of dissociating our beliefs from our interests and passions.

It is almost commonplace to insist on the way in which our hopes and desires determine our beliefs. As Pascal observed:

> All men whatsoever are almost always led into belief not because a thing is proved but because it is pleasing.[106]

He sought to explain this phenomenon by insisting on the fact that:

> Things are true or false according to the aspect in which we look at them. The will, which prefers one aspect to another, turns away the mind from considering the qualities of all that it does not like to see; and thus the mind, moving in accord with the will, stops to consider the aspect which it likes and so judges by what it sees.[107]

William James justified the beliefs that further our desires, as by strengthening them they make the desires more likely to be fulfilled.[108] Other more rationalistic writers discount the effect of this desirability factor, regarding it as responsible for the irrational character of our beliefs.[109] But both views merely represent hypotheses of a general nature, which are difficult to verify in the absence of criteria for an "objectively based" belief. Thus a study of the kind made by Lund,[110] showing a correlation of 0.88 between the desirability of given theses and the degree of conviction they inspired, while the correlation between conviction and knowledge, or between conviction and elements of proof, was low, has been criticized in ironical terms by Bird, the American sociologist:

> I fear, however, that analysis of the coefficients of correlation leaves much to the imagination, so that desire may have determined the belief that desire determines belief.[111]

---

[106] Pascal, *On Geometrical Demonstration*, Section II: "Concerning the Art of Persuasion," GBWW, vol. 33, p. 440.

[107] Pascal, *Pensées*, GBWW, vol. 33, p. 191.

[108] James, *Essays in Pragmatism*, First Essay: "The Sentiment of Rationality" (1960), p. 31.

[109] Crawshay-Williams, *The Comforts of Unreason*, pp. 8 et seq.

[110] Lund, "The Psychology of Belief," *Journal of Abnormal and Social Psychology*, XX, (1925) 13-21.

[111] Bird, *Social Psychology*, p. 211.

Whenever it is necessary to refute the accusation that our desires have determined our beliefs, it is essential that we furnish proof, not of our objectivity, which is not possible, but of our impartiality, and that we indicate the circumstances in which, in a similar situation, we acted contrary to what might appear to be our interest, specifying, if possible, the rule or criteria we are following, which would be valid for a wider group comprising all the interlocutors, and identifiable, at the limit, with the universal audience.

We must not, however, forget that, even in this case, we are putting forward our own conception of the universal audience and that the theses we claim should be valid for everybody may have their detractors who are not necessarily stupid or dishonest. Failure to admit this would lay us open to the charge of fanaticism. There can be no question of fanaticism where we are dealing with truths established by appealing to criteria which are recognized as beyond discussion, since we are not then in a situation where it is possible to resort to argumentation. The fanatic is a person who adheres to a disputed thesis for which no unquestionable proof can be furnished, but who nevertheless refuses to consider the possibility of submitting it for free discussion and, consequently, rejects the preliminary conditions which would make it possible to engage in argumentation on this topic.

Equating adherence to a thesis with recognition of its absolute truth sometimes leads, not to fanaticism, but to scepticism. The man who requires that argumentation provide demonstrative proof of compelling force and will not be content with less in order to adhere to a thesis misunderstands as much as the fanatic the essential characteristic of argumentative procedure. For the very reason that argumentation aims at justifying choices, it cannot provide justifications that would tend to show that there is no choice, but that only one solution is open to those examining the problem.

Since rhetorical proof is never a completely necessary proof, the thinking man who gives his adherence to the conclusions of an argumentation does so by an act that commits him and for which he is responsible. The fanatic accepts the commitment, but as one bowing to an absolute and irrefragable truth; the sceptic refuses the commitment under the pretext that he does not find it sufficiently definitive. He refuses adherence because his idea of adherence is similar to that of the fanatic: both fail to appreciate that argumentation aims at a choice among possible theses; by proposing and justifying the hierarchy of these theses, argumentation seeks to make the decision a rational one. This role of argumentation in decision-making is denied by the sceptic and the fanatic. In the absence of compelling reason, they both are inclined to give violence a free hand, rejecting personal commitment.

PART TWO

The Starting Point of Argumentation

CHAPTER 1

Agreement

§ 15. *The Premises of Argumentation*

Our analysis of argumentation will deal first with what is taken as the starting point of arguments and afterwards with the way in which arguments are developed through a whole set of associative and disassociative processes. This division of the subject is indispensable to our examination and should not be misunderstood. The unfolding as well as the starting point of the argumentation presuppose indeed the agreement of the audience. This agreement is sometimes on explicit premises, sometimes on the particular connecting links used in the argument or on the manner of using these links: from start to finish, analysis of argumentation is concerned with what is supposed to be accepted by the hearers. On the other hand, the actual choice of premises and their formulation, together with the adjustments involved, are rarely without argumentative value: it is a preparation for argument which not only establishes the elements but constitutes the first step in the utilization of these elements for persuasive purposes.

When a speaker selects and puts forward the premises that are to serve as foundation for his argument, he relies on his hearers' adherence to the propositions from which he will start. His hearers may, however, refuse their adherence, either because they do not adhere to what the speaker presents to them as being accepted, or they may see that his choice of premises is one-sided, or they may be shocked by the tendentious way in which the premises were advanced. Since the criticism of a single statement may bear on three different aspects, premises will be discussed in three chapters, devoted respectively to *the agreement on the premises, the choice of the premises,* and *the presentation of the premises.*

We shall begin by considering the question of what sort of agreements can serve as premises. Our treatment of this question will obviously not attempt to draw a complete list of everything capable of constituting an object of belief or adherence: we shall merely inquire into the types of objects of agreement that play different roles in the arguing process. We think it convenient to divide these objects of agreement into two classes: the first concerning the *real*, comprising facts, truths, and presumptions, the other concerning the *preferable*, comprising values, hierarchies, and lines of argument relating to the preferable.

The conceptions people form of the real can vary widely, depending on the philosophic views they profess. However, everything in argumentation that is deemed to relate to the real is characterized by a claim to validity vis-à-vis the universal audience. On the contrary, all that pertains to the preferable, that which determines our choices and does not conform to a preexistent reality, will be connected with a specific viewpoint which is necessarily identified with some particular audience, though it may be a large one.

It is open to anyone to question the merits of our scheme for classifying types of objects of agreement, but we think it difficult, without recourse to such a scheme, to attempt a technical analysis of argumentation as it actually occurs. Each audience will, of course, allow only a certain number of objects belonging to each of the various types. But objects of each type occur in the most varied kinds of argumentation. Further, these objects turn up also as types of objects of disagreement, that is, as points round which a dispute may arise.

Besides the question of agreements, we shall deal, in this first chapter, with considerations of two different orders: we will examine the state of the premises, either in view of special agreements that govern certain audiences, or in view of the state of the discussion. Considerations of the first order are rather static, inasmuch as they involve studying the character of the agreements of certain set audiences; the others are of a more dynamic nature, since they have to do with the agreements as they are linked to the progress of the discussion. Since we are concerned with premises, our interest in this dynamic process will focus on the speaker's effort to detect the explicit or implicit manifestations of an adherence on which he can depend.

a) TYPES OF OBJECTS OF AGREEMENT

§ 16. *Facts and Truths*

Objects of agreement relating to the real can be divided into two main groups: the first consists of facts and truths, the second, of presumptions. It is not possible—nor would it be consistent with our purpose—to define "fact" in a way that would enable us, at any time or place, to classify this or that concrete datum as a fact. On the contrary, we must stress that, in argumentation, the notion of "fact" is uniquely characterized by the idea that is held of agreements of a certain type relating to certain data, those which refer to an objective reality and, in Poincaré's words, designate essentially "what is common to several thinking beings, and could be common to all."[1] This quotation suggests at once what we have called the agreement of the universal audience. The way in which the universal audience is thought of, and the incarnations of this audience that are recognized, are thus determining factors in deciding what, in a particular case, will be considered to be a fact, characterized by adherence of the universal audience, an adherence such as to require no further strengthening. Facts are withdrawn, at least for the time being, from argumentation, that is to say, there is no need to increase the intensity of the adherence or to generalize it, and it requires no justification. For the individual, adherence will simply be a subjective reaction to something that is binding on everybody.

From the standpoint of argumentation, we are confronted with a fact only if we can postulate uncontroverted, universal agreement with respect to it. But it follows that no statement can be assured of definitively enjoying this status, because the agreement can always be called in question later,[2] and one of the parties to the debate may refuse to qualify his opponent's affirmation as a fact. Normally, there are thus two ways in which an event can lose the status of fact: either doubts may have been raised within the audience to which it was presented, or the audience may have been expanded through the addition of new members who are recognized as having the ability to judge the event and who will not grant that a fact is involved. The latter process comes into play as soon as it can effectively be shown

[1] Poincaré, *La valeur de la science*, Introduction, p. 65.
[2] Cf. Perelman and Olbrechts-Tyteca, *Rhétorique et philosophie*, pp. 2 et seq. and Perelman, *The Idea of Justice and the Problem of Argument*, pp. 169 et seq.

that the audience admitting the fact is only a particular audience and that its views are in opposition to those of an enlarged audience.

We do not hope to find a criterion that enables us, under all circumstances and independently of the hearers' attitude, to affirm that something is a fact. Nevertheless, we may recognize that there are certain conditions favoring this agreement, rendering the fact easily defensible in the face of an opponent's mistrust or ill will. This will be the case, in particular, when there is agreement on conditions for verification. However, by the time such an agreement has to be brought into effective operation, argumentation is in full swing. A fact serving as premise is an uncontroverted fact.

Mere questioning of a statement is thus sufficient to destroy its privileged status. However, if an interlocutor wishes to combat the prestige attaching to what has been admitted as a fact, he will not be satisfied in most cases with a simple denial that might be considered just ridiculous. He will endeavor to justify his attitude either by showing the incompatibility of the statement in question with other facts and attacking it for its inconsistency with the coherence of reality or by showing that the so-called fact is simply the conclusion of an argument which, by its very nature, is not compelling.

A fact loses its status as soon as it is no longer used as a possible starting point, but as the conclusion of an argumentation. It can recover this status only by being detached from the context of the argument; in other words, there must once again be an agreement that does not depend on the terms of the argument for its proof. It is to be observed that a fact's loss of status, due to its insertion in an argumentative context of which it is no longer the basis but one of the conclusions, often occurs in philosophy, where the construction of a system of argumentation often leads to connecting facts—previously casually admitted as such—with a line of argument that claims to establish them.

Accepted facts may be either observed facts—this is perhaps the case for most premises—or supposed, agreed facts, facts that are possible or probable. There is thus a considerable mass of elements that is compelling to the hearer or which the speaker strives to make compelling. They may all be challenged and, so, lose their status as facts. But, as long as they enjoy this status, they must conform to those structures of the real that are accepted by the audience, and they will have to be defended against other facts that may compete with them in the same argumentative context.

Everything just said about *facts* is equally applicable to what are called *truths*. The term "facts" is generally used to designate objects of precise, limited agreement, whereas the term "truths" is preferably applied to more complex systems relating to connections between facts. They may be scientific theories or philosophic or religious conceptions that transcend experience.

As Piaget has pointed out,[3] currently known psychological data will not warrant our conceiving the possibility of arriving at isolated facts. Nonetheless, the distinction between *facts* and *truths* seems to us helpful and legitimate for our purpose, since it corresponds to the usual practice in argumentation of relying at one point on facts and at another on systems of wider import. We have no desire to settle, once and for all, the philosophic problem of the relationship between facts and truths: this relationship characterizes the conceptions of various audiences. For some people, fact is opposed to theoretical truth as the contingent is to the necessary, for others, as the real is to the schematic. It is also possible to so conceive their relationship that the statement of a fact is a truth and that any truth enunciates a fact.

When a primacy either of facts or of truths follows from the way in which their relationship is considered, facts and truths cannot be utilized on quite the same footing as a starting point in argumentation. Only one of the two is considered to have the full agreement of the universal audience. It must be remembered, however, that the primacy of one over the other is usually invoked only when the two types of objects are confronted. In everyday practice, on the other hand, facts and systems can both equally be considered as a starting point for argumentation.

In most cases, facts and truths (scientific theories or religious truths, for instance) are used as separate objects of agreement, between which there are, however, connections that enable a transfer of the agreement to be made: certainty of fact A combined with belief in system S leads to the certainty of fact B; in other words, acceptance of fact A plus theory S amount to acceptance of B.

The connection between A and B, instead of being regarded as established, may be only a probability: it will be admitted that the appearance of A entails, with a certain degree of probability, the appearance of B. When the degree of probability of B can be calculated in terms of facts and of a theory that are the subject of unquestioned agreement, the probability in question is the object of an agreement of exactly the same nature as the agreement concerning the definite fact. This is why we treat agreements on the probability of events

---

[3] Piaget, *Traité de logique*, p. 30.

of a certain kind as equivalent to agreements on facts, insofar as agreements of the former kind involve probabilities that are calculable.

Kneebone[4] quite rightly stresses, in this connection, that "likelihood" attaches to propositions and especially to inductive conclusions, and hence is not a measurable quantity, whereas probability is a numerical relation between two propositions that apply to specific, well-defined, and simple data of an empirical nature. The domain of probability is then connected with that of facts and truths, and it is in terms of these that it is characterized for each audience.

§ 17. *Presumptions*

In addition to admitting facts and truths, all audiences admit presumptions. But, although presumptions also enjoy universal agreement, adherence to them falls short of being maximum, and hearers expect their adherence to be reinforced at a given moment by other elements. In fact, those who admit a presumption ordinarily reckon on this reinforcement.

Preliminary argumentation may strive to establish the existence of certain presumptions, just as it may strive to show an audience that it is faced with a fact. But as it is in the very nature of presumptions to be reinforced, an important distinction must be made. Whereas there is always a risk that justification of a fact will lessen its status, this is not true of presumptions. In order to preserve their status, there is, accordingly, no need to detach them from a possible preliminary argumentation. However, in most cases, presumptions are admitted straight away as a starting point for argumentation. We shall even see that certain presumptions can be imposed upon audiences governed by conventions.

Use of presumptions yields statements whose likelihood is not derived from a calculation based on factual data and could not be so derived even if the calculation were perfected. It is true, of course, that the boundary between likelihood and probability that can be calculated (at least theoretically) may vary with different philosophic conceptions. But, in order to reduce statements resulting from presumptions to statements with calculable probability, it would, in any case, be necessary to change the formulation and the scope of the argument. Let us mention some common presumptions: the presumption that the quality of an act reveals the quality of the person responsible for it; the presumption of natural trustfulness by which

---

[4] Kneebone, "Induction and Probability," *Proceedings of the Aristotelian Society*, New Series, L (1950), 36.

our first reaction is to accept what someone tells us as being true, which is accepted as long and insofar as we have no cause for distrust; the presumption of interest leading us to conclude that any statement brought to our knowledge is supposed to be of interest to us; the presumption concerning the sensible character of any human action.

In each particular instance, presumptions are connected with what is normal and likely. A more general presumption than all those that we have mentioned is the existence, for each category of facts, and particularly for each category of behavior, of an aspect regarded as normal and capable of serving as a basis for reasoning. The existence of this connection between presumptions and what is normal is itself a general presumption accepted by all audiences. Until there is proof to the contrary, it is presumed that the normal will occur, or has occurred, or rather that the normal can safely be taken as a foundation in reasoning.[5] Is this foundation one that can be defined statistically in terms of rate of occurrence? Doubtless, it cannot. And that is one reason why we are compelled to talk about presumptions and not about calculated probability. The most that can be said is that, broadly speaking, the idea we form of the normal, in our reasonings, oscillates between certain different aspects. (We exclude cases in which the calculation of frequency of occurrence is effectively carried out, and the common concept of what is normal is abandoned in favor of the idea of distribution characteristics.) Using statistical language to describe these different aspects, we may say that the concept of *normal* usually covers simultaneously, and with a different emphasis in each particular case, the ideas of mean, of mode, and of more or less extensive portion of a distribution.

The normal, where the capacity required of a driver is concerned, is everything exceeding a minimum; in the case of a vehicle that has knocked down a pedestrian, it is everything below a maximum. In other cases, attention centers on the whole central portion of a distribution curve, and the normal is opposed to the exceptional. Thus, if we suppose a binomial distribution, the normal usually refers to the mode, together with a certain margin in both directions.

Where characteristics of a population (in the broad sense of the term, for all sorts of elements, animate or inanimate, objects or behavior) are concerned, it is the *mode* rather than the *mean* which is dominant in all presumptions based on what is usual. The *mode* is likewise the point of comparison in estimates of what is *big* or *small*. It forms also the basis of all reasoning concerning behavior, of the

[5] Cf. Gonseth, "La notion du normal," *Dialectica*, 3 (1947), 243-252.

presumptions that may justify *Einfühlung* which are so profusely used by orators when they beg their listeners to put themselves in the place of those for whom they are pleading.

Although a presumption based on the normal can rarely be reduced to an evaluation of frequencies or to the use of definite characteristics of statistical distribution, it is nevertheless useful to clarify the usual concept of "normal" by showing that it always depends on a reference group, that is, on the whole category for whose benefit it was established. It is to be observed that this group—which is often a social group—is hardly ever explicitly described, perhaps because interlocutors rarely think about it; it is clear, however, that all presumptions based on what is normal imply agreement on this reference group.

In most cases, this group is highly unstable. Indeed if certain individuals diverge in behavior from what is regarded as normal, their conduct may modify the norm (statistically, we will say it may modify the mean). But if a person deviates beyond certain limits, he will be excluded from the group, and thus, the reference group will be modified. The individual will be considered mad and be excluded from the community, or he will be regarded as too ill bred to be admitted to the company of respectable people. The following dialogue seems to involve an exclusion of this kind:

> "You, sir," said Bloch, turning to M. d'Argencourt, to whom he had been made known, with the rest of the party, on that gentleman's arrival, "you are a Dreyfusard, of course; they all are, abroad."
> "It is a question that concerns only the French themselves, don't you think?" replied M. d'Argencourt with that peculiar form of insolence which consists in ascribing to the other person an opinion which one must, obviously, know that he does not hold since he has just expressed one directly its opposite.[6]

The interlocutor is excluded from the ranks of well-bred persons for whom this opinion is normal, so that one can legitimately presume that they hold it.

The reference group, besides being unstable, may be considered in different ways. Sometimes one thinks of the real or fictitious group acting in a certain manner, sometimes of the common opinion held with respect to those who act in this way or of the opinion of those regarded as spokesmen for this common opinion or of what is commonly considered to be the opinion of these spokesmen. These different conceptions of the reference group will often work against one another in argumentation.

Variations in the reference group enter into all legal argument. The longstanding opposition between argument from the motives

[6] Proust, *The Guermantes Way*, pt. I, pp. 337-338.

of the crime and argument from the conduct of the accused corresponds to two different reference groups. The reference group relating to motives is wider; that relating to conduct is more specific in the sense that the presumptions are derived from what is normal for men who, all their life, have behaved like the accused.

In general, any addition to the available information may bring about a change in the reference group and thereby modify our conception of what is extraordinary or shocking. It will often be the task of the speaker to promote such a modification by communicating fresh information. When counsel for the accused urges extenuating circumstances, he is suggesting a change in the reference group: thenceforth the presumed behavior, which will serve as criterion for judging the defendant, will be the normal behavior of this new reference group. Again, if the circle of our relationships is extended, natural gifts that seem to us extraordinary no longer appear so, because we shall have occasion to encounter them more often. Conversely, a death among the inhabitants of a big city is an absolutely routine matter, but, if it strikes the small circle of our acquaintances, we find it extraordinary. Opposition between the two reference groups enables some to be astonished that a mortal being should be dead and others to be astonished by this astonishment.

Since, then, presumptions attached to the normal are an object of agreement, there must also be a subjacent agreement with respect to the reference group for this normal. Most arguments striving to show that it is extraordinary and contrary to any presumption that man should have been able to find a world scaled to his needs, assume (without usually saying so) that the reference group, that of habitable worlds, is extremely limited. On the other hand, an astronomer, such as Hoyle, who considers that there are exceedingly numerous habitable worlds, can humorously remark that, if our world were not habitable, we would be somewhere else.[7]

Often the very concepts used in argumentation assume that the normal is determined by one or more reference groups, without this being explicit. This is so, for instance, with the juridical concept of negligence: the existence of the different groups will emerge only from the discussions relating to this concept.

Agreement based on the presumption of the normal is supposed to have the same order of validity for the universal audience as agreement upon established facts and upon truths so that agreement on presumptions is often not easily distinguishable from agreement on facts. At a given moment, presumed facts are treated as equivalent

---

[7] Hoyle, *The Nature of the Universe*, p. 90.

to observed facts and can serve, with equal authority, as a premise for argument. This is only true, of course, until the presumption is subjected to discussion. There is thus a jump, whereby the normal comes to coincide with something unique, that happened only once and will never happen again. It is to be observed that, by specifying in more and more detail the conditions that must be satisfied by the members of the reference group, one might actually end up by reducing the group to a single individual. Nevertheless, even then, the presumed behavior of this individual and his actual behavior do not merge, and the strange jump of which we have spoken, making it possible to reason on presumed facts in the same way as on observed facts, still remains.

§ 18. Values

Besides facts, truths, and presumptions, characterized by the agreement of the universal audience, our classification scheme must also find a place for objects of agreement in regard to which only the adherence of particular groups is claimed. These objects are the values, hierarchies, and *loci* of the preferable.

Agreement with regard to a value means an admission that an object, a being, or an ideal must have a specific influence on action and on disposition toward action and that one can make use of this influence in an argument, although the point of view represented is not regarded as binding on everybody. The existence of values, as objects of agreement that make possible a communion with regard to particular ways of acting, is connected with the idea of multiplicity of groups. In antiquity, statements about what we term values, insofar as they were not treated as unquestionable truths, were included with any sort of likely statement in the undifferentiated group of *opinions*. They were still considered in this way by Descartes when he laid the maxims of his provisional code of morals:

> And thus since often enough in the actions of life no delay is permissible, it is very certain that, when it is beyond our power to discern the opinions which carry most truth, we should follow the most probable; ...and afterwards consider it as no longer doubtful in its relationship to practice, but as very true and very certain, inasmuch as the reason which caused us to determine upon it is known to be so.[8]

In this maxim, Descartes shows well the precarious nature of values, as well as their indispensability. He speaks of opinions that are probable,

---

[8] Descartes, *Discourse on the Method*, GBWW, vol. 31, p. 49.

but what is really involved is a choice with reference to what we would today call values. What he calls a very true and very certain reason is indeed, until philosophic certainty is attained, the apparently unquestionable value attaching to efficacious human conduct.

Values enter, at some stage or other, into every argument. In reasoning of a scientific nature, they are generally confined to the beginning of the formulation of the concepts and rules that constitute the system concerned and, insofar as the reasoning aims at the truth value, to the conclusion. As far as possible, the actual unfolding of the argument is free from values, and this exclusion is at a maximum in the exact sciences. But in the fields of law, politics, and philosophy, values intervene as a basis for argument at all stages of the developments. One appeals to values in order to induce the hearer to make certain choices rather than others and, most of all, to justify those choices so that they may be accepted and approved by others.

In a discussion, it is not possible to escape from a value simply by denying it. Just as someone who contests that something is a fact must give reasons for his allegation ("I don't see that," which is the same as saying, "I see something else"), so, when a value is in question, a person may disqualify it, subordinate it to others, or interpret it but may not reject all values as a whole: this would amount to leaving the realm of discussion to enter that of force. The gangster who rates his personal safety above anything else can do so without any need for explanation as long as he confines himself to the domain of action. But, if he wants to justify this primacy to others or even to himself, he must acknowledge the other values marshaled against it in order to be able to fight them. In this respect, values are comparable to facts: for, when one of the interlocutors puts forward a value, one must argue to get rid of it, under pain of refusing the discussion; and in general, the argument will imply that other values are accepted.

Various objections are raised to our conception that values are objects of agreement which do not claim the adherence of the universal audience.

In making this distinction, are not more fundamental differences overlooked? Is it not enough to say that facts and truths express the real, whereas values are concerned with an attitude toward the real? But, if the attitude toward the real were universal, it could not be distinguished from truths. It is only its nonuniversal aspect that makes it possible to confer on it a status of its own. It is indeed hard to see how purely formal criteria can be relevant. For a statement can be understood as relating to what is commonly considered a fact or to what is considered a value, depending on its place in the speech, on what it enunciates, refutes, or corrects. Also, the status of statements evolves: when inserted into a system of beliefs for which universal validity is claimed, values may be treated as facts or truths. In the course of the argumentation, and sometimes by a rather slow process, it may perhaps come to be recognized that one is dealing with objects of agreement that cannot make a claim to the adherence of the universal audience.

But if this is, as we claim, the characteristic of values, what about such things as the *True*, the *Good*, the *Beautiful*, and the *Absolute*, which are readily considered as universal or absolute values?

The claim to universal agreement, as far as they are concerned, seems to us to be due solely to their generality. They can be regarded as valid for a universal audience only on condition that their content not be specified; as soon as we try to go into details, we meet only the adherence of particular audiences.

According to E. Dupréel, universal values deserve to be called "values of persuasion" because they are

> *means of persuasion* which, from a sociological viewpoint, *are that and no more than that*; they are, as it were, spiritual tools which can be completely separated from the material they make it possible to shape, anterior to the moment it is used, and remaining intact after use, available, as before, for other occasions.[9]

This conception displays extremely well the role of these values in argumentation. These tools, as Dupréel calls them, can be used for all audiences: the particular values can always be connected to the universal values and serve to make the latter more specific. The actual audience will be able to consider itself all the more close to a universal audience as the particular value seems to fade before the universal value it determines. It is thus by virtue of their being vague that these values appear as universal values and lay claim to a status similar to that of facts. To the extent that they are precisely formulated, they are simply seen to conform to the aspirations of particular groups. Their role is accordingly to justify choices on which there is not unanimous agreement by inserting these choices in a sort of empty frame with respect to which a wider agreement exists. Though this agreement is reached over an empty form, it is nonetheless of considerable significance: it is evidence of the fact that one has decided to transcend particular agreements, at least in intention, and that one recognizes the importance attaching to the universal agreement which these values make it possible to achieve.

[9] Dupréel, *Sociologie générale*, pp. 181-182.

§ 19. *Abstract Values and Concrete Values*

In argumentation concerning values, there is a fundamental, but too often neglected, distinction to be made between abstract values, such as justice or truth, and concrete values, such as France or the Church. A concrete value is one attaching to a living being, a specific group, or a particular object, considered as a unique entity. There is a close connection between the value attached to what is concrete and to what is unique: by displaying the unique character of something we automatically increase its value. By revealing to us the unique character of certain beings, groups, or moments in history, the romantic writers have brought about, even in philosophical thought, a reaction against abstract rationalism, a reaction characterized by the prominent position assigned to that preeminently concrete value— the human person. Though Western morality, insofar as it is based on Greco-Roman ideas, values most the obedience to rules that are valid for all people and under all circumstances, there exist virtues and forms of behavior that can be conceived only in relation to concrete values. Such notions as obligation, fidelity, loyalty, solidarity, and discipline are of this kind. Likewise Confucius' five universally binding obligations—between rulers and ruled, father and son, husband and wife, older brother and younger brother, friend and friend[10]— reflect the importance attached to personal relations among beings who constitute concrete values for one another.

Whatever the dominant values may be in a cultural milieu, the life of the mind cannot avoid relying on abstract values as well as concrete ones. It seems that there have always been people who attach more importance to one set than to the other; perhaps they form characterial families. In any case their distinctive trait would not be complete neglect of values of one kind, but subordination of these values to those of the other. We may contrast Erasmus who preferred an unjust peace to a just war with the man who rated the abstract value of truth higher than Plato's friendship.

Argumentation is based, according to the circumstances, now on abstract values, now on concrete values: it is sometimes difficult to perceive the role played by each. When a person says that men are equal because they are children of the same God, he seems to be re-

---

[10] Kou Hong Ming and Borrey, *Le Catéchisme de Confucius*, p. 69, following the *Tchoung-young*, chap. XX, § 7, Pauthier, *Confucius et Mencius*, p. 83. See also the *Hsiao King* or classic of filial piety in Legge, *The Sacred Books of the East*, vol. 3, p. 482.

lying on a concrete value to find an abstract value, that of equality; but it could also be said that really only the abstract value is expressed, by appealing, through analogy, to a concrete relationship; in spite of the use of *because*, the starting point would lie in the abstract value.

This motion back and forth from concrete to abstract values is nowhere better seen than in reasonings involving God, considered both as absolute abstract value and perfect Being. Is God perfect because he is the incarnation of all abstract values? Is a quality perfection because certain conceptions of God make it possible to grant perfection to that quality? In this matter it is difficult to establish any kind of priority. The contradictory positions taken by Leibniz on this question are very instructive. He knows God is perfect, but he wishes that this perfection should be justifiable and that all God's decisions should not be considered good solely for the very reason that they are God's decisions.[11]

The universality of the principle of sufficient reason requires that there be a sufficient reason, a conformity to a rule, justifying God's choice. On the other hand, belief in the perfection of God precedes any proof that Leibniz may be able to provide and is the starting point for his theology. For a great number of thinkers, God is the model who must be followed in all things. Thus Kenneth Burke was able to draw a lengthy list of all the abstract values which found their origin in the perfect Being.[12]

Some ideologies unwilling to recognize God as the foundation of all values have had to turn to notions of a different order, such as the State or Mankind. These notions also can be conceived either as concrete values of the personal type or as the outcome of reasonings based on abstract values.

The same reality, a social group, for instance, will sometimes be treated as a concrete value and as an entity and sometimes as a multiplicity of individuals which will be opposed to one or several others, by means of argumentations in terms of number which are completely removed from any idea of concrete value. That which is, under certain circumstances, a concrete value is not always such: for a value to be concrete, it must be envisaged in its aspect of unique reality; to say that a particular value is, once and for all, a concrete value is to take an arbitrary stand.

Concrete values are most frequently used as the foundation of abstract values, and conversely. In order to establish which conduct

---

[11] Leibniz, *Discourse on Metaphysics*, pp. 2-3.
[12] Burke, *A Rhetoric of Motives* (Braziller) pp. 299-301.

is virtuous, we often turn to a model whom we strive to imitate. The relationship of friendship and the actions it prompts provide Aristotle with a criterion for evaluation:

> Also, the things which we like to do to our friend are more desirable than those we like to do to the man in the street, e.g., just dealing and the doing of good rather than the semblance of them; for we would rather really do good to our friends than seem to do so, whereas towards the man in the street the converse is the case.[13]

Fénelon, on the other hand, is indignant that certain virtues are extolled over others because of the wish to praise a man who practised them; in his view, "a hero must be praised only in order to teach his virtues to the multitude and to incite it to imitate them."[14]

The need for reliance on abstract values is perhaps essentially connected with change. They seemingly manifest a revolutionary spirit. We have seen the importance the Chinese attached to concrete values, and this attitude would tie in with China's imperviousness to change.

Abstract values can readily be used for criticism, because they are no respectors of persons and seem to provide criteria for one wishing to change the established order. On the other hand, where change is not wanted, there is no reason to raise incompatibilities. Now concrete values can always be harmonized; the very existence of the concrete implies that it is possible, that it achieves a certain harmony. Abstract values, on the other hand, when carried to extremes, are irreconcilable: it is impossible to reconcile, in the abstract, such virtues as justice and love. Perhaps in the West the need for change has been the stimulus for argument on abstract values, as such argument is better suited for raising incompatibilities. At the same time, the confusion of these abstract notions would allow us, after these incompatibilities have been raised, to form new concepts of these values. An intense activity in the realm of values is thereby made possible; they are constantly being recast and remodeled.

Leaning on concrete values would thus be much easier when one wishes to preserve than when one wishes to renovate. The reason conservatives consider themselves realists is perhaps that they put these values in the foreground. The notions of fidelity, loyalty, and solidarity, which are connected with concrete values, do in fact often characterize conservative argumentation.

[13] Aristotle, *Topics*, III, 2, 118a.
[14] Fénelon, "Dialogues sur l'Eloquence," *Œuvres*, vol. XXI, pp. 24-25.

§ 20. *Hierarchies*

Argumentation relies not only on values, both abstract and concrete, but also on hierarchies, such as the superiority of men over animals, of gods over men. Justification for these hierarchies can doubtless be found with the help of values, but as a general rule the question of finding a basis for hierarchies will only arise when they need to be defended. Such hierarchies often remain implicit, as is the case with the hierarchy of persons and things in the passage where Scheler first shows that values can be ranged in a hierarchy depending on their supports and then concludes that, by their very nature, values relating to persons are superior to those relating to things.[15]

The accepted hierarchies occur in practice with two distinct aspects: next to concrete hierarchies, like that expressing the superiority of men over animals, there are abstract hierarchies, like that expressing the superiority of the just over the useful. Concrete hierarchies may of course refer, as in the above example, to classes of objects; but each one of them is considered in its concrete unicity.

In a hierarchy with several elements, one can conceive that *A* might be superior to *B*, and that *B* might be superior to *C*, without necessarily being able to adduce the same basis for these two superiorities or even without giving any justification for them. But if one resorts to abstract principles, these generally introduce into the relationships between things an order that transforms simple superiority, a matter of preference, into systematic hierarchy, into hierarchy in the strict sense of the term. In these cases, a single abstract principle, capable of repeated application, can establish the whole hierarchy: for instance, anteriority, the fact of engendering or of containing, may constitute the criterion for the hierarchical structure.

A hierarchy of this kind is clearly distinguishable from the merely preferable in that it assures an ordering of everything subject to its governing principle. Thus, according to Plotinus, all the elements of the real form a systematized hierarchy, in which that which is cause or principle must be ranked higher than that which is effect or consequence.[16] In some cases, a second principle may establish a hierarchy among terms that cannot be ordered by application of the first principle: thus, a hierarchic grouping of the animal genera by following one principle may be completed by ordering the species within each

---

[15] Scheler, *Der Formalismus in der Ethik und die Materiale Wertethik*, pp. 98-99.

[16] Plotinus, *Enneads*, V, 5, § 12.

genus by following a different principle. Curious applications of this duality of principles can be found in St. Thomas, particularly where he deals with the hierarchies of angels.[17]

One of the most common principles for setting up a hierarchy is the greater or smaller amount of something. Thus, together with hierarchies of values based on the preference given to one of these values, there will be true hierarchies based on the quantity of a value: the higher rank corresponds to a larger quantity of the chosen characteristic.

To these quantitative hierarchies we can oppose the heterogeneous hierarchies. The hierarchic ordering of abstract values that are not ranked quantitatively does not mean that these values are independent of one another. Quite the opposite. We shall see that values are generally considered to be interconnected, and this very connection between them is often the basis of their subordination: for instance when the "end" value is deemed superior to that which is "means" or when the "cause" value is deemed superior to that constituting "effect." In many cases, however, the accepted hierarchic structure might well have been drawn up by recourse to connecting schemes, but these are not explicit, and we cannot be sure that the hearers are aware of them. For instance, some people will grant that the true is superior to the good, in the absence of any explicit statement of the possible bases for this superiority, or of any effort to establish the connection involved in the subordination of one to the other, or even without any indication as to the nature of this connection.

Value hierarchies are, no doubt, more important to the structure of an argument than the actual values. Most values are indeed shared by a great number of audiences, and a particular audience is characterized less by which values it accepts than by the way it grades them.

Values may be admitted by many different audiences, but the degree of their acceptance will vary from one audience to another. A hierarchy which should not be disregarded is established by the intensity with which one value is adhered to as compared to another. If this intensity is not known with sufficient exactness, the speaker may use each value more or less freely, without necessarily having to justify the preference given to one of them, since he does not wish to upset an established hierarchy. But this situation is rather exceptional. In most cases, not only are the values adhered to with different degrees of intensity, but the audience admits principles by which the values can be graded. Many of the philosophers dealing with values have failed to draw attention to this point. Studying

---

[17] Gilson, *The Christian Philosophy of St. Thomas Aquinas*, pp. 170-173.

the values in themselves, as it were, independently of their practical use in argumentation, they have rightly stressed the convergence of values, but have too often neglected the question of their hierarchy, which solves the conflicts between them.

It is to be observed, however, that these hierarchies do not prevent the values from being relatively independent. Their independence would be endangered if the principles establishing the hierarchic structure were fixed once and for all: this would lead to a monism of values. But this is not how hierarchies actually occur: their bases are as multifarious as the values they coordinate.

As an illustration of our thesis, let us examine different ways of considering the relationships that exist between the certainty of a particular item of knowledge and the importance or interest that it may possess. Isocrates and St. Thomas rank the importance higher than the certainty. According to Isocrates, "it is better to have a reasonable opinion about useful matters than exact knowledge of things which are useless."[18] We find a heightened and dramatized echo of this view, though in a totally different perspective, in St. Thomas' thought:

> To minds tormented by the divine thirst, it is useless to offer the most certain knowledge of the laws of numbers and the arrangement of the universe. Straining for an object which eludes their grasp, they endeavor to lift a corner of the veil, only too happy to perceive, sometimes even under heavy shadows, glimmerings of the eternal light which must one day shine upon them. To such the slightest knowledge touching the highest realities is far more desirable than the most absolute certitude touching minor objects.[19]

On the other hand, Julien Benda recalls the following passage in an unpublished letter from Lachelier to Ravaisson: "The subject I will take as my thesis is not that which I told you about; it is a more limited subject, *that is to say, more serious.*"[20]

The reason why one feels obliged to order values in a hierarchy, regardless of the result, is that simultaneous pursuit of these values leads to incompatibilities, obliges one to make choices. This is indeed one of the basic problems confronting almost all scientists. As an illustration we may cite an observation made by researchers in the field of "content analysis," which aims at an objective, systematic, and quantitative description of the actual contents of any sort of communication.[21]

[18] Isocrates, *Helen*, § 5.
[19] Gilson, *The Christian Philosophy of St. Thomas Aquinas*, p. 24, citing *Summa Theologica*, I, 1, 5, ad 1; *ibid.* I, II, 66, 5 ad 3; *Sup. lib. de Causis.* I.
[20] Benda, *Du style d'idées*, p. 82, note.
[21] Berelson, "Content Analysis," *Handbook of Social Psychology*, pp. 488-522.

In general a recurring problem of content analysis is the proper balance to be struck between reliability and significance. We can be completely reliable about the frequency of occurrence of any selected word, but this may be of very trivial importance.[22]

In these different examples, the problems, as well as the context in which they arise, are different, and the justification for the hierarchic structure, if it is given, may vary, but there are striking analogies in the argumentative procedure. In all cases it assumes the existence of values which are accepted, though incompatible in a certain situation; the hierarchic structure, whether it be the result of an argumentation or has been established from the start, will indicate which value will be sacrificed.[23]

§ 21. *Loci*

When a speaker wants to establish values or hierarchies or to intensify the adherence they gain, he may consolidate them by connecting them with other values or hierarchies, but he may also resort to premises of a very general nature which we shall term *loci*. These are the τόποι of Greek writers, from which come the *Topics*, treatises devoted to dialectical reasoning.

As used by classical writers, *loci* are headings under which arguments can be classified. They are associated with a concern to help a speaker's inventive efforts and involve the grouping of relevant material, so that it can be easily found again when required.[24] *Loci* have accordingly been defined as storehouses for arguments.[25] Aristotle made a distinction between the *loci communes*, or "common places," which can be used indiscriminately for any science and do not depend on any, and the special topics, which belong either to a particular science or a particular type of oratory.[26]

Originally, then, *loci communes* were characterized by their extreme generality, which made them available for use in all circumstances. But the degeneration of rhetoric, and the lack of interest shown in

---

[22] Lasswell, Leites, and Associates, *Language of Politics*, p. 66, note citing Geller, Kaplan, and Lasswell, "The Differential Use of Flexible and Rigid Procedures of Content Analysis," *Experimental Division for the Study of War Communications*, Library of Congress, Document no. 12.

[23] Cf. § 46 infra.: Contradiction and Incompatibility.

[24] Aristotle, *Topics*, VIII, 14, 163b.

[25] Cicero, *Topics*, II, § 7; *Partitiones Oratoriae*, § 5; Quintilian, V, x, 20.

[26] Aristotle, *Rhetoric*, I, 2, 1358a; cf. Viehweg, *Topik und Jurisprudenz*, and Stroux, *Römische Rechtswissenschaft und Rhetorik*.

the study of *loci* by logicians, lead to the unexpected result that oratorical expositions aimed against luxury, lust, sloth, and the like, after
endless repetition in school exercises, were classified as commonplace
despite their very specific character. Quintilian already had tried
to react against this abuse, but without much success.[27] Increasingly,
the term *loci communes* is used to mean what Vico calls oratorical
themes, in contradistinction to the themes dealt with in the *Topics*.[28]
The triteness characteristic of what we today call commonplace does
not in any way exclude specificity. Our commonplaces are really
merely applications of "commonplaces" in the Aristotelian sense of
the term to particular subjects. But because the application is made
to a frequently treated subject, developed in a certain order, with
expected connections beween the *loci*, we notice only its banality
and fail to appreciate its argumentative value. The result is a tendency to forget that *loci* form an indispensable arsenal on which a
person wishing to persuade another will have to draw, whether he
likes it or not.

In his *Topics*, Aristotle studies every kind of *locus* that can serve
as premise for dialectical or rhetorical syllogisms. He classifies them,
according to the viewpoints established in his philosophy, as *loci* relating to accident, species, property, definition, and sameness. Our
approach is different. First of all, we do not wish to bind our viewpoint to any particular metaphysical system. Secondly, as we distinguish the types of objects of agreement which relate to the real
from those which relate to the preferable, we shall only apply the
term *loci* to premises of a general nature that can serve as the bases
for values and hierarchies. *Loci* of this kind are treated by Aristotle
under the heading of *loci* relating to accident.[29] Such *loci* form the
most general premises, actually often merely implied, that play a
part in the justification of most of the choices we make.

It is debatable whether it would be possible to draw up a list of
the *loci* representing primary agreements in the sphere of the preferable, from which all others could be deduced, and consequently
in terms of which they could be justified. Even if it were feasible,
such an undertaking would involve metaphysics or axiology and take
us beyond our present purpose, which is limited to the examination
and analysis of concrete arguments. Arguments break off at different
levels. When agreement occurs, we can assume it is based on more
general *loci* accepted by the interlocutors; however, in order to show

[27] Quintilian, V, x, 20.
[28] Vico, *Delle instituzioni oratorie*, p. 20.
[29] Cf. Aristotle, *Topics*, III, 116a-119a, and *Rhetoric*, I, 6, 7, 1362a-1365b.

what these *loci* are, we would have to resort to hypotheses that are any-thing but certain. Thus one might feel justified in reducing the affir-mation that what is more lasting or durable is more desirable than that which is less so, to the apparently more general *locus* affirming the su-periority of the whole to a part: but it should be observed that the latter *locus* is not expressed in the *locus* relating to the lasting, that a ques-tion of interpretation is involved, to which the parties to the argument might not give their assent. However, when some *locus* has been used by the interlocutor, he can always be required to justify it.

Although the more general *loci* primarily claim our attention, it is undoubtedly worthwhile to examine the more specific *loci* which are accepted in various societies and are thus characteristic of them. On the other hand, it is amazing that even where very general *loci* are concerned, each *locus* can be confronted by one that is contrary to it: thus, to the classical *locus* of the superiority of the lasting, one may oppose the romantic *locus* of the superiority of that which is pre-carious and fleeting. It is accordingly possible to characterize societies not only by the particular values they prize most but by the intensity with which they adhere to one or the other of a pair of antithetical *loci*.

We do not think it necessary, for a general understanding of ar-gumentation, to provide an exhaustive list of the *loci* which are used. It seems to us, moreover, that this would be a very difficult task. Our concern is with the fact that all audiences, of all kinds, have to take *loci* into account. We will classify *loci* under a few very general headings: *loci* of quantity, quality, order, the existing, essence, and the person. Our justification for this classification lies in the im-portance of considerations relating to these categories in the actual practice of argumentation. We are obliged to discuss them at some length so that the concept of *locus* will be, for all our readers, more than just an empty frame.

§ 22. *Loci of Quantity*

By *loci* relating to quantity we mean those *loci communes* which affirm that one thing is better than another for quantitative reasons. More often than not, a *locus* relating to quantity constitutes a major, though implied, premise, without which the conclusion would have no basis. Aristotle mentions some of these *loci*: a greater number of good things is more desirable than a smaller;[30] a good thing useful

---

[30] Aristotle, *Topics*, III, 2, 117a.

for a comparatively large number of ends is more desirable than one useful to a lesser degree;[31] that which is more lasting or durable is more desirable than that which is less so.[32] We note also that the superiority in question attaches to negative as well as positive values, so that a lasting evil is greater than one that is momentary. Isocrates declares that the merit of a person is proportional to the number of those to whom he is of service:[33] athletes are inferior to those who teach, since their strength benefits only themselves, whereas those who think soundly are useful to all.[34] Timon uses the same argument to emphasize the value of pamphlets:

> An orator speaks to the deputies, the publicist to the statesmen, the newspaper to its subscribers, the pamphlet to everyone. ... Where books do not reach, the newspaper enters. Where the newspaper does not reach, the pamphlet circulates.[35]

The statement "the whole is better than a part" seems to be a translation in terms of preference of the axiom "the whole is greater than a part." Even Bergson, when he wishes to establish the superiority of becoming, of evolution, over what is fixed and static, does not hesitate to use a *locus* relating to quantity:

> We said there is *more* in a movement than in the successive positions attributed to the moving object, *more* in a becoming than in the forms passed through in turn, *more* in the evolution of form than the forms assumed one after another. Philosophy can therefore derive terms of the second kind from those of the first, but not the first from the second. ... How, then, having posited immutability alone, shall we make change come forth from it? ... So at the base of ancient philosophy lies necessarily this postulate: that there is more in the motionless than in the moving, and that we pass from immutability to becoming by way of diminution or attenuation.[36]

A *locus* of quantity, the superiority of that which is accepted by the greater number of people, forms the basis of certain conceptions of democracy and also of conceptions of reason which equate reason with *"common sense."* Even when certain philosophers such as Plato contrast truth with the opinion of the greater number, it is by means of a *locus* of quantity that they justify the preference they accord to truth, for they hold it to be something commanding the assent

---

[31] *Ibid.*, III, 3, 118b.
[32] *Ibid.*, III, 1, 116a.
[33] Isocrates, *To Nicocles*, § 8.
[34] Isocrates, *Panegyrics*, 2.
[35] Timon, *Livre des orateurs*, pp. 90-91.
[36] Bergson, *Creative Evolution* (Modern Library), pp. 343-344. The italics are Bergson's.

of all the gods, something which should win the assent of all men.[37]
The quantitative *locus* of durability justifies also the high value attached to truth as being that which is eternal in contrast to opinions
that are passing and unstable.

Another *locus* of Aristotle makes this affirmation:

> That is more desirable which is more useful at every season or
> at most seasons, e.g., justice and temperance rather than courage:
> for they are always useful, while courage is useful only at times.[38]

Rousseau is fond of this kind of reasoning. Similar considerations
of universality are at the basis of the superiority of the system of education that he recommends:

> In the social order where each has his own place, a man must
> be educated for it. If such a one leaves his own station he is fit for
> nothing else. ... In the natural order men are all equal and their
> common calling is that of manhood, so that a well-educated man
> cannot fail to do well in that calling and those related to it. ...
> We must therefore look at the general rather than the particular and
> consider our scholar as man in the abstract, man exposed to all
> the changes and chances of mortal life.[39]

The general validity of something good is sometimes defined also
as that whose use cannot be made superfluous by any other good
thing; this slant provides another justification for the preference given
to justice over courage. According to Aristotle:

> That one of two things which if all possess, we do not need the
> other thing, is more desirable than that which all may possess and
> still we want the other as well. ... If everyone were just, there
> would be no use for courage, whereas all might be courageous,
> and still justice would be of use.[40]

We may regard the preference given to the probable over the improbable, to the easy over the difficult, and to that which is less likely
to be taken from us, as *loci* relating to quantity. Most of the *loci* which
aim at showing the effectiveness of a means will be quantitative. Thus
the following *loci* are listed by Cicero in his *Topics* under the heading
of efficacity (*vis*):

> An efficient cause is superior to one that is not; those things
> which are complete in themselves are superior to those which stand
> in need of the other things; those which are in our power are pre-
> ferable to those which are in the power of another; those which

[37] Plato, *Phaedrus*, 273d-e.
[38] Aristotle, *Topics*, III, 2, 117a.
[39] Rousseau, *Émile* (Dent), pp. 9-10.
[40] Aristotle, *Topics*, III, 2, 117a-b.

are stable surpass those which are uncertain; those that cannot be taken from us are better than those that can.[41]

That which occurs most often, the usual, the normal, is the subject of one of the most commonly used *loci*, so much so that for many people the step from what is done to what should be done, from the normal to the norm, is taken for granted. But only the *locus* of quantity justifies this assimilation, this passage, from the normal, which expresses a frequency, a quantitative aspect of things, to the norm, which states that this frequency is favorable and should be conformed to. While all people can agree on the normal character of an occurrence, provided they agree on what is to serve as the criterion for normality, presentation of what is normal as the norm requires, in addition, the use of the *locus* of quantity.

Assimilation of the normal with the normative leads Quetelet to consider his imaginary average man as the very model of the beautiful,[42] and Pascal deduced some paradoxical thoughts from it, such as: "men are so necessarily mad that not to be mad would amount to another form of madness."[43]

The passage from the normal to the normative, which is common among those who base ethics on experience, has rightly been considered an error of logic.[44] Nevertheless, it should be recognized as one of the valid foundations of argumentations, inasmuch as this passage is implicitly admitted, whatever the domain under consideration. It has left its mark in the German word *Pflicht*, which is close to *man pflegt*. It is found also in all those terms which cover both membership in a group and the usual behavior of the individuals in this group: thus, depending on circumstances, the words "American" and "socialist" may refer either to a behavioral norm or to a normal behavior.

The passage from the normal to the norm is a phenomenon of common occurrence and seems to be taken for granted. On the other hand, dissociating them and opposing them by claiming primacy of the norm over the normal would require justification by argumentation: this argumentation will aim at lowering the value of the normal, mostly by using *loci* other than those of quantity.

The exceptional is not trusted unless its value is demonstrated. Descartes goes so far as to make distrust of the exceptional a rule in his provisional code of morals:

---

[41] Cicero, *Topics*, XVIII, § 70.

[42] Quetelet, *Physique sociale*, vol. II, p. 386.

[43] Pascal, *Pensées*, GBWW, vol. 33, p. 242.

[44] Ossowska, *Podstawy nauki o moralności*, The Foundations of a Science of Morality, p. 83.

And amongst many opinions all equally received, I chose only
the most moderate, both because these are always most suited
for putting into practice, and probably the best (for all excess has
a tendency to be bad). ...[45]

Any exceptional situation is deemed precarious: "The Tarpeian
rock is close to the Capitol." Thus, the abnormal character of a situation, though it may even be favorable, can become an argument
against this situation.

§ 23. *Loci of Quality*

Loci of quality occur in argumentation when the strength of numbers
is challenged, and it is in such a context that they are most readily
perceived. They are used by reformers or those in revolt against the
commonly held opinions: thus Calvin warning King Francis I against
those who would attack his doctrine with the argument that it "has
long since been condemned by the verdict of both estates."[46] Calvin
rejects custom, for "the affairs of men have scarcely ever been so well
regulated that the better things pleased the majority."[47] To numbers
he opposes the quality of the truth guaranteed by God:

> Against the whole tribe of the prophets, Jeremiah alone is sent
> from the Lord to announce that "the law was going to perish from
> the priest, counsel from the wise, the word from the prophet."[48]

The leaders themselves may thus be mistaken. In the extreme
position adopted by Calvin, it is not a question of superior knowledge
granted to an elite nor of a knowledge of the truth corresponding,
as in Plato, to what a universal audience of gods and men would accept. It is the struggle of one in possession of the truth, guaranteed
by God, against the multitude that is in error. The truth cannot be
subdued however numerous its adversaries: we are dealing with a
value of a higher order, beyond compare. The protagonists of the
locus of quality cannot fail to emphasize this aspect: at the limit,
the *locus* of quality leads to a high rating of the unique which, just
like the normal, forms one of the axes of argumentation.

The unique is linked to a concrete value: what we consider as a
concrete value seems to us unique, but it is what appears unique that
becomes precious to us. As Jouhandeau says,

[45] Descartes, *Discourse on the Method*, GBWW, vol. 31, p. 48.
[46] Calvin, *Institutes of the Christian Religion*, Library of Christian Classics,
vol. XX, p. 10. Prefatory Address to King Francis.
[47] *Ibid.*, p. 23.
[48] *Ibid.*, p. 26.

his resemblance to me, that which brings us together and makes us alike, does not interest me; what matters to me and impresses itself upon me is the particular sign isolating X, his "singularity."[49]

To consider people as interchangeable, to fail to see what makes the particular quality of their personality, is to lower them. A mere inversion of terms will sometimes suffice to show the colorless character of those to which they refer: "Thanks, Rosencrantz and gentle Guildenstern," says the King; "Thanks, Guildenstern and gentle Rosencrantz," adds the Queen.[50]

These examples tend to show that the uniqueness of a creature or thing depends on the manner in which we conceive our relationship with that creature or thing: to one man a certain animal is just one specimen of a species; to another the same animal is a unique being with which he has a special relationship. Such philosophers as Martin Buber and Gabriel Marcel rebel against the fungible and mechanical, against that which can be universalized. Buber would rather have

force exercised on a being that one has really possessed than indifferent solicitude for faceless numbers.[51]

For G. Marcel, the value of an encounter with another being originates in the fact that the meeting is "unique of its kind."[52] That which is unique cannot be priced, and its value is increased by the very fact that it cannot be estimated. Thus we find Quintilian advising orators not to charge for their collaboration, since "most things can seem without importance by the very fact that a price is set upon them."[53]

The value of what is unique can be expressed by opposing it to the usual, the ordinary, the vulgar. These would be the belittling form of the multiple as opposed to the unique. The unique is original, stands out from other things and for this reason it is remarkable and pleasing even to the masses. High estimation of the unique, or at least of what appears to be unique, is the basis of the maxims of Gracian and of his advice to courtiers. They should avoid repeating themselves and should appear to be unfathomable, mysterious, and not easily classifiable:[54] a unique quality becomes the means for winning the approval of the majority. Even the multitude appreciates that

[49] Jouhandeau, Essai sur moi-même, p. 153.
[50] Shakespeare, Hamlet, act II, scene ii.
[51] Buber, I and Thou, p. 24.
[52] Marcel, Le monde cassé, followed by Position et approches concrètes du mystère ontologique, pp. 270-271.
[53] Quintilian, XII, vii, 8.
[54] Gracian, L'homme de Cour, pp. 2, 8, 102, 113, etc.

which stands out, that which is rare and difficult to attain. Aristotle says that the more difficult is preferable to the easier, "for we appreciate better the possesssion of things that cannot be easily acquired."[55]

We note that Aristotle is not content just to mention the *locus*. He outlines an explanation. He links it to the person, to the effort. What is rare relates mainly to the object, and what is difficult, to the subject as an agent. A sure way of setting value on a thing is to put it forward as something difficult or rare.

Precariousness can be considered as the qualitative value opposed to the quantitative value of duration; it is correlative with the unique, the original. As we know, anything that is threatened acquires great value: *Carpe diem.* The poetry of Ronsard skillfully plays on this theme which touches us so closely. Precariousness is not always the threat of death, it can involve a situation: the situation of lovers compared with that of husband and wife exemplifies the opposition of the value of the precarious to the value of that which is stable.

This *locus* is connected with another very important *locus* mentioned by Aristotle: that of timeliness.

> Also, everything is more desirable at the season when it is of greater consequence; e.g., freedom from pain in old age more than in youth: for it is of greater consequence in old age.[56]

If we reverse Aristotle's example and stress things important to the child or adolescent, we can see that, by making value dependent on a transitory state of affairs, we lay stress on the precariousness of this value and, at the same time, increase the store set on it while it lasts.

The *locus* of the irreparable presents itself as a limit, which accentuates the *locus* of the precarious: the effect of argument which makes use of it can be overwhelming. A good example is the famous peroration of St. Vincent de Paul while showing the orphans under his protection to some pious women and appealing to them in these terms:

> You have been their mothers by grace since the time when their mothers by nature abandoned them. Consider now whether you too wish to abandon them forever...; their life and death are in your hands. ... If you continue to give them your charitable care, they will live; but I tell you before God, they will all be dead tomorrow if you forsake them.[57]

---

[55] Aristotle, *Topics*, III, 2, 117b.
[56] Aristotle, *Topics*, III, 2, 117a.
[57] Cited by Baron, *De la Rhétorique*, p. 212.

If this peroration was so successful (it led to the foundation of the Hôpital des Enfants-Trouvés), it was thanks to the *locus* of the irreparable.

If we care to examine the bases of the value of the irreparable, we shall find that it is connected with quantity: the infinity of time which will elapse after the irreparable has been done or established, the certitude that the effects, whether or not they were wanted, will continue indefinitely. But it can be connected also with quality: the event qualified as irreparable acquires uniqueness. Whether the results of it be good or evil, the irreparable event is a source of terror for man; to be irreparable, an action must be one that cannot be repeated: it acquires a value by the very fact of being considered under this aspect.

The irreparable applies sometimes to the subject, sometimes to the object. A thing may be irreparable in itself or in relation to a particular subject: you may plant a new oak tree in my garden, but it is not I who will sit in its shade.

We see that the irreparable, in argumentation, is indeed a *locus* relating to the preferable, in this sense that it can bear only on the object to the extent that the latter is of value. The irreparable or irremediable will never be mentioned when the irreparability does not affect behavior. The second law of thermodynamics may be referred to in a scientific address, but this will be considered an appeal to the irreparable in argumentation only if value is attributed to a certain state of the universe.

A decision entailing irremediable consequences is important by that very fact. Generally, in action, one pays particular attention to what is urgent: intensity values connected with the unique, the precarious, and the irremediable are preponderant. Thus Pascal uses quantatitive *loci* to show us that we should prefer eternal life to life on earth, but, when he urges us to make a decision, he tells us we have begun the voyage and must choose our course, that there is no time for hesitation, that there is urgency, and that we must fear shipwreck.

Besides the uses of the *locus* relating to the unique as original and rare, with precarious existence and the loss of which is irremediable, thus opposing it to that which is fungible and common, in no danger of being lost and easily replaceable, the *locus* of unique is used, in an entirely different connection, in opposition to the diverse. Here the unique is that which can serve as norm, and the latter takes on qualitative value compared with the quantitative multiplicity of the diverse. The uniqueness of truth is set against the diversity of opinions. The superiority of the classical humanities, compared with the modern ones, says one author,[58] is due to the fact that the ancient authors offer fixed, recognized models, which are eternal and universal. Modern authors, even if they are as good as the ancient ones, have the disadvantage that they cannot serve as a norm, as a model beyond dispute: the multiplicity of the values represented by modern writers makes them pedagogically inferior. This same *locus* is used by Pascal to justify the value of custom:

> Why do we follow the ancient laws and opinions? Is it because they are more sound? No, but because they are unique and remove from us the root of difference.[59]

That which is unique is certain of enjoying prestige: following Pascal we find in this the explanation of a phenomenon of adherence, by grounding it on this positive value which is taken as the basis of an argumentation, without having to be grounded also. There seems to be a very general acceptance of the inferiority of that which is multiple, be it the fungible or the diverse, regardless of the very varied justifications that might be found for it.

§ 24. *Other Loci*

It would be possible, perhaps, to reduce all *loci* to *loci* of quantity or quality, or even to a single category, and we shall consider such attempts later. But in view of the role they have played, and continue to play, as *starting points* in argumentation, we think it more useful to consider separately *loci* relating to order, the existent, essence, and the person.

Loci of order affirm the superiority of that which is earlier over that which is later, sometimes the superiority of the cause, of the principle, sometimes that of the end, of the goal.

The superiority of laws and principles to facts, to the concrete, which seem to be an application of the laws or principles, is admitted in nonempirical thought. The cause is the justification of the effects, and is thereby superior to them. Thus we find Plotinus saying:

> If these produced forms . . . existed alone, they would not rank last; [if they do, it is because] beyond are the primitive things, the producing causes which, because they are causes, rank first.[60]

Many great philosophical disputes have turned on the question of knowing what is anterior and what is posterior in order to deduce

---

[58] Baron, *ibid.*, note 5, p. 451.
[59] Pascal, *Pensées*, GBWW, vol. 33, p. 227.
[60] Plotinus, *Enneads*, V, 3, § 10.

conclusions concerning the preponderance of one aspect of reality over another. In order to give greater value to the goal, finalistic theories see in it the real cause and origin of a process. Existentialist thought, with its insistence on the importance of action turned toward the future, connects the plan with the structure of man and hence "always seeks to return to the originating source."[61]

The *loci* relating to the existent affirm the superiority of that which exists, of the actual, of the real, over the possible, the contingent, or the impossible. Samuel Beckett's *Molloy* expresses as follows the advantage which the existing has over that which has still to be brought about, over the project:

> For being in the forest, a place neither worse nor better than the others, and being free to stay there, was it not natural that I should think highly of it, not because of what it was, but because I was there.[62]

Use of *loci* relating to the existent presupposes agreement as to the form of the real to which they are applied: in a large number of philosophical disputes, though one admits that agreement has been reached on these *loci*, one tries to get an unexpected advantage from them, either by changing the level at which the *loci* are applied or by introducing a new concept of the existent.

By *locus* of essence, we do not mean the metaphysical attitude which affirms the superiority of the essence to each of its incarnations—which is based on a *locus* relating to order—but the fact of according a higher value to individuals to the extent that they embody this essence. We are comparing concrete individuals: we immediately value highly a rabbit which exhibits all a rabbit's qualities: we consider him "a fine rabbit." That which best incarnates a type, an essence, or a function acquires value by this very fact. To King Francis, Marot speaks thus:

> King more than Mars by men renowned,
> King the most kingly that was ever crowned.[63]

Proust makes use of the same *locus* to praise the Duchesse de Guermantes:

> ... the Duchesse de Guermantes, who, to tell the truth, by dint of being a Guermantes, became to a certain extent something different and more attractive. . . .[64]

---

[61] Wahl, "Sur les philosophies de l'existence," *Glanes*, 15-16 (1950-51), p. 16; cf. Wahl, *A Short History of Existentialism*, p. 5.

[62] Beckett, *Molloy* (Minuit), p. 132; English translation (Grove), p. 116.

[63] Quoted by La Houssaie in his letter to Louis XIV preceding his translation of Gracian's *El Discreto* (*L'homme de Cour*).

[64] Proust, *The Guermantes Way*, pt. II, p. 181.

An ethical or aesthetic code could be based on the superiority of the thing that best incarnates the essence and on the obligation to attain it and the beauty of that which does attain it. Because man is made in order to think, thinking properly is, according to Pascal, the first principle of morality. It is because, to Marangoni, distortions are inherent to the essence of art, that one cannot find any work of art without distortions among those which are recognized as successful.[65]

In the heroic life, according to Saint-Exupéry, the leader's justification of his ruthlessness, of the sacrifices he demands of his men, is not what he gets out of them nor his authority over them, but the fact that those under him realize their highest possibilities, achieve what they are capable of.[66] The whole attraction and prestige of the morality of the superman derives from the *locus* of essence.

We shall conclude this brief inventory by examining a few *loci* derived from the value of the person, concerning his dignity, his worth, his autonomy. Aristotle affirms that "what cannot be got from another is more desirable than what can be got from another, as is the case of justice compared with courage."[67]

It is by virtue of this *locus* that Pascal can criticize diversion:

> Is it not to be happy to have a faculty of being amused by diversion? No; for that comes from elsewhere and from without. . . .[68]

The same *locus* confers a value on that which is done with care and demands effort.

The *loci* we have considered are those in most common use. Many others, of more limited significance, could be cited. However, as *loci* get more specific in character, there is a gradual, but imperceptible, shift into the realm of those agreements which we would prefer to consider as agreements on values or hierarchies.

§ 25. *Use and Systematization of Loci; Classical Outlook and Romantic Outlook*

It would be interesting to list, at different times and in different circles, the *loci* which are most commonly accepted, or at least appear to be accepted, by the audience, as conceived by the speaker. It would

---

[65] Marangoni, *Apprendre à voir*, p. 103.
[66] Saint-Exupéry, *Night Flight*, pp. 135-136.
[67] Aristotle, *Topics*, III, 2, 118a.
[68] Pascal, *Pensées*, GBWW, vol. 33, p. 203.

be a task requiring considerable discernment, as the *loci* that are regarded as beyond discussion are used without being explicitly stated. On the other hand, the speaker will insist on those he wishes to refute or to introduce in a slightly altered form.

The same goal can be attained by using a wide variety of *loci*. In order to emphasize the horror of a heresy or of a revolution, a speaker may sometimes use *loci* relating to quantity, showing that the heresy caps all the heresies of the past, that the revolution causes more disorder and upheaval than any other, and sometimes *loci* relating to quality, showing that it entails a completely new deviation, or a system that has never before existed.[69]

It should be observed, however, that the use of certain *loci* or of certain lines of argument does not necessarily characterize a well-determined cultural milieu but may be, and frequently is, due to the particular argumentative situation in which the speaker finds himself. Arguments which Ruth Benedict, in her interesting work on Japan,[70] regards as characteristic of the Japanese mentality are, in our interpretation, explained by the fact that Japan was the agressor: those who want to change the existing state of affairs will tend, in justifying the change, to introduce a normative element, such as the substitution of order for anarchy or the establishment of a hierarchy.

The argumentative situation, which is essential in the choice of *loci*, embraces both the goal the speaker has set himself and the arguments he may encounter. The two elements are actually closely connected; the desired goal, even when this is the initiation of a well-determined action, is simultaneously the alteration of certain convictions and the refutation of certain arguments, alteration and refutation which are essential to starting the action. The choice between different *loci*, between *loci* of quantity and *loci* of quality for instance, may, then, be due to one or the other of the components of the argumentative situation: in some cases it will be clear that the choice is being influenced by the attitude of the opponent; in others, on the contrary, we will clearly see the connection between the choice of *loci* and the desired action. Calvin frequently uses *loci* relating to quality. Their use, as we have mentioned, is often characteristic of the argumentation of those who wish to change the established order. To what extent, we may ask, did Calvin use these *loci* because his opponents resorted to *loci* of quantity?

[69] For examples, see Rivadeneira, *Vida del bienaventurado padre Ignacio de Loyola*, p. 194, and Pitt, *Orations on the French War*, p. 42, Fox's Fourteen Resolutions, May 30, 1794.

[70] Benedict, *The Chrysanthemum and the Sword*, pp. 20 et seq.

Our opponents take great pains to heap up Scriptural passages: and they do this so unremittingly that, although they cannot prevail by having better and more suitable ones than we do, in the numbers at least they can bear us down.[71]

A much more general example of this type of opposition can be found in the effort made by the Romanticists to overthrow certain positions of classicism: where the Romanticists saw that classicism could defend itself by means of *loci* of quantity, they quite naturally turned to *loci* of quality. Whereas the Classicists aimed at the universal audience, which is, in a sense, an appeal to quantity, it was quite normal that the Romanticists, whose aim was, as a rule, limited to persuading a particular audience, should resort to such *loci* of quality as the unique, the irrational, the elite, and genius.

In the area of *loci*, even less than in that of values, is the speaker anxious to completely remove certain elements in order to enhance others: he rather tries to subordinate them, to reduce them to those he considers fundamental.

When *loci* relating to order are reduced to *loci* of quantity, that which is anterior is regarded as more durable, more stable, and more general; when they are reduced to *loci* of quality, the principle will be regarded as the original source, as possessing a higher reality, as a model, as determining the extreme possibilities of a line of development. If value is placed on the old as having had a longer existence and embodying a tradition, the new will be valued as being original and rare.

Loci relating to the existent can be linked to quantitative *loci*, connected with what is lasting, stable, habitual, normal. But they can be linked also to qualitative *loci*, connected with the unique and the precarious: that which exists derives its value from its compelling nature as an experience, as something irreducible to anything else, as something actual. It could be maintained that the existent, as that which is concrete, provides the basis of the *loci* relating to quality, and gives the unique its value, and that the existent, as that which is real, is at the basis of the *loci* relating to quantity and gives their meaning to the lasting and the universally recognized.

The *locus* of essence can be connected with the normal, which, for the empirical thinkers, is the only possible basis for establishing types and building structures, whose perfect embodiment is appreciated in some of its representatives. To a rationalist like Kant, however, the

---

[71] Calvin, *Institutes of the Christian Religion*, Library of Christian Classics, vol. XX, p. 323.

only valid foundation for normality is the ideal, the abstract archetype.[72] It is another problem whether this archetype is valued as being the source and origin or as a reality of a higher kind, as universal or as rational. The superiority of that which best embodies the essence might be based now on the classical and universally valid aspect, now on the exceptional aspect of this achievement considered as rare and difficult.

Loci relating to the person can be based on those of essence, of autonomy, of stability, but also on the uniqueness and originality of that which is connected with human personality.

These associations and justifications of loci are sometimes the product of circumstances, but such an endeavor may result from the adoption of a metaphysical position and may be characteristic of a certain outlook. Thus the primacy accorded to loci of quantity and the attempt to reduce all other loci in terms of quantity characterize the outlook of the Classicists; on the other hand, the Romanticists, when they argue, reduce all loci to those of quality.

The universal and eternal, the rational and universally valid, that which is stable, durable, essential, that which concerns the largest number will be considered as superior and as the basis of value by the Classicists.

The loci of the Romanticists are the unique, the original and the new, that which is outstanding in history and bears the mark of eminence, that which is precarious and irremediable.

To the classical virtues of truth and justice, the Romanticist opposes the virtues of love, charity, and loyalty. The Classicists are attached to abstract or, at least, universal values, while the Romanticists advocate particular, concrete values. The Classicists maintain the superiority of thought and contemplation, the Romanticists that of effective action.

The Classicists will even try to justify the value they attach to loci of quality by presenting them as an aspect of quantity. Thus, the superiority of an original personality will be justified by the inexhaustible nature of his genius, the influence of his personality on a large number of people, the magnitude of the changes for which it is responsible. The concrete will be reduced to the infinity of its components, and the irremediable to the length of time during which it cannot be replaced.

As for the Romanticists, the quantitative aspects that are taken into consideration may be reduced to a purely qualitative hierarchy: we will then have a more important truth, constituting a reality at

---

[72] Kant, *The Critique of Pure Reason*, GBWW, vol. 42, pp. 173 et seq.

a higher level. When the Romanticist contrasts the will of the multitude and the individual will, the former may be conceived as a manifestation of a superior will, that of the group, which will be described as a unique being, with its own history, originality, and genius.

Thus systematizing *loci*, conceiving them in terms of *loci* that one considers fundamental, can give *loci* a variety of aspects and the same locus, the same hierarchy, when given another justification, may lead to a different vision of reality.

b) AGREEMENTS PARTICULAR TO CERTAIN ARGUMENTATIONS

§ 26. *Agreements of Certain Special Audiences*

What we usually call *common sense* consists of a series of beliefs which are accepted within a particular society and which the members of that society suppose to be shared by every reasonable being. But, beside beliefs of this kind, there are agreements that are peculiar to the members of a particular discipline, whether it be of scientific or technical, juridical or theological nature. Such agreements constitute the body of a science or technique. They may be the result of certain conventions or of adherence to certain texts, and they characterize certain audiences.

These audiences are usually distinguishable by their use of a technical language of their own. It is in the formalized disciplines that this special language is furthest removed from the language of the members of such an audience in everyday relations, which they understand as members of a more general audience. But even disciplines such as law, which borrow many of their technical terms from everyday language, sometimes seem an impenetrable mystery to the uninitiated. For such technical terms, which are supposed to be as univocal as possible in the context of the discipline, in fact summarize an aggregate of acquired knowledge, rules, and conventions. Because he is not familiar with these, the layman completely fails to understand these terms, as technical terms.

Entry into a specialized group requires initiation. While a speaker must normally adapt himself to his audience, this is not true of a teacher responsible for teaching students what is accepted by the particular group they wish to join, or at least which those responsible for their education wish them to join. In this case, persuasion is preliminary to initiation. It must secure submission to the requirements of the specialized group, for which the teacher is spokesman. Initiation into a given discipline consists of communicating its rules, techniques, specific ideas, and presuppositions, as well as the method of criticizing its results in terms of the discipline's own requirements. These characteristics distinguish initiation from popularization, which aims at the public at large for the purpose of acquainting it, in nontechnical language, with certain interesting results, without enabling it, however, to use the methods which made it possible to reach these results, or, *a fortiori*, to attempt to criticize them. The results are presented, so to speak, independently of the science that produced them: they have acquired the status of truths, of facts. The difference between enlightened knowledge, that of scholars, and accepted knowledge, which becomes that of the universal audience, is characteristic of the difference between initiation and popularization.[73]

It is not always easy to determine whether an argumentation is being carried out for the benefit of an audience whose members are bound by special agreements, or for a nonspecialized audience. In certain controversies regarding archeological frauds, for example, appeal is made both to specialists and to public opinion.[74] The same thing often happens in criminal trials where the matter is debated both at the legal and the moral levels.

Moreover, there exist areas which, depending on the idea one has of them, are said either to be specialized or to be free of any convention or special agreement: philosophy is an outstanding example.

Whereas classroom philosophy, developed within a systematic framework worked out by the teacher, may be considered as specialized and close to a theology, may we say that an independent philosophic effort presupposes the initiation prerequisite to a scientific technique, in this case, the technique of professional philosophers? This view is expressed by a young German writer, E. Rogge, in a very profound book, published posthumously, in which the author contrasts a "popular philosophy," such as Nietzsche's, with the contemporary philosophies which all presuppose a thorough knowledge of the history of philosophy, in relation to which, in one way or another, they are forced to see themselves.[75]

But does a philosopher altogether renounce speaking to the universal audience when he adopts a position vis-à-vis the history of philosophy, attributing a certain meaning to that history, thence-

---

[73] Cf. Perelman, "La vulgarisation scientifique, Problème philosophique," *Revue des Alumni*, XXI (1953), 4 (reprinted in *Justice et raison*, pp. 118-120).

[74] Cf. Vayson de Pradenne, *Les fraudes en archéologie préhistorique*, especially at p. 637.

[75] Rogge, *Axiomatik alles möglichen Philosophierens*, pp. 100 et seq.

forward having to admit that his own ideas are a function of this meaning? May we not say that the universal audience, as seen by the philosopher, is one which admits certain facts, particularly the acquired knowledge of the sciences, and more particularly that of the scientific history of philosophy, but which nonetheless retains the sovereign power of inserting these facts into new arguments and even of overthrowing them? In this case, any philosopher continues to address the universal audience, on the same footing as the popular philosopher, and it does not seem that philosophy can claim an aggregate of acquired knowledge, rules, and techniques comparable to the body of a scientific discipline which is common to all those who practice it.

The example of philosophy shows that the question of knowing which are the specialized audiences is a factual one that must be settled in each particular case. But there are audiences for which this question is settled by formal considerations; audiences of jurists and theologians belong in this category. In contrast with natural law and rational theology, positive law and positive theology, which are governed by well-defined texts, constitute special fields of argument.

What is essential is that texts of positive law or positive theology, regardless of their origin or basis—a problem with which we are not at present concerned—form the starting point of new reasonings. Legal or theological argumentation has to be developed within a definite system; this brings certain problems to the foreground, namely those relating to the interpretation of texts.

In disciplines in which texts form the connecting link, certain notions, such as those of self-evidence and fact, acquire a special meaning. If, when arguing before an audience which is not bound by texts, we say that a certain proposition is self-evident, it is because we neither entertain the wish nor possess the means to reject this proposition. But if we say that a certain rule of law is self-evident, this is because we think no question can arise as to its applicability to a particular case. The lack of self-evidence attributed to certain rules, the so-called necessity for justifying them, is the consequence of immediately converting the possibility of challenging them into a search for their bases. This is because, even if the values protected by the law are not disputed, any difficulty in applying the rules threatens to set in motion a whole chain of argumentation in which the possible foundations of the rule will probably have to be considered. If we say that a sacred text is self-evident, we are claiming that there is only one way to interpret it, since rejecting it is out of the question.

The agreements of specialized audiences may comprise special definitions of certain types of object of agreement, for example of what is a fact. They involve also the way in which these may be invoked or criticized.

Theologians and jurists consider as a fact not that which can claim agreement of the universal audience, but that which their texts require or permit them to consider as such. A theologian cannot question facts or truths attested by dogmas without shutting himself out of the particular audience that regards them as established. In law there exist fictions which require that something, even if it does not exist, should be treated as though it did or that something that does exist should not be considered as existing. What common sense accepts as a fact may be devoid of any legal consequence. Thus a judge "has no authority to declare a fact established simply because he has acquired positive knowledge of it outside the proceeding."[76] The judge's intervention might modify the claims put forward by the parties, and it is the parties who determine the outcome of the trial, within the framework of the law. For certain audiences, then, a fact is connected with the proof that the speaker wishes, or is able, to submit.

In contemporary natural sciences, facts are increasingly subordinated to the possibility of measurement, in the broad sense of that term. The natural sciences display a resistance to any observation which cannot be fitted into a system of measurement. Again, a scientist verifying the conclusions reached by another scientist, after certain experiments, will take into account all the facts that occur and that are relevant to the soundness of the proposed theory but does not feel he has the right, in the controversy, to introduce other facts that are not relevant within the set limits. The situation differs, however, from that in law, in that science does not have rules of procedure giving a relative fixity to the claims put forward by the parties: the scientist, when acting as judge, is always also a party, and before long he will put forward new claims. It is accordingly only by analogy with what happens in law that we can discern phases in the discussion, phases in which certain facts are provisionally treated as irrelevant.

Even in daily life, certain facts are considered not to have occurred, for the reason that it would be bad taste to bring them forward. The speaker cannot bring forward certain kinds of information about his opponent without lowering his own value: a multitude of rules of morality, ethics, and etiquette prevent the introduction of certain facts into a discussion. The juridical audience enjoys a special privilege in this regard only because the restrictions are codified and bind-

---

[76] Aubry and Rau, *Cours de droit civil français*, vol. XII, pp. 73-74.

ing on all parties: this is the essential distinction between judicial proof and historical proof.[77]

There is an equally important distinction concerning presumptions: the law may consider the connection linking certain facts to certain others to be "so strong that the probability that this is accompanied by that amounts to judicial certainty of the latter."[78]

Legal presumptions are often of the same nature as the presumptions recognized in everyday life. Thus, the law often lays down what it regards as normal. The origin of these legal presumptions is, however, of little importance: the presumption of the innocence of the accused, in criminal matters, is probably due to fear of the social and moral consequences of a different convention, rather than adoption by the law of a common-sense presumption based on what is normal.

The usual characteristic of legal presumptions is the difficulty there is in overcoming them: they are often irrefragable or can be rebutted only by following very precise rules. Sometimes they concern only the burden of proof. Before any audience, this is almost always a function of the accepted presumptions, but the choice of these presumptions is not prescribed, as it is in certain legal situations.

These observations regarding special agreements particular to certain audiences show sufficiently how arguments that are valid for some people have no validity for others, who may even find them very strange. As Jouhandeau has remarked,

> a layman present at a theological discussion comes close to thinking that he has discovered a world where people work hard at talking nonsense together with the same imperturbable logic manifested by the inmates of a lunatic asylum.[79]

It follows from what we have said that it might be to a speaker's advantage to choose a particular audience. Unless circumstances determine the audience, an argument can be presented first to one group of people, and then to another, and gain by the adherence of the first, or, more oddly, by their rejection of it: the choice of audiences and interlocutors, as well as the order of presentation of the argumentations, have a great influence in political life.

The fact that there is a mingling of specialized and nonspecialized audiences has an effect on the argumentation. Schopenhauer mentions as an expedient available when scholars are engaged in discussion before a public without competence in their field, the raising of an objection which is not pertinent but which the opponent cannot

---

[77] *Ibid.*, p. 63, note 2b by Bartin.
[78] *Ibid.*, p. 100, note 1b by Bartin.
[79] Jouhandeau, *De la grandeur*, p. 98.

refute without entering into lengthy technical explanations.[80] This tactic puts the opponent in a difficult position as it forces him to use arguments his hearers cannot follow. However, the opponent might denounce the maneuver and discredit the one who used it, and this disqualification, which requires no technical premises, may be of weight for all members of the audience, scholars as well as laymen. Similarly, in a legal proceeding, the tendency to judge according to the law is combined with that of judging on the basis of equity. Although a judge concerned with technicalities may attach relatively little importance to the latter, he is not entirely immune to arguments addressed to him as a member of a particular, but not specialized, social group or as a member of the universal audience: this appeal to his moral sense may lead him to discover new arguments that are valid in his conventional framework, or to see in a new light the arguments already before him. On the other hand, concern with the present or future opinion of specialized audiences has an effect on speeches addressed to nonspecialized audiences: thus, in the discussion and making of such everyday transactions as purchases and sales, one considers not only the immediate implications of the act, but the possibility that it may one day be brought up in a legal context. In the same way an ordinary person observing natural phenomena may, in so doing, take into consideration what he thinks would be of significance to an audience of scientists. Arguments between nonspecialists are thus formulated in such a way as either to escape the opinion of the specialist or to be subject to his decision: in any case, many controversies between laymen are affected by the possibility that a specialist will enter into the discussion.

§ 27. *Agreements Particular to Each Discussion*

The premises in argument consist of propositions accepted by the hearers. When the hearers are not bound by exact rules that compel them to recognize certain propositions, the whole structure raised by the speaker has no other basis than a factor of psychological nature, the adherence of the hearers. And more often than not, the speaker only presumes that this adherence exists. When his interlocutors disagree with the speaker's conclusions, they can, if they see fit, challenge the presumed agreement on the premises with a denial which will undermine the whole argument at its base. However, the re-

[80] Schopenhauer, *Sämtliche Werke* (Piper), vol. 6: "Eristische Dialektik," p. 418, Kunstgriff 28.

jection of the premises is not always without disadvantages for the hearers. We shall have more to say of this when we come to deal with the ridiculous in our analysis of techniques of argument.[81]

Sometimes a speaker is guaranteed the express adherence of his interlocutors to the propositions on which he builds his argumentation. This adherence is not an absolute guarantee of stability, but it does increase it, without which we would lack the minimum of confidence necessary for living in society. When Alice, in talking with the inhabitants of Wonderland, wants to take back an affirmation, she is met with the objection: "When you've once said a thing, that fixes it, and you must take the consequences."[82] This is an odd retort if we examine it from the standpoint of truth; at this level, change is always permissible, as one might plead a mistake. In the realm of action, however, it is a profound observation; for at this level propositions constitute a kind of commitment which cannot be violated without good reason without threatening to destroy all possibility of social life.

A speaker is accordingly eager to receive tokens of adherence, either explicit or implicit: a whole series of techniques is used to underscore adherence or to recognize it. These techniques are particularly developed in the case of certain audiences, in particular juridical audiences, but are not limited to them.

As a rule, the formality surrounding the promulgation of certain texts and the pronouncement of certain words aims at making it more difficult to repudiate them and at increasing social confidence. In particular, an oath gives a religious or quasi-religious sanction to the expressed adherence. An oath may concern the truth of facts, the adherence to norms, or it may extend to a whole set of dogmas: the relapsed heretic was subject to the severest punishment because he had transgressed an oath.

The technique of the closed case aims at stabilizing certain judgments, at preventing certain decisions from being discussed anew. In science certain propositions are set apart and qualified as axioms and are thus explicitly granted a privileged position within the system: an axiom cannot then be revised except by an equally explicit repudiation; revision cannot be effected by an argument developed within the system to which the axiom belongs.

In most cases, however, a speaker has no firmer support for his presumptions than psychical and social inertia which are the equivalents in consciousness and society of the inertia of physics. It can

---

[81] Cf. infra, § 49: The Ridiculous and Its Role in Argumentation.
[82] Carroll, *Through the Looking Glass*, p. 293.

be presumed, failing proof to the contrary, that the attitude previously adopted—the opinion expressed, the behavior preferred—will continue in the future, either from a desire for coherency or from force of habit. According to Paulhan, the strange thing about our condition is that it is

> easy to find reasons for strange acts, but difficult to find them for ordinary acts. A man who eats beef does not know why, but if he gives up beef forever in favor of frogs or salsify he will think up a thousand proofs, each more ingenious than the last.[83]

Inertia makes it possible to rely on the normal, the habitual, the real, and the actual and to attach a value to them, whether it is a matter of an existing situation, an accepted opinion, or a state of regular and continuous development. Change, on the other hand, has to be justified; once a decision has been taken, it cannot be changed except for sufficient reason. It is very common in arguing to insist that there is nothing in the circumstances to warrant a change. Thus, Pitt, who favored continuation of the war with France, opposed any idea of negotiation in these terms:

> Have the circumstances and situation of the country materially altered since the last motion on this subject, or since my honourable friend first found himself an advocate of negociation? Has the posture of affairs varied since that time so as to make negociation more eligible at the present moment than it was at any former period?[84]

To justification of the change one will often substitute an effort to prove that there has been no real change. This effort is sometimes made necessary by the fact that change is prohibited: thus, a judge who is unable to change the law may maintain that his interpretation does not modify it but corresponds better to the intention of the legislator; similarly, reform of the Church will be presented as a return to primitive religion and to Scripture. In theory, justification for change and argument tending to show that there has been no change are not aimed at the same audience. But they both have the same objective, to respond to the demands of inertia in the life of society.

The change will be justified by pointing out either an objective modification to which the subject has had to adapt or a change in the subject, seen as an improvement. In this way, change, which always has a somewhat devaluating effect because it shakes social confidence, can nevertheless be appreciated as a proof of sincerity. A change

---

[83] Paulhan, *Les fleurs de Tarbes ou la terreur dans les lettres*, p. 212.
[84] Pitt, *Orations on the French War*, p. 93, On Wilberforce's Motion in Favour of a General Pacification, May 27, 1795.

which has been successful for its originator is likely to become a model
for those who would hesitate to enter upon the same course: thus W.
Lippmann presents as a model to the United States Republicans
the evolution of Senator Vandenberg from his traditional isolation-
ism to his postwar position of ardent and convinced supporter of international cooperation.[85]

Theoretically, inertia can be opposed to all new proposals and *a
fortiori* to proposals which have been known for a long time but have
not yet been accepted. What Bentham calls the fallacy of the fear
of innovation or also the fallacy of universal veto, which consists of
opposing any new measure just because it is new, is not a fallacy at
all, but the effect of inertia which operates in favor of the existing
state of affairs. What exists should not be changed unless there are
reasons for reform.

Actually Bentham understands this very well, for to someone who
argues that, if a measure had been a good one, it would have been
taken long before, he retorts that particular interests might have
been opposed to it or that a particular degree of ingenuity might be
required to adapt it to its purpose. In effect, Bentham is assuming
the burden of proof.[86] In this connection, it is to be observed that
the law is conforming to the principle of inertia in putting as a rule,
the burden of proof on the plaintiff. The attitude of the law is to
ratify facts as they are, until further information is available.[87]

It is through inertia that the technique of the closed case is extended,
so to speak, into the technique of the precedent. The only difference
between the repetition of a precedent and the continuance of an existing state is that in the former the facts are seen as discontinuous.
With this very small shift in perspective, we can still see inertia at
work: it is as necessary to prove the expediency of changing behavior
when confronted with the repetition of a situation as it is to prove
the utility of changing an existing state of affairs.

In countries where traditionalism is strong, precedent becomes
an integral part of the judicial system and provides a model that can
be availed of on condition that one can show that the new case is sufficiently similar to the old one. This explains the fear of creating a
precedent which crops up in so many decisions: "You are going to
decide not about Isocrates, but about the value of the whole profession

---

[85] *New York Herald Tribune*, Paris edition, 12 March, 1948.
[86] Bentham, *Works*, vol. II: *The Book of Fallacies* (Tait) p. 410, pt. I, chap. IV,
No-Precedent Argument.
[87] Cf. Demogue, *Les notions fondamentales du droit privé*, p. 543.

of philosophy."[88] The mere fact of doing certain acts, whether they be appraisals or decisions, is regarded as an implicit consent to the use of these acts as precedents, as a sort of promise to behave in the same way in similar situations.

In like manner, by observing a rule and especially by proclaiming that he observes it, a person is showing that it is a good rule to follow. Taking up a position in this way is similar to an *admission*, with which one may be taxed if the occasion should arise. Thus Demosthenes attacks Aeschines by citing what the latter had once said about the way in which a trial should be conducted:

> ... He employed in his prosecution arguments that are now valid against himself. For surely the principles which you, Aeschines, laid down when you prosecuted Timarchus ought to have equal weight for others against you.[89]

It is very effective for a speaker to bring up, for use against his opponent, anything that can be considered, because of the adherence displayed in it, to have been admitted by the latter. Such immediate response to the interlocutor's words is the essence of what is ordinarily called *repartee*.

In law, when only the private interest of the parties is at stake, an admission by one party, just as an agreement between them, provides a stable element on which the judge can depend. But, in cases in which public order is involved, an admission does not have the same convincing character because it is the judge, and not the parties, who then decides what can be regarded as established.

Sometimes, instead of relying on statements of the opponent, one will make use of mere signs of his admission, particularly of his silence.

Silence can be taken either as a sign that no objection or refutation has been found or as a sign that the matter is beyond question. The first interpretation affirms the agreement of the interlocutor as to a fact, while the second derives the legal consequence. To Quintilian "that which the opponent does not deny" is an element which the judge can use.[90]

It is because of the danger that silence will be taken for consent that a person will so often elect to make some reply, even if the objection he can bring up at the time is a weak one.

The association made between silence and admission can prove detrimental to some affirmations: thus, absolute silence in the face of

---

[88] Used by Aristotle (citing Isocrates, *On the Exchange*, 173) to illustrate the *locus* relating to antecedents and results in his *Rhetoric*, II, 23, 1399b.

[89] Demosthenes, *On the Embassy*, § 241.

[90] Quintilian, V, x, 13.

measures taken by public authorities seems suspicious, as it is difficult to interpret it as unanimous approbation; in order to explain it, one more readily resorts to the hypothesis of intimidation. The signs that can be taken to constitute an admission are manifold. Admission can be unearthed in an abstention or, better still, in an apparent shift of opinion. Thus a legislator's rejection of a clause in a bill he is examining will later be treated as an admission, namely the implicit affirmation that he thought about the point involved and rejected it.

The dialectical use of question and answer essentially aims at securing explicit agreements which can be used later; this is a characteristic of the Socratic method. One application of this method is to try to reach explicit agreement as to the point which is to be decided, the one which, in the opponent's view, will settle the outcome of the debate, or as to the proofs he will accept and consider as conclusive. We have mentioned in another work[91] the case of the American factory owner who spent a whole day asking the workers' representatives for their objections and had these carefully listed on a blackboard. By this tactic, he obtained their explicit agreement on the points he would have to answer. If fresh points were to be raised subsequently, this could be interpreted as a sign of lack of good faith. By fixing the object of the controversy, one narrows it down: the interlocutor can find a loophole which will justify his refusing agreement once the admitted conditions have been fulfilled only at the risk of going back on his word. Since third parties usually decide on the issue of the debate, such a disavowal can hardly have any consequences other than discrediting its author.

Quintilian gives this advice to lawyers:

> It will accordingly be wise to conceal some of our weapons. For the opponent insistently clamors for them and often makes the whole issue of the case depend on them, in the belief that we do not possess them. By calling for our proofs, he gives them authority.[92]

An agreement made prior to discussion may relate not to the object of debate or to the proofs, but to the manner of conducting the discussion. This agreement may be more or less ritual, as is the case in judicial, parliamentary, or academic discussions; but it can result, at least partially, from the particular discussion in progress and from

---

[91] Perelman and Olbrechts-Tyteca, *Rhétorique et philosophie*, p. 20, based on Carnegie, *L'art de parler en public* (Desoer) p. 344.

[92] Quintilian, VI, IV, 17.

an initiative taken by one of the parties. Thus, Demosthenes describes to Aeschines the modalities of his defence:

Now it is an honest and straightforward defence to prove either that the acts alleged were never committed or that, if committed, they were for the advantage of the state.[93]

Fearing that the accused will divert the attention of the assembly to secondary points, Demosthenes prescribes to him, as it were, the technique of his defence and, by so doing, binds himself to recognize its value. Thus the interlocutor who in a controversy takes up point by point the allegations of his predecessor, accepting the order followed in his speech, is proving his sincerity in the debate.

Securing agreement on, or rejection of, certain points is hence an objective which will determine the order to be followed in argumentation. A speech is not exclusively built up by developing the original premises; it consists also of establishing premises and of making agreements unambiguous and stable.[94]

Thus each argument exhibits stages, marked out by the agreements that should be reached. These agreements sometimes are the result of the attitude of the parties, and sometimes they are institutionalized by virtue of established custom or the existence of explicit rules of procedure.

§ 28. *Argumentation* ad Hominem *and* Begging *the* Question

The possibilities for argumentation depend on what each participant is ready to concede, on the values he recognizes, on the facts on which he indicates his agreement: for this reason, any argument is an argument *ad hominem* or *ex concessis*. The frequent opposition of argument *ad hominem* to argument *ad rem*,[95] the first relating to opinion, the second to the truth or the thing itself, is due to the fact that people forget that the truth in question has to be accepted. In terms of our theory, argument *ad rem* corresponds to an argument that is claimed to be valid for all reasonable beings, that is, *ad humanitatem*. Argument *ad humanitatem* would be a special, but important, case of argument *ad hominem*.

Argumentation aiming at the universal audience, argument *ad humanitatem*, will avoid, as far as possible, the use of arguments that

---

[93] Demosthenes, *On the Embassy*, § 203.

[94] Cf. infra: § 103, Order and Persuasion.

[95] Cf. Schopenhauer, *Sämtliche Werke* (Brockhaus), vol. 6: *Parerga und Paralipomena*, II, p. 29.

would be valid only for particular groups. Philosophical argument, in particular, should be careful about this.

It would be possible to distinguish as many different types of arguments *ad hominem* as there are audiences to hear them. We propose to apply the term argument *ad hominem*, in the narrow sense, to arguments which the speaker knows would be without weight for the universal audience, as he conceives it.

Here is a very simple example. There will be eleven people for lunch. The maid exclaims, "That's bad luck!" Her mistress is in a hurry, and replies, "No, Mary, you're wrong; it's thirteen that brings bad luck." The argument is unanswerable and puts an immediate end to the dialogue. This reply can be considered as a type of argument *ad hominem*. It does not question any personal interest of the maid, but is based on what she accepts. It is more immediately effective than a speech on the ridiculous character of superstitions and makes it possible to argue within the framework of the prejudice instead of opposing it.

Arguments *ad hominem* are often termed "pseudoarguments" : these are arguments which obviously persuade some people, although they should not, for the good reason, in the opinion of the person who belittles them in this manner, that he himself would not in any way be influenced by them. In fact, the person who treats them so contemptuously believes, on the one hand, that the only true argumentation is that adressed to the universal audience and, on the other hand, considers himself a legitimate representative of that audience. The reason some take the effectiveness of arguments *ad hominem stricto sensu* as a sign of human weakness is that for them all argumentation should appeal to the universal audience. Schopenhauer applies the term "artifice" (*Kunstgriff*) to the use of argument *ad hominem* that consists of making the interlocutor contradict his own affirmations, the teachings of a party he approves, or his own acts.[96] But there is nothing improper in this mode of procedure. We can even qualify argument of this kind as rational, while admitting that the premises under discussion are not accepted by everyone. These premises fix the framework within which the argument unfolds: it is for this reason that we link the examination of this question with agreements particular to certain argumentations.

Argument *ad hominem* must not be confused with argument *ad personam*, which may be defined as a personal attack on the opponent and which aims essentially at disqualifying him. Such confusion may

---

[96] Schopenhauer, *Sämtliche Werke* (Piper), vol. 6: "Eristische Dialektik," p. 415, Kunstgriff 16.

arise, since these two kinds of argument are often interacting. A speaker whose thesis has been refuted by use of an argument *ad hominem* sees his prestige diminished, but let us remember that this is a consequence of any refutation, irrespective of the method used. La Bruyère already pointed out that "an error of fact makes a wise man ridiculous."[97]

On the other hand, by using the technique of admission which we have just examined, one can deduce, from a person's acts, the rules of conduct which that person seems implicitly to sanction and which can then be used as the basis for an argument *ad hominem*. Argument *ad personam* and argument *ad hominem* are then closely mingled, as in the following dialogue described by Stevenson:

> A: You are much too hard on your employees.
> B: But you, certainly, are not the one to say so. Your own factory would bear investigation far less easily than mine.[98]

The nature of "begging the question," or *petitio principii*, can be understood in terms of argumentation in general and particularly of argument *ad hominem*.

Begging the question is often regarded as an error in the technique of demonstration and Aristotle deals with it not only in his *Topics* but also in the *Prior Analytics*[99]: it consists of postulating what one wishes to prove.

We must state at the outset that on the level of formal logic the accusation of begging the question is meaningless. It could indeed be maintained that any formally correct deduction consists of a *petitio principii* and the principle of identity, affirming that any proposition implies itself, then becomes a formalization of the *petitio principii*.

Actually, the *petitio principii*, which does not concern the truth but the adherence of the interlocutors to the presupposed premises, is not an error of logic, but of rhetoric. Its nature becomes apparent, not in the context of a theory of demonstration, but in relation to the technique of argument. *Petitio principii* consists of the use of argument *ad hominem* where it cannot be used because it supposes that the interlocutor has already given his adherence to a proposition which the speaker is in fact endeavoring to make him accept. Also, the two propositions, the principle and the conclusion, which are never exactly the same, must be sufficiently close to one another for the accusation of *petitio principii* to be justified. Consequently, a dispute

---

[97] La Bruyère, "Les caractères. Des jugements," 47, *Œuvres Complètes*, p. 379.
[98] Stevenson, *Ethics and Language* (Yale), p. 127.
[99] Aristotle, *Prior Analytics*, II, 16, 64b-65a.

almost always arises as to whether or not the accusation is legitimate.

The hearer cannot claim that there really was *petitio principii* unless the premise he is challenging has, on that occasion, no other basis than the very conclusion the speaker wished to draw from it and for which the premise would be an indispensable link in the chain of reasoning. It is extremely rare that this dependence is sufficiently certain for the accusation to go unanswered. Indeed, such an accusation implies that it is possible, in an argument, to tell with precision not only whether or not the statement of a premise is distinguishable from the statement of the conclusion, but also what share can be exclusively attributed to a particular type of argument in the "conclusion-premise-conclusion" relationship. It is because of the complexity of this relationship that discussion might arise as to whether or not there is begging of the question.

The importance of the way in which the relationship between premises and conclusion is considered is shown clearly in this example involving the relationship between a person's acts and his nature. If one wants to get an admission that X is a courageous person and, with this end in view, if one presents an action of his as a manifestation of his courage, the interlocutor can claim that here is a begging of the question. But the accusation will be harder to maintain if this same action is considered as an example justifying a generalization. In order to show that there was no begging of the question, the speaker will accordingly stress that the premise under attack has a basis other than the conclusion and that its argumentative relationship with the conclusion is of a different kind than that which had been supposed. It is therefore very much to the advantage of the person accusing his interlocutor of being guilty of a *petitio principii* to put the reasoning in proper form.

Blass and, following him, Navarre, have drawn attention to this *petitio principii* occurring in Antiphon's speech on the murder of Herodes:

> I would have you know that I am much more deserving of your pity than of punishment. Punishment is indeed the due of the guilty, while pity is the due of those who are the object of an unjust accusation.[100]

The order of the major premise and of the conclusion is reversed. The implied minor premise, "I am the object of an unjust accusation," cannot be accepted by the hearers because, if it were, the case would

[100] Navarre, *Essai sur la rhétorique grecque avant Aristote,* p. 141, note 1. Cf. Blass, *Die attische Beredsamkeit,* I, p. 122.

be decided. For this reason Antiphon, instead of advancing the right to pity, which he claims to have, as the conclusion of a syllogism, makes his assertion before the major premise, so as to give it a sort of independent validity. We note in this connection that the ancient writers like, in their speeches, to present the problems as settled in their favor and make ingenious use of formal devices to hamper efforts to charge them with begging the question. And very often they are successful. Neither Blass nor Navarre considers as a *petitio principii* the argument found in the exordium of the same speech by Antiphon [1 to 8], although its structure is very similar to that of the argument just analyzed.

Bentham qualified the use of a single eulogistic or dyslogistic term in describing certain phenomena as *petitio principii* concealed in a "single appellative."[101] Schopenhauer was condemning this procedure when he remarked that what would be regarded as a "phenomenon of worship" by a neutral observer will be termed an "expression of piety" by a supporter of religion and a "superstition" by an opponent.[102] But we do not think that one can speak of begging the question in such cases, unless the qualifications are supposed to be accepted by the interlocutor who is actually challenging them. Without this limitation, every assertion of value would have to be regarded as a *petitio principii*.

Summing up, we can say that a *petitio principii* is an error in argumentation. It has to do with argument *ad hominem* and presupposes it, for its sphere is not truth, but adherence. If it is recognized as illegitimate to indulge in begging the question, that is, to base one's argument on premises that the audience rejects, the implication is that one may use those premises that it accepts. When truth is in question, and not adherence, argument *ad hominem* should be rejected, but in that case begging the question is impossible. Argument *ad hominem* and *petitio principii* are correlative: it is only within the framework of a theory of argumentation that one can take an accusation of *petitio principii* into consideration and examine whether or not the implied criticism is legitimate.

[101] Bentham, *Works*, vol. II, *The Book of Fallacies*, p. 436, pt. IV, chap. I, Question-Begging Appellatives.

[102] Schopenhauer, *Sämtliche Werke* (Piper), vol. 6: "Eristische Dialektik," p.414, Kunstgriff 12.

CHAPTER 2

The Choice of Data and Their Adaptation
for Argumentative Purposes

§ 29. *Selection of Data and Presence*

One datum in argumentation consists of the agreements available
to the speaker as supports for his argument. But this element is so
large and capable of being used in so many different ways, that the
manner in which one makes use of it is of paramount importance.
Accordingly, before examining the use of this datum in argumentation, it is essential that we say something of the part played by
preliminary selection of the elements that are to serve as the starting
point of the argument and by the adaptation of these elements to
its purposes.

We must make it clear, however, that being able to choose from
among data does not imply that the elements which are not utilized
can be totally disregarded. For each audience there is a set of things
that are admitted, and all of them are liable to have an effect on its
reactions. This set can be determined fairly easily if the audience
is a specialized one: it will be the corpus of knowledge recognized
by those trained in a scientific discipline;[1] it will be the whole juridical
system within which a legal decision is fitted.[2] Except where a for-

---

[1] Cf. Kneebone, "Induction and Probability," *Proceedings of the Aristotelian
Society*, 50 (1949-50), 35. In the field of mathematics, cf. Wilder, "The Origin
and Growth of Mathematical Concepts," *Bulletin of the American Mathematical
Society*, 59 (1953), 424-425.

[2] Cf. Cossio, "Phenomenology of the Decision," in *Latin-American Legal Philos-*

115

malized field which can be completely isolated is involved, the aggregate of things admitted is fluid and remains open. Its boundaries are especially vague where the audience is not a specialized one, although at certain periods the elaboration of philosophical ideas may help to make its content slightly more definite. In any case, it provides each audience with a frame of reference by means of which arguments can be tested.

The part that is played by selection is so obvious that when facts are mentioned, we must always ask ourselves what it is that their use can strengthen or weaken. The press, whether it supports the government or is in opposition to it, has made us accustomed to this selection of the facts either for the purposes of explicit argument or for those of argument which it is hoped the reader will carry out himself. In the traditional systems of rhetoric under the heading of "narration," there is no dearth of advice on the methods of choosing the facts of the case.[3] But this choice is also a dominant factor in scientific debates: choice of the facts deemed relevant, choice of hypotheses, choice of the theories that should be confronted with facts, choice of the actual elements that constitute facts. The method of each science implies such a choice, which is relatively stable in the natural sciences, but is much more variable in the social sciences.

By the very fact of selecting certain elements and presenting them to the audience, their importance and pertinency to the discussion are implied. Indeed, such a choice endows these elements with a *presence*, which is an essential factor in argumentation and one that is far too much neglected in rationalistic conceptions of reasoning. What we have in mind is illustrated by this lovely Chinese story:

> A king sees an ox on its way to sacrifice. He is moved to pity for it and orders that a sheep be used in its place. He confesses he did so because he could see the ox, but not the sheep.[4]

Presence acts directly on our sensibility. As Piaget shows, it is a psychological datum operative already at the level of perception: when two things are set side by side, say a fixed standard and things of variable dimensions with which it is compared, the thing on which the eye dwells, that which is best or most often seen, is, by that very

---

ophy, p. 399. Cited by Goldschmidt, *Le système stoïcien et l'idée de temps*, p. 97, note 7.

[3] *Rhetorica ad Herennium*, I, 12; Cicero, *De Inventione*, I, § 30; Quintilian, IV, II, especially § 57.

[4] Pareto, *The Mind and Society*, vol. II, § 1135, p. 671, summarizing a story of Meng-Tseu, bk. I, § 7, in connection with his treatment of pity as a residue. Cited in Pauthier, *Confucius et Mencius*, pp. 230 et seq.

circumstance, overestimated.[5] The thing that is present to the consciousness assumes thus an importance that the theory and practice of argumentation must take into consideration. It is not enough indeed that a thing should exist for a person to feel its presence. This is true even of the disputes of scholars, witness the role played in the Gassendist dispute by the book in which Jean de Launoy pointed out the variations in the Church's attitude toward Aristotle:

> To be sure, says the Abbé Lenoble in this connection, no one is unaware that the Church is much older than the Aristotelianism of the thirteenth century. All the protagonists know this, but nobody thinks of it.[6]

Accordingly one of the preoccupations of a speaker is to make present, by verbal magic alone, what is actually absent but what he considers important to his argument or, by making them more present, to enhance the value of some of the elements of which one has actually been made conscious.

In Bacon's view, rhetoric, envisaged as a technique making it possible "to apply reason to imagination, for the better moving of the will,"[7] is essentially connected with the effects of presence:

> ... The affection beholdeth merely the present; reason beholdeth the future and sum of time. And therefore the present filling the imagination more, reason is commonly vanquished; but after that force of eloquence and persuasion hath made things future and remote appear as present, then upon the revolt of the imagination reason prevaileth.[8]

Bacon is expressing, in the philosophical language of his day, an idea not far removed from ours: presence, at first a psychological phenomenon, becomes an essential element in argumentation.

Certain masters of rhetoric, with a liking for quick results, advocate the use of concrete objects in order to move an audience: Caesar's bloody tunic which Antony waves in front of the Roman populace, or the children of the accused brought before his judges in order to arouse their pity. The real thing is expected to induce an adherence that its mere description would be unable to secure; it is a precious aid, provided argumentation utilizes it to advantage. The real can indeed exhibit unfavorable features from which it may be difficult to distract the viewer's attention; the concrete object might also turn

---

[5] Piaget, *Introduction à l'Épistémologie génétique*, vol. I, pp. 174-175.

[6] Lenoble, "Histoire et physique," *Revue d'histoire des sciences et de leurs applications*, 1953, p. 125.

[7] Bacon, *Advancement of Learning*, bk. II, xviii, § 2, GBWW, vol. 30, p. 66.

[8] *Ibid.*, bk. II, xviii, § 4, p. 67.

his attention in a direction leading away from what is of importance to the speaker. Presence, and efforts to increase the feeling of presence, must hence not be confused with fidelity to reality.

On the other hand, one should not either, as one might be tempted to by overrationalizing thought, want to reduce presence to certitude and treat events that are more remote from the present as less important because they are less probable. Lewis considers that this is the only solution that makes propinquity and remoteness—put forward by Bentham as a dimension of pleasures—compatible with utilitarian calculus.[9] However abnormal it may be in his system, the introduction by Bentham of this supplementary dimension is, for us who interpret it in terms of presence, perfectly justified since it conforms to undeniable psychical tendencies.

In an appendix to his work on rhetoric, Whately[10] reproduces a lengthy note by Campbell dealing with the conditions of time, place, relation, and personal interest by means of which an event affects us: these conditions are also those which determine presence. Presence is thus not exclusively linked to proximity in time, although such proximity is an essential element. It should also be observed that the effort to make something present to the consciousness can relate not only to real objects, but also to a judgment or an entire argumentative development. As far as possible, such an effort is directed to filling the whole field of consciousness with this presence so as to isolate it, as it were, from the hearer's overall mentality. And this is essential. If one finds that a properly developed syllogism, which was accepted by the hearer, does not necessarily induce him to act in accordance with the conclusions, it is because the premises, which were isolated during the demonstration, might have encountered obstacles once they entered the mental circuit of the person they were supposed to persuade.[11]

The importance of presence in argumentation has a negative as well as a positive aspect: deliberate suppression of presence is an equally noteworthy phenomenon, deserving of detailed study. We will give only an indication, which we consider essential, of the unreal character of all that which is not a part of our actions, which is not connected with our convictions. Stephen Spender makes the following accurate remark:

> ... Nearly all human beings have an extremely intermittent grasp on reality. Only a few things, which illustrate their own interests

---

[9] Lewis, *An Analysis of Knowledge and Valuation*, p. 493.
[10] Whately, *Elements of Rhetoric* (Harper), Appendix H, pp. 328 et seq.
[11] Cf. § 6, supra: Persuading and Convincing.

and ideas, are real to them; other things, which are in fact equally real, appear to them as abstractions... Your friends are allies and therefore real human beings... Your opponents are just tiresome, unreasonable, unnecessary theses, whose lives are so many false statements which you would like to strike out with a lead bullet. ...[12]

Applying this conception to the reactions he felt during the civil war in Spain when confronted with the atrocities committed by the pro-Franco and Republican sides, he adds: "In the first case I saw corpses, in the second only words."

In the same book, Koestler, writing about executions required by the cause, makes this observation:

> Now these two individuals had become more real to me than the cause in the name of which they were to be sacrificed. ...[13]

The individual whom one is ready to sacrifice to the system is not only unreal *de jure* because he has lost his ontological status, but also *de facto* because he is not present. Shock is experienced either because of theoretical doubts or when, in a concrete situation, the presence of the man one is going to sacrifice can no longer be kept out of the consciousness.

This notion of presence, which we are speaking of here and which we consider to be of paramount importance for the technique of argumentation, is not a philosophical formulation. A philosophy that considers presence as a cornerstone of its structure—that of Buber or Sartre, for example— would connect it with an ontology or an anthropology. That is not our purpose. We are interested only in the technical aspect of this notion, which leads to the inevitable conclusion that all argumentation is selective. It chooses the elements and the method of making them present. By doing so it cannot avoid being open to accusations of incompleteness and hence of partiality and tendentiousness. And we must bear this criticism in mind when we want argumentation to be convincing, that is, valid for the universal audience. A tendentious argument, deliberately put forward on behalf of a party it is one's interest or duty to favor, will have to be completed by the adverse argument in order to reach a balance in the appraisal of the known elements. The judge will not make a decision before he has heard both parties. But going beyond this requirement to the assertion that the totality of informational elements must be presented, giving to each element the emphasis it deserves, would imply the existence of a criterion for determining these relevant elements and would imply also that the totality de-

---

[12] Crossman, *The God That Failed* (Bantam), p. 257.
[13] *Ibid.*, p. 72.

fined in this way can be exhausted. We think this is an illusion and that passage from the subjective to the objective can be accomplished only by successive enlargements, none of which can be regarded as final. The person who effects a new enlargement will necessarily emphasize that the previous statements had involved a choice of data, and he will probably be able to show quite easily that this was indeed the case. We must add that in the social as well as in the natural sciences this choice is not mere selection, but also involves construction and interpretation.[14]

All argumentation presupposes thus a choice consisting not only of the selection of elements to be used, but also of the technique for their presentation. Questions of form and questions of substance are intermingled in order to achieve presence. For clarity of treatment, we will deal with them later in succession.[15]

§ 30. *The Interpretation of Data*

The utilization of data for argumentative purposes is impossible without a conceptual development which gives them meaning and makes them relevant to the progression of the discourse. A consideration of the aspects of this development—of this formulation— helps us to grasp more clearly what distinguishes argumentation from demonstration.

Every demonstration requires that the elements on which it is based should be univocal. They are supposed to be understood by everyone in the same way, by virtue of means of knowledge which are assumed to be intersubjective, and, if this is not the case, the object of reasoning is reduced artificially to those elements alone from which all ambiguity seems to be removed. Either the datum is presented immediately as something clear and significant, in a rationalistic conception of deduction, or attention is directed only to the form of the signs which is supposed to be perceived by all in the same way, such that handling of these signs does not lead to ambiguity; this is the conception of the modern formalists. In all these cases, interpretation does not raise any problems, or, at least, the problems it does raise are eliminated from the theory. Things are different in argumentation.

The study of argumentation compels us to take into account not only the choice of data but also the way in which they are interpreted,

---

[14] Cf. Aron, *Introduction à la philosophie de l'histoire*, p. 115.
[15] Cf. § 37, infra: Technical Problems in the Presentation of Data, and § 42, infra: Figures of Choice, Presence, and Communion.

the meaning attributed to them. It is to the extent that it constitutes a conscious or unconscious choice between several modes of meaning, that the interpretation can be distinguished from the data being interpreted, and can be opposed to them. This does not, of course, mean that we adhere to a metaphysics that separates immediate, irreducible data from the theoretical constructions developed out of them. If we were to adopt a metaphysical position, we would be more inclined to admit the existence of an indissoluble link between theory and experience, as expressed in F. Gonseth's principle of duality.[16] However, for the time being, we are not so ambitious. We wish only to insist on the fact that, in the practice of argumentation, data constitute elements on which there seems to be an agreement that is, at least provisionally or conventionally, considered to be univocal and undisputed. To these data we will consciously oppose their interpretation, when the latter appears as a choice between meanings which are not an integral part, so to speak, of that which they interpret. It is precisely when incompatible interpretations make us hesitate as to how we are to conceive the datum that the problem of interpretation is very important; it falls into the background as soon as one of the interpretations has appeared most adequate and is therefore the only one present in our consciousness.

The problem we are dealing with can be seen in its full extent only by one who realizes that interpretation does not consist merely in the choice, at a well-defined level, between interpretations that seem incompatible—as where one wonders if it is the train one is in or the neighboring one which has started to move—but also in the choice of the level on which the interpretative effort will be conducted. The same process can indeed be described as the action of tightening a bolt, assembling a vehicle, earning a living, or helping the export drive.[17] On the other hand, an act can be considered in itself, pinpointed as much as possible, considered in its most contingent aspect, and isolated from the situation. But it can also be interpreted as a symbol, a means, a precedent, a step in a direction. Whether they present the phenomenon at such and such a level of abstraction or whether they connect it to an overall situation—and we note in this connection that interpretation can be not merely a simple choice but also a creation, an invention of significance—these various interpretations are not always incompatible, but emphasizing one of them and setting it in the foreground of consciousness often pushes the others into the

---

[16] Cf. Gonseth, "Les comptes rendus des Troisièmes Entretiens de Zurich sur le principe de dualité," *Dialectica*, 22-25 (1952-1953).
[17] Gellner, "Maxims," *Mind*, 60, new series, (1951), 393.

shadow. The core of many arguments is formed of this play of innumerable interpretations and of the struggle to impose some of them and get rid of others.

The infinite complexity of interpretations, coupled with their mobility and interaction, sufficiently explain the impossibility of reducing all statements to propositions with a numerical probability that can be evaluated. Even if an increase in our knowledge enables us to estimate these probabilities more precisely, it will be only as long as we remain within the framework of a particular interpretation. Conventionally there is nothing against this, but there is also nothing to prevent a new interpretation from being brought forward or suggested implicitly: the possibilities of interpretation seem inexhaustible.

Sometimes those who argue aim not so much at imposing a particular interpretation as at showing the ambiguity of the situation and the various ways of understanding it. The mere fact of giving a preference to a certain interpretation, or even of believing in the existence of a single valid interpretation, may indicate a particular system of beliefs, or even a conception of the world. Uniqueness of interpretation can indeed be postulated not only in a specific case, but also as a general rule. In Pascal's view, it is our corrupted will that prevents us from recognizing truths[18]: it is impossible to conceive of any possible rational justification for the multiplicity of interpretations. The ancient authors applied the term *color* to interpretations that were favorable to a viewpoint: to them the term had a pejorative meaning, due to the fact that one admits that the facts have a truth, which the advocate knows, and *color* would be an alteration of this truth.[19]

For the ancients, whether philosophers, jurists, or theologians, interpretation normally had to do with texts: it is mostly modern psychologists who have insisted on the ubiquity of interpretation, which is not absent even at the level of perception.[20] To reduce somewhat the confusion that these multiple uses of the notion of interpretation must inevitably lead to, we suggest a distinction— which seems essential in a theory of argumentation—between the interpretation of *signs* and the interpretation of *indices*. By *signs* we mean all phenomena capable of evoking another phenomenon, to the extent that they are used in an act of communication, for this evocative purpose. Whether or not they are linguistic, the important thing, to us, is the

---

[18] Pascal, *On Geometrical Demonstration*, GBWW, vol. 33, pp. 439 et seq.
[19] Quintilian, IV, II, 88.
[20] Cf. Claparède, "La genèse de l'hypothèse," *Archives de Psychologie* XXIV (1934); Merleau-Ponty, *Phénoménologie de la perception*.

intention to communicate which characterizes them. An *index*, on the other hand, makes it possible to evoke another phenomenon in what we may call an objective manner, independently of any intentionality. The same act, that of closing a window, may, according to the circumstances, be a prearranged sign or an index of someone's being cold. The order "Go out" can be simultaneously interpreted as a request for someone to leave and as an index of the anger of the person making the request. Our distinction, though comparable to Jasper's distinction between expression and symptom,[21] differs from it in that it is strictly technical. Indeed, interpretation as a sign or as an index presents distinct problems, although these two kinds of interpretation are sometimes inextricably entangled.

§ 31. *The Interpretation of the Discourse and Its Problems*

Our study has displayed the ambiguity surrounding the argumentative datum that is to be interpreted and the manifold and constantly interacting aspects under which it can be interpreted. Current studies on language as a means of communication are dominated by the problems raised by this matter of interpretation. In no other period has there been such amazement at the fact that a person can communicate to another something which has, for the hearer, a foreseeable meaning. Incomprehension and error in interpretation ceased to be regarded as an avoidable accident, but were seen as an essential condition of language. Letter and spirit were no longer distinguished for the mere purpose of setting them in opposition and claiming the right to make an interpretation other than that literally authorized: the letter itself came to be seen as a mirage that dissolved, so to speak, between the possible interpretations. From this point on, we witness an effort to find rules which would make it possible to limit the excessively wide possibilities of interpretation that are theoretically admissible.

No one has worked at this task with more zeal than I. A. Richards. To him rhetoric is not, as it is to us, essentially connected with argumentation; it is, as it is to Jean Paulhan, a study of expression and, more particularly, of linguistic interpretation. According to Richards, rhetoric ought to be the study of misunderstanding and of ways of remedying it.[22]

Having freed thought from the so-called single meaning of words, Richards puts forward a technique of interpretation. It consists of

---

[21] Jaspers, *Psychopathologie générale*, chap. III.
[22] Richards, *The Philosophy of Rhetoric*, p. 3.

seeking a meaning close to that which the speaker would attach to his own words if he could listen to his own speech.[23] The hearer finds this meaning by looking for what gives him "satisfaction,"[24] a criterion that is applicable because author and hearer have in common both experiences and ways of reacting. A good interpretation of an expression is thus one that the author could approve, given the context.

According to Richards, it is always the context that gives a word its meaning, and it is only through the context that we can discover what the word does.[25] But what elements of the situation does this context—which cannot be purely verbal—embrace? When the boy cries "wolf" for the tenth time and fails to get attention although, this time, the danger is real, this happens because the interpretation of his cries has been determined by the entire situation, which includes his earlier warning cries. The boy does not desire this extension of the context. In other circumstances, however, the author himself endeavors to have certain elements included in the context. One playwright, for instance, will make a caretaker's lodge the setting for his dialogue, while another will take the total expanse of the natural and supernatural world.[26]

Every writer has to be able to rely on the interpreter's goodwill,[27] and the more prestige the text has, the greater the effort the interpreter will be ready to make. But is there not a danger, from this very fact, of imposing on the writer an interpretation that will really be a function of the reader's own convictions? When the believer interprets a passage in the Bible, he assumes the text to be not only coherent, but truthful. As Pascal says: "When the word of God, which is really true, is false literally, it is true spiritually."[28] But the person who is determined to reject nothing in the Scriptures can interpret them only in terms of the truths to which he already adheres. In a lesser degree, as soon as a writer enjoys a certain renown, the goodwill applied to the interpretation of his text is not independent of that which is admitted by the interpreter, because the latter has to incorporate the writer's contribution with his own convictions. Now, the theses admitted will vary from one interpreter to another. Hence every so-called internal rule of interpretation, such as coherence, is

---

[23] Richards, *Principles of Literary Criticism* (Harcourt, Brace) pp. 226-227.
[24] Richards, *Interpretation in Teaching* (Harcourt, Brace), p. 68.
[25] *Ibid.*, pp. viii, 48, 62; Richards and Gibson, *Learning Basic English*, p. 88.
[26] Cf. Burke, *A Grammar of Motives* (Prentice-Hall), p. 77.
[27] Richards, "A Symposium on Emotive Meaning," *The Philosophical Review*, (1948), p. 145.
[28] Pascal, *Pensées*, GBWW, vol. 33, p. 299.

inescapably mixed up with criteria set by the interpreter. Rejection of incoherent interpretations is *a priori* a thing to be recommended, but paying attention to this does not provide a rule of behavior that is sufficient to guide us in each case toward the interpretation that would objectively be the best.

If the interpretation of a text is to translate the totality of the author's intentions, one must take into consideration the fact that the text often includes an implicit argument as its essential component. Thus, when Isocrates has the son of Alcibiades say

> everyone knows that the same men brought about the destruction of democracy and the exile of my father[29]

he offers verifiable facts, but the words mean: "my father's exile was a political act as condemnable as the destruction of democracy." The whole meaning of the sentence lies in the implicit argument that is to lead to this final conclusion. Although the statement seems only to concern facts, what it suggests is an evaluation. Now the distinction between what is said and what is only a superadded construction subject to debate depends on agreement or disagreement with respect to the interpretation: just as the speaker's choice of an interpretation of facts can be distinguished from them only when a different interpretation seems possible, so the interpretation of the text is superadded to it as a distinct element when there are reasons for distinguishing the two.

Besides the cases which cannot be excluded *a priori*, in which the ambiguity of a text is deliberate, and any effort to make it univocal is due to a misunderstanding, it is rare in a nonformalized language that a text appears absolutely clear to everybody. In most cases the impression of clarity, linked with univocity, is the product of ignorance or of lack of imagination. Locke called attention to this when he wrote:

> Many a man who was pretty well satisfied of the meaning of a text of Scripture or clause in the Code, at first reading, has, by consulting commentators, quite lost the sense of it and by these elucidations given rise or increase to his doubts and drawn obscurity upon the place.[30]

The clearness of a text is conditioned by the possibilities of interpretation that it offers. But for attention to be drawn to the existence of nonequivalent interpretations, the consequences of one interpretation must in some way differ from those of another; now it may be that it is only in a particular context that the differences between

---

[29] Isocrates, *Concerning the Team of Horses*, § 4.
[30] Locke, *An Essay Concerning Human Understanding*, bk III, chap. IX, § 9, GBWW, vol. 35, p. 287.

them can become apparent. Clarity in a text or a concept can therefore never be absolutely assured, except conventionally, by voluntary limitation of the context in which the interpretation should be made. The necessity for interpretation is thus the rule, while the elimination of all interpretation is part of an exceptional and artificial situation.

§ 32. *Choice of Qualifiers*

Dealing with data for argumentative purposes involves not only their interpretation, the meaning attributed to them, but also the presentation of certain aspects of these data, thanks to the agreements underlying the language used.

The most obvious way in which this choice becomes apparent is through the use of the *epithet*. The epithet results from the visible selection of a quality which is emphasized and which is meant to complete our knowledge of the object. This epithet is used without justification because it is supposed to set forth unquestionable facts; only the choice of the facts will seem tendentious. It is permissible to call the French Revolution "that bloody revolution," but this is not the only way of qualifying it and other epithets could equally well be chosen. The role of epithets in argumentation is most clearly seen when two symmetrical qualifications with opposite values appear equally possible: by calling Orestes a "mother slayer" or the "avenger of his father," by referring to a mule as a "half donkey" or a "daughter of a storm-footed steed,"[31] the speaker unmistakably chooses a viewpoint which is perceived to be tendentious because one can immediately see how it might be corrected. But not all epithets appear as a choice between two points of view which require, so to speak, to be completed by each other: generally, the various aspects of a reality are situated on different planes, and a more complete vision of reality can consist only of a progressive multiplication of aspects to which attention is drawn.

Where choice of epithet is concerned, tendentiousness in presentation is fairly easily detectable. Its discovery is more difficult when an individual is merely inserted into a class and designated simply as a member of it.[32] When someone is called "the murderer," the choice is not as apparent as in the expression "Orestes, the murderer," because the choice seems to identify with the very use of the concepts.[33]

---

[31] Aristotle, *Rhetoric*, III, 2, 1405b.

[32] Cf. Perelman and Olbrechts-Tyteca, "Les notions et l'argumentation," *Archivio di Filosofia*, vol. *Semantica* (1955).

[33] These considerations relative to the epithet and the insertion of an individual

But actually existing classifications used in making a qualification are numerous, and it is impossible to qualify without at the same time choosing the classification to which preeminence will be afforded. This choice is rarely devoid of argumentative intent. Classes are indeed characterized not only by the features common to their members but also, and sometimes mostly, by the attitude adopted toward them, the manner of judging and treating them. The various laws govern this relationship: to declare that someone has committed a theft is also to determine the punishments to which he may be subjected. Similarly, if someone is declared to be suffering from a particular disease, this involves, at least partially, an advance judgment of the treatment that will be applied to him.

Thus every conceptual thought is inserted into frameworks that are already completely formed,[34] which one must use and manipulate so as best to serve the necessities of action upon others.

Not only does concrete argument imply the existence of classifications, but sometimes even, on the strength of the latter, one disqualifies what does not fit into them, and accordingly seems defective. The marxists classify all philosophies as either materialist or idealist; thus metaphysicians who do not come under one of these categories are accused of lack of courage.[35]

These classifications can be disputed, modified, and adapted, but in the majority of cases, one will merely oppose to them other classifications deemed more important, interesting, or fruitful. Instead of dividing people into rich and poor, it is enough to bring to the fore the contrast between black and white for the poor white to feel his stock rise. "Similarly," Simone de Beauvoir tells us, "the most mediocre of males considers himself a demigod as compared with women"[36]: a dominant classification, made the center of attention, pushes into the background the other classifications and the consequences attaching to them.

into a class hold good, *mutatis mutandis*, for adverbs and verbs, which both permit a choice of certain aspects of the data with a view to bringing them into the forefront. The choice expressed by an adverb will be more visible than that expressed by a verb. Instead of saying "advancing with difficulty," it will often be much more effective to use the verbs "creep" and "thread one's way." Cf. Weaver, *The Ethics of Rhetoric*, p. 135. However, the effectiveness is rather due to hidden metaphor. (Cf. § 88, infra: Dormant Metaphors or Expressions with a Metaphorical Meaning.)

[34] Cf. Whorf, "The Relation of Habitual Thought and Behavior to Language," in Hayakawa, *Language, Meaning, and Maturity*, p. 225.

[35] Lefebvre, *A la lumière du matérialisme dialectique, I: Logique formelle, logique dialectique*, p. 25.

[36] Beauvoir, *Le deuxième sexe*, vol. I, p. 25, Introduction.

To quote Simone de Beauvoir again:

> a sincere faith greatly helps the little girl to avoid an inferiority complex: she is neither male nor female, but the creature of God.[37]

Saint Thomas uses a similar procedure to suggest the superiority of knowledge pertaining to salvation over knowledge of sensible phenomena: as Gilson puts it, he invites man to look rather toward another kingdom which is not merely that of man, but that of the children of God.[38]

The proper noun, as well as the common noun and adjective, can be used to bring about this change in viewpoint. For instance, when, after the defeat of the English forces in Holland, Pitt asks in Parliament "whether it was not of immense advantage to Europe in general, that Holland was not added to France without a struggle,"[39] he modifies the appraisal of events by relating the disaster not to the limited group formed by Holland, and not to England upon whose own particular interests he did not dare to dwell, but to a notion embracing both England and Holland and providing the victim with a measure of consolation by linking its destiny with a continent that was far from defeated.

Qualifications sometimes are of such an unexpected character that one sees in them rather a figure than a choice. The important thing is to see what makes them an argumentative figure.[40] It is the classifying form which yields a striking result. This passage from Bossuet provides an example :

> In these deplorable conditions [of poverty] may we even think of adorning our bodies? Do we not tremble at the thought of wearing the sustenance, the life, and the patrimony of the poor?[41]

The ornaments are qualified, without further ado, as the sustenance of the poor: the classifying form considers as already accepted what is precisely the aim of Bossuet's sermon.

Qualification, insertion into a class, may be expressed by use of a coordinating conjunction, such as "and," "or," or "nor," instead of by use of a notion already developed. We can illustrate this by two excerpts from a book by Gide: first he attacks a certain procedure, which he does not disdain to use a few pages later :

> And I would not even mention it [Stirner's book] to you, my dear Angela, if there were not some who by a process worthy of *vil-*

---

[37] *Ibid.*, vol. II, p. 449.

[38] Gilson, *The Christian Philosophy of Saint Thomas Aquinas*, p. 378.

[39] Pitt, *Orations on the French War*, p. 90.

[40] Cf. § 41, infra: Rhetorical Figures and Argumentation.

[41] Bossuet, *Sermons*, vol. II: *Sur l'intégrité de la Pénitence*, p. 616.

lainous laws would now like to link the fate of Nietzsche with that
of Stirner, and, by considering them together, bring them under
a common mantle of admiration or reproach. ... You should be
just as indignant to hear people say, "Stirner and Nietzsche," as
Nietzsche himself was to hear people say, "Goethe *and* Schiller."[42]

But the spurned technique is soon used by Gide himself:

> One may love the Bible or not understand it, love the Thou-
> sand and One Nights or not understand it, but, if you please, I
> will divide the whole mass of thinking people into two classes, be-
> cause of two irreconcilable types of mentality: those who are moved
> by these two books, and those who are and will remain unaffected
> by them.[13]

The word "and" is not actually used, but it might as well be; the two
books are put into a single class to which the reaction will be identical.
Here also there is homogenization and, thereby, equalization of values.
In neither case is there argumentation in favor of this equalization.
But the two terms are presented as if their insertion into the same class
went without saying, and there is a formation of a class *ad hoc* through
the union of the two terms on a plane of equality. This process of qualifying by coordination can be applied to any object. All that is necessary to effect such a qualification is to treat the objects in the same
way. Humorists and creators of utopias often manage to produce a
comic effect by treating alike behavior that is governed by social conventions and behavior that is not.

Treatment of this sort does not necessarily lead to the formation of
technically developed classes. In most cases there is no notion permitting their designation: it is enough that the elements placed side by
side in this way to form a class should react on each other in the hearer's
mind, and it is because of this that the technique assumes its argumentative value. It is not, however, a matter of indifference whether or
not insertion into a class is effected by use of a qualifier. The notion
that one uses often plays an essential role, if only because of the suggestion of praise or blame that attaches to it. We have already seen the
tendentious use of such qualifiers as "tyrant" or "pirate" condemned
by Bentham as being a *petitio principii* "by the employment of a single appellative."[44] This role played by notions leads us to consider
what is perhaps the most profound aspect of choice, that is, its most
insidious and ineluctable aspect.

---

[42] Gide, *Prétextes*, p. 135.
[43] *Ibid.*, p. 175.
[44] Cf. § 28, supra: Argumentation *Ad Hominem* and Begging the Question.

§ 33. *On the Use of Notions*

The qualification of the data and their insertion into classes are two aspects of a single activity, seen at one time as comprehension, and at another as extension and which is the application of notions to the object of discourse. As long as their use does not give rise to difficulties, these notions appear also as data on which one thinks one can depend and on which one depends indeed effectively. But the nature of this agreement, the consciousness of its precarious nature, of its limitations, and also of the argumentative possibilities concealed in it can be interpreted in different ways.

Univocal passage from the word to the idea it represents was seen by the theoreticians of the past as a phenomenon resulting from the good use of language. One assumes also that this idea can be precisely determined by resort to other ideas that are themselves expressed by univocal terms or that it can be the object of a rational intuition.[45] For centuries many good minds have found in the artificial language of mathematicians an ideal of clarity and univocity that natural languages, with their lesser development, should strive to imitate. From this viewpoint, any ambiguity, obscurity, or confusion is considered an imperfection that can be eliminated not only in theory but also in fact. Because of the univocity and the exactness of its terms, scientific language is held to be the best instrument for demonstration and verification, and one would like to impose these characteristics on all language.

But are all the functions of language linked in the same way to these qualities of univocity and exactness, and is it even possible to say that scientific language is really free from all ambiguity? Discussion[46] in *Philosophy of Science* of an article by M. Black[47] led A. Benjamin to the conclusion that vague ideas are an integral part of science and that any theory of meaning which denies their existence is not a theory of science.[48]

How is this change to be explained? It seems to follow from the fact that one has come to see that a notion can be considered univocal only if its field of application is wholly determined, which is possible only in a formal system from which every unforeseen element has been excluded: the notion of "bishop" in the game of chess satisfies this condi-

---

[45] Cf. Pascal, *On Geometrical Demonstration*, GBWW, vol. 33, pp. 430 et seq.

[46] See articles by Hempel, Copilowish, and Benjamin in *Philosophy of Science*, 6 (1939).

[47] Black, "Vagueness," *Philosophy of Science*, 4(1937), 427-455.

[48] Benjamin, "Science and Vagueness," *Philosophy of Science*, 6(1939), 430.

tion. But the situation is different where one is dealing with notions developed within a scientific or juridical system and which must apply to future events whose nature cannot always be completely determined. In a remarkable article, F. Waismann asks that this be recognized and that the idea be abandoned that scientifically utilizable notions can be reduced to *sense data,* because their use presupposes a texture adaptable to the requirements of a future experience. He writes:

> For instance, we define gold in contrast to some other metals such as alloys. This suffices for our present needs, and we do not probe any further. We tend to *overlook* the fact that there are always other directions in which the concept has not been defined. And if we did, we could easily imagine conditions which would necessitate new limitations. In short, it is not possible to define a concept like gold with absolute precision, i.e., in such a way that every nook and cranny is blocked against entry of doubt.[49]

To the extent that future experiences and the way in which they are to be examined are not entirely foreseeable, it is essential to conceive even the most precisely stated terms as surrounded by a fringe of indefiniteness sufficient to enable them to be applied to reality. A perfectly clear notion is one of which all cases of application are known so that it does not admit of a new unforeseen use.[50] Only divine knowledge or knowledge limited by conventions satisfies such a requirement.

For these reasons it is not possible to do as Bobbio suggests, and compare the exactness of law with that of mathematics.[51] Nor can we follow Kelsen's proposal to regard law simply as a closed order.[52] A judge cannot do as a formal logician does and limit the field of application of his system once and for all. He is in danger of being guilty of a denial of justice if he refuses to make a decision "on the ground of the silence, obscurity, or deficiency of the law" (Code Napoléon, art. 4). In each case, he must be able to decide whether or not the provision that is invoked can be used under the circumstances, even if these circumstances were not foreseen by the legislature. This compels him to make a decision based on specific reasons as to the way he will define one or another juridical category.[53]

[49] Waismann, "Verifiability," in Flew, *Essays in Logic and Language,* p. 120.

[50] Cf. Perelman, "Problèmes de logique juridique," *Journal des Tribunaux,* Apr. 22, 1956, p. 272.

[51] Cf. Bobbio, "Scienza del diritto e analisi del linguaggio," *Saggi di critica delle scienze,* p. 55.

[52] Kelsen, *Reine Rechtslehre.*

[53] Cf. Perelman, *The Idea of Justice and the Problem of Argument,* p. 90.

When the use of notions has not been formalized, their application presents problems connected with the formulation and determination of the concepts. These problems inevitably get more difficult as the notions used get vaguer and more woolly. This is the case, in particular, with notions which can be referred explicitly or implicitly to indeterminate groupings, such as negative phrases like "that which is not living" and "those who do not pay taxes." The difficulty is greatest with vague notions—*justice*, for example[54]—which can be made precise and applied only by selecting and bringing to the fore certain of their aspects that are incompatible with others or with notions—of which *merit* is one—whose use can be conceived only in terms of their vagueness: an evaluation has to be made by referring both to the subject who acts and to the result obtained.[55]

Use of the notions of a living language thus very often appears not as a simple choice of data applicable to other data, but as a construction of theories and as an interpretation of reality by means of the notions which they make it possible to develop. And that is not all. Language is not only a means of communication: it is also an instrument for acting on minds, a means of persuasion. Now, the influence of the needs of argumentation on the malleability of notions has not received the emphasis it deserves.[56]

Where the basic notions of morality and philosophy are concerned, only argumentation and controversy can explain why nuances are introduced and why distinctions are brought in that show the ambiguity of what had previously been considered clear. And it is precisely because the notions used in argumentation are not univocal and have no fixed meaning that will not change that the conclusions of an argumentation are not binding.

The values accepted by the audience, the speaker's prestige, and the very language he uses, all these elements are in constant interaction when one wishes to gain the adherence of minds. Formal logic has eliminated all these problems from its demonstrative technique, thanks to a set of conventions that are well founded in a field of purely theoretical knowledge. But to be unaware of the influence exerted on language

[54] *Ibid.*, pp. 1 et seq.

[55] Cf. Dupréel, "Sur les rapports de la logique et de la sociologie ou théorie des idées confuses, *Revue de métaphysique et de morale,* July 1911, pp. 517-522; *Le rapport social*, pp. 227 et seq.; "La logique et les sociologues," *Revue de l'Institut de Sociologie Solvay* 1-2 (1924), 71-116, 215-238; "La pensée confuse," *Annales des Hautes Études de Gand,* vol. III, pp. 17-26, reprinted in *Essais pluralistes.*

[56] Cf. Perelman and Olbrechts-Tyteca, "Les notions et l'argumentation," *Archivio di Filosofia,* vol. *Semantica* (1955).

and thought by the need to decide and act is to keep oneself in darkness and to disregard certain fundamental aspects of human thought.

§ 34. *Clarification and Obscuration of Notions*

The necessity for a univocal language, which dominates scientific thought, has made clarity of concepts an ideal which one feels bound to try and achieve, forgetting that this very clarity may stand in the way of other functions of language.[57] The existence of this ideal accounts for the endeavors at the technical level to achieve this clarification of notions and at the theoretical level to describe it, without paying attention to the practices and occasions that cause notions to be obscured, just as in a well-kept garden one does not bother about how the weeds grow: one simply pulls them up. We believe on the contrary that, from the use of notions and from the rules governing this usage in particular circumstances, we should gain an understanding of how notions are clarified and obscured and how sometimes the clarification of certain notions can bring about the obscuring of others.

We have seen that a concept can be perfectly clear only if it is within a formal system. As soon as certain experiments are brought into contact with a formal system which ought to enable us to describe and forecast them, a certain indetermination is introduced due to the fact that it is not said, *a priori*, how this integration of the experiment will be achieved. Once the integration is achieved, the system in question will comprise, in addition to the formal rules, semantic rules about the interpretation of the signs, their application to a specific aspect of reality, considered as a model of the system in question. Consequently, outside a pure formalism, notions can remain clear and univocal only in relation to a field of application that is known and determined. A notion, that of number for instance, whose use is completely univocal in a formal system will cease to have this limpidity when used in ontology. Conversely, a highly ambiguous notion, like that of freedom, has some of its uses clarified in a juridical system where the status of free men is defined as opposed to that of slaves. But we must note that although agreement on particular clear uses of an ambiguous notion is unquestionably of service in a specific field, it is of no use in the majority of cases in which the ambiguous notion was employed before. This emerges clearly from such an analytical study as that made by Dupréel of the notion of merit.[58]

---

[57] Cf. Parain, *Recherches sur la nature et les fonctions du langage*, p. 96.
[58] Dupréel, "La pensée confuse," *Essais pluralistes*, pp. 328-329.

Salvador de Madariaga reminds us, in this connection, of what has often been said of the English:

> The sense of the complexity of life which tends to make English thought concrete, tends to make it also vague.

And, further on, he writes:

> The complex and vital character of English thought demands therefore a standard somewhat more complicated and at the same time more elastic than mere reason. This standard is wisdom.[59]

It should be noted, however, that this vague use of notions is completed by the specification of situations governed by tradition, in which the utilization of these same notions is laid down in as much detail as possible.

But an ambiguous notion cannot be exhausted by simply enumerating the cases to which it applies. This means that the successive criticism of a series of its aspects cannot turn our thoughts away from it: final devaluation of the notions of justice, liberty, and wisdom cannot be achieved by showing that all the forms of these notions that one considers are but a fraud.

When their system of reference is not indicated and cannot be supplied in a univocal way or even when they are integrated into widely differing ideological systems, ambiguous notions do make possible the crystalization of a global effort of goodwill; but, in each instance that they are applied with a view to concerted action, they will require suitable adjustments. Thus, as J. Maritain has pointed out, the adoption of a universal declaration of human rights by the supporters of very different ideologies has resulted in practical norms which, "although justified in different ways by different persons, are principles of action with a common ground of similarity for everyone."[60] This agreement was possible only by the use of ambiguous notions understood and interpreted by each in accordance with his own values. Its principal merit is that it encourages a continuation of the dialogue. When the time comes that third parties are appointed as judges or arbitrators to settle disputes on the basis of the adopted charter, the different interpretations by each of the signatories will count for less than the fact that there was acceptance of a text whose interpretation is not univocal, and the judges' power of appraisal will be correspondingly increased.

As the meaning of notions depends on the systems in which they are used, all that is necessary, in order to change the meaning of a notion,

---

[59] Madariaga, *Englishmen, Frenchmen, Spaniards*, pp. 55, 63.
[60] Maritain, Introduction, *Human Rights*, p. 10.

is to put it in a new context and particularly to integrate it in new lines of argument. This thought has been well expressed by Kenneth Burke where he speaks of Descartes' proofs of the existence of God:

> It has been said by one of Descartes' editors, John Veitch, that when Descartes questioned an old dogma, rather than attacking it head on, he aimed at "sapping its foundations." And he got rid of traditional principles "not so much by direct attack as by substituting for them new proofs and grounds of reasoning." Veitch quotes also a defender of Descartes who says ironically that his enemies called him an atheist "apparently because he had given new proofs of the existence of God." But these new proofs were in effect new qualifications of God. And in this capacity they subtly changed the nature of "God" as a term for motives. ...[61]

Every time a traditionally confused notion is put forward as an element of a carefully structured system, the reader may get the impression that one is after expressing what he has always thought, if he did not have himself a sufficiently precise context which would provide this notion with certain of its determinations. But, if this context were to exist, the reader is more likely to think there is treason, like the scholastics who were enraged by Descartes' audacity.

Ambiguous notions present the person who uses them with difficulties whose solution calls for a handling of concepts, for a decision as to how they are to be understood in a given case. This decision, once agreed upon, results in a clarification of the notion in certain of its uses in which it can exercise the role of a technical notion. A notion seems clear enough as long as one sees no situation in which it would lend itself to differing interpretations. When such a situation arises, the notion becomes obscure, but after a decision as to its univocal application it will seem clearer than it was before *on condition that this decision is unanimously accepted*, if not by everybody, at least by all the members of a specialized, scientific or juridical, group.

The likelihood that the notions will be obscured increases with the apparent difficulty of rejecting the propositions in which they are inserted, either because these confirm certain universal values or because they are compulsorily valid either as sacred texts or as legal prescriptions. In such cases, the whole effort has to be directed only to the interpretation of the propositions.

We are reminded of a thought of La Bruyère:

> The dying who speak in their wills can expect to be listened to like oracles: everyone draws them to his side and interprets them in his own way, I mean in accordance with his desires or interests.[62]

[61] Burke, *A Grammar of Motives* (Prentice-Hall), p. 55.
[62] La Bruyère, "Les caractères, De quelques usages," 56, *Œuvres complètes*, p. 442.

The motives prompting different interpretations may be nobler than those cited by La Bruyère: the theologian may be concerned with coherency, the judge with equity. The important thing, for us, is to indicate the circumstances in which differing interpretations might occur and might contribute to obscuring notions.

Notions are obscured also by the confusion that new situations may bring into accepted relationships between their different aspects. If certain individuals behave in a particular way, a connection will normally be established between their nature and their behavior: the latter will be regarded as the expression of their essence. One and the same adjective gets to express ambiguously a determination in space or time, membership in a party, and a manner of appearing: the words "European," "mediaeval," and "liberal" qualify a culture, an art, a political outlook by means of their spatial and temporal determinations and by the nature of their manifestations. If these cease to coincide, if European culture spreads to other continents, if gothic churches are built in the twentieth century, if members of other parties adopt a liberal policy, or, conversely, if people in Europe get influenced by the culture of India, if manifestations of classical art are found in the Middle Ages, or if members of the liberal party advocate socialistic measures, then the notions become obscured, and one wonders whether it would not be a good thing to try afresh to find a criterion that will enable the epithets to be applied univocally.

Also, since the use of notions is connected with their practical consequences, a change in the consequences has repercussions affecting the use. In Belgium, a large number of legal measures were enacted after 1939 in the form of decrees containing a provision that they would cease to be in effect on the date, to be fixed by royal decree, for the "restoration of the army to a peacetime footing." In 1947, two years after the end of hostilities and a long time after the demobilization of the Belgian army, this royal decree had still not been issued. As M. Lilar, Minister of Justice at that time, explained:

> If the restoration of the army to a peacetime footing has not up to the present been achieved, this is exclusively due to difficulties of a juridical nature. The restoration of the army to a peacetime footing is an act of considerable juridical import, necessitating the revision, measure by measure, of all the wartime legislation and particularly of all the decrees which were made pursuant to the extraordinary powers of March 20, 1945, and would become void by virtue of the restoration of the army to a peacetime footing.[63]

[63] *Annales parlementaires de Belgique*, Chambre des Représentants, sitting of Feb. 5, 1947, p. 6.

The limitation on the validity of the special powers pursuant to which measures were taken was fixed more exactly by reference to a specific fact, the restoration of the army to a peacetime footing, than it would have been by a mere reference to "return to normal conditions of life." But the use made of the notion of "restoration of the army to a peacetime footing" was not without a reaction on this notion: clear enough to begin with, it became obscure because of the interdependence established between it and the totality of its juridical consequences.

Any analogical or metaphorical use of a notion tends to render it obscure. Indeed, in order that there be an analogical use, the notion must be applied to a sphere other than its normal field of application and this use therefore cannot be regulated and made specific.[64] Future uses will, whether one wants it or not, retain a trace of this analogical use, a trace which, since it is not necessarily the same for every user, can only make the notion more indeterminate.

All these situations, to which we must add the very numerous instances in which the notion is modified by the needs of the argument itself[65] and which we will consider in the next section, contribute to what is called the life of language and of thought, which leads to an evolution in the meaning of words.

This evolution can in turn be utilized to obtain poetic effects that are themselves capable of reacting on linguistic usage. Charles Chassé has shown that Mallarmé used many words in their initial, obsolete, meaning; he goes so far as to write, "The key to Mallarmé is in Littré"[66]; according to him, all that need be done to understand certain poems that are generally deemed obscure is to refer to this archaic meaning. But we agree with G. Jamati and R. Caillois[67] that one cannot just be satisfied with the archaic meaning of words to understand texts of this kind. For one does not expect the reader to forget the present meaning of the words; it coalesces with the old one to create an evocative conceptual entity that does not correspond to any moment of semantic development and is more hazy than the meanings that are already known.

In conclusion, we observe that the evolution of notions, consequent upon their use, will hinder all the more a univocal comprehension of these notions as, for most people, all this evolution presents only fragmentary aspects, formulations and approximations of a single concept

---

[64] Cf. § 82, infra: What Is Analogy?

[65] Cf. § 35, infra: Argumentative Usage and Plasticity of Notions.

[66] Chassé, "La clé de Mallarmé est chez Littré," *Quo Vadis*, March - May (1950); *Les clés de Mallarmé*.

[67] Jamati, "Le langage poétique," in *Formes de l'art, formes de l'esprit*, pp. 271, 272; Caillois, *Poétique de St-John Perse*, pp. 22 et seq.

that react upon one another. Each time, the speaker will have to emphasize certain of these aspects, to make them present, at the expense of others. More often than not, he will achieve this result by making use of their plasticity and adapting the notions to the needs of the argument. It is with these techniques of adaptation that we propose to deal in the next section.

§ 35. *Argumentative Usage and Plasticity of Notions*

The manner of presenting fundamental notions in a discussion often depends on the fact that these notions are connected with the theses defended by the speaker or his opponent. In general, when a notion characterizes his own position, the speaker presents it as being not at all ambiguous but very flexible and rich, that is, with great possibilities of being highly rated, and, above all, as capable of resisting the assaults of new experiences. The notions connected with his opponent's theses will, on the contrary, be fixed and presented as unchangeable. By proceeding in this way, the speaker makes the force of inertia work for him. The flexibility of the notion, postulated at the outset and claimed as inherent to it, makes it possible to minimize, and at the same time underline, the changes that the new experience would impose, that objections would demand: this basic adaptability to new circumstances will enable the speaker to maintain that he is keeping the same notion alive. Here are some examples.

In the following passage, H. Lefebvre defends a flexible and fertile materialism, while presenting the concept of idealism as something fixed:

> To modern materialism, the *onesidedness* of idealism is at once its defining mark and the ground for its criticism. But the materialists must not let the basic truths of materialism be simplified, or allow them to fall back to the level of vulgar materialism, by forgetting the valuable results obtained by the idealists in the history of knowledge and particularly in logic.[68]

Materialism can and must embrace everything that is of value; it enjoys the advantage of a plasticity that is explicitly denied to idealism, which, as the writer says, is marked by its "onesidedness."

The same rigidity is attributed to the notion of "metaphysics," which is regarded as expressing an outmoded state of knowledge; the writer even wonders how metaphysics was possible[69]: his attitude assumes

---

[68] Lefebvre, *A la lumière du matérialisme dialectique, I: Logique formelle, logique dialectique*, pp. 38, 39.
[69] *Ibid.*, p. 20.

that metaphysics is incapable of adaptation and renewal, that its bounds are set once and for all, and that its functions are definitively fixed. In opposition to this view we could set down the reflections on metaphysics developed by one of the authors of this book, who described the successive enlargements of metaphysics and sought to show its permanence: metaphysics as an ontology, then as an epistemology, then as an elucidation of the reasons for axiological choice, and finally the metaphysics of the future, with boundaries that cannot be foretold.[70] Quite unintentionally he has provided an example of how a notion is made flexible.

It seems that the technique often develops at two levels. On the one hand, we actually make the notions flexible, thus enabling them to be used in circumstances far removed from their original usage; on the other hand, we qualify the notions in question as flexible.

The fixed character of the concepts of the opponent makes it easier to refute them and makes it possible to consider them as annulled, unadaptable, and, in consequence, outmoded. The conceptions which the speaker himself is defending stem from a living, flexible, and adaptable thought, and they are therefore up-to-date. These various procedures, however spontaneous they may be, are often interpreted by the opponent as a sign of misunderstanding or insincerity, against which he will, of course, protest.

Making notions more flexible or more rigorous is a technique adopted when the valuation put upon them is to result, at least in part, from the argument. But when the value indicated by a notion is clearly established before the argumentation, use will be made of another technique which has to do rather with the extension of notions. It consists simply of enlarging or restricting the sphere of a notion so that it does or does not embrace certain beings, things, ideas, or situations. For instance, the pejorative term "fascist" may be extended to include certain opponents; whereas the appreciative term "democratic" may have its range restricted in order to exclude these same opponents. Conversely, the meaning of "fascist" can be limited to exclude the friends one is supporting, and the meaning of "democratic" can be extended to embrace them. This technique is not confined to politics; it is found even in scientific controversies. Thus Claparède has observed that when the psychologists gave up associationism, they turned to criticizing one another as associationists, progressively extending this

---

[70] Perelman, "Philosophies premières et philosophie régressive," *Rhétorique et philosophie*, pp. 85 et seq.

idea to make it include the opponent. Claparède concludes his amusing analysis with the remark, "One is always someone's associationist."[71]

From what we have said, it can be seen that the use of notions on the basis of a wish to appreciate or depreciate what they qualify profoundly influences the meaning of the notions. There is no question here, as some studies would have us believe, of a juxtaposition of two elements, one of which is descriptive and the other emotive. What has been called the "emotive meaning" of notions[72] is a component that the theoretician concerned with registering the complexity of the effects of language is obliged to introduce when he wishes to correct, subsequently, the idea that the meaning of notions is essentially descriptive, that is, when they have been envisaged in a static manner. But if the meaning is viewed dynamically, in terms of the uses of the notion in argumentation, it will be seen that the field of application of the notion varies according to these uses and that the plasticity of notions is related to them. The "emotive meaning" is an integral part of the notion's meaning, not just an adventitious addition that does not belong to the symbolic character of language.[73] Thus the use of notions in argumentation influences their ambiguity. The difficulty in reaching agreement as to their use rises in proportion as they serve as instruments of persuasion. It is not surprising, therefore, that the universal values, which are regarded as the instruments of persuasion *par excellence*, are designated by the notions which are most confused in our mind.

These remarks are sufficient, for the moment, to call attention to the fact that the presentation of data does not consist of a simple choice between preliminary elements but of a more comprehensive treatment which explains, at least in part, the dynamism of language and thought.

The choice of premises had the particular advantage for our study that it was permissible and useful to recognize it under various avatars: the selection of data which, as a corollary, make them present, the role of interpretation, the choice of particular aspects of data by use of epithets and by the insertion of phenomena into this or that class already known to the hearers, and, finally, the choice involved in the use and transformation of the notions themselves. We deliberately presented these topics as a series, in order that our analysis may appear as reaching deeper and deeper. At the same time, there is no hiding

---

[71] Claparède, "*La genèse de l'hypothèse,*" *Archives de psychologie,* XXIV (1934).

[72] Ogden and Richards, *The Meaning of Meaning*; Stevenson, *Ethics and Language.* Cf. also "A Symposium on Emotive Meaning," *Philosophical Review,* 57 (1948) 111-157.

[73] Cf. Perelman and Olbrechts-Tyteca, "Les notions et l'argumentation," *Archivio di Filosofia,* vol. *Semantica.*

the fact that in our treatment of selection of data, of interpretation, of the use of epithets, of insertion into a class, and of resort to the plasticity of notions we have often examined, under new aspects, what is but a single fundamental process. But, in our view, one cannot neglect the study of any one of the aspects we have considered if one refuses to carry out a philosophical, or even simply technical, systematization which would, at the very least, be premature. The order adopted in our study led us to consider last the use and transformation of notions, that is, the aspect of the problem of choice that forces us to consider anew from a rhetorical viewpoint most of the semantic problems.

Thus the form in which data are stated is necessarily involved in everything said so far. And one is led to inquire whether, from the viewpoint of reasoning, other problems more particularly concerned with form should not be considered. This question will be taken up in the next chapter, dealing with the presentation of data and the form of the discourse. How will this chapter differ most from those that precede it? Only in that, instead of starting from points of view that traditionally concern reasoning, belief, adherence, in short all that is the object or aim of persuasion, we will start from points of view which traditionally involve the form, the expression of thought, and we will endeavor to see the role that various characteristics of expression may play in the presentation of data. In other words, the term "form" will be used with a meaning much closer to that given it by the writer than to that given it by the logician.

CHAPTER 3

Presentation of Data and Form
of the Discourse

§ 36. *Content and Form of the Discourse*

We indicated in the last chapter the importance that should be attributed in argumentation to the role of presence, to the displaying of certain elements on which the speaker wishes to center attention in order that they may occupy the foreground of the hearer's consciousness. Before even starting to argue from particular premises, it is essential that the content of these premises should stand out against the undifferentiated mass of available elements of agreement: the choice of premises can be identified with their presentation. Effective presentation that impresses itself on the hearers' consciousness is essential not only in all argumentation aiming at immediate action, but also in that which aspires to give the mind a certain orientation, to make certain schemes of interpretation prevail, to insert the elements of agreement into a framework that will give them significance and confer upon them the rank they deserve.

This technique of presentation has even developed to the point that its study came to form the whole material of rhetoric, considered as the art of good speaking and good writing, as an art of expressing thought, a purely formal art. We rebel against this conception, which is at the source of the degeneration, sterility, and verbalism of rhetoric as well as of the contempt one generally feels for it. We refuse to separate the form of a discourse from its substance, to study stylistic structures and figures independently of the purpose they must achieve in the argumentation. We shall go even further. We know that there are forms of expression capable of producing an aesthetic effect, connected with harmony, rhythm, and other purely formal qualities and that such forms of expression can be of influence through the admiration, delight, relaxation, excitement, and the rise and fall of attention that they provoke without its being possible to analyze them directly in terms of the argumentation. Nevertheless, despite their unquestionable importance in oratorical practice, we shall not deal further with these mechanisms in our present study of argumentation.

In examining the form of discourse, insofar as we find it possible to distinguish the form from the content, we shall direct our attention to the means whereby a particular presentation of the data establishes agreement at a certain level, impresses it on the consciousness with a certain intensity, and emphasizes certain of its aspects. It is by thinking of variations of the form, of different presentations of the same content, which is actually not quite the same when presented differently, that it will be possible to track down the choice of a particular form. The existence of more than one possible interpretation saves us from confusing the text with the meanings given to the text; in a similar way, by thinking of the different means that the speaker might have employed to communicate the matter of his discourse to his audience, we shall be able, for the purpose of exposition, to distinguish the problems raised by the presentation of data from those pertaining to their choice.

§ 37. *Technical Problems in the Presentation of Data*

Every speech has a time limitation, and this is also true in practice for any writing addressed to third parties. The time limitation may be imposed by convention or it may depend on opportunity, on the attention or interest of the hearers, on the space available in a newspaper or review, or on the cost of printing a text. But, whatever the cause of the limitation, the form of the discourse cannot but take it into account. The general problem of the length of a speech immediately affects the place to be given to the exposition of the premises, the choice and the presentation of these elements. A person making a speech that aims at persuasion—in contradistinction to the requirements of formal demonstration where as a rule nothing should remain implicit — must take care to make the best use of his time and to hold the attention of his hearers: the length of each part of his speech will usually be in proportion to the importance he would like to see it occupy in the minds of his hearers.

When a particular premise is familiar to everybody and is not being questioned, it may seem ridiculous to state it. As Aristotle wrote:

If any of these propositions is a familiar fact, there is no need even to mention it; the hearer adds it himself. Thus, to show that Dorieus has been victor in a contest for which the prize is a crown, it is enough to say, "For he has been victor in the Olympic games," without adding "and in the Olympic games the prize is a crown," a fact which everybody knows.[1]

Two comments must be made on this unquestionably correct observation. It is not always so easy to indicate the implied premise, and this premise is not always as secure as in Aristotle's example. Speakers are often quick to seize on this circumstance and keep quiet about premises which are really very questionable, but to which they do not wish to draw their hearers' attention. On the other hand, a speaker will do well sometimes to expatiate at length on the significance and importance of certain unquestionable elements, instead of implying or merely mentioning them. By dwelling on them longer, the speaker increases their presence in the minds of his hearers. The classical writers on rhetoric offered specific advice on this matter of accentuating a point by spending more time on it. Thus Quintilian tells us,

I made a practice of extracting the points on which my opponent and I were in agreement ... and of not only drawing out all the possible consequences of his admissions, but of multiplying them by a process of division.[2]

Aristotle's advice is sound when one is dealing with a fact that serves exclusively as a link in a chain of argument, but the advice of Quintilian should be followed when the facts are unquestionable but one wishes to enhance them by making the hearer familiar with them. While a rapid style is effective in reasoning, a slow style creates emotion, for "love is formed by habit. ... Which explains why those who speak briefly and concisely enter only a little way into the heart and stir their hearers less."[3]

The simplest way of creating this presence is by repetition; accentuation of certain passages, either by tone of voice or by pausing before them, has the same purpose. Accumulating stories, even contradictory ones, on a given subject may create the impression that it is an important one. An avalanche of books on a particular country influences not only by their content but also by the effect of increased presence. The plays and novels of romantic literature restored the Middle Ages to a place of honor and, by giving them presence, acted, as Reyes justly observes, as a spur to historical thinking.[4]

[1] Aristotle, *Rhetoric*, I, 2, 1357a.
[2] Quintilian, VII, I, 29.
[3] Vico, *Delle instituzioni oratorie*, p. 87.
[4] Reyes, *El Deslinde*, vol. I, p. 101.

There are also less direct methods of insisting on a point: one wonders whether one of the benefits resulting from the obscurity of certain texts is not that it quickens the attention; "presence of mind" confers presence on what the writer desires to communicate.[5] Sometimes a writer speculates that the reader will attach increased importance to a sign that belies his expectations. Aragon has analyzed this mechanism in connection with two lines of his hymn to Elsa:

> Ce ne sont plus les jours du vivre séparés
>
> *   *   *
>
> Et jamais tu ne fus si lointaine à mon gré. ...

You will grant that the plural *séparés*, implying two people, adds to the expression. If I had then used a plural word to rhyme with it, the final "s" of *séparés* would be taken for a mistake or a stopgap, and the fact that its presence is intentional would be overlooked.[6]

The accumulation of contradictory accounts of a subject impresses not only by its bulk, as we mentioned just now, but also by the problem which this multiplicity presents.

The technique of accumulating, of insisting, is often connected with another technique, that of evoking details. These two techniques are often so closely connected as to be indistinguishable. In treating a subject, its overall, synthetic description will be followed by analysis or enumeration of its details. In his funeral oration for Turenne, Fléchier describes the reactions provoked by the Marshal's death:

> What a host of sighs, lamentations, and praises arise from town and countryside! One man, seeing his crops come safe to harvest, blesses his memory. ... Another wishes eternal peace to him who. ... In one place, one offers a mass for the soul of him who. ... In another, a funeral celebration is held for him. ... So the whole kingdom weeps for the death of its defender. ... [7]

In other cases, a speaker will give a detailed account of the successive stages of a phenomenon, setting out the way in which he got his knowledge of it. The stages cited may be those of an action to be accomplished. Publicity agents know that, if they indicate in detail the necessary steps for placing an order, they get the idea of ordering into the customer's consciousness and make it easier for him to decide. An impression of reality is similarly conveyed by piling up all the conditions preceding an act or by indicating all its consequences. Here are two examples of these procedures taken from Proust:

[5] Cf. Cocteau, *La difficulté d'être*, p. 177.
[6] Aragon, *Les yeux d'Elsa*, p. 23.
[7] Fléchier, *Oraison funèbre de Henri de La Tour d'Auvergne, Vicomte de Turenne*, pp. 100-101.

[Aunt Léonie has just announced her intention to make an excursion.] The incredulous Françoise was told not only to prepare my aunt's clothes in advance, to air those that had been put away too long, but to order a carriage, and to arrange, to within a quarter of an hour, all the details of the day.[8]

* * *

In the same way, so that Albertine might not think I was exaggerating and to have her go along as far as possible in the idea that we were to separate, drawing myself the deductions that followed from what I had just proposed, I had begun to anticipate the time that was to begin next day and was to last forever, the time in which we should be separated, giving Albertine the same injunctions as if we were not going to be reconciled in the near future.[9]

There is a striking parallelism between these procedures which establish the presence and methodology of the hypothesis. Formulation of a hypothesis does not consist of an isolated assertion, for an assertion can be made explicit only by enumerating the conditions imposed on it and the consequences deduced from it. This explains how, alongside scientific hypotheses that are useful for invention, we find also argumentative hypotheses. In one of his speeches, Demosthenes supposes hypothetically that Aeschines is the prosecutor, Philip the judge, and himself the defendant.[10] He imagines what the behavior and reactions of each of the three would be in this fictitious situation in order to deduce the correct behavior and reactions in the real situation. Sometimes, on the contrary, a hypothesis is described in full detail in order to make it strongly undesirable or shocking. These two possibilities indicate the two customary uses in argumentation of all forms of utopia. As R. Ruyer rightly maintains, utopia aims less at the truth than at an increase of awareness; it confronts reality with an imaginary presence which it thrusts on the hearer in order to secure longer lasting reactions.[11] That is why utopias are usually described in such very great detail: one does not hesitate to keep the audience in this new environment for hours on end. Success is possible only if the logical structure of the imaginary environment is the same as that of the reader's usual environment and if events normally bring about the same consequences in both. Collective myths, legendary tales which are part of a common cultural heritage, have this advantage over hypotheses and utopias that they can much more readily take advantage of presence. Plato combats the belief in the superiority of the right

---

[8] Proust, *A la recherche du temps perdu*, vol 12: *La prisonnière*, II, p. 190.
[9] *Ibid.*, p. 191.
[10] Demosthenes, *On the Embassy*, § 214.
[11] Ruyer, *L'utopie et les utopies*, chap. II.

hand over the left with the statement, "If a person had the nature of Geryon or Briareus he ought to be able with his hundred hands to throw a hundred darts."[12] He goes thus from the ancient structure in which there is a qualitative difference between the two hands to a structure in which the hands are of the same kind. Plato's hypothesis commands attention more readily because it can be related to mythology: it seems less arbitrary, less abstract.

To create emotion, it is essential to be specific.[13] General notions and abstract schemes have hardly any effect on the imagination. Whately relates how an audience that had remained unmoved by a general description of the carnage that occurred at the battle of Fontenoy was moved to tears by a little detail concerning the death of two young men.[14] To give an impression of actuality it is good to specify the time and place of an action. Whately even advises that wherever possible the concrete rather than the abstract term should be used. The more specific the terms, the sharper the image they conjure up, and, conversely, the more general the terms, the weaker the image. Thus in Antony's speech in Shakespeare's *Julius Caesar*, the conspirators are not referred to as those who "killed Caesar" but as those "whose daggers have stabbed Caesar."[15] The concrete term increases the sense of actuality.

The advice seems sound, as a general rule, but if the opposition between abstract and concrete terms is examined in detail, it will be found that there are several types of abstractions which undoubtedly vary in their effect on the feeling of actuality. Attempts are often made to define these kinds of abstractions either in terms of their departure from the concrete, or in terms of their constructive features: "man" is an instance of the first type, "truth" of the second.[16] But we see immediately that the line of cleavage between concrete and abstract depends in all cases on what we take as our point of departure, and this is dictated by our conception of reality.

Renouncing to oppose concrete and abstract, we can try to arrange given levels of abstraction in a graduated order. With reference to

[12] Plato, *Laws*, VII, 794ᵈ et seq. Cf. Schuhl, *Le merveilleux, la pensée et l'action*, p. 186.

[13] There is a close connection between emotion and presence if we assume as D. O. Hebb does in *The Organization of Behavior* that emotion slows down the process of thinking, thus making the object "interesting." Cf. Hebb and Thompson, *Handbook of Social Psychology*, vol. I, p. 553.

[14] In a footnote to p. 130 of the 1828 edition of *Elements of Rhetoric*.

[15] Shakespeare, *Julius Caesar*, Act III, scene 2, cited by Whately, *Elements of Rhetoric* (Harper), p. 195.

[16] Cf. Schopenhauer, *Sämtliche Werke* (Brockhaus), vol. 2: *Die Welt als Wille und Vorstellung*, Band I, § 9, p. 49.

Korzybski's scale of rising levels of abstraction, Hayakawa has pointed out that at lower levels of abstraction facts themselves act directly on our affectivity.[17] But this is not always true as we see that, to Korzybski, the cow we perceive is more abstract than the atoms, the electrons of which it consists and which science apprehends.[18]

To appreciate how complex the problem is, one has only to think of the effect produced on our imagination by the same facts when presented in their quantitative aspect, now in absolute figures, now in relative figures. Generally speaking, absolute figures have a greater impact on the imagination, for though the things are seen under their purely quantitative aspect, they are in effect independent individualities which are present to the highest degree. But the converse is also possible, namely when the relative figure, which is certainly not more concrete than the absolute figure, refers to an event that affects us, such as the probability of dying from this or that disease within the year. The same numerical relation can seem more or less concrete depending on our interest in it. It would seem that presence determines the degree of abstraction rather than the other way round. And instead of solving the problem under discussion with the help of ontological considerations, would it not be more correct to make our idea of the concrete depend on the impression of presence aroused in us by certain levels of presentation of the phenomena?

The intuitive manner of expression, the use of striking terms, is sometimes not without disadvantages. Schopenhauer observed that certain writers do their best to avoid the more definite expression in favor of more abstract notions making it easier for them to avoid objections.[19] The observation is accurate, and instructive. For though the precise, concrete term makes agreement possible by contributing to presence and favoring univocity, it must not be forgotten that there are cases in which it is only by the use of an abstract term that the possibility of agreement is kept open. At the limit, the most concrete, the most actual term may correspond to what is inexpressible, and be no more than the fleeting demonstrative of an infinitely unstable presence. The desire to express the concrete in its unicity, if carried to excess, may, instead of being the basis for good agreement, mean the renunciation of any agreement at all. The presentation of data must in every case be adjusted to the conditions for effective argumentation.

---

[17] Hayakawa, *Language in Thought and Action*, p. 127.

[18] *Ibid.*, p. 169.

[19] Schopenhauer, *Sämtliche Werke* (Brockhaus), vol. 6: *Parerga und Paralipomena*, Band II, § 283, p. 552.

§ 38. *Verbal Forms and Argumentation*

The presentation of data is necessarily connected with problems of language. Choice of terms to express the speaker's thought is rarely without significance in the argumentation. It is ony where argumentative intent has been deliberately or unconsciously suppressed that one can allow that synonyms exist which can be used indifferently in place of each other; only then is the choice of one term rather than another a mere matter of form, dictated by such considerations as variety, euphony, and oratorical rhythm. It can be said that this negative intention exists whenever the argumentative intention cannot be known, as in a dictionary where terms appear to be interchangeable because they are put there for whatever use can be made of them. But as regards their use by a speaker in a particular speech, the equivalence of synonyms can only be assured by taking account of the total situation into which the speech is fitted, and, more particularly, of the social conventions to which the speech may be subject. Sometimes the choice of a term will merely be an indication of distinction, of familiarity, or of simplicity. Sometimes it will serve the argumentation more directly, by fitting the object of discourse into a category more satisfactorily than would a synonym: an example would be the choice of the word "hexahedron" rather than "cube."

In general, an indication of the argumentative intent is given by the use of a term representing a departure from ordinary language. Naturally, selection of the ordinary term may also have argumentative value; on the other hand, one would have to specify when and where use of a particular term can be regarded as ordinary; broadly speaking, a term that passes unnoticed may be considered ordinary. There is no neutral choice—but there is a choice that appears neutral, and this can serve as a starting point for the study of modifications for the purpose of argument. What term is neutral clearly depends on the environment. For instance, in Belgium, under the German occupation, it was probably the normal thing in certain circles to refer to a German as a "boche." Consequently, the use of the term "German" could indicate either a general relaxation of the hostile attitude toward the enemy or particular regard for an individual German deserving this consideration. Similarly, the purpose in using the periphrasis "person having a tendency to mislead" to designate "a liar" may be as far as possible to strip the term of depreciative significance, and to turn it into a descriptive term and make the judgment of which it is an element appear as a judgment of fact.[20] Thus the periphrasis has an argumentative significance not possessed by the term "liar." These two examples show that the term we call neutral—the term that goes unnoticed—is by no means always the one that is generally called descriptive or factual. Nothing could be more arbitrary than the distinction made in textbooks between factual, neutral, descriptive speech, and sentimental, emotive speech. These distinctions have the sole advantage of drawing the student's attention to the fact that value judgments are very obviously introduced into argumentation, but they are harmful in that they imply that there are ways of expressing oneself that are per se descriptive, that there are speeches in which only facts, with their unquestionable objectivity, find a place.

In order to discern the argumentative use to which a term is being put, it is important to know the words or expressions the speaker might have used and to which he preferred the word he selected. Following the terminology of the Dutch significists, the totality of available locutions may be called a *word-family*; the words composing it are not connected by a system of derivations, but are expressions related by their meaning.[21] The composition of such a family of words is not, of course, entirely free of arbitrariness, for the sole criterion of admission to it is the idea we have at the outset of the concept that the family will make it possible to elucidate. The development of the concept would depend on variations in the use of each of the quasi-synonyms[22] belonging to the family; these terms would form an interacting system.[23] There is no reason why terms from several different languages should not be considered as belonging to the same *word family*, provided the different linguistic circles have sufficient contacts. It is perhaps in this little-studied field that the introduction of the notion of *word*

---

[20] We shall have occasion more than once to use the notions "value judgment" and "judgment of fact" in the meaning generally accepted today. Our study aims at showing that there is no clear-cut and fundamental distinction between these two kinds of judgments.

[21] Cf. Mannoury, *Handboek der analytische significa*, I, pp. 43, 126; Stokvis, *Psychologie der suggestie en autosuggestie*, p. 19.

[22] The term "quasi-synonym" is to be taken here in its broadest sense, because it can embrace words differing widely in grammatical form, e.g., "necessary" and "on account of."

[23] The notions of *Sprachfeld* (linguistic field), and of *Bedeutungsfeld* (field of meaning), introduced by structural linguistics, could also be of use in the study of argumentative choice. Cf. Trier, *Der deutsche Wortschatz im Sinnbezirk des Verstandes*, pp. 1-26; "Sprachliche Felder," *Zeitschrift für deutsche Bildung*, Jan 1932, 417-427; "Das Sprachliche Feld," *Neue Jahrbücher für Wissenschaft und Jugendbildung* 5(1934), 428-480. Concerning these "semantic fields," cf. Ullman, *Précis de sémantique française*, pp. 303-309.

family could be most fruitful. One would doubtless see that the introduction of a foreign term, with its particular nuances of meaning, can lead to modification of an already existing concept, and give each of the quasi-synonyms a new background. The meaning of the term "honor" is certainly influenced today both by the French *honneur* and the Spanish term *honor*, at least in the minds of the learned, who consider them as members of the same word family.

The terms comprising a family form an aggregate by relation to which any given term is specifically determined : they are, so to speak, the background against which the selected term stands out. On the other hand, terms which are related by derivation influence each other directly. The writers of antiquity liked to speak of argument by flections,[24] which consists of applying the same predicate to terms derived from one another, like "justly" and "just." This kind of argument is open to many objections, particularly on the score that it overlooks differences in semantic evolution. It is nonetheless true that before any argumentation it is often important to make a statement in terms capable of evoking other terms that are, or are fancied to be, linked with them through derivation.

It is still more effective to bring the terms together in the same context. If a writer dismisses a theory as simplistic and then goes on to qualify another theory as hardly less simple,[25] a pejorative note attaches to the second qualification, although under ordinary circumstances the simplicity of a scientific theory is undeniably a quality. A splendid example of the interaction of terms—achieved by purely formal means—is found in Jouhandeau. To a German general who, in 1940, had commandeered her mansion and who was singing the praises of France, an elderly aristocrat replied:

> En effet, monsieur, mon pays est un grand pays, mais qui a connu depuis si longtemps de si petits régimes que, pour employer le langage de Mme du Deffand, après les trompeurs et les trompés, il fallait s'attendre (et nul n'en est moins surpris que moi) à voir vos trompettes.[26]

Where the relationship between ordinary forms is not sufficient, one may resort to anagrams and other mutations to bring about the desired associations.

Analysis of the argumentative role of certain variations in expression can be carried out only in terms of divergence from the expression that

---

[24] Cf. Aristotle, *Rhetoric*, II, 23, 1397a. Cf. also "related" arguments, Cicero, *Topics*, § 12; Quintilian, V, x, 85.

[25] Nogaro, *La valeur logique des théories économiques*, p. 155.

[26] Jouhandeau, *Un monde*, p. 17.

goes unnoticed. Taken literally, this method gives the impression that making ˙use of expressions that pass unnoticed is not an argumentative procedure. This is of course not the case. But any study concerned not with divergences but with what goes unnoticed will be of a global nature. It cannot deal with the effect of any given modality of expression: the most it can do is to inquire why it is desirable for a speaker to express himself in a neutral manner, and not how he will succeed in doing it. For if the manner can be grasped, it must be because it exhibits special characteristics, which can be defined by elements different from mere neutrality.

When we ask ourselves why a speaker expresses himself in a neutral manner, we imply that he might not have done so, and that he must have a reason for doing it. We have here one of the many aspects of the problem of procedure. We shall meet it at every turn: absence of technique can be a method; even being natural can be deliberate behavior.

We confine ourselves here to a few remarks on the effects of restraint from the point of view of argumentation. In a study of Gide's style, Yves Gandon observes:

> Some would even say that a more brilliant style would not have served him equally well. The smooth vocabulary, the statement aiming to give nothing but the essential, where one might think the author's intent would be subdued in phrases lacking in contrast, locutions devoid of aggressive meaning—these would be the ideal tools for the writer in quest of an atmosphere of fever or of doom.[27]

Gandon refutes this argument as being "too obviously manufactured just for M. Gide's benefit" and as one "which the example of a Mauriac is sufficient to destroy." But Gandon is mistaken when he compares the fevered atmosphere of Mauriac with that of Gide. Mauriac is in the Christian tradition, wheras Gide tries to promote new standards: he is feverish in what he approves, not in what he describes. Now it seems that within an orthodoxy, all methods can be used; but when one is trying to advance new and shocking value judgments, these are more readily admitted when the style employed is not shocking. So it is not impossible that Gide's neutral style really helped him in his persuasive effort. We have mentioned Gandon's observations because they immediately draw attention to one of the advantages of a neutral style: it suggests the transition from general approbation given to the language to approbation of the standards enunciated. It must not indeed be forgotten that among the various elements of agreement lan-

---

[27] Gandon, *Le démon du style*, p. 16.

guage is one of the first. Following Cicero, Quintilian wrote that "the worst fault in speaking is to shun ordinary speech and generally admitted ideas."[28] The relationship between ordinary language and admitted ideas is not fortuitous: ordinary language is by itself the manifestation of agreement, of a community of thought, by the same right as the received ideas. Ordinary language can help to promote agreement on the ideas.

Resort to a neutral style can also be regarded as an instance of renunciation tending to enhance the credence given to the premises.[29] A neutral style increases credibility by contrast with a more emphatic style of argument that could have been used. It achieves its effect through our knowledge, from other sources, of the argumentative force of certain stylistic variations.

This brings us to a phenomenon of the utmost importance: the fact that generalized—or at least intuitive—knowledge of the techniques of argument, of the conditions for their application, and of their results underlies many of the mechanics of argument; the hearer is not considered as an ignoramus, but rather as a well-informed person.

To illustrate this relation between art and argumentation, let us take first the rough draft and then the final version of a passage from Bossuet. We purposely select from a passage cited in a treatise on rhetoric.[30] The author of the treatise emphasizes the stylistic improvement:

> First version: "When people attend funeral ceremonies, or hear of an unexpected death, they talk to one another. ..."
> Second version: "At funeral ceremonies one hears nought but expressions of astonishment that a mortal man has died. ..."[31]

Progress with regard to number of words, harmony, force, and compactness. Artistic enjoyment is thus increased. But, most of all, Bossuet has found and incorporated in his speech an argument used by Epictetus: Why be astonished that a fragile jar breaks, that a mortal dies? By the use of classification, by setting the dead man among all mortals, an argument that was only implicit in the first sketch is explicitly introduced into the finished version. There is also an exaggeration, a strengthening of the observation: people do not just talk to one another about an unexpected death, but "one hears nought but expressions of astonishment": the absurdity is made to seem all the greater by its more frequent occurrence. We can say that Bossuet, while appearing to choose a new form for his thought, has actually altered the signifi-

---

[28] Quintilian, VIII, Preface, 25.
[29] Cf. § 96, infra: Rhetoric as a Process.
[30] Saint-Aubin, *Guide pour la classe de rhétorique* (La Procure), p. 136.
[31] Bossuet, *Sermons*, vol. II, p. 449.

cance of the premises underlying his argument; indeed, he has gone further, and has included the argument in the expression of the premises. We must not forget that separation of premises and argument is an artificial operation for the convenience of analysis; in reality, there is already argumentation in the very setting of the premises. This becomes particularly apparent if certain variations of form in expressing these premises are juxtaposed: without these variations the argumentation would pass unnoticed. But the very fact that study of these variations enables us to bring out the argumentative element proves that even where the expression seems neutral and passes unnoticed there is often already a choice of terms and an outline of argument.

§ 39. *Modalities in the Expression of Thought*

The way in which we formulate our thought brings out certain of its modalities, which modify the reality, the certainty or the importance of the data. One generally agrees today that modalities of meaning are preferably expressed by particular grammatical forms, but that these forms can also serve to express other modalities. Both the new schools of semioticians[32] and those who favor the old philological disciplines[33] emphasize this relative independence. Awareness of this flexibility gave rise to a search for categories of meaning, or "affective categories," that do not correspond to the grammatical categories and can be expressed by different grammatical means. However, parallel with this effort to trace the modalities of thought underlying variable grammatical forms, one finds efforts in the opposite direction tending to connect clearly defined behavior with a particular category of verbal expression. Fr. Rostand, for instance, has attempted a psychoanalytical exposition of grammatical forms and their acquisition by children.[34]

We feel it is important to draw attention to the argumentative role played by certain forms of expression that may be ascribed to modalities, in the broad sense of the term. Our observations will not be exclusively confined either to grammatical form or to psychological or logical categories.

One and the same idea can be formulated affirmatively or negatively. If a quality is attributed to something, this involves choice of this

---

[32] Cf. Morris, *Signs, Language and Behavior*, pp. 62 et seq., 82, 93, 103 note A, 257.

[33] Cf. Brunot, *La pensée et la langue*.

[34] Rostand, *Grammaire et affectivité*.

quality from among many others because it is considered important or characteristic. Any description is built up on a background from which it is desired that the thing described shall stand out, in a way that takes on significance only in terms of the end pursued. But this reference to the situation and to the way of handling it might not be grasped by someone who does not recognize the connection between thought and action. If a negative formulation is made, the reference to something else is quite explicit: a negation is a reaction to an actual or virtual affirmation by someone else.[35] In Bergson's view, the thought that hugs reality can only be expressed affirmatively:

> Give knowledge back its exclusively scientific or philosophical character, suppose in other words that reality comes itself to inscribe itself on a mind that cares only for things and is not interested in persons: we shall affirm that such or such a thing is, we shall never affirm that a thing is not. ... That which exists may come to be recorded, but the nonexistence of the nonexisting cannot.[36]

According to him, negative thought only comes into play if one's concern is with persons, that is, if one is arguing.

It is only in certain well-defined cases, when but two possibilities are present to the mind, that the negative rejection of one of them is tantamount to choosing the other, which is thus often presented as the lesser evil. Sometimes the negative does not correspond to any definite affirmation, but reveals an order of preoccupations. Let us consider, with Empson and Britton, the meaning of Othello's phrase: "Yet I'll not shed her blood."[37] In a case like this the hearer has to guess whether a generic or a specific rejection is involved, in other words, whether the rejected action is to be interpreted in terms of a class of acts of which it is a specimen, one way of killing elected from among others or one way of taking vengeance elected from among others, or whether the statement represents a class, with the further question of what class, that is whether no murder will be done, no vengeance carried out. Depending on which interpretation is adopted, the negative can promise either vengeance or forgiveness. But the advantage of the negative form is that, whatever the interpretation, death is irresistibly evoked.

The same ambiguity is encountered when the negative is applied not to an assertion but to a notion, by the apposition of a prefix. Thus, the negative in the word "inhuman" may apply to the genus, and designate that which is completely extraneous to man, or it may designate the

---

[35] Cf. Guillaume, *Manuel de psychologie*, p. 261.

[36] Bergson, *Creative Evolution*, pp. 316, 318.

[37] Shakespeare, *Othello*, Act V, scene 2, cf. Empson, *Seven Types of Ambiguity*, pp. 185, 186; Britton, *Communication*, p. 12.

species of men or of human behavior which fall short of the human ideal. The negative formulation leaves undetermined the concept within which the exclusion takes place.

When we have a number of data at our disposal, we have immense possibilities with regard to the connections that can be established between them. The problem of the coordination or subordination of elements often depends on the hierarchy of the admitted values. However, within the frame of these hierarchies of values, we can establish between the elements of the discourse connections which will modify the premises considerably; the choice among these possible connections is just as important as the choice made in classification or in qualification.

Grammarians distinguish between coordinate conjunctions such as "and," "or," "but," "for," "therefore," "nor" and subordinate conjunctions like "although," "since," and "despite that." But if we examine the nature of the connections made by conjunctions, we find that subordination of one proposition to another is the rule, regardless of the type of conjunction that is used.

Such coordinate conjunctions as "and" "or" "nor", and "therefore," may indeed be considered as expressing a logical relation. But it is only under certain very definite conditions that this logical relation will leave the propositions connected by these conjunctions on a footing of equality. Generally we find that in actual speaking practice an intention to subordinate almost always underlies the use of the coordinate form.

Let us take the very simple case of a succession of events: "I met your friend yesterday; he did not mention you." The first proposition is a fact that my interlocutor does not dispute, and so is the second. They are coordinate, and could be joined by the conjunction "and." But in certain situations the normal interpretation would be: "Your friend did not mention you, *although* he had the opportunity." Placing the first statement in this position, before the second one, to which it is actually subordinate, modifies considerably the impression produced by the affirmation of these two facts by simple coordination. The judgments of fact are thereby colored by an implicit interpretation which gives them their whole meaning.

Subordination is not exclusively expressed by means of conjunctions; other grammatical forms can play the same role. Fr. Rostand has established the relationship between expressions such as "beautiful, for modest," "beautiful, because modest," "beautiful through modesty," "beautified by modesty," and "with a beauty created by modesty."[38]

[38] Rostand, *Grammaire et affectivité*, p. 66.

The interdependence of beauty and modesty is expressed, though in a slightly different way, by each of these formulas.

Effects of subordination are often obtained by the use of qualification. Depending on the subordination we are establishing, we shall speak of "pious sorrow" or "sorrowing piety."

The various techniques of presentation enable us, when different elements are present, to direct attention to those of them that are of weight. The formulas "for the love of," "in consideration of," and "on account of" show what terms are being accorded primacy: "All things work together for good to the elect, even the obscurities of Scripture; for they honour them because of what is divinely clear."[39] The same primacy is expressed elsewhere through the relative proposition: "the clearness, which requires us to reverence the obscurities."[40] The preposition "except" or the prepositional phrase "with the exception of" is often used to minimize an element. The benevolently forbearing attitude of Julian the Apostate vis-à-vis the Jews is expressed in these peculiar terms:

> They agree with the Gentiles with the exception of their belief in one God. That is special to them and foreign to us. Everything else is common to us both.[41]

Finally, such expressions as "although," "in spite of," and "doubtless" indicate that one is making certain concessions, but their main function, depending particularly on their position in the phrase, is to show the degree of importance attached to what is conceded.

With the help of these techniques, the speaker can very effectively guide the hearer toward what he wants to get him to admit. Auerbach has correctly stressed, in this connection, the strategic character[42] of the construction—termed "hypotactic"—which establishes precise relations between the elements of discourse. Opposed to it is the "paratactic" construction characterized by the absence of precise connection between the parts. The typical example presented by Auerbach is this sentence from the Vulgate: *Dixitque Deus: fiat lux, et facta est lux*.[43] The hearer is left free to imagine between the events a relationship that by its very lack of precision, assumes a mysterious, magical character: in this way moreover it can sometimes produce a highly dramatic effect. We feel that enumeration, in some of its uses at least, exemplifies paratactic construction. E. Noulet is struck by the enumeration in

---

[39] Pascal, *Pensées*, GBWW, vol. 33, p. 275.

[40] *Ibid.*, p. 273.

[41] C. Gal. 306 B. Quoted by Bidez, *La vie de l'empereur Julien*, p. 305.

[42] Auerbach, *Mimesis*, p. 92.

[43] *Ibid.*, p. 74.

Rimbaud's sonnet on the vowels. An extreme expression of movement ?[44] This may be so. But it is also a way of expressing the triumphant mystery of relationships that the poet knows exist, though he does not know their exact nature.

The hypotactic construction is the argumentative construction par excellence. Auerbach considers it to be characteristic of Greco-Roman literature in contradistinction to the paratactic construction favored in Hebrew culture. Hypotaxis creates frameworks, constitutes the adoption of a position. It controls the reader, forces him to see particular relationships, restricts the interpretations he may consider, and takes its inspiration from well-constructed legal reasoning. Parataxis leaves greater freedom, and does not appear to wish to impose a particular viewpoint. It is probably because of its paratactic construction that the carefully composed and balanced sentence of eighteenth century English authors gives an impression that R. M. Weaver terms philosophical[45] but that we prefer to call descriptive, contemplative, impartial.

It is generally agreed that the modalities, in the linguist's technical meaning of this word, are four in number: the assertive, the injunctive, the interrogative, and the optative.

The assertive modality is suitable for argumentation of all kinds, and there is no need to discuss it.

In our western languages the injunctive modality is expressed by the imperative.

Contrary to appearances, the imperative does not have persuasive force: all its power comes from the hold of the person commanding over the one carrying out his orders; the relation is one of relative forces, without any implication of adherence. When actual force is lacking or when one does not consider using it, the imperative assumes the tone of a prayer.

On account of the personal relation which it implies, the imperative form is very effective for increasing the feeling of presence. A radio reporter, describing some sport contest, will sometimes tell the players to do this or that. These imperatives are not heard by the players, nor do they apply to the hearers, but while, communicating indirectly to the hearers' judgments on the players—admiration for their courage, for example, or disapproval of their hesitation—they also give the scene a high degree of presence owing to the fact that the speaker appears to be participating in the action he is describing.

---

[44] Noulet, *Le premier visage de Rimbaud*, p. 183.
[45] Weaver, *The Ethics of Rhetoric*, p. 125.

The interrogative is a modality of considerable rhetorical importance. A question presupposes an object to which it relates and suggests that there is agreement on the existence of this object. To answer a question is to confirm this implicit agreement. The Socratic dialogues tell us a lot about both the usefulness and the dangers of this dialectical technique.

The classical writers, particularly Quintilian, made a number of practical observations on the role played by interrogation in legal proceedings, and what they said is still applicable. The purpose of asking a question is sometimes to obtain a confession of an act the existence and circumstances of which the speaker presumes, without actual knowledge of it. The question "What did you do that day in such-and-such a place?" already implies that the person questioned was at the place indicated at a certain moment; if he answers, he indicates his agreement on this point. But very often the questioning, though concerned with real events, is intended not so much to enlighten the questioner as to lead his opponent into inconsistencies. Questions are often merely a clever way of initiating a line of reasoning, particularly by the use of the alternative, or of division, with the complicity, so to speak, of the interlocutor who, by answering, is giving his endorsement to this mode of argument.

Because of the presuppositions implicit in certain questions, the interrogative form may be regarded as a rather hypocritical way of expressing certain beliefs. When one says *"Whatever* could have led the Germans to start so many wars in recent times?" the suggestion often is that the answers that spontaneously come to mind must be rejected. The question is less concerned with search for the motive than with search for the reason for not finding a motive; it is rather an affirmation that there is no motive that is sufficiently explanatory. For this reason Crawshay-Williams detects in questions of this kind the warning signs of an irrational turn of mind.[46]

According to Wittgenstein, interrogation amounts to a simple judgment in such a phrase as "Isn't the weather glorious today?"[47] And to Sartre, in these lines by Rimbaud—

O saisons, o châteaux,
Quelle âme est sans défauts?[48]

interrogation has turned into "thing," "substance." In fact, the interrogative form admits of appeal to communion with an audience, even if it is the subject himself.[49]

---

[46] Crawshay-Williams, *The Comforts of Unreason*, p. 176.
[47] Wittgenstein, *Philosophische Untersuchungen*, p. 10.
[48] Rimbaud, *Œuvres complètes, Poésies*, LXXXIII, p. 139.
[49] Sartre, *Situations*, II, pp. 68-69.

Sometimes one question can be used to dismiss another. An instance is Gide's dream in which not knowing the right thing to say in answer to the question, "What do you think of Russia?", he adopted the effective device of replying, "How can you ask?", thereby putting his agreement with his interlocutor beyond all doubt.[50]

The optative modality is perhaps the one that lends itself best to the expression of standards. The action in the wish "May he succeed!" is of the same order as the action of epidictic discourse. A wish expresses approval, and, indirectly, a standard; in that respect it is close to the imperative when the latter expresses a prayer, a supplication.

An audience can also be influenced by the use of tense. Each language group offers possibilities along this line which merit detailed study.

It can be said that in French the past tense stands for the irrefragable fact; the imperfect is the tense of transiency; the present expresses the universal, the law, the normal. The present is the tense of maxims and proverbial sayings, of that which is always timely and never out of date. Hence the present seems to have the most equivocal role; it expresses best the normal in its progress toward the norm. In a phrase such as "Women like to talk," one insists on the normal to the extent of making it a general characteristic: at first sight such a statement is indistinguishable from the affirmation "Man is subject to death." If we were to replace the present by "It has been stated that women like to talk" there would be much less confusion with the distributive meaning. One would get away from law and remain in the sphere of observation.

The present has the further property of conveying most readily what we have called "the feeling of presence." The rhetoricians have often ascribed this role to the present.[51] And its use by contemporary novelists is perhaps due to this property. Nelly Cormeau draws attention to the abrupt switch to the present in this passage from Mauriac:

> After an inner debate, she left her bed, slipped her swollen feet into a pair of old shoes, and wearing a brown dressing gown, went out of the room, candle in hand. She goes down the staircase, follows a corridor, crosses the expanse of the hallway.[52]

In Yves Gandon's study on style there are a number of interesting remarks about the use of tenses by writers. In Flaubert and the naturalists the imperfect takes over from the past definite (past historic). The narrative present is discovered or, at least, given preeminence by

[50] Gide, *The Journals* (Knopf), vol. IV, pp. 70-71.

[51] Cf. Longinus, *On the Sublime*, pp. 108-111.

[52] Cormeau, *L'art de François Mauriac*, pp. 348, 349, from Mauriac, *Génitrix*, p. 42.

contemporary writers: Jules Romains, for instance, shows a fondness for it. As Gandon says, "the illusion of life is secured at less cost."[53]

It is not of course certain that the feeling of presence is best conveyed by the present tense in every language. In the Slavonic languages, for instance, the grammatical form of the present of verbs of perfect action actually expresses the future, and is used only with this meaning. The influence of the verbal form on the way of expressing passage from the normal to the normative, on the feeling of presence, can only be studied for a given linguistic system at a given moment. Here it is enough to mention the possibilities offered by the use of these verbal forms when they are used, for argumentative purposes, within the framework of existing conventions.

We shall conclude this section with some observations on the argumentative use of pronouns, articles, and demonstratives.

The indefinite "one" is often used to put forward a standard. "One does this" is more or less equivalent to "This should be done." Sometimes "one" may simply designate that which applies to particular people in particular situations: "One cannot see clearly the shape of this tree." As the passage from the normal to the normative is a *locus* this turn of speech is of distinct interest from an argumentative viewpoint.

The substitution of "one" for "I" is, according to the Chevalier de Méré, sometimes agreeable, sometimes out of place:

> ... I see that a lady will rather say "One does not hate you," or "One loves you," than "I do not hate you," or "I love you." ... And because this expression is due to modesty, it cannot help but be well received. But if it is used out of a false sense of delicacy, as in "one asserts," or "One does not remain in agreement," it is disagreeable. And I know people who cannot stand it.[54]

In both sets of instances the subjective is transformed into the normal; the speaker somehow decreases his responsibility for the statement. Nevertheless, the "one" is understood as "I", and not just as an expression of the normal. If the first use is agreeable, and the second is not, this is less a matter of modesty and false delicacy than of the difference in the effect produced by generalizing a flattering opinion or a personal disagreement one wishes to emphasize.

The use of the third person, even when definite, in place of the first person may have the same effect as the use of "one," of diminishing the subject's responsibility, of making the speaker remote from what he says. Jouhandeau provides a nice example of this:

[53] Gandon, *Le démon du style*, pp. xv, 86.
[54] Méré (Chevalier de), *Œuvres complètes,* vol. II, p. 34.

> At the moment of her intoxication with the pride and admiration she felt for herself, the poor old woman ceased to say "I"; out of deference, perhaps, she began to speak of herself in the third person, addressing herself firmly as "Madame Robillard." Or else it was to separate herself, out of modesty from her glory or, maybe, it was to be more truthful by making herself, all of a sudden, objective.[55]

Even if the substitution is simply a return to childhood behavior—it is known that most children use their name before the personal pronoun in the first person[56]—one of its chief effects on the audience seems to be that the statement becomes more objective.

The ambiguity of an indefinite pronoun or adjective sometimes warrants its use for argumentative purposes. Such assertions as "Some people know too much about it" or "One does not enjoy oneself here" may or may not include the speaker or his interlocutor. These formulas are deliberately ambiguous: an excessively exact statement, allowing of no doubt in its interpretation, is sometimes carefully avoided, for a great variety of reasons.

On the other hand, the substitution of expressions designating one or more specified persons for the indefinite pronoun can give a strong impression of presence. That is why "the teller of tales ... calls as witnesses to his story obscure persons who cannot be found and convicted of falsehood."[57]

Noteworthy argumentative results sometimes come from the use of the singular instead of the plural, and of demonstratives.

Use of the singular instead of the plural in the terms "the Jew" or "the Russian" has an undeniable import.[58] We find in this substitution both an impression of presence due to the change of the group into a person, and a unification of viewpoint, the impossibility of distinguishing between the good and the bad that follows from this transformation.

Unusual use of the demonstrative can create a very vivid impression of presence: Here is one of the many examples found in the works of François Mauriac:

> He gazed at the big bed with the twisted columns, in which eight years earlier his elder brother, Michel Frontenac, had endured *that* interminable death-struggle.[59]

---

[55] Jouhandeau, *Un monde*, p. 80.

[56] Pichon, *Le développement psychique de l'enfant et de l'adolescent*, p. 96.

[57] La Bruyère, "Les Caractères de Théophraste, Du débit des nouvelles," *Œuvres complètes*, p. 51.

[58] Cf. Klemperer, *L. T. I., Notizbuch eines Philologen*, p. 186.

[59] Mauriac, *Le mystère Frontenac*, p. 11; cf. Gandon, *Le démon du style*, p. 65.

Gandon describes this contrivance as "inacceptable as measured by pure logic," while recognizing that it is "excellent as regards romantic technique." The demonstrative in the passage cited above refers to something known to only one of the characters, himself merely described by the author, and all this is on the first page of the novel. Yet the feeling of presence is undeniable.

All these forms of presentation have an influence on what the logicians regard as modalities: certainty, possibility, and necessity of a proposition. Adverbs, of course, are normally well suited to exercise such an influence, but from the few remarks above it is clear that one would be doing less than justice to the realities of argument to imagine that these modalities can be expressed through adverbs only.

What is required in argumentation is not so much the exactness of specific logical modalities attributed to what is asserted, as the means of obtaining the adherence of the audience through variations in the way of expressing thought.

§ 40. *Form of the Discourse and Communion with the Audience*

The form in which data are presented, besides aiming at producing argumentative effects in relation to the object of discourse, may also exhibit a set of characteristics connected with communion with the audience.

Every linguistic system involves formal structural rules which bind those who use it, but the practical application of the system can be reconciled with various styles, with particular formulas, characterizing a milieu, the speaker's place in it, a particular cultural atmosphere.

The role played by vocabulary in the differentiation of environments is well known. In certain societies there are languages for nobles or divinities alone;[60] the use of archaic terms, of dialects, very often signifies a separation, which may be an opposition of classes or an opposition of another nature. The significance of these differences lies in the fact that the language reserved to the privileged or the dialect coexists with the language of a larger group, to which those who speak it also belong. Restricted languages accordingly have a quite different segregative role than that exercised by the languages of people who are foreign to one another. It may happen that the restricted language is the ordinary language of a wider external group, as where a society adopts as its language of culture and refinement the language of another

[60] Cf. Porzig, *Das Wunder der Sprache*, pp. 187-188.

group. Examples are the use of Latin by the Gallo-Romans and, in the nineteenth century, of French by the inhabitants of Flanders.

We are all familiar with the role played by carelessness in expression: mutilation of a proper name or distortion of a text usually attest to a certain contempt for the person or thing referred to. These negligences can create a complicity with the hearer, emphasize a hierarchy. To take a rather trite example: a doctor who has to read a financial report seems to hesitate, as he reads, between *milliers* (thousands) and *millions* (millions) of francs, indicating a contempt for these material questions and communion with the members of the audience who share this attitude. Use of a deliberately poor or clumsy vocabulary may serve the same purpose.

And there is more. One is beginning to recognize that to each social structure there correspond particular modes of expressing social communion. Lasswell has emphasized this problem in his writings on propaganda. So far two main styles in the transmission of thought seem to have been distinguished: the style of democratic societies and the style of hierarchic societies. Studies in this field are still embryonic. However, it is interesting to note, as Lasswell has done, the almost ritual character of the style of certain hierarchic societies. It has been pointed out that the proclamations of the King of England as Emperor of India were much more ritualistic in style than his proclamations as King of England. Various hypotheses have been advanced: it would appear that certain linguistic structures are more suited to a society based on equality, on individual initiative; others would be more suited to societies with a hierarchic structure.

Heinz Paechter has endeavored to indicate these two structural types in his interesting study of Nazi German.[61] The grammar of equalitarian societies seems to accentuate predicates, evaluations by the subject, whereas the language of hierarchic societies would be evocative, its grammar and syntax would have a magical quality :

> The verbal symbols cease to be representative of things, and tend to become things in themselves, with a well-defined place in the hierarchy of values, and participation in the ritual at their own independent level.[62]

In an equalitarian society language belongs to everybody and evolves quite freely; in a hierarchic society it congeals. Its expressions and formulas become ritual and are listened to in a spirit of communion and total submission.

---

[61] Paechter et al, *Nazi-Deutsch*, quoted by Lasswell et al, *Language of Politics*, p. 385, note.

[62] Paechter et al, *Nazi-Deutsch*, p. 6.

But it is sufficient that the formulas be no longer compulsory, that one no longer listens to them in the same spirit of communion, for them to become stereotyped. The imitation of biblical style sometimes found in sermons and the attempts made with varying success to reproduce a fine line of Racine—the well-known passages of classical literature have something of a ritual quality— seem hackneyed, for the very reason that they claim originality.

If, since the time of Romanticism, the cliché has been run to ground in our culture bent on originality at any price—Jean Paulhan has well described this reign of terror in literature—this is due to the fact that the hackneyed formula is valueless except as an easy, sometimes too easy, way of entering into communion with one's audience. The cliché is the result of an agreement as to the way of expressing a fact, a value, a connection between phenomena, or a relationship between people. There are poetical clichés and political clichés. These formulas are an aid to interpretation: we know that the use of the word "charger" shows a poetic intention, while "your glorious country" is a formula for after-dinner speakers. The terms "right," "liberty," "democracy" can bring about communion in the same way as the unfurling of a flag.

For these words or formulas to be recognized as clichés, there has to be a separation; the hearer must no longer identify himself, from every point of view, with those who use and accept the words and formulas. Two sets of considerations (which may reinforce one another) appear to promote this recoil. The cliché is both form and content. It is an object of agreement regularly expressed in a certain way, a repeated formula of a stereotyped character. All that is necessary, then, for an expression to be recognized as a cliché is the realization that the same thing can be said as well, or even better, in another way. The hearer who reaches this conclusion has effected a dissociation between content and form and has drawn back at the linguistic level. But it is also sufficient to reject the values expressed by the cliché. In this case, the hearer will draw back at the level of thought. In either case, the hearer perceives an inadequacy which makes him aware of the presence of something that is ready-made and not perfectly adapted to the situation.

Though admission of the stereotyped formula can advance discussion through the communion it makes possible, its rejection may mean that certain arguments will be disqualified, certain speakers discredited.

The importance of a recognized formulation is clearly seen when it is a question of expressing a norm more or less explicitly. *Maxims* not only condense the wisdom of the nations—they are also one of the most effective means of promoting this wisdom and causing it to develop: the use of maxims makes us put our finger on the role played by the accepted values and on the procedures for transferring these values. It is true that a maxim can always be rejected, that the agreement it calls forth is never compulsory, but so great is its force, so great the presumption of agreement attaching to it, that one must have weighty reasons for rejecting it.

A maxim or *gnōmē*, as described by Aristotle,[63] is what we today would call a value judgment. "It invests a speech," he says, "with moral character."[64] Its significance comes from its social elaboration. It is uttered in order to suggest its applicability to a particular situation. The more its form is traditionally known, the readier will be the acceptance of the statement and of the consequences it involves.

The dictionary tells us that a proverb is a short maxim that has become popular. According to Schopenhauer, proverbs are *loci* with a practical bent.[65] We would like to emphasize what we consider to be an essential feature of this kind of maxim: the proverb expresses a particular occurrence and at the same time suggests a standard; whence, probably, its easy diffusion, its popular character, that sets it in contrast to the scholarly, bookish character of certain maxims. We must add, as Estève has rightly pointed out, that the imperativeness of proverbs is due, at least in part, to their rhythm.[66]

Because a proverb is recognized as illustrating a standard, it can be used as a starting point for a line of argument, provided, of course, the standard is one admitted by the audience. But one should not conclude from this that proverbs can be of use only if it has become virtually unnecessary to state them. The litany of proverbs teeming from the lips of Sancho Panza are so many calls to order for the benefit of those who may be forgetful of values that it is advisable not to completely neglect.

Although proverbs record traditional agreement, new ones can still come into being. But they immediately derive their status *qua* proverbs from existing proverbs, either by virtue of purely formal imitation or because the new proverb is simply a new illustration of a standard already illustrated by an earlier proverb. Jean Paulhan has described the poetical competitions of the Madagascans in which the contest is carried out by volleys of proverbs and of what are called "proverbial images."[67] These are stylized phrases expressing standards,

---

[63] Aristotle, *Rhetoric*, II, 21, 1394a et seq.

[64] *Ibid*, 1395b.

[65] Schopenhauer, "Eristische Dialektik," *Sämtliche Werke* (Piper), vol. 6, p. 401, note.

[66] Estève, *Études Philosophiques sur l'expression littéraire*, p. 217.

[67] Paulhan, *Les hain-tenys*, p. 37.

but only the initiate can distinguish a proverb from a mere proverbial image.

Slogans and catchwords are maxims developed to meet the requirements of a specific action.[68] They are designed to secure attention through their rhythm and their concise and easily remembered form, but they are adapted to particular circumstances, require constant renewal, and are too recent to enjoy the wide traditional agreement accorded to proverbs. They may be able to stimulate action, but they are much less effective in inducing beliefs; their function is essentially that of compelling our attention to certain ideas, by means of the form in which they are expressed.

§ 41. *Rhetorical Figures and Argumentation*

From antiquity, and probably from the moment man first reflected on language, one has noticed certain modes of expression which are different from the ordinary, and they generally have been studied in the treatises on rhetoric: hence their name, *rhetorical figures*. Because of the tendency of rhetoricians to restrict their study to problems of style and expression, rhetorical figures increasingly came to be regarded as mere ornaments that made the style artificial and ornate. When Latro, the orator, expressed the opinion that figures were not invented as ornaments, his view was considered worthy of comment.[69] The opinion commonly held among the theoreticians of persuasive discourse was that of Quintilian who regarded figures as an important factor in obtaining variety and polish, "although it seems to matter very little for the proof that the arguments be presented in the form of this or that figure."[70] Is this really the case? Let us look at the definition of *hypotyposis* (*demonstratio*) found in the *Rhetorica ad Herennium*: it is a figure "which sets things out in such a way that the matter seems to unfold, and the thing to happen, under our eyes."[71] It is, then, a way of describing things which makes them present to our mind: can one deny the importance of its role as a persuasive factor? If the argumentative role of figures is disregarded, their study will soon seem to be a useless pastime, a search for strange names for rather farfetched and affected turns of speech. Already Quintilian was weary at the thought of the multiplicity of names and classifications proposed

---

[68] Cf. Bellak, "The Nature of Slogans," *Journal of Abnormal and Social Psychology*, 37 (1942), 496-510.

[69] Seneca, *Controverses et suasoires*, bk. I, Preface, § 24.

[70] Quintilian, IX, I, 19-21.

[71] *Rhetorica ad Herennium*, IV, § 68; cf. Quintilian, IX, II, 40.

by the rhetoricians, their entanglement with one another, and the differences of opinion even on the question of what is a figure.[72] Jean Paulhan declares that if one confines oneself to what one can get out of the authors, "the sole characteristic of figures is the views expressed about them and the studies made of them by the writers on rhetoric."[73] In the face of this paradox, Paulhan finds himself compelled to reconsider the problem of the relation between thought and its expression.

For us, more concerned with the techniques of persuasive discourse than with the justification of a literary mode of expression, the important thing seems not so much to study the problem of figures in its totality as to show *how and in what respects the use of particular figures is explained by the requirements of argumentation.* We note, in this connection, that Cournot had already seen that figures do not act only on the feelings. It is easy to see, he writes, that "the language of philosophers is no less figurative than that of orators and poets."[74]

In order that there may be a figure, the presence of two characteristics would seem essential: a discernible structure, independent of the content, in other words a form (which may, under the divisions recognized by modern logicians, be syntactic, semantic, or pragmatic), and a use that is different from the normal manner of expression and, consequently, attracts attention. At least one of these requirements can be found in most of the definitions of figures that have been advanced over the centuries; the other is generally there indirectly. Thus Omer Talon defines a figure as "an expression in which the appearance of speech differs from pure and simple custom." But he brings in the idea of form by the medium of etymology:

> The name "figure" seems to be derived from the mask and costume of actors, who uttered different kinds of speech under different external guises (*variis corporis figuris*).[75]

Anyone who studies speeches from a structural viewpoint will encounter some forms that are seen right away to be figures (repetition, for instance), but he will also find figures that seem normal (interrogation, for instance), but can nevertheless be regarded as figures under some circumstances. The fact that they may or may not be considered as figures immediately raises the most delicate aspect of the problem.

---

[72] Quintilian, IX, i, 10; IX, iii, 99.

[73] Paulhan, "Les figures ou la rhétorique décryptée," *Cahiers du Sud*, 295 (1949), 387.

[74] Cournot, *Essai sur les fondements de nos connaissances*, vol. II, p. 12.

[75] Talon, *Audomari Talaei Rhetoricae Libri Duo P. Rami Praelectionibus Illustrati*, p. 16.

Theoretically, there is no structure incapable of becoming a figure by the way it is used, but the mere fact that a use of the language is uncommon does not justify our regarding it as a figure.

In order that a structure be a possible object of study, it must be possible to isolate it, to recognize it as a structure; it is also necessary to know in what respect a use must be regarded as unusual. Exclamatory phrases, phrases that repeat words after a hesitation, are structures; but they would only be figures of speech outside their normal use, that is, only when they do not express real surprise or real hesitation.

Is there not thus a direct connection between the use of figures and pretense? According to Volkmann, this was the opinion of the classical authors.[76] It is certain, at all events, that there is a figure only when dissociation can be effected between the normal use of a structure and the use to which it is put in the speech, and when the hearer makes a distinction, which seems to him imperative, between form and substance. The whole of the argumentative significance of figures arises at the moment when this distinction, which was immediately noticed, is dissolved through the effect produced by the speech.

It may be that the purpose in using a given structure, under unusual conditions, is simply that of giving a thought more life, of feigning emotion, of creating a dramatic situation that does not exist in reality. If, for instance, a speaker introduces objections into his sentence in order to answer them himself, we have a figure of speech, *prolepsis*, which is simply a feint. These objections may be clearly imaginary, but it can be important for a speaker to show that he had himself foreseen possible objections and had taken them into account. There is, as a matter of fact, a whole series of degrees separating a real objection and a pretended objection. One and the same structure can go from one degree to another simply by the effect produced by the speech. Forms which seem at first to be used in an unusual manner may come to appear normal if their use is justified by the speech taken as a whole. We consider a figure to be *argumentative*, if it brings about a change of perspective, and its use seems normal in relation to this new situation. If, on the other hand, the speech does not bring about the adherence of the hearer to this argumentative form, the figure will be considered an embellishment, a figure of style. It can excite admiration, but this will be on the aesthetic plane, or in recognition of the speaker's originality.

It is apparent, then, that it is impossible to decide in advance if a given structure is or is not to be regarded as a figure, or if it will be

---

[76] Volkmann, *Hermagoras oder Elemente der Rhetorik*, p. 275.

an argumentative or a stylistic figure. The best one can do is to point out some structures that are liable to become figures.

Certain figures, such as *allusion*, can never be recognized independently of their context, for their structure is neither grammatical nor semantic, but depends on a relationship with something that is not the immediate object of discourse. If this mode of expression strikes the hearer as unusual, there is a figure ; the type of figure will depend on the impression made by the speech and on the hearer's adherence to the form of argument which is promoted in this way. We already note that allusion will nearly always have argumentative value because it is essentially an element of agreement and communion.

The importance of the movement of the speech can be better appreciated by considering certain *metaphors*. Adam Smith, in a well-known passage, shows by what mechanism the individual serves the general interest while pursuing his private gain:

> ... He intends only his own gain, and he is, in this, as in many other cases, led by an invisible hand to promote an end which was no part of his intention.[77]

The famous expression "invisible hand" used by Smith does not generally strike the reader as the normal expression of thought, in the sense that few readers will think that the author is referring to a hand of flesh and blood. The reader feels that the invisible hand is there to persuade him that the harmony between individual interest and social interest is not due to chance, that he is at liberty to explain it by a supernatural intervention, that the foresight denied to man may be that of a supreme being. We shall not analyze here the mechanism of this figure, but we wish to show that because it is possible to adhere to the argumentative value it contains it may properly be regarded as a figure, though not as a figure of style. We may observe, in this connection, that a figure may be seen as argumentative without its necessarily bringing about adherence to the conclusions of the discourse : all that is required is that the argument should be seen in its full value. It is of little importance if other considerations stand in the way of acceptance of the thesis involved.

It follows that a figure which has failed in its argumentative effect will fall to the level of a stylistic figure. Accordingly, if a critic wishes to deny to a philosophical theory any value other than literary, he will claim that it is only a figure of speech. Thus Sartre writes :

> This Past of Bergson's, which clings to the present and even penetrates it, is scarcely more than a rhetorical figure. And it

[77] Adam Smith, *The Wealth of Nations*, GBWW, vol. 39, p. 194.

shows well the difficulties which Bergson encountered in his theory of memory.[78]

If the writers who have concerned themselves with figures have been inclined to see only their stylistic aspect, this is due, in our opinion, to the fact that the moment a figure is detached from its context and pigeonholed, it is almost necessarily perceived under its least argumentative aspect. In order to perceive its argumentative aspect, it is necessary to conceive of a step from the common to the uncommon, and a return to another order of commonness, that created by the argument at the moment of its completion. Further, and this is perhaps the most important point, it is necessary to understand that the normal expression is relative not only to a milieu, an audience, but to a particular moment in the discourse. If one admits, on the contrary, that there is a way of expressing oneself that is the good, authentic, true, and normal way, then one can conceive of a figure only as something static: an expression is or is not a figure; one cannot imagine that it may or may not be a figure, depending on the hearer's reaction. Only a more flexible conception, which considers the normal in all its changing facets, can do full justice to the place argumentative figures occupy in the phenomenon of persuasion.

We concur thus, by the relativization of the normal, with an observation by the author known to us as Longinus:

> No figure is more excellent than the one which is entirely hidden, so that it is no longer recognized as a figure. There is no more wonderful aid and succor in preventing its appearance than sublimity and pathos, for artifice thus enclosed in the midst of something great and dazzling has everything it lacked, and becomes free from any suspicion of deception.[79]

Party dresses are in order in certain surroundings, and do not attract attention.

§ 42. *Figures of Choice, Presence, and Communion*

In dealing with rhetorical figures, and seeing what each of them contributes to argumentation, we shall readily refer to them by their traditional names. This will facilitate an understanding with the reader, as we shall be speaking of structures that have already attracted attention in the past. Even the examples will often be traditional. On the other hand, the customary classifications of figures cannot be of help

[78] Sartre, *Being and Nothingness*, p. 135.
[79] Longinus, *On the Sublime*, chap. XV.

to us. We believe, on the contrary, that the major distinction between figures of thought and figures of speech, which was unknown to Aristotle but has been apparently obligatory since the second century B.C., has helped to obscure the whole conception of rhetorical figures.

Our view is that a given figure, recognizable by its structure, does not always produce the same effect in argumentation. And it is this effect which is our principal concern. Instead of embarking on an exhaustive examination of all the traditional figures, we shall inquire, in the context of a given argumentative procedure or scheme, if certain figures are of such a nature as to fulfil the function we have attributed to this procedure, if they can be regarded as one of its manifestations. This approach involves a sort of dismembering of figures. For not only will figures range over different chapters of our study, but examples of a particular figure may occur in more than one chapter. We feel that it is this dismembering itself that best conveys the argumentative significance of figures.

To illustrate our method of proceeding, we shall make a quick survey of certain figures relating to choice, presence, and communion. These terms do not represent families in which certain traditional figures appear as members. They simply indicate that the effect, or one of the effects, certain figures have in the presentation of data is to impose or to suggest a choice, to increase the impression of presence, or to bring about communion with the audience.

One of the essential modes of choice, interpretation, can give rise to an argumentative figure. We are inclined to regard as an instance of this the procedure described by Seneca in the dispute about the son who provided for his uncle although his father had forbidden it. One defender of the son claims that the son believed that his father's orders did not correspond to his real wishes. But Cestius with greater boldness has the son address his father thus :

You wished it and you still wish it today.[80]

This highly audacious interpretation is presented as a fact and will be considered an argumentative figure or a stylistic figure depending on the effect it has on the audience.

Oratorical definition is a figure relating to choice, because it makes use of the structure of a definition not to give the meaning of a word, but to bring to the fore certain aspects of the facts which might otherwise remain in the background of our consciousness. We are told by Baron

---

[80] Seneca, *Controversiae*, I, § 15.

that when Fléchier wanted to emphasize the qualities a general must
have, he formulated his definition of the army

> ... in such a way that each proposition was one of the premises
> of a syllogism which had as its conclusion: therefore it is difficult
> to command an army.

The definition runs as follows:

> What is an army? It is a body animated by an infinity of different
> passions which a clever man sets in motion for the defense of his
> country. It is a band of armed men who follow blindly the orders
> of a leader whose intentions are unknown to them. It is a multitude
> of souls, for the most part vile and mercenary, who without thought
> for their own glory labor for the glory of kings and conquerors.
> It is a confused assemblage of libertines. ...[81]

We can see clearly in the case of oratorical definition that the abnor-
mality of a structure can be considered from two different viewpoints.
On the one hand, oratorical definition, though it exhibits the structure
of definition, does not play the usual role of the latter. On the other
hand, choice—an effect ordinarily produced by means of an epithet, by
qualification— is effected here through use of the oratorical definition.
If the first viewpoint were emphasized, we would deal with oratorical
definition as a definition. It is because we refer to the second viewpoint,
to the functional aspect, to its effect on the audience, that we think of
it as a figure relating to choice.

Periphrasis may exercise the same function as oratorical definition:
"the three goddesses who, according to myth, weave the web of our
existence" to indicate the Fates, will be a periphrasis if, instead of
being used to define the word "Fates," it is used to replace it, which
presupposes knowledge of the existence of the word for which the longer phrasing is substituted. The argumentative role of assertion in these
lines from *Athalie* stands out clearly, yet the first of the two lines may
be considered to be a periphrastic description of God:

> He who curbs the fury of the waves
> Can also foil the plots of the wicked.[82]

Many periphrases can be analyzed in terms of such figures as *synecdoche* or *metonymy*, whose function is not essentially that of choice,[83]
though they may serve that function. The use of "mortals," for
instance, in place of "men," is a way of drawing attention to a par-

[81] Baron, *De la rhétorique*, p. 61.
[82] Racine, *Athalie*, Act I, scene i, *Œuvres complètes*, vol. I, p. 896.
[83] Cf. § 75, infra: The Symbolic Relation.

ticular characteristic of men. We also mention here, as a figure of choice, *antonomasia*, which Littré defines as "a kind of synecdoche which consists of using a common name for a proper name, or a proper name for a common name." The purpose of the first form of antonomasia is sometimes to avoid the mention of a proper name, but it may also be to qualify someone in a manner that helps the argument. The latter purpose may be detected in the use of "the grandchildren of Africanus" in place of "the Gracchi."

Prolepsis or *anticipation* (*praesumptio*) can be a figure relating to choice when its aim is to hint that there are grounds for substituting one qualification for another that might have raised objections:

> Although that was not a punishment, but merely a prevention of crime.[84]

The hesitation expressed when checking oneself (*reprehensio*) simply serves to stress the legitimacy of a choice:

> Citizens, I say, if I may call them by that name.[85]

The same purpose is served by correction (*correctio*) which replaces a word by another:

> If the accused had requested it of his guests or, rather, if he had merely given them a sign. ... [86]

The effect of figures relating to presence is to make the object of discourse present to the mind.

The first of these figures is *onomatopoeia*. Whether or not spontaneous onomatopoeia was at the origin of certain words in the language is of little consequence to our study. Onomatopoeia is seen as a figure when there is creation of a word or unusual use of existing words to evoke an actual noise. It does not much matter whether the sound is an exact or only a fairly close reproduction of the noise one wishes to make more present. The only thing that seems to count is the intention to imitate. It is amusing to note, in this connection, that Dumarsais gives as an example of onomatopoeia the Latin *bilbit amphora*, which he translates as *la petite bouteille fait glouglou*[87] (the little bottle goes glug-glug).

The simplest figures for increasing the feeling of presence are those depending on *repetition*. Repetition is important in argumentation,

---

[84] Quintilian, IX, II, 18.
[85] *Ibid.*
[86] *Rhetorica ad Herennium*, IV, 36.
[87] Dumarsais, *Des tropes*, p. 161.

whereas it is of no use in demonstration or scientific reasoning in general. Repetition can act directly; it may also accentuate the breaking up of a complex event into separate episodes which, as we know, promotes the impression of presence. Thus in this example of *anaphora*, the repetition of the first words in two successive sentences:

> Three times I flung my arms around his neck,
> Three times the empty image fled away.[88]

But most of the figures classified by the rhetoricians under the heading of figures relating to repetition[89] seem to have a much more complex argumentative effect than merely giving feeling of presence. Though they have the form of a repetition, they really aim at suggesting distinctions: expressions of the type "Corydon ever since has for me been Corydon" are seen to be figures on account of this abnormal use of repetition.[90]

Somewhat closer to figures relating to presence are the *conduplicatio* of the *Rhetorica ad Herennium* and Quintilian's *adjectio*:

> Wars, C. Gracchus, civil and intestine wars are what you provoke. ... [91]

> I have killed, yes, I have killed. ...[92]

Here again the effect of the repetition is not merely to add to the feeling of presence; because of the repetition, the second statement of the term seems to be much more weighty; the first one, by reaction, seems to refer exclusively to a fact, whereas normally and alone it would have been felt to contain both fact and value. The effect of presence is thus subordinated to other purposes. In consequence, we cannot agree with Chaignet's explanation, though it does attempt to find a meaning for the use of repetition:

> It is obvious that if one has a lot to say about a person or thing, one is compelled to call him or it by its name several times. Conversely, if one names a person or thing several times, it seems that one has said a lot about them.[93]

Far more instrumental than mere repetition of words in obtaining the feeling of presence is the use of *amplification*: by this we mean the oratorical development of a theme, irrespective of the exaggeration that people generally associate with it.

---

[88] Quoted by Vico, *Delle Instituzioni Oratorie*, p. 142.
[89] *Ibid.* pp. 142 et seq.
[90] Cf. § 51, infra: Analyticity, Analysis, and Tautology.
[91] *Rhetorica ad Herennium*, iv, 38.
[92] Quintilian, IX, iii, 28.
[93] Chaignet, *La Rhétorique et son histoire*, pp. 515-516.

When and why is amplification a figure? Mainly, it seems, when it makes use of forms that normally have another aim than presence: this is the case, in particular, for amplification through enumeration of parts, which recalls a quasi-logical argumentation.[94] Here is an example of *aggregation* given by Vico:

> Your eyes are made for impudence, your face for effrontery, your tongue for false swearing, your hands for plunder, your belly for gluttony ... your feet for flight: so you are all malignity.[95]

Similarly *synonymy* (*metabolè*)—the repetition of a single idea by means of different words—conveys presence by using a form that suggests progressive correction. In the line

> Go, run, fly and avenge us ....[96]

terms that seem increasingly appropriate are used one after the other. Synonymy would be an abbreviated correction, or even an abbreviated prolepsis: it would convey presence through a form that was essentially intended for choice.

A very similar figure to this is *interpretatio*, the explanation of one expression by another, not so much for purposes of clarification as to increase the feeling of presence:

> It is the republic you have completely upset, the State that you have completely destroyed.[97]

Imaginary direct speech increases the feeling of presence by the fictitious attribution of words to a person (*sermocinatio*) or to a group of persons engaged in conversation (*dialogism*).[98] Imaginary direct speech can have a variety of purposes, but they all have to do with hypothesis. Now we have already seen the role of the latter in creating the feeling of presence.[99] The use of imaginary direct speech will reveal the intentions ascribed to a person, or what is thought to be the opinion of other people regarding those intentions. It can be presented as half spoken and half thought. Robert Browning makes ample use of this last very equivocal form of imaginary speech in his poem *The Ring and the Book*.

There are also figures connected with the grammatical tenses. It is sudden passage from the past tense, the narrative tense, to the present, the

---

[94] Cf. § 56, infra: Division of the Whole into Its Parts.
[95] Vico, *Delle instituzioni oratorie*, p. 81.
[96] Corneille, *Le Cid*, Act I, scene 6.
[97] *Rhetorica ad Herennium*, iv, 38.
[98] Cf. Vico, *Delle Instituzioni Oratorie*, p. 151.
[99] Cf. § 37, supra: Technical Problems in the Presentation of Data.

descriptive tense, which often makes it appear as the figure of *hypotypo-sis*,[100] which we have previously mentioned; the example generally mentioned is the account of the death of Hippolytus, in which all the verbs are in the present tense.[101]

The syntactical substitution of one tense for another, contrary to normal practice, that is, *enallage of tense*, can produce a very strong impression of presence: "If you speak, you are dead" suggests that the consequence of disobeying the injunction will be instantaneous.

The figures that relate to communion are those in which literary devices are used to try and bring about or increase communion with the audience. Often this communion is achieved through references to a common culture, tradition or past.

Allusion, which many writers treat as a figure, certainly has this function. There is allusion when the interpretation of a passage would be incomplete if one neglected the deliberate reference of the author to something he evokes without actually naming it; this thing may be an event of the past, a custom, or a cultural fact, knowledge of which is peculiar to the members of the group with whom the speaker is trying to establish the communion. There is generally a special affectivity attached to these cultural facts: the emotion created by memories, or community pride. Allusion increases the prestige of the speaker in possession of this treasure, and able to utilize it. Thus Mirabeau in this passage quoted by Baron:

> I did not need this lesson to know that it is but a step from the Capitol to the Tarpeian rock.[102]

Quotation can be regarded as a figure relating to communion only when it is not fulfilling its normal role of backing up a statement with the weight of authority.[103]

Maxims and proverbs can also be considered to be quotations: when their use does not seem to arise from the requirements of argument, and their content becomes of secondary importance, they are seen as figures. In Sancho Panza or Tevye the Dairyman[104] maxims and proverbs are a sign of how rooted they are in a culture. Quotation, like the cliché, may be conceived as a mere formalism. But the person of whom La Bruyère says:

---

[100] Cf. Longinus, *On the Sublime*, chap. XXV.

[101] Racine, *Phèdre*, Act V, scene vi, *Œuvres complètes*, vol. I, pp. 817-818.

[102] Baron, *De la rhétorique*, p. 335.

[103] Cf. § 70, infra: Argument from Authority.

[104] Sholom Aleichem, *Tevye's Daughters*.

> It is not to give more authority to what he says, nor perhaps to
> plume himself on what he knows. He wants to quote.[105]

is undoubtedly still seeking communion with his audience.

Communion is also increased by all those figures whereby a speaker
endeavors to get his audience to participate actively in his exposition,
by taking it into his confidence, inviting its help, or identifying himself with it.

Apostrophe, and the *oratorical question* which aims neither at getting
information nor at securing agreement are often figures relating to
communion. In *oratorical communication* the speaker asks his opponent, or the judge, to think about the situation under discussion and
invites them to take part in the deliberation which he appears to carry
on in front of them,[106] or he may also try to merge himself in his audience, as Massillon does in this passage:

> Now I request this of you, and I request it stricken with terror,
> not separating my fate from yours in this matter. ...[107]

The same effect is obtained by *enallage of person*, in which "I" or
"he" is replaced by "thou," making "the hearer imagine he sees himself
in the midst of the danger,"[108] and which is a figure relating both to
presence and to communion. And also by *change in the number of persons*, in which "I" or "thou" is replaced by "we." A mother uses this
figure when she tells her child, "We are going to bed."

An excellent example is to be found in Massillon, who is constantly
concerned with identification with his audience:

> And there, dear listener, is matter to instruct and confuse you
> at the same time. You complain of your misfortunes. ... Yet what
> could be a greater consolation in our trouble? God sees me, counts
> my sighs, weighs my afflictions, beholds my flowing tears. ...[109]

In this passage "you," "us," and "me" are the stages by which the
speaker identifies himself with his audience. In the final stage, there
is, along with the change in number, the use of imaginary direct speech
which can thus also be a figure relating to communion.

These few indications as to the role of some of the rhetorical figures
in the presentation of data are sufficient, we think, to show the connec-

---

[105] La Bruyère, "Les caractères. Des jugements," 64, *Œuvres complètes*, p. 385.

[106] Vico, *Delle instituzioni oratorie*, p. 147.

[107] Quoted by Saint-Aubin, *Guide pour la classe de rhétorique*, p. 91. Massillon,
Carême, Sermon XIX: *Sur le petit nombre des élus*, vol. I, col. 722.

[108] Longinus, *On the Sublime*, chap. XXVI.

[109] Massillon, Sermon IV. Pour le second dimanche de l'Avent. *Sur les afflictions*,
vol. I, col. 241.

tion existing between their effects and factors of a general kind that enter into persuasion. Our study of figures is thus made subordinate to an earlier study of argumentation. The objection may be made that by this approach we shall never deal with what some would deem essential aspects of the study of figures.

We believe, nonetheless, that it is advantageous to treat the matter in this way, and we shall accordingly revert to our present approach in the course of this work whenever the occasion arises.

§ 43. *Status and Presentation of the Elements of the Argumentation*

One of the most important results of the presentation of the data is the alteration of the status of the elements of the discourse.

We know that the various types of objects of agreement enjoy different prerogatives. Facts, truths, and presumptions are assumed to command the agreement of the universal audience, whereas values, hierarchies, and *loci* only command the agreement of particular audiences. The precariousness of these various objects of agreement is not dependent on the same conditions. This explains the importance ascribed to fixing the status of the elements used, to the transfer of certain elements into another category, to the possibility of emphasizing objects of agreement of one type rather than another.

The speaker and his audience are normally assumed to grant the same status to the elements of the discourse, at least until an explicit disagreement makes it necessary to modify this hypothesis. But it very often happens that in the interests of his argument a speaker will endeavor to get the discussion on the plane he considers most favorable to himself by modifying the status of particular data as he finds necessary. Presentation plays an essential role in this process.

As a general rule, the speaker's effort will be directed to assigning the highest possible status, the status enjoying the widest agreement, to the elements upon which he is basing his argument. He may accordingly seek to confer the status of value on personal feelings, and the status of fact on values.

Personal feelings and impressions are often expressed as widely shared value judgments. Typical instances would be the tourist's "How nice it is to travel in France !" or the young lover's "How lovely the moon is tonight !" Such expressions, as Britton points out,[110] are more effective in conversation carried on before an audience of close friends than in writings intended for just any reader. What is involved

---

[110] Britton, *Communication*, p. 48.

is not so much a value judgment that the speaker is prepared to defend, as an impression that he is asking a kindly disposed audience to share.

Value judgments, and even purely subjective feelings, can be transformed into judgments of fact through certain tricks of presentation. The use of the formula "These apples do not appeal to me" instead of "I do not like these apples" makes it possible to effect a sort of shift of responsibility. The thing involved is reproached with not making an appeal, and the unfavorable reaction to it is considered to result from its behavior. Naturally, this assertion refers to an unverifiable fact, and the hearer could refuse his agreement. But no one thinks about this until the time comes when he wants to contradict the speaker and defend the high quality of the apples.

If the term "liar" is replaced by that of "person having a tendency to mislead deliberately,"[111] one gets the impression that the value judgment contained in the designation "liar" has been transformed into a jdgment of fact because in its new form the statement seems more exact and because the conditions governing its verification are emphasized. Furthermore, the avoidance of the term "liar" stresses the intent to avoid a disparaging appraisal. Terms that ordinarily serve to describe facts can be advantageously used to prompt value judgments without their being explicitly stated, where the audience is one that is distrustful of anything that does not seem verifiable. The person who, instead of saying "I have acted well," says "I have acted in such and such a way" seems to limit himself to an undeniable and objective statement of fact. However, in a roundabout way he secures, in the eyes of someone disposed to approve this way of acting, the same result as he would by the assertion of a value. The transposition is indubitably advantageous because the value, not having been stated, is not needlessly laid open to question. Similarly, instead of praising someone's fine qualities, it is sufficient to call attention to certain facts, avoiding the mention of the ensuing valuation, letting the hearer take care of this.

Value judgments can also be converted into expressions of fact by attributing them to someone: this change of status is generally put forward to give weight to an assertion. But it can also have the effect of limiting its impact: a standard that is buttressed with the authority of some famous person runs the risk of being transformed into a simple cultural fact.

Another technique is to present as a fact of experience what is really only the conclusion of an argumentation. In his book on archeological frauds, Vayson de Pradenne pays considerable attention to the argu-

---

[111] Cf. § 38, supra: Verbal Forms and Argumentation.

ments used by the different sides in the controversies, and points out that Chierici defended the authenticity of the Breonio flints with this statement: "The mere inspection of these flints excludes any suspicion of recent workmanship."[112] Vayson de Pradenne considers this a form of argument from authority. But really the interesting feature of the statement is precisely that it is not put forward as an argument from authority, but as a testimony concerning a verifiable fact.

When someone qualifies the solution he considers to be the best as the sole solution, he is effecting a similar transposition of a value judgment into a judgment of fact.

Sometimes disagreement with respect to values is presented as a disagreement over facts, because it is easier to correct a factual error than a value judgment of which one disapproves. Typical of this technique of argument is the appeal from a badly informed authority to a better informed authority: one assumes that the disagreement is due to insufficient information and that when all the facts are known the badly informed person will change his opinion. Similarly, the value of a disputed law will be increased if it is proclaimed that if it was transgressed, this could only have occurred through ignorance. The implication is that anyone who knew of the law would not hesitate to follow it.

A funny example of this mode of argument, funny precisely because it is a feint, is given by Quintilian. When a Roman knight was charged by Augustus with squandering his patrimony, his answer was "I thought it belonged to me," as if the sole basis of the reproach was a factual error.[113]

Some figures, particularly *metalepsis*, can facilitate the transposition of values into facts. "He forgets benefits" for "he is ungrateful," or "remember our agreement" for "keep our agreement," are ways of attributing a certain behavior to a phenomenon of memory, of allowing the interlocutor to modify his attitude though one seems merely to have improved his knowledge of the facts. Similarly, replacement of "I despise you" by "I do not know you"[114] turns a value judgment into an existence judgment.

Sometimes a hypothesis will change a value judgment into a factual situation, as in this passage from a speech by Schollaert, the Belgian Catholic leader:

> Gentlemen, I would like to be able to take a Christian woman up on a mountain high enough for her to be able to take in at a single

[112] Vayson de Pradenne, *Les fraudes en archéologie préhistorique*, p. 244.
[113] Quintilian, VI, iii, 74.
[114] Examples quoted by Dumarsais, *Des Tropes*, p. 70.

glance all the women and all the peoples of the earth. And there ...
I would say to her: "Look around you, and after you have looked,
answer me. ... Who made you pure, beautiful, regal, and superior
to all the unfortunate sisters traipsing beneath you?"[115]

The factual situation imagined by the speaker entails a possibility of
downward gaze which suggests a superiority of value.

Finally, certain grammatical constructions, such as noun-phrases,
can be utilized to convey factual status. Caillois notes the frequency
of their use by St.-John Perse, and interprets this as the tone of one
who is sparing with his words, in affirmations that are on account of
their self-evidence or of his authority undisputed.[116] Noun-phrases
are, rather, an effort to make a statement timeless and, in consequence,
beyond the limits of subjectivity and bias.

In presenting premises it can however be desirable to lower the status
of certain objects of agreement.

In order to minimize the seriousness of opposition to a fact, of a twist
given to the truth, one will transform a fact into an opinion. A very
good example of this transposition can be found in Browning's poem,
Bishop Blougram's Apology, where the bishop tries to play down the
significance of his unbelief:

> All we have gained then by our unbelief
> Is a life of doubt diversified by faith,
> For one of faith diversified by doubt:
> We called the chessboard white, —we call it black.[117]

Sometimes standards are reduced to the level of individual caprice
or the expression of a personal feeling. The aim of such a formulation
is to show that the speaker is not seeking to impose his standards on
others. In Jacques Rivière's novel, *Aimée*, the heroine's lover is shocked
by certain aspects of her behavior. First he reproaches her with them,
then he is angry with himself:

> What was my justification for making my tastes and opinions
> the rule she should follow? Why did my values have to be preferred
> to her own?[118]

By calling his standards "my tastes" Aimée's lover excuses her and
forbears to condemn her in the name of rules not adopted by her.

The most interesting case of transposition is the one in which argumentation is deliberately reduced to the level of value judgments,

---

[115] Speech on all stages of women's education, March 22-23, 1871, cited by Descamps, *Études d'art oratoire et de législation*, p. 40.
[116] Caillois, *Poétique de St.-John Perse*, pp. 33-34.
[117] Browning, *Complete Poetical Works*, p. 351.
[118] Rivière, *Aimée*, p. 131.

where one reverses the process of appeal from a badly informed authority to a better informed one, the object being to show that it is only
differences of value that matter, and that the debate is centered on
them. Thus, in dealing with art under a totalitarian regime,[119] Bobbio
refuses to consider whether the artist is freer in the United States than
in the Soviet Union, whether the aesthetic quality of Russian works
of art is satisfactory or not, because in his opinion these are factual
questions, irrelevant to the discussion, and Bobbio terms everything
a fact that does not involve the value under debate, namely freedom.

It is rather rare for the desire to reduce the discussion to a question
of values to be so clear-cut: it implies a technique and a mode of thinking about values that correspond to contemporary preoccupations.
But it is common for a speaker deliberately to bring only values to the
fore. A well-known instance is Brutus' speech to the crowd in Shakespeare's *Julius Caesar*. Everything extraneous to the value of freedom
is eliminated from it:

> Had you rather Caesar were living, and die all slaves, than that
> Caesar were dead, to live all free men?[120]

Brutus' speech has often been regarded as the speech of a cold logician
in comparison with that of Antony. Yet it is characterized not by the
elimination of values, but on the contrary by a very decided intention
to transpose the debate to a selected value to the exclusion of all others.

These few observations regarding the status of objects of agreement,
and the modification of this status through the way in which data are
utilized, bring us back to what we said earlier about the simultaneous
solidity and precariousness of the leaning posts of argumentation.
Our description of the objects of agreement intimated that these can
be recognized only within the entire context. We have just seen that
this status can be affected by the form in which they are expressed,
and by the way in which the discussion is conducted. We have purposely used the ambiguous term "transposition" to indicate that this may
be seen either as a mere shift in the agreement or as a profound modification. Circumstances and differences of viewpoint will dictate which
interpretation will be preferred. The important thing, in our opinion,
was to stress the influence of these extremely complex phenomena of
transposition on the development and effectiveness of argumentation.

---

[119] Bobbio, "Libertà dell'arte e politica culturale," *Nuovi argomenti* (1953), 245-
259. Republished in *Politica e cultura*, Einaudi, Torino, 1955.
[120] Shakespeare, *Julius Caesar*, Act. III, scene 2.

PART THREE

Techniques of Argumentation

§ 44. General Remarks

Persuasive discourse is effective because of its insertion as a whole into a situation which is itself usually rather complicated. Since the various elements of the discourse interact with each other, both the scope of the argumentation and the order of the arguments give rise to problems which we shall discuss at the end of our study. But before examining these synthetic aspects of our subject we must analyze the structure of the isolated arguments.

This procedure, indispensable as a first approximation, will oblige us to distinguish components (*articulations*) which are really integral parts of one and the same discourse and which together constitute a single argument. Now the meaning and the scope of an isolated argument can rarely be understood without ambiguity: the analysis of one link of an argument out of its context and independently of the situation to which it belongs involves undeniable dangers. These are due not only to the equivocal character of language, but also to the fact that the springs supporting the argumentation are almost never entirely explicitly described.

In establishing the structure of an argument, we must interpret the words of the speaker, supply the missing links, which is always very risky. Indeed it is nothing more than a plausible hypothesis to assert that the real thought of the speaker and of his hearers coincides with the structure which we have just isolated. In most cases, moreover, we are simultaneously aware of more than just one way of conceiving the structure of an argument.

Another objection should be added whenever our analyses deal with arguments taken, not from oral discourse, but from written texts. What guarantee do we have that these imagined discourses are not as far removed from reality as creatures of mythology? There is indeed an undeniably artificial character to certain ceremonial speeches and school exercises left to us by the rhetors.

These two objections would certainly be difficult to set aside if, on the one hand, it were a matter of analyzing some particular discourse in conformity to some particular historical reality and, on the other hand, if one claimed to offer as models of persuasive discourse arguments which have proved effective in the past. But our task is a different one. What we wish to analyze in the following chapters are argumentative schemes of which the particular cases examined serve only as examples, examples which could have been replaced by countless others. We have borrowed them from texts with which we believe ourselves sufficiently familiar to reduce the risk of misunderstanding. However we are convinced that these same arguments could be analyzed differently, in accordance with other planes of cleavage. And this because there is no reason why a single statement cannot be regarded as capable of expressing several schemes which would act at the same time on the minds of different persons—even on a single hearer. It is possible, moreover, that these schemes are effective without being clearly perceived and that only an attempt at clarification, which is rarely performed, would enable the speaker, and especially his hearers, to become aware of the mental schemes which they are using or which are acting upon them. In this connection literary works—novels, plays, speeches—often have the advantage of presenting the arguments in a simplified, conventionalized, or exaggerated manner. Taken out of an actual context, in which all the elements of the rhetorical situation are blended, they appear with greater clarity. We can be assured, moreover, that, if we recognize them as arguments, it is because they correspond to familiar patterns.

To clarify our analysis we shall make use of a number of humorous illustrations. We do not believe that a study of humor in the art of oratory is directly pertinent to our task— although humor is a very important factor in winning over the audience or, more generally, in establishing a communion between the speaker and his hearers, in reducing value, in particular making fun of the opponent, and making convenient diversions. But our interest will center not so much on humor *in* rhetoric as on the humor *of* rhetoric. We understand thereby the humorous use of certain types of argumentation. If, as we believe, there is a humor of rhetoric, the humorous elements can help us discover certain processes of argumentation which it would be more difficult to distinguish in their usual and customary form. Every procedure can easily become a source of humor; the procedures of rhetoric are no exception. In certain cases isn't the humorous effect due precisely to the fact that habitual processes of reasoning are seen to be caricatured for the occasion and that irrelevant, improper, or awkward use is made of the argumentative scheme?

From the beginning, we must also insist that discourse is an act which, like every other act, can, for the hearer, become an object of thought.

While the speaker is arguing, the hearer in turn tends to argue on his own account about the speech in order to take his own stand, to determine the credibility he ought to attach to it. The hearer who listens to the arguments not only understands them in his own way, but also creates new arguments of his own, which are usually unexpressed but which nevertheless intervene to modify the final results of the argumentation.

This mental activity of the hearer can often be guided by the speaker either by supplying certain arguments bearing on the nature of his own theses or by supplying certain items of information which will encourage his hearers to reason in some particular way. These arguments which take the discourse itself as their object, and these items of information likely to arouse such arguments, can also come from a third party: the speaker's opponent, particularly in legal debate, or perhaps from a mere spectator.

In principle all the argumentative schemes that we shall meet can thus be applied to the speech itself. In some cases, we shall be led to show this in some depth, especially with arguments based on the relation between the speaker as a person and his speech and with the treatment of the speech as an oratorical process. But these are only outstanding cases among those in which the argument which has the discourse as an object is superimposed upon the actual argument of the speaker. It would certainly be possible to attempt a similar study for every type of argument. In any case we must never lose sight of this observation.

The levels at which this observation apply are, moreover, very diverse. It can consider the discourse as an act, as a sign, as a means; it can deal with its content alone or neglect none of the factors it involves. In particular it may deal with the use of language: while the speaker describes what he has "seen," the hearer can perhaps think about the psychological or physiological meaning of vision; with Ryle, he can also note that the verb "to see" does not indicate a process or a state, but a result.[1] Normally these linguistic considerations will have no repercussions on the effect of the speech because the latter will aim at a level where they are irrelevant; but this is not always the case. It should be noted, moreover, that these considerations can be the fruit of personal ideas or of ideas suggested by a theorist. But

[1] Ryle, *Dilemmas*, p. 102.

the latter usually claims only to point out what is the verbal consciousness of most men.[2]

It is by taking this superimposition of arguments into account that we can best explain the practical, actual effect of the argumentation. Any analysis which would neglect it would, we think, be doomed to failure. Indeed, contrary to what happens in a proof, where demonstrative processes operate within an isolated system, argumentation is characterized by a constant interaction among all its elements. Doubtless, logical proof can itself be the object of the hearer's attention: he admires its elegance, deplores its heaviness, notices its adequacy to the end that is pursued. But that argument which has demonstration as its object will not itself be a demonstration. It does not superimpose itself on the demonstration to modify the latter's validity. It will develop at an argumentative level in which we shall find the very rhetorical arguments that we are analyzing.

The schemes we shall try to examine—which can also be considered as *loci* of argumentation because only agreement on their validity can justify their application to particular cases—are characterized by processes of *association* and *dissociation*.

By processes of association we understand schemes which bring separate elements together and allow us to establish a unity among them, which aims either at organizing them or at evaluating them, positively or negatively, by means of one another. By processes of *dissociation*, we mean techniques of separation which have the purpose of dissociating, separating, disuniting elements which are regarded as forming a whole or at least a unified group within some system of thought: dissociation modifies such a system by modifying certain concepts which make up its essential parts. It is in this way that these processes of dissociation are characteristic of all original philosophical thought.

Psychologically and logically, all association implies dissociation, and, conversely: the same form which unites various elements into a well-organized whole dissociates them from the neutral background from which it separates them. The two techniques are complementary and are always at work at the same time; but the argumentation through which a datum is modified can stress the association or the dissociation which it is promoting without making explicit the complementary aspect which will result from the desired transformation. At times these two aspects are present together in the consciousness of the speaker, who may wonder to which one it is better to draw attention.

[2] Cf. Wittgenstein, in *Philosophical Investigations.*

On the other hand, what is given before argumentation can seem more firmly established than what results from it alone: should separate elements be tied together, or should they be presented as already forming a whole? These questions and the problems they present to the speaker can be made more understandable by this characteristic passage from Bossuet:

> In my plan to devote the whole of this week's discourse to the sad fate of the sinner, I had first thought to give two pictures, as it were, one of which would represent his evil life, and the other his unhappy end. But I thought that if I were to make this division, sinners, who are always favorable to what puts off their conversion, would too easily be persuaded that they also could separate these things, which, much to our misfortune, are only too closely linked.[3]

Rejecting the idea which had occurred to him of unifying them through association, Bossuet presents the life and death of a sinner as forming an indissoluble unity:

> Death [he says] has no distinct being which separates it from life; it is nothing but a life coming to an end.

If it is therefore permissible to consider an argument as constituting, from one point of view, an association and, from another, a dissociation, it will still be useful to examine both kinds of argumentative schemes.

We shall first analyze, as association schemes, the quasi-logical arguments, which are best understood by comparing them with formal thought and then the arguments based upon the structure of the real, which are alleged to be in agreement with the very nature of things. It is to be noted that the distinction between these two kinds of reasoning could be compared with Husserl's distinction between formalizing abstraction and generalizing abstraction, with Piaget's distinction between schemes derived from operations and schemes derived from things, and with Gurwitsch's double perceptive thematization.[4] But all these distinctions have a genetic aspect which is foreign to our study.

Next we shall examine the arguments which aim at establishing the structure of the real: arguments taking the particular case into account, arguments by analogy which attempt to reconstruct certain elements of thought in conformity with schemes admitted in other domains of the real.

And finally we shall devote a whole chapter to the techniques of dissociation, which are mainly characterized by the modifications which

---

[3] Bossuet, *Sermons*, vol. II: *Sur l'impénitence finale*, pp. 221-222.
[4] Cf. Gurwitsch, *Actes du XIe Congrès international de Philosophie*, vol. II, pp. 43-47.

they introduce into notions, since they aim less at using the accepted language than at moving toward a new formulation.

One must not believe that these classes of argumentative schemes are isolated entities. We are often allowed, as we have said, to interpret an argument in accordance with one scheme or another. But, beyond this, we can even consider an argument as belonging to one of the classes of structure as well as to another. A statement, such as "If the world is ruled by Providence, the state requires a government," which Quintilian treats as an "argument by association or by comparison,"[5] can be considered as quasi-logical (what is true for the whole is true for the part) or as an analogy or indeed as based on relations of coexistence.

It would even be possible with some plausibility to reduce all the classes of schemes to one of them, which would be considered as fundamental, underlying all the others. But this would distort the first results of our analysis for the benefit of a preconceived idea. Let us then examine in succession the various classes of arguments in their most characteristic forms.

[5] Quintilian, V, x, 89.

CHAPTER 1

Quasi-Logical Arguments

§ 45. *The Characteristics of Quasi-Logical Argumentation*

The arguments we are about to examine in this chapter lay claim to a certain power of conviction, in the degree that they claim to be similar to the formal reasoning of logic or mathematics. Submitting these arguments to analysis, however, immediately reveals the difference between them and formal demonstrations, for only an effort of reduction or specification of a nonformal character makes it possible for these arguments to appear demonstrative. This is why we call them quasi-logical.

In every quasi-logical argument it is necessary first of all to set forth the formal scheme on the model of which the argument is constructed and after that to display the operations of reduction which make it possible to insert the data into this scheme and which aim at making the data comparable, similar, homogeneous.

Our technique of analysis may seem to give primacy to formal reasoning over argumentation, which would only be an approximate and imperfect form of it. However this is not our intention. On the contrary, we believe that formal reasoning results from a process of simplification which is possible only under special conditions, within isolated and limited systems. But, since there are formal proofs of recognized validity, quasi-logical arguments derive their persuasive strength from their similarity with these well-established modes of reasoning.

What characterizes quasi-logical argumentation, therefore, is its nonformal character and the effort of thought which is required to formalize it. It is over the latter aspect that disagreement will even-

193

tually arise. When it is a matter of justifying some reduction which presentation of the elements of the discourse did not suffice to make convincing, one will often resort to other forms of argumentation than the quasi-logical ones.

Quasi-logical arguments are presented in a more or less explicit manner. Sometimes the speaker will mention the formal reasoning to which he makes reference, availing himself of the prestige of logical thought; sometimes the formal reasoning provides only an underlying texture. There is no necessary correlation between how explicitly the formal reference schemes are described and the magnitude of the reductions required to base the argumentation on them.

Anyone who criticizes an argument tends to claim that what he has before him has to do with logic; the charge of having committed a logical error is often itself a quasi-logical argument. By making this charge, one takes advantage of the prestige of rigorous thought. The charge can be specific (a charge of contradiction, for example) and takes place at the very level of argumentation. It can also be general (the charge of giving an impassioned speech instead of a logical one). In this case the hearer sets up in opposition to the speech he has actually heard the concept of a better speech made up of logical patterns to which the datum would be reduced.

The reductions required to submit argumentation to formal schemes have to do partly with the terms of the speech, which are treated as homogeneous entities and partly with the structures which are likened to logical or mathematical relations, these two aspects of reduction being moreover closely related.

Among the quasi-logical arguments, we shall first analyze those which depend on logical relations—contradiction, total or partial identity, transitivity; we shall then analyze those which depend on mathematical relations—the connection between the part and the whole, the smaller and the larger, and frequency. Many other relations could obviously be examined.

It should be repeated in this connection that one and the same argument can be understood and analyzed differently by different hearers, and logical structures can be regarded as mathematical, and *vice versa*. Moreover, almost every quasi-logical argument also makes use of other kinds of argument, which to some may seem more important. The examples we shall give here are analyzed as quasi-logical because this aspect of them is readily recognized.

In this connection it is surprising that quasi-logical argumentation explicitly based on mathematical structures was formerly esteemed, particularly by the ancients, much more highly than it is today. Just as the development of formal logic permitted demonstration to be distinguished from argumentation, so the development of the sciences doubtless resulted in reserving to them the use of computation and measurement by making clear the conditions required for applying them. It should be added that, during periods in which the *loci* of quantity are prevalent, the use of mathematical relations is naturally favored and that the classifying mode of thinking of the ancients is entirely geometrical. However that may be, quasi-logical arguments were formerly developed with a kind of joy, of virtuosity, which stress clearly their modalities.

§ 46. *Contradiction and Incompatibility*

To assert a proposition and its negation within one and the same system, bringing out a contradiction which the system contains, makes the system inconsistent and thereby unusable. To display the inconsistency of a group of propositions is to expose it to a condemnation without appeal, to require anyone who wants to avoid the charge of absurdity to abandon at least certain elements of the system.

When the statements are perfectly univocal, as is the case with formal systems, where the signs alone are sufficient, by their combination, to make the contradiction undeniable, one can only bow to the evidence. But this is not the case with statements in ordinary language, whose terms can be interpreted in different ways. Normally, when someone asserts a proposition and its negation simultaneously, we do not think he is trying to say something absurd, and we wonder how what he says should be interpreted in order to avoid inconsistency. The language used in argumentation can indeed rarely be considered as entirely univocal, as would be that in a formal system. Logical contradiction, recognizable in a purely formal fashion, becomes part of the system and is independent of our will and of contingencies, for it is inescapable within the framework of the preassigned conventions. This is not the case for argumentation, where the premises are only rarely explicit and, when they are, are rarely defined in an entirely univocal way; the limits and the conditions of application vary with circumstances, to which belong the very decisions of the participants in the debate.

For all of these reasons, it is permissible only in exceptional cases—when the speaker happens to borrow several links of his argument from a formal system—to claim the presence of a contradiction in the opponent's system. Usually the line of argument tries to show that the theses one is disputing lead to an *incompatibility*, which resembles a contradiction in that it consists of two assertions between which a choice must be made, unless one rejects one or the other. The incompatibility of these theses is not due to purely formal reasons as is the case with contradictory assertions. Although the attempt is often made to explain incompatibility as determined by reason or logic, that is, as necessary, it depends either on the nature of things or on a human decision. Therefore one of the means of defense to be used against the quasi-logical argument which claims a contradiction is to show that it is not a matter of contradiction but of incompatibility. In other words, one will display the reduction which alone has made possible the likening to a formal system of the system under attack, which in fact does not exhibit the same rigor.

The case where the incompatibility depends on a personal decision seems furthest removed from formal contradiction, since, instead of imposing itself, this incompatibility is imposed and since it can be hoped that a new decision will eventually remove it. The head of a government who asks for a vote of confidence creates an incompatibility between his remaining in office and the rejection of the action he advocates. An ultimatum creates an incompatibility between the refusal to yield and the preservation of peace between two states. The leaders of a faction can decide or affirm at a given time that there is an incompatibility between belonging to their faction and belonging to another, while the leaders of the latter need not realize it or may assert the contrary.

From certain points of view it is therefore possible to determine the existence of an incompatibility, but for the third party, who cannot modify this decision, the incompatibility which is presented can have an objective aspect, which must be taken into account, as of a law of nature. Willfully to ignore this obligation to choose can lead to grave miscalculations. As La Bruyère puts it so well:

> Neutrality between women toward whom one is equally friendly, even when they have broken with each other for reasons that have nothing to do with us, is a difficult matter: often we must choose between them, or lose them both.[6]

Neutrality between nations in time of war or great tension is no less difficult to maintain. As E. Dupréel has observed in his chapter on the logic of conflicts, "Every dispute tends to expand to a third party, who increases it by taking sides."[7]

Incompatibilities can result from the application of several moral or legal rules, or of legal or sacred texts, to definite situations. While

---

[6] La Bruyère, "Les caractères. Des femmes," *Œuvres complètes*, 50, p. 142.
[7] Dupréel, *Sociologie Générale*, p. 143.

contradiction between two propositions implies a formal system, or at least a system of univocal concepts, incompatibility is always relative to contingent circumstances, whether the latter be determined by natural laws, particular events, or human decisions. Thus it was, according to William Pitt, that the approval of a certain motion could make two aspects of a desired peace incompatible:

> ... the considerations "speedy and honourable," then become separated. —We must in that case choose the alternative; if we adopt the motion, a peace "speedy and honourable" we cannot have.[8]

§ 47. *Procedures for Avoiding Incompatibility*

Incompatibilities oblige one to make a choice, which is always difficult. One of the two rules, one of the two values, must be sacrificed—unless both of them are given up, which often involves further incompatibilities—or else one must resort to various techniques for removing the incompatibility. These we call compromises, in the broadest sense of the term, but they also involve a sacrifice. Thus life presents us with numerous and important examples of behavior whose essential aim is not to remove an incompatibility between two rules, or between an action and a rule, but to prevent this incompatibility from arising.

As the incompatibilities are not formal, but only exist in relation to certain situations, it is understandable that there might be three quite different approaches to the treatment of the problems that are presented to the theorist and the man of action by this confrontation of rules and situations.

The first, which may be called *logical*, is that in which the primary concern is to resolve beforehand all the difficulties and problems which can arise in the most varied situations, which one tries to imagine, by applying the rules, laws, and norms one is accepting. This is usually the approach of the scientist, who tries to formulate laws which appear to him to govern the area of his study and which, he hopes, will account for all the phenomena which can occur in it. It is also the usual approach of someone who is developing a legal or ethical doctrine and who proposes to resolve, if not all the cases where it applies, at least the greatest possible number of those with which one might be concerned in practice. The person who in the course of his life imitates the theorists we have just referred to is regarded as a logical man, in the sense in which it is said that the French are logical and the English are prac-

---

[8] Pitt, *Orations on the French War*, Feb. 15, 1796, p. 116.

tical and realistic. The logical approach assumes that one can clarify sufficiently the ideas one uses, make sufficiently clear the rules one invokes, so that practical problems can be resolved without difficulty by the simple process of deduction. This implies moreover that the unforeseen has been eliminated, that the future has been mastered, that all problems have become technically soluble.

Opposed to this approach is that of the *practical* man, who resolves problems only as they arise, who rethinks his concepts and rules in terms of real situations and of the decisions required for action. Contrary to the approach of the theorists, this is the approach of practical men, who do not want to commit themselves more than is necessary, who want to keep as long as possible all the freedom of action that circumstances will permit, who wish to be able to adjust to the unexpected and to future experience. This is the normal attitude of a judge who, knowing that each of his decisions constitutes a precedent, seeks to limit their scope as much as he can, to pronounce his verdicts without giving any more reasons than are necessary as a basis for his decision, without extending his interpretative formulas to situations whose complexity might escape him.

Finally, the third approach we shall label the *diplomatic* approach, with the expression "diplomatic disease" (maladie diplomatique) in mind. Here, in order to avoid, at least at a certain time and under certain circumstances, coming into conflict with a principle or solving, in any way, the conflict between two incompatible principles which apply to a particular situation, procedures are invented for preventing an incompatibility from arising or for postponing the moment of decision until a more convenient time. Here are some examples.

Proust, following Saint-Simon, reminds us of the subterfuges used by the nobility to avoid solving difficult problems of precedence when no established tradition provided for settling the question satisfactorily.

> In certain cases, in view of the impossibility of arriving at a decision, a compromise is arranged by which the son of Louis XIV, Monseigneur, shall entertain certain foreign sovereigns only out of doors, in the open air, so that it may not be said that in entering the house one has preceded the other; and the Elector Palatine, entertaining the Duc de Chevreuse at dinner, pretends, so as not to have to make way for his guest, to be taken ill and dines with him indeed, but dines lying down, thus avoiding the difficulty.[9]

It is the rule in Japan to receive visitors only in proper clothing. If a farmer is interrupted in his work by an unexpected visitor, the

---

[9] Proust, *The Guermantes Way*, pt. II, pp. 176, 177.

latter acts as if he didn't see him until he has changed his clothes, which can be done in the very room where the visitor is waiting.[10]

It is apparent in this case, as in the preceding one, that fiction plays a role as a technique for avoiding an incompatibility. Fiction is a process consisting of a pretense, accepted by both parties, by convention, or by the social system, that makes it possible to act, and especially to reason, as if certain things had or had not happened, contrary to reality. When the pretense is only unilateral we are dealing with falsehood. Those who avoid making unpleasant decisions are often obliged to lie to others, as well as to themselves. Sometimes silence has no other purpose than to avoid making a decision when faced with an incompatibility. To quote Proust once more:

> Do you know, Ma'am [says the Duc de Guermantes to the Princesse de Parme], I should really prefer not to mention to Oriane that you have spoken to me about Mme de Souvré. My wife is so devoted to your Highness, she will go round at once to invite Mme de Souvré to the house; that will mean another call to be paid[11]....

By pretending not to tell his wife that the Princesse de Parme has spoken of Mme de Souvré, the duke avoids an incompatibility; actually he probably will mention the occurrence, but he spares his wife the task of choosing between her aversion to Mme de Souvré and her deference toward the Princesse de Parme.

Fiction, falsehood, and silence help avoid an incompatibility on the level of action so that it will not have to be solved on the theoretical level. The hypocrite gives the appearance of adopting a rule of conduct in agreement with that of others in order to avoid having to justify some action which he prefers and which he adopts in reality. It has often been said that hypocrisy is the homage that vice pays to virtue: more precisely, hypocrisy is an homage to a certain value, that which one sacrifices while pretending to follow it, because one refuses to confront it with other values. Incompatibility is thus removed in the action, but this is obviously at the cost of new incompatibilities, between hypocritical conduct and conduct that is frank and sincere, between a manner of thinking which is more or less systematic and one which has given up the search for defensible solutions. In this connection we may recall the comparison which V. Jankélévitch has made between almsgiving and lying: "Almsgiving, like telling a lie, pushes the problem away without solving it, makes the difficulty greater by postponing it."[12] This last observation seems obvious to us; how-

---

[10] Benedict, *The Chrysanthemum and the Sword*, p. 156.
[11] Proust, *The Guermantes Way*, pt. II, p. 201.
[12] Jankélévitch, *Traité des vertus*, p. 435.

ever we must realize that these are new difficulties: we all know of the problems encountered by a liar in keeping his fictitious system consistent. But the immediate problem has really been solved. On this ground lying is hardly distinguishable from all the other solutions we shall meet : they too raise new problems, but problems whose solution may, however, not be as pressing as that of the problem they have solved.

Whereas hypocrisy consists in letting it be believed that one has adopted a course of conduct which agrees with what is expected, that is, in letting it be believed that a decision has been made in a certain way, there are other techniques which consist, on the contrary, in letting it be believed that no decision has been made. "Diplomatic disease" makes it possible to avoid certain decisions, but it serves also to conceal the fact that a decision has been made: having decided not to attend a particular reception, one pretends not to be in a position— because of illness or absence—to choose whether or not one will go.

Sartre has developed a theory of bad faith, as "a certain art of forming contradictory concepts."[13] These concepts "unite in themselves an idea and the negation of that idea." It appears clearly from the examples which he gives that Sartre is not talking about contradictions but that his bad faith is the refusal to recognize incompatibilities: witness the example of the woman to whom words of a spiritual nature are spoken while her hand is being held. Starting from this refusal, Sartre develops a conception of bad faith which is applied to belief itself[14] and which we will not examine. But the distinction which he makes at the outset between facticity, what the words and gestures mean, and transcendence, that toward which they tend, a distinction which bad faith refuses to coordinate, can be useful in describing certain incompatibilities and the refusal to recognize them.

Incompatibilities differ from contradictions because they exist only in terms of the circumstances: in order that a conflict imposing a choice arise between two principles, they must be applicable simultaneously to the same reality. As soon as the incompatibility can be spread out in time, as soon as it appears possible to apply the rules successively rather than simultaneously, the sacrifice of one of them can be avoided. That is why the approach which we have called "practical" does not attempt to solve all possible conflicts ahead of time. The diplomatic approach tries to delay their solution, so as to avoid having to make immediately a sacrifice considered to be painful, in the hope that later circumstances will be such that the choice can be avoided or the deci-

[13] Sartre, *Being and Nothingness*, p. 56.
[14] *Ibid.*, p. 67.

sion taken with a better understanding of the issues. But we have already said, and we repeat, that avoiding the present incompatibility can create new and more serious ones in the future.

§ 48. *Techniques for Presenting Theses as Compatible or Incompatible*

Since two propositions are not incompatible but become so as the result of a certain determination of notions with respect to particular circumstances, the techniques making it possible to show that statements are incompatible and the techniques for reestablishing compatibility are among the most important ones in any argumentation.

In a formal system two propositions are said to be contradictory when, one being the negation of the other, it is assumed that whenever one of them is relevant to a situation, the other is also. To present propositions as being contradictory is to treat them as if, by being negations of each other, they formed part of a formal system. To point out the incompatibility of two statements is to point out the existence of circumstances which make unavoidable a choice between the two propositions involved.

Any formulation which, in the statement of propositions, tends to present them as negations of each other might suggest that the responses which are attached to them are incompatible. The world "in which there is being" and the world without being are for G. Marcel the ontological presuppositions of two ways of life, that of personality and that of function, one "full," the other "empty," which, having been described as incompatible, seem to be so described judiciously because of these very presuppositions.[15] On the other hand, to assert that a choice has been made will help, as it were retrospectively, to establish the incompatibility of the theses which have influenced that choice.

Theses are thus presented as being incompatible by emphasizing— in the aggregate to which they are bound—the point where they can most easily be interpreted by an affirmation or a negation. But setting theses in opposition to each other is never independent of the conditions in which they are applied.

One of the techniques for presenting incompatibilities consists in affirming that of two mutually exclusive theses at least one is always applicable, which makes the conflict with the other inevitable on condition that they both refer to the same object. The two theses become

---

[15] Marcel, *Position et approches concrètes du mystère ontologique,* in *Le monde cassé.*

compatible if a division in time or a division in the object makes it possible to avoid conflict. Two assertions by the same person at different times in his life can be presented as incompatible if all the statements by that person are regarded as forming a single system; if the different periods of his life are regarded as not being intimately connected with one another, the incompatibility disappears. Statements by different members of a group are treated as incompatible if the group is considered as a unit and the theses of the members are considered to form a single system; if it can be shown that one of the statements does not represent an authorized point of view, the incompatibility no longer exists. In principle there is no objection to having the behavior of members of different groups governed by different rules. Difficulty arises if a member of both groups is put in a situation where the two different rules prescribe incompatible lines of behavior.

It is perfectly possible that a head of state, wishing to preserve peace, may do so without compromising national honor. But it is possible that these two standards which he invokes in directing political affairs may become incompatible in a specific situation. What situation will be detrimental to national honor? Politicians will have differing opinions on the subject: their freedom of choice is correlated with the vague nature of the concepts used in describing the situation.

The person who refuses to kill a living creature can be faced with an incompatibility if he also grants that anyone who is ill with an infection ought to be treated. Will he, or will he not, use penicillin, which might destroy a vast number of microbes? To avoid incompatibility between the two principles he wishes to follow, he will perhaps be forced to make certain terms clearer, so that the particular situation he is faced with does not fall under one of these principles. Just as extension of the field of application of the rules increases the risk of incompatibility, so the narrowing of the field lessens it.

Bentham points out the fallacy committed by those who put forward the danger of increasing the influence of government as an argument against the establishment of any new office. According to him the entire system of government would be destroyed if this reasoning were consistently applied.[16] The fallacy results from the incompatibility between that argument, when it is extended not only to all new proposals but also to existing situations, and the maintenance of some form of government. But to bring out this incompatibility, Bentham is forced to extend the argument's field of application far beyond what his adversaries would ever have attempted.

---

[16] Bentham, *Works*, vol. II: *The Book of Fallacies*, p. 472, pt IV, chap. xv, "Rejection Instead of Amendment."

It is often by extension to cases which have escaped the opponent's attention that evidence of incompatibility can be offered: to someone who refuses to admit that a truth can be in the mind if one has never thought about it, it may be replied by extension that truths which are no longer being thought about would likewise not be in the mind;[17] the birth of the gods can be likened to their death in order to impute impiety as much to those who say the gods were born as to those who say that they die.[18]

These extensions are not simple generalizations; they obviously bring into play an identification about which we shall have occasion to speak again.[19] Locke emphasizes this identification when he writes:

> For it will be very difficult to persuade men of sense that he who with dry eyes and satisfaction of mind can deliver his brother to the executioners to be burnt alive, does sincerely and heartily concern himself to save that brother from the flames of hell in the world to come.[20]

Certain standards can be incompatible through the fact that one of them applies to a situation which the other excludes. Ruth Benedict notes that Japanese prisoners were very cooperative during interrogation because they had received no instructions about what they could or could not disclose when they were made prisoners. She remarks that this was due to Japanese military code which required soldiers to fight to the death.[21] This concept was incompatible with instruction in the rules of conduct to be followed by prisoners.

It would certainly be permissible to expatiate on many other instances of incompatibility. We should like also to indicate several situations of particular interest in which the incompatibility is not between two opposed rules, but between one rule and the consequences resulting from the very fact that it has been affirmed. We shall designate this kind of incompatibility, which is found in various forms, under the generic term of *autophagia*. Generalizing a rule, applying it without exception, may lead to preventing its application, indeed to destroying the rule itself. To take an example from Pascal:

> Nothing fortifies scepticism more than that there are some who are not sceptics; if all were so, they would be wrong.[22]

---

[17] Leibniz, *Die philosophischen Schriften*, vol. V, *Nouveaux essais sur l'entendement*, pp. 79-80.
[18] Aristotle, *Rhetoric*, II, 23, 1399b.
[19] See § 53, infra: Arguments of Reciprocity.
[20] Locke, *A Letter Concerning Toleration*, GBWW, vol. 35, p. 8.
[21] Benedict, *The Chrysanthemum and the Sword*, pp. 30 and 41.
[22] Pascal, *Pensées* GBWW, vol. 33, p. 237.

Retort, which in the Middle Ages was known as *redarguitio elenchica*, is the best known example of autophagia. It is an argument which claims to show that the act by which a rule is attacked is incompatible with the principle which supports that attack. Retort has often been used since the time of Aristotle to prove the existence of first principles.[23] It is what Ledger Wood aptly describes as the "method of affirmation by attempted denial."[24]

Thus to anyone who objects to the principle of contradiction it may be retorted that his very objection, through the fact that he claims to speak the truth and draw from it the consequence that his opponent is affirming what is false, presupposes the principle of contradiction: the very act implies what the words deny. The argument is quasi-logical, because, in order to make the incompatibility evident, an interpretation must be made of the act by which the opponent opposes a rule. And this interpretation, necessary to retort, could itself become the object of controversy.[25]

An amusing case of the application of retort, which suggests the possibility of avoiding it, is supplied by the story of the policeman in a provincial theatre who, when the audience was about to sing the "Marseillaise," climbed on the stage to warn that anything not announced on the play-bill was forbidden. "How about you?" asked one of the audience, "are you on the play-bill?" In this example the policeman by his announcement contradicted the very principle he was announcing, whereas in cases of retort one presupposes the principle one rejects, but the structure of the argument is the same.

Another circumstance which can lead to autophagy is that in which, instead of opposing a statement to the act by which it is affirmed, one applies the principle to itself: the autophagy results from *self-inclusion*. The positivists, who insist that every proposition is either analytical or empirical, may be asked whether what they have just said is an analytical proposition or an empirical one. The philosopher who insists that every judgment is a judgment of reality or of value, may be asked what is the status of his assertion. The person who argues against the validity of any nondemonstrative reasoning may be asked what is the value of his own argumentation. Not all self-inclusion leads to autophagy, but it does require thinking about the validity of the frame-

---

[23] Cf. Isaye, "La justification critique par rétorsion," *Revue Philosophique de Louvain*, 52 (1954), 205-233. Cf. also *Dialectica*, 21, p. 32.

[24] Wood, *The Analysis of Knowledge*, pp. 194 et seq.

[25] In this connection see Gonseth, "Réponse au R. P. Isaye," *Dialectica*, 21 (1952), 61, and Feigl, "De Principiis non Disputandum ... ?" in Black, *Philosophical Analysis*, p. 125.

work of classification which is to be set up, and thereby leads to an increase of awareness. Often the author makes the first move either to show that self-inclusion creates no difficulty or to indicate the reasons which prevent self-inclusion from occurring.

Another form of autophagy is that which opposes a rule with the consequences that appear to flow from it. In his *Anarchical Fallacies* Bentham criticizes the French constitution, which justifies insurrection:

> By justifying it, they invite it. ... In justifying the demolition of existing authorities, they undermine all future ones, their own consequently in the number. ... They imitate in their conduct the author of that fabled law, according to which the assassination of the prince upon the throne gave to the assassin a title to succeed him.[26]

Any theory forwarded by an invalid advocating the elimination of invalids would fall by the same principle. In this same class of arguments can be placed the reply made by Epictetus to Epicurus, who was holding for the abandonment of children:

> Why, I think that if your father and mother had foreseen that you were going to talk thus, even then they would not have cast you away from them.[27]

All these instances of autophagy weaken a thesis by showing the incompatibilities which are brought out by reflecting on conditions or consequences of its affirmation. Neither here nor in the other cases of incompatibility is there a *reductio ad absurdum*, a purely formal contradiction. Nevertheless these arguments must be taken into account if one wants to avoid ridicule. It is the ridiculous and not the absurd[28] which is the principal weapon of argumentation: it is therefore indispensable that we give that concept a more detailed treatment.

§ 49. *The Ridiculous and Its Role in Argumentation*

The ridiculous is what deserves to be greeted by laughter, that laughter which has been designated as "exclusive laughter" (rire d'exclusion) by E. Dupréel in his excellent analysis.[29] Exclusive laughter is the response to the breaking of an accepted rule, a way of condemning

---

[26] Bentham, *Works* (Tait), vol. II: *Anarchical Fallacies*, p. 496, "A Critical Examination of the Declaration of Rights—Preliminary Observations."

[27] Epictetus, *Discourses*, I, 23, 7.

[28] Cf. the use of these terms in Pascal, *Pensées*, GBWW, vol. 33, p. 222.

[29] Dupréel, "Le problème sociologique du rire," *Essais pluralistes*, p. 41.

eccentric behavior which is not deemed sufficiently important or dangerous to be repressed by more violent means.

A statement is ridiculous as soon as it conflicts, without justification, with an accepted opinion. A person who sins against logic or is incorrect in stating facts is ridiculous at the outset, assuming that he is not considered insane or so lacking in credibility that nothing he did could disqualify him more. An error of fact, says La Bruyère, is enough to make a wise man ridiculous.[30] The fear of ridicule and the discredit that results from it is often used as a means of education; so powerful a means is it that psychiatrists have even emphasized the adverse effects of its use on the stability of an anxious child.[31] Ridicule is usually connected with the fact that a rule has been unconsciously violated or opposed,[32] through ignorance either of the rule itself or of the disastrous consequences of a thesis or of an action. Ridicule works toward the preservation of what is accepted; a simple unwarranted change in opinion, that is, an opposition to what he had previously stated, makes the speaker liable to ridicule.

Ridicule is a powerful weapon at the disposal of a speaker against those who might undermine his argument by refusing, without cause, to accept some premise of his discourse. This is the weapon that must be used against those who take it into their heads to hold and persist in holding two incompatible points of view without trying to remove the incompatibility: ridicule affects only the person who allows himself to be entangled in the system forged by his adversary. Ridicule is the penalty for blindness and is apparent only to those for whom this blindness is obvious.

The person who stands in opposition to logic or experience is not alone in being ridiculous; so is anyone who sets forth principles whose unforeseen consequences put him in opposition to ideas which are accepted in a given society, and which he himself would not dare to contravene. Opposition to what is normal or to what is reasonable can be considered as a special case of opposition to an accepted standard. For example, it is laughable if one's efforts are out of all proportion to the importance of their object.[33]

---

[30] La Bruyère, "Les caractères, Des jugements," 47, Œuvres complètes, p. 379.

[31] Sullivan, The Interpersonal Theory of Psychiatry, p. 268; cf. on the other hand the relation between anxiety and incompatibility, pp. 170, 190, 346, and for selective inattention for avoiding these incompatibilities, Stanton, "Sullivan's Conceptions," in Mullahy, The Contributions of Henry Stack Sullivan, p. 70.

[32] Plato is by no means unaware of this. He foresees correctly the laughter which will be provoked by some of his ideas which are markedly different from current notions. Plato, Republic, V, 452, 457b, 473c.

[33] Plato, Republic, VI, 504e. For argumentation by double hierarchy see § 76, infra.

To say of a writer that his views are inadmissible because their consequences are ridiculous is one of the strongest objections that can be made in argumentation. This is how La Bruyère, in his dialogues on quietism, makes fun of that doctrine by showing that its supporters would have to be as much opposed to the duty of charity as to devotional exercises—a consequence to which no Christian could subscribe.[34] In Belgium in 1877 when the Catholic Minister of Justice decided, despite a law which protected the freedom of the voter, not to prosecute the priests who had threatened the punishments of Hell against their parishoners who had voted for the liberal party, Paul Janson ridiculed the Minister: by raising doubts about the gravity of such threats, he was "really committing religious heresy."[35]

Ridicule is often achieved through clever deductions drawn from what one is attempting to criticize. In geometry, *reductio ad absurdum* begins with the assumption that the proposition *A* is false, in order to show that the consequences are incompatible with what was already known, and thereby infers the truth of *A*. Similarly the most characteristic form of quasi-logical argumentation by the ridiculous consists in temporarily accepting a statement contradictory to that one wishes to defend, deducing its consequences, showing their incompatibility with what is accepted on other grounds, and thereby inferring the truth of the proposition being defended. This is what Whately attempted in an anonymous pamphlet. He began by admitting as established the kind of objections raised against the truth of the Scriptures and, by developing the consequences, he arrived at a denial of the existence of Napoleon. The argument which, by ridiculing the methods of biblical criticism, aspired to restoring confidence in the text of the Scriptures, was not as successful as he had hoped, but it was thought clever.[36]

The provisional assumption with which arguments of this sort begin can be expressed in the rhetorical figure of *irony*. In irony "one seeks to convey the opposite of what one actually says."[37] Why this roundabout way? Because we are really dealing with an indirect argument. Here is a good example drawn from Demosthenes:

> The people of Oreus have good reason to rejoice over having come into the power of Philip's men and having thrust Euphraeus aside! The Eretrians have good reason to rejoice at having dismissed

[34] La Bruyère "Dialogues sur le quiétisme," I, p. 532; V, p. 576 in *Œuvres complètes.*

[35] Janson, *Discours parlementaires*, vol. I, p. 19. (June 6, 1877)

[36] Cf. Whately, *Elements of Rhetoric* (Harper), pt. I, chap. III, é 7, p. 118.

[37] Dumarsais, *Des tropes*, p. 131.

your ambassadors and having given themselves over to Clitarchus! Slaves now, they are beaten and massacred![38]

The irony here has a didactic purpose,[39] for, even if the people of Oreus and the Eretrians can no longer do anything, the people of Athens can still make a choice. In this connection, let us recall the uproar in Belgium, in 1940, caused by a speech in which Paul Reynaud spoke of "the neutrality which has twice served Belgium so well."[40] The speaker declared that he had not intended to criticize Belgium but to show that neutrality was no safeguard. He granted that there had been strong material and psychological reasons in favor of Belgian neutrality; the ridicule was aimed at his French hearers, who were still free to decide.

Irony always presupposes supplementary information on facts, or norms. In the example given by Dumarsais—"I therefore declare that Quinaut is a Virgil"[41]—the assertion is incompatible with accepted and well-known standards. Thus irony cannot be used if there is uncertainty about the speaker's opinions. This gives irony a paradoxical character: using it implies that argumentation is necessary; but in order to be able to use it, a minimum of agreement is required. That is doubtless what led Baroja to say that irony has a more social character than humor.[42] This apparent paradox is only one of the aspects, carried to the extreme, of all argumentation.

Irony is all the more effective when it is directed to a well-defined group.[43] Only by having some idea of the beliefs held within certain social environments can we guess whether or not a given text is ironical.[44]

Irony may be used in all argumentative situations. But some of them seem particularly to invite it. Vayson de Pradenne observes that, in controversies dealing with archaeology, irony is freely used by those who are defending authenticity: thus Th. Reinach describes a gang of forgers, its decisions based on the majority, which might have made the tiara of Saitapharnes.[45] It is understandable that irony should

---

[38] Demosthenes, *Third Philippic*, § 66.

[39] For its role in the dialogues of Plato, cf. R. Schaerer, "Le mécanisme de l'ironie dans ses rapports avec la dialectique," *Revue de métaphysique et de morale*, July 1941, pp. 181-209.

[40] Cf. the newspaper *Le Soir*, June 3, 1950.

[41] Boileau, *Satire IX*, cited by Dumarsais, *Des tropes*, p. 132.

[42] Baroja, *La caverna del humorismo*, p. 96.

[43] Cf. Auerbach, *Mimesis*, pp. 213-214, an excellent analysis of an ironic passage from Boccaccio.

[44] For example, the letter from Zhdanov to Stalin, in Huxley, *Soviet Genetics and World Science*, pp. 230-234, Postscript II.

[45] Vayson de Pradenne, *Les fraudes en archéologie préhistorique*, p. 538.

primarily be a tactic of defense, since, if it is to be understood, irony requires a previous knowledge of the position of the speaker; now this position has been described in his attack.

If it is true that the ridiculous plays, in argumentation, a role analogous to that of the absurd in demonstration, still ridicule may be defied by squarely taking issue with a generally accepted principle—and this is the proof that argumentation is never coercive. Whoever defies ridicule sacrifices this principle and incurs condemnation by the group. But this sacrifice may be only provisional if the group is willing either to admit exceptions or to modify the principle.

Courage is required to defy ridicule, a certain capacity for rising above anxiety, but this is not sufficient for success: in order not to founder in ridicule, one must have sufficient prestige, and one can never be sure that it will be sufficient. To defy the ridicule which is always provoked by unjustified opposition to an accepted standard, one implicates one's whole person, united with this perilous deed, one hurls defiance, one provokes a showdown between values where the issue is uncertain.

Those who adopt an insulting name and glory in it; those who advocate a new way or refuse, like Gandhi, to conform, even when they are in the West, to the mores of the West; those who hold opinions or adopt modes of behavior which depart from the ordinary, these cease to be ridiculous when others fall into step. The prestige of a leader is measured by his ability to impose rules which seem ridiculous and to have them accepted by his subordinates.[46] In order that a statement which is contrary to accepted opinion become a principle worth discussing, it has to gain the support of some eminent philosopher.[47] A superhuman prestige would be necessary to take up position against fact or reason: whence the significance of the *credo quia absurdum*. Argumentation, an activity of human beings, is normally opposed only to what is not considered objectively valid. The opinions it deals with are not beyond all discussion, the authorities who offer them or combat them are not beyond all attack, and the solutions which will finally be accepted are not known beforehand.

The most common method of attacking an accepted rule or standard does not consist simply in a test of strength, in setting the prestige enjoyed by the opponents of the rule against the prestige of the rule. Normally, a justification will be given for this opposition, reasons found for which in certain circumstances, in concrete situations, the rule

[46] Cf. Isocrates, *Busiris*, § 26.
[47] Aristotle, *Topics*, I, 2, 104b.

should not be applied: its scope and meaning are limited by means of appropriate argumentation, whose result is a break with accepted ties, a modification of concepts. We shall examine these processes of argumentation at length in the part of our treatise devoted to dissociations.

§ 50. *Identity and Definition in Argumentation*

One of the essential techniques of quasi-logical argumentation is the identifying of various elements which are the object of the discourse. Any use of concepts, any application of a classification, any recourse to induction involves a reduction of certain elements to what they have in them that is identical or interchangeable. But we call this reduction *quasi-logical* only when we consider this identification of entities, events, or concepts as neither arbitrary nor obvious, that is, when it is justifiable by argument. Among these procedures of identification we distinguish those which are aimed at making a complete identity from others which claim only a partial identity of the elements being compared.

The most characteristic method of complete identification consists in using *definitions*. These, when they are not part of a formal system and when, nevertheless, they claim to identify the *definiens* and the *definiendum*, we shall consider as quasi-logical argumentation. We cannot grant that such definitions are based on the self-evidence of conceptual relations, for that would presuppose the perfect clarity of all the terms compared.

In order that a definition should not suggest to us that the terms which are being offered as equivalent are identical, it must insist on the distinction between the terms, as is the case with definitions by approximation or example, in which the reader is expressly asked to attempt to purify or generalize, thus enabling him to bridge the gap which separates what is being defined from the means used to define it.

Among the definitions leading to identification of what is defined with what defines it, we shall distinguish, with Arne Naess,[48] the following four kinds:

1. Normative definitions, which indicate the manner in which a word is to be used. This norm can result from an individual decision, from a command given to others, from a rule of which one believes that it should be followed by everyone.

---

[48] Cf. Naess, *Interpretation and Preciseness*, chap. IV.

2. Descriptive definitions, which indicate what meaning is given to a word in a certain environment at a particular time.

3. Condensed definitions, which point out the essential elements of a descriptive definition.

4. Complex definitions, which combine, in various ways, elements of the other three types.

These various definitions are either prescriptions or empirical hypotheses concerning the synonymy of the *definiens* and the *definiendum*.

Among the normative definitions only those which are offered as necessary rules are likely to be supported or challenged by means of argumentation. The same is true of condensed definitions, about which one might ask whether the particulars they supply are essential or not. As for descriptive definitions, they enjoy the status of facts so long as they remain unchallenged.

All these definitions and the argumentative possibilities they provide are still misunderstood by most logicians, whose thought continues to operate within the framework of the classical dichotomy between real and nominal definitions, the former being regarded as propositions which may be either true or false, and the latter as purely arbitrary.

Here is a typical passage from J. S. Mill, one to which a good number of contemporary logicians would still subscribe:

> Assertions respecting the meaning of words, among which definitions are the most important, hold a place, and an indispensable one, in philosophy; but, as the meaning of words is essentially arbitrary, this class of assertions is not susceptible of truth or falsity nor, therefore, of proof or disproof.[49]

Mill opts for the nominal, hence conventional and arbitrary, character of definitions, which by that very fact avoid both proof and refutation. But is this really the case? If it is correct that definitions are arbitrary in the sense that one does not have to accept them, must we consider them as being arbitrary in a much stronger sense, which would claim that there was no reason to select one definition rather than another and that there is hence no possibility of arguing in their favor? Now not only can one find in Mill's work a series of arguments supporting his definitions of cause, inference, and induction, but in his work on utilitarianism there is even a definition of proof broad enough to cover reasonings of this sort.[50]

What gives credibility to the conventional nature of definitions is the possibility of introducing new symbols out of nothing in all languages, even the common ones. But if these new signs are called on to

[49] Mill, *A System of Logic*, bk ii, chap. 1, § 1, p. 103.
[50] Mill, *Utilitarianism*, GBWW, vol. 43, p. 446.

fill, entirely or partially, the role of existing terms, the arbitrariness of their definition is illusory —even if it is a matter of symbols created *ad hoc*. It is even more so if the *definiens* and the *definiendum* are both borrowed from common language. When Keynes proposes in his writings[51] a series of technical definitions,[52] these can be so far removed from the idea common sense has of the concepts thus defined that they appear to be merely a convention. The author even modifies them from one work to another.[53] But when he defines "savings," on the one hand, and "investment," on the other, in such a way that his views and analyses finally show that their likeness is more essential than their transient differences, the interesting thing about his reasoning is that we compare the terms he has defined with concepts that are usual or already specified by the economists, which his analysis helps to clarify.

A theory can claim to be purely conventional and on this claim it can base the right to define its symbols as it wishes. But as soon as it tries to deal with the real world, as soon as an attempt is made to apply it to situations which have occurred before, the problem of identifying the notions it defines with those of ordinary language cannot be avoided. The difficulty one was trying to avoid has only been transposed to another level. Here lies the whole problem of formalism: either formalism provides a system which is isolated not merely from its applications, but even from the living thought which must understand and manipulate it, that is, integrate it into preexistent mental structures; or it will have to be interpreted and will effect identifications which can be ascribed to quasi-logical argumentation. Even if these identifications are not contested during a given period of scientific evolution, it would be dangerous for ulterior progress of thought to regard them as necessary and to grant them the self-evidence one attributes to assertions which are no longer open to discussion. This is one of the reasons for our acceptance of the principle of revisability, defended with such vigor by F. Gonseth.[54]

The argumentative character of definitions is clearly apparent when various definitions occur of some term in ordinary language (or even of equivalent terms in different languages). These multiple definitions are indeed either successive parts of a single descriptive definition— in which case the user of the term must make his choice among them—

---

[51] Keynes, *A Treatise on Money* (1930); *The General Theory of Employment, Interest, and Money* (1936).

[52] Which could be compared with Carnap's concept of "explanation"; cf. Hempel, *Fundamentals of Concept Formation in Empirical Science*, pp. 11-12.

[53] In this connection, see Keynes, *The General Theory* ..., pp. 60-61.

[54] Gonseth, *Dialectica*, 6 (1948), 123-124.

or they are descriptive definitions which are opposed to each other and incomplete, normative or condensed definitions which are incompatible. To make their task easier, and sometimes to avoid undesired discussions, some authors provide, not necessary and sufficient conditions, but sufficient conditions for the application of a term;[55] but the statement of these conditions, together with what is otherwise known about the term in question, nevertheless constitutes a choice of definition.

The argumentative character of definitions always presents two closely connected aspects which must nevertheless be distinguished, since they deal with two phases of the reasoning: definitions can be supported or validated by argument; they themselves are arguments. They can be justified by the most diverse methods: one method is to fall back on etymology;[56] the other is to substitute a definition by conditions for a definition by consequences or vice versa.[57] But all those who argue in favor of some definition want it, through some slant or other, to influence the use which would probably have been made of the concept had they not intervened and mostly to influence the relations of the concept with the whole system of thought, and this without causing the former usages and relations to be completely forgotten. Now the same thing is true when the definition is given as natural or is imposed, legal definitions for instance, and when the reasons supporting it are not explicit. The use of the concept one wishes to modify is generally what is called the normal use of this concept, so that defining an idea borrowed from common language gives rise by implication to all the difficulties inherent in double definition.

When Spinoza at the beginning of his *Ethics* defines "cause of itself" as "that whose essence involves existence or [*sive*] that whose nature cannot be conceived unless existing," when he defines substance as "that which is in itself and is conceived through itself; in other words [*hoc est*] that the conception of which does not need the conception of another thing from which it must be formed,"[58] the words *sive* and *hoc est* indicate the interchangeable character of two different definitions of the same idea. Actually, the identity of three concepts is involved, the third consisting of the way the term was used—particularly among the Cartesians—in Spinoza's own day. Usually such an identification requires, if not a proof, at least an argument in order that it be accepted. When the identification is simply posited, we have a typical case of

---

[55] E.g. Morris, *Signs, Language, and Behavior*, p. 12 and note G, p. 250.
[56] Quintilian, V, x, 55; Paulhan, *La preuve par l'étymologie*.
[57] Cf. the definition of miracle in Weil, *The Need for Roots* (Putnam), p. 266.
[58] Spinoza, *Ethics*, pt I, definitions I and III, GBWW, vol. 31, p. 355.

quasi-logical procedure. But what Spinoza does explicitly, and which can therefore be observed and even criticized by a logician who restricts himself to the actual text without comparing it with the common use of the terms, can, in a manner which it is more difficult to observe, also be found in the writings of anyone who defines the words of the language in a seemingly univocal manner, while the reader cannot help also identifying the word defined in this way with the same word as it is understood in the tradition of the language.

These observations tend to show that the use of definition in argumentation implies the possibility of several definitions, borrowed from common usage or created by the writer, among which a choice must be made. It is also brought out that related terms themselves are constantly interacting, not only with a set of other terms in the same language or in other languages which can be related to the original, but also with the totality of other possible definitions of the same term. These interactions cannot be eliminated; generally they are even essential to the significance of the reasoning. However, once the choice is made, whether it be presented as self-evident or whether it be supported by arguments, the definition which is used is regarded as an expression of an identity, indeed as the only satisfactory one under the circumstances, and the equivalent terms, detached in a sense from their ties and their background, can be considered as logical substitutes for each other. Therefore the use of definition in carrying on an argument appears to us as typical of quasi-logical argumentation.

§ 51. Analyticity, Analysis, and Tautology

When a definition is accepted, the equality which has been established between the two allegedly synonymous terms may be looked on as analytic. But this analyticity has, in the knowledge, the same status as the definition on which it depends. It is immediately obvious that if, by analytical judgment, asserting the equivalence of two expressions, we wish to understand a judgment permitting the expressions to be substituted for each other, without ever changing the truth-value of the propositions in which they appear, then the analyticity of such a judgment can be affirmed with constancy, without risk of error, only in a language where there is no longer a threat of new linguistic usages— that is, in a formalized language.

In spite of these restrictions we are witnessing in Great Britain the development of a philosophical movement, initiated by G. Moore, whose principal task is the analysis of propositions. J. Wisdom has distinguished three forms of analysis: material analysis, formal analysis, and philosophical analysis.[59] Material analysis (e. g. "*A* is the child of *B*" means that "*A* is the son or daughter of *B*") and formal analysis (e. g. "The King of France is bald" is equivalent to "There is one and only one being who is King of France and who is bald") would remain at the same level of discourse, while philosophical analysis—for this reason called "directional" by L. S. Stebbing[60] (e. g. "The forest is very thick" is equivalent to "The trees in this area are very close to one another")— would go in a certain direction; for Stebbing it leads toward fundamental facts, for J. Wisdom toward sensory data.

To us the distinctions made by Wisdom appear to presuppose a philosophical attitude. From the point of view of argumentation, it must, on the contrary, be emphasized that *all* analysis is directional, in the sense that it tends in a certain direction. The choice of the latter is determined by the quest for the interlocutor's agreement. Outside of treatises on logic, there never occurs an analysis which doesn't have a definite purpose.[61] When it is a technical analysis conforming to the requirements of some discipline, such analysis is directed toward the elements which are deemed to be fundamental within that discipline; a nontechnical analysis is adapted to the hearer and may therefore proceed in widely differing directions depending on what the hearer agrees to. To try to impose on the philosophical hearer standards of fact or value which must be accepted without discussion is already to depend on a particular philosophy and to carry on the reasoning within its framework.[62]

To the degree, then, that it is not purely conventional, all analysis can be regarded as quasi-logical argumentation, using either definitions or an enumerative procedure, which limits the extension of a concept to the elements which have been spelled out.

This is why analysis outside of a formal system can never be definitive or exhaustive. Max Black rightly takes Moore to task for not showing the method of arriving at the analyses that he recommends or of evaluating their exactitude.[63] In reality, this exactitude could not even be postulated if an attempt is made to reproduce the meanings of the notions of an ordinary language.

[59] Wisdom, "Logical Constructions," *Mind*, 1931 to 1933, and Coombe-Tennant, "Mr. Wisdom on Philosophical Analysis," *Mind*, XLV (1936), 432-449.
[60] Stebbing, "The Method of Analysis in Metaphysics," *Proceedings of the Aristotelian Society*, XXXIII (1932-33), 65-94.
[61] Cf. Britton, *Communication*, p. 139.
[62] Cf. the discussion of facts and truths in § 16.
[63] Black, *Philosophical Analysis*, Introduction.

If analysis were entirely certain and beyond all discussion, could not the charge be made that it teaches us nothing new? All quasi-logical argument whose evidential and even necessary nature is recognized runs thus the risk that, instead of being criticized as weak and inconclusive, it will be criticized as being totally uninteresting, since it teaches us nothing new: such an affirmation is called a *tautology*, because it derives from the very meaning of the terms which are used.

Here is a passage from Nogaro illustrating this process:

> For a long time the classical economists insisted that the depreciation or diminishing of the value of money *brought about* an increase in prices, without realizing that the diminishing of the value of money (with relation to goods) and the increase in prices are two inverse ways of describing the same phenomenon, and that consequently what we really have is not a relation of cause and effect, but a tautology.[64]

The charge of tautology amounts to presenting an assertion as the result of a definition, of a purely linguistic convention, which tells us nothing about the empirical relations which one phenomenon may have with another, relations whose study would require empirical research. It presupposes that the definitions are arbitrary, devoid of scientific interest, and independent of experience. But inasmuch as this is not the case, inasmuch as definitions are connected with a theory which can provide original insights, the charge of tautology loses its force. Britton even identifies natural law with tautology. He gives the example of an unknown metal newly identified through the use of certain tests which make it possible to detect its presence; finally the metal is isolated and its melting point is determined; the new property is incorporated into the definition and thus takes on a primary importance: "The great discovery," writes Britton, "has become a simple tautology."[65] Once it has become tautological, the assertion becomes incorporated into a deductive system, it may be regarded as analytical and necessary, and no longer appears to be subject to the hazards of empirical generalization.

Thus the designation of tautology applied to a proposition divorces the latter from the very context which has permitted the elaboration of the very concepts on which it has bearing. When these concepts are integrated in the living thought which has made their development possible, it is observed that they are characterized neither by the necessity particular to a formal system nor by the triviality with which they are charged in a nonformal discussion. Rather their status is tied to that of the definitions on which they are based.

[64] Nogaro, *La valeur logique des théories économiques*, pp. 12-13.
[65] Britton, *Communication*, p. 179.

When in a nonformal discussion a tautology is obviously intended, as in expressions such as "A penny is a penny," or "Boys will be boys," it will be considered as a figure. Use is made of a formal identity between two terms which cannot be identical if the statement is to be of any interest. The interpretation of the figure, which we shall call an *apparent tautology*, therefore requires a certain amount of goodwill on the part of the hearer.

Statements like these have long attracted the attention of theorists of style. Observing that the two terms must have different meanings, they have interpreted these tautologies as special cases of other figures. According to Vico, in the figure known as *ploce* ("Since then Corydon is Corydon to me") the same term is used for the person and for the way he acts (or for a thing and its properties).[66] According to Dumarsais, in "A father is always a father" the second term is used adjectively.[67] According to Baron, it is an *oratorical syllepsis*, one of the words being understood in its usual sense, and the other figuratively.[68]

Being less concerned with figures, the moderns analyze this kind of expression in terms of their own interests. Among the most interesting comments we cite those of Morris, who emphasizes the distinction between formal mode and function of evaluation,[69] those of Hayakawa, for whom it is a way of applying directives of classification,[70] and finally those of J. Paulhan, who has well grasped the argumentative value of such expressions, but who sees in them a paradox of reason.[71]

These propositions, because they are tautological, lead to making a distinction between the terms, but it would be incorrect to think that the exact meaning of the terms is fixed in advance or that the relation between the terms is always the same. The formulation of an identity puts us on the track of a difference, but does not specify to what we should set our attention. It is nothing but a formal example of the procedure which consists in evaluating something positively or negatively by use of a pleonasm. A happy example is given in *Les Ana de Madame Apremont:*

When I see everything I see, I think what I think.[72]

Here, as in repetition, it is the second use of the term which bears the value.[73]

---

[66] Vico, *Delle instituzioni oratorie*, p. 142.
[67] Dumarsais, *Des tropes*, p. 173.
[68] Baron, *De la rhétorique*, p. 337.
[69] Morris, *Signs, Language and Behavior*, p. 171.
[70] Hayakawa, *Language in Thought and Action*, pp. 213-214.
[71] Paulhan, *Entretien sur des faits divers*, p. 145.
[72] Jouhandeau, *Les Ana de Madame Apremont*, p. 61.
[73] Cf. § 42, infra: Figures of Choice, Presence, and Communion.

It should be noted that the need to differentiate between terms, instead of arising from a concern to give a meaning to a tautology expressing an identity, can arise from another quasi-logical figure, based on the *negation of a term by itself*, therefore on a contradiction: "A penny isn't a penny" can play the same role as "A penny is a penny." *The identity of contradictories* should be put on the same level, for example the famous aphorism of Heraclitus:.

We step and do not step into the same river.[74]

Tautologies and contradictions have a quasi-logical character because at first sight the terms are treated as univocal, as capable of being identified, of excluding each other. But, after interpretation, differences arise. These can be known before the argumentation. In the figure of *antanaclasis* we have nothing more than the use of a homonym:

Being loved is very dear to me if it doesn't cost dear.[75]

Here a knowledge of linguistic usages supplies the solution immediately. But in tautologies of identity the difference is not generally determined. By following models which are already known we can make a great variety of differentiations and establish a great variety of relations between the terms.

If some of these identities can serve as maxims ("A woman is a woman" can be a way of saying that all women are the same, but may also mean that a woman ought to act like a woman) they acquire their argumentative value only when they are applied to a concrete situation, which alone gives to these concepts the particular meaning which is appropriate.

§ 52. *The Rule of Justice*

The arguments we are about to examine in this section and the following one deal, not with reducing to complete identity the elements which are being compared, but with a partial reduction which allows them to be regarded as interchangeable from a limited point of view.

The rule of justice requires giving identical treatment to beings or situations of the same kind. The reasonableness of this rule and the validity that it is recognized as having derive from the principle of

---

[74] Burnet, *Early Greek Philosophy*, p. 139. See § 94, infra: Statements Prompting Dissociation.

[75] Vico, *Delle instituzione oratorie*, p. 142.

inertia, from which originates in particular the importance that is given to precedent.[76]

For the rule of justice to serve as the basis of a rigorous demonstration, the objects to which it applies ought to be identical, that is, completely interchangeable. However, this is never the case. These objects always differ in some respect, and the great problem, which gives rise to most controversies, is to decide whether the observed differences are negligible or not, or, in other words, whether the objects differ in essential characteristics, that is in the only ones which must be taken into account in the administration of justice. The rule of justice recognizes the argumentative value of what one of us has called *formal justice*, according to which "beings in the same essential category should be treated in the same way."[77] Formal justice does not tell when two objects belong to the same category; neither does it specify the treatment they should be given. Indeed in every concrete situation a prior classification of the objects and the existence of precedents as to the manner of treating them is indispensable. The rule of justice furnishes the foundation which makes it possible to pass from earlier cases to future cases. It makes it possible to present the use of precedent in the form of a quasi-logical argument.

Here is an example of the use of the rule of justice in argumentation; we take it from Demosthenes:

> Would they claim, perhaps, that a treaty which is unfavorable to our city is binding, and yet refuse to recognize it if it gives us any guarantees? Do you find this just? What? If a clause of the treaty is favorable to our enemies but unfavorable to us, they insist that it is valid; but if, on the contrary, they find in it a clause which is just and advantageous for us and disadvantageous to them, they think they must oppose it vigorously.[78]

If neither the Athenians nor their adversaries occupy a privileged position, the rule of justice requires that, since they are parties to an agreement, their behavior toward each other should not be different. Appeal to this rule has an undeniably rational character. When the consistency of a course of action is accounted for, reference is almost always made to the rule of justice.

This rule presupposes the partial identification of beings by putting them in a category and applying the treatment foreseen for members of that category. Now criticism can be brought to bear on each of these points, and prevent the conclusion from being coercive.

---

[76] Cf § 27, supra: Agreements Particular to Each Discussion.
[77] Perelman, *The Idea of Justice and the Problem of Argument*, p. 15.
[78] Demosthenes, *On the Treaty with Alexander*, § 18.

Gheorghiu's whole novel *The Twenty-Fifth Hour* is a protest against the mechanization of men, against destroying their individuality by putting them into bureaucratic categories. Here is a passage in which his macabre humor rises in revolt against such dehumanization:

> These broken fragments of men, who have only pieces of flesh remaining, get the same amount of food as the prisoners who are entirely sound. This is a great injustice. I suggest that prisoners should receive food rations in proportion to the amount of body they still have.[79]

To show the arbitrary character of all bureaucratic classifications, the author makes a farcical suggestion: he proposes to introduce a horrible element, mutilation; he intends thus to make ridiculous the established categories which treat men, not as individuals in a spirit of charity and love, but as interchangeable members of a class.

The other criticism, which deals with the way in which the rule of justice is applied, can be illustrated by the reasoning by which Locke hopes to bring about more tolerance on the part of his countrymen:

> No man complains about the ill-management of his neighbor's affairs. No man is angry with another for an error committed in sowing his land or in marrying his daughter. Nobody corrects a spendthrift for consuming his substance in taverns. ... But if any man do not frequent the church, if he do not there conform his behavior exactly to the accustomed ceremonies, or if he brings not his children to be initiated in the sacred mysteries of this or the other congregation, this immediately causes an uproar.[80]

Locke would like the same rule to be applied in religious and civil affairs, and he makes use of the tolerance in civil affairs which was common in his time to encourage the same tolerance in religious questions. But today there would be some hesitation about likening these two situations to each other, for fear that it might lead to the State's intervention in matters of conscience, similar to the authoritarianism characteristic of several areas of economic life. Application of the rule of justice, following upon a prior likening of two types of situations, can lead to results which are very different from those which were desired. The rule, which is purely formal, requires, for its application, a foundation in the concrete, anchored to opinions and agreements which are rarely beyond argument.

---

[79] Gheorghiu, *La vingt-cinquième heure*, p. 274.
[80] Locke, *A Letter Concerning Toleration*, GBWW, vol. 35, p. 8.

§ 53. *Arguments of Reciprocity*

Arguments of reciprocity aim at giving the same treatment to two situations which are counterparts of each other. Here the identification of the situations, necessary in order that the rule of justice be applicable, is indirect, in the sense that it requires using the concept of symmetry.

In formal logic a relation is symmetrical when its converse is identical with it, that is, when the relation between b and a is the same as that between a and b. The order of the antecedent and the consequent can therefore be inverted.

Arguments of reciprocity show that the situations are similar by regarding certain relations as symmetrical. This intervention of symmetry evidently introduces special difficulties in the application of the rule of justice. But, on the other hand, symmetry makes it easier to show that actions, events, and things are identical, since it emphasizes a certain aspect which seems to stand out on account of the very symmetry which is exhibited. This aspect is then claimed to be essential.

Among the examples which Aristotle considers to be drawn from "reciprocal relations" we find that of the tax-farmer Diomedon speaking on the subject of taxes:

> If it is no disgrace for you to sell them, it is no disgrace for us to buy them.[81]

Quintilian supplies an example of the same sort of propositions "which confirm one another":

> What it is honorable to learn is also honorable to teach.[82]

By a reasoning of the same nature, La Bruyère condemns the Christians who attend plays, since the actors are condemned for performing in these plays.[83]

These arguments by reciprocity, based on the connections between the antecedent and the consequent of the same relation, appear, more than any other quasi-logical arguments, to be at once formal and based on the nature of things. Symmetry is most often assumed in the very qualification of situations.

This influence of qualification is apparent in certain arguments where it is the only ground for the symmetry that is invoked—such as in this argument from Rousseau:

[81] Aristotle, *Rhetoric*, II, 23, 1397a.
[82] Quintilian, V, x, 78.
[83] La Bruyère, "Les caractères. De quelques usages," 21, *Œuvres complètes*, p. 432.

> No mother, no child; their duties are reciprocal; and, when ill done by the one, they will be neglected by the other.[84]

Arguments based on reciprocity can also result from the transposition of points of view, which makes it possible through their symmetry to recognize the identity of certain situations.

The possibility of making such transpositions is regarded by Piaget and, following him, by certain psychiatrists, as one of the basic human aptitudes.[85] It makes it possible to consider as relative situations which had previously been thought to be privileged if not unique. Since we find the customs of the Persians strange, shouldn't they be surprised at ours? The ridiculous customs of utopian countries, described so entertainingly, lead us to reflect on their counterparts in our own civilizations, and to find them every bit as ridiculous.

Let it be noted that in the guise of doing justice to someone else's point of view, these arguments often adopt the point of view of a third party, with respect to which symmetry would be set up; it is the intervention of this impartial party which makes it possible to eliminate such factors as the prestige of one of the interested parties, which might disturb the symmetry.

Often a transposition, emphasizing the symmetry (Put yourself in his place!) provides a basis for what is deemed to be a well-founded application of the rule of justice: he who has been generous in his wealth and merciful in his power has the right, so it seems, to appeal for generosity and mercy when fortune is unfavorable to him.[86]

A number of moral rules are set up on the basis of symmetry. Isocrates praises the Athenians for the fact that:

> They require of themselves toward their inferiors the same feelings that they ask of their superiors.[87]

The precepts of humanistic ethics, whether they be Judeo-Christian maxims ("Therefore all things whatsoever ye would that men should do to you, do ye even so to them") or the categorical imperative of Kant ("Act only on that maxim whereby thou canst at the same time will that it should become a universal law") require that neither the individual nor his rules of action may claim any privileged position, that, on the contrary, he is governed by a principle of reciprocity which appears rational because it is quasi-logical.

---

[84] Rousseau, *Émile* (Dent, Dutton), p. 14.

[85] Piaget, *Le jugement et le raisonnement chez l'enfant*, pp. 252 et seq; cf. Odier, *Les deux sources, consciente et inconsciente, de la vie morale*, pp. 263-268.

[86] Cf. *Rhetorica ad Herennium*, II, 25.

[87] Isocrates, *Panegyric of Athens*, § 81.

This principle of reciprocity, based on a symmetry of situations can be used as an argument even when the situation to which one refers is presented merely as an hypothesis. In this way Demosthenes, urging the Athenians to take action against Philip, pictures what the latter would have done against them if he had been in their place:

> ... wouldn't it be shameful for you, having the opportunity but not the courage, not to inflict on him the harm that he would inflict on you if he could?[88]

Elsewhere he asks the Athenians to consider the hypothesis that, if Aeschines were the accusor and Philip the judge, he, Demosthenes, would do as Aeschines did and judge Aeschines as he himself would have been judged by Philip.[89]

The portrait which La Bruyère draws of a diplomat, whose purpose is always deception, corresponds to a fairly common view. But the deceptions so described are nothing but ways of using the symmetries of the situation; the task of the diplomat is to get what he wants by means of good reasons: the reciprocity argument, if it is not always expressed, is one of the pivots of diplomacy, operating from equal to equal; this, at least, is the ideal case, corresponding to the classical description of La Bruyère.[90]

Sometimes this identity of situations results from the fact that two entirely distinct acts have jointly brought about the same effect.

> "I have accused; you have condemned," is the famous reply of Domitius Afer.[91]

Two actions which are complementary, in the sense that they both constitute a necessary condition for bringing about a certain effect, can provide an occasion for using the argument from symmetry. An example of this sort of argument is found in the position taken by the United States minister to The Hague, who was in Brussels during the first weeks of the Revolution of 1830. He was trying to obtain from the Belgian government the release of goods belonging to neutrals and stored in Antwerp. To be effective this authorization would also have to be granted by the King of Holland. Accordingly the argument of the American diplomat to the Belgians went: "If you grant this authorization and the King of Holland refuses, what moral prestige will result for you! If you refuse the authorization and the king of Holland grants

---

[88] Demosthenes, *First Olynthiac*, § 24.
[89] Demosthenes, *On the Embassy*, § 214.
[90] La Bruyère, "Les caractères. Du Souverain ou de la République," 12, *Œuvres complètes*, 295 et seq.
[91] Quintilian, V, x, 79.

it, what prestige will accrue to him!"[92] The quasi-logical argument becomes possible through disregarding everything that makes the situations different and reducing them to what makes them symmetrical.

Quasi-logical arguments can make use of another type of symmetry, resulting from the fact that two actions, two courses of behavior, two events, are presented as the inverse of each other. It is concluded that what applies to one—means necessary to achieve it, evaluation of it, nature of the event—likewise applies to the other.

Here is a passage from the *Pro Oppio* cited by Quintilian:

> How could those whom he could not summon to the province against their will be kept there against their will?[93]

The well-known thought of Pascal:

> A mere trifle consoles us, for a mere trifle distresses us.[94]

draws its persuasive force from this same kind of symmetry.

In the same way Calvin, beginning with the dogma of the redemption of mankind by the death of Christ, finds there an argument enabling him to indicate the scope of the dogma of original sin, the effects of which would be overcome by the sacrifice of Christ:

> What nonsense will the Pelagians chatter here? That Adam's sin was propagated by imitation? Then does Christ's righteousness benefit us only as an example set before us to imitate. Who can bear such sacrilege? But if it is beyond controversy that Christ's righteousness, and thereby life, are ours by communication, it immediately follows that both were lost in Adam, only to be recovered in Christ; and that sin and death crept in through Adam, only to be abolished through Christ.[95]

When the use of the argument by reciprocity leads to incompatibilities, it is necessary to reconsider the situation as a whole. Pascal urges this with regard to the Jesuits:

> You imagine that it would tell considerably in their favor to show that some of their fathers are as friendly to Evangelical maxims as others are opposed to them; and you would conclude from that circumstance, that these loose opinions do not belong to the whole Society. That I grant you; for had such been the case, they would not have suffered persons among them holding sentiments so diametrically opposed to licentiousness. But, as it is equally true

[92] Letter, dated Nov 16, 1830, from the Minister, W. P. Preble, to Martin van Buren, Secretary of State, published in Sophie Perelman, "Introduction aux relations diplomatiques entre la Belgique et les États-Unis," *Bull. de la Commission royale d'histoire*, 1949, p. 209.

[93] Quintilian, V, x, 76.

[94] Pascal, *Pensées*, GBWW, vol. 33, p. 196.

[95] Calvin, *Institutes of the Christian Religion*, (Westminster) vol. I, p. 248.

that there are among them those who hold these licentious doctrines, you are bound also to conclude that the Spirit of the Society is not one of Christian severity, for had such been the case, they would not have suffered persons among them holding sentiments so diametrically opposed to that severity.[96]

Most of the examples of *argument by contraries* given to us by the ancients end up with a generalization, starting from some particular situation and requiring that the same treatment be applied to the symmetrical situation:

> For if not even evil-doers should
> Anger us if they meant not what they did,
> Then can we owe no gratitude to such
> As were constrained to do the good they did us.[97]

We find an analogous argument in an 18th century treatise:

> How can it be maintained that on sufficient proof the judge ought to give a verdict against an innocent man whose innocence happens to be known to him, and that in the absence of sufficient proof he ought to absolve the guilty, even though he happens to have knowledge of his crime?[98]

Use of the argument by reciprocity is the basis of a generalization frequently encountered in philosophy, such as that which asserts that all that is born dies, thus going from the birth of a being to his contingency.[99] Montaigne draws a moral lesson from this:

> And therefore to lament and take on that we shall not be alive a hundred years hence, is the same folly as to be sorry we were not alive a hundred years ago.[100]

Is this reasoning valid? Is the argument from symmetry being abused? What are the limits beyond which the argument is not admissible? The limits are obviously exceeded when the use of the argument produces a ludicrous effect. Here is one of those rare tales which seem to have caused Kant to laugh:

> At Surat an Englishman is pouring out a bottle of ale which is foaming freely. He asks an Indian who is amazed at the sight what he finds so strange. "What bothers me," replies the native, "isn't

---

[96] Pascal, *The Provincial Letters* (Letter V), GBWW, vol. 33, p. 27.

[97] Aristotle, *Rhetoric*, II, 23, 1397a.

[98] Gibert, *Jugemens des savans sur les auteurs qui ont traité de la Rhétorique*, vol. III, p. 154.

[99] Cf. Quintilian, V, x, 79, and Aristotle, *Rhetoric*, II, 23, 1399b, enthymeme xvii. Cf. § 48, supra: Techniques for presenting Theses as Compatible or Incompatible.

[100] Montaigne, *Essais*, bk. I, chap. xx, p. 105.

what is coming out of the bottle, but how you got it in there in the first place."[101]

This amusing story recalls the passage from *Pro Oppio* quoted above. It seems like a caricature of it.

Lawrence Sterne consciously explores the same vein of comical argument in a passage from *Tristram Shandy*:

> "But whoever thought," cried Kysarcius, "of lying with his grandmother?"
>
> "The young gentleman," replied Yorick, "whom Selden speaks of, who not only thought of it, but justified his intention to his father by the argument drawn from the law of retaliation. 'You lay, Sir, with my mother,' said the lad. 'Why may not I lie with yours?' 'Tis the *argumentum commune*," added Yorick.[102]

As is obvious from these humorous examples, arguments by reciprocity cannot always be used, since making situations identical, while valid from a given point of view, may nevertheless neglect essential differences. Proof of the asymmetry of two situations makes this kind of argument invalid. Already Aristotle emphasized certain fallacies of reciprocity in connection with acts which were performed or undergone.[103] Others will show that there are concepts which can normally be applied only in certain situations, such as (according to Ryle) the notion of a voluntary act which the philosophers would have improperly extended from blameworthy to meritorious acts.[104] Symmetry is often rejected because a higher value is attached to one of the situations: what brings about a good is generally less appreciated than what avoids an evil.

The conditions under which arguments of this sort may be applied are not purely formal. They are the result of an evaluation of the importance of the elements which distinguish situations, which are, however, deemed to be symmetrical from a certain point of view. Sometimes the symmetry of the situation is complacently brought out for the sole purpose of denying it. This is the case in this statement recorded by Jouhandeau:

> Levy, if I had known you were so rich, I would not have loved you. But you, rather than Raymond, would have married me; and I would have betrayed you with him until, by dint of stealing from you, when we could be happy together without you, I would have left you. But everything happened otherwise: I am his wife and

---

[101] Quoted from Lalo, *Esthétique du rire*, p. 159.
[102] Sterne, *The Life and Opinions of Tristram Shandy*, bk IV, chap. 29, p. 298.
[103] Aristotle, *Rhetoric*, II, 23, 1397a.
[104] Ryle, *The Concept of Mind*, p. 71-74.

even if you were richer than you are, neither for gold or silver would I betray Raymond with you.[105]

§ 54. *Arguments by Transitivity*

Transitivity is a formal property of certain relations which makes it possible to infer that because a relation holds between a and b and between b and c, it therefore holds between a and c; the relations of equality, superiority, inclusion, and ancestry are transitive.

The transitivity of a relation allows formal demonstrations, but when the transitivity is debatable, or when affirming it requires precautions, specification, the transitivity argument is structurally quasilogical. Thus the maxim, "Our friends' friends are our friends," really involves an assertion that in the mind of the person proclaiming the maxim, friendship is a transitive relation. If objections are raised—based on observation or on an analysis of the concept of friendship—the defender of the maxim can always reply that this is his conception of true friendship and that true friends ought to act in conformity to the maxim.

We have here also a good example of the diversity of the argumentative structures which can be involved. Instead of an inference of the type

$$a \text{ R } b, \qquad b \text{ R } c, \qquad \text{therefore } a \text{ R } c,$$

we can recognize in this example an inference of the type

$$a = b, \qquad b = c, \qquad \text{therefore } a = c$$

(assuming that friendship establishes an equality among the parties—and this equality can be conceived not as a relation but as the belonging to a class). We can also recognize here an inference of the type

$$a \text{ R } b, \qquad c \text{ R } b, \qquad \text{therefore } a \text{ R } c$$

(assuming that friendship is both transitive and symmetrical). This latter aspect of friendship was expressed by the young man who was driven out in turn by his father and by his uncle, who were enemies, for having helped one and then the other:

O that they should love one another! They both loved me ![106]

The arguments combining transitivity and symmetry seem to have had a great attraction for the Latin rhetoricians. In the same controversy, another defender of the son offers this argument:

---

[105] Jouhandeau, *Un monde*, p. 251.
[106] Seneca, *Controversiae*, I, i, 7.

> I have deserved well from the father of both of you, although his age has prevented my knowing him. He also owes me a kindness: I have given bread to his two sons.[107]

Since the father and the uncle are antagonists, it is preferable not to limit oneself to considering only them as relayers of the relationship of kindness: the argument assumes two transitive symmetrical relations between the son and the father, the son and the uncle, and relations of the same kind between the father and the grandfather, the uncle and the grandfather, to conclude to a similar relation between the grandfather and the grandson.

Most of these arguments can be interpreted not merely by means of quasi-logical schemes, but can be supported also by arguments based on the structure of the real (for example, the relation of means to end: since the well-being of our friends is an end, we value everything that can help them). However it would seem at first glance that what we have is the use of a quasi-logical scheme. It is only upon reflection, if the quasi-logical argument is attacked, that a justification of the argument would first be given, and afterwards probably arguments based on the real and capable of supporting the same statements. The strength of many arguments results from the fact that a relative, precarious, doubtful validity is supported by the validity—which is of course just as precarious—of arguments of another sort. As soon as the quasi-logical scheme is made explicit, the supporting arguments are suppressed: formalization, while providing a coercive element, makes the argument thereby appear poorer and weaker than it is in reality. One might be tempted to think that its value is illusory, when the reductions which have been made are denounced but this is because, by formalizing it, the argument has been detached from the other arguments which could bolster it, and which for certain hearers and at certain times are perhaps more important.

In the following example it is seen that an interpretation by consequences can be superimposed on a quasi-logical interpretation:

> Although you think that your best allies are those who have sworn to have the same friends and enemies as you, you think that in political matters those whom you know for certain to be supporters of the enemies of the city are the ones to be trusted the most.[108]

The quasi-logical aspect is here emphasized by the explicit passage from one relation to another, from the maxim "the enemies of our enemies are our friends" to the conclusion "the friends of our enemies are our enemies."

---

[107] Ibid., I, i, 8.
[108] Demosthenes, For the Liberty of the Rhodians, § 33.

Arguments based on relations of friendship or antagonism between persons and between groups easily take on a quasi-logical appearance since the social mechanisms on which they rest are known and accepted by everyone. E. Dupréel has even tried to systematize what he calls the *logic of conflicts* by formulating, on this subject, five theorems which, he emphasizes, deal only with probabilities.[109] These theorems deal with the spread of antagonisms and the formation of alliances; although they are put in the form of algebraic equations, the statement of these theorems seems to us to be of a quasi-logical nature.

These arguments are applied to all forms of cooperation and antagonism, not merely to relations between persons and groups: the relations between values are often represented as giving rise to new relations among values without recourse to any other justification than transitivity, combined, if necessary, with symmetry.

The use of transitive relations is valuable in cases where it is a matter of ordering beings and events which cannot be directly compared with each other. On the model of such transitive relations as *greater than, heavier than, broader than* relations which are considered as transitive can be established between things whose nature cannot be known except through their effects. Thus, if player *A* has beaten player *B* and player *B* has beaten player *C*, we consider that player *A* is better than player *C*. It is possible that, in an actual contest, player *C* might beat player *A*. But this contest is often impossible to arrange; a knock-out tournament does not provide for it, in any case. The hypothesis of transitivity is thus necessary if one wishes to avoid a direct contest between all the players. The classification which results from these transitive relations is made possible only because conclusions are drawn about the person on the basis of his performance.

The transitive relation *to live on* seems to underlie the following passage, which aims at exhibiting an incompatibility:

> If a vegetable diet is best for the child, how can meat food be best for his nurse? The things are contradictory.[110]

The reasoning here is almost comical, since the term "nurse" suggests a transitivity, foreign, no doubt, to the mind of Rousseau, who couldn't have forgotten that the nurse's milk is not a vegetable food.

Finally, one of the most important transitive relations is that of implication. In actual practice, argumentation does not make use of

---

[109] Dupréel, *Sociologie générale*, pp. 140-145.
[110] Rousseau, *Émile* (Dent, Dutton) p. 26.

all the implications which can be defined in formal logic. But it does make considerable use of the relation of logical consequence. Syllogistic reasoning is essentially based on transitivity. It is not surprising that the ancient writers tried to put the arguments they encountered into syllogistic form. The terms *enthymeme* and *epicheirema* correspond roughly to quasi-logical arguments presented in syllogistic form. The syllogism of rhetoric is called *enthymeme* by Aristotle[111] and *epicheirema* by Quintilian.[112] We shall not go into the details of their terminology— one would have, in all probability, to show how it was modified under the influence of Stoic logic[113]—but we do insist on the fact that the assimilation of certain arguments with formal reasoning imposes on them in the main the role of quasi-logical arguments. The attempts of the jurists to cast their reasoning into syllogistic form should be understood in the same way. Our study of quasi-logical arguments makes it possible to see that such arguments are more varied than one might have thought.

It should be noted in this connection that the syllogistic chain, as a relation of logical consequence, is one of the transitive chains that seem to be of great interest to quasi-logical argumentation; but the syllogism can introduce relations of equality, the relation of the part to the whole. The transitive relation of implication is itself but the resultant of other transitive relations. Transitive chains can thus be constructed on diverse relations of logical consequence: this is the normal practice with most reasoning.

However there is a type of reasoning which is distinctive in this connection and which is found abundantly in Chinese writings. Some authors call it a *sorites* (a term that is reserved by others for the paradox of the heap of grain [σωρός] ; for convenience we shall call one the *Chinese sorites* and the other the *Greek sorites*, and we shall not deal with the question of the relation they have to each other).[114] Here is an example, taken from the *Tá Hio*:

> The Ancients, who desired intelligence to play its educative role through the whole country, first established order in their own principality; desiring to establish order in their own principality, they first regulated their family life; desiring to regulate their family life, they first improved their own characters; desiring to improve their own characters, they first purified their hearts; desiring to purify their hearts, they sought for sincerity in their thoughts; seeking for sincerity in their thoughts, they applied themselves first

[111] Aristotle, *Rhetoric*, I, 1, 1335a; II, 22, 1395b.
[112] Quintilian, V, xiv, 14.
[113] Cf. Cicero, *Topics*, § 54 et seq.
[114] Cf. § 66, infra: The Argument of Direction.

to perfect knowledge; this perfect knowledge consists in acquiring a sense of reality.[115]

This reasoning is very strict in form, in the sense that the last term of each proposition is the first term of the following one—in Chinese the rhythm also accentuates the relation between the propositions. It is shown that there is a possible chain between the value that is being extolled (the knowledge of things) and the other values that are recognized. But the passage from condition to consequence is based at each stage on different relations. Therefore the transitivity, to our occidental eyes at least, is only loose and weakly formal.

§ 55. *Inclusion of the Part in the Whole*

The relation of inclusion gives rise to two groups of arguments between which it will be important to differentiate: those restricted to dealing with this inclusion of the parts in the whole, and those dealing with the division of the whole into its parts and with the relations between the parts which result from this division.

The quasi-logical arguments of the first group, limited to comparing the whole with one of its parts, ascribe no special quality either to the parts or to the whole: the whole is treated as similar to each one of its parts. Nothing is considered but the relations which make possible a quasi-mathematical comparison between the whole and its parts. This permits arguments to be presented which are based on the principle "what is true of the whole is true of the part," for example this assertion of Locke:

> For whatsoever is not lawful to the whole Church cannot by any ecclesiastical right become lawful to any of its members.[116]

Usually the relation of the whole to its parts is dealt with quantitatively: the whole includes the part and is consequently more important. Often the value of the part will be considered to be proportional to the fraction of the whole which it constitutes. In this way Isocrates uses the argument of the superiority of the whole to its parts to emphasize the importance of the role of the teachers of princes:

---

[115] The *Tá Hio*, pt I, § 4. The translation is close to those of Legge, *The Sacred Books of the East*, vol. XXVIII, pp. 411-412; and *The Chinese Classics* (Macmillan), vol. I, 2d ed, pp. 357-358. The other interpretations, particularly that of Pauthier, *Les Sse Chou ou les quatre livres de philosophie morale et politique de la Chine*, pp. 21-23, preserve the general trend of the reasoning, but the commentators, ancient and modern, are in debate as to what is the main point of this passage.

[116] Locke, *A Letter Concerning Toleration*, GBWW, vol. 35, p. 7.

Masters who direct the education of private persons serve only their pupils; but whoever would incline the people's leaders toward virtue would serve both those who are in power and those who are under their authority.[117]

Much philosophical reasoning, especially that of the rationalists, is based on similar argumentation. For H. Poincaré this is what establishes the superiority of the objective over the subjective:

What we call objective reality is, in final analysis, what is common to several thinking beings, and could be common to all; ... [118]

One type of reasoning based on inclusion which is frequently used involves the relation between the one who understands and what is understood, what contains and what is contained. In its simplest form it consists in declaring that the liar is superior to the person who is deceived because "he knows he is lying": what his interlocutors know is only part of what he knows. In a more subtle form this is the scheme used by Plato to prove the superiority of the lover of wisdom over the lover of honors or riches.[119] In philosophy we have the superiority that comes from understanding, knowing, explaining the other, without the reverse being true. Thus, for Merleau-Ponty, empiricism is suffering from a kind of intellectual blindness; it is

... the system which is least capable of exhausting revealed experience, while reflection [that is, criticism] understands its subordinate truth, putting it where it belongs.[120]

The philosopher, as related to the scientist—particularly the critical philosopher—is thus tempted to attribute a superiority to himself deriving from the fact that his subject includes science and the principles that govern it, while science constitutes only part of the interests of man. This implies that science, or specialized knowledge, is no more than a part of what the philosopher understands. Many of Pascal's aphorisms dealing with the superiority of the honnête homme express this point of view.[121] But this presupposes a kind of homogeneity between the part and the whole, a mere denial of which puts this superiority of the nonspecialist in doubt. This denial, however, requires vigorous argumentation, while the quasi-logical scheme has no trouble

---

[117] Isocrates, To Nicocles, § 8. Cf. also Panegyricus, § 2; Archidamus, § 54; Antidosis, § 79.

[118] Poincaré, La valeur de la science, Introduction, p. 65; cf. § 16, supra: Facts and Truths.

[119] Plato, Republic, IX, 582b-583b.

[120] Merleau-Ponty, Phénoménologie de la perception, p. 33.

[121] Pascal, Pensées, GBWW, vol. 33, p. 177.

in ascribing greater value to the whole, to that which includes, to that which explains the part.

Arguments based on the inclusion of the part in the whole give rise to the problem of their relationship with the *loci* of quantity which we have examined among the premises of argumentation. Quasi-logical arguments are always at our disposal to support the *loci* of quantity if these should be questioned. On the other hand, the *loci* of quantity can act as premises for an argumentation of quasi-logical appearance. This makes it possible to consider an argument sometimes as an application of the *locus* of quantity and sometimes as a quasi-logical argument.

Let us consider this passage from Vl. Jankélévitch:

> Economy operates in accordance with a temporal sequence just as diplomacy operates in terms of coexistence. Just as this one requires the sacrifice of the part for the whole, of local interest for total interest, so that one, by its temporal arrangements, decides on the sacrifice of the present to the future, of the transitory moment to the longest duration possible. Could you without absurdity want to endanger, by pleasure of a moment, the superior interests of a whole life?[122]

One might wonder whether we have here a *locus* of quantity or a quasi-logical argument: it is only the allusion to the absurdity of a certain choice that makes us incline toward the latter. Instead of a *locus* of quantity, a *locus* of quality could indeed always be supplied which would prevent the part and the whole from being considered as homogeneous. This is what the same author notes, a few pages later, when, to bring out the superiority of "today" over "any tomorrow," he writes:

> The pleasurable experience, by its very effectiveness, contains an irrational and *quodditive* element which all the good reasons of reason cannot define.[123]

Do we have homogeneity or heterogeneity among the elements that are being compared? Nothing but an argument which compares the *loci* and the reasons and tests them in the light of a consciousness illuminated in this way will enable us to decide and to justify our decision in our own eyes and in the eyes of others.

---

[122] Jankélévitch, *Traité des vertus*, p. 18.
[123] *Ibid.*, p. 28.

§ 56. *Division of the Whole into Its Parts*

The concept of the whole as the sum of its parts provides the basis of a series of arguments that can be called arguments of *division* or of *partition*, such as the enthymeme of Aristotle:

> All men do wrong from one of three motives: *A*, *B*, or *C*; in my case *A* and *B* are out of the question, and even the accusers do not allege *C*.[124]

This may be compared with the following enthymeme:

> Another line of argument consists in taking separately the parts of a subject. Such is that given in the *Topics*: what *sort* of motion is the soul? for it must be this or that.[125]

Why does Aristotle say that the second enthymeme consists in taking the parts separately while the first consists in a division? At first sight they do not appear to be different. However by referring to the *Topics*, according to Aristotle's instructions, it can be verified that the second enthymeme is directed primarily toward a division into *genus* and *species*:[126]

> It must be examined whether, in accordance with one of the kinds of motion, the soul can move: whether it can, for example, increase, or be corrupted, or become, or have some other kind of motion.[127]

In this last example we are presented with an argument which, though it is nearly an argument from division, nevertheless differs from it by being based clearly on the relation between genus and species: anything that is to be affirmed about the genus must be established for one of the species; what does not belong to any species cannot belong to the genus. An echo of the distinction between these two enthymemes is found in Cicero—although the terminology is somewhat different from that of Aristotle—in dealing with definition by enumeration of parts (*partes*) or by analysis dealing with the species (*formae*).[128] Quintilian also takes the matter up, insisting on the fact that the number of parts is indeterminate but the number of species, on the contrary, is determined: it cannot be said how many parts make up a State, but it can be said that there are three species of State: democracy, oligarchy, or monarchy.[129]

---

[124] Aristotle, *Rhetoric*, II, 23, 1398a.
[125] *Ibid.*, II, 23, 1399a.
[126] Aristotle, *Topics*, II, 4, 111a.
[127] *Ibid.*, II, 4, 111b.
[128] Cicero, *Topics*, § 28-30.
[129] Quintilian, V, x, 63.

We see a constant effort to distinguish between what—judging by this effort—one has a tendency to confuse. We shall consider that in the argument by *division* the parts must be exhaustively enumerable, but that they can be chosen at will in a variety of ways on condition that by adding them up the given whole may be reconstituted. In the argument by *species* we are dealing with divisions on which there is agreement, divisions which antedate the argument, which seem natural, and which one does not have to enumerate exhaustively in order to be able to argue. The argument by species, which presupposes a similarity in kind between the parts and the whole, can be connected with the arguments by inclusion which we considered in the previous section. But usually it becomes an argument by division, for the species are viewed as adding up to form the genus. This is why we consider them here under the same heading as the argument by division.

To use the argument by division effectively, the enumeration of the parts must be exhaustive. Quintilian tells us:

> If we omit a single hypothesis in our enumeration, the whole edifice falls to the ground and we invite ridicule.[130]

This caution draws our attention to the fact that the argument by division is not purely formal; it requires a knowledge of the relations which the parts actually have with the whole in the particular case under consideration. This technique of argumentation assumes, moreover, that the classes formed by the subdivision of a set are not ambiguous: now this is not always the case. If one seeks the motives of a crime and one wonders whether the murderer acted through jealousy, hatred, or greed, one is not only unsure of having exhausted all the possible motives, but one is unsure of being in a position to reply unambiguously to each of the particular questions raised by this reasoning. The latter requires a structure of the real which is univocal, spatialized so to speak, from which would be excluded overlappings, interactions and fluidity, which, on the contrary, are never absent from the arguments we will examine later in the chapter dealing with reasonings founded on the structure of the real.

What can argumentation by division give us? In principle everything that is derived from the operations of addition, subtraction, and their combinations.

Its use may tend essentially to prove the existence of the wholes this is the case in Aristotelian induction and in a series of argument;

---

[130] *Ibid.*, V, x, 67.

by enumeration of parts. It should be noted in this connection that these forms of argumentation can give rise to rhetorical figures: we have cited an example of amplification by *aggregation*, borrowed from Vico, in which the enumeration of parts has the effect of increasing presence.[131] Depending on the case, a statement can be an argument by division or by amplification: one might prove to someone who doubts it that a city has been completely destroyed by enumerating exhaustively the districts that have been destroyed. But if the hearer does not question the fact, or is not acquainted with the city, the same enumeration will be an argumentative figure of presence.

The most characteristic arguments by division are directed toward proving the existence or nonexistence of one of the parts. One argues by exclusion. Here is an example, taken from Bergson, in which he asks what force in moral aspiration can play the role that is played in social ethics by group pressure:

> We have no choice. Beyond instinct and habit there is no direct action on the will except feeling.[132]

The same scheme can explain the use of tables of presence and absence, as recommended by Bacon and Mill, although in most cases these ought to be connected with tables of concomitant variation.[133]

Argument by division lies at the basis of the dilemma, a form of argument in which two hypotheses are examined, with the conclusion that no matter which one of them is chosen the result is a statement, a course of action, which amounts to the same thing in either case, and this for one of the following reasons: either they lead to the same result, or they lead to results amounting to the same thing (usually two dreaded events), or they both imply an incompatibility with some already accepted principle.

We borrow from Pascal an example of the first kind of dilemma:

> What could the Jews, His enemies, do? If they receive Him they give proof of Him by their reception; for then the guardians of the expectation of the Messiah receive Him. If they reject Him, they give proof of Him by their rejection.[134]

In order that the two horns of the dilemma lead to the same conclusion, the equivalence of the alleged means of proof must be granted, for in the first case the reasoning is based on the authority of the Jews and in the second on the authority of the Scriptures. But if the two

---

[131] Cf. § 42, supra: Figures of Choice, Presence and Communion.

[132] Bergson, *The Two Sources of Morality and Religion*, p. 39.

[133] Cf. § 76, infra: The Double Hierarchy Argument.

[134] Pascal, *Pensées*, GBWW, vol. 33, p. 322.

authorities are equivalent, would not the inverse reasoning, which would lead to two conclusions against the Messiah, be equally admissible? The ancients had already examined such a refutation of the dilemma under the name of *conversion*.[135]

That two contradictory possibilities lead to the same conclusion seems to result more from a preconceived idea in favor of that conclusion than from the argument that is offered. That is why such a dilemma is often attributed to the opponent as a proof of his bad faith. In the controversy over the authenticity of the tiara of Saitphernes, Héron de Villefosse, who defended the tiara, exclaimed:

> When M. Furtwängler discovers on some ancient monument one of the figures or one of the motifs of the tiara, he declares for that reason that the tiara is a fraud; when he doesn't discover an example of the same motif or figures, ... he likewise concludes that the tiara is a fraud. This is a most extraordinary way of arguing.[136]

The second kind of dilemma tends to restrict the scope of the debate to two solutions, both disagreeable, but between which a choice seems unavoidable. The remainder of the argument consists in proving that the proposed solution is the lesser of two evils:

> In a word, fellow Athenians, you must not lose sight of this fact: you have the choice between attacking Philip in his own land or being attacked by Philip in yours. Is it necessary to show the difference between making war in his land and in yours?[137]

We find an amusing example of the third kind of dilemma in the reflections Sterne attributes to the jurisconsults of Strasburg concerning the nose of a foreigner:

> Such a monstrous nose, said they, had it been a true nose, could not possibly have been suffered in civil society—and if false—to impose on society with such false signs and tokens, was a still greater violation of its rights, and must have had still less mercy shown it.
> The only objection to this was, that if it proved anything, it proved the stranger's nose was neither true nor false.[138]

To reduce a situation to a dilemma, the two alternatives must be presented as incompatible, because they refer to a situation unaffected by time and which, for that reason, contains no possibility of change. This static character of the dilemma is very clear in the following examples. The first, which the *Rhetorica ad Herennium* attributes to

---

[135] Cicero, *De Inventione*, I, § 83.
[136] Vayson de Pradenne, *Les fraudes en archéologie préhistorique*, p. 533.
[137] Demosthenes, *First Olynthiac*, §§ 25, 27.
[138] Sterne, *The Life and Opinions of Tristram Shandy*, bk. IV, Slawkenbergius's Tale, p. 231.

a hard-working author, is the argument of a daughter whose father is trying, against her will, to separate her from her husband.

> You are treating me, Father, more harshly than I deserve. Indeed, if you consider Chresphontes to be an evil man, why did you give him to me as a husband? If, on the other hand, he is a good man, why do you force me, against my will and his, to leave him?[139]

The other dilemma is that which Demosthenes uses against Aeschines:

> I would like to ask Aeschines whether, when all this was going on and the city was full of pride, joy, and self-congratulation, he joined in the sacrifices and celebrations of the mass of the people or stayed at home, grieving, groaning, and angry at his fellow-citizens' happiness. If he was present and seen among all the others, does he not now act in a scandalous, even sacrilegious manner, in asking you, who have taken an oath by the gods, to vote that these acts were not excellent, these very acts to the excellence of which he made the gods his witnesses? If he was not present, does he not deserve to die a thousand times over for suffering at the sight of the things which brought joy to others?[140]

Reducing the situation to a quasi-logical scheme, which excludes both nuances and the effect of change, makes it possible to hem in the adversary with the alternatives of the dilemma, from which he can break out only by alleging a change or nuances, which must each time be justified.

Since the argument by division presupposes that the sum of the parts equals the whole and that the situations which are being considered exhaust the possibilities, when the parts or the possibilities are limited to two, the argument becomes an application of the exclusion of a third party. This form of division is used in debate when the solutions are limited to two: that of the adversary and that of the speaker himself. After pointing out the absurdity of the adversary's thesis—which is sometimes completely fabricated to suit the argument—the speaker then proposes his own thesis as the only remaining possibility. A somewhat different technique consists in presenting a thesis as the answer to the problem, all other hypotheses being tossed aside *en bloc*. Only the thesis which the speaker is developing is made present. Sometimes, after having set it forth, he asks his hearers if they have a better solution to offer. This appeal, known classically as the *argumentum ad ignorantiam*, derives its force essentially from its very urgency, for it excludes the possibility of pausing for thought: the debate is limited

---

[139] *Rhetorica ad Herennium*, II, 38.
[140] Demosthenes, *On the Crown*, § 217.

to the thesis that has been offered and to what might possibly be opposed to it immediately. Thus this argument, to be useful, places the interlocutors in a limited framework which recalls that of the dilemma.

All the arguments by division obviously imply relations between the parts such that their sum can reconstitute the whole. These relations can be connected with a structure of the real (for example, the relation between the different sections of a city); they can also be primarily logical in character. In this respect negation plays an essential role; it is negation that seems to guarantee that the division is exhaustive. This is true in the eristic argument (*Kunstgriff* 13) that Schopenhauer sets forth in these terms:

> To make the opponent accept a proposition, its contrary must be presented with it and the adversary given a choice. The contrary is formulated in a rather crude way, so that the interlocutor, not wishing to be paradoxical, accepts our proposition, which by contrast with the other appears quite plausible. For example, to get the adversary to grant that a son ought to do everything his father asks him to, one asks, "should one in all matters obey or disobey one's parents?"[141]

The thesis offered as a foil is formed by the negation of the other—or at least by the negation of certain of its elements. The trick is obvious. But let us note that Pascal does not hesitate to recommend argument by division between the two possibilities presented by a proposition and its contrary.

> ... Whenever a proposition is inconceivable, we must suspend our judgment and not deny it for that reason, but examine its contrary; and if we find that this is manifestly false, we may boldly affirm the original statement, however incomprehensible it may be.[142]

Used as Pascal used it to prove the infinite divisibility of space, this quasi-logical argumentation is itself based on the exhaustive division of a given whole.

Such argumentation is usually considered as a matter of course. La Bruyère writes:

> The very impossibility of my proving that God does not exist persuades me of his existence.[143]

On this type of reasoning, as E. Dupréel has shown, is generally based the concept of necessity in philosophy.[144]

The disjunction asserted between two terms which are not formally contradictory often indicates that the speaker assumes the identity of

[141] Schopenhauer, *Sämtliche Werke* (Piper), vol. 6: "Eristische Dialektik," p. 414.
[142] Pascal, *On Geometrical Demonstration*, GBWW, vol. 33, p. 436.
[143] La Bruyère, "Les caractères. Des esprits forts," 13, *Œuvres complètes*.
[144] Dupréel, *Essais pluralistes*, "De la nécessité," p. 77.

one of the alternatives with the negation of the other. When Gide in the example cited above[145] says about the Bible and *The Thousand and One Nights*, "One can love it or not understand it," he identifies "not understand" with "not love," thereby disqualifying this negative alternative.

And when H. Lefebvre writes

> Logical and scientific thought is *objective* ... or it is nothing. Similarly it is *universal* ... or it is nothing.[146]

he seems, by identifying "nothing" with "not objective," "not universal," to give an absolute value to the definition he has proposed.

This identification of the negative alternative with something despicable can itself be expressed in a dilemma. Condemning religious wars and the intolerance of Christian priests, Locke writes:

> And if anyone that professes himself to be a minister of the word of God, a preacher of the gospel of peace, teach otherwise, he either understands not or neglects the business of his calling and shall one day give an account thereof unto the Prince of Peace.[147]

Such a dilemma can be used as a figure of speech. The *Rhetorica ad Herennium* gives the following example of *hesitation* (*dubitatio*):

> At that time the republic suffered great wrong because of the consuls, should we say because of their stupidity or because of their perversity or because of both.[148]

This is not simply a matter of hesitation about how to qualify something; we are dealing with a figure of presence rather than a figure of choice. We already know that the amplification is recognized as a figure when it makes use of characteristic argumentative schemes.[149] Here the dilemma is resolved into a nonexclusive disjunction

The two parts forming a whole can also be complementary.

What is necessary to explain, justify, and allow the use of a concept is complementary to it: this is what E. Dupréel calls a "crutch-concept." Also complementary, however, is that which, when added to the notion, always reconstitutes a whole, whatever variation there may be in the application of the notion. These two aspects of complementariness are related.

Bishop Blougram shows that belief and unbelief are complementary:

---

145 Cf. § 32, *supra*: Choice of Qualifiers.
146 Lefebvre, *A la lumière du matérialisme dialectique*, I, p. 43.
147 Locke, *A Letter Concerning Toleration*, GBWW, vol. 35, p. 8.
148 *Rhetorica ad Herennium*, IV, 40.
149 Cf. § 42, *supra*: Figures of Choice, Presence, and Communion.

All that we have gained then by our unbelief
Is a life of doubt diversified by faith,
For one of faith diversified by doubt:
We called the chessboard white,—we call it black.[150]

An affirmation and its negative are in a sense always complementary, but, in putting the emphasis on this quality, one eliminates the idea of opposition and of unavoidable choice, ending instead with the idea that the choice is indifferent. The negations used in dilemmas could in this way be related to complementariness.

The manner of understanding the relation between the parts forming a whole is particularly important in the arguments *a pari* and *a contrario*, which are well known in the juristic tradition. These arguments deal with the application or nonapplication to another species of the same genus of what can be asserted about some particular species. Let us take an example. A law requires certain procedures relative to male heirs; by use of the argument *a pari* one tries to extend these procedures to women. The argument *a contrario*, on the other hand, makes it possible to claim that they do not apply to persons of the female sex. In the first case the law is regarded as an example of a rule which covers the whole genus; in the second it is conceived as an exception to an implied rule concerning the genus.

The argument *a pari* is conceived as an identification; the argument *a contrario* as a division. It must be noted, however, that insofar as the identification *a pari* is said to be a likening of two species of the same genus, it gives a foothold to the argument *a contrario*: the quasi-logical argument instigates the quasi-logical argument of the opponent. To the degree that the identification is made by other means it runs a lesser risk of provoking a reply by the argument *a contrario*.

How must legal texts and decisions in jurisprudence be interpreted? It is not possible to know *a priori*. Only the context, the evaluation of the situation, the determination of the end sought by legal decisions or jurisprudence will allow us to choose one or the other technique of argument, to prefer to identify two species rather than oppose them, or conversely. This conclusion provides good evidence of the difference between quasi-logical argument and formal proof.

---

[150] Browning, *Complete Poetical Works*, p. 351: Cf. § 43, supra: Status and Presentation of the Elements of the Argumentation.

§ 57. *Arguments by Comparison*

Argumentation could not proceed very far without making use of comparisons, where several objects are considered in order to evaluate them through their relations to each other. In this sense arguments by comparison should be distinguished both from arguments by identification and from arguments by analogy.

In saying "Her cheeks are as red as apples," or "Paris has three times as many inhabitants as Brussels," or "He is handsomer than Adonis" we are comparing realities and doing it in a way which seems much more susceptible of proof than a simple statement of similarity or of analogy. This impression is due to the concept of measure underlying these statements, even though any standard of measurement is completely lacking; this is how arguments by comparison are quasi-logical. They are often presented as a statement of fact, whereas the relation of equality or inequality which is asserted is often nothing more than a claim of the speaker. Thus:

> It is the same crime, whether it is stealing from the state or giving bribes contrary to public interest.[151]

is an assertion which compares with an established crime an action which has no legal qualification, and whose equivalence to the other is therefore not preliminary to the argumentation.

The idea of measure, which underlies arguments by comparison, is often conveyed by the statement of certain criteria.

Comparisons can be made by opposition (the heavy and the light), by ordering (heavier than), and by quantitative ordering (the weight in terms of units of weight).[152] When it comes to concepts taken from common usage, the criteria are generally complex. Breaking down an idea as statisticians do (for example, measuring the level of education on the basis of the number of literate persons, the number of libraries, publications, etc.) amounts to an attempt to do justice to the various measurable elements. The criteria are combined in various ways. Thus, in St. Thomas, we find the following combination:

> The lower beings are naturally incapable of attaining complete perfection. But they do attain a mediocre degree of excellence by means of certain movements. There are higher beings which acquire a complete perfection by means of a large number of movements.

---

[151] Cicero, *De Oratore*, bk II, § 172.
[152] Hempel and Oppenheim, *Der Typusbegriff im Lichte der neuen Logik*.

Still higher beings attain their complete perfection by a small number of movements; and the highest among these are those which possess their perfection without executing any movements in order to acquire it.[153]

This gradation, which correlates the degrees of perfection with the means of acquiring it, allows St. Thomas to put God at the summit, then the angels, men, and animals. This metaphysical construction is based on an analogy in which this double criterion also comes into play: the degrees of health, compared by reference to the result obtained and the remedies necessary to obtain it.

The criteria are often in conflict: St. Thomas' procedure establishes for each level of one of the criteria a hierarchy based on the second criterion,[154] which obviously implies a predominance of the first over the second. However the very need to introduce the second shows that the first was recognized as insufficient.

Combinations of the most diverse character can be considered; they will never reflect the complexity of unformalized notions. Moreover in many cases there is an inverse ratio between the criteria which are used; merit, from the common sense point of view, is a matter of inner disposition toward the good and of sacrifice: establishing a hierarchy of merits requires the introduction of these incompatible factors.

As soon as there is a comparison of elements which are not integrated into a system, the terms of the comparison, whatever it may be, interact with each other. They do this in two ways.

On the one hand, the absolute value of the term which is used as a standard influences the value of the terms belonging to the same series which are compared with it. This effect is observed in perception; let us note that the repetition of the terms which are compared all seem to concur in establishing a neutral level of adaptation.[155] The same thing probably happens in argumentation where the terms already set forth form a background which influences new evaluations.

On the other hand, the comparison can bring together two terms which were considered, with good reason, to be incommensurable. The comparison between God and man will work both to the advantage of the lower and to the detriment of the higher term. Even as the believers in heavenly love are contemptuous of earthly love, they cannot but give value to the latter by comparing them:

---

[153] Gilson, *The Christian Philosophy of St. Thomas Aquinas*, p. 200. Cf. *Summa Theologica*, I, 77, 2, ad Resp; Tr. in Pegis, *Basic Writings of Saint Thomas Aquinas*, p. 722.

[154] Cf. § 20, supra: Hierarchies.

[155] Cf. Helson, "Adaptation Level as a Basis for a Quantitative Theory of Frames of Reference," *Psychological Review*, Nov 1948, p. 302.

> But one day coming to hate her shame, she (the soul) puts away the evils of earth, once more seeks the father, and finds her peace.
> Those to whom this experience is strange may understand by way of our earthly longings and the joy we have in winning what we most desire—remembering always that here what we love is perishable, hurtful, that our love is of mimicries and turns awry because all was a mistake; our good was not here, and this was not what we sought.[156]

This valuation of the lower is emphasized by such orators as Bossuet to bring about certain argumentative effects:

> ... pious sovereigns are willing that all their glory disappear before that of God; and, far from being saddened that their power is thereby diminished, they know that they are never more profoundly revered than when they are humbled by comparison with God.[157]

Similarly it is an honor for a mediocre poet to be declared inferior to a famous master: from then on, even if he will not take up an honored position in it, he joins the fraternity of illustrious poets.

On the other hand, anything that is compared to objects which are far inferior cannot but suffer through this comparison. That is why Plotinus, after emphasizing the superiority of the One over any other reality, but fearing the resulting loss of value, adds:

> Let us separate him from everything else. Let us not even say that things depend on him and that he is free ... he must have absolutely no connection with anything. ... [158]

An effective method for belittling someone is to compare him with that of which he is contemptuous, even if it is to grant that he is superior to it. It remains that from then on the things that are compared belong to the same class.

The interaction between the terms of a comparison may be due to an awareness of real connections between the things which are being compared. But their origin is of little importance. The result of these interactions is that in comparisons, when a distinction between the terms is sought, a constant effort is required to maintain the distance between them. Only precise methods of measurement can assure the persistence of the relations which have been evoked.

Arguments by comparison, however, do not fail to consider these relations as established and transposable. Here is an amusing example: A pretty girl and an ill-tempered old woman are waiting for the bus. The latter indignantly refuses a cigarette:

---

[156] Plotinus, *Enneads*, VI, ix, § 9.
[157] Bossuet, *Sermons*, vol. II: *Sur l'ambition*, p. 395.
[158] Plotinus, *Enneads*, VI, viii, § 8.

"Smoke on the street? I'd rather kiss the first man who comes along!"
"So would I. But while we're waiting, why not light up?"[159]

The humor is due to the fact that the same hierarchy of preference is located in an entirely different range of the scale of values.

A choice of the terms of comparison which is adapted to the hearer can be an essential element in the effectiveness of an argument—even when dealing with a comparison that can be evaluated numerically. It is advantageous in certain cases to describe a country as nine times larger than France rather than half as large as Brazil.

The characteristics of the term of reference give their particular appearance to a series of arguments.

A typical form of comparison is that which makes use of a loss that was not sustained to enhance the advantages of the adopted solution. When he was asked what had been gained by the war, Pitt's answer was, "all that we must have lost without it."[160] The term of reference is hypothetical, but, thanks to the tautology, a real though indeterminate importance is given to it. Often, however, it is necessary to evaluate this term of reference, which is presented in a manner favorable to the conclusions of the argument. Pitt, again, criticizes Fox for conveying the disadvantages of the war with France by recalling the prosperity which had existed prior to its outbreak, "though it seemed little to affect him at the time it was enjoyed."[161] In general, pictures of a golden age, past or future, of paradise lost or hoped for—whether it is a matter of the good old days or of happiness to be found elsewhere — work to the disadvantage of the time or the country in which one is actually living. On the other hand, an enthusiastic description of the present circumstances seems to lessen efforts to ameliorate or even modify them; the relative increase in happiness would be minimum, and the loss of happiness would be considerable. All persuasion by threat is therefore all the more effective as the conditions now enjoyed are valued.

Argument by comparison can also occur as a use of the superlative. This is done by considering some object either as superior to all the members of a series, or as beyond compare and therefore unique of its kind. Let us not forget that this last qualification requires a prior attempt at comparison whose impossibility is acknowledged. It is in this way that uniqueness can be the result of a superlative, as in Leib-

---

[159] Quoted from *Le Soir*, 20 June 1950.
[160] Pitt, *Orations on the French War*, p. 123.
[161] *Ibid.*, p. 133.

niz, where the uniqueness of contingent truths is based upon the principle of the best. This technique allows beings to be individualized by qualifying them with the superlative—a procedure which Giraudoux does not hesitate to use frequently.[162]

Moreover, judgments making use of the superlative are much more impressive, partly because of their quasi-logical aspect, than more moderate judgments. They often dispense with showing that the comparison is made with something which has a value: witness the abundance of superlatives in advertisements. Their peremptory nature makes it easy to dispense with proof. The charge of having committed "the most infamous act" is generally less supported by proof than that of having "done wrong." This hierarchy can be expressed without using the comparative form at all through the use of such expressions as "execrable," "miraculous." La Bruyère has noted the peremptory nature of these terms.[163]

The superlative can also be suggested by certain processes of amplification, such as the one of which Quintilian gives an example:

> It is your mother whom you have struck. What more can be said?
> It is your mother whom you have struck![164]

When there is nothing to be added which could increase the gravity of an offense or emphasize the importance of an act, it is no longer necessary to compare it with anything else to realize how outstanding it is.

Sometimes the effect of a superlative is reinforced by some particular restriction. This gives the impression of having truly made an effective comparison, and the superlative is not to be considered merely as a manner of speaking or as a figure of style. Virgil speaks of Lausus:

> ... who far excelled
> All others in personal beauty except for Laurentine Turnus.[165]

Here the superlative is not the same as the unique. On the other hand, the impression of uniqueness is conveyed when in speaking of a thing nothing but itself can be found as a term of comparison. It belongs, so to speak, to a class apart, it is incomparable. As La Bruyère said:

> V ... is an artist, C ... a musician, and the author of *Pyramus* is a poet; but Mignard is Mignard, Lulli is Lulli, and Corneille is Corneille.[166]

---

[162] Cf. Gandon, *Le démon du style*, p. 140.

[163] La Bruyère, "Les caractères. De la société et de la conversation," 19, *Œuvres complètes*, p. 176.

[164] Quintilian, VIII, IV, 7.

[165] Virgil, *Aeneid*, VII, 649-650. Cited in Quintilian, VIII, IV, 6.

[166] La Bruyère, "Les caractères. Du mérite personnel," 24, *Œuvres complètes*, p. 118.

Every comparison, as we see by this example, is discrediting in some way, because it makes light of this uniqueness of things which are incomparable. To treat *my* country, *my* family, as *a* country, *a* family is to deprive it of part of its prestige: this accounts for the slightly blasphemous character of rationalism, which refuses to consider concrete values in their uniqueness. This is why all love, to the degree that it results from making a comparison leading to the choice of the best of the things being compared, is suspect and not highly valued. There are feelings which exclude any choice, no matter how flattering that choice might be.

The very concept of choice, of a good choice, always implies a comparison. Nevertheless expressions relating to choice show the coming and going between the domain of the comparative and that of the absolute. "We have made a good choice" is often a sign of contentment, of the desire not to compare. The idea that something is good, especially if this something exists and if inertia is at work, is easily expressed by the idea that it is the best, that better could not be found, that is, by a superlative. An implicit justification would be that the object appears capable of withstanding any amount of comparison. These assertions dealing with a good choice can be compared with many assertions that are quantitative (for example the amount of business brought in by a certain advertisement). It is suggested that this amount is greater than any other to which it might be compared. On the other hand, if some event is given huge headlines in the papers, its importance may be minimized by pointing out that every day some event is played up: the absolute value is reduced to a relative value.

These interpretations seem to move in two stages from absolute value to relative value, or the converse. However this is the result of analysis. On the other hand, there are arguments in two stages which make this transition explicitly. Blougram[167] maintains that once an end is chosen, the means must be the best means possible. But this comparison at the level of the means has an effect on the entire situation: in this case it gives greater value both to the religion which is most effective in acting on the world and to the chosen end, to act on the world. We shall meet these interactions again when we study the arguments based on the structure of the real.

All these analyses tend to show how much arguments by comparison differ from comparisons between values which can actually be measured, whose place in a series or in a system is established once and for all. Nevertheless it is their connection with mathematical structures which provides a great part of their power of persuasion.

[167] Browning, *Complete Poetical Works*, p. 351.

§ 58. Argumentation by Sacrifice

One of the most frequently used of the arguments by comparison is that which is based on the sacrifice which one is willing to make in order to achieve a certain result.

This argument lies at the basis of every system of exchange, whether it be barter, sale, or hire of services—though it is certainly not the sole factor in the relation between seller and buyer. But it is not limited to economic matters. The mountain climber, debating whether he is prepared to make the effort necessary to scale a mountain, has recourse to the same form of evaluation.

In every weighing of alternatives, the two terms determine each other. Therefore Sartre is right in saying that we can never know whether the world, by the obstacles it presents, tells us about itself or about us. It is we who freely set the limits of our efforts.[168] But to take this effort into account, it must be described, or known in some other way which, provisionally at least, appears adequate. In this connection we must avoid a number of illusions. Klages makes a disstinction between quantitative faculties, which could be measured by comparing different individuals, and motives, which could be measured reciprocally in the same individual.[169] This is perhaps a fruitful distinction, but we must not forget that this reciprocal evaluation is useful only on condition that, for some particular individual, we know whether a given motive has a normal intensity or we have some kind of estimate of it.

In argumentation by sacrifice, the sacrifice is a measure of the value attributed to the thing for which the sacrifice is made. This is the argument Calvin uses to guarantee the importance which the Protestants—as opposed to the Catholics—attach to their religion:

> But however much they may belittle its uncertainty, if they had to seal their doctrine in their own blood, and at the expense of their own life, one could see how much it would mean to them. Quite the opposite is our assurance, which fears neither the terrors of death nor even God's judgment seat.[170]

Directed against the Catholics, this is the well-known argument based on the existence of confessors of the faith; and the absence of sacrifice

---

[168] Sartre, *Being and Nothingness*, pp. 509 et seq.

[169] Klages, "Notions fondamentales de la caractérologie," in *Le diagnostic du caractère*, p. 16.

[170] Calvin, *Institutes of the Christian Religion* (Westminster), vol. I, p. 16, Prefatory Address to King Francis.

is a measure of the scanty importance attached to something which one otherwise claims to revere.

If, in the argument by sacrifice, it is the person who consents to the sacrifice who does the weighing, the meaning of this sacrifice in the eyes of others depends on the esteem enjoyed by this person. When Pascal writes:

> I believe only those stories for which the witnesses would readily die.[171]

the witnesses, who serve as an element of reference, must enjoy a certain prestige. The greater the prestige, the greater the force of the argument. Pauline expresses this well when she says:

> My husband in dying has left me his ideals;
> His blood with which your executioners have just covered me
> Has unsealed my eyes and opened them.[172]

The sacrifice of a divine being is the extreme case; it is evoked by Bossuet:

> And in truth, fellow Christians, Jesus Christ, who is truth itself, loves the truth no less than his own body; on the contrary, it was to seal with his own blood the truth of his words that he was willing to sacrifice his own body.[173]

The confessors of the faith may be humble, but they will be neither mad nor contemptible. Their great number can make up for the lack of individual prestige, as in the legend of the 11,000 virgins who accompanied St. Ursula. The weighing which led to the sacrifice, which was made in all sincerity, is moreover an element that might increase this prestige.

However, if the object of the sacrifice is known and if its value is not great, the prestige of those who have sacrificed themselves will be decreased by a kind of reaction. In his eulogy of Helen, Isocrates glorifies her because of the sacrifices the Greeks made to get her back.[174] Fénelon criticizes him:

> Nothing is seriously established. In all this there is no moral truth. He judges the value of things only by men's passions.[175]

The sacrifice of the Greeks seems futile to him because of the futility of its object; but the technique of the proof is no different from that

---

[171] Pascal, *L'œuvre, Pensées*, n° 397, p. 932 (n° 593 ed. Brunschvicg).
[172] Corneille, *Polyeucte*, V, v.
[173] Bossuet, *Sermons*, II: *Sur la parole de Dieu*, p. 157.
[174] Isocrates, *Eulogy of Helen*, §§ 48 ff.
[175] Fénelon, *Œuvres*, vol. XXI: *Dialogues sur l'éloquence*, p. 75.

used by the confessors, that which was used by Plotinus to prove the value of the mystic state:

> Once there she [the soul] will barter for This [the One] nothing the universe holds; not though one would make over the heavens entire to her; than This there is nothing higher, nothing more good. ... All that she had welcomed of old—office, power, wealth, beauty, knowledge—of all she tells her scorn as she never could had she not found their better.[176]

But let us note that in order to prove the value of the One by the greatness of the sacrifice, the asceticism which results therefrom must rest upon a positive prior evaluation of worldly goods, without which the renunciation would hardly prove anything. A grave objection can always be made to the argument by sacrifice. The emphasis which contemporary psychology places on the ambivalence of feelings allows us to formulate it in extreme terms: could it not be that the man who sacrifices his son to honor really bears an unconscious hatred toward him? The value of honor would in no way be increased by this immolation. To measure something by sacrifice presupposes that there are constant elements placed in a quasi-formal framework, elements which in fact are subject to variation. In proof of this, the concept one has of some sacrifice can in practice be very different depending on the conclusions one wishes to draw. Suppose it is a matter of giving or not giving an office to a person for whom all the participants in the discussion have a high regard. Those who favor the candidate can make a point of the humiliation he would suffer if he were not appointed; the opponents, on the other hand, would try to minimize his disappointment. And does not the very fact of renouncing something work by a kind of recoil to change the value of what is being renounced? Clearly we find ourselves confronted here by a quasi-logical argument, since the term of reference has no fixed value, but interacts constantly with the other elements.

The value of the end which is sought by sacrifice is likewise modified during the action by the very sacrifices themselves. On this point Simone Weil has rightly observed:

> Too high a degree of suffering in relation to what the heart prompts can produce one or other of two attitudes: either the violent rejection of the object to which too much has been sacrificed, or else the clinging to it in a sort of despair.[177]

In the first case one does not wish to be fooled again and one turns others away from this false value; in the second, one increases the

---

[176] Plotinus, *Enneads*, VI, 7, § 34.
[177] Weil, *The Need for Roots*, p. 129.

desirability of the end, so that its importance exceeds the sacrifice. In this latter case we are dealing with another argument which we shall analyze later on as the *argument of waste*.[178]

The argument from sacrifice, used in a hypothetical fashion, can indicate the price that is attached to something. It is often accompanied by the assertion that such a sacrifice, which one would be ready to make, is either unnecessary, because the circumstances do not require it, or ineffectual, because it would not really achieve the desired result.[179]

Useless sacrifice, which is not a mere hypothesis but a tragic reality, often leads to the disrepute of those who have made it. Here is the comment of one of the combatants about the dead who fell in an unsuccessful attack:

> ... all in all, they had become unattractive to us. They were the useless dead who hadn't succeeded. Ferrer expressed it by saying: "those we must start all over again."[180]

The pathos of useless sacrifice inspires some of Bossuet's poignant effects in his sermon on the compassion of Our Lady. The mother of God resigns herself to the sacrifice of her son in the hope of saving mankind, but the impenitence of Christians is a grief greater than she can bear:

> ... when I see you wasting the blood of my Son and making his sacrifice useless. .,. [181]

Related to this process of evaluation in terms of deliberate sacrifice are the techniques of evaluation by a sacrifice which is a consequence, of the crime by the punishment, the retaliation, or the remorse, of the virtue by the glory or the reward, of the loss by the sorrow.

By reason of their causal character, arguments of this type are related to arguments based on the structure of the real. But they also constitute a weighing; and one often tries to make it easier by giving a homogeneous structure to one of the elements being put on the scales, so that it can be described quantitatively.

The severity of the punishment indicates the gravity of the crime: the damnation of the human race is better known than original sin in Christian theology; the sufferings of Job give a measure of his guilt.

Retaliation brings out the importance of an act:

---

[178] Cf. § 65, infra: The Argument of Waste.

[179] Cf. Epictetus, *Discourses*, I, 4, § 27; Crossman, *Palestine Mission, with Speech Delivered in the House of Commons, 1st July, 1946*, p. 250.

[180] Paulhan, *Le guerrier appliqué*, pp. 132-133.

[181] Bossuet, *Sermons*, vol. II: *Sur la Compassion de la Sainte Vierge*, p. 645.

> Here is, as it were, a certain characteristic of the divine Word, that it never comes forth without Satan working up and causing trouble.[182]

The intensity of regret is a measure of the value of what is lost. A curious application of this argument is to be found in the phantasms of burial, which, according to Odier, can be a powerful mechanism for finding security: the "abandonnien" imagines his own burial and measures his worth by the intensity of the regrets which his own death would cause.[183]

The quasi-logical argument from sacrifice can also be applied to the whole field of the relationship between ends and means,[184] the means being a sacrifice, an effort, an expenditure, a suffering. The quasi-logical character is especially pronounced when in order to give something greater value some other thing is transformed into a means calculated to bring it about and measure it. Thus Isocrates in the *Panegyric of Athens* writes:

> In my view it is some god who has brought about this war out of admiration for their courage, in order to prevent them from being unrecognized and ending their lives in obscurity.[185]

The procedure is also clear when the importance of what is at stake is measured by the size of the forces which have been called in. Paul Janson reproaches his Catholic opponents for having used this technique to convince the people that their faith would be endangered by the vote on the school law of 1879.

> No doubt they get tired of praying to God; they decide to call in the saints. So here they all are, requisitioned to intervene, so that the left won't vote for this accursed law.[186]

The old argument, which is eternally repeated, about the difficulty of expressing oneself is likewise a quasi-logical form of measurement:

> ... it is no less difficult to praise those who surpass all others in virtue than those who are good for nothing. With the latter there is nothing to praise; with the former no words are adequate.[187]

All these arguments are effective only if the value that is being measured is not dependent on some other more convincing factor.

---

[182] Calvin, *Institutes of the Christian Religion*, (Westminster), pp. 27-28. Prefatory Address to King Francis.

[183] Odier, *L'angoisse et la pensée magique*, p. 214.

[184] Cf. § 64, infra: Ends and Means.

[185] Isocrates, *Panegyric of Athens*, § 84.

[186] Janson, *Discours parlementaires*, vol. I, p. 124, Séance de la Chambre des Représentants, Feb 26, 1880.

[187] Isocrates, *Panegyric of Athens*, § 82.

If this is not the case, the argument by sacrifice can become ludicrous, as in the anecdote of the employer who was questioning an applicant for a job. "You're asking a very high salary," he exclaimed, "for a man of no experience." "Well," replied the applicant, "the work is all the harder when you don't know how to do it."[188]

Since the argument by sacrifice, like any argument by comparison, makes possible the evaluation of one term by the other, the way in which the comparison is made can itself give rise to an interesting argument.

From Jankélévitch:

> The Devil is strong only through our weakness; let him then be weak through our strength.[189]

From Bossuet:

> Wretched are you if your bonds are so strong that the love of God cannot break them; wretched, too, if they are so weak that you will not break them for the love of God.[190]

The first example is limited to indicating a possible inversion; one of the terms, the Devil, is considered to have a constant value. But in Bossuet's example neither of the two terms is constant: the difference between them remains, in the same direction, in two different standards of measurement. The use of *can* and *will* indicates that in the first case the strength of passions is being measured, and in the second the weakness of the love for God is shown by the sacrifice that one is unwilling to make.

It seems, indeed, that measuring by sacrifice is often connected with the idea of a movable boundary between the two elements. When the elements add up to a fixed entity, the argument from sacrifice is sometimes the same as the argument by division. This is the case when two qualities are such that, to obtain a given result, the quantity of one varies inversely as that of the other. The sacrifice then measures the importance to be attributed to the complementary elements.

Aristotle used this measurement of one good through the sacrifice of the other in this passage from the *Topics*:

> Also, if of two things we repudiate the one in order to be thought to possess the other, then that one is more desirable which we wish to be thought to possess; thus we repudiate the love of hard work in order that people may think us geniuses.[191]

---

[188] *Fun Fare*, p. 62.
[189] Jankélévitch, *Traité des vertus*, p. 795.
[190] Bossuet, *Sermons*, vol. II: *Sur l'ardeur de la pénitence*, p. 588.
[191] Aristotle, *Topics*, III, 2, 118a.

Complementariness is offered sometimes as a compensation. This also presupposes a constant total to which one refers. But the idea of compensation is more complex than that of complementariness. It presupposes, first of all, a series of reciprocal evaluations. Weakness, for example, can become the standard for election:

> ... an exquisite sense of her own weakness had brought her wondrous comfort and consolation, for it seemed like an ineffable sign of the presence of God ....[192]

Weakness is a value only in an ethics of compensation. But for the reader it also becomes an argument in favor of this ethics of compensation. It may become an argument in the eyes of a whole civilization.

These arguments of complementariness, of compensation, involving the idea of a totality, are widely used to promote a certain stability. Montesquieu argues in favor of a bicameral system by showing that compensation must be made for the numerical weakness of men who are distinguished by birth, riches, or honor through increasing the power of their votes.[193] His reasoning is based neither on a hierarchy of classes nor on experience: it is based on the maintenance of a balance.

The compensatory element can become a measure of the imperfection of what is to be completed by it. Thus, for St. Thomas, God introduces his likeness into things. But

> it is evident that no one species of creatures can successfully express the Creator's likeness. ... On the contrary where it is a question of finite and created beings, it will take many such to express under the greatest possible number of aspects the simple perfection from which they proceed.[194]

Here again, let it be noted, the argument is based on a totality, which is perfect in this instance, and therefore invariable, which the compensatory element must, at best, try to reconstitute.

The compensatory elements can sometimes both be of the same nature. It is by bringing compensation into play that Bertrand Russell, arguing against violence, but recognizing the necessity of some form of constraint, tries to lessen the incompatibility between these two positions:

> There is probably one purpose, and only one, for which the use of force by a government is beneficent, and that is to diminish the total amount of force in the world.[195]

---

[192] Bernanos, *La joie*, p. 35.

[193] Montesquieu, "De l'esprit des lois," XI, vi, *Œuvres complètes*, p. 267.

[194] Gilson, *The Christian Philosophy of St. Thomas Aquinas*, p. 153; cf. *Cont. Gent.*, II, 45, ad Cum enim, *Summa Theologica*, I, 47, 1, ad Resp.

[195] Russell, *Political Ideals*, cited by Hayakawa, *Language in Thought and Action*, p. 139.

He reasons as if the violence in the world formed a total to which no addition is lawful unless it is compensated for by at least an equal subtraction. Actually the force which is used becomes deducted from future force, which is not yet known.

In conclusion, let us insist again on the fact that arguments by sacrifice and allied arguments compare the terms and establish an interaction between them. In one of his letters, St. Jerome is addressing Pammachius who, after the death of his wife, gave all his property to the poor:

> Other husbands scatter violets, roses, lilies, and purple flowers on the graves of their wives: they are consoled in the grief of their hearts by these pious duties. My Pammachius, however, bedews the sacred ashes and honored bones with the balm of charity.[196]

Auerbach, who cites this passage, rightly notes that the flowers which are not strewn still give their scent. In this way the critic draws our attention to the flowery style of St. Jerome.[197] But for us his comment has a much more general bearing. It applies to most sacrifices. Even if they had not been dwelt upon so lovingly, the flowers which had not been strewn would already have cast their perfume. Auerbach's phrase, "die Blumen duften mit" serves to remind us that in quasi-logical argumentation an interaction between the terms is always going on.

§ 59. *Probabilities*

The increasing use of statistics and the calculus of probabilities in all areas of scientific research should not make us forget the existence of arguments, which cannot be quantified, based on the reduction of the real to series or collections of beings or events, similar in some ways and different in others. Thus Isocrates pleads against Euthynus:

> Even if Nicias had been able and willing to make a false accusation, it is obvious that he would not have made an attack against Euthynus. Those who want to do that kind of thing do not begin with their friends. If it were just to make a complaint, there is everyone to choose from. But if it is a matter of theft, you can only defraud someone who has trusted you.[198]

Since chance fails to explain the action of Nicias, Isocrates suggests that there must be another reason, namely the cogency of the accusation.

[196] St. Jerome, *Epistolae*, XVI, 5; *Patrologie Latine*, vol. XXII, col. 642.
[197] Auerbach, *Mimesis*, p. 70.
[198] Isocrates, *Against Euthynus*, §§ 8, 10.

The technique of the calculus of probabilities today enables Lecomte du Noüy to show in an analogous way that, given the very small probability that molecules as complex as the protein molecules necessary for life should form on earth, some other hypothesis is required to explain their appearance.[199]

All these arguments, which seem to move from the past to the present, take their start from a real situation or fact, whose noteworthy character they emphasize and whose argumentative value and interest they likewise increase.

Another important group of arguments is based on the concept of variability and on the advantage offered, from that point of view, by a more extensive collection of items. From Isocrates again we quote the following argument in favor of letting the young take part in deliberations:

> Since the quality of our judgments does not depend on our age but on our temperament and our faculty of attention, why not make it obligatory to call on the experience of two generations in order to make possible the choice of the wisest counsel on all matters?[200]

Similarly, in *Phaedrus*, Lysias uses this argument, among others, for preferring the nonlover to the lover:

> If you choose the best from among the lovers, you will have to choose from a small number; but if, from among all the others, you choose the one who will be most useful to you, your choice will be from a greater number, and your hope of finding someone worthy of your friendship will therefore be greater.[201]

This sort of argument could be regarded as an instance of the relation between the whole and the parts. But the parts here are the values of a variable, the useful, and the argument is aimed at increasing the range of this variable.

Also based on variability, but with somewhat different conclusions in mind, is this argument of Locke's against the tyranny of princes in matters of religion:

> For there being but one truth, one way to Heaven, what hope is there that more men would be led into it if they had no rule but the religion of the court and were put under the necessity to quit the light of their own reason? ... The narrow way would be much straitened. ... One country alone would be in the right.[202]

[199] Lecomte du Noüy, *Human Destiny*, pp. 34 et seq.
[200] Isocrates, *Archidamus*, § 4.
[201] Plato, *Phaedrus*, 231d.
[202] Locke, *A Letter Concerning Toleration*, GBWW, vol. 35, p. 4.

It should be noted that in this argument it is presupposed that all individuals are equally competent to find the right road. Without any explicit comparison, it is recommended that a system which is certainly bad be abandoned in favor of one which will probably be more advantageous.

Quasi-logical argument by the probable takes on all its special character when the evaluations are based both on the importance of events and on the probability of their occurrence—that is on the magnitude of the variables and on their frequency, on mathematical expectation. Pascal's bet is a typical case.[203] This argument compares the chances of winning or losing combined with the magnitude of what is at stake, treating all the elements involved as quantitative. In this connection we should note immediately that when comparisons bring probabilities into the reckoning, the comparisons are subject to all the interactions we have called attention to in the previous paragraphs; the introduction of probabilities merely gives them an additional dimension; when sacrifice is concerned with something which in any case there is only one chance in two of keeping, all that we have said about argumentation by sacrifice holds true nonetheless.

Application of the calculus of probabilities to behavioral problems is most often—it must be said—expressed as a wish. Adopting Locke's classification of the degrees of assent, Leibniz would have liked to recast the art of discussion and dispute by making these degrees of assent proportional to the degrees of probability of the propositions at issue. The distinction which the jurists have established between the different kinds of proof—*preuve entière, preuve plus que à demi-pleine, à demi-pleine*, and others—seemed to him to be an effort in this direction which would be worth pursuing.[204] Bentham has similar hopes, especially in evaluating the convincing power of testimony.[205] Many writers at the present time, particularly those who, more or less directly, are carrying on the utilitarian tradition, resort to arguments from probability to explain our behavior.[206] Those concerned with the theory of decision functions try, for their part, to formulate problems of choice so that they can be dealt with by means of this calculus. There is nothing against this, in spite of the technical difficulties, which have so

[203] Pascal, *Pensées*, GBWW, vol. 33, pp. 214-215.
[204] Leibniz, *Die philosophischen Schriften*, vol. V, *Nouveaux essais sur l'entendement*, pp. 445 et seq.
[205] Bentham, *The Works of Jeremy Bentham*, vol. 6: *Rationale of Judicial Evidence*, p. 220.
[206] Cf. Good, *Probability and the Weighing of Evidence*.

far been admirably surmounted—on condition that for a precise problem there be provided precise criteria of choice, particularly regarding what is considered to be an acceptable risk. Wherefore many expositions of these mathematical techniques are accompanied by a revival of Leibniz' ambitions.[207]

Indeed in every discussion where probability enters the argument—except where we are dealing with conventionally circumscribed scientific areas—objections are made to the reductions which had to be effected to insert the question into the scheme which has been proposed. J. S. Mill has already emphasized that a rough measurement of statistical frequency is no basis for confidence in the credibility of a witness. In the domain of conjecture, application of the rule of historical criticism according to which the likelihood of a text's not having been altered is greater the fewer the number of copies between it and the original[208] will be tempered by whatever may be conjectured about these copies on other counts. The argumentation is even more open to objection when it deals with behavioral problems. Of course these objections are themselves never coercive, but they can be developed on very different levels.

More particularly, it can be shown that reasoning by probabilities is but an instrument which requires for its application a series of prior agreements. Leibniz seems to have been unaware of this when he proposed (he was the first, according to Keynes) that mathematical expectation be applied to problems of jurisprudence: if two persons claim a certain sum, the sum should be apportioned according to the probabilities of their respective claims.[209] The reasoning is based on a certain conception of equity which is far from being necessarily accepted, for usually the whole sum is awarded to the person whose claim appears best founded. Van Danzig draws attention to this factor, which is independent of the calculus, in analyzing two problems presented to Pascal by the Chevalier de Méré.[210] While the first could be completely solved by the calculus, the second (which has to do with the fair division of the pot between two gamblers who do not finish the game, but whose relative standing is known) presupposes that there be an understanding about the meaning of the expression "fair division." It is indeed possible to imagine that this is proportional to the chances of each of the players, or else that the one whose probability of winning is greater should receive the whole pot.

[207] Cf. for instance Bross, *Design for Decision.*

[208] Cf. Halkin, *Initiation à la critique historique*, p. 22.

[209] Cf. Keynes, *A Treatise on Probability*, p. 311, note.

[210] Van Danzig, *Blaise Pascal en de Betekenis der Wiskundige Denkwijze voor de Studie van de Menselijke Samenleving*, p. 12.

In another connection it will be shown that argument by probability entails a reduction of the data—even when it is not a matter of quantifying them—to elements which seem more easily comparable. It was only by substituting for the moral and philosophical concepts of "good" and "bad" concepts which seemed more precise and definite, like "pleasure" and "pain," that the utilitarians could hope to base their ethics on a calculus. Other kinds of reduction are possible, but they always end up in a monism of values which by some twist makes it possible to give homogeneity to the elements that are being compared. Thus the philosophers of Port Royal, in their efforts to expose the fallacies of Jesuit probabilism—which was inclined to excuse certain acts when a favorable result might eventually arise from them— introduced the idea that it was necessary to consider not only good and evil, but also the probability they had of occurring.[211] This is a powerful argument against the probabilism of the Jesuits. But such a comparison of consequences is possible only if the consequences belong to the same order of things. Unless this is so, a favorable consequence, even of low probability, can influence the decision. Now the distinction between these orders is not one that can be taken for granted; it is generally the result of argumentation. Pascal's introduction of the concept of infinity in his bet is similar to the introduction of a concept of order. It makes the possible gain so far superior to what is put at stake that there can be no hesitation about it. But at the same time this prevents all effective comparison and puts all the weight of the argument on this concept of order.

Finally, on a more technical level, it can be shown that the complexity of the factors which must be taken into account can be extended indefinitely: the importance of a good, the probability of attaining it, the amount of information on which this probability is based, the certitude of our knowledge that something actually is a good. Each of these elements will follow from a set of reasonings which are, in most cases, of a quasi-logical nature. And, because of the very discussion, some of the important elements it deals with, such as reality, might be modified.

Let it be remembered that, in a concrete argument, the statements themselves become the object of spontaneous reasonings which interfere with the stated reasonings. In this case, there are numerous arguments by probability which deal with the truthfulness of the speaker. For some hearers these arguments can become tied up with questions

---

[211] Cf. Keynes, A Treatise on Probability, p. 308.

about the basis for the probabilities, which in turn interfere with the stated arguments.

Reasoning which is based on probabilities, whatever theoretical support may be given to the probabilities, has the general effect of imparting an empirical character to the problems. Such quasi-logical reasonings can modify the concept one has of certain fields. According to Cournot the philosophy of the probable would have been retarded by the discovery of the calculus of probabilities, because the calculus seemed inapplicable to philosophy.[212] In any case, the use of certain forms of reasoning cannot help but have a profound effect on the very conception of the data which are their object.

---

[212] Cournot, *Essai sur les fondements de nos connaissances et sur les caractères de la critique philosophique*, vol. I, pp. 171-172.

CHAPTER 2

Arguments Based on the Structure
of Reality

§ 60. *General Considerations*

Whereas quasi-logical arguments lay claim to a certain validity owing to their rational appearance, which derives from their more-or-less close relation with certain logical or mathematical formulae, the arguments based on the structure of reality make use of this structure to establish a solidarity between accepted judgments and others which one wishes to promote. How is this structure presented? On what is belief in its existence founded? These are questions which are not supposed to arise as long as the agreements which sustain the argumentation do not provoke discussion. The essential thing is that they appear sufficiently secure to allow the unfolding of the argumentation. Here is a passage in which Bossuet endeavors to increase the respect due to the teaching of preachers:

> The temple of God, Christians, contains two august and venerable places, I mean the altar and the pulpit. ... There is a very close alliance between these two holy places, and the things that are transacted in them have a wonderful relationship. ... It is because of this wonderful relationship between the altar and the pulpit that some ancient divines did not hesitate to preach to the faithful that they ought to approach both of them with equal veneration. ... That man is no less blameworthy who listens carelessly to the holy word than he who by his own fault lets fall the very body of the Son of God.[1]

---

[1] Bossuet, *Sermons*, vol. II: *Sur la parole de Dieu*, pp. 143-145.

In establishing a connection between preaching and communion, Bossuet does not believe for an instant that the prestige of the latter can suffer by it; he knows both that his hearers will in fact admit the connection which he establishes between the altar and the pulpit and how strong is their veneration for the body of Christ.

One way of displaying the close connection between various elements is to present them as inseparable parts of a single whole:

> Is the Gospel of Jesus Christ only a great assemblage of truth and falsehood, and does one have to take one part of it and reject the other? *Totus veritas*: it is all wisdom, all light, and all truth.[2]

Sometimes this connection is the result of human will, but of one which appears unshakable; one takes it or one leaves it.

> If she is pleasing to you [says old Charmides in one of Plautus' comedies] the dowry she brings to you must please you too. In short, you won't get what you want if you don't take what you don't want.[3]

Under the circumstances, the argument is comical because the dowry appears scarcely less desirable than the girl. Normally the solidarity serves to overcome a resistance, to bring about acceptance of what one does not want in order to obtain what one wants.

In the present chapter we shall analyze successively different types of arguments, classified according to the structures of reality to which they apply and which one can find in common usage. In other words we are not assuming any ontological position. What we are interested in here is not an objective description of reality, but the manner in which opinions concerning it are presented. These can, moreover, be treated as facts, truths, or presumptions.[4]

We shall examine, to begin with, the arguments which apply to relations of succession, which unite a phenomenon to its consequences or causes, as also the arguments which apply to the relations of co-existence, which unite a person to his actions, a group to the individuals who form it, and, in general, an essence to its manifestations. We shall see, after that, to what extent the symbolic tie, which links the symbol to what it symbolizes, constitutes a relation of coexistence. We shall close this chapter with an analysis of more complex arguments, for which these connections can serve as a basis, that is, arguments of double hierarchy, as well as those relating to differences of degree or of order.

---

[2] Bossuet, *Sermons*, vol. II: *Sur la soumission due à la parole de Jésus Christ*, p. 133.

[3] Plautus, *The Three Penny Day* (*Trinummus*), Act V, scene 2, 1159-1160.

[4] Cf. § 16, supra: Facts and Truths; § 17, supra: Presumptions.

Let us emphasize that we are convinced that the various types of relations we have mentioned do not exhaust the riches of living thought, and that one kind of relation shades into another. The speaker can conceive a certain reality in accordance with different types of relations. Moreover, nothing guarantees that these connections are always understood in the same way by the speaker and his hearers.

Finally, in discourse considered as reality, the meaning attributed to the connection of the argument, to what justifies the "therefore," will vary according to what the speaker says, and also according to the hearer's opinion on the subject. If the speaker claims that such a connection is compelling, the effect of the argument can be strengthened by it. It can, however, be weakened by this very claim, from the moment the hearer finds it inadequately founded and rejects it.

a) SEQUENTIAL RELATIONS

§ 61. *The Causal Link and Argumentation*

Among the sequential relations, the causal link plays, without dispute, an essential role, and its argumentative effects are as numerous as they are varied. It is immediately apparent that the causal link must allow argumentation of three types:

(a) argumentation tending to attach two given successive events to each other by means of a causal link;

(b) argumentation tending to reveal the existence of a cause which could have determined a given event;

(c) argumentation tending to show the effect which must result from a given event.

If an army, provided with an excellent information service, is very successful, one might be inclined to attribute this to the efficiency of the service in question; one can, from its actual success, infer that it possesses a good information service; one can also find support, in the efficiency of the latter, for one's expectation of future successes.

We leave the examination of the first of these three types of arguments to the sections in which we shall analyze argumentation by example and the problems which arise from inductive reasoning. For the moment we shall limit ourselves to argumentation which relies on the intervention of the causal link to try, with a given event as starting point, to increase or decrease the belief in the existence of a cause which would explain it, or of an effect which would result from it. The term "event" should moreover be used in its widest sense. Actually the relation between a principle and its consequences is often treated as a relation of succession belonging to the structure of reality.

The policeman, trying to identify the murderer in a crime committed without witnesses or other helpful clues, will direct his investigation toward those who had some interest in the death of the victim and also an opportunity to commit the crime. One must suppose that the crime had not only a cause but a motive: an accusation founded on assumptions would have to show both how and why the criminal act was committed. The *how* or the *why* will dominate the argumentation according to the interpretation one gives to certain events which are difficult to explain. In *The Ring and the Book* one half of Rome claims that Guido Franceschini was sleeping at the time of his wife's departure because she had drugged him;[5] the other half suggests that Guido simulated sleep so as not to have to intervene.[6]

Argumentation by cause presupposes, where human acts are concerned, that they are reasonable. One would not easily admit that someone had acted in a certain way if the accuser did not explain the reasons for the alleged behavior; he may even have to explain why a certain act was committed and not another which might seem preferable. Thus Aristotle says:

> In the *Medea* of Carcinus the accusers allege that Medea has slain her children; at all events, they say, they are not to be seen. ... In defense she argues that it is not her children, but Jason, whom she would have slain; for it would have been a mistake on her part not to do this if she *had* done the other. This special line of argument for enthymeme forms the whole of the *Art of Rhetoric* in use before Theodorus.[7]

To be effective this argumentation requires agreement between the interlocutors concerning the motives for action and their precedence.

It is by reason of such agreements that argumentations can arise which aim at excluding anything that seems too improbable to have happened. When an event nevertheless asserts itself as incontestable, it will have to be set in a frame which will explain its appearance. Thus, in a game of chance, the person who wins time after time will be suspected of cheating, which would make his success less improbable. In the same way, if the evidence of different witnesses agrees, this calls for an explanation other than pure chance: if the risk of collusion has

---

[5] Browning, *The Ring and the Book*, p. 56.
[6] *Ibid.*, p. 97:

"—who knows?
Sleeping perhaps, silent for certain, ..."
[7] Aristotle, *Rhetoric* II, 23, 1400b.

been excluded, one will have to recognize that the testimonies relate to an event that was really observed.

The causal link plays an important part in historical reasoning, which appeals to *retrospective probability*. Aron, following Weber, writes: "Every historian, in order to explain what has been, asks himself what could have been."[8] The cause, considered as a necessary condition for producing the phenomenon, is eliminated, in a purely theoretical construction, and the modifications which would result from this elimination are examined. Sometimes the emphasis is put especially on this modification of the effect: the lawyer defending a scientist convicted of spying will say that had there not been a war, his client, instead of being in the dock, would have been eligible for the Nobel Prize.[9]

A caricature of argumentation by causal link—wherein proof of an event is given by its cause, and vice versa—is found in an admirable episode in the second *Don Quixote*. Speaking of the wonders the hero claims to have witnessed in Montesino's cave, the disbelieving Sancho Panza exclaims:

> Now Heaven defend us ! ... Who could ever have believed that these devilish enchanters and enchantments should have so much power as to bewitch my master at this rate, and craze his sound understanding in this manner.[10]

The comical element springs here from the antinomy between the reflections on the cause by proceeding from a certain interpretation of the event and reflections on the event by proceeding from a certain interpretation of the cause.

In other circumstances, the search for the effect corresponds to the search for the cause. The argumentation develops here in a similar fashion: the event guarantees certain consequences; foreseen consequences, if they come to pass, help to prove the existence of the event which conditions them.

Finally, let us draw attention to the reasonings derived from the universal validity of the principle of causality or of the corresponding principle of responsibility. Starting from the principle that every event has a cause, people argue in favor of the eternity of a world which would never have begun. Similarly, from the fact that every act is considered either the reward for, or the punishment of, an act which preceded it, the Hindus conclude that the soul is eternal; other-

---

[8] Aron, *Introduction à la philosophie de l'histoire*, p. 164.
[9] Curtis-Bennett, defending Dr. Fuchs at his trial in April 1950.
[10] Cervantes, *Don Quixote*, vol. 2, pt. II, chap. xxiii, p. 152.

wise it would be "the bearer of a *karman* for which it would not itself be responsible."[11]

§ 62. *The Pragmatic Argument*

Value transfers between elements of the causal chain are carried out by going from cause to effect and from effect to cause. But in the first case, that of the relation we shall term descending, the link between terms—especially when dealing with persons—is normally not given by the causal relation but by a relation of coexistence.[12] Thus the devaluation of a norm by showing that it derives from a primitive custom of man on the ground that he is descended from animals, or the placing of a higher value on a child because of his parents' nobility, is brought about more by a relationship of coexistence, by the idea of essence, than by a relationship of succession.

We call that argument *pragmatic* which permits the evaluation of an act or an event in terms of its favorable or unfavorable consequences. This argument plays such an essential part in argumentation that some have wished to see in it the sole scheme of the logic of value-judgments: to judge an event one must refer to its effects. Locke, for instance, has such effects in mind when he criticizes the spiritual power of Princes:

> No peace and security, no, not so much as common friendship, can ever be established or preserved amongst men so long as this opinion prevails, that dominion is founded in grace and that religion is to be propagated by force of arms.[13]

For utilitarians, such as Bentham, there is no other satisfactory way of arguing:

> What is it to offer a *good reason* with respect to a law? It is to allege the good or evil which the law tends to produce. ... What is it to offer a *false reason*? It is the alleging for or against a law something else than its good or evil effects.[14]

The pragmatic argument seems to develop without great difficulty, for the transfer of the value of consequences to the cause comes about by itself. However, the man accused of having committed an evil act can try to break the causal link and throw the blame on another person or on circumstances.[15] If he succeeds in proving his innocence, he will,

[11] Annambhatta, *Le Compendium des Topiques*, p. 46.
[12] Cf. § 68, infra: The Person and His Acts.
[13] Locke, *A Letter Concerning Toleration*, GBWW, vol. 35, p. 7.
[14] Bentham, *The Theory of Legislation*, pp. 66-67.
[15] Cf. Cicero, *De Inventione*, II, 86; *Rhetorica ad Herennium*, II, 26.

by that very fact, have transferred the unfavorable judgment onto what will appear, at that moment, to be the cause of the action.

The pragmatic argument, which allows a thing to be judged in terms of its present or its future consequences, is of direct importance for action.[16] No justification is necessary for it to be accepted by common sense. The opposite point of view, on the contrary, requires argumentation every time it is defended. An instance is the affirmation that the truth is to be commended, whatever the consequences may be, because its value is absolute, independent of them.

The consequences, which are the basis for the value attributed to the event which causes them, can be observed or merely foreseen; they can be positive or purely hypothetical; they will influence behavior or only judgment. The connection between a cause and its consequences can be perceived with such sharpness that an immediate, emotive, unexplained transfer is brought about from the latter to the former, in such a way that one believes one prizes something for its own value, whereas in actual fact the consequences are the important thing.[17]

Argumentation by consequences may apply either to generally accepted connections, whether they are verifiable or not, or to connections known only to one person. In the latter case the pragmatic argument can be used to justify the behavior of this person. Thus in his book about anxiety neuroses Odier summarizes the reasoning of a superstitious person as follows:

> If we are thirteen at table, if I light three cigarettes with one match, well, I am disturbed and cannot do a thing. ... If, on the other hand, I insist on our being twelve or refuse to light the third cigarette, then I feel reassured and recover all my faculties. *Therefore* this insistence and this refusal are legitimate and reasonable. In short, they are logical and I behave logically.[18]

From the moment a *fact-consequence* connection is apparent, the argumentation is valid, whatever the merits of the connection itself. We note that the superstitious man rationalizes his conduct, the rationalization consisting of the use of arguments which can be accepted by his interlocutor. The superstitious man will be justified if the inter-

---

[16] Cf. Feigl, "De Principiis non Disputandum?" in *Philosophical Analysis*, edited by Max Black, p. 122, on the opposition between *justificatio actionis*, which he calls "vindication" and *justificatio cognitionis*, or "validation."

[17] Cf. remarks by Van Danzig in *Democracy in a World of Tensions*, edited by McKeon, p. 55.

[18] Odier, *Le rôle des fonctions du moi dans l'évolution psychique*, vol. I: *L'angoisse et la pensée magique*, p. 121.

locutor recognizes the usefulness of an action which spares its author discomfort or psychic distress. In general, pragmatic argument can be developed only in terms of agreement on the value of the consequences. Argumentation founded mostly on other techniques will be called to the rescue, if dispute arises and the importance of the alleged consequences has to be discussed.

The pragmatic argument is not limited to transfer of a given quality from the consequence to the cause. It makes it possible to pass from one kind of value to another, from a value inherent in the fruit to another value inherent in the tree, to infer the superiority of a particular behavior from the usefulness of its consequences. It can also, and this is when it seems most interesting from the point of view of philosophy, regard the good consequences of a thesis as proof of its truth. Calvin gives an example of this kind of reasoning, concerning the relation of free will and grace:

> But in order that the truth of this question may be more readily apparent to us, I shall presently set a goal to which the whole argument should be directed. The best way to avoid error will be to consider the perils that threaten man on both sides.[19]

A characteristic use of the pragmatic argument consists in proposing success as a criterion of objectivity, of validity. In many philosophies and religions happiness is presented as the ultimate justification of their theories, as the indication of conformity with the real, of harmony with the universal order. Stoicism does not hesitate to use such an argument. Even some existentialist philosophies, which claim to be antirationalistic, see in the failure of an existence the evident sign of its "nonauthentic" character. Contemporary drama likes to dwell on this idea.[20] The same argument is made use of in the most varied traditions, ranging from that in which the better cause is proved by the triumph of its paladin to the Hegelian realism which sanctifies history by conferring on it the role of ultimate judge. It is this bias which makes reality a guarantee of value and causes what has been born, has developed and survived, to present itself as success, as a promise of future success, as a proof of rationality and objectivity.

The pragmatic argument often takes the form of a mere estimate of something by means of its consequences. But it is very difficult to combine all the consequences of an event in a single cluster, and, on the other hand, to determine the part played by a single event in the bringing about of an effect.

[19] Calvin, *Institutes of the Christian Religion* (Westminster), vol. I, bk. II, chap. II, § 1, p. 255.
[20] Cf. Marcel, *Un homme de Dieu*; Puget, *La peine capitale*.

In order that the transfer of value may take place clearly an effort will be made to show that a certain event is the necessary and sufficient condition for another. Here is an example of such argumentation; it aims at depreciating earthly, and therefore perishable, possessions:

> Is it hard for you to have lost this or that? Do not then try to lose; for it is trying to lose to want to get what cannot be preserved.[21]

Nevertheless, apart from the cases in which cause and effect can be considered as mutually defining—when we are confronted with quasilogical argumentation—the event to be evaluated will be only a partial cause or a necessary condition. In order to place on it the whole weight of the effect, it will be necessary to reduce the importance and influence of the complementary causes, by considering them as mere occasions, pretexts, or apparent causes.

Also, when it is a question of transferring the value of an effect to the cause, to which link in the causal chain can one go back? Quintilian states that "by going back thus from cause to cause, and by selecting them, one can arrive wherever one wants."[22] But the further back one goes, the easier it will be for one's opponent to refuse his agreement. By imputing the consequences to a too distant cause, one might destroy all possibility of transfer.

Another complication of the pragmatic argument results from the obligation to take into consideration a great number of consequences, good or bad. The existence of divergent consequences formed the subject matter of the "Art" of Callippus, Aristotle tells us, and he gives the following example:

> Education exposes to envy, which is bad, and makes men wise, which is good.[23]

A sure means of fostering controversy, this consideration of favorable and unfavorable consequences seems to find a solution in the utilitarian calculus. But objections of principle have been opposed to such a philosophy.

The opponents of pragmatic argument claim the right to choose from amongst the consequences those which they think worthy of consideration in view of the object of the debate. Over and above this, the pragmatic argument is criticized by those who believe in an absolutist or formalist conception of values and, especially, of morals.

---

[21] Guigues, *Meditaciones*, chap. ii, *Patrologie latine*, vol. CLIII, col. 610b, quoted in É. Gilson, *L'esprit de la philosophie médiévale*, p. 268.
[22] Quintilian, V, x, 84.
[23] Aristotle, *Rhetoric* II, 23, 1399a.

These people accuse the pragmatic argument of reducing the sphere of moral or religious activity to a utilitarian common denominator, which eliminates the specific element in the concepts of duty, fault, or sin. Montaigne has this to say on the matter:

> ... for this sentence is justly received: That we should not judge of counsels by events. The Carthaginians punished the ill counsels of their captains, though the issue was successful. And the people of Rome often denied a triumph for great and very advantageous victories because the conduct of the general was not answerable to his good fortune.[24]

These reflections, opposed to the pragmatic argument, assume that moral and religious values are not subject to discussion, that the rules of truth and falsehood, of good and evil, of expediency and inexpediency are recognized in some other way, independently of their consequences, or at least of their actual and immediate consequences.

S. Weil is indignant that several arguments in favor of Christianity should be of the nature of "publicity for Dr. Pink's pills" and of the type of "before-and-after use." They consist of saying:

> See how mediocre men were before Christ. ...[25]

But is an argument poor because it is successful in business? Neither Calvin nor Pascal was averse to arguments of this kind. And Leibniz, an unexpected precursor of pragmatism, does not hesitate to judge the processes of argumentation themselves in terms of their consequences:

> Now this truth of the immateriality of the soul is doubtless important. For it is of infinitely greater advantage to religion and morality, especially in our time (when many people pay scant respect to miracles and revelation), to show that souls are naturally immortal and that it would be a miracle if they were not, than to maintain that our souls must, by nature, die but that, thanks to a miraculous grace, founded solely on the promise of God, they do not die. Besides, it has long been known that those who have wished to destroy natural religion and reduce everything to revelation, as if reason had nothing to teach us in this matter, are looked upon with suspicion, and not always without reason.[26]

§ 63. The Causal Link as the Relation of a Fact to Its Consequence or of a Means to Its End

The same event will be interpreted, and differently evaluated, according to the idea formed of the nature—intended or involuntary—

---

[24] Montaigne, *Essais*, bk. III, chap. VIII, 904-905.

[25] Weil, *L'enracinement*, p. 213; *The Need for Roots*.

[26] Leibniz, *Die philosophischen Schriften*, vol. V, *Nouveaux essais sur l'entendement*, pp. 60-61.

of its consequences. The cries of the new-born draw the mother's attention, but at a given moment they become a means to this end; the mother's reaction will depend very often on the intention which she attributes to them. In a general way, the fact of considering or not considering a particular behavior as a means to an end can have very important consequences and can accordingly constitute the essential object of argumentation. Depending on whether one thinks of causal succession in its aspect of the "act-consequence" relation or of the "means-end" relation, the accent will be put on the first or on the second of the two terms; if one wishes to minimize an effect, it is enough to present it as a consequence; if one wishes to enhance its importance, it should be presented as an end. It is of little moment that the increase in value is ascribable, in the first case, to the setting of the singleness of the act against the plurality of its consequences and, in the second case, to the setting of the singleness of the end against the multiplicity of the means. In any case, this consideration justifies a double criticism of the pragmatic argument: it shows that the value of the consequences is not of fixed magnitude and also seems to justify those who insist on the disqualification which the use of this argument entails for all that appears solely from then on as a means toward the results to be obtained.

The distinction between ends and consequences makes it possible to impute to an agent only some of the effects of his acts. St. Thomas justifies the existence of evil in the world in this manner:

> Now the principal form which God clearly intends in created things is the good of the universal order. But the order of the universe demands, as we already know, that certain things be deficient. God, therefore, is the cause of corruptions and defects in all things, but only because He wills to cause the good of the universal order, and, as it were, by accident. In sum, the effect of the deficient secondary cause can be attributed to the first cause, free from all defect, in what concerns the being and perfection of such an effect, but not in what concerns evil and defectiveness.[27]

Sometimes irony consists in reversing the interpretation of an event. Quintilian gives this example:

> Augustus, when the inhabitants of Tarraco reported that a palm had sprung up on the altar dedicated to him, replied, "That shows how often you kindle fire upon it."[28]

Augustus interprets the facts not as a miraculous sign, but as the consequence of neglect.

---

[27] Gilson, *The Christian Philosophy of St. Thomas Aquinas*, p. 158. Cf. *Sum. Theol.*, I, 49, 2, Ad Resp.
[28] Quintilian, VI, III, 77.

Since a single act may have several consequences, these may conflict, and the unwanted consequences may come to outweigh the desirable ends of some action, which can then appear comically inappropriate. Here is a story which Kant found very amusing:

> A rich heir paid his servants handsomely to cut dignified figures at the funeral of his father. But, the rascals, the more they were paid to look sad, the happier they became![29]

Paulhan analyzes as a "prevision of the past"[30] expressions such as "a murderer for a hundred francs" which result from the transformation of the sequence "deed-consequence" into the sequence "means-end." The debasing and shocking character of this transformation is readily apparent. But the same transformation appears less shocking when it is a matter of integrating a large number of these important though unsolicited consequences into the ends of some enterprise. This is the case, for example, when a war brings about consequences which surpass anticipations and it is affirmed afterwards that the country took up arms for the purpose of defending its existence.

Different techniques will be employed to maintain a *deed-consequence* interpretation as opposed to a *means-end* interpretation. It will be shown, for example, that the event which took place could not be an end, considering how little interest it evoked when it happened, the little fuss made of it, or the few advantages derived from it. Or else it will be shown that the act which was bound to lead to it was not a means, as it was already a consequence of a definite fact. Thus in order to prove that the division of labor was not intended by men as a means to certain ends, Adam Smith presents it as the consequence of their propensity for exchange.[31]

The transformation of an act into a means often destroys the fortunate effects it could have: it is disqualified as merely a "device." This passage from Proust illustrates the point:

> In the same way, if a man regrets that he is not sought out enough by people, I would not advise him to pay more visits and to have a still better equipage; I would tell him not to accept any invitation, to live shut up in his room, to let no one enter it, and then there will be a queue forming outside his door. Or rather I would not tell him. For this is an assured way of being sought after, which, like the way to be loved, brings results only when it is not adopted purposely, if, for instance, one keeps to one's room because one is

[29] As related by Lalo, *Esthétique du rire*, p. 159.
[30] Paulhan, *Entretien sur des faits divers*, p. 54; cf. on this point Lefebve, *Jean Paulhan*, pp. 91 et seq.
[31] A. Smith, *The Wealth of Nations*, GBWW, vol. 39, p. 6.

very ill or thinks one is, or is keeping a mistress inside, whom one prefers to the world. ...[32]

To avoid the accusation of "device," a better explanation of the behavior must be given: it may be said perhaps that it is a consequence of an act independent of the will or a means to another end than the one at issue. Thus the cult of spontaneity in art, and the presentation of art as a means to social or religious ends, are different ways of showing that the techniques of the artist are not devices, an accusation which threw discredit on rhetoric in the 19th century.[33]

When an act, the end of which is already established, produces appreciable consequences that particularly affect others, the latter can see in the act in question only a means to those consequences. In Pagnol's *César*, it will be recalled, the doctor pushes the priest carrying the holy oil away from Panisse's bed, with the words:

... And the streetcar employee with his leg cut off by the second car? After the blood transfusion he had a good chance. But when you came: it didn't take long. When he saw you, he thought he was dead and he died from thinking himself dead. ... So let me tell you it isn't your business to kill my patients. I already kill enough of them all by myself, without doing it on purpose.[34]

This disconnection of an act from its normal purpose, in favor of its consequences, can become so habitual that the original relation passes into the background. Hunting, the purpose of which was the quest for food, has become primarily a means of maintaining certain social distinctions.[35]

If an end itself brings about certain ulterior consequences, these may be taken as the real end. The agent can be made to appear ridiculous when the two phases of the events destroy each other, as may be seen in this passage from Cicero:

Your iniquity has not inflicted a miserable exile on me, but has prepared a glorious return instead.[36]

Many *antitheses* are of this type.

§ 64. *Ends and Means*

The logic of values, in its early elaborations, assumed a clear distinction between ends and means, with ultimate ends corresponding to

[32] Proust, *A la recherche du temps perdu*, vol. 12: La prisonnière, II, p. 210, in *Œuvres complètes*.
[33] Cf. § 96, infra: Rhetoric as a Process.
[34] Pagnol, *César*, p. 60.
[35] Amy, *Hommes et bêtes*, pp. 106 et seq. *Rev. de l'Inst. de Sociol.*, no. 1 (1954), 166 et seq.
[36] Cicero, *Paradoxa Stoicorum* IV, 29.

absolute values. But in practice there exists an interaction between the aims pursued and the means used to realize them. The ends are progressively constituted, made more precise, and transformed with the evolution of the situation of which the available and accepted means are a part. Certain means can be identified with ends, and can even become ends, by leaving the purpose they may serve in the vague, shadowy realm of possibility.

Modern techniques of publicity and propaganda have thoroughly exploited the plasticity of human nature which makes possible the development of new needs and the disappearance or transformation of old ones. These changes confirm that only ends stated in a general and vague manner remain invariant and universal and that the end is often made clear by examination of the means.[37]

Some ends appear desirable because the means to realize them are created or become easily accessible. To encourage sinners to repent Bossuet points out that God provides them with the means of salvation.

> He [God] refuses to sinners nothing that they need. They require three things: divine mercy, divine power, and divine patience.[38]

Some ends appear all the more desirable as their realization is easy. It is therefore useful to show that if, up to the present, no success has been obtained, the reason is either ignorance of the right means or neglect to use them. Let us note, in this regard, that the impossible and the difficult or their opposites, the possible and the easy, do not always concern technical impossibilities and difficulties, but also moral ones, that which stands in opposition to demands, that which entails sacrifices one is not willing to make. These two points of view, though they may usefully be distinguished, are not, as Sartre's analyses have shown, independent of one another.[39]

In certain cases, the means can become an end to be pursued for itself. Goblot gives a good example taken from the realm of love:

> One loves already when one senses in the loved one a source of inexhaustible, vague, unknown happiness. ... Then the loved one is still a means—a means that is unique and impossible to replace, to countless, vague ends. ... One really loves, one loves one's friend *for himself*, as the miser loves his gold, when, the end having ceased to be considered, the means have become the end, and the value of the beloved has ceased to be relative and has become absolute.[40]

---

[37] Cf. Barnes, "Ethics without Propositions," *Aristotelian Society*, Suppl. vol. XXII (1948), 16.

[38] Bossuet, *Sermons*, vol. II: *Sur la pénitence*, p. 71.

[39] Sartre, *Being and Nothingness*, pp. 464 et seq.

[40] Goblot, *La logique des jugements de valeur*, pp. 55-56.

In social life, it is more often than not agreement on a means, capable of realizing different ends, not equally appreciated by all, which leads to the separation of this means from the ends which confer on it its value and to its use as an independent end.[41] Moreover, the best technique for enlarging this agreement is to see in it an agreement on ends, that is, on what appears to be the most important. To insist that the agreement concerns only a means leading to various ends is to insist on what is temporary, precarious, and secondary in the agreement.

In the same spirit, in order to show that in future the worker's well being and joy in his work ought to be of first importance, S. Weil would like these to be considered as an end in themselves and not as a simple means to increase the output:

> Up to now the technicians have never had anything else in view but the needs of production. If they began always to have the needs of the workers in mind, the whole technique of production would have to be gradually changed.[42]

The appeal for a change of goal has something generously revolutionary about it.

The reverse process which would turn an end into a means has a depreciative effect. It is against the reduction of morality to a simple technique directed to an end—however important—that Jankélévitch rebels, for the essential thing is not the end but the method, "the interval is the all-important thing":

> You say: it is not necessary to suffer, but to get well. ... In this identification of moral activity with techniques, who does not recognize the philosophy of the pharisaic approximation, that is, of trickery? Certainly if one can get well without cutting and cauterizing, one can go right ahead. But moral law tells us that we shall have to labor in pain and that anesthesia would be the most serious trickery, because it does not recognize this means which is the end itself.[43]

In order to avoid disqualification of the values he is dealing with, without, however, sacrificing a good argument involving the usefulness of the values as a means toward an end which is recognized independently to be good, many a speaker will mention this usefulness, but will at the same time stress the redundant character of the argument and protest that he uses it only because of the audience he is addressing. In this connection it is to be observed that before certain audiences and in certain circumstances mention of too lofty values might reduce them to the rank of means.

[41] Cf. Stevenson, *Ethics and Language* (Yale), p. 193.
[42] Weil, *L'enracinement*, p. 57; *The Need for Roots*.
[43] Jankélévitch, *Traité des vertus*, p. 38.

It is to be noted also that choosing among values and giving a preference to those one favors often leads to treating, or appearing to treat, them as means. Thus Ignatius de Loyola, when he entreats the Pope not to give a bishopric to a Jesuit, says:

> I do not wish cupidity and ambition to take away from us everything that up to now has grown by charity and scorn of the world.[44]

When two activities confront each other, the one one wishes to subordinate to the other, and so devaluate, will be presented as the means, as in the maxim: "One should eat to live, and not live to eat." Very pungent argumentation sometimes results from such a reversal, which can occur whenever the causal chain presents a continuous succession of two alternate elements. This explains the search for, and construction of, similar schemes expressly for the purposes of argumentation. Often the interaction between elements will be expressed by such alternations, making it possible to treat what gains adherence most readily as an end.

An activity may, however, be evaluated as a means. This evaluation does not result from the transformation of an end into a means, but from the importance something of a completely neglected or even negative value is recognized to possess as an instrument. In the following passage, Demosthenes hesitates to speak about himself in self-congratulatory terms, but decides to do so because it is an effective means:

> While I am well aware, Athenians, that to talk in this assembly about oneself and one's own speeches is a very profitable practice, if one has the necessary effrontery, I feel it is so vulgar and so offensive that, though I see the necessity, I shrink from it. I believe, however, that you will form a better judgment of what I am going to propose, if I remind you of a few things that I have said on former occasions.[45]

We should be careful not to praise ourselves, "unless we have in prospect some great advantage to our hearers or to ourselves."[46]

It must not be forgotten that, though it may be true that the end justifies the means, this is not always the case, for the use of the means may be blameworthy in itself or have disastrous consequences outweighing the end one wished to secure. Nevertheless, the attribution of a noble purpose to a crime will reduce the horror felt with respect not only to the criminal, but also to his act. Political murders and the

---

[44] Rivadeneira, *Vida del bienaventurado padre Ignacio de Loyola*, p. 277.
[45] Demosthenes, *On the Peace*, § 4.
[46] Plutarch, *Moralia: On Praising Oneself Inoffensively*, 547.

crimes of idealists, even when they are punished more severely than a sordid crime, are not met with unreserved moral condemnation.

The choice of a certain end makes it possible to place a high value on an act which is ordinarily condemned. Thus, Claudel, far from presenting woman as the instrument of original sin, sees in her a condition for Redemption.[47]

The choice is often made between ends situated apart in time. But there are a great many other ways of substituting one end for another, of subordinating them. The distinction made by the Stoics between the purpose of the action and the goal of the agent places both ends in the present, but makes the former a means toward the latter.[48] The replacement of an apparent end by a real one[49] will have all the greater an argumentative effect as the audience is taken by surprise. It is said that Harry Stack Sullivan deterred certain mental cases from suicide by showing them that their suicidal tendency was nothing else than an attempt to be born again differently.[50]

The substitution of ends in order to enhance the means may reduce itself to the choice of the end most favorable to the argumentation, without any claim that one is better than the others. We may appeal, as Quintilian says,

> ... to the interests of the State, of a number of persons, of our opponent himself, or finally, at times, of ourselves. ... Under the same heading as the appeal to public or personal interest comes the plea that the act in question has prevented the occurrence of something worse.[51]

All we have just said about enhancing the value of the means through the end is, with a change of sign, equally applicable to what is regarded as an obstacle to the realization of this end.

If the value of the means is to be enhanced by the end, the means must obviously be effective; but this does not mean that it has to be the best. The determination of the best means is a technical problem, which requires various data to be brought into play and all kinds of argumentation to be used. The means which prevails—the means requiring the smallest sacrifice for the end anticipated—enjoys a value which is, this time, inherent in this superiority.

---

[47] Cf. Beauvoir, *Le deuxième sexe*, p. 343.
[48] Cf. Goldschmidt, *Le système stoïcien et l'idée de temps*, pp. 146-149.
[49] Cf. § 92, infra: The Role of Philosophical Pairs and Their Transformations.
[50] Mary White, in *The Contributions of Harry Stack Sullivan*, edited by Patrick Mullahy, p. 147.
[51] Quintilian, VII, iv, 9, 12.

The possible danger in treating something as a means is thus increased by the fact that one can always find a means that is more effective for a given end.

It is evident that the determination of the best means depends on the exact definition of the end pursued. And then the man arguing in terms of the best means will be tempted to divide the problems in such a way as to eliminate all consideration of values other than those that relate to the end in view. Certain technical disciplines are geared in this direction. On the other hand, everyday reasoning can rarely avail itself of this kind of schematic approach.

Since technical discussion about the best means depends on agreement as to the end, the speaker will sometimes ask his interlocutor for specific agreement on the end, while at other times he will attribute to his interlocutor an end which the latter would not dare to repudiate, and the means will be discussed in terms of it. Then again, if a means is recognized as ineffective for producing the proclaimed end, a person insisting on and using this means will always be suspected and accused of seeking an unavowed end. Thus, assertion of the ineffectiveness of a means often influences much more the discussion of the ends than the technical problem of the best means.

An outstanding instance of the technical problem of the best means is provided by arguments considered as means of persuasion. Nothing makes it permissible to assert that there is an argument that is the best for everyone. As St. Theresa puts it:

> Some people make progress by meditating on hell, others by meditating on heaven, as they are disturbed by the thought of hell; others again are distressed by the thought of death.[52]

Hence the close relationship between the technical problem of effective argumentation and the problem of the audience.

The discourse itself can, as we know, become the object of reflection. It can be treated as a fact producing consequences, as a consequence, as a means, as an end. The thoughts of the hearer in this matter will sometimes modify strongly the effect produced by the discourse. And, to be more precise, the hypothesis that any intentional act whatever must have a reason, that it constitutes a means toward a certain end, will justify the rejection of any interpretation of the discourse which would make the latter ridiculous or useless. This is the concept that serves as basis for the arguments *ab absurdo* and *ab inutili sensu* that are used in the theory of interpretation.[53]

---

[52] Santa Teresa de Jesús, *Vida*, p. 115.
[53] Berriat Saint-Prix, *Manuel de logique juridique*, 47-48.

§ 65. *The Argument of Waste*

The following arguments refer to the succession of events, of situations, in a manner which, though it does not put the idea of causality in the foreground, does not necessarily exclude it.

The argument of waste consists in saying that, as one has already begun a task and made sacrifices which would be wasted if the enterprise were given up, one should continue in the same direction. This is the justification given by the banker who continues to lend to an insolvent debtor in the hope of getting him on his feet again in the long run. This is one of the reasons which, according to Saint Theresa, prompt a person to pray, even in a period of "dryness." One would give up, she says, if it were not

> ... that one remembers that it gives delight and pleasure to the Lord of the garden, that one is careful not to throw away all the service rendered, and that one remembers the benefit one hopes to derive from the great effort of dipping the pail often into the well and drawing it up empty.[54]

By giving them a certain twist, the arguments of the possible and the easy can be linked up with the argument of waste. It is not the person concerned, but the deity or nature or fortune which seems to have taken pains which should not be scorned. Hence also the advice to fall into step and carry forward a development which has already begun: one is asked not to hinder these natural or social forces which have already been manifested and constitute a sort of outlay.

Bossuet uses the argument to reproach impenitent sinners for squandering the sacrifice made by Jesus by not profiting from the possibilities of salvation he offered.[55]

One can assimilate to this argument all those which stress an opportunity not to be missed or a means which exists and should be used.

The same argument will be used to incite someone with talent, skill, or an exceptional gift, to use it to the fullest extent. For an analogous reason, Volkelt refuses to consider two words that exist in a language as identical: to do so would be to waste the richness of the means of expression.[56]

Similarly, one feels regret when one sees an almost successful effort or a nearly perfect work, which does not reach full completion. This is what Polyeucte is saying of Pauline:

---

[54] Santa Teresa de Jesús, *Vida*, p. 96.
[55] Bossuet, *Sermons*, vol. II: *Sur la pénitence*, p. 72.
[56] Volkelt, *Gewissheit und Wahrheit*, p. 169, note 1.

> She has too many virtues not to be Christian:
> It pleased you to form her with too much merit
> For her not to know and love you,
> For her to live as the unfortunate slave of Hell.[57]

Particularly valued is the thing whose presence will nicely round off a whole, which can then be considered as being in the very nature of things. In an optimistic conception of the world, the idea of waste encourages the completion of structures, by embodying in them the thing whose absence is felt to be a lack.[58]

The feeling of loss can play a part even when one does not exactly know of what the lost opportunity consists. This harrowing aspect of the argument is well expressed by the hero of *Quand le navire* ...:

> "Missing," "What you miss." I heard again these words. I admitted to myself that they were poignant. To nearly touch something, to be within two inches of something. To miss it. Even without knowing what one misses, one can feel very well the essential tragedy of one's situation.[59]

As soon as the conviction of missing something is established, it reinforces the value of the effort that is squandered in this way.

Ignorance is an important instance of loss. It is felt to be responsible for the loss of what nature, effort, and suffering might achieve. The tragedy of waste echoes in this line from Arvers' sonnet:

> And she who did it never knew anything of it.

The argument of waste is thus an encouragement to knowledge, study, curiosity, and investigation.

The argument of waste recalls that of the useless sacrifice. The sacrifice is the measure of its determining value, but if this value is minimal, the sacrifice is depreciated in turn. In *Le guerrier appliqué*, Sièvre, when wounded, says simply and stoically: "What must be, must be." Comments Jacques Maast:

> Though there were good reasons for fighting, nothing less [than this wound] was required to have him realize it.[60]

The sacrifice, when realized and accepted, increases and enhances the reasons for the struggle and prompts one to continue fighting.

It was by an analogous process that certain Nazi torturers tried to explain how they reached the point of treating their prisoners with

---

[57] Corneille, *Polyeucte*, Act IV, scene III.
[58] Cf. § 74, infra: Other Relations of Coexistence, Act and Essence.
[59] Romains, *Psyché*, vol. III: *Quand le navire* ..., pp. 194-195.
[60] Lefebve, *Jean Paulhan*, p. 165. Paulhan, *Le guerrier appliqué*, pp. 122 and 125.

bestiality: the first pain inflicted on a man makes the perpetrator a sadist unless torture is continued up to the point when the victim talks.

The preference given to that which is *decisive* can be connected also with the argument of waste. There is a temptation to give one's vote to a candidate, if one believes that this vote could bring victory. The argument does not consist in saying that the winner must be followed, but in advising a person to act in such a way that, by virtue of the suggested action, there will be a winner. The action, which, under the circumstances, can attain its full bearing and should thus not be considered a waste, will thereby gain in value, and this militates in favor of its being done.

Conversely, an action may be devaluated by stressing its *unnecessary* character. The superfluous, by virtue of being superfluous, decreases in value. While the argument of waste prompts one to continue the action begun until final success, the argument of redundancy prompts one to abstain from action, since any additional action would be of no avail. Thus, for Leibniz, if one is to imagine an intelligent creator of the world, this intelligence must not appear redundant:

> When one is seriously involved in these sentiments which ascribe everything to the necessity of matter or to chance happening, ... it is difficult to recognize an intelligent creator of nature. For the effect must correspond to its cause and is even better known through knowledge of its cause, and it is unreasonable to introduce a sovereign intelligence that orders things and then, instead of using its wisdom, use the properties of matter only to explain the phenomena.[61]

In the field of axiomatics, the attempt to make axioms independent is justified by the same reasoning: a system is less elegant if it contains a superfluous axiom.

In political economy, the loss in value of commodities partly destined for quasi-superfluous needs is attacked under the theory of marginal utility. This loss in value has sometimes served as a basis of argument in favor of socialism where the issue was promotion of an order in which riches gained in value through a more equal distribution and which discouraged their useless accumulation in a relatively few hands.

§ 66. *The Argument of Direction*

The causal link, the connection between ends and means, has up to now been dealt with in a global and static way. But it is possible to

---

[61] Leibniz, *Die philosophischen Schriften*, vol. IV, *Discours de métaphysique*, pp. 445-446.

split up the pursuit of an end into several stages and to consider the manner in which the situation is transformed: the viewpoint will be incomplete, but dynamic. It is often found to be better not to confront the interlocutor with the whole interval separating the existing situation from the ultimate end, but to divide this interval into sections, with stopping points along the way indicating partial ends whose realization does not provoke such a strong opposition. Though the passage from point A to C may cause difficulties, it might happen that no objection may be seen to passing from point A to B, from which point C will appear in a quite different light. We may call this technique the *device of stages*. The structure of reality conditions the choice of these stages but never imposes it.

The argument of direction consists, essentially, in guarding against the use of the device of stages: if you give in this time, you will have to give in a little more next time, and heaven knows where you will stop. This argument is used frequently in negotiations between states and between representatives of management and workers when a party does not want to seem to yield to force, threats, or blackmail.

The argument of direction can be used whenever an end can be made to look like a stopping point, marking a stage in progress in a certain direction. This argument answers the question: What are you driving at? For we frequently break up a problem in order to make acceptable a solution which at first sight seems disagreeable. If we wish somebody to make a speech on a certain occasion, but he is reluctant to do so, we shall first convince him that a speech has to be made and then go on to find the best speaker, or, conversely, we shall show him first that, if a speech must be made, he is the only one to make it, and, later, that it is indispensable that the speech be made.

It is, however, possible for the division to be not only useless, but actually damaging. This would be the case, if Mr. X loves speaking in public. In this situation, it will be better to propose to him, all in one, that he make a speech on a certain occasion.

The manner in which division will be made depends on the speaker's estimate of the relative ease with which certain stages can be negotiated. The order in which the speaker envisages the stages will seldom be a matter of indifference. Once a first stage is passed, the interlocutors find themselves facing a new configuration of the situation which modifies their attitude toward the final issue. In certain cases, one of the characteristics of this new situation will be the opportunity to use the argument of waste, the first stage being considered as an outlay.

Any argument by degrees could be related to a device of stages. However, it will be condemned as a device, and will be fought by use of the argument of direction, only when a decision is asked for at each phase of the argumentation, and this decision is capable of modifying the way in which a later decision is considered.

Further, it is advisable to distinguish the argument of direction from the fear of precedent, which resembles it in that it is opposed to an action from fear of its repercussion on other actions in the future. But whereas fear of precedent concerns other actions of the same kind, the argument of direction evokes actions which, although different from the action under consideration, will bring about a change in the same direction. Nevertheless, there are cases which lie between fear of precedent and the argument of direction: the cases where recurrence comes into play, with the same operation repeating itself, though in a modified situation. Such a tendency to recurrence is often put forward as a reason for guarding against certain constructions. Thus G. Ryle, criticizing the intellectualist doctrine, according to which an intelligent act is one which is preceded by an intelligent theoretical activity, tells us that this requirement will be followed by a series of others:

> Must we then say that, for the hero's reflections how to act to be intelligent, he must first reflect how best to reflect how to act?[62]

The device of stages can become a positive argument in favor of a measure regarded as a first step in a direction one wants to take. This argument may, however, be only a feint, a delaying maneuver; the speaker may pretend to regard a reform, a measure, as a steppingstone in a certain direction, while he has secretly made up his mind not to continue or at least only to continue with "prudent" slowness. Bentham examines, among the delaying fallacies, the use of the snail's pace argument. The instrument of deception here, he writes:

> consists in holding up to view the idea of graduality or slowness. ... To the epithet *gradual*, are commonly added such eulogistic epithets as *moderate* and *temperate*.[63]

Here the fact of presenting as a steppingstone what in the eyes of its promoters is, if they could have their way, a final measure had no other purpose than to enhance this first step in the eyes of partisans of more drastic reforms.

The argument of direction always aims at making a stage and later developments interdependent. The person defending himself against this argument seeks to isolate the proposed measure and to have it

---

[62] Ryle, *The Concept of Mind*, p. 31.
[63] Bentham, *Works*, vol. II: *The Book of Fallacies*, pt III, Fallacies of Delay, p. 433.

examined separately; he assumes that it will not bring about any changes in the total situation and asserts that the situation can be considered in the same state of mind after the measure is adopted as it could before. If, then, the argument of direction is to be challenged, the action under debate must exhibit an advantage in itself and be capable of evaluation independently of the direction it leads to. May not the great art in intellectual or moral education consist in the capacity for selecting stages, each of which presents an interest of its own, independent of the fact that they facilitate passage to a later stage? The order of the arguments in discourse will have to allow for this same consideration.

The argument of direction, conjuring up the slippery slope or the toe over the threshold, insinuates that there can be no stopping on the way. More often than not, past experience alone makes it possible to decide, in this matter, between the antagonists.

Here is a good example of the use of the argument of direction, in connection with experiments on animals:

> Experimental medicine practiced on animals accepted the idea that, for the furtherance of human medicine, animals might be sacrificed. Soon the idea arose that, for the benefit of all mankind, some human beings could be sacrificed. At first this idea certainly raised strong inner defenses, but habit always finally prevails. People begin by accepting the idea of experimenting on men under sentence of death, then comes the idea of experimenting on ordinary prisoners, and finally there arises the idea of experimenting on one's enemies! The progress of ideas is, as one sees, extremely formidable and at the same time very insidious.[64]

When he brings up the idea of familiarization, Dr. Baruk furnishes a reason in support of the thesis which forms the essence of the argument of direction, namely, that we are not in control of our subsequent behavior and that we will not be able to stop at a particular stage of a development in a certain direction.

The argument of direction implies, then, the existence of a series of stages toward a certain—usually dreaded—end and, with it, the difficulty, if not the impossibility, of crying halt once one has started on the road leading to that end. The retorts to this argument will therefore bear on one or the other of these points.

The first obvious reply to the argument of direction consists in showing developments arising out of the first stage that are different from those that might be feared. Stress will be laid on the ambiguity of

---

[64] Baruk, "Le psychiatre dans la société," *La Semaine des Hôpitaux de Paris*, 74(1949), 3046-3047.

development and, consequently, on the arbitrariness of seeing only a single possible direction.

This reply can, it must be added, raise other objections and, more especially the fear of not knowing toward what one is heading; one fears the unforeseeable consequences of the first disturbance:

> But the novelty, Philonus, the novelty! There lies the danger. New notions should always be discountenanced; they unsettle men's minds, and nobody knows where they will end.[65]

One may show also that there is a qualitative difference between the stage under discussion and the following ones of which one is apprehensive. Thus B. S. Chlepner insists on the difference existing between the nationalization of certain concerns and the socialist economy to which nationalization seems to lead:

> Hence it can be maintained that the nationalization of a concern, or even of a whole industrial branch, is not a socialist measure since the rest of the economy continues to be based on the principle of private initiative and of the market economy and since the nationalized branch is itself subject to the discipline of the market, particularly by paying its way by means of sales rather than by means of subsidies from the state.
> ... The only point we want to stress is that, between a socialized economy and one certain branches of which have been nationalized, there is more than a quantitative difference. The atmosphere is different, or, at least, might be different.[66]

The second kind of reply concerns the possibility of stopping after a certain stage is reached. Ordinarily the halt will be guaranteed by the creation of a formal, juridical framework which will prevent going beyond what has been decided. The main thing is to know to what extent a formalism is able to oppose a natural evolution. Another customary way of anticipating the halt is to show a balance of forces which will prevent an indefinite progress in a certain direction. It is assumed that a pluralism exists which justifies the hope of a resistance that will progressively grow as movement in a certain direction continues. This argument is suitable for those who are opposed to extreme solutions.

Finally, there is yet another argument, which consists in showing that one is already on the fatal slope one fears, and that it is essential to take a first step in a certain direction, so as to be able to stop after that step has been taken. This is Demosthenes' favorite argument.

---

[65] Berkeley, *The Works of George Berkeley*, vol. II: "Three Dialogues between Hylas and Philonous," Third Dialogue, p. 243.

[66] Chlepner, "Réflexions sur le problème des nationalisations," *Revue de l'Institut de Sociologie*, (1949), p. 219.

Thus, his reply to those who would not aid Megalopolis, when it was threatened by Sparta, because the city was an ally of Thebes, was the following:

> If the Lacedemonians take Megalopolis, Messene will be imperiled. If they take Messene too, I predict that we shall become allies of Thebes. Is it not then a far more advantageous and honorable course to spontaneously welcome the allies of Thebes, thus thwarting the cupidity of the Lacedemonians, than to shrink from protecting a city because it is an ally of Thebes, and so sacrifice it, only to have to rescue the Thebans themselves later and, in addition, be afraid for our own safety?[67]

According to Demosthenes, then, one has to take a step in order not to be led into taking another, which would be much more serious.

One might ask whether these two kinds of answers—those that put the accent on the nature of the course, and those which bear on the possibility of calling a stop—can be combined for the benefit of a single hearer. It would seem that they can. The hearer would be effectively reassured by a combined argumentation, which would show him that something else was involved than what he feared and would also show him the possibility of stopping.

The argument of direction can take different forms. One of these is the *propagation* argument. One cautions against certain phenomena, which, through the medium of natural and social mechanisms, would tend, by a process of gradual transmission, to multiply and, by the very fact of this growth, become harmful.

If the initial phenomenon is itself already considered a bad thing, one will usually resort to the notion of *contagion*. So we find Pitt advising that the revolutionary principles be nipped in the bud:

> If once the principles of jacobinism should obtain a footing in the French West-India islands, could we hope that our own would be safe from contagion?[68]

In the contagion argument there is therefore a collusion between two devaluating points of view; what is feared as a stepping-stone is at the same time stigmatized as an evil.

In the *popularization* argument, the perspective is quite different. The warning is against a propagation which would lower the value, by making it appear common and vulgar, of that which is distinctive because it is rare, limited, and secret. Conversely, but in an analogous

---

[67] Demosthenes, *For the People of Megalopolis*, §§ 20, 21.
[68] Pitt, *Orations on the French War*, "On Wilberforce's Peace Amendment," Dec. 30, 1794, p. 61.

perspective, the *consolidation* argument warns against repetitions which give full significance and value to what was a mere sketch, an inarticulate whisper, a fantasy, but will become a myth, a legend, a rule of behavior.

Finally, there are a number of variations of the argument of direction which lay stress on the *change of nature* between the first stage-and the conclusion. The typical example of this is the sorites of the Greeks in which the step from a pile of wheat to a pile minus one grain, continuously repeated, ends in the nonexistence of the heap. The change may be interpreted as a real change of nature or as the revelation of the real nature of the first steps. It does not much matter. But it is something to which attention must be paid. As Camus says:

> Each concession made to the enemy and to the spirit of accommodation led to another. This one was no worse than the first, but the two together constituted an act of cowardice. Two acts of cowardice put together became dishonor.[69]

The humorous aspect of these changes of nature gives rise to such jests as the remark of P. Oppius about the family of the Lentuli, to the effect that since the children were always smaller than their parents, the race would perish by propagation.[70]

All these developments, whether identified with the notion of contagion, of popularization, of consolidation, or of change of nature, show that a phenomenon, when inserted in a dynamic series, acquires a different significance from what it would have if taken separately. This significance varies according to the part it is made to play in the series.

§ 67. *Unlimited Development*

Contrary to the argument of direction, which raises the fear that an action will involve us in a process with an outcome that fills us with alarm, arguments with *unlimited development* insist on the possibility of always going further in a certain direction without being able to foresee a limit to this direction, and this progress is accompanied by a continuous increase of value. As a peasant woman says in one of Jouhandeau's stories: "The more it is good, the better it is."[71] Thus Calvin asserts that one can never go too far in the direction which attributes all glory and all virtue to God:

---

[69] Camus, *Actuelles*, p. 57.
[70] Quintilian, VI, iii, 67.
[71] Jouhandeau, *Un monde*, p. 251.

But we do not read of anyone being blamed for drinking too deeply of the fountain of living water.[72]

By presenting it in this light, it is possible to defend behavior which the hearers would be tempted to blame, were it not assigned a place in the protraction of that which they approve and admire: for example, nationalist fanaticism in the eyes of patriots, or religious fanaticism in the eyes of believers. *Unlimited development* can also be used to depreciate a state or situation which could have given satisfaction, but to which a more favorable condition is supposed to be able to follow. Pitt made this reply to those who thought the military situation sufficiently good to open peace negotiations with France:

> That something more of this security exists at the present moment, I not only admit, but contend that the prospect is improving every day, and that this becomes more and more ascertained.[73]

What is important is not the achievement of a certain objective, the arrival at a certain stage, but continuing, going further, passing beyond, in the direction indicated by two or three stepping-stones. The important thing is not a well-defined end: Each situation, on the contrary, serves as a stepping-stone or springboard permitting indefinite advance in a certain direction.

This kind of reasoning is used not only to promote a certain behavior but also, particularly in philosophical works, to define certain "purified" notions, stemming from common-sense conceptions which are presented as a starting point. Thus Sartre, starting from a concept of bad faith which, to begin with, is inspired by common sense, ends up, by virtue of *unlimited development*, with a concept which is far removed from it, under which every social or rational commitment is found to be more or less tainted with bad faith.[74]

In the same way, Claparède shows in an amusing analysis, to which we have alrady referred elsewhere, how the meaning of the word "associationism" is always gradually evolving in a certain direction. This evolution recalls the attitude of the person of revolutionary temperament who does not define himself in terms of a rigid program, but by the fact of being always more to the left.[75]

---

[72] Calvin, *Institutes of the Christian Religion* (Westminster), vol. I, p. 13, Prefatory Address to King Francis.

[73] Pitt, *Orations on the French War*, "On Wilberforce's Motion in Favour of a General Pacification," May 27, 1795, p. 93.

[74] Sartre, *Being and Nothingness*, pp. 67 et seq. Cf. § 48, supra: Techniques for Presenting Theses as Compatible or Incompatible.

[75] Claparède, "La genèse de l'hypothèse," *Archives de Psychologie*, vol. XXIV (1934), p. 45; cf. Perelman and Olbrechts-Tyteca, "Les notions et l'argumentation," *Archi-*

In order to provide a basis for this conception of an *unlimited direction* with hierarchized terms, one will present at the end an ideal which is unrealizable, but whose realizable terms will constitute incarnations that are ever more perfect, ever purer, and ever closer to the ultimate term.[76] The realizable terms will be the "mirror," the "image" of the ultimate term. In other words, there is a descending movement from the ideal to them which guarantees the inaccessible character of that ideal, whatever the progress achieved.

In other instances the ideal is conceived only through the inferior terms which are opposed and surpassed. Thus to Lecomte du Noüy:

> Biologically, therefore, man remains an animal. Later on, we shall see that this was necessary, for it is by fighting against his instincts that he humanizes himself.[77]

This technique is often employed to transform arguments "against" into arguments "for," to show that what was up to that point regarded as an obstacle is in reality a means for reaching a superior station, like the illness which makes an organism more resistant by giving it immunity.

The refutation of an argumentation by means of *unlimited development* lies in the statement that it is impossible to go indefinitely in the direction indicated, either because one encounters an absolute or because one ends up with an incompatibility. To end up with an absolute, perfect term is to recognize that the hope of further progress must be abandoned. Pascal, who adopts the Cartesian point of view in his manner of treating definitions, asserts:

> As we proceed ever further with our investigations, we come of necessity to primitive words which can no longer be defined and to principles so clear that it is no longer possible to find others more clear for their demonstration.[78]

Under these conditions, it is out of the question to further pursue an ideal, to increase a value, since the perfection reached stands in opposition to the capacity for improvement. Another thing which can stand in the way of continued progress and an *unlimited development* is the danger of appearing ridiculous as a result of incompatibility with values one is loath to give up: one must accordingly seek an equilibrium which will make it possible to harmonize values, which, if carried to

---

vio di Filosofia, vol. *Semantica,* pp. 260-261; and § 35, supra: Argumentative Usage and Plasticity of Notions.

[76] Cf. Plotinus, *Enneads,* I, 2, § 6.

[77] Lecomte du Noüy, *Human Destiny,* p. 84.

[78] Pascal, *On Geometrical Demonstration,* GBWW, vol. 33, p. 431.

their furthest limit, would come in conflict. Cautioning against the excesses to which unlimited fidelity to a maxim, or a line of behavior, may lead always involves the introduction of other values for which respect is demanded. Thus, the Stoics warn against an excess of contempt for the body, which would lead to unreasonable suicide. And the theologian who asserts that the ways of God are inscrutable is obliged to modify this assertion in one way or another, or theology becomes impossible. He will say, for instance, that the ways of God are inscrutable by the light of nature or without revelation.

In argumentation using unlimited development, the hearers are often more interested in the value which such argumentation confers on certain terms which fall short of the ultimate term, but are really the center of the debate, than they are in the ultimate, always receding, term in a given direction.

This becomes clear when one looks at the figures that are intended to serve the purposes of unlimited development. We have in mind, particularly, *hyperbole* and *litotes*.

Hyperbole is an extreme form of expression. As Dumarsais put it:

> We use words which, taken literally, go beyond the truth and represent the most or the least in order to convey some excess up or down. Our hearers discount from our words what needs to be discounted.[79]

Hyperbole differs from the usual argumentation by means of unlimited development in that it is not justified or prepared, but fired with brutality: its role, however, is to give a direction to thought, to guide it toward a favorable evaluation of this direction, and only by a return shock is it intended to give an indication of the significant term. Hence the enormous margin of liberty in statements, be they simple assertions of fact, as in this example, taken from the *Aeneid*:

> Twin rocks threaten heaven[80]

or be they in the form of similes, as in this example, from Bossuet's oration at Condé's funeral:

> ... In his bold leaps and light steps, like to those vigorous, bounding animals, he advances only in lively and impetuous spurts, and neither mountains nor precipices can stop him.[81]

---

[79] Dumarsais, *Des tropes*, p. 98.

[80] Quoted by Quintilian, VIII, vi, 68, *Aeneid*, I, 162-163.

[81] Quoted by Saint-Aubin, *Guide pour la classe de rhétorique*, p. 90. Text based on Bossuet, "Oraison funèbre de Louis de Bourbon, Prince de Condé," *Oraisons funèbres. Panégyriques*, p. 216.

Hyperboles using concrete expressions do not, as Erdmann has already pointed out,[82] try to create an image. Their role is to provide a reference which draws the mind in a certain direction only to force it later to retreat a little, to the extreme limit of what seems compatible with its idea of the human, the possible, the probable, with all the other things it admits.

Dumarsais, who sees in hyperbole only the element of exaggeration, and not that of unlimited development which seems to us essential, feels loathing for this manner of expressing oneself which is characteristic of "orientals" and "young people." He recommends the use of hyperbole only with such rhetorical precautions as "so to speak," and "if one may say so," which would reduce it to a mere figure of style. Now the very person who uses these oratorical precautions does not want them taken too seriously. For unlimited development is certainly what hyperbole aims at, when it has an argumentative purpose, as it almost always does. This is seen in this maxim of Audiberti which is quoted by Paulhan as an example of hyperbole:

Nothing will be but what has been.[83]

Unlimited development is used to give positive value to the past.

It is to be noted that the ancients often distinguished between two kinds of hyperbole—hyperbole by exaggeration and hyperbole by attenuation— which they considered to be very different. An example of hyperbole by attenuation is the Virgilian

Scarce cling they to their bones.[84]

But with its abstract character, Audiberti's maxim can be interpreted in either way, and it shows clearly that diminution and enlargement form in hyperbole a single process of unlimited development.

Litotes is generally defined in contrast to hyperbole, as a manner of expression which seems to weaken the thought.[85] The classic example is Chimène's "Go, I do not hate you."[86] Dumarsais mentions among other examples "He is not a fool," "Pythagoras is not an author to be scoffed at," and "I am not misshapen."

If litotes can be set in opposition to hyperbole, it is because, when it seeks to establish a value, it relies on something that falls short of the value, instead of something beyond it.

---

[82] Erdmann, *Die Bedeutung des Wortes*, p. 224.
[83] Paulhan, "Les figures ou la rhétorique décryptée," *Cahiers du Sud*, 295 (1949), 370.
[84] Quintilian, VIII, vi, 73.
[85] Dumarsais, *Des tropes*, p. 97.
[86] Corneille, *Le Cid*, Act III, scene IV.

More often than not, litotes is expressed by a negative. Doubtless there are litotes that take the form of an assertion, such as "it is quite good," when this expression refers to a highly appreciated value. But we feel that litotes by negation displays best the typical mechanism of this figure. The term which is mentioned and rejected has to serve as a springboard to lead thought in the desired direction. There is the suggestion that this term could normally have been admitted as adequate, in the circumstances prevailing and given the information available to the hearer. Chimène is asserting that she should have hated, that it would have been normal to hate, and that her hearer might believe so. With this negation of the normal as departure point, the thought is directed toward other terms. Now the rejected term is often itself a hyperbole. In the phrase "Pythagoras is not an author to be scoffed at," the effect of surprise is achieved by this hyperbole, which is used only to be rejected immediately afterwards.

Even more than hyperbole, litotes requires that the hearer be acquainted with a certain number of data to guide him in his interpretation. "He is not a fool" can be taken in a static sense, or as a start in a direction. Hence the interest there is in using a litotes that is based on the rejection of a hyperbole.

The relations between these two figures are therefore much more complex, we feel, than commonly appears. The function of hyperbole is often to prepare for litotes, the purpose of which might otherwise be missed. And so litotes is not always, as has been said, a whispered confession.[87]

In this connection it is to be observed that litotes can be converted into *irony* by suppressing the negation. Of the same misshapen man of whom one would say, using litotes, "He is no Adonis," one might say ironically, "He is an Adonis." In the first case, we have a movement of thought through a scale of values; in the second, there is a confrontation of a qualification with an apparent reality. In the first case, the direction is dominant; in the second, one does not want to bring about a sudden turnabout of the mind, but one wants the mind to take note of the ridicule arising from an incompatibility.

Hyperbole, which is often involuntarily funny, may be made so deliberately. Let us quote this quip related by the pseudo-Longinus:

Smaller his field was than a Spartan letter.[88]

Here we see the comic aspect of argumentation. But would the writer have thought of this amusing witticism if serious hyperboles did not exist?

---

[87] Estève, *Etudes philosophiques sur l'expression littéraire*, p. 87.
[88] Longinus, *On the Sublime*, p. 141.

b) The Relations of Coexistence

§ 68. *The Person and His Acts*

In sequential connections, the terms brought together are on the same phenomenal plane, but connections of coexistence unite two realities that are not on an equal level, one of them being more basic and more explanatory than the other. It is by the more highly structured character of one of the terms that connections of coexistence are distinguished; the order of the elements in time is of quite secondary importance. We speak of relations of coexistence, not for the purpose of emphasizing the simultaneity of the terms, but in order to oppose connections of reality of this kind to sequential connections, in which order in time is of prime importance.[89] The fundamental connection of coexistence in philosophy is the one which connects the essence and its manifestations. It seems to us, however, that the prototype of this theoretical construction is found in the relationship existing between a person and his acts. We shall begin our analysis by examining this relationship.[90]

The construction of the human person, which underlies his acts, is connected with a distinction between that which is regarded as important, natural, and peculiar to the being under discussion and that which is regarded as transitory, as an external manifestation of the subject. As this connection between the person and his acts does not constitute a necessary relation and does not possess the same characteristics of stability as the relation existing between an object and its qualities, the mere repetition of an act can bring about either a reconstruction of the person or an intensified adherence to the previous construction.

The concept of the person will naturally vary a great deal, depending on the period and the metaphysical system adopted. The argumentation of primitive people would use a much wider concept of the person than ours. They would doubtless include in it all its *appurtenances*, such as shadow, totem, name, and detached fragments of the body, whereas we would establish only a symbolic connection between these elements and the totality of the person. The single example of wo-

---

[89] For a similar approach, see Angyal, *Foundations for a Science of Personality*, chap. VIII.
[90] As regards §§ 68-71,cf. Perelman and Olbrechts-Tyteca, *Rhétorique et philosophie*, pp. 49-84, "Acte et personne dans l'argumentation."

man's beauty suffices to show how one and the same phenomenon can be considered either as an integral, essential part of the person or as one of the transitory manifestations of the person, that is, as a mere act.

Considering a phenomenon as part of the person's structure endows it with a higher status: that is, the way of constructing the person may be an object of limited and transitory agreements, peculiar to a given group, and susceptible of revision under the influence of a new religious, philosophic, or scientific outlook.

The concept of "person" introduces an element of stability. Any argument about the person has to do with this stability: it is assumed when an act is interpreted as a function of the person, and it is failure to respect this stability which is deplored when someone is reproached for incoherence or unjustified change.

Very many arguments are devoted to proving that the person has not changed, that the change is only apparent, that only the circumstances have changed, and so on.[91]

Nevertheless, the stability of the person is never completely assured: linguistic techniques will help to stress the impression of permanency, the most important of these being the use of the proper noun. Designation of the person in terms of certain traits (your miser of a father), hypostasis of certain emotions (she whose fury pursued you through childhood), can also help. Qualification and the use of epithet (this hero, Charlemagne, with the white flowing beard) aim at rendering certain characteristics immutable so that their stability will reinforce that of the person referred to. It is through this stability that a merit that is acquired or to be acquired can be attributed to someone in a timeless way. As Kenneth Burke accurately remarks:

> A hero is first of all a man who does heroic things; and his "heroism" resides in his acts. But next, a hero can be a man with the potentialities of heroic action. Soldiers on the way to the wars are heroes in this sense. ... Or a man may be considered a hero because he *had done* heroic acts, whereas in his present *state* as a hero he may be too old or weak to do such acts at all.[92]

But this stability of the person, which makes him somewhat resemble an object, with his properties fixed once and for all, is opposed to his freedom, to his spontaneity, to the possibility of his changing. One is therefore much more inclined to stabilize others than oneself:

> The others may, and often do, have qualities far superior to mine, but their qualities cling to them far more closely than my defects

---

[91] Cf. Leites, "The Third International, on its Changes of Policy," Lasswell, *Language of Politics*, pp. 293-333.

[92] Burke, *A Grammar of Motives* (Prentice-Hall), p. 42.

cling to me. If they are generous, intelligent, hardworking, charming, they will remain so, just as they will remain miserly, stupid, lazy, dull, if they are made that way. But not I. I am not a poet, but in a moment I may possibly become one. Nothing prevents me from doing tomorrow the work which I have not been able to do today. Sylvia also possessed this plasticity, a mixture of fact and doubt.[93]

A real privilege is conferred on Sylvia, after a first meeting, by seeing in her this plasticity, which everyone allows spontaneously to himself, while just as spontaneously denying it to others. Any jeopardizing of this faculty of renewal is much resented. This probably explains why we feel uncomfortable if we hear our friends speak of our future behavior, even in eulogistic terms.[94]

Existentialism has succeeded in working out an original ontology by putting the accent on the freedom of the person, which places him in clear opposition to things. Pages of what seems to be complicated metaphysics assert uniquely the refusal to see in the relation of the person to his acts a simple replica of the relation between an object and its properties.[95] The object, defined in terms of its properties, provides the model for a concept of the person, stabilized on the basis of certain of his acts, which are transformed into qualities and virtues and which are integrated into an unvarying essence. But if the person did not have the power of self-transformation, of change, of conversion and could not somehow turn his back on the past, education would be a farce, morality would be without meaning, and the ideas of responsibility, of guilt, and of merit, which are bound up with the idea of freedom of the person, would have to be abandoned in favor of a simple pragmatic appraisal of behavior.

In argumentation, the person, considered as the support for a series of qualities, the author of a series of acts and judgments, and the object of a series of appraisals, is a durable being, around whom is grouped a whole series of phenomena to which he gives cohesion and significance. But the person as a free subject possesses the spontaneity, the power to change and transform himself, the possibility of submitting to or resisting persuasion, which make man an object of study *sui generis* and make the social sciences disciplines that cannot merely copy faithfully the methodology of the natural sciences.

Thus, for example, morality and law need the concepts of *person* and *act* in their relationship and in their relative independence. Morality and law judge both the act and the agent: they could not merely con-

---

[93] Berl, *Sylvia,* p. 86.
[94] Cf. Paulhan, *Entretiens sur des faits divers,* p. 67.
[95] Cf. Sartre, *Being and Nothingness,* pp. 114 et seq.

sider one of these two elements. By the very fact that one judges the individual and not his acts, there is an admission that he and his acts are solidary. However, if one is concerned with him, it is because of his acts, which can be qualified independently of his person. While the notions of responsibility and of guilt or merit are related to the person, the notions of norm and of rule are primarily concerned with the act. However, this dissociation of the act and the person is never more than partial and precarious. The merit of a person can be considered independently of his acts, but this would only be possible within a metaphysic in which reference to the acts would be provided in the context. On the other hand, if rules prescribe or prohibit certain acts, their moral or juridical significance resides in the fact that they are meant for persons. The terms of the *act-person* relation are independent enough to permit, when necessary, the use of each one on its own, but they are sufficiently connected for entire spheres of social life to be characterized by their joint intervention.

§ 69. *Interaction of Act and Person*

After these considerations of a general nature, we shall examine in turn the influence of acts on the concept of person and that of the person on his acts, and we shall conclude by indicating situations where the interaction is so pronounced that even analysis cannot award primacy to the one element rather than the other.

The reaction of the act on the agent is such as to modify constantly our concept of the person, whether one is dealing with new acts attributed to him or old acts to which reference is made. Both kinds of acts play a similar role in argumentation, although more recent acts are made preponderant. Except in borderline cases, which we shall examine later, the construction of the person is never finished, not even at his death. But it stands to reason that the further an individual recedes in history, the more rigid becomes his image. As Raymond Aron has put it:

> The *other*, when present, constantly reminds us of his capacity
> for change; when absent he is the prisoner of the image we have
> made of him. ... While we may still be able to distinguish in our
> friends what they are from what they do, this distinction progress-
> ively wears away as men get swallowed up in the past.[96]

The person will then coincide with the structured aggregate of his known acts. More precisely, we may say, the relation between what

---

[96] Aron, *Introduction à la philosophie de l'histoire*, p. 80.

must be considered the essence of the person and the acts which are but the manifestation of that essence is fixed once and for all. However, this rigidity is only relative: not only may new documents bring about a revision, but, quite apart from any new facts, a change in public opinion or a different conception of history may modify the conception of the individual by bringing into his structure acts that had previously been neglected or by minimizing acts which were until then thought to be important.

The act cannot be considered as a simple indicator revealing the intimate character of the person, which would be invariable, but inaccessible without the help of the act. We are somewhat shocked by this passage from Isocrates, who compares men to poisonous mushrooms:

> The best thing would actually be, if bad men were marked with a distinguishing sign, to punish them before they have committed a crime against one of their fellow citizens. But since it is impossible to recognize them before they have wronged someone, at least everyone should detest them as soon as they are discovered and should regard them as the enemies of all men.[97]

It follows that punishment should be in proportion, not to the seriousness of the offense, but to the wickedness of the nature the offense reveals.

In our usual conception, an act is not so much an indicator as an element making it possible to construct and reconstruct our image of the person and to classify him into categories to which certain qualifications may be applied, as in this well-known passage from Pascal:

> There are only three kinds of persons: those who serve God, having found Him; others who are occupied in seeking Him, not having found Him; while the remainder live without seeking Him and without having found Him. The first are reasonable and happy, the last are foolish and unhappy; and those between are unhappy and reasonable.[98]

The value we attribute to the act prompts us to attribute a certain value to the person, but this is not a random assignment of value. In a case when an act brings about a transfer of value, this transfer is correlative to a modification of our conception of the person, to whom we shall explicitly or implicitly attribute certain new tendencies, aptitudes, instincts, or feelings.

By act we mean everything that can be considered an emanation of the person, be it an action, a mode of expression, an emotional reaction, an involuntary twitch, or a judgment. The inclusion of this

---

[97] Isocrates, *Against Lochites*, § 14.
[98] Pascal, *Pensées*, GBWW, vol. 33, p. 220.

last item is essential for what we are going to say. For, by attributing a certain value to a judgment, we are actually thereby making an appraisal of its author. Sometimes the judgment even enables us to pass a judgment on the judge himself.

> *Philanthus* is a man of merit, wit, charm; he is exact in his duties, faithful and attached to his master, but his master does not much care for him. He is not liked, he is not appreciated. "Tell me, is it Philanthus you are condemning or the great man he serves?"[99]

Judging the judge presupposes a certain agreement about the value of the object which the judge dealt with; it is questioning this agreement that the judgment passed on the judge may be modified. On the other hand, if one claims to judge a person by the expressions he uses, shifting of the discussion onto the object is much more difficult. Theodore Reinach takes Furtwängler to task for using the expressions "gross fraud" and "despicable inventions," in the controversy about the authenticity of the tiara of Saïtapharnes, and concludes:

> Such excessive judgments most of all judge the person who makes them.[100]

Here the disqualification of the adversary seems connected with an absence of impartiality; in other cases the charge will be lack of seriousness. Of course, a person can be charged with partiality or lack of seriousness in what he says only if there is agreement on the subject matter. However, reference is usually not made to the subject, but to a generally recognized standard of measure, of propriety, which makes it possible, whatever the circumstances, to disqualify an opponent who departs from this standard. Hence the well-known danger of defending a good cause by too violent expressions.

Only rarely is the reaction of the act on the person limited to an upward or downward appraisal of the person himself. More often than not the person serves as a kind of relay permitting the passage from known acts to unknown acts, from the knowledge of past acts to the prediction of future acts. This technique is constantly used, especially in legal discussions. Sometimes this process will involve acts of the same nature— "He who has never been seditious will not contrive the overthrow of kingdoms"[101]; sometimes it will allow passage from a particular act to another similar one— "Whoever has borne false witness will not hesitate to call false witnesses in his own favor"[102];

[99] La Bruyère, "Les caractères. Des Grands," 8, *Œuvres complètes*, p. 270.
[100] Vayson de Pradenne, *Les fraudes en archéologie préhistorique*, pp. 536-537.
[101] Calvin, *Institutes of the Christian Religion*, (Westminster), vol. I, p. 30, Prefatory Address to King Francis.
[102] Isocrates, *Against Callimachus*, § 57.

and sometimes it will be complicated by an argument *a fortiori*—"The man who has killed will not hesitate to lie."[103]

Acts which serve as premises may be ordinary ones, or they may be rare. The important thing is that they should be regarded as characteristic. Special techniques are needed to prevent a unique act from reacting on the person, and these will be discussed later. The accumulated errors of the opponent may disqualify him; a single error can also serve this purpose.

This guarantee of one act by another is also applicable to a person's opinions. To mark her defiance of Thomism, so saturated with Aristotelian thought, Simone Weil attacks Aristotle for what he writes on the subject of slavery:

> Even if we reject that particular notion of Aristotle, we are necessarily led in our ignorance to accept others that must have lain in him at the root of that one. A man who takes the trouble to draw up an apology for slavery cannot be a lover of justice. The age in which he lived has nothing to do with it.[104]

What is invoked here is doubtless the coherence between certain ideas. But this coherence is postulated through the medium of the person, for our "ignorance" prevents us from taking it in any other way.

Past acts and their effect end up by assuming a kind of consistence and form extremely harmful liabilities or highly useful credits. The reputation a person enjoys should be taken into consideration, and Isocrates does not fail to invoke it to defend his clients:

> I would be the most unfortunate of men, if, after spending a great deal of my money for the state, I should be accused of coveting that of others and of not caring for your bad opinion, when people can see that I set less store, not only on my property but even on my life, than on your good opinion of me.[105]

The fact of having been careful of one's good reputation in the past is a guarantee that one will do nothing that might cause one to lose it. Former acts, and the good reputation resulting from them, become a sort of capital incorporated in the person, an asset which one can rightfully invoke in one's defense.

Often, the idea one has of a person, instead of being the outcome of argument, is rather its starting point and is used either to foresee certain unknown acts, or to interpret known acts in a particular way, or else to transfer to the act the judgment passed on the agent. A caricature of the last-mentioned process is given by La Bruyère:

---

[103] Cf. also Quintilian, V, x, 87.
[104] Weil, *The Need for Roots*, pp. 243-244.
[105] Isocrates, *Against Callimachus*, § 63.

> ... certain women who swear by you and your word will say: "That is charming! What was it he said?"[106]

This transfer mechanism does not necessarily follow a chronological order. The valuation process can be extended equally well to acts antedating the moment when the person acquired a high value. "What genius does not rescue his childhood?"—as Malraux has so aptly put it.[107] And it is true that when we judge the early works of a great artist we cannot help seeing in them the precursory signs of his future greatness. The author of works of genius, created at different periods, is a genius: this qualification relates the acts to a stable quality of the person which radiates as much on the years previous to the period when he produced great works as on the later years. It is no longer sufficient to say that the past guarantees the future. Now we must say that the stable structure of the person permits us to prejudge his acts. This reaction of the person on the act is most clearly apparent when a qualification, an epithet, places this character of stability particularly in evidence.

Pascal uses this transfer from person to act to pose the following dilemma:

> The Koran says Saint Matthew was an honest man. Therefore Mahomet was a false prophet for calling honest men wicked or for not agreeing with what they have said of Jesus Christ.[108]

In a parallel way the neurotic, whom Odier mentions, is incapable of upholding a point of view in a discussion:

> How could he place a value on his ideas without having previously placed a value on himself?"[109]

An ambiguous act often achieves its full significance and meaning through what we know of its author. Thus Isocrates relates, in his *Helen*, that Theseus carried off Helen while she was still a child and adds:

> Certainly, if the man responsible for these exploits had been one of a crowd and not of an exceptional nature, my speech could not yet show proof whether it was a eulogy of Helen or an attack on Theseus. ... It seems to me proper to talk of him now more at length, for I believe that, in order to give all necessary authority to praise of Helen, it is best to show that her friends and admirers were themselves more worthy of admiration than other men.[110]

[106] La Bruyère, "Les caractères, De la societé et de la conversation," 66, *Œuvres complètes*, pp. 188-189.

[107] Malraux, *Saturne, Essai sur Goya*, p. 18.

[108] Pascal, *Pensées*, GBWW, vol. 33, p. 278.

[109] Odier, *Le rôle des fonctions du moi dans l'évolution psychique*, vol. I: *L'angoisse et la pensée magique*, p. 128.

[110] Isocrates, *Helen*, §§ 21, 22.

A long eulogy of Theseus follows.

Nor is this all. In certain cases our knowledge of the person permits us not merely to place a value on an act but constitutes the only criterion by which to judge it. Thus, for Pascal:

> There is a great difference between not being for Jesus Christ and saying so, and not being for Jesus Christ and pretending to be so. The one party can do miracles, not the others.[111]

Miracles performed by enemies of Jesus Christ are possible, for they are clearly the devil's work; the others are impossible, for God would not permit the faithful to be deceived.

The intervention of the person, as a context for the interpretation of an act, comes about most frequently through the medium of the notion of intention, which has the function of both expressing and justifying the reaction of the agent on the act.

When one passes from the knowledge of a man's past acts to the consideration of his future ones, the role of the person is important, but it is only a privileged link in the totality of the facts invoked. On the other hand, as soon as appeal to intention is introduced, the accent is placed essentially on the person and his permanent character. Intention is closely bound to the agent; it is, as it were, an emanation, the result of his will, of his intimate [character. As another person's intention cannot be known directly, it can be presumed only from what is known of the permanent aspects of the person. Sometimes intention is revealed by repeated, concordant acts, but there are cases in which it can be determined only from the idea one has of the agent. The same act, done by someone else, will be considered different and will be differently assessed because it will be deemed to have been done with a different intention. Appeal to intention will then constitute the crux of the argument, and there will be a subordination of the act to the agent, whose intention will make it possible to understand and appraise the act. Thus, Calvin will conclude, when he recalls the afflictions of Job that can be attributed simultaneously to God, Satan, and men, that God acted rightly, but Satan and men acted in a condemnable fashion, because their intentions were not the same.[112] The idea we have of these intentions depends essentially on what we know of the agents.

All moral argumentation based on the intention involves the morality of the agent as opposed to the morality of the act, which is much more formalistic. The example given above, in which we consider such clearly differentiated agents as God and Satan shows the mechanism

---

[111] Pascal, *Pensées*, GBWW, vol. 33, pp. 334-335.
[112] Calvin, *Institutes of the Christian Religion* (Westminster), vol. I, pp. 229-230.

of these arguments particularly well, but there is no moral controversy where they are not used. The intentions of the agent, the motives which determined his action, will often be considered as the reality hidden behind the purely external manifestations, a reality which one must try to find beyond the appearances, for they alone, in final analysis, are important. The ambassador of an Asiatic country who is invited to dine in the private dining room of an American restaurant is at first flattered by this mark of distinction, but he protests indignantly when he finds out that the real reason for putting him there is that the city he is in practices racial segregation and he has been taken for a Negro.

This technique of interpretation by intention makes it possible to judge the agent, and not only one or other of his works. The two ways of judging—the one having reference to a formal criterion and the other passing beyond this criterion—may lead to opposite judgments. As A. Lalande says:

> We speak of intelligent errors, and not without reason: Descartes is full of them; of honorable crimes or misdemeanors, like Saint Vincent de Paul cheating for the poor. ... An unsuccessful novel can make one say: "That is no good, but it is the work of an artist."[113]

How can one prove the existence of the alleged intention? Chiefly by establishing correspondences between various acts by the same person and by suggesting that they were determined by the same intention.

> All know indeed that the same men have caused the destruction of democracy and the banishment of my father.[114]

Going beyond the actual facts, the assertion hints that the same political intention animated them.

Search for the real intention is one of the central problems of the contemporary theatre. Sometimes the main character is groping for it and his partners enlighten him gradually as to the meaning of his acts. In G. Marcel's Le chemin de crête, neither the central character nor his partners, nor the spectators, succeed in disentangling the intentions. Only a knowledge of the agent—possessed by God alone— could give the acts their meaning with full certainty.

It is the ambiguity of human behavior, when interpreted in terms of intention, which marks one of the essential points in which any science dealing with man differs profoundly from the natural sciences.

---

[113] Lalande, La raison et les normes, pp. 196-197.
[114] Isocrates, Concerning the Team of Horses, § 4; cf. § 31, supra: The Interpretation of the Discourse and Its Problems.

Hence the effort of the behaviorists to eliminate this factor of uncertainty, and subjectivism, but at the cost of what distortion of the very object under examination! Psychoanalysis has preferred the risk of error to renouncing the study of the whole man.

The reaction of the person on his acts is influenced by a factor to which social psychology has attributed very great importance, the factor of prestige.

Prestige is a quality of the person which is known by its effects. E. Dupréel can thus define it as the quality of those who arouse in others the inclination to imitate them; it is thus closely bound up with the relation of superiority of one individual over another and of one group over another group.[115] To Lippitt and his collaborators, prestige is referable to those who, in their circle, are most apt to become the leaders and to get others to do what they want.[116] Psychologists and sociologists endeavor to recognize its forms,[117] to reveal its origins, to describe it as the resultant of a field of force, and to establish the relationship between the prestige accorded to others and that accorded to oneself. What interests us in these efforts is that most of the analytical elements introduced are also the factors which, in argumentation, make it possible to defend and explain prestige and to attach a value to it. Sociological description more often than not coincides with argumentative practice. If, in certain cases, one postulates or believes he observes a discordance between the reasons alleged for the prestige and its real origin, it is in terms of the alleged reasons that any investigation is made, by the members of a concrete group, into the criteria of the prestige, these criteria differing from group to group.

However, except where the prestige is called into question, it is not customary to justify it. It works for good or for evil.

> The example of the great—says Gracian—is a rhetorician of such power that it can persuade people to commit the most infamous acts.[118]

It is possible, on the other hand, for a person to have such a bad reputation that everything he says or does bears a negative mark and is lowered in value by its association with the person.

---

[115] Dupréel, *Sociologie générale*, p. 66.
[116] Lippitt, Polansky, and Rosen, "The Dynamics of Power," *Human Relations*, V, (1952), 37-64.
[117] Cf., for instance, Stokvis, *Psychologie der suggestie en autosuggestie*, pp. 36 et seq.
[118] Gracian, *L'homme de Cour*, p. 217.

This phenomenon, which is so characteristic of social psychology, explains what at first might seem strange—what we may call the polarization of virtues and vices. This is how Méré describes it:

> Do we not observe that merit appears to us of greater value in a beautiful body than in an ugly one? Just as when merit is well recognized we find the person to whom it attaches more charming. The same thing happens with things that are solely in the realm of the senses. When we are pleased by someone's face, the sound of his voice sounds more agreeable.[119]

The characters in popular novels, who are all black or all white, are simply exaggerations of a spontaneous tendency of the mind which is inclined to dispel certain scruples in action. This polarization of virtues and vices can extend to the social aspects of the person: merit attaches to the privileged social position; everything is divided into opposing camps. As Walter White has written:

> I was a Negro, I belonged to that which, in history, is opposed to the good, to the just, to the light.[120]

Argumentative technique uses these connections. Panegyric unifies, in a common eulogy, all the aspects of the person, which thus reinforce each other's value.

But these techniques based on solidarity are rather weak if they are not envisaged as a continuous interaction of act and person. This interaction has a truly snowballing effect. For instance, argumentation by sacrifice[121] becomes more powerful thanks to the enhanced prestige of those who have sacrificed themselves: the blood of the martyrs testifies all the more to the value of the religion for which it was shed as the confessors of the faith previously enjoyed a greater prestige, and this prestige itself cannot fail to grow following their sacrifice.

The snowballing effect is most pronounced when one's whole idea of a person is derived from certain acts, and yet the idea reacts on one's opinion of these acts. This is illustrated in the case of the false autographs presented to the Academy by M. Chasles. Each time M. Chasles had countered an objection raised by his opponents, he was encouraged to incrase his confidence in the man who supplied him with the documents, and this confidence in turn increased their value. On the other hand, the forger, whom Chasles cannot even imagine, acquires such capabilities in his eyes that when figures borrowed from the third

---

[119] Méré, *Œuvres complètes*, vol. II: *Des agrémens*, p. 20.
[120] Walter White, "Deux races se rencontrent en moi," *Echo*, June 1948, p. 417.
[121] Cf. § 58, supra: Argumentation by Sacrifice.

edition of Newton's *Principia* turn up in a supposed letter of Pascal, Chasles affirms:

> The alleged forger would have been too intelligent to commit the error of copying from the third edition of the *Principia*.[122]

This extreme case of interaction, involving the destruction of all critical faculty, is possible only because interpretations of documents at one moment as genuine and at another moment as false help equally to bolster confidence in the documents through the instrumentality of a conception of the person, which is exclusively based on the documents.

§ 70. *Argument from Authority*

Many arguments are influenced by prestige, including, as we have seen, argument by sacrifice. But there is a series of arguments whose whole significance is conditioned by prestige. A man's word of honor, given by him as the sole proof of an assertion, will depend on the opinion held of that man as a man of honor. The respect inspired by Brutus' integrity is the chief basis of his argumentation in Shakespeare's *Julius Caesar*.[123]

The *Rhetorica ad Herennium* picks out, as an example of weak argumentation, based on what one is going to do and not on what one should do, these sentences placed by Plautus in the mouth of the old dotard Megaronides:

> To criticize a friend for a fault ... is a thankless task, but there are times when it is useful and profitable: I myself am going to reproach a friend of mine for a fault that soundly deserves it.[124]

If the argumentation is weak or even comic, it is not because of its underlying structure, but because it is an argument from a model that is misapplied because the model in question did not enjoy any prestige at all.[125]

The prestige argument appears in its most characteristic form in the argument from authority, which uses the acts or opinions of a person or group of persons as a means of proof in support of a thesis.

The argument from authority is the method of rhetoric reasoning that has been most heavily attacked, because it was the one most

---

[122] Vayson de Pradenne, *Les fraudes en archéologie préhistorique*, pp. 398-399.
[123] Shakespeare, *Julius Caesar*, Act III, scene II.
[124] *Rhetorica ad Herennium*, II, 35. Cf. Plautus, *The Three Penny Day* (Trinummus), Act I, scene 1, 23-27; also quoted by Cicero, *De Inventione*, bk I, § 95.
[125] Cf. § 80, infra: Model and Anti-Model.

widely used in circles hostile to free, scientific research and used more-over, in an abusive, peremptory way, that is, it was considered to be compelling, as if the authorities invoked were infallible:

> Whoever backs his tenets with such authorities thinks he ought thereby to carry the cause and is ready to style it impudence in any one who shall stand out against them. This I think may be called *argumentum ad verecundiam*[126]

Certain positivist thinkers have attacked this argument—though recognizing its enormous importance in practice—by accusing it of being fraudulent. Thus, Pareto thinks this argument should be con-sidered as "an instrument for logicalizing nonlogical actions and the sentiments in which they originate."[127] The argument from authority is, in this view, a pseudo-argument, intended to camouflage the irra-tionality of our beliefs and win for them the consent of everybody or of the majority by appeal to the authority of eminent persons.

To us, on the contrary, the argument from authority is of extreme importance, and, although in any given argument it is permissible to question its value, it cannot be dismissed as irrelevant without further ado, except in certain special cases which we shall examine in the following section. The argument from authority has been at-tacked in the name of truth. And indeed, insofar as any proposition is considered to be true or false, the argument from authority no longer holds a legitimate place in our intellectual arsenal. But is this always the case, and can all the legal problems, for instance, be reduced to scientific problems where only truth is involved? It is because of this kind of conception that a writer dealing with legal logic is led to see a fallacy in the argument from authority, which he equates with precedent:

> A judicial precedent exerts an inevitable, though unfortunate, influence on the judge considering a claim. ... *Authors* must keep their independence and search for truth through logic.[128]

But is it not perhaps a sad illusion to think that the jurists are con-cerned only with truth and not also with justice and social peace? But the quest for justice and the maintenance of an equitable order, of social trust, cannot neglect considerations based on the existence of a legal tradition, which appears just as clearly in legal doctrine as in the actual holdings of courts. Recourse to argument from authority is inescapable if the existence of such a tradition is to be attested.

---

[126] Locke, *An Essay Concerning Human Understanding*, bk IV, chap. XVII, § 19, GBWW, vol. 35, pp. 379-380.

[127] Pareto, *The Mind and Society*, § 583, vol. I, pp. 349-350.

[128] Berriat Saint-Prix, *Manuel de logique juridique*, pp. 77, 85, 89.

On the other hand, the comic aspect of the argument from authority is evoked when resort to this type of argument appears unnecessary, as, for instance, in this reply of a child to his big sister who was inquiring how Princess Elizabeth knew that she was going to have a baby:

"Well, she can read, can't she? It was in all the papers."[129]

Often *argument from authority* seems to be under attack, but the challenge is really to the *person chosen as authority.* Thus, Pascal derides argument from authority when the authority is that of "men of influence,"[130] but has no hesitation in invoking the authority of St. Augustine.[131] Similarly, Calvin rejects the authority of the Church, but admits that of the prophets.

As the authorities contradict each other, we may, like Descartes, decide to discard them all in favor of other means of proof. Generally, we are content to enumerate the authorities that are trustworthy, or to indicate those we shall prefer in case of conflict (cf. Theodosius' law of citations). In any case, the person invoking an authority commits himself: there is no argument from authority without some repercussion on its user.

The authorities invoked vary considerably. Sometimes, the authority will be "unanimous opinion" or "general opinion." Sometimes it will be certain categories of men, such as "scientists," "philosophers," "the Fathers of the Church," "the prophets." At other times, the authority will be impersonal: "physics," "doctrine," "religion," or "the Bible." At yet other times, the authorities will be designated by name.

More often than not, the argument from authority will not constitute the only proof, but will round off well-developed argumentation. The same authority comes to have a high or low value set on it, depending on whether it agrees or does not agree with the opinion of the speaker. To his conservative opponent who exclaims disdainfully: "That is pure Condorcet," the liberal speaker will oppose the views of "renowned Condorcet."[132] To express contemptible thoughts, says Pascal, is to follow the maunderings of ill-bred persons:[133] the argument from authority is here invoked not merely negatively but, so to speak, backwards and is used as much to qualify the source of a proposition as to refer to it.

The role of the argument from authority in argumentation is considerable. But it must not be forgotten that, like any argument, it fits in

[129] Cf. *Fun Fare*, p. 21.
[130] Pascal, *Pensées*, GBWW, vol. 33, p. 232.
[131] *Ibid.*, pp. 330, 344.
[132] Janson, *Discours parlementaires*, vol. I, p. 82, 17-19 May, 1879.
[133] Pascal, *Pensées*, GBWW, vol. 33, p. 209.

among other agreements. On the one hand, one resorts to it when agreement on the question involved is in danger of being debated. And, on the other hand, the argument from authority may itself be challenged. As to the first point, we note the tendency to support axiological norms by transforming them into thetic norms. On the second point, we note that very often the argument from authority is not clearly seen as such, because we think at once of possible justifications.

When the authority is that of large numbers, the argument of the normal often underlies the argument from authority. Thus Lefebvre writes in defense of the materialist viewpoint:

> Materialism explicitly bases its theory of knowledge on this naive, practical conviction held by all human beings [that things exist independently of our sensation].

He speaks also of "the normal man, who has not passed through a lunatic asylum or a group of idealistic philosophers."[134]

The authority of numbers can take the form of qualification, as where Plotinus writes:

> Indeed, those who possess them [the civil virtues] are held to be divine.[135]

So, when a person is presented as being notoriously "wise" or "learned," the particular authority invoked is, at it were, guaranteed by the large number of people who, by implication, endorse this designation.

Often, before someone is involved as an authority, his standing will be buttressed; one shows that he is a competent witness. For the greater the authority, the more unquestionable does his pronouncement become. The extreme case is the divine authority which overcomes all the obstacles that reason might raise:

> ... A master [Jesus] who enjoys such great authority, even though his doctrine may be obscure, deserves to have his word believed: *ipsum audite.* ... You can recognize his authority when you consider the respect Moses and Elijah pay to him, i. e., the law and the prophets, as I have explained. ... Do not let us search for the reasons for the truths he teaches us: The whole reason is that he has spoken.[136]

The peremptory and absolute aspect of this argument from authority is found in the conclusion. However, we note that this authority is further attested by the respect which other authorities, namely Moses

[134] Lefebvre, *A la lumière du matérialisme dialectique*, vol. I, p. 29.

[135] Plotinus, *Enneads*, I, 2, § 1.

[136] Bossuet, *Sermons*, vol. II: *Sur la soumission due à la parole de Jésus-Christ*, pp. 117, 120, 121.

and Elijah, have paid to him. Its power is revealed by the obstacles placed on the path of belief, which can be nonetheless overcome. This is *credo quia absurdum* in another form.

Except when an absolutely perfect being is in question, the authorities invoked are usually specific authorities, that is, persons whose authority is recognized by the audience in a particular field, and it is only in this field that they can be used. But what authority do they have outside their own field? What is the influence of the expert's opinion when it is opposed to the opinion of large numbers? In which fields should expert opinion count more than popular opinion and vice versa? Much research has been devoted to these questions, particularly in the United States.[137]

As soon as there is a conflict between authorities, the problem of the basis of the authority is raised. The basis should help to determine what credit each of the respective authorities deserves. At the present time, the foundation most frequently alleged in favor of an authority is his competence, but this does not hold good for every milieu and every period. The struggle against the argument from authority (which, as we have seen, is sometimes simply a struggle against certain authorities in favor of others) can also be due to the desire to replace the traditional basis of authority by a different one. This will often bring about a change of authority.

There is a curious case in which argument from authority gives undeniable argumentative value to statements which express ignorance or incomprehension. When the master says to his pupil, "I don't understand what you say," this usually means: "You have expressed yourself badly" or "Your ideas on this point are not very clear." Pretended incompetence and affected ignorance were condemned by Schopenhauer[138] and by Bentham.[139] There are some nice examples of these practices in Marcel Proust.[140]

The incompetence of the competent may serve as a criterion for disqualifying all those whom there is no reason to think more competent than the person who called himself incompetent. This form of argumentation can have notable philosophical significance, for it can aim at destroying not only the competence of an individual or a group, but that of the whole of humanity. When eminent thinkers are de-

---

[137] Cf. Bird, *Social Psychology*, pp. 284 et seq.
[138] Schopenhauer, *Sämtliche Werke*, (Piper), vol. 6: "Eristische Dialektik," p. 423, Kunstgriff 31.
[139] Bentham, *Works*, vol. II: *The Book of Fallacies*, p. 411, pt 1, chap. v, 1. "Self-Assumed Authority."
[140] Proust, *The Guermantes Way*, pt II, pp. 58 et seq.

nounced for deficiency of reasoning, it is often for the purpose of maintaining the deficiency of reason in general, and it is only the authority of these thinkers which permits such an extrapolation.

However, nothing prevents a person from having certain deficiencies which actually increase his authority. We can see this if we put side by side an argument based on competence (expert opinion) and an argument based on innocence (the evidence of a child or an intoxicated person).[141] After an accident, the opinion of the expert and that of the child can be invoked together; in both cases the opinion is evaluated through the characteristics of the person, which are quite different from those of just any witness.

The foundations of competence—for competence should itself also be capable of justification—are of many kinds. They will be sought in rules of conditioning and acquisition of skills and in rules governing verification of aptitudes and confirmation of competence.

Who is competent to judge and make a decision? As disagreement on competences often leads to a question's being left undecided, a legal system concerned with avoiding denial of justice must decide who are, in cases of conflict, the competent magistrates with the authority to judge in the matter and settle the dispute.

§ 71. *Techniques of Severance and Restraint Opposed to the Act-Person Interaction*

Techniques which sever or restrain the interaction of the act and the person must be used when there is a contradiction between what we believe of the person and what we think of the act and when we decline to make the modifications which would be necessary, either because we wish to shield the person from the influence of the act or the act from the influence of the person. In other words, the techniques we are going to describe have the effect of transforming the interaction into action which goes only one way and not the other.

The most effective technique for preventing the reaction of the act on the agent is to consider the latter as a perfect being, perfect in good or perfect in evil, a god or a devil. A most effective technique for preventing the reaction of the agent on the act is to consider the act as a truth or the expression of a fact. We shall call these two processes *severance techniques.*

When the person who is the agent is thought to be a perfect being, the idea formed of his acts will obviously benefit from the opinion

---

[141] Cf. Cicero, *Topica*, § 75.

held of the agent, but the converse ceases to be true. Leibniz explains this process, which he finds consistent with a "sound logic of probabilities,"[142] by imagining

> ... that there is found something similar among men to what there is with God. A man may give such great and strong proofs of his virtue and saintliness that all the most apparent reasons which can be mustered against him to accuse him of a supposed crime, for instance of stealing or killing, will deserve rejection as calumnies of false witnesses or as an extraordinary play of chance, which sometimes makes the most innocent people suspect. So that in a case in which anybody else would be in danger of being convicted or subjected to the rack (depending on the law of the place), this man would be unanimously found innocent by his judges.[143]

This justification, which he considers to be rational, of the technique that consists of refusing to admit any unfavorable effect of the act on the agent, Leibniz explains by means of a human example, but it is clear that the process cannot be attacked when applied to God:

> I have indicated already that the things which can be opposed to the goodness and justice of God are only appearances, which would have weight against a man, but which are naught when applied to God and when weighed against the demonstrations which assure us of the infinite perfection of his attributes.[144]

That which can be opposed to God is neither true nor real: that which can be considered as incompatible with the divine perfection is by that very fact disqualified and considered an illusion.

We also find this independence of the person with respect to the act when we are dealing with evil spirits:

> However, let us recognize, Christians, that neither the sciences nor wisdom nor other gifts of nature are of great advantage since God has granted them also to the devils, his chief enemies.[145]

Instead of upgrading the person, these recognized qualities are devaluated and minimized by the fact that they constitute attributes of devils: the act-person interaction ceases to operate. The nature of the person alone influences our opinion of the value of the act.

When the quality of the person does not seem good enough to shield him from the interaction, recourse to this same type of argument can appear comical or even blasphemous, as is seen in this reflection concerning St. Mary the Egyptian:

---

[142] Leibniz, *Die philosophischen Schriften*, vol. VI, *Essais de Théodicée*, p. 71.
[143] Ibid, pp. 70-71.
[144] Ibid, p. 74.
[145] Bossuet, *Sermons*, vol. II: *Premier sermon sur les démons*, p. 11.

One has to be as saintly as she to do as much without sinning.[146]

The opposite severance technique stresses the act, which then no longer depends on the opinion held of the person. This independence follows from the fact that the act expresses a fact or a truth. Nobody's prestige (apart from that of the perfect Being) could make us admit that $2 + 2 = 5$ or gain our adherence to testimony contradicting experience. On the other hand, "an error of fact makes a wise man look ridiculous,"[147] and there is the danger that all one's prestige will be lost if one supports something which is considerecd contrary to nature. As witness, consider this misadventure of a Dutch ambassador who

> ... entertaining the king of Siam with the particularities of Holland, which he was inquisitive after, amongst other things told him that the water in his country would sometimes, in cold weather, be so hard that men walked upon it and that it would bear an elephant if he were there. To which the king replied, "Hitherto I have believed the strange things you have told me, because I look upon you as a sober, fair man, but now I am sure you lie."[148]

In this story, experience and the generalizations it seems to authorize are considered as a fact which surpasses all influence the person might have. His act, because it is judged incompatible with the convictions gained from experience is considered to be a lie; it casts discredit on its author and impairs the credit accorded to all his earlier testimony.

A fact imposes universal recognition; no authority can affect it. A fact's status as such will therefore be overthrown if something which should be independent of the person is made dependent on the quality of the person bearing witness to it. Let us recall again the anecdote of the court magician who gave the King a suit of clothes which, he alleged, could be perceived only by the morally irreproachable. Neither the King nor his courtiers dared to confess that they did not see anything, until a child, in his innocence, exclaimed: "Why does the King walk about naked?" The spell was broken. The prestige of the magician was sufficient to confer on perception the value of a criterion of morality up to the moment when the unquestionable innocence of the child destroyed the credit of the magician.

If it is undeniable that facts and truths, as long as they are recognized as such, are outside the range of argumentation— and this is the well-founded side of the opposition which Pareto draws between

---

[146] France, *La rôtisserie de la reine Pédauque*, p. 45. Communicated by R. Schaerer.

[147] La Bruyère, "Les caractères. Des jugements," 47, *Œuvres complètes*, p. 379.

[148] Locke, *An Essay Concerning Human Understanding*, bk IV, chap. xv, § 5, GBWW, vol. 35, p. 366.

the logico-experimental sphere and the sphere of authority[149]—when is it possible to say that one is confronted with a fact or a truth? As we have already seen, we can say so as long as the assertion is considered as valid for a universal audience. To avoid all discussion on this question, it is encased in a discipline, the bases of which are assumed to be accepted and whose criteria can form the object of an explicit or implicit agreement of universal scope. In this case, and in this case alone, does the validity of the fact lie beyond the reach of all argument from authority.

> From the logico-experimental standpoint, the soundness of the proposition $A = B$ is independent of the moral qualities of the person who asserts it. Suppose tomorrow it should be discovered that Euclid was a murderer, a thief, in short the worst man that ever lived. Would such a thing in the remotest degree affect the validity of the proofs in his geometry?[150]

But is it permissible to extend the example of geometry into all fields, as Pareto's reasoning suggests?

> "A certain proposal, A, can be sound only if it is made by a good man. The person who is making it is not an honest man (or, he is being paid to make it). Therefore the proposal A is detrimental to the country." That, of course, is absurd; and anyone so arguing abandons the rational domain therewith.[151]

Although Pareto may be right in criticizing this peremptory way of rejecting a proposition on the grounds of the personality advancing it, he is wrong in totally neglecting the influence of the person on the act. We must agree with Whately who, to a similar remark by Bentham:

> If the measure is a good one, will it become bad because it is supported by a bad man? If it is bad, will it become good because supported by a good man?

replies:

> It is only in matters of strict science and too in arguing with scientific men that the character of the advocates (as well as all other probable arguments) should be wholly put out of the question.[152]

Though facts and truths may escape all influence by the person, this technique of severance should not be abused by granting this very special quality to statements on which there is not only no agreement

---

[149] Cf. § 70, supra: Argument from Authority.
[150] Pareto, *The Mind and Society*, vol. III, § 1444, p. 917.
[151] *Ibid*, § 1756, pp. 1220, 1221.
[152] Whately, *Elements of Rhetoric* (Harper), pt II, chap. III, § 4, pp. 170, 171.

314 THE NEW RHETORIC

but for which there can be no recognized criteria which could confer on them the unanimity alone capable of guaranteeing their status as facts or truths.

Scientific and practical techniques aim at objectivity by detaching the act from the agent in order either to describe it or to judge it. Behaviorism is one instance of this; another is provided by all the competitions in which the contestants are judged on the basis of measurable performance or in which, at least, the work done is judged without revealing the name of its author. In law, a great number of provisions aim at qualifying acts without regard to the person committing them or to his intention. This formalism is, however, seldom found in ethics, although Japanese morality seems to provide certain examples.[153]

These modes of procedure often exhibit undeniable advantages, the greatest advantage being that they promote agreement on the criteria. But we must never forget that these are only techniques, which sometimes turn out to be fraught with drawbacks which have later to be remedied. The best proof of this is the recent endeavor in the field of penal law, to adjust punishment to the individual case.

The cases in which the influence of the act on the person or of the person on the act is completely severed are relatively rare in argumentative practice, for they represent extremes. Most of the techniques used in argument aim at reducing influence, rather than at suppressing it. This is why we call them *techniques of restraint.*

One of these techniques is prejudice or, better, bias. The act is interpreted and judged in terms of the agent, the latter providing the context which makes for better understanding of the act. Thereby an equivalence is maintained between the act and the conception we had of the person. It is to be observed, however, that, though the bias may suffice to remove the threat of an incompatibility, it cannot remove an incompatibility when it is too obvious.

Since bias, prejudice, for or against, often leads to blindness as to the value of an act and transfers to the act other values stemming from the agent, offsetting bias will take the form of making beneficial severance between act and person. But, if we take the standpoint we consider to be primodial, namely that of the permanence of the person, bias appears as a restraining technique directed against the continuous revision of our conception of a person and contributing greatly to its stability. While prestige can be considered the factor which guarantees the influence of the person on the act and has an active positive

[153] Benedict, *The Chrysanthemum and the Sword, Patterns of Japanese Culture,* p. 151.

role, bias corrects an incompatibility and operates when the person is in need of protection. Prestige and bias can operate in the same direction, but they come into play at different times in the argumentation.

If one wishes to avoid giving the impression of judging certain acts in terms of the person, of seeming prejudiced, one must often take precautions. One precaution is to preface an unfavorable opinion of the act by some praise of the person and vice versa. This praise may sometimes relate to other acts of the same person, but its aim is to praise him and to prove our impartiality. Praise of an adversary is therefore more often than not something more than just politeness: it can play a role in the argumentation.

When, between the act and the image one has formed of the person, there is a discordance of such flagrancy that bias cannot abolish it by a satisfactory interpretation, various devices are still available to prevent the act from affecting the person.

It is possible to make a separation between different spheres of activity in such a way that an act depending on some of the spheres will be deemed irrelevant to the idea one has of the person. The determination of which spheres are of importance will be made differently in different societies and environments. Steady application to work, marital fidelity, piety, or irreligiousness, for instance, may in some cases be determining factors with respect to the image of the person, while in others these considerations will fall into the nonoperative spheres. The extent of these inactive areas is a matter of agreement, for the most part tacit, and a social group can even be characterized in terms of them. The sphere of irrelevant acts will clearly vary with the person involved: acts that are unimportant in the case of a prince will be judged essential to the idea we form of persons of a lesser rank and vice versa. The same applies to acts covering a certain period of life, childhood, for example. Schopenhauer considered that our image of the person should be determined by minor acts. Indeed, according to him, acts which are performed with caution, just because of their possible repercussions, would have a much lower representative value.[154] It is also possible to retain only a particular aspect out of the diversity of acts; and sometimes the person can be fragmented without interaction between the parts. Sometimes again, the influence of an act on the person is counteracted by congealing the person at a certain stage of his existence, as in the case of this character of Jouhandeau, who says to his customer:

---

[154] Schopenhauer, *Sämtliche Werke* (Brockhaus), vol. 6: *Parerga und Paralipomena*, II, Zur Ethik, § 118, p. 245.

I am in the past. ... It is only my mummy, sir, who is mending your shoes.[155]

Besides these techniques of a general character, whose rich variety we are far from having exhausted, there are techniques with a more restricted range which apply only to certain specific acts. One of them is resort to the notion of exception. One pleads the exceptional character of the act in order to lessen its repercussion on the image of the person.

Sometimes an act will be described as clumsy or ineffective in order to suggest that the person did not give himself wholly to it, with all his might, with the best part of himself, and that therefore it is not a true manifestation of him.

Conversely, in order that an act should not suffer from the image held of the person, one will claim that the fact does not proceed from him and that he is merely a spokesman, a witness. Thus Bossuet asks:

Can corrupt preachers bear the word of eternal life?[156]

And he answers, using a simile of St. Augustine:

The shrub bears a fruit which does not belong to it but is no less the fruit of the vine though the shrub supports it. ... Do not scorn this grape on the excuse that you see it among thorns; do not reject this doctrine because it is surrounded by bad morals; it still comes from God.

The attribution of an act not to its author but to good luck or the attribution of an opinion to a third party or to an impersonal "they" are only some of the many well-known devices that, for a great variety of reasons, seek to reduce the solidarity between act and person.

All these techniques are very commonly and widely used in judicial debates, particularly in trials. The classical treatises on rhetoric rarely fail to point out that the defendant's best chance of getting off lightly may be to admit his crime and ask for mercy on the grounds of his past.[157] He will try to strengthen his solidarity with his praiseworthy acts and to weaken his solidarity with the acts for which he is on trial. The role of his counsel will be to present an image of his person calculated to arouse pity in the judges.

§ 72. *The Speech as an Act of the Speaker*

In treating the relationship between act and person, the speech, considered as an act of the speaker, deserves special attention, both be-

---

[155] Jouhandeau, *Un monde*, p. 35.

[156] Bossuet, *Sermons*, vol. II: *Sur les vaines excuses des pécheurs*, p. 489.

[157] Cf. *Rhetorica ad Herennium*, I, 24.

cause, for many people, speech is the most characteristic manifestation of the person and because the interaction between speaker and speech plays a very important part in argumentation. Irrespective of his wishes and whether or not he himself uses connections of the act-person type, a speaker runs the risk that the hearer will regard him as intimately connected with his speech. This interaction between speaker and speech is perhaps the most characteristic part of argumentation as opposed to demonstration. In formal deduction, the role of the speaker is reduced to a minimum; it increases progressively as the language used is more removed from univocity and as context, intentions, and ends gain in importance.

It is true, as Pareto pointed out, that Euclid's morality in no way influences the validity of his geometrical proofs, but, if the person who recommends a candidate hopes to draw a considerable personal advantage from his nomination or election, the weight of his recommendation will inevitably be greatly affected by it.[158] We must not overlook that the person is the best context for evaluating the meaning and significance of an assertion, especially when the statements are not integrated in a more or less rigid system, in which case the place they occupy and the role they play in the system provide sufficient criteria for interpretation.

Even the words of other people, when repeated by a speaker, have changed their meaning, for in the process of repetition he always adopts toward them a position that is in some way new, even if only in the degree of importance he attaches to them. This applies to statements made in arguments from authority. It is also true of children's remarks. Lewis Carroll was right when he wrote to a friend that irreverent remarks which are assumed to be innocent when made by children lose their innocent character when repeated by grown-up persons.[159] Conversely, an abusive remark by a member of parliament for which he should be called to order ceases to appear so serious to persons who thought he was quoting someone else.[160]

In this connection, let us mention an interesting American study[161] criticizing the procedures ordinarily used in social psychology to determine the influence of prestige. The subjects are first asked how far

---

[158] Cf. Stevenson, *Ethics and Language* (Yale), p. 128.

[159] Carroll, *Alice's Adventures in Wonderland*, Introduction by Alexander Woollcott, p. 6.

[160] Debate in the House of Commons on Oct. 4, 1949, as reported in *New York Herald Tribune*, Oct 5, 1949, Paris edition.

[161] Asch, "The Doctrine of Suggestion, Prestige and Imitation in Social Psychology," *Psychological Review*, 55 (1948), 250-276. Cf. the same author's *Social Psychology*, pp. 387-449.

they agree with a series of opinions. Later they are shown the same opinions along with references to their authors. The results do not prove, as is generally believed, that the subjects modify their evaluation only in terms of the prestige enjoyed by the author, all other factors remaining the same. The statement made is in fact not the same coming from one person as from another; its meaning does change. There is not just a simple transfer of values, but a reinterpretation in a new context, which is provided by what one knows of the presumed author. It follows that the influence due to prestige, and the power of suggestion it exercises, are manifested in a less irrational and more complex way than had been thought.

The ancient masters of rhetoric derived practical recommendations from the relation they recognized to exist between the opinion held of a speaker and the manner of judging his speech. They recommended speakers to give a good impression of themselves as persons, to gain the respect, goodwill, and sympathy of their hearers.[162] The speaker's opponents, on the other hand, should do their best to depreciate him by attacking his person and intentions.

In short, a speaker should inspire confidence: without it, his speech does not merit credence. In order to refute an accusation, Aristotle advises

> ... accusing, in our turn, whoever accuses us, for it would be the height of absurdity that the accuser should be deemed unworthy of confidence, but that his words should be deemed worthy of it.[163]

Those who are presumed to be untrustworthy are not even allowed in the witness box, and rules of judicial procedure very clearly aim at their exclusion.

Today, the advice to refute one's opponent by attacks *ad personam* can perhaps be followed in certain very special cases—for instance when it is a question of disqualifying an unreliable witness—but in the great majority of cases personal attack is likely to bring discredit on its user. The prestige of science and its methods of verification has diminished the credit of all argumentation which does not deal directly with the subject and attacks the opponent rather than his point of view. But the distinction between the speaker and what he has to say applies only where established criteria make this separation possible, through use of the techniques of severance. In many cases, and especially when it is a matter of edification, the person of the speaker plays a prominent part:

---

[162] Cf. § 104, infra: The Order of the Speech and Conditioning of the Audience.
[163] Aristotle, *Rhetoric*, III, 15, 1416a.

A worldly or irreligious cleric who goes up into the pulpit is just a phrasemonger. On the other hand, there are saintly men whose character, alone, carries the power of persuasion. They appear, and the whole multitude which is going to hear them is already moved and, as it were, persuaded by their presence. The sermon they are about to preach will do the rest.[164]

The same words provide quite a different effect according to who pronounces them. As Quintilian says:

> The same language is often natural when used by one speaker, foolish in the mouth of another, and arrogant in that of a third.[165]

The office of a speaker, no less than his person, forms a context which has an undeniable influence. The members of a jury will judge the same remarks quite differently according as they are pronounced by the judge, the counsel for the defense, or the prosecutor.

If the person of the speaker provides a context for the speech, conversely the speech determines the opinion one will form of the person. What the ancients used to call *oratorical ethos* can be summed up as the impression which the speaker, by means of his words, gives of himself.[166] Isocrates has this to say:

> Never support to defend a bad cause, for people will suspect that you yourself do the things which you aid others in doing.[167]

Although it is desirable that the speech should contribute to the good opinion which the audience may form of the speaker, he is very seldom permitted to achieve this by singing his own praises. The cases in which self-praise is permissible have been minutely examined by Plutarch.[168] They are the situations in which self-praise constitutes only an indispensable means to attain a legitimate end.[169] In all cases where its use seems determined by vanity, self-praise has a deplorable effect on the hearers. Plato represented all the sophists as braggarts because, thinking, as he did, that truth was more important than gaining the adherence of others, he could not see how the prestige of the speaker could be relevant. But, as soon as these procedures are examined from the angle of argumentation, a justification can be found for them which makes them less offensive.

---

[164] La Bruyère, "Les caractères. De la chaire," 24, *Œuvres complètes*, p. 464.

[165] Quintilian, XI, i, 37.

[166] Aristotle, *Rhetoric*, I, 2, 1356a; II, 21, 1395b; *Topics*, VIII, 9, 160b; Cicero, *Partitiones Oratoriae*, § 2; Quintilian, VI, ii, 8 et seq. Cf. Süss, *Ethos, Studien zur älteren griechischen Rhetorik*.

[167] Isocrates, *To Demonicus*, § 37.

[168] Plutarch, *Moralia, On Praising Oneself Inoffensively*.

[169] Cf. § 64, *supra*: Ends and Means.

Today self-praise by a speaker would appear to us more often than not as out of place and ridiculous. Ordinarily, the chairman of the meeting does the praising, but in most cases the speaker is known, either because he is speaking to a familiar audience or because he is known through the press and all the modern methods of publicity. The speaker's life, insofar as it is public, forms a long prelude to his speech.[170]

Because of the constant interaction between the opinions held of the speaker and of his speech, a person who is arguing constantly involves his prestige to a certain extent, and it will increase or decrease depending on the effect of the argumentation. A shameful, weak, or unintelligible argumentation can only damage the speaker. Vigorous reasoning and clarity and nobility of style, on the other hand, will act in his favor. Because of the unity between speech and speaker, most discussions, especially if before witnesses, partake somewhat of the nature of a duel, in which victory rather than agreement is sought: the abuses to which eristic argument has led are well known. The quest for victory is not, however, merely a sign of puerile ambition or a manifestation of pride, it is also a means by which the speaker can create for himself better conditions for persuasion.

The speaker will make every effort to conciliate his audience, either by showing his solidarity with it or his esteem for it or by demonstrating his trust in its judgment. A figure of speech, *permissio*, a term often translated as *surrender*, is illustrated by the following passage from the *Rhetorica ad Herennium*:

> Since everything has been taken away from me, and only my soul and my body remain, even these ... I deliver up to you.[171]

This is a figure of speech because the speaker cannot avoid having judgment passed on him, while at the same time he has no intention, in reality, of submitting to it.

Since a speaker must often assume the role of a mentor who advises, reprimands, and directs, he must be careful not to rouse a feeling of inferiority and hostility toward himself in his public: the audience must get the impression that it has full freedom of decision. In some very beautiful pages, Jouhandeau explains the divine discretion as the exercise of God's respect for the human ego: in spite of his power, God renounces everything which might seem to infringe on the independence of human judgment, to the point of wanting to appear absent.[172]

---

[170] Cf. § 104, infra: The Order of the Speech and Conditioning of the Audience.
[171] *Rhetorica ad Herennium*, IV, 39.
[172] Jouhandeau, *Essai sur moi-même*, p. 146.

Every technique promoting the communion of the speaker with his audience will decrease the opposition between them—an opposition which is harmful when the task of the speaker is to persuade. Ceremonial, a technique that enhances a speaker's glamor by emphasizing rank, can promote persuasion if the listeners consider it a ritual in which they themselves also take part.

When it is a matter of communicating facts, the personality of the speaker seems much less involved than when it is a matter of expressing evaluations. But, even then the attitude of the speaker can indicate his respect for the audience: discretion, restraint, refusal to pronounce on a point on which he is knowledgeable, and brevity in presentation[173] can all serve as tokens of esteem for his audience.

When it comes to initiation into a discipline, the feeling of inferiority on the part of the audience does not come into play, because the audience has previously wished to assimilate the discipline. The role of the teacher is really much closer to that of the priest than to that of the propagandist.[174]

In conclusion, it is to be observed that the connection between act and person exists also in the case of the audience. We have already seen that the value of arguments will be gauged in terms of the value of the audience giving the credence.[175] Conversely, an audience can be praised or blamed depending on the kind of speech to which it will listen, the kind of speakers it likes to hear, and the kind of reasoning which meets with its approval. The interdependence of act and person in the audience influences the effect of the argumentation. Reference to this connection between act and hearer can be superimposed on the arguments expressed, as well as on the connection between speaker and speech, and can interfere with these elements.

§ 73. *The Group and Its Members*

The connection between a person and his acts, with all the argumentation it may occasion, may be regarded as the prototype of a series of links which give rise to the same interactions and lend themselves to the same types of argumentations. The most common of these is per-

---

[173] Cf. Ogden and Richards, *The Meaning of Meaning*, p. 225.

[174] Cf. § 12, supra: Education and Propaganda.

[175] Cf. § 5, supra: Adaptation of the Speaker to the Audience; § 6, supra: Persuading and Convincing. Cf. also § 97, infra: Interaction and Strength of Arguments. In Hovland, Lumsdaine, and Sheffield, *Experiments in Mass Communication*, pp. 166-168, 190-194, 275-278, an attempt is made to characterize and classify opinions according to the audiences which accept them.

haps the relationship established between a group and its members, the members being the manifestation of the group just as the act is the expression of the person.

We must at once observe that there is no question here of advancing an "organicist" or Durkheimian sociology which would lead to the personification of the group and would attribute to it all the properties of a person. Such theories are merely particular conceptions of the relationship we are speaking about, which is one that is implicit in any statement concerning a group designated otherwise than by the enumeration of its members.

Thus we can repeat here what we have said about the relationship between the person and his acts. Individuals influence our impression of the group to which they belong, and, conversely, what we think of the group predisposes us to a particular impression of those who form it. If an academy sheds luster on its members, it is equally true that each of them contributes to the renown of the academy of which he is the representative.

The value of an individual reflects on the group. Fault in an individual can in certain cases compromise the reputation of the whole group, particularly if one refuses to make use of the techniques of severance. Jouhandeau relates this anecdote:

> Elise called a Moroccan to unload her firewood, and he noticed a Frenchman supposed to be helping him but who does it so badly that he finally exclaims, to Elise's delight: "To think I was colonized by 'that.'"[176]

Conversely, the prestige of the group can promote the spread of its ideas, habits, and customs and of its products and methods; everyone knows that hostility felt toward a group can become a serious handicap to the spread of these things.

Argumentation concerning a group and its members is far more complex than that concerning a person and his acts, in the first place, because a person always belongs to a number of different groups, but mainly because the notion of group is vaguer than the notion of person. There may be doubt not only as to the limits of the group, but as to its very existence.

Certain groups—national, family, religious, or occupational—will be recognized by everybody and may even enjoy institutional guarantees. But other groups arise out of the behavior of their members; for instance, within certain classes of children in a school, subdivisions may arise on the basis of age, sex, race, or religion, subdivisions which are more or less clearly patterned on existing social categories. Oppo-

[176] Jouhandeau, *Un monde*, p. 251.

sition can also arise between the small and the big, and these will form two quite distinct and closely knit groups.

Although the reality of a group may depend on the attitude of its members, it depends as much and even more on the attitude of outsiders. These like to think that a social group exists, whenever they themselves behave differently toward the members of the group. Thus, the notion of group serves to describe, explain, or justify this different behavior, as well as to support the arguments with which we are dealing here. It is to be observed that it is the needs of argument which explain the tendency to form into a group and so band together all those who are seen to share the same attitudes, the supporters and opponents of a certain viewpoint, a certain person, or a certain way of acting. This claim will not always be accepted. In short, the concept of group is an argumentative element of a highly controversial and unstable nature, but of the utmost importance.

The interaction between the individual and the group can be used to raise or lower the value of either. Stress may, for instance, be laid on the errors of particular archeologists in order to disqualify them all.[177] Conversely, although a man may not praise himself directly, he can present himself as belonging to this or that political party or church, and this might constitute a strong recommendation.[178] This constitutes an application of a very effective technique, which consists in the introduction of unexpressed positive value judgments under the cover of indisputable judgments of fact.[179] The speaker does not stress the value set implicitly by the hearers on all those who belong to the group in question: the more natural it seems, the more effective it will be.

Membership in a given group can, in fact, raise the presumption that certain qualities will be found in its members and this presumption will gain in strength as the feeling of class or of caste is more pronounced. Accordingly, Racine tries to make Phaedra seem a little less odious than in the Greek tragedy, on account of her rank. In his *Préface à Phèdre*, he writes:

> I thought that calumny was something too ignoble and black to put in the mouth of a princess who otherwise displays such noble and virtuous sentiments. Such low feelings seemed to be better suited to a nurse who could have more servile inclinations.[180]

---

[177] Vayson de Pradenne, *Les fraudes en archéologie préhistorique*, p. 314.
[178] Whately, *Elements of Rhetoric* (Harper), pt. II, chap. III, § 3, pp. 168, 169.
[179] Cf. § 43, supra: Status and Presentation of the Elements of the Argumentation.
[180] Racine, "Préface à Phèdre," *Œuvres complètes*, vol. I: *Théâtre*, p. 763.

Certain ways of behaving conform to the idea a person has of the members of a group. The behavior of aristocrats is aristocratic; that of serfs is servile; that of Christians is Christian; that of men is human. The behavior is often described by the name of the group, and it reacts on the image that is formed of the group.

We know that the value of an act depends on the prestige of the individual, and the value of the individual depends on the value placed on the group. The relation of the person to the act is similar to the relation of the group to the individual, and the two sets of relations can combine. The group will be proud of the conduct of those it considers its members and will often disregard those who are outside it.

> The examples of the noble deaths of the Lacedaemonians and others scarce touch us. For what good is it to us? But the example of the death of the martyrs touches us, for they are "our members" [Rom. 12:5].[181]

In the individual-group connection, the techniques of severance seem less developed than they are in the act-person connection, in the sense that we do not encounter an extreme where all reaction is suspended, as in the case of the perfect Being, or of opinion regarded as a fact. There is no group perfect enough in the sense required here: neither the society of the gods of antiquity nor Christian society nor the princely family can qualify. Closest to the notion of the perfect group is the notion of a humanity characterized solely by what is common to all men and unaffected by the behavior of any number of men.

On the other hand, would not the reasonable man, the man who obeys only the universal order, be detached from all groups,[182] and would not his behavior possess an objectivity corresponding to the objectivity of a fact? However, agreement on the universal order is far from being assured at any time.

Therefore the only technique permitting severance of the interaction between the group and the individual is the exclusion of the latter. This exclusion can be effected either by the individual himself or by the other members of the group or by third parties. If anyone expresses an opinion violently opposed to that of other members of the group and there is refusal to allow this opinion to be considered as that of the group, a breach will be necessary: there will be incompatibility between adherence to a certain thesis and membership in the particular group. The person who no longer shares the opinions of the group, while showing clearly that he does not wish to detach himself from it, will have to use dissociations that oppose, for example, the true doctrine

---

[181] Pascal, *Pensées*, GBWW, vol. 33, p. 257.
[182] Dupréel, *Essais pluralistes*, pp. 71-72, "De la nécessité."

to that of the majority.[183] But it goes without saying that the majority may not be of the same opinion and may proceed to exclude the non-conforming member. Such a procedure can be applied for any kind of action deemed incompatible with the interests or the honor of the group. Nearly always the exclusion results in the member's joining another group, and this act of joining is sometimes what shows that there has been a severance from the first group.

It may happen that exclusion is sought by the individual himself. In this case, the man who possesses certain outward characteristics usually serving as the criterion for recognizing membership in a group will bring about his exclusion—particularly in the eyes of third parties— by disagreeing with the beliefs of the group, or by adopting the beliefs of another group. It follows that an identical criticism of a group will have a very different significance according as it comes from a person who remains bound up with the group, from a person who wishes to be dissociated from the group, or from people who have nothing to do with it.

It is to be observed that the problem of the connection individual-group, in argumentation, is complicated, as compared to the problem act-person, by the possible inclusion of an individual in a group to which he has hitherto not belonged. If individual A defends the opinions of group B, he may be placed by third parties in this group. Henceforward, his arguments and opinions will be interpreted as those of a member of group B and not as those of an outside observer. It is accordingly sometimes a good thing, for argumentative purposes, to keep a distance between the individual and certain groups he may favor.

A group which rejects immediately, and more or less automatically, any nonconforming member, and which never accepts responsibility for its members, comes closest to the situation of the perfect person. But this requires constant criticism at least as severe as that of third parties, and this must entail a modification of the group, if only in its composition. This modification may be viewed as a simple mathematical operation, but it will more often be considered as a reshaping.

More frequently used than the techniques of severance are the techniques of restraint. One way in which law has progressed has been in the substitution of individual responsibility for collective responsibility, by ceasing to make the group liable for acts prohibited by legislation and subject to prosecution. But this is only a juridical technique, one which a moralist or a sociologist can repudiate.

[183] Cf. § 90, infra: The "Appearance-Reality" Pair.

The techniques of restraint with the widest application are resort to bias and the use of exceptions. The latter technique is more successful in the degree that the individual is thought less representative of the group: if leaders, delegates, or official spokesmen are often taken as incarnating the group, this is because it is more difficult to put their views or opinions aside as being exceptional. It has been pointed out that Bismarck, in his parliamentary speeches, attacked parties in the persons of their leaders.[184]

The claim is sometimes made that it is a fallacy to attribute to the group the ridiculous or stupid statements made by one member.[185] This amounts to requiring the hearer to make a distinction and not consider the individual whose assertions are incorrect or untenable as representative of the group.

Another technique of restraint, intended to show that the individual does not represent the group and does not identify himself with any fixed group, is to associate part of him with some of them, and part of him with others. Thus, according to Bernanos:

> A man of the *Ancien Régime* had a Catholic conscience, a monarchist heart and brain, and a republican temperament.[186]

All these techniques of restraint have repercussions on the two components of the individual-group relation. Resort to the exception not only tends to restrain the influence which the behavior of the individual exerts on the group, but can also have the effect of heightening or lowering the value set upon the individual, by presenting him as unique, by intentionally producing an effect of surprise.

> This exemption from the common fault is all the more esteemed as no one expects it.[187]

The more unfavorable the prejudice against the group, the more difficult it seems to imagine an exception and the harder the members of the group who do not want to fall under the general condemnation must work for recognition of this exceptional status. This explains the following disillusioned remarks of a Negro:

> I have often heard this reasoning. Did not my mother repeat a hundred times that it is bad enough to be black and that I must avoid committing the smallest mistake? Yes, I know that both Whites and Blacks are agreed on the fact that a Negro, who can claim

---

[184] Wunderlich, *Die Kunst der Rede in ihren Hauptzügen an den Reden Bismarcks dargestellt*, p. 85.

[185] Bentham, *Works*, vol. II: *The Book of Fallacies*, pp. 416-417.

[186] Bernanos, *Scandale de la vérité*, p. 27.

[187] Gracian, *L'homme de Cour*, p. 8, Maxime IX: "Démentir les défauts de sa nation."

so little indulgence on account of his color, is tolerable only as long as he behaves like a saint.[188]

§ 74. *Other Relations of Coexistence: Act and Essence*

The same interactions found in the relationship between act and person, and individual and group, recur whenever events, objects, beings, or institutions are grouped in a comprehensive way, are considered characteristic of a period, style, regime, or structure. These intellectual constructions try to connect and explain particular, concrete, individual phenomena by treating them as manifestations of an essence which is also expressed by other events, objects, beings, or institutions. History, sociology, and aesthetics are the favorite field for explanations of this type: events characterize a period, works a style, and institutions a regime. Even the behavior and manners of men can be explained not only by their membership in a certain group, but also by the period or the regime to which they belong: to speak of medieval man or of capitalist behavior is to try to show how this man or that behavior partakes of and expresses an essence, and how they, in turn, help to characterize it.

The philosophical notion of essence is one that is also quite familiar in common-sense thinking, and its relationship with everything that expresses it is conceived on the model of the relation of the person and his acts. We have seen how a person gets classified as a hero on the basis of certain characteristic acts which, so to speak, stabilize our view of him.[189] By a similar process, using a verb, adjective, or an expression designating a relation as starting point, essences come to be formed ("the gambler," "the patriot," "the mother") which characterize and explain the behavior of certain classes of beings.

Whenever act and essence seem to be in opposition, instead of interpreting one another, devices will be used that make possible a justification of the incompatibility: the man who does not fit in with his period will be a precursor or else will be behind the times, a work exhibiting characteristics foreign to the usual style of the author will have been developed under outside influence or will already show signs of degeneration, and not be a really pure expression of his style. Whatever does not correspond to the image of the essence becomes exceptional, and this exception will be justified by one or the other of innumerable possible explanations.

Recourse to the notion of essence will permit a variety of events to be connected to a stable structure which alone will be of importance.

---

[188] Zobel, *La rue Cases-Nègres*, p. 292.
[189] Cf. § 68, supra: The Person and His Acts.

328 THE NEW RHETORIC

The *philosophia perennis* is a classic example of this. Recourse to the notion of essence may also be implicit and may serve to account for certain changes. For instance, changes in a country's customs tariff will be considered the result of an endeavor to maintain a certain economic structure.[190] Politics become the economic structure in action: the variations of politics, which can be explained by occasional causes, are only accidental.

In this connection it is to be noted that what corresponds to essence—outside biological phenomena—can in most cases be determined with a freedom which surpasses that of the relation between act and person. But it is, of course, in reference to this essence, however defined, that all the phenomena of severance and restraint will be used with the purpose of reestablishing a compatibility between the essence and its manifestations.

Two interesting notions, that of *abuse* and that of *deficiency*, are correlative to the notion of essence, which expresses the normal way things occur. A speaker has only to mention abuse and deficiency for the hearer to refer to an essence which is implicitly understood.

Thus, according to Bentham, the maxim "from the abuse argue not against the use" is fallaciously used to avoid taking account of the bad effects of an institution.[191] The bad effects resulting from it should be considered as the *abuse*, while the ideal inspiring the promoters of the institution is the *use*, which would correspond to its essence.

It is often held that essence is determined by the element that was intentional, while the remainder, that which contravenes what was intended, is regarded as abuse or accident. The connection between intention and essence is made clear in this passage from Bossuet:

> You find it strange perhaps that I should give such great praise to the rebel and deserting angels; but I ask you to remember that I speak of their nature and not of their malice, of what God made them to be and not of what they have made themselves.[192]

Normal use conforms to the essence. Abuse must be detached from it or it will modify it profoundly. However, as long as the term "abuse" is used, it is a sign that one wishes to preserve the essence, that it is not at issue. If liberal supporters of capitalism favor the control of profits, they will say that they do so in order to correct an abuse of capitalism and to keep an essentially healthy economic structure. The socialists will support the same measure in order to attack and weaken capitalism,

---

[190] Cf. Weiler, *Problèmes d'économie internationale*, vol. II, pp. 282-300.

[191] Bentham, *Works*, vol. II: *The Book of Fallacies*, p. 469.

[192] Bossuet, *Sermons*, vol. II: *Premier sermon sur les démons*, p. 6.

which by its very mode of operation produces revolting inequalities. On the other hand, the liberal who is against the measure will say that there is a danger of its profoundly altering the structure of the system, while the communist, if he opposes it, will say that the measure is an illusory one, a mere palliative which makes no essential change in the system. Who is right in this case? It is difficult to say without having an exact idea of what the essence of capitalism is. The advocate of each course conceives capitalism in such a way as to justify his own point of view. What are considered, traditionally, to be value judgments determine conceptual structures which permit a better elaboration of the meaning and content of what are called judgments of fact. When revolution and reform are qualified, not in terms of the means employed, but in terms of the amount of change brought about in a system, the same discussion can arise, bearing on the essence of the changed system.

On the knowledge level, the notion of "distortion" corresponds to that of "abuse." Thus, according to Chester Bowles, the Indians have a distorted idea of capitalism.[193] This idea relates actually to the idea of deficiency as well as to the idea of abuse.

Like abuse, deficiency can be claimed only if one has an idea, be it vague or precise, of the essence in relation to which the deficiency is determined. The criterion which makes it possible to prove the deficiency is completely dependent on the conception held of the essence. A curious application of the idea of deficiency is found in the descriptions of woman in psychoanalysis: woman's characteristics are interpreted as a reaction to the lack of external genital organs, with the implication that man is considered to represent the essence.[194]

Deficiency is, even more than negation, to which it may be related, characteristic of argumentation on values, on what should be done. The notion of *deficiency*, unlike that of negation, cannot be reduced to formal characteristics, which are reversible and static, for it is defined in relation to a norm, whether it be the normal or the ideal. It corresponds to what J.-P. Sartre calls the internal negation as opposed to the external negation.

> By an internal negation we understand such a relation between two beings that one which is denied to the other qualifies the other at the heart of its essence—by absence.[195]

When essence is considered to be totally incapable of alteration, a deficiency, viewed as a deception, may suggest that the gap will be

---

[193] Bowles, *Ambassador's Report*, p. 106.
[194] Cf. Klein, *The Feminine Character, History of an Ideology*, pp. 72, 83.
[195] Sartre, *Being and Nothingness*, p. 175.

filled. It will provide an argument for claiming that there is something to look forward to:

> ... he is well aware that it is impossible that our nature, the only one which God created in his image, should be the only one left to chance. Thus, since he is convinced by his reason that there must be order among men, and since he sees, by experience, that it is not yet established, he comes to the necessary conclusion that man has something to look forward to.[196]

That which is *too much* is also defined in relation to essence, either a particular essence or just any essence. That which is too much in this latter meaning, being inexplicable by any structure or any order, will have neither weight nor significance.

> Consciousness exists like a tree, like a bit of grass. It drowses, it is bored. ... And this is the meaning of its existence: it is conscious of being redundant. ... [197]

The techniques for suggesting that there is a deficiency or a redundancy are very varied. One of them is the wish: a wish can lower the value of the person to whom it is addressed by summoning an essence to which the person does not conform. The safest way, Sterne says, to counter the force of a wish

> ... is for the party wished at, instantly to get upon his legs—and wish the wisher something in return, of pretty near the same value.[198]

Sometimes mere qualification, by evoking the essence, can make clear how far the reality is separated from it. In this way an imperfection will be revealed which without this reference might perhaps pass unnoticed. Antony will hold up Brutus as a friend of Caesar, in order to show how far he failed in the essence of friendship.[199] Sometimes certain modes of expression will be used to suggest the deficiency: a passionate style may convey that the scene described is not at all passionate enough.

These techniques are found also in *allusion* and *irony*. Allusion refers implicitly and irony explicitly to the essence which serves as a criterion for devaluation.

We conclude this section with an observation intended to reinforce our conception that the various relations of coexistence result from the generalization, or rather the transposition, of the act-person relationship, namely, that the categories of essence and of person can be

---

[196] Bossuet, *Sermons*, vol. II: *Sur la providence*, p. 208.
[197] Sartre, *La nausée*, p. 213.
[198] Sterne, *Tristram Shandy*, bk. III, chap 1, p. 140.
[199] Shakespeare, *Julius Caesar*, Act III, scene 2.

used to interpret the same phenomena. Whenever arguments based on deficiency are used, the notion of essence is applied, even to the person. On the other hand, whenever one wishes to make a group or an essence stable, concrete, and present, *personification* will be used. This argumentative figure makes it possible to stabilize the boundaries of the group and to give it coherence. The figure can be applied also to certain traits of the individual, as in this sentence of Demosthenes:

> In truth, it is your softness and your negligence which Philip has conquered, but he has not conquered the republic. ... [200]

Here we have two kinds of personification, the personification of softness and negligence and the personification of the republic. The first constitutes a technique of severance. Its effect is to isolate by making them distinct entities, the faults which the citizens of Athens have displayed and, by so doing, to shield them from the excessively devaluating effect of their acts and enable them to regard themselves as members of an unconquered republic in spite of their momentary lapses. The personification of the republic, on the other hand, reinforces its importance as a group that is more stable than the individuals who are merely its manifestation and that is strongly opposed to the accidents and vicissitudes occasioned by events.

Personification will often be stressed by the use of other figures. By the use of *apostrophe*, a speaker will address that which is personified and has therefore become capable of being made a hearer. By means of *prosopopoeia*, the thing personified is turned into a speaking and acting subject.

§ 75. *The Symbolic Relation*

It will be useful, we think, to compare the symbolic relation with the relations of coexistence. It seems to us that the symbol differs from the sign in that it is not purely conventional. If it has meaning and representational value, these derive from the fact that between the symbol and what it evokes there is a relation, which, for lack of a better term, we will call the relationship of *participation*. It is the almost magic, and in any case irrational, nature of this relationship which distinguishes the symbolic connection from the other connections, be they sequential or of coexistence. The symbolic connection, like these other connections, is considered part of reality, but it does not refer to a definite structure of reality. By reason of the fact that the symbol and the thing symbolized are often conceived to belong to different

[200] Demosthenes, *Third Philippic*, § 5.

strata of reality, to different spheres, their relation may be called one of analogy. But to view them in this way means destroying the most striking aspect of the symbolic connection, for it cannot play its part unless the symbol and the thing symbolized are integrated into a mythical or speculative reality in which they are mutual participants.[201] In this new reality there exists a relation of coexistence between the elements of the symbolic relation even when, in fact, the symbol is separated in time from the thing symbolized.

This happens when certain persons or events are treated as "figures" of other persons or events. Between Adam or Isaac or Joseph and Christ, of whom they are a prefigure, there is no sequential connection in a causal sense, but there is an indefinable relation of coexistence, a participation at the level of the divine vision of reality.

The symbolic connection brings about transferences between the symbol and the thing symbolized. When the cross, the flag, the monarch are viewed as symbols of Christianity, the fatherland, the state, these realities excite love or hate, veneration or contempt, which would be incomprehensible and ridiculous if these symbols, in addition to having a representative character, did not constitute a bond of participation. This bond is indispensable for arousing patriotic or religious fervor.[202] Ceremonies of communion require a material support on which emotion can fasten, for it is difficult to arouse and nourish emotion with a mere abstract idea. This link between the support and the thing for which it stands is not provided by a connection which is admitted by all, that is, by an objective connection, but by one that is recognized only by the members of the group: belief in these structures of participation is in itself an aspect of their communion.

The establishment of these immaterial bonds, of these invisible harmonies and solidarities, is characteristic of a poetic or religious or, we may simply say, a romantic conception of the universe. The romantic authors were fond, as we know, of describing events in such a way that human emotions and physical setting seemed intertwined. Even as realistic a writer as Balzac did not eschew this romantic view of things, as is shown by this portrait of Mme Vauquer in *Le Père Goriot*:

> Her round, elderly face, in which the salient feature is a nose, shaped like a parrot's beak, her little fat hands, her body as plump as a church mouse, and her gown that hangs too loosely about her are all in harmony with the room smelling of misery and tainted

---

[201] According to Cassirer, in the mythical view the part is identified with the whole so that the symbol and the thing symbolized are indistinguishable. Cf. Cassirer, *The Philosophy of Symbolic Forms*, vol. II: *Mythical Thought*.

[202] Lasswell et al, *Language of Politics*, Introduction, p. 11.

with the love of sordid gain, the close, foetid air of which she can breathe without nausea. Her face is as fresh as the first autumn frost, and the expression of her wrinkled eyes passes quickly from the forced smile of a ballet dancer to the sour scowl of the discounter. In short, her whole personality explains the boardinghouse, as the boardinghouse suggests her personality. The jail cannot exist without the jailer; you cannot conceive one without the other.[203]

It is to be noted that a speaker often has great freedom in the choice of connections. Thus, although in *The Divine Comedy* everything seems to indicate that souls here on earth are considered to be "figures" of what they will be in the world beyond,[204] this is a way of conceiving the relationship between present and future life that is by no means imperative. And, in Balzac's case, precise connections of the causal or act-essence type could have been invoked to interpret the relationship between the individual and environment. But it is only in a setting presented as unitary by simple description, without any justification, with a relation of participation postulated between persons and the environment, that the smallest event can assume a symbolic value.

Symbolic acts will play an entirely different role, and will have quite another meaning than acts which are not symbolic: they react more violently on beings who are bound up with them and who are responsible for them. The techniques of severance or restraint between act and person cannot be applied when the act is considered to be symbolic, for these techniques imply a certain rationality.

It is therefore important in argumentation to know to what extent a thing and everything related to it partake of this symbolic nature. In view of the indeterminate and objectively indefinite character of the symbolic connection, every thing, act, or event can be given a symbolic value, and its measure and importance can thereby be modified. The less plausible any other interpretation is, the greater the readiness to accept the symbolic aspect of an act.

Certain signs can become symbolic of a situation, of a way of life, of a social class, like the possession of a car of a certain make or the wearing of a top hat. Similarly, if an individual who is a member of a group has become a symbol of this group his behavior will be regarded as more important, because it is more representative, than that of other members of the same group. This symbolic person, representing the group, will sometimes be chosen to play this representative role either

[203] Quoted by Auerbach, *Mimesis*, p. 146. Cf. also Poe, "The Fall of the House of Usher," *Tales of Mystery and Imagination*; Villiers de l'Isle Adam, "L'intersigne," *Contes Cruels*, pp. 238-262.
[204] Cf. Auerbach, *Mimesis* pp. 183-196.

because he is the best in a given field, as, for example, a boxing champion, or because he is an average person whom nothing, not even his name, distinguishes, as in the case of the unknown soldier.

The man who is the spokesman for a group is, by this very fact, acknowledged as its representative. For a person to consider himself, or be considered, the symbol of a group is a fact which can exercise a decisive influence on his behavior. Recourse, in argumentation, to the concept of honor is always bound up with the idea that the individual is the symbol of a group. Honor varies from group to group and, moreover, assumes a certain superiority of the group. If one speaks of the honor of the person, it is as a symbolic representative of mankind. Giving one's word of honor is not a reference to the value of the individual, but to his symbolic relation to the group.

The behavior of an individual can dishonor the group; if it dishonors also the individual, this is because it entails his exclusion from the group and, in an extreme case, from the whole of mankind. He is regarded as a carrier of plague, by which one fears to be symbolically contaminated. The legal interpretation of this is civil death, and in some cases moral pressure will drive a person to suicide.

Resort to symbol can play an important role in the presentation of premises as well as in the body of the argumentation. Everything that concerns the symbol is supposed to relate to the thing symbolized. Although the relationship between them is not strictly reversible[205] — this has been seen to be a characteristic of all connections, except certain formal connections in quasi-logical argumentation—the symbol is modified by its use as such. Whatever may be the origin of the generally accepted symbolic connection between the lion and courage, each fresh use of this connection in argumentation confers on the lion certain characteristics and a certain value attached to courage.

The symbol is generally more concrete, more manageable, than the thing symbolized. This makes it possible to exhibit in concentrated form toward the symbol an attitude toward the thing symbolized which would require long explanations in order to be understood. The act of saluting the flag is an illustration. The technique of the scapegoat simplifies behavior by making use of the symbolic relation of participation between individual and group.

Not only is the symbol easier to handle, it can impose itself with a presence that the thing symbolized cannot have: the flag which is seen or described can wave, flap in the wind, and unfurl. In spite of its

---

[205] Cf. Ceccato, "Divagazioni di animal semioticum," *Sigma*, 4-5 (1947), pp. 294-302.

bonds of participation, the symbol maintains a kind of individuality which makes possible a great variety of manipulations. "There are no longer any Pyrenees" does not merely express a political idea; it evokes also the fatigues and dangers of a frontier and the enormous efforts needed to abolish it.

Any symbol can be used as a sign, and serve as means of communication, on condition that it is integrated into a language understood by the audience. But since the symbolic connection is neither conventional nor based on a universally known and acknowledged structure of reality, the meaning of a symbolism may be understood solely by the initiated and remain quite incomprehensible to everyone else: a symbol will lose the character of symbol where this initiation is lacking.

It can nevertheless happen that, after having lost their symbolic aspect, certain realities continue to be used as signs, as purely conventional means of communication. They will be, so to speak, desacralized and will then play a quite different role in spiritual life. The symbol that has become a sign designates the object signified more adequately than it did before; it is better adapted to the needs of communication because it has lost some of the aspects which were peculiar to it and gave it a reality independent of that of the thing symbolized. But this advantage enjoyed by the symbol that has become a sign is balanced by the fact that action on the sign no longer brings about action on the thing of which it is the sign.

We must not forget, however, that, like any connection, the symbolic connection can apply to speech itself. Whether or not it has a symbolic origin, the verbal sign may be regarded as having a magical connection with what it signifies: speech acts on what it states. On the other hand, the action on the sign can symbolize action on the thing of which it is the sign: carelessness in pronouncing a proper noun, the suppression of certain endings, the substitution of certain consonants for others, these are all actions which, intentionally or not, can indirectly influence the conception which the hearer forms of the thing signified.

The precariousness of the symbolic connection, along with its evocative power and its emotional strength, is doubtless due to the fact that it is virtually not subject to justification. Symbols have an indisputable effect on those who recognize the symbolic connection, but none at all on others. They are characteristic of a particular culture, but cannot be used for the universal audience, which confirms their irrational aspect.

Symbolic connections are extremely varied, precarious, and particular, but the same cannot be said of the existence of symbols themselves and of the importance attached to them. The symbolic value *in abstracto*, unlike particular symbols, can therefore be the subject of rational argumentation with a universal aim. The same holds good of all argumentation which demands that the symbolic connections belonging to a certain milieu should neither be neglected nor underestimated when one is addressing it: the demand here is simply for respect for a fact, namely the part played by given symbols in a particular society.

The figures of substitution, *metonymy* and *synecdoche*, have been variously described and defined by different writers.[206]

What seems to us to deserve attention, together with the structural relationship between the terms that are substituted for one another, is the question of whether there is a real connection between them and, if so, what it is. An important distinction between figures of sbstitution will emerge at this level.

There appears to be a symbolic connection in this example of metonymy taken from Fléchier by Dumarsais:

> This man (Maccabeus) ... who gave joy to Jacob by his virtues and his deeds.[207]

"Jacob" for the Jewish people, "John Bull" for England, "blackshirts" for Fascists, these are so many symbols. In the same way, we find "the scepter" for royal authority, "the hat" for the cardinalate, "Mars" for war, and perhaps even "the bottle" for wine, "a Persian" for a rug from Persia, and "a Philippe" for a coin bearing the head of Philippe.

In the synecdoches, on the other hand, like the use of "the sail" for the ship and "mortals" for men, we find that the substituted term is no longer united to the term it replaces by a symbolic connection, but points to a characteristic aspect of the designated object. Sometimes this aspect is a part of the thing sufficient for its recognition (as in the case of "the sail"); sometimes it is the class to which the thing belongs, but a class which makes it possible to characterize the thing as aptly as possible ("mortals" as opposed to "gods").

If attention is focused mainly on the connection between terms, there may well often be hesitancy in interpreting the figure as a metonymy rather than a synecdoche or vice versa. Let us simply note that if all figures are subject to certain cultural conventions (it would

---

[206] Cf. Baron, *De la Rhétorique*, pp. 341-345; Estève, *Études philosophiques sur l'expression littéraire*, pp. 223-225.

[207] Dumarsais, *Des tropes*, p. 53, cf. Fléchier, *Oraison funèbre de Turenne*, p. 4.

sound ridiculous, Dumarsais says, to say that a fleet of battleships is composed of a hundred masts[208]), figures based on the symbolic connection are the most precarious—unless they become signs and so lose their nature of figure.

§ 76. *The Double Hierarchy Argument as Applied to Sequential Relations and Relations of Coexistence*

Hierarchies, like values, belong to the agreements which serve as premises to discourse. But hierarchies can also be the subject of argumentation; there can be discussion as to whether a hierarchy is well founded and where some one of its terms belongs. One may wish to show why a particular term should occupy a particular place rather than another.

Different arguments can be used in this connection. In most cases, however, one will introduce a correlation of the terms of the contested hierarchy with those of an accepted hierarchy: one will be resorting to what we will call the double hierarchy argument. Sometimes the hierarchies are presented as so closely related that one hierarchy serves as criterion or definition for the other. When we hear the assertion that a certain man is stronger than another because he can lift heavier weights, we are not always sure if this latter hierarchy serves as foundation or as criterion for the first.

The double hierarchy argument is often an implicit one. For behind any hierarchy there may be discerned the outline of another hierarchy; this is a natural and spontaneous occurrence because we realize that this is how the interlocutor would probably try to sustain his assertion. And this to the extent that meditation on hierarchies often leads us to denying that any simple hierarchies can exist. We must however be careful not to think that the hierarchy which the interlocutor will use as justification is necessarily that which we have in mind. When we inquire why an item of news appears under a bigger heading than another, we may be able to answer that it is more important, more interesting, or more unexpected, but we shall find that the hierarchy on which the hierarchy of headings would be based remains implicit and vague.

Double hierarchy normally expresses an idea of direct or inverse proportionality, or at least a term-to-term relation. Nevertheless, in many cases, the connection, when closely examined, can be reduced to a statistical correlation in which the hierarchical terms of one of the

[208] Dumarsais, *Des tropes*, p. 85.

series are coupled to an average derived from terms belonging to the other. This is the case, for instance, when, from the respective heights of two men, the probable respective length of their limbs is calculated.

But it is evident that many hierarchies cannot be described or established by means of homogeneous elements capable of being counted or measured. It is when we are confronted with qualitative hierarchies, which exclude counting or measuring, that argumentation has the most important role and that other hierarchies often borrowed from the physical world, have to be called in to support these qualitative hierarchies. We may, for instance, use notions of depth, height, size, and consistency.

The quantitative hierarchy, which seems to underlie the qualitative one, is perhaps itself governed by a hierarchy of values. Thus, when Saint Anselm concludes that the freedom of not being able to sin is greater than the freedom of being able to sin or not to sin, the hierarchy of intensity is derived from our attribution of greater value to the first freedom.[209] Certain maxims, such as "He who can do more, can do less," which exhibit a quasi-logical form of argument— the inclusion of the part into the whole—can be justified or applied only by resorting to double hierarchies, the majority of which, despite appearances, are qualitative.

It is true that the origin of many of these double hierarchies is of little importance for their use. However, in order to justify using them, an effort will be made to discover a relationship between the two hierarchies that is based on reality, often by resorting to the concept of symbol. Or perhaps one will try to see a still closer connection between the two series, so that they form a single reality: to Cassirer, for instance, all activity of thought must express itself in spatial forms.[210] To many contemporary thinkers, such as Sartre, Merleau-Ponty, and Minkowski, moral qualities and physical qualities have one and the same root of meaningfulness,[211] and when Gabriel Marcel affirms that the life of a believer is superior to that of an unbeliever because it is "fuller," he states explicitly that this expression is to be understood to mean "metaphysical" fulness,[212] and he thereby excludes, as a mat-

---

[209] Saint Anselm, De Libero Arbitrio, chap. I, Patrol. Latine, vol. CLVIII, col. 490c-491a.

[210] Cassirer, The Philosophy of Symbolic Forms, vol. I: Language (Yale), p. 199.

[211] Sartre, Being and Nothingness, pp. 604 et seq; Merleau-Ponty, Phénoménologie de la perception, p. 329; Minkowski, "Le langage et le vécu," in the volume Semantica of Archivio di Filosofia, pp. 358, 362.

[212] Marcel, Le monde cassé, and Position et approches concrètes du mystère ontologique, p. 259.

ter of principle, any reference to a more or less full receptacle or to a more or less dense matter.

All relations, whether sequential or of coexistence, founded on the structure of reality, can be used to connect two hierarchies and to provide a basis for the double hierarchy argument.

Through the relation of cause and effect, variations in the volume of a body can be ranged in a hierarchical order in accordance with variations in temperature. Conversely, a hierarchy of ends can help to establish a hierarchy of means, in conformity with this observation of Aristotle's:

> Of two productive agents, that one is more desirable whose end is better.[213]

A reasonable being cannot but recognize this double hierarchy. This explains the strength of Leibniz' argument, which he borrowed from the Gospels:

> ... Since he [God] cares for the sparrows, he will not neglect reasonable creatures who are far dearer to him.[214]

Bossuet uses the same argument in one of his sermons:

> You have so often overcome yourselves to serve your ambition or your wealth, overcome yourselves sometimes to serve God and reason.[215]

He uses it elsewhere in the form of a hierarchy of ends based, not on the value of those ends, but on the ease with which they can be reached:

> If he [the demon] struggles with such steadfastness against God, although he knows that all his efforts will be in vain, what will he not undertake to do to us, of whose weakness he has so often had experience?[216]

This argument is of the same kind as this *locus* of Aristotle:

> Of two means, the one most related to the end is the more desirable.[217]

The double hierarchy is more frequently based on connections of coexistence than on sequential connections. Thus, setting persons in a hierarchy leads to the grading of their feelings, actions, and every-

---

[213] Aristotle, *Topics*, III, 1, 116b.

[214] Leibniz, *Die philosophischen Schriften*, vol 4, *Discours de métaphysique*, XXXVII p. 463.

[215] Bossuet, *Sermons*, vol. II: *Sur l'efficacité de la pénitence*, p. 567.

[216] Bossuet, *Sermons*, vol. II: *Premier sermon sur les démons*, p. 16.

[217] Aristotle, *Topics*, III, 1, 116b.

thing else that emanates from them. This is expressed in this *locus* of Aristotle:

> The attribute is more desirable which belongs to the better and more honorable subject, e.g., to a god rather than to a man and to the soul rather than to the body.[218]

Antigone's famous reply to Cleon is another illustration:

> I did not think your edicts strong enough to overrule the unwritten unalterable laws of God and Heaven, you being only a man.[219]

The attitude of Antigone is legitimate, but the opposite attitude is ridiculous:

> It is a singular thing to consider that there are people in the world who, having renounced all the laws of God and nature, have made laws for themselves which they strictly obey, as, for instance, the soldiers of Mahomet, robbers, heretics, etc.[220]

Argumentation of this kind assumes, of course, previous agreement on the hierarchy of persons, or it will not be effective. Thus, when Iphicrates, after asking Aristophon if he would hand over some ships for money and getting a negative answer, exclaims:

> Very good, if you who are Aristophon would not betray the fleet, would I, who am Iphicrates?

This argument has value only for a person who does not doubt the moral superiority of Iphicrates.[221]

Aristotle makes some curious applications of double hierarchy, based on the relationships which exist in his metaphysics between an essence and its incarnations. He has no hesitation in saying:

> If A be without qualification better than B, then also the best of the members of A is better than the best of the members of B; e.g., if Man is better than Horse, the best man is better than the best horse.

And conversely:

> ... If the best man be better than the best horse, then also Man is better than Horse, without qualification.[222]

He reasons in the same way about the stature of men and women,[223] implicitly allowing that distribution in the different groups always remains statistically the same.

---

[218] Aristotle, *Topics*, III, 1, 116b, 10-15.
[219] Sophocles, "Antigone," *The Theban Plays*, p. 151.
[220] Pascal, *Pensées*, GBWW, vol. 33, p. 240.
[221] Aristotle, *Rhetoric*, II, 23, 1398a.
[222] Aristotle, *Topics*, III, 2, 117b.
[223] Aristotle, *Rhetoric*, I, 7, 1363b.

Again, in contemporary biology, it is the relation of coexistence, far more than the causal relations, which underlies the relationships between hierarchies of different characteristics found in an individual—for instance, size and weight—or between the hierarchy of species and the hierarchy of a given characteristic—for example, place in the line of evolution and weight of the brain.

Double hierarchies are often used to extrapolate one of the hierarchies:

> If it pleases the barbarians to live from day to day, our own purpose must be to contemplate the eternity of the centuries.[224]

However, it is difficult to say whether the extrapolation is strictly limited to only one of the hierarchies. The length of time to be anticipated is stretched to cover eternity, but is man not also carried here beyond his condition? The following example shows clearly that an extrapolation can involve both hierarchies:

> Consciousness is generally imprisoned in the body; it is concentrated in the centers of the brain, the heart, and the navel (mental, emotional, and sensory centers). When you feel that consciousness or a part of it rises and remains above the head, ... then it is the mental in you which is rising to that spot and making contact with something that is above ordinary mentality.[225]

Extrapolation can consist also in passing from positive to negative degrees of a quality or situation or vice versa. It would seem that the double hierarchy argument formed the basis of what the ancients called "argument from contraries." Here are two examples of this mode of arguing:

> Temperance is beneficial, for licentiousness is harmful.

> If war is the cause of our present trouble, peace is what we need to put things right again.[226]

Analysis of these arguments in terms of subjects and predicates seems artificial and lacks reliability, but the arguments are justified if one admits a double hierarchy extending over the negative as well as the positive degrees of a quality or situation; the use of opposite terms is no more than a linguistic convenience intended to indicate approximately the respective position of the terms.

---

[224] Cicero, *De Oratore*, II, § 169.
[225] Shrî Aurobindo, *Œuvres complètes*, vol. III: *Le guide du Yoga*, p. 90.
[226] Aristotle, *Rhetoric*, II, 23, 1397a; cf. Quintilian, V, x, 73.

The double hierarchy argument makes it possible to base a contested hierarchy on an accepted hierarchy. It is therefore most useful when rules of conduct require justification. Since what is preferable ought to be preferred, the determination of what is preferable dictates our behavior. If certain laws are preferable to others, it is the former that we should obey and not the others; if certain virtues are objectively superior, we should strive to acquire them during our lives. It is by the expedient of double hierarchies that metaphysical considerations supply a foundation for ethics, as they do in this characteristic example from Plotinus:

> We are in search of unity; we are to come to know the principle of all, the Good and First; therefore we may not stand away from the realm of Firsts and lie prostrate among the lasts: we must strike for those Firsts, rising from things of sense which are the lasts.[227]

An ethical hierarchy of conduct will correspond to an ontological hierarchy.

By a rather understandable rebound, if there is unwillingness to accept rules of behavior which follow from the acceptance of a double hierarchy, the double hierarchy itself will be battered. This is the bent of Iphicrates' rejoinder to those who were trying to force his son, who was tall for his age, to take part in religious ceremonies for which he was not old enough:

> If you count tall boys men, you will next be voting short men boys.[228]

This example shows that argumentation by double hierarchy is sometimes used to lead to ridicule: one shows that an inadmissible double hierarchy is concealed in the opponent's assertion.

The refutation of a double hierarchy is made either by challenging one of the hierarchies or by contesting the connections—which presupposes a change in the view of reality which was put forward—or by showing that another double hierarchy counters the effects of the first one. On the other hand, acceptance of a double hierarchy generally strengthens the structure of reality invoked for uniting the two series.

In this connection, presence and absence tables, which might be considered a special case of double hierarchies limited to 0 and 1, might from another point of view be considered a very general case, referring to connections without a precise structure, but capable of elaboration through observation.

[227] Plotinus, *Enneads*, VI, 9, § 3.
[228] Aristotle, *Rhetoric*, II, 23, 1399a.

It seems to us that the double hierarchy argument forms the basis of certain well-known techniques of *amplification*, witness this example from Quintilian:

> The size of the ancient heroes may be judged by their weapons, as witness the shield of Ajax and Achilles' spear, Pelias.[229]

Another technique, based on the correlation between a hierarchy of acts and that of their qualifications, consists of performing a displacement of the whole second hierarchy. This operation seems to provide the best general explanation for certain modes of arguing described by the classical writers:

> After presenting particularly atrocious deeds under the most odious light, we extenuate them purposely, so that subsequent deeds may appear still darker. This is what Cicero did, when he said in a well-known passage: "But for the defendant I am prosecuting these are only peccadilloes."[230]

If the displacement of qualifications takes the form of an amplification, it is normal that a point should be reached where words can no longer be found to describe the most atrocious crimes:

> It is an indignity to put a Roman citizen in irons, a crime to beat him with rods, practically parricide to execute him. What shall I term the act of crucifying him?[231]

One of the two hierarchies therefore seems unable to follow the other. This deficiency can be claimed to be definitive, and the terms exceeding a certain degree of the hierarchy and exhibiting values of another order may stand for what is inexpressible or incapable of comparison.

Nearly all double hierarchy arguments can be treated as arguments *a fortiori*. The intention is then not so much to find the exact place of an element in a hierarchy with the aid of another hierarchy, but to determine a limit *a quo*. Thus in the argument quoted earlier, Leibniz affirms that God's care for men will be at least as great as that he bestows on sparrows. "If even the Gods are not omniscient, certainly men are not"[232]; the sacrifices made by a more distant relative should *a fortiori* be made by a closer relative.[233]

However, the term "argument *a fortiori*" in its strict sense will be confined to arguments like that which appears in this passage from

---

[229] Quintilian, VIII, ɪv, 24.
[230] *Ibid.*, VIII, ɪv, 19.
[231] *Ibid.*, VIII, ɪv, 4.
[232] Aristotle, *Rhetoric*, II, 23, 1397b.
[233] Cf. Proust, *A la recherche du temps perdu*, vol 8: *Le côté de Guermantes*, III, p. 234.

Isocrates where the limit is strengthened by another double hierarchy to which it also belongs:

> Is it not shameful that in those days single men among us were strong enough to protect the cities of others, but now all of us together are not able, nor do we attempt, to save our own city?[234]

Nowadays *a fortiori* arguments are often used more discreetly:

> I believe that a great power should be magnanimous, and, as to some extent this Government is in the wrong, it should show more magnanimity.[235]

A third hierarchy that comes into play—which we will call the *confirmative* hierarchy—is not derived from the first, term by term, as may occur in such a series of hierarchies as Gods, men—divine laws, human laws—obedience to divine laws, obedience to human laws. It therefore does not run entirely parallel to the first one, but enjoys a relative independence. To assess a line of behavior, one will relate it to such different factors as cause, effects, and conditions, which will make it possible to establish several double hierarchies working in the same direction. In the example given by Isocrates the greater importance of the end pursued and the superiority of the available means are calculated to enhance the shame evoked by the confrontation of the two situations.

Certain antitheses—and, in particular, the figure called *contrarium* in the *Rhetorica ad Herennium*, which "of two opposite statements uses one so as to neatly and directly to prove the other"[236]—are really nothing else than *a fortiori* arguments. Here is an illustration:

> Now why should you think that one who is, as you have learned, a faithless friend can be an honorable enemy?

Though it is the harmony of the sentence which prompts us to see a figure here, it is essentially an argumentative figure.

Double hierarchy arguments applied to the speech itself can give it a setting by the use of either sequential connections or of connections of coexistence. These connections will have reference to its aims, to the means it uses, to the speaker from whom it emanates, and to the audience he addresses. All these elements can belong to hierarchies. One of the main hierarchies will be the classification of audiences according to their size. It is not impossible for such a hierarchy to arise

---

[234] Isocrates, *Archidamus*, § 54.

[235] Crossman, *Palestine Mission. A Personal Record with Speech Delivered in the House of Commons*, 1st July, 1946, p. 254. (Hansard, vol. 424, column 1876).

[236] *Rhetorica ad Herennium*, IV, 25.

spontaneously in the hearers' minds and for it to influence their judgment on the speech and modify its effects.

§ 77. *Arguments Concerning Differences of Degree and of Order*

In examining the double hierarchy argument, we have stressed the fact that the hierarchies which serve as its basis can be either *quantitative* or *qualitative*. It is even possible for one of them to be qualitative and the other quantitative as, for example, in the correlations established in physics between colors and wavelengths.

Quantitative hierarchies exhibit between their terms only numerical differences, differences of degree or intensity, without any hiatus between one term and the next due to passage to another order.

The importance of this distinction between degree and order is well illustrated by the remark of Ninon de Lenclos on being told that St. Denis, after being beheaded, walked over a mile with his head in his hand: "It is only the first step that is hard." Her answer brings out admirably the great importance of a difference of order in comparison with a difference of degree.

The introduction of considerations relative to order, whether they result from the opposition of a difference of degree to a difference of nature, or from that of a difference of modality to a difference of principle, has the effect of minimizing differences of degree, of more or less equalizing terms which differ from one another only in intensity, and of accentuating that which separates them from the terms of another order. On the other hand, transformation of differences of order into differences of degree has the reverse effect; it brings terms which seemed to be separated by an impassable boundary closer together and emphasizes distances between the degrees.

Here is a passage in which Cicero takes up certain ideas of the Stoics:

> Wicked actions should not be judged by their results, but by the wickedness which they imply. The substance of the wrongdoing may be greater or smaller, but the act in itself comprises neither the greater nor the smaller. If a pilot loses a vessel loaded with gold rather than a barge loaded with straw, there will be some difference in the amount of the loss, but none in the incompetence of the pilot. ... It is with evil-doing as it is with stepping over a boundary: once outside, the deed is done; however far you go beyond the fence, you add nothing to the wrong of having crossed it.[237]

The decision to take account only of the vices of the agent, and not to classify wrongdoing by its consequences, tends to establish an axio-

---

[237] Cicero, *Paradoxa Stoicorum*, III, § 20.

logical hierarchy between actions that is characterized by a sharp division between what is permitted and what is forbidden. The degree of seriousness of the wrongdoing is of no importance: they all belong to the same order. What counts most is the quality of the human nature revealed by the act in question.

The following passage from Demosthenes' *Third Philippic* recalls Cicero's reasoning:

> Philip ... occupied Serrium and Doriscus and expelled your troops from the fortress of Serrium and from the Sacred Mountain, where your own general had posted them. What was he getting at in acting thus? For he had already sworn peace. Let no one say to me, "But what are these places?" or "Of what importance are they to us?" For whether they were small places and of no importance to you is another matter. But the sanctity of an oath and of justice, whether violated in a small matter or in a great one, have always the same value.[238]

This technique of equalization is often used where it is feared that something will hardly seem worth attention in its lower degrees. In order to obviate this possibility, the lower degrees are made to participate in the value which would normally attach to the higher degrees. The matter, by being placed in the realm of principles, is no longer solely assessed from a utilitarian point of view. The assertion of a fundamental distinction prevents strict application of the pragmatic argument.

There is perhaps an application of this technique of equalization in certain legal defense procedures. A small fragment of the facts will be admitted and told, in the anticipation that a difference of degree will, if necessary, be considered less serious than a difference of nature, and that one will not be put ill at ease by the accusation of having lied or of having suppressed facts.

By transformation of a difference of nature into a difference of degree, things that might appear to stem from incommensurable orders are brought into proximity with one another.

Here is a significant passage from Bergson:

> The difference [between ancient and modern science] is profound. In fact, in a certain aspect it is radical. But from the viewpoint from which we are regarding it, it is a difference of degree rather than of kind. The human mind has passed from the first kind of knowledge to the second through gradual perfecting, simply by seeking higher precision. There is the same relation between these two sciences as between the noting of the phases of a movement

---

[238] Demosthenes, *Third Philippic*, §§ 15, 16.

by the eye and the much more complete recording of it by instantaneous photography.[239]

Pomponazzi rejects any difference of order between the spiritual and the material, and consequently rejects one of the bases for the immortality of the soul, by his assertion that nature proceeds in a gradual fashion and that the lower forms of life, even vegetable forms, already have a more or less developed soul:

> There are animals that are intermediate between plants and animals, such as the marine sponges which are stationary like plants, but sentient like animals. There is the ape of which we do not know whether he is animal or man. And there is the intellective soul half way between the temporal and the eternal.[240]

The same result is obtained by an evolutionistic hypothesis which cannot consider the human species as belonging to a different order than the rest of the animal realm.

When we are confronted with two realms of a different order, the establishment of degrees within one of them is often for the purpose of diminishing the break between them. The way is thus prepared for reducing a difference of order to a difference of degree. The hierarchy set up in one realm is so established that its extreme degree forms a bridge between the two realms: thus the certain and the uncertain are more easily joined when there are degrees within the uncertain. Similarly, value judgments and judgments of reality are brought closer together by establishing gradations in the value judgments.[241] This technique sometimes benefits the material order, sometimes the spiritual:

> The natural sciences have grown a great deal toward the spiritual sciences. As a result, the differences are perhaps rather of degree than of principle.[242]

If we assert that we have a difference of order, we shall focus attention on what might have caused or might explain or certify or, at least, evidence the leap from one order to another. But if we assert that there is only a difference of degree involved, we shall not stress these factors. Often, therefore, the arguments relative to differences of order pave the way for, or presuppose, considerations bearing on the phenomenon which marks the break: mutation and emergence will be invoked to account for the leap from one order to another in the chain of evolution, while religious conversion will raise an individual from the natural order to the state of grace. In general, this key-event is obscure, unforeseeable, and irrational. In reducing differences of nature

---

[239] Bergson, *Creative Evolution*, pp. 360, 361.
[240] Cf. Garin, *L'umanesimo italiano*, pp. 175-177.
[241] For instance, Polak, *Kennen en keuren in de Sociale Wetenschappen*, pp. 95, 180.
[242] *Ibid.*, p. 171.

to differences of degree, one tends to use these vague elements sparingly and to confine the mind to what is known, familiar, and rational.

Among sequences, that of passing time plays an important role. The phenomena guided by this succession assume an aspect of continuity and homogeneity that is often also quantifiable: duration, growth, ageing, forgetting, and improvement can be quantified in terms of time elapsed. But successive phenomena are often cut up in such a way as to make them heterogeneous. We have already mentioned that certain periods of history are thought of as essences, of which particular phenomena are merely the manifestations.[243] In the present context, these essences thus assume the role of natures, principles. This means that whenever such essences are utilized, there will be a tendency to accentuate the importance of the events which are the source of, or the occasion marking, the discontinuity: a revolution, a war, the act of a prince, the work of a great thinker, in short, any phenomenon capable of justifying the break between two phases of history. Conversely, whenever essences are passed over, the importance of these events will be reduced.

In order to reduce in importance the idea held of a phenomenon connected with a break, we are led not merely to replace a difference of order by a difference of degree, but also to introduce new differences of order which will be deemed more important. When he argued against the fear of death, Montaigne presented the whole of life as a succession of "leaps" leading us toward death and showed that the last moments of life are not the most painful:

> We feel no shock when our youth dies in us, though in essence and in truth this is a harder death than the final dissolution of a languishing body in the death of old age. For the leap from uncomfortable being to none at all is not as hard as it is from a flourishing, sprightly being to one that is full of pain and trouble.[244]

By dividing life into several periods which die one after the other, Montaigne superimposes on the image of death creeping up imperceptibly a division into orders, different from the opposition "life-death," and consequently diminishes the sharpness of the break this latter contrast suggests. On the other hand, those people who insist on the importance of death and who would like to make it the center of our preoccupations will have to reject all other distinctions and hierarchies as nothing but vanity. So Bossuet declares:

> Thus man, small in himself and ashamed of his smallness, works to increase and multiply himself by his titles, his possessions, and

---

[243] Cf. § 74, supra: Other Relations of Coexistence, Act and Essence.
[244] Montaigne, *Essais*, bk. I, chap. xx, p. 104.

his vanities; so many times a count, so many times a lord, owner of so much wealth, master of so many people, minister to so many councils, and so on. However, though he multiply himself as often as he will, but a single death suffices to lay him low. ... He never thinks to measure himself against his coffin, which is, nevertheless, the sole true measure of him.[245]

It seems to follow from what has been said that there is a very clear opposition between quantitative series and hierarchies among terms which stem from two different orders. Yet, at a given moment, there may be a purely quantitative difference that brings about the passage to phenomena of another order. Here is an illustration which we have used already elsewhere.[246] When in the years following World War II, the Marshall plan for aiding Europe was being debated, its advocates claimed that a 25% reduction in the loans to be made would transform what was meant to be a reconstruction program into an assistance program. In other words, a quantitative change would bring about a change in the very nature of the plan. The obvious aim of this assertion was to secure a minimum of credits, below which the desired objectives could not be attained.

That a quantitative change can bring with it a change of nature was demonstrated long ago by the reasoning which the Greeks called *sorites*.[247] At a certain moment, grains added to grains make a heap, and hairs pulled out one by one transform a man with a head of hair into a bald one. But at what point is the boundary to be fixed, as fixed it must be however difficult the task? There is no objective criterion for this; there has to be a decision. When the decision is made, the break acquires an importance which a merely quantitative determination would not warrant.

The establishment of the break is made easier by the presence of certain concepts. Thus, the negative and positive aspects of a hierarchy, when indicated by a term and its negation—such as temperance and intemperance, or tolerance and intolerance—will often be interpreted as a difference of order.[248]

Every original conceptual development in some way modifies accepted hierarchies, either by reducing a difference of order to a difference of degree or, conversely, by replacing one hierarchical system by another considered to be more fundamental. These different ways of constructing and reconstructing reality have an undeniable effect on valuations and on the way in which they are made.

[245] Bossuet, *Sermons*, vol. II: *Sur l'honneur*, p. 173.
[246] Perelman and Olbrechts-Tyteca, *Rhétorique et philosophie*, p. 35 ("Logique et rhétorique").
[247] Cf. § 66, supra: The Argument of Direction.
[248] Cf. in § 76, supra: the Argument by Contraries.

CHAPTER 3

The Relations Establishing the Structure
of Reality

a) Establishment Through the Particular Case

§ 78. *Argumentation by Example*

The first half of this chapter is devoted to the analysis of the relations that establish reality by resort to the particular case. The latter can play a wide variety of roles: as an example, it makes generalization possible; as an illustration, it provides support for an already established regularity; as a model, it encourages imitation. We shall examine these three types of argument in turn.

Argumentation by example—by the very fact that one has resorted to it— implies disagreement over the particular rule the example is invoked to establish, but assumes earlier agreement on the possibility of arriving at a generalization from particular cases or, at the very least, on the effects of inertia.[1] This preliminary agreement may be challenged at some moment, but at this level of the discussion it will not be countered through argumentation by example. Accordingly, the philosophical problem of induction does not enter into our present discussion.

When is a phenomenon introduced into discourse as an example, that is, as the starting point of a generalization? For what rule does the

---

[1] Cf. § 27, supra: Agreements Particular to Each Discussion.

cited example constitute an argument? These are the two obvious questions that arise.

A description of a phenomenon does not necessarily have to be regarded as providing an example. To certain theorists in the field of history, the essential characteristic of history is its attachment to that which is unique in the events studied, by virtue of the particular place they occupy in a series which in its totality forms a continuous process characterized by the events themselves.

In the sciences, particular cases are treated either as examples that are to lead to the formulation of a law or the definition of a structure or else as specimens or illustrations of a recognized law or structure. When a precedent is invoked in law, the precedent is treated as an example that establishes a rule which in at least certain of its aspects is new.[2] And a legal provision is often regarded as an example of general principles that are recognizable from that provision.

On many occasions a speaker will clearly show his intention to present facts as examples, but this is not always the case: Certain American magazines like to describe the career of this or that big businessman, politician, or movie star without explicitly drawing a lesson from it. Are the facts retailed just a contribution to history or a sidelight on it? Are they examples suggesting a spontaneous generalization? Are they illustrations of well-known recipes for social success? Or are the central figures in these narratives put forward as remarkable models to be emulated by the public? It is impossible to be sure. Probably a story of this kind is meant to—and does indeed effectively—fulfil all these roles for different classes of readers.

Nonetheless, when particular phenomena are invoked one after the other we are inclined to regard them as examples. This is particularly the case when the phenomena exhibit some similarity. On the other hand, the description of a single phenomenon is more likely to be taken as a mere item of information. A single attorney, appearing on the stage, may be taken as a particular, rather than a representative, character. But if two attorneys are introduced in the same play, their behavior will seem to exemplify the whole profession.[3] It is to be observed in this connection that merely putting an event in the plural is of significance. Caillois makes this interesting observation about the plural:

> It brings about the poetic development, the generalization, which by giving an unimaginable event an archetypal value enables the event to take its place in human annals. This is just what the writer

---

[2] Cf. § 52, supra: The Rule of Justice.
[3] Cf. Aymé, *La tête des autres*.

does when he speaks of the Coliseums, Castiles, and Floridas or writes that "the land sings of its King Renés" [*Vents*, IV, 5] or multiplies—without naming it—the utterly unique Easter Island [*Vents*, IV, 2].[4]

We can be most fully certain that we have argumentation by example when a statement exhibits the strict form of this mode of argument. The extreme case is the phrase with five terms of the logicians of ancient India:

> The mountain blazes
> Because it smokes.
> All that smokes blazes, just like the hearth;
> This one likewise,
> Hence thus.[5]

When, on the other hand, the speaker does not himself draw any conclusion from the facts he advances, we can never be sure that he wishes them to be taken as examples. Schopenhauer mentions a stratagem consisting in extracting from the speaker's words conclusions that run counter to his thought.[6] A speaker can be highly embarrassed when something is treated as an example when he did not intend it to be.

Even when it is made quite apparent that argument by example is being used, there is a tendency to lead the hearer from the example to a particular conclusion, without any rule being stated. This is termed arguing *from the particular to the particular*:

> We must prepare for war against the king of Persia and not let him subdue Egypt. For Darius of old did not cross the Aegean until he had seized Egypt; but once he had seized it, he did cross. If therefore the present king seizes Egypt, he also will cross, and therefore we must not let him.[7]

This form of reasoning, as well as passage from example to rule, appeals to inertia. The notions used in describing the particular instance that serves as example implicitly operate as the rule enabling the passage from one instance to another. This curious piece of reasoning by Simone Weil sheds light on the process involved:

> Just as the only way of showing respect for somebody suffering from hunger is to give him something to eat, so the only way of

---

[4] Caillois, *Poétique de Saint-John Perse*, p. 152.

[5] Annambhatta, *Le compendium des topiques*, pp. 128 et seq.

[6] Schopenhauer, *Sämtliche Werke* (Brockhaus), vol. 6: *Parerga und Paralipomena*, Zweiter Band, *Zur Logik und Dialektik*, § 26, "Achtes Stratagem," p. 31.

[7] Aristotle, *Rhetoric*, II, 20, 1393b.

showing respect for somebody who has placed himself outside the law is to reinstate him inside the law by subjecting him to the punishment ordained by the law.[8]

The rule implicit in this argument is that the only means of showing respect to a human being is to give him what he lacks. But whereas the example of the hungry man is not liable to be disputed, because there is a coincidence of objective and subjective viewpoints (the hungry man is "suffering from hunger"), application of the rule to the case of the criminal lets the objective viewpoint prevail, without paying much attention to the wishes of the person who is the object of our solicitude.

Criticism of argument from the particular to the particular, which is characteristic of the Socratic dialogues, will center on the conceptual material by means of which passage is made from one situation to another.

Whatever the way in which an example is presented, whatever the field in which the argumentation takes place, the example chosen must, in order to be accepted as such, enjoy the status of a fact, at least provisionally. The greatest advantage to be got from the use of an example is the focusing of attention on this status. Thus, most of Alain's observations start with a concrete statement which the reader has no reason to question. If the example is rejected either as being contrary to historical truth or because convincing reasons can be found for opposing the suggested generalization, adherence to the thesis that is being promoted will be considerably weakened. For the choice of example, considered as an element of proof, commits the speaker as if he had made an admission. The hearers have the right to assume that the soundness of the thesis is closely related to the argument that seeks to establish it.

What generalization can the example yield? This question is closely connected with that of knowing what cases can be considered examples of the same rule. It is by their relation to a given rule that phenomena become interchangeable, and, on the other hand, it is by their enumeration that the point of view from which they have been compared to one another emerges. For this reason, when one wishes to clarify a rule with many different applications, it is good to provide examples that are as different as possible, as by doing so it can be shown that the differences are without importance on this occasion. Thus we find Berkeley writing:

> I further observe, that sin or moral turpitude doth not consist in the outward physical action or motion, but in the internal devia-

[8] Weil, *The Need for Roots*, p. 21.

tion of the will from the laws of reason and religion. This is plain, in that the killing an enemy in a battle, or putting a criminal legally to death, is not thought sinful, though the outward act be the very same with that in the case of murder.[9]

By giving more than one example, Berkeley makes his thought more precise as though by a comment. Systematization of this procedure leads to the classical rules concerning the variation of conditions in induction. Application of these rules can yield a principle that is quite general in its bearing and significance. Thus, the principle of the lever can be used in such a wide variety of forms that it is hardly possible to find a physical characteristic that is common to them all.[10]

Instead of merely cumulating a number of different examples, a speaker will sometimes strengthen the argumentation by example by resorting to the double hierarchy argument which makes *a fortiori* reasoning possible. This is what we call resort to the hierarchically arranged example:

> [Everyone honours the wise.] Thus, the Parians have honoured Archilochus, in spite of his bitter tongue; the Chians Homer, though he was not their countryman; the Mytilenaeans Sappho, though she was a woman; the Lacedaemonians Chilon ..., though they are the least literary of men.[11]

Whately was apparently recommending resort to the hierarchically arranged example when he speaks of "argument from progressive approach."[12]

Selection of the example that is most convincing because of the rarity of its occurrence may give rise to caricature. If, in order to prove that grief can turn the hair of some victims white overnight, a speaker relates that this infrequent accident befell a merchant who lost a cargo at sea, and that his wig suddenly turned gray,[13] the effect produced is ascribable to the humor of argumentation. Many of the tall stories for which Marseilles is famous are but hierarchically arranged examples which try to be too convincing.

It is to be observed that there is an interaction between the examples, in the sense that the mention of a further example modifies the meaning of the examples previously given, making it possible to define accurately the point of view from which the facts given earlier should be regarded. In the field of law, for instance, although the term "precedent" is sometimes reserved for the first decision made pursuant

---

[9] Berkeley, *The Works of George Berkeley*, vol. II: "Three Dialogues between Hylas and Philonous," Third Dialogue, pp. 236-237.

[10] Cf. on this question, Polanyi, *The Logic of Liberty*, p. 21.

[11] Aristotle, *Rhetoric*, II, 23, 1398b.

[12] Whately, *Elements of Rhetoric*, pt. I, chap II, § 6, (Harper), pp. 65-68.

to a certain interpretation of a statute, the full bearing of the decision may emerge only gradually, after a number of later decisions have been made. Thus, it would appear that being content with a single example in argument is an indication that no doubt is felt as to the manner of generalizing it. From this standpoint, the situation is similar where numerous instances are lumped together under a single rubric like "One often sees that. ..." They may doubtless be assumed to differ a little from each other, but, for the purposes of the generalization, they are treated as a single example. Multiplication of undifferentiated instances becomes important, on the other hand, when a speaker does not want to make a generalization, but to establish the frequency of an occurrence and to reach a conclusion as to the probability of observing it in the future. Here again the undifferentiated nature of the occurrences nonetheless presupposes a certain variability in the conditions. The choice of cases for observation must accordingly be made in such a way that the representative character of the samples taken from reality is guaranteed.

In many statements, including the passage from Berkeley quoted earlier in this section, an essential role is also played by the invalidating case, the *exemplum in contrarium*, which prevents an unwarranted generalization by showing the incompatibility of the generalization with it and thereby indicates in which direction only it is permissible to generalize.

According to Karl Popper, it is the weakening of a rule by the invalidating case, with the subsequent rejection or modification of the rule, which provides the sole criterion making it possible to verify a law of nature empirically.[14]

But does the invalidating case, even when it is unchallenged, always result in rejection of the law? It does, if by law is meant a statement applicable to an aggregate of cases that includes the invalidating case. This implies, at the limit, that the invalidating case could be foreseen before the rule was formulated, which wouldn't make sense. In reality, a particular observed case can never be in absolute contradiction with a judgment of empirical universality. It can only strengthen or weaken it.[15] The law can always be retained by slightly changing its scope to take into account the newly introduced case.

The law can also be maintained by restricting its field of application, through resort, for instance, to the concept of *exception*: the relation between events connected by the law ceases, as in grammar and lin-

---

13 Cf. Lalo, *Esthétique du rire*, pp. 159-160.
14 Popper, *Logik der Forschung*, particularly pp. 12-14.
15 Cf. Waismann, "Verifiability," Flew, *Essays on Logic and Language*, p. 125.

guistics, to be an absolute one. Sometimes an effort will be made to replace a deterministic law by a more or less strict correlation.

Both solutions presuppose that the occurrences requiring a modification or restriction of the law are admitted and are even theoretically at least, capable of enumeration. When enumeration is inconceivable, other solutions must be found. One solution commonly adopted is to leave the rule standing, but to list the categories to which it is not applicable. Resort to the concept of miracle is a device of this kind. The existence of the miraculous event does not bring about a modification of the laws of nature. On the contrary, for a miracle to exist, the miraculous occurrence and the law must coexist, each in its own sphere.

Another technique is to transform a rule that is threatened into a conventional rule. This is what happens when determinism is regarded as a methodological rule and not as a scientific law[16] or when legal presumptions are established.

Argumentation is to a considerable extent concerned with getting audiences to be conscious of the invalidating fact, that is, to recognize that the facts admitted by them contradict rules which they also admit. We know from certain experiments of Eliasberg that there is an interaction between the perception of invalidating facts and the awareness of the rule. A child is asked to find cigarettes placed under certain cards (blue ones); when a tendency to choose blue cards has been established, the child is subjected to a test in which there are no cigarettes under *one* of the blue cards. At this point the rule is brought to the level of full consciousness, and the child rapidly formulates it.[17] It is not surprising, then, that it is possible in argumentation to use invalidating cases, not only to cause the rejection of the rule, but also to define it. This is particularly true in law, where provisions dealing with an exception are the only source for making known a rule that has otherwise never been stated.

Language plays an essential role in argument by example. When two phenomena are subsumed under a single concept, their assimilation seems to derive from the very nature of things, while their differentiation appears to require justification. This is why persons engaged in argumentation frequently adapt the notions they use to suit their exposition, except in those disciplines in which the use of concepts is accompanied by a technique defining their field of application. Particularly in argument by example are the meaning and scope of notions influenced by the dynamic aspects of their use. Moreover, this adaptation,

---

[16] Cf. Kaufmann, *Methodology of the Social Sciences.*

[17] Guillaume, *Manuel de psychologie,* p. 274. Cf. also Eliasberg, "Speaking and Thinking," in Révész, *Thinking and Speaking,* pp. 98-102.

this modification of notions usually seems so natural and so in harmony with the needs of the situation that it goes almost completely unnoticed.

The stronger the desire to subsume the examples under a single rule without modifying it, the greater the importance of the role played by the use of language for assimilating the different cases. This is especially true in law. In the making of a legal decision, the assimilation of new instances is not just a matter of passing from the general to the particular. It also contributes to the foundation of juridical reality, that is, of norms, and, as we have already seen, new examples react on earlier ones and modify their meaning. It has rightly been emphasized that through what is called *projection* this assimilation of new cases that were unforeseeable or not taken into consideration when the law was elaborated is effected quite easily, without recourse to any technique of justification.[18] Language is often one step ahead of the jurist. In turn, the jurist's decision—for language does not impose a decision on him, but facilitates his task—may react on the language. In particular, his decision may have the result that two words which could, at a given time, be regarded as homonyms will be interpreted as stemming from a single concept.

§ 79. *Illustration*

The difference between illustration and example lies in the status enjoyed by the rules they support.

Whereas an example is designed to establish a rule, the role of illustration is to strengthen adherence to a known and accepted rule, by providing particular instances which clarify the general statement, show the import of this statement by calling attention to its various possible applications, and increase its presence to the consciousness. Though there may be situations where it would be hard to say what is the function of a particular case cited in the course of argumentation, the suggested distinction between illustration and example seems to us nonetheless important and meaningful, for, as they have different functions, different criteria will be used in their selection. While an example must be beyond question, an illustration need not be, as adherence to the rule does not depend on it. On the other hand, it should strike the imagination forcibly so as to win attention.

Aristotle had already differentiated two uses of the example depending on whether or not a general principle was involved. (Use as an

---

[18] Cf. for instance, Drilsma, *De Woorden der Wet of de Wil van de Wetgever*, pp. 116 et seq.

358 THE NEW RHETORIC

element of induction, use as testimony.) But according to him, the use made of particular cases will differ according as they precede or follow the rule to which they relate. He says:

> If you put your examples first you must give a large number of them; if you put them last, a single one is sufficient; even a single witness will serve if he is a good one.[19]

However, the order in the speech is not an essential factor. Examples may follow the rule they are used to prove, and illustrations of a rule that is fully accepted may precede the statement of that rule. At the very most, the order will incite one to consider a fact as an example or as an illustration—and as Aristotle correctly points out the hearer is more demanding in the first case.

Bacon, emphasizing that it was not just a question of the order, but of the substance of the discourse, affirms that an example "should be set down with all circumstances," when used inductively, because circumstances can play a role of paramount importance in the reasoning, whereas when examples are used in a "servile" manner thay can be cited succinctly.[20] On this point, we shall not follow Bacon, for an illustration designed to create presence will sometimes have to be developed with a wealth of concrete and vivid detail, whereas an example should be carefully pruned in order that the mind should not be distracted and depart from the aim the speaker has set himself. An illustration runs much less risk than an example of being misinterpreted, since we are guided by the rule, which is known to us—sometimes very well indeed.

Whately brings out very clearly that some examples are not introduced to further proof, but "for illustration."[21] He speaks, in this connection, of the passage in the De Officiis where Cicero maintains that "nothing is expedient which is dishonorable," and adduces the example of the proposed design of Themistocles to burn the allied fleet, which Cicero, unlike Aristides at the time, disapproved of as being inexpedient, because unjust.[22] Whately points out that the instance cited by Cicero would be a plain begging of the question if it were intended as an example introduced to establish the rule, since it presupposes the rule. But this would not be the case if the instance were meant to illustrate the scope of the rule.

Although the difference between example and illustration may be subtle, it is not unimportant, as it enables us to see, not only that par-

[19] Aristotle, *Rhetoric*, II, 20, 1394a.
[20] Bacon, *Advancement of Learning*, bk II, xxiii, § 8, GBWW, vol. 30, p. 85.
[21] Whately, *Elements of Rhetoric*, pt I, chap. iii, § 3, (Harper), p. 102.
[22] Cicero, *De Officiis*, III, xi, 49.

ticular cases are not always introduced to establish a rule, but that sometimes the rule is stated in order to lend support to the particular cases that appear to corroborate it. In their tales of fantasy, Poe and Villiers de l'Isle-Adam often begin the story by stating a rule, and the rest of the story is simply an illustration of it. The purpose of this is to make the events more credible.

When at the beginning of Part II of the *Discourse on the Method,* Descartes maintains that

> there is very often less perfection in works composed of several portions, and carried out by the hands of various masters, than in those on which one individual alone has worked,[23]

he goes on to enumerate some particular instances. A building designed by a single architect is more beautiful, the layout of a city is better; a constitution framed by a single legislator, like the true religion "whose ordinances are of God alone," is incomparably better organized; the reasoning of a man of sense with respect to matters that are only probable is closer to the truth than knowledge found in books; the judgments of those led only by reason from birth are more excellent and solid than those of men governed by several masters. According to Étienne Gilson,[24] Descartes gives these examples to support his thesis that the thing made or done by a single person is superior, and to justify the intention he conceived of reconstructing the whole body of knowledge on the basis he propounded. But are the different instances he cites all examples? When closely examined, the last two seem rather to be illustrations of a rule that has already been established by the preceding examples. It may be conceded that the idea of the beautiful, the harmonious, and the systematic held by Descartes' contemporaries permitted them to accept the value of his reflections on buildings, cities, constitutions, and religion, but his two last assertions are distinctly paradoxical and could be favorably received only by someone who saw them as illustrations of a previously accepted rule, as they presuppose a conception and criterion of truth and method that form the original contribution of Cartesian thought. The particular cases enumerated for the purpose of sustaining a rule do not all have the same role, for, while the first ones must be beyond question in order to count as heavily as possible in the discussion, the following ones profit by the credit attaching to the first, and the last ones may only serve as illustrations. This not only explains why all cases are not on the same plane and why the order in which they are presented is not reversible, but also how it is that the passage from example to illustration often occurs almost

---

[23] Descartes, *Discourse on the Method,* GBWW, vol. 31, p. 44.
[24] Descartes, *Discours de la méthode* (Vrin), p. 55, note 1.

imperceptibly, and that controversy is possible as to the manner of understanding and qualifying the use of each particular case and its relation to the rule.

Because an illustration seeks to increase presence by making an abstract rule concrete by means of a particular case, there is a tendency to see an illustration as "a vivid picture of an abstract matter."[25] But unlike an analogy, an illustration does not lead to replacement of the abstract by the concrete, or to the transposition of structures into another sphere.[26] It really *is* a particular case, it corroborates the rule, it can even, as in proverbs, actually serve to state the rule.[27] Illustrations are undoubtedly often chosen for their affective impact. The illustration used by Aristotle in the following passage is clearly of this nature. He is contrasting periodic style with free-running style, which has the disadvantage that it has no definite end in itself:

> ... one always likes to sight a stopping-place in front of one: it is only at the goal that men in a race faint and collapse; while they see the end of the course before them, they can keep on going.[28]

Very often the purpose of an illustration is to promote understanding of the rule, by means of an unquestionable instance of its application. Illustrations often have this function in the writings of Leibniz, as in the following passage:

> [Moral evil] should be admitted or *permitted* only insofar as it is regarded as the necessary consequence of an indispensable duty, in circumstances such that the person who would like to prevent another's sin would fail in his own duty if he did; as if an officer with the duty of guarding an important post were to leave it, particularly at a time of danger, in order to stop a quarrel in the town between two soldiers of the garrison who were on the point of killing one another.[29]

Comparable to the hierarchically arranged example is the amazing, unexpected, and prestigious illustration which depends on its startling nature to bring out the significance of a rule. Méré gives the following illustration of his assertion that only the lovable man is loved:

> When I reflect how it is that the Lord loves one man and hates another without our knowing why, I see no other reason than that he finds things to please him in the first and not in the second,

---

[25] Thouless, *How to Think Straight*, p. 103.
[26] Cf. § 82, infra: What is Analogy?
[27] Cf. § 40, supra: Form of the Discourse and Communion with the Audience.
[28] Aristotle, *Rhetoric*, III, 9, 1409a.
[29] Leibniz, *Die philosophischen Schriften*, vol. VI, *Essais de Théodicée*, p. 117.

and I am convinced that the best and perhaps the only means of salvation is to please him.[30]

The inadequate illustration does not play the same role as the invalidating case, because the rule is not called in question and hence the inadequate statement of the illustration reflects on the person using it, testifying to his misunderstanding or misinterpretation of the rule.

However, a deliberately inadequate illustration can constitute a form of *irony*. The speaker who in one and the same breath says: "You must respect your parents; when one of them rebukes you, answer back promptly," raises a doubt as to whether the rule is to be taken seriously.

This ironic use of the inadequate illustration is particularly striking by reference to qualifications. It will be observed in this connection that the "rule" is any statement that is general with respect to that which is an application of it. The qualification assigned to a person can be considered a rule of which his behavior provides illustrations.[31] Antony is using a deliberately inadequate illustration when, along with repeated assertions that Brutus is a honorable man, he enumerates his acts of ingratitude and betrayal;[32] Montherlant uses it also in *Les jeunes filles* where he has Costals declare that Andrée Hacquebaut is intelligent, but page after page testifies to her stupidity.[33] Certain classical figures like *antiphrasis* are often just an application of this same device.

Just as an example not only provides a foundation for a rule but also makes it possible to go from one particular instance to another, a comparison, when it is not an evaluation,[34] is often an illustration of one case by means of another, both being considered as applications of the same rule. Here is a typical example of its use:

> Difficulties are what show a man's character. Therefore, when you encounter a difficulty, remember that God, like a gymnastics teacher, has pitted you against a young and formidable partner.[35]

In a passage like the following, reference to a rule, though it is completely implicit, is also unmistakably present, so that we are indeed dealing with an illustration:

---

[30] Méré, *Œuvres complètes*, vol. II: *Des agrémens*, p. 29.
[31] Cf. also, qualification as an expression of essence, in § 74, supra.
[32] Shakespeare, *Julius Caesar*, Act III, scene 2.
[33] Cf. Beauvoir, *Le deuxième sexe*, vol. I, p. 315.
[34] Cf. § 57, supra: Arguments by Comparison.
[35] Epictetus, *Discourses*, I, 24, § 1.

No dead, no dying; the area close to the ambulance is the part of the battlefield that is kept clean and tidy for the sake of hygiene. The nearest hedges and haystacks are stripped of wounded, as are the low branches in an orchard of their fruit.[36]

Some comparisons illustrate a general qualification through the use of a concrete instance well known to the hearer, as in such expressions as "proud as Lucifer" or "rich as Croesus." Expressions of this kind seek to transfer to the person to whom they are applied some of the characteristic quality of the chosen illustration, but they rapidly degenerate into "clichés," and at the most have the value of a superlative.

What part is played in argumentation by the fictitious particular case, by mental experimentation? Mach, Rignano, Goblot, Ruyer, and Schuhl are some of those who have investigated this problem, which arises mostly in connection with illustration.[37] For a situation that will illustrate a rule can be most easily constructed when the rule is familiar; for example, the rule prescribing the selection by lot of the responsible leaders, is illustrated by the story of the sailors choosing their captain by lot.[38] Fictitious cases are not to be confused in this connection with cases that are made up by a speaker to suit his cause, but could very easily have occurred.

The author of *Rhetorica ad Herennium* explains why he considers it better to devise his own illustrations for the rules of rhetoric he lays down, rather than to borrow them, as the Greeks did, from great writers.[39] The manufactured case has a closer connection with the rule than an observed case, and shows better than the latter that success is possible to one who conforms to the rule, as well as what the rule consists of. However, this guarantee is to some extent illusory. The manufactured case resembles an experiment conducted in a school laboratory, but it may be devised rather in imitation of an outstanding model than as an application of the rule it is supposed to illustrate.

§ 80. *Model and Anti-Model*

In the realm of conduct, particular behavior may serve, not only to establish or illustrate a general rule, but also to incite to an action inspired by it.

[36] Giraudoux, *Lectures pour une ombre*, p. 216.

[37] Cf. Mach, *Erkenntnis und Irrtum*; Rignano, *Psychologie du raisonnement*; Goblot, *Traité de logique*; Ruyer, *L'utopie et les utopies*; Schuhl, *Le merveilleux, la pensée et l'action*.

[38] Plato, *Republic*, VI, 488b-489b; cf. Aristotle, *Rhetoric*, II, 20, 1393b; Whately, *Elements of Rhetoric*, pt I, chap. 2, § 8, p. 80.

[39] *Rhetorica ad Herennium*, iv, 1-10.

Some imitative behavior is entirely spontaneous. Accordingly, the tendency toward imitation has often been considered to be an instinct, and one to which sociologists attach very great importance.[40] And everyone is familiar with the importance contemporary psychology attaches to the identification processes.[41] We have ourselves stressed the role played by inertia, the fact that repeated behavior differs from deviating or changed behavior in that it requires no justification, and the consequent importance of precedent.[42]

However, imitation of behavior is not always spontaneous. One person may seek to induce it in another. Argument can be based either on the rule of justice[43] or on a model that one will be asked to follow, as in this example given by Aristotle:

> It was a strange thing that the Dread Goddesses could without loss of dignity submit to the judgement of the Areopagus, and yet Mixidemides could not.[44]

Persons or groups whose prestige confers added value on their acts may be used as models. The value attaching to the person, which is previously recognized, is the premise from which will be drawn the conclusion encouraging some particular behavior. One does not imitate just anybody; the person chosen as model must enjoy some measure of prestige.[45] According to Rousseau,

> The monkey imitates man, whom he fears, and not the other beasts, which he scorns; he thinks what is done by his betters must be good.[46]

If someone serves as a model, he must therefore possess a certain prestige, and his serving as model is proof that he does.[47] Thus Isocrates writes to Nicocles:

> Let your own level-headedness stand as an example to the rest, realizing that the manners of the whole state are copied from its rulers. You will have evidence of the value of your royal authority when you see that your subjects enjoy easier circumstances and more civilized habits because of your activity.[48]

---

[40] Tarde, *Les lois de l'imitation*; Dupréel, *Sociologie générale*, pp. 66 et seq.

[41] Cf. the very interesting example of verbalized identification in Sechehaye, *Journal d'une schizophrène*, p. 118.

[42] Cf. § 27, supra: Agreements Particular to each Discussion.

[43] Cf. § 52, supra: The Rule of Justice.

[44] Aristotle, *Rhetoric*, II, 23, 1398b.

[45] Cf. § 70, supra: Argument from Authority.

[46] Rousseau, *Émile* (Firmin-Didot), p. 95.

[47] Cf. the striking use of increased value due to being a model in De Vivier, *Le mal que je t'ai fait*, p. 155. "Sebastian Galois, may eternity resemble you or not be."

[48] Isocrates, *To Nicocles*, § 31; cf. also *Panegyricus*, § 39.

Ordinarily the model extolled is held up for imitation by everyone, but sometimes the model is restricted to a few or even just the person proposing him, and sometimes it is a pattern to be followed under particular circumstances: in this situation behave like a good father, love your neighbor as yourself, regard as true only propositions as clearly and distinctly conceived as the proposition "I think, therefore I am."[49]

A man, a social class, a period can be typified by the models they adopt and their way of looking at them. It is worth noting, as an indication of the intellectual revolution which took place in France at the turn of the seventeenth century, that whereas Petrus Ramus, in developing his dialectic, seeks his models among poets, orators, philosophers, and jurists,[50] Descartes offers himself as model to his readers.[51]

A model shows what behavior to follow, and also serves as a guarantee for an adopted behavior. To justify his sarcastic references to the Jesuits, Pascal cites a series of fathers of the Church and even God himself who on occasion did not scruple to treat error with derision.[52]

Close adherence to a recognized model guarantees the value of the behavior. The person following the model enjoys an enhanced value, and can thus, in turn, serve as model: the philosopher will be held out as model to the city because he himself has the gods as his model.[53] Saint Theresa inspires the conduct of Christians because she herself had Jesus as model.[54]

It is to be noted, however, that indifference to a model may itself be given as a model. A person may be held up as model for his capacity to avoid the temptations of imitation. The fact that argument by a model can be favorable to originality shows clearly that modes of argument are applicable to a wide variety of circumstances. In other words, argumentative technique is not bound up with this or that particular social situation or with respect for this or that particular value.

On the one who is a model inspiring others rests an obligation which more often than not will determine his behavior. We have seen that Isocrates used this argument when instructing Nicocles. It is also the central theme of a contemporary play, in which the elder of two brothers,

---

[49] Descartes, *Discourse on the Method*, GBWW, vol. 31, p. 51.

[50] Ramus, *Dialecticae Libri Duo* (1566), note p. 9.

[51] Descartes, *Meditations on the First Philosophy*, Preface to the Reader, GBWW, vol. 31, pp. 71-72. Cf. Husserl, "La crise des sciences européennes et la phénoménologie *transcendantale*," *Études Philosophiques*, 1949, no. 2, p. 143.

[52] Pascal, *Provincial Letters*, Letter XI, GBWW, vol. 33, pp. 81 et seq.

[53] Plato, *Republic*, VI, 500c, d.

[54] Don Quixote may be a model for some people, as one who was able to follow with intense devotion the model he had chosen.

because he is the model for the younger, finds his behavior being inspired by the latter:

> It is in him that I confront the image I have formed of myself with his image of me, and that I model the one image on the other. Without him I am nothing, for it is through him that I prove myself.[55]

A model must keep careful watch on his behavior, for the least deviation will be the justification for a thousand other deviations, a justification which is often reinforced by use of an *a fortiori* argument. Pascal is quite right when he says:

> The example of Alexander's chastity has not made so many continent as that of his drunkenness has made intemperate. It is not shameful not to be as virtuous as he, and it seems excusable to be no more vicious.[56]

The person to whom prestige attaches will be described in terms of his role as model. In order that people may be more easily inspired by his conduct, emphasis will be laid on some particular characteristic or act of his, or even a particular slant may be given to his image or situation:

> An honorable man [de Méré writes] must live almost like a great prince who finds himself in a foreign country without subjects and retinue and who is reduced by fortune to behaving like an honorable private person.[57]

The attribution of good qualities to superior beings makes it possible, if it is accepted, to argue from the model, and, if it is challenged, to enhance the value of the quality as being at least worthy of attribution to the model. Thus according to Isocrates,

> ... it is said that even the gods are ruled by Zeus as king. If the saying is true, it is clear that the gods also prefer this regime; but if, on the other hand, no one knows the truth about this matter, and we by our own conjecture have simply supposed it to be so, it is a proof that we all hold monarchy in the highest esteem.[58]

Similarly, Montesquieu puts these words into the mouth of Usbek:

> Accordingly, even if there were no God, we should always love justice. That is to say, we should make every effort to resemble this being who is so nobly conceived by us, and who, if he existed, would necessarily be just.[59]

---

[55] Puget, *La peine capitale*, Act II, p. 64.
[56] Pascal, *Pensées*, GBWW, vol. 33, p. 192.
[57] Méré, *Œuvres complètes*, vol. II: *Des agrémens*, p. 21.
[58] Isocrates, *Nicocles*, § 26.
[59] Montesquieu, *Lettres persanes*, LXXXIV, Usbek to Rhedi, *Œuvres complètes*, p. 58.

Although it is a mark of prestige to serve as model, the reduction in the distance between the model and those— almost always his inferiors— who are inspired by him and imitate him can detract somewhat from the value attaching to the model. We have already seen that any comparison brings about interaction between the two terms.[60] Moreover, the popularization of the model robs him of the value arising from his distinctiveness. The phenomenon of changing fashions is explained, as we know, by the desire of the masses to be like those who set the fashion and by the desire of those who are copied to escape from the mass and be different. So we find Isocrates, who advises Nicocles to serve as a model to the people, telling him also to distinguish himself from the multitude:

> You, who are ... a king over the multitude ought not to be of the same mind as men at large, convinced that you do not appraise what things are worthy or what men are wise by the standard of the pleasure they bring you, but that you test them in the light of their practical value.[61]

The multitude has become the anti-model.

Whereas reference to a model makes it possible to encourage a particular kind of behavior, reference to an *anti-model* or foil serves to deter people from it. Some feel, like Montaigne, that the anti-model exerts a more powerful influence:

> There may be some of my complexion, who better instruct myself by contrariety than by similitude, and more by avoiding than imitating. The elder Cato was referring to this sort of discipline when he said that "the wise may learn more of fools than fools of the wise." And Pausanias tells us of an ancient lyre player who used to make his students go to hear one that lived across the street and played very badly, so that they might learn to hate his discords and wrong notes.[62]

Is the deterrent effect brought about by arguing from the anti-model or because the hearers evaluate the action by its deplorable consequences? Two different arguments are involved, although there is inevitably interaction between them: is the agent judged by his acts, or vice versa? Only in the latter case shall we see the effect of the anti-model as described by the Chevalier de Méré:

> I notice too that we do not merely avoid people we do not like, but hate everything connected with them and wish to resemble them

---

[60] Cf. § 57, supra: Arguments by Comparison.

[61] Isocrates, *To Nicocles*, § 50.

[62] Montaigne, *Essais*, bk III, chap. VIII, p. 893.

as little as possible. If they praise peace, they make us wish for war; if they are pious and lead well-ordered lives, we want to be dissolute and disorderly.[63]

At first sight, everything we have said about the model is applicable, *mutatis mutandis*, to the anti-model. Sometimes, when he is deliberating, a person will be prompted to choose a particular behavior because it is the opposite of that of the anti-model. The repulsion may even be such that it brings about change of a previously adopted attitude for no other reason than it is also the anti-model's attitude.[64] An important feature nevertheless distinguishes this form of argument from argument by a model. Whereas in the latter there is the intention to pattern oneself, be it even in a clumsy way, on someone, and the conduct to be adopted is relatively well known, in argument by the anti-model one is trying to get others to be different from someone without its being possible always to infer precise positive behavior from the distinction. Often only through an implicit reference to a model will it be possible to establish a definition of what this conduct should be. Thus, only he who knows the figure of Don Quixote can envisage holding himself aloof from Sancho Panza, and only one who knows the behavior of the disciplined Spartan can have his behavior determined by the picture of the Helot.

Because the anti-model turns us away from his course of action, adoption by him of a particular behavior turns that behavior, whether he intends it or not, into a parody and, sometimes, a provocation. This is the case with the demons described by Bossuet:

> I learn also from Tertullian that the demons not only had vows and sacrifices which are the proper offerings to God offered to their idols, but they had these decked out with the clothes and ornaments worn by the magistrates, and had wands and staffs of office and other insignia of public authority carried in front of them, because, as this great man says, "the demons are the magistrates of the world." ... And what insolence, my brethren, has this rival of God not committed ? He has always affected to do what God did, not in order to draw nearer to saintliness, which is his chief enemy, but as a rebellious subject who out of scorn or insolence affects the same pomp as his sovereign.[65]

Is Bossuet alluding here to the Fronde? Perhaps, but the importance of the passage to us is that it reveals clearly the mechanism of argument by the anti-model.

---

[63] Méré, *Œuvres complètes*, vol. II: *Des agrémens*, pp. 30-31.

[64] Cf. Marcel, *Rome n'est plus dans Rome*, Act III, scene IV.

[65] Bossuet, *Sermons*, vol. II: *Premier sermon sur les démons*, p. 13.

The anti-model is often presented in a conventional and deliberately false manner so as to bring about the revulsion desired. The characteristics conventionally ascribed to the Saracen in the French chanson de geste are not due to ignorance of Moslem society.[66]

However, an anti-model may be introduced, not for the purpose of bringing about revulsion, but as the starting point of an argument *a fortiori*, in which case the anti-model represents a minimum below which it is improper to go. Moreover, since the anti-model is often simultaneously an adversary to be fought and eventually to be overcome, the same abhorred figure can play a very complex role in argumentation. As we know, competition develops resemblances between opponents,[67] as over a period of time they borrow each others' effective devices: certain techniques can be recommended for use just because they are those used by the opponent. However, when the opponent is also the anti-model, the speaker will often be at pains to distinguish means from ends, or the temporary from the permanent, the superfluous from the necessary, the permissible from the unlawful.[68]

When a speaker proposes a model or an anti-model, it is generally implied, unless the role is specifically restricted to particular circumstances, that he himself strives to emulate the one or to shun the other. This opens the door to humorous rejoinders, as where a father tells his son who is doing poorly at school: "At your age, Napoleon was top of his class," and the son replies, "At your age, he was emperor."

Argument by model or anti-model can be applied spontaneously to the discourse itself. The speaker who asserts his belief in something does not support it merely with his authority. His behavior toward the thing, if he enjoys prestige, can also serve as model, and prompt others to behave as he does. Conversely, if he is the anti-model, the hearers will avoid doing as he does.

§ 81. *The Perfect Being as Model*

The disadvantages of arguing by model or anti-model appear when the model exibits undesirable characteristics, or the anti-model desirable ones that are worthy of imitation. Any attempt to discriminate between the various acts of the model or anti-model presupposes a criterion other than the person or group being extolled or denigrated,

---

[66] Cf. Meredith-Jones, "The Conventional Saracen of the Songs of Geste," *Speculum*, XVII (1942), 202.

[67] Dupréel, *Sociologie générale*, p. 157.

[68] Cf. Giraudoux writing on the establishment of the Information Board (Commissariat à l'Information), *La Française et la France*, pp. 234-237, 241.

and recourse to such a criterion makes it impossible to use argument by model or anti-model, as it then becomes unnecessary or even dangerous.

To obviate these difficulties, writers feel the necessity to embellish or blacken reality, to create heroes and monsters, all good or all bad, and to transform history into myth or legend. But even then, the multiplicity of models or anti-models makes it impossible to extract a single clear rule of conduct. It is for this reason that, according to Kant, things derived from the realm of experience cannot be regarded as models or archetypes:

> He who would make (as many have really done) that, which at best can but serve as an imperfectly illustrative example, a model for the formation of a perfectly adequate idea on the subject, would in fact transform virtue into a nonentity changeable according to time and circumstance, and utterly incapable of being employed as a rule.[69]

Kant holds, on the contrary, that every incarnate being must be confronted not merely with the idea of virtue but with an ideal, like the wise man of the Stoics:

> ... a human being existing only in thought and in complete conformity with the idea of wisdom. As the idea provides a rule, so the ideal serves as an *archetype* for the perfect and complete determination of the copy. Thus the conduct of this wise and divine man serves us as a standard of action with which we may compare and judge ourselves, although the perfection it demands can never be attained by us. Although we cannot concede objective reality to these ideals, they are not to be considered as chimeras; on the contrary, they provide reason with a standard, which enables it to estimate, by comparison, the degree of incompleteness in the objects presented to it.[70]

Kant realizes the importance of the model for behavior, but thinks that the model is simply an ideal borne by each man within himself and that natural limitations prevent the phenomenal realization of the ideal.

This archetype, which Kant finds in "this divine man we bear within ourselves," is set before men by the religions by means of the idea or image they present of God, the perfectly good Being, or, at least, of his representative and spokesman on earth. Tarde has shown the importance of Jesus, Mahomet, and Buddha as models for humanity.[71] Their role of model is facilitated by the fact that, notwithstanding their supernatural qualities, these beings behave like men living among

---

[69] Kant, *Critique of Pure Reason*, GBWW, vol. 42, p. 114.
[70] *Ibid.*, p. 173.
[71] Tarde, *La logique sociale*, p. 308.

other men. From one standpoint, the incarnation of the divinity represents already a correction of the model so as to bring it closer to those who are to be edified. However, we find that those who use this form of argument adapt their model much more directly to the conclusions they want to promote. We will cite some pertinent examples in which Jesus is put forward as the model.

Here are two passages where Bossuet presents Jesus as the model of absolute monarchy:

> Jesus Christ, Lord of lords, and Prince of the kings of the earth, though raised upon a throne of sovereign independence, has elected to subject himself to the rules he has made and the laws he has established, in order to give all monarchs who depend on his power an example of moderation and justice.[72]

And in another sermon he declares:

> This great God needs no man, and yet he would win over all men to him. ... This great God knows all things and sees all things, and yet he would that all men speak to him; he listens to everything, his ear is always open to the complaints laid before him, and he is ever ready to do justice. There is the model for kings.[73]

To Locke, Jesus is the model of tolerance, which should inspire the acts of his priests and followers:

> If, like the Captain of our salvation, they sincerely desired the good of souls, they would tread in the steps and follow the perfect example of that Prince of Peace. ... Though if infidels were to be converted by force, if those that are either blind or obstinate were to be drawn off from their errors by armed soldiers, we know very well that it was much more easy for Him to do it with armies of heavenly legions than for any son of the Church, how potent soever, with all his dragoons.[74]

And he concludes with this supreme cry:

> Nay God Himself will not save men against their wills.[75]

The Chevalier de Méré, who, as we have seen, did not scruple to use divine grace in order to illustrate the importance of being lovable, maintains that the love of pleasant things was taught to us by Jesus:

> It seems to me also that the most perfect model, and the one we should imitate the most, loved everything done graciously, like those fine perfumes with which he was anointed. And can one imagine anything more pleasant than the least of his sayings or the least of his acts?[76]

[72] Bossuet, *Sermons*, vol. II: *Sur la prédication évangélique*, p. 50.
[73] Bossuet, *Sermons*, vol. II: *Sur l'ambition*, p. 411.
[74] Locke, *A Letter Concerning Toleration*, GBWW, vol. 35, p. 2.
[75] *Ibid.*, p. 8.
[76] Méré, *Œuvres complètes*, vol. II: *Des agrémens*, p. 28.

Certain stories in the Gospels will even be interpreted solely in the light of Jesus' role as model, as otherwise they would be incomprehensible because incompatible with divine perfection:

> In his prescience Jesus sees into how many and great perils we are led by the love of greatness; and so he flees from it in order that we may fear it. ... He tells us that the essential duty of a Christian is to repress his ambition.[77]

He himself, who is God, has no reason to flee. Only the model has.

Also the milieu in which the model lives can be invoked to increase the model's influence, by bringing him closer to those to whom he is proposed and thus enhancing themselves in their own eyes:

> Just as the young *Jocistes* feel exalted at the thought of Christ as a workingman, so the peasants should take a similar pride in the part devoted in the New Testament parables to the life of the fields and in the sacred function ascribed to bread and wine, and derive therefrom the feeling that Christianity is something which belongs to them.[78]

These different examples show how argument from a model, even when limited to the extolment of the life of a single person, can have varied uses and adaptations, according as some particular aspect of the perfect Being is singled out and offered to men for imitation.

The perfect Being lends himself more than any other model to this adaptation, because by his very nature and essence there is something about him that cannot be grasped, that is unknown, and because, moreover, he is not valid just for one time or one place. Where, then, it is found possible to use a model independently of circumstances and the model is not just a pattern of limited application, the charge of anachronism has no foundation. The interpreter's role is then essential, for it is through him that an unquestioned model can serve as guide in every circumstance of life.

b) Reasoning by Analogy

§ 82. *What Is Analogy?*

No one will deny the importance of analogy in the workings of the intellect. Yet, though everyone recognizes it as an essential factor

---

[77] Bossuet, *Sermons*, vol. II: *Sur l'ambition*, p. 394.
[78] Weil, *The Need for Roots*, p. 90. Jocistes: members of the J.O.C. (*Jeunesse Ouvrière Catholique*).

in imaginative thinking, it has been viewed with distrust when used as a means of proof. It is true that some philosophies—notably those of Plato, Plotinus, and Saint Thomas Aquinas— have justified the use of analogy in argumentation because of their particular conceptions of reality, but in such cases the use of analogy has been linked to a metaphysical conception, with which it stands or falls. The empiricists, on the other hand, for the most part look on analogy as a resemblance of quite minor importance because of its weak and uncertain character.[79] It is more or less explicitly accepted that analogy constitutes the least significant member of the series identity-resemblance-analogy. Its sole value is that it makes it possible to formulate a hypothesis for verification by induction.[80]

Far be it from us to suggest that an analogy cannot serve as point of departure for subsequent verifications. But in this it is no different from any other form of reasoning, since the conclusions of all of them can always be subjected to further testing. And have we any warrant for denying analogy any power to convince when the mere fact that it can make us prefer one hypothesis to another shows that it has argumentative value? Any complete study of argumentation must therefore give it a place as an element of proof.

It seems to us that the argumentative value of analogy can be most clearly seen if it is envisaged as a resemblance of structures, the most general formulation of which is: A is to B as C is to D. This conception of analogy is in line with a very ancient tradition, still followed by Kant,[81] Whately,[82] and Cournot.[83] Nor is it entirely forgotten today, as is witnessed by this opinion of M. Cazals, quoted by Paul Grenet in a recent work:

> What gives an analogy originality and distinguishes it from a partial identity, that is, from the rather banal notion of resemblance, is that it is a *resemblance of relationship* rather than a *relationship of resemblance*. This is not just a play upon words. The purest type of analogy is found in a *mathematical proportion*.[84]

We agree with everything in this passage, except for the last point. Though etymology may encourage one to find the prototype of analogy in mathematical proportion,[85] we consider the latter to be merely a

[79] Hume, *A Treatise on Human Nature*, pp. 142, 147.
[80] Mill, *A System of Logic*, pp. 364-368.
[81] Kant, *Prolégomènes à toute métaphysique future*, pp. 146-147.
[82] Whately, *Elements of Rhetoric* (Harper), p. 316, Appendix to p. 74 (E).
[83] Cournot, *Essai sur les fondements de nos connaissances*, vol. I, pp. 93-94.
[84] Grenet, *Les origines de l'analogie philosophique dans les Dialogues de Platon*, p. 10. Cf. Solages, *Dialogue sur l'analogie*, p. 15.
[85] Cf. Dorolle, *Le raisonnement par analogie*, chap. I.

particular instance of similarity of relationship, and by no means the most significant one. For we do not find in mathematical proportion the characteristic that we feel is peculiar to analogy and bears on the difference between the relations involved.

To make our point clearer, we will take a rather simple but typical analogy given by Aristotle:

> For as the eyes of bats are to the blaze of day, so is the reason in our soul to the things which are by nature most evident of all.[86]

A and *B* together, the terms to which the conclusion relates (reason in the soul, obviousness), we shall call the *theme*, and *C* and *D* together, the terms that serve to buttress the argument (eyes of bats, blaze of day), we shall call the *phoros*.[87] In the ordinary course, the phoros is better known than the theme of which it should clarify the structure or establish the value, either its value as a whole or the respective value of its components. This will, however, not always be the case. Thus Catherine of Genoa tries at the end of her *Traité du Purgatoire* to describe the state of her soul by drawing an analogy with the state of souls in Purgatory, of which it can hardly be said that it is better known but to the description of which she has previously devoted considerable space:

> This purgative form which I see in the souls of Purgatory I have felt in my own soul, particularly during the last two years. Every day I feel and see it more clearly. My soul lives in this body of mine as in a Purgatory.[88]

There is, at any rate, an asymmetrical relation between theme and phoros, arising from the position they occupy in the reasoning.

For an analogy to exist, it is also necessary that the theme and the phoros belong to different spheres. When the two relations encountered belong to the same sphere, and can be subsumed under a common structure, we have not analogy but argument by example or illustration, in which the theme and the phoros represent two particular cases of a single rule. Accordingly, we can say that some arguments are quite unquestionably cases of reasoning by analogy (this is very often the case when the phoros is drawn from the sphere of the senses, and the theme from the spiritual sphere), but there may be some doubt about others, as in this passage where Colette is dealing with her relations with a flock of sparrows:

> ... it was not long before I would discover in a small undifferentiated flock the special, preferred individual who would prefer me.

[86] Aristotle, *Metaphysics*, II, 993b.
[87] Coined from the Greek *phoros*, bearing, which is found in *metaphora*.
[88] Catherine de Gênes, *Les œuvres*, "Traité du purgatoire," p. 150.

Each time the animal faces the same danger as ourselves. Choosing, being chosen, loving: immediately afterward come anxiety, the risk of loss, the fear of sowing the seeds of regret. Such big words about a sparrow? Yes, about a sparrow. In love, no thing is small.[89]

Is this an analogy with human love, or is it an example leading to a generalization? The final words suggest the latter interpretation. But until we came to them we were inclined to read it as an analogical development with human love as its theme. In some cases, we may add, wavering between the two forms of reasoning can be very effective.

The impression that two different spheres are involved may depend on the proclivities of the hearer. But the discourse itself often paves the way for seeing the spheres as one or as separated. Everything depends on the choice of terms, and we might repeat here what we have already said about differences in nature and degree. Everything that shows a difference in nature, in order, tends to establish separate spheres which can be respectively occupied by a theme and a phoros. Thus, opposition between finite and infinite constitutes a difference of order that favors the development of reasoning by analogy.

Does one find true analogies within a single discipline? It is a tricky question, but we think it can be said that there are. Biologists use two notions that can shed light on this problem: homology (e. g., arm and wing) and analogy (e.g., resemblances caused by an aquatic existence in individuals of different species). In the first case, we have a structural theme which forms a natural system, under which are subsumed the individual related instances falling within it. And this system is determined by anatomy, embryology, and paleontology which together unite the individuals in a single sphere. In the second case, thought proceeds from one animal species to another, each being viewed in relative isolation.

In the field of law, reasoning by true analogy appears to be restricted to comparison as to particular points of systems of positive law separated by time, place, or content. On the other hand, whenever resemblances between entire systems are sought, the systems are regarded as examples of a universal system of law. Similarly, whenever someone argues in favor of the application of a given rule to new cases, he is thereby affirming that the matter is confined to a single domain. Accordingly, if pursuant to the wish of certain jurists to see in analogy something more than the term by which one's opponent's example is disqualified, there is to be a rehabilitation of analogy as a device for wider interpretation, this result can be achieved only if analogy is given a different meaning from the one we have proposed.[90]

---

[89] Colette, *Le fanal bleu.*

[90] Cf. Bobbio, *L'analogia nella logica del diritto*, particularly at p. 34.

§ 83. *Relations Between the Terms of an Analogy*

When we say that every analogy involves a relation among four terms, we are, of course, giving a schematized picture of things. In fact, each term may correspond to a complex situation, and such a situation is precisely what makes a *rich analogy*.

The resemblance in analogy being one of relations, the differences between the terms of the theme and the phoros can be as great as one likes. At first sight, at any rate, the nature of the terms is of secondary importance. Often their exact meaning emerges only from the role that they play in the analogy. When Ezekiel declares:

> I will put a new spirit within them, and I will take the heart of stone out of their body and will give them a heart of flesh,[91]

flesh is to stone as godliness is to rebelliousness, whereas in very many analogies flesh is to spirit as a state of sin is to a state of grace. One and the same term can accordingly be conceived in very different ways, and thus be capable of insertion into analogies with quite opposite meanings.

Although the typical analogy comprises four terms, an analogy will quite often have only three terms. One of the three will appear twice in the scheme, which then will have the form: *B* is to *A* as *C* is to *B*. Leibniz provides this example:

> ... All other substances depend on God just as thoughts emanate from our substance. ...[92]

And there is this saying of Heraclitus:

> In the sight of the divinity man is as puerile as a child is in the sight of a man.[93]

The common terms "substance," "man," invite the reader to locate the theme in an extension of the phoros, and to arrange them hierarchically. Nevertheless, the distinction between spheres, which is essential for the existence of an analogy, is maintained. For, though the common term is formally the same in both theme and phoros, it is dissociated by being differently used, and this makes it ambiguous. It is, indeed, not hard to foresee that the common term, through being related to

---

[91] Ezekiel, XI, 19.
[92] Leibniz, *Die philosophischen Schriften*, vol. IV, *Discours de Métaphysique*, XXXII, p. 457.
[93] Grenet, *Les origines de l'analogie philosophique dans les Dialogues de Platon*, p. 108, note 367. (Fragments Diels 79, Bywater 97).

terms of a different order in the theme and the phoros, would assume a more or less different meaning in the two places.

It might be concluded from this that any three-term analogy could be analyzed as a four-term analogy. It is as well, however, to distinguish analogies in which the phoros and the theme are a sort of prolongation of each other from those in which the emphasis is rather on the parallelism between them. The interpretation of the two, from an argumentative viewpoint, could well be very different.

This possibility may be illustrated by looking at two analogies used by Gilson in his work on Thomism. The first passage runs as follows:

> When a master instructs his disciple, his own knowledge must include whatever he would introduce into the soul of the disciple. Now our natural knowledge of principles comes from God, since he is the author of our nature. These principles themselves are also contained in the wisdom of God. Whence it follows that whatever is contrary to these principles is contrary to the divine wisdom and, consequently, cannot come from God.[94]

In the second passage Gilson writes:

> Like a child, understanding when the master teaches what it would not have been able to discover alone, the human intellect takes easy possession of a doctrine whose truth is guaranteed by more than human authority.[95]

In both cases, there is a phoros taken from daily life, that of teaching; n both cases there is a considerable difference of value both between the terms belonging to each sphere and between the two spheres themselves. But in the first case this difference in value is not what is most important, and we are conscious rather of the parallelism between the two relations (the wisdom of God is to natural knowledge as the knowledge of a master is to that of his disciple). In the second passage, on the other hand, the differences in value are the most important thing, and the passage strikes us rather as a three-term analogy (divine authority is to the human intellect what the master is to the child), in spite of the fact that the common term is not formally identical ("master," "human intellect.")"[96]

We should add that, in addition to three-term analogies that exhibit a hierarchic structure, one also finds analogies that follow the pattern "A is to B as A is to C." Demosthenes provides this good example of this type of analogy:

---

[94] Gilson, *The Christian Philosophy of Saint Thomas Aquinas*, p. 18; cf. *Contra Gentiles*, I, 7.

[95] *Ibid.*, p. 20.

[96] Cf. a passage in Pascal where in a single piece of reasoning he draws a four-term analogy and a three-term analogy exhibiting a hierarchic structure: *Pensées*, GBWW, vol. 33, p. 216.

For as soon as you put money alongside a decision, as if in the pan of a scale, the money rapidly pulls the decision down with it and draws reason to itself, so that the taker becomes incapable of any sound calculation.[97]

Although money is understood exclusively in a material sense, it here fulfils two different functions. The speaker takes advantage in a sense of a fortunate coincidence; this makes possible the fusion of one of the terms of the phoros and one of the terms of the theme. We shall see later how an analogy of this kind resembles certain metaphors.

In an analogy the essential feature is the confrontation of theme and phoros; it does not at all imply that there was any preexisting relationship between their respective terms. But when a relation does exist between A and C and between B and D, the analogy can be developed in many directions, which is one of the characteristics of a rich analogy. Tarde liked to devise astonishingly full analogies in which the relations between homologous terms were scarcely less well developed than those within the theme and phoros.[98] Sometimes these relations between homologous terms are even given preference, and the analogy is primarily conceived as an affinity between terms of the theme and the phoros. The structural resemblance between the two spheres is inferred from this affinity. It was reasoning of this kind that led Girolamo Fracastoro, in the middle of the 16th century, to assert that the agents responsible for our infectious diseases were both multiple and specific.[99]

Rich analogies can be drawn with the aid of double hierarchies, as these are characterized by complex relations both horizontal and vertical—the former based on the structure of reality, the latter exhibiting a hierarchic progression. In our view, a double hierarchy is very different from an analogy, since the first is based on a real connection, while the second suggests the comparison of relations belonging to different spheres. But it is often possible to argue from analogy by distributing the successive terms of a double hierarchy between theme and phoros. Thus, the double hierarchy which concludes to the superiority of divine justice over human justice from the superiority of God over men can be replaced by the analogy wherein divine justice is to God as human justice is to men. Conversely, when an analogy develops two lengthy hierarchies, one of which belongs to the phoros and the

[97] Demosthenes, *On the Peace*, § 11.
[98] Cf. in particular, Tarde, *La logique sociale*, pp. 98-99.
[99] Fracastoro, *Opera Omnia*. "De Sympathia et Antipathia Rerum," chap II, *De Analogia Rerum in Agendo*, pp. 65b et seq; "De Contagione," chap. 8, *De Analogia Contagionum*, pp. 81a et seq. Cf. also *Sifilide*, bk I, vv 258-306.

other to the theme, and the two spheres are unequal in value, the analogy can readily be replaced by a series of double hierarchies. This process is well illustrated by the passage in Plotinus where from the hierarchic order found in a royal procession he draws conclusions concerning the realities that depend on the One and which are more or less close to it.[100]

Although analogy is reasoning that deals with relations existing within the phoros and within the theme, what distinguishes analogy fundamentally from simple mathematical proportion is that in analogy the nature of the terms is never a matter of indifference. For the effect of an analogy is to bring the terms A and C and B and D closer together, which leads to an interaction and, more specifically, to increasing or decreasing the value of the terms of the theme. The mechanism of this interaction appears more clearly from this passage from Calvin's writings:

> That election of Amadeus [Duke of Savoy], duly solemnized by the authority of a general and holy council, went up in smoke, except that the aforesaid Amadeus was appeased by a cardinal's hat, as a barking dog by a morsel.[101]

The devaluation of the terms of the theme is brought about by the choice of terms for the phoros; but the value attached to these terms is itself derived, in part at least, from their use in the analogy. The attitude of a barking dog is not one that necessarily calls for a depreciatory judgment.

If the interaction is overlooked, one gets one of those comic effects to which Sterne was so partial:

> "Brave! brave, by heaven!" cried my uncle Toby, "he [King William] deserves a crown."
> "As richly, as a thief a halter," shouted Trim [the faithful corporal].[102]

Interaction between terms of an analogy is what often makes it possible to fit into the phoros elements which would be without significance if the theme, which gives them significance, were not in mind. Thus, to describe the road leading to salvation, Locke employs as phoros the picture of a road leading straight to Jerusalem, and he goes on to inquire why the pilgrim should be molested because he does not wear buskins, because his hair is not of the right cut, or because he

---

[100] Plotinus, *Enneads*, V, 5, § 3.

[101] Calvin, *Institutes of the Christian Religion* (Westminster), Prefatory Address to King Francis, pp. 26-27.

[102] Sterne, *The Life and Opinions of Tristram Shandy*, bk. VIII, chap. 19, p. 517.

does or does not follow a guide clothed in white or crowned with a mitre.[103] These details have importance only because they make the reader think of the quarrels between the members of different churches.

Sometimes the influence of the theme on the phoros is such that certain elements of the phoros undergo modification. For example, we may find details with respect to such Old Testament figures as Adam or Moses being changed in order that they may prefigure Christ more adequately. Réau points out this technique:

> Contrary to the verse in Exodus which says that Moses, on his return to Egypt, set his wife and sons upon an ass, a panel of the enamel reredos at Klosterneuburg (12th century) shows the prophet astride the ass while his wife Sephora follows on foot. ... This variation is simply due to symbolical considerations as this scene was to match the *Entry of Christ into Jerusalem*. Moses had accordingly to be shown mounted on the ass so as to be exact counterpart of Jesus whom he prefigures.[104]

Often the terms of the phoros will be endowed with qualities that are the product of the imagination, but bring them nearer to the theme. An example is the attribution of the faculty of speech to animals in fables.

Modification of the phoros to fit the needs of the theme is well shown in this analogy of Bossuet's:

> There remained the redoubtable infantry of the Spanish army, whose close-set big battalions, like so many towers—towers, though, that could repair the breaches made in them—stood steadfast when all around them were in flight.[105]

This description by likening the battalions to towers in a besieged fortress, endeavors to characterize the role of the infantry in battle-without, however, losing sight of the quality that constitutes their superiority.

To relate the phoros more closely to the theme Plotinus makes frequent use of a technique which a French translator of his works, É. Bréhier, has referred to as "correction of images."[106] This technique does not involve any actual modification of the phoros, but consists in its purification by means of a rectifying statement to raise it to a higher degree of perfection:

---

[103] Locke, *A Letter Concerning Toleration*, GBWW, vol. 35, pp. 8-9.

[104] Réau, "L'influence de la forme sur l'iconographie médiévale," *Formes de l'art, formes de l'esprit*, pp. 91-92.

[105] Bossuet, "Oraison funèbre de Louis de Bourbon, Prince de Condé," *Oraisons funèbres. Panégyriques*, p. 218.

[106] Plotinus, *Ennéades*, vol. V: Introductory note to Fifth Ennead, Eighth Tractate, p. 129.

Here is one example, out of many, of this particular procedure:

> Thus when a man enters a richly furnished house, he might gaze
> about and admire the varied splendor before the master appears;
> but the moment he sees and loves the master—no thing of ornament
> but calling for the truest attention—he would ignore everything else
> and look only to the master. ... Our analogy would be closer perhaps
> if instead of a man appearing to the visitor who had been admiring
> the house we were to say it was a god which cannot be seen but fills
> the soul with his presence.[107]

Here the phoros continues, after its correction, to have the desired
effect, without diminishing the plausibility of the theme. Often the
correction is put forward as a hypothesis, and Plotinus will preface
it, as in the present example, with the conditional "if we were to say."

Kant is also using a hypothesis in his famous analogy of the dove:

> The light dove cleaving in free flight the thin air, whose resistance
> it feels, might imagine that her movements would be far more free
> and rapid in airless space. Just in the same way did Plato, aban-
> doning the world of sense because of the narrow limits it sets to the
> understanding, venture upon the wings of ideas beyond it, into the
> void space of pure intellect. He did not reflect that he made no
> real progress by all his efforts; for he met with no resistance which
> might serve him for a support, as it were, whereon to rest, and on
> which he might apply his powers, in order to let the intellect acquire
> momentum for its progress.[108]

Plato's endeavor is compared to that of the dove, and is described in
terms that recall the dove's behavior. But the interaction between the
terms is, so to speak, caught in the act, as the dove's behavior is itself
no more than a hypothesis conditioned by the theme.

But sometimes correction of the phoros may render it ludicrous
by making it completely incompatible with reality. Quintilian mentions these expressions which he often heard when he was young:

> "Even the sources of mighty rivers are navigable," and "The
> generous tree bears fruit while it is yet a sapling."[109]

What are these but analogies in which the theme has reacted excessively
on the phoros? The desire to relate phoros and theme more closely,
instead of making the analogy more convincing, turns against the speaker. Caution is therefore necessary when a phoros is being modified.
It is permissible to make it fantastic, but not to state an untruth,
even as a hypothesis. Rather than state an untruth, it is better to use
the terms of the phoros but make it absolutely clear that the modifica-

---

[107] Plotinus, *Enneads*, VI, 7, § 35.
[108] Kant, *Critique of Pure Reason*, GBWW, vol. 42, p. 16.
[109] Quintilian, VIII, III, 76.

tion deals with the theme, as in this passage from Bossuet in which the analogy of childbirth is used to describe penitence:

> In the performance of these acts of penance, imagine, brethren, that you are giving birth, and that what you are giving birth to is yourselves. If it is such a lively consolation to have brought another to the light of day and given him life, that it wipes out all past suffering, what rapture must a man feel to have illuminated himself, and to have begotten himself for everlasting life![110]

§ 84. *Effects of Analogy*

In the interaction which occurs in analogy, action on the theme is the more pronounced, but, as we have seen, action in the opposite direction is by no means unimportant. Interaction—in either direction—manifests itself structurally and through transfers of value deriving from the structure. These will be transfers of value from phoros to theme and vice versa, or the transfer of the relative value of the two terms of the phoros to the relative value of the two terms of the theme.

Let us consider this celebrated analogy of Epictetus:

> If a child puts his hand into a narrow-necked jar to pull out figs and nuts and fills his hand, what will happen to him? He will not be able to pull it out, and he will cry. "Let a few go" someone will tell him, "and you will get your hand out." So I say to you, do the same with your desires. Wish only for a small number of things, and you will obtain them.[111]

The normative conclusion with regard to the behavior of him who desires more than is within his grasp is simply the transfer onto him of the judgment passed on the childish behavior of the boy who could not withdraw his hand when it was too full. But the transfer takes place because the phoros is made the starting point for reconstructing the behavior of the adult. In this example, as in all cases where the phoros is taken from the domain of senses and the theme from the spiritual domain, the analogy makes it possible to build the theme with a structure that seems plausible, and this is particularly helpful since the structure cannot be known directly. This explains why the constantly recurring arguments about the relations between human free will and divine grace always have selected the phoros of vision, which requires both visual organs and a source of light:

[110] Bossuet, *Sermons*, vol. II: *Sur la pénitence*, p. 83.
[111] Epictetus, *Discourses* (Arrian's), bk III, chap 9.

Indeed, just as a man when surrounded by thick darkness, though he possesses the sense of sight, sees nothing, because he cannot until there comes from without the light, which he feels even when he keeps his eyes shut, and which he sees, together with all that surrounds him, when he opens his eyes, so is the will of man, as long as he remains in the shadow of original sin and of his own sins, hemmed in by his own darkness. But when the light of divine mercy appears, it not only disperses the night of sin and its guilt, but it heals the sick will, gives it sight, and makes it able to contemplate this light by cleansing it through good works.[112]

The analogy makes it possible to understand better the relationship between grace and free will and the relative importance of man and God in sin and salvation.

The value of the terms of an analogy is very often determined by the structure of the analogy. We find, for instance, that three-term analogies in which the terms are respectively drama, earthly life, and beyond-earthly life, often aim at depriving earthly life of all serious import compared with that which lies beyond, and it achieves this purpose by making earthly life a kind of game or spectacle in which each person plays a role while he waits for true life to begin.[113]

Such terms as *light, height, depth, full, empty,* and *hollow*, though borrowed from the physical world, seem to be of value just as they stand. This may well be the case. But it could be that they have so often served in the past as elements of a phoros in analogies whose theme deals with the spiritual world, that it is no longer possible to detach from them the value derived from this role, as a consequence of interaction with certain terms of the theme. Sometimes one feels that one has succeeded in grasping exactly how the transfer of value was effected, but one can never be really sure. How, for instance, does the transfer take place in this analogy drawn by Plotinus, in which the phoros is composed of the relation of the center to the circumference:

> Outside him [the First] are reason and intelligence, which circle round and touch him and are wholly dependent on him or, rather, it is intelligence only because it touches him. ... It is accepted that a circle derives its properties from the center because it touches the center; it has something of the nature of that center in that the radial lines converging on that one central point assimilate their impinging ends to that point of convergence and of departure. ...[114]

---

[112] Scotus Erigena, *Joannis Scoti Liber de Praedestinatione,* IV, 8. *Patrol. Latine,* vol. CXXII, columns 374-375.

[113] Cf. Plotinus, *Enneads,* III, 2, § 15.

[114] Plotinus, *Enneads,* VI, 8, § 18.

The world of Plotinus may get its structure from the circle, but it is its principle, the One, by interaction and whatever geometrical reasons one may give, which has enhanced the idea of the center, to which continuing value attaches in our civilization.

The numerous parables found in the Bible, and the paradigms of Plato and Platonistic writers, are not necessarily drawn from the realm of matter. They may be drawn from daily life in order to illuminate aspects of social, political, or moral life and to endow them with a particular structure or value. An analogy of this kind is used by Demosthenes in one of his speeches:

> And you know very well too that all the wrongs the Greeks suffered from the Lacedaemonians or from us, they at least suffered at the hands of true-born sons of Greece. It was just what happens in a noble house when a legitimate son manages his estate badly. He certainly deserves blame and reproach, but it cannot be said that he was not the legitimate heir, or had no rights to the property. But if some slave or supposititious son were ruining and spoiling property to which he had no title, how much more scandalous and intolerable everybody would have thought it! Yet they show no such feeling with regard to Philip and his present actions, although not only is he not a Greek, and has nothing in common with the Greeks, but is not even a barbarian with an honorable origin.[115]

Since the analogy specifies the place occupied by Philip in the Greek world, it cannot do otherwise than strengthen the feelings of scorn and indignation at his conduct, but on condition, of course, that one has previously been convinced that Philip was not entirely Greek. We see from this that analogies could be differentiated according to the degree of previous adherence to the theme. Some analogies would have a reinforcing role, like illustrations, while others, likely to carry greater persuasive force, would play a role closer to that of an example. But one must not forget that this comparison with illustration and example is itself merely an analogy.

One of the effects of analogy is to help to determine one or both of the terms of the theme. This use of analogy is most common in three-term analogies with the structure B is to X as C is to B. To convey the nature of the divine Word, Plotinus uses the following analogy:

> As spoken language is but a splintering of words compared to the inward language of the soul, so the language of the soul which interprets the divine Word is but a fragment when it is compared to the Word.[116]

---

[115] Demosthenes, *Third Philippic*, §§ 30, 31.
[116] Plotinus, *Enneads*, I, 2, § 3.

It can sometimes happen that both terms of the theme are unknown, so that its structure can be formulated only from the relationship assumed to exist between the domain of the theme and the domain of the phoros. The basis for reasoning about God and his characteristics are the known relations between man and his characteristics and the idea held of the distance separating God from man. When one admits that divine goodness and human goodness do not belong to the same sphere of reality, one will be saying that between these two characteristics there is no relation of resemblance, despite their designation by means of a single concept, but only a relation of analogy.

The idea that there are two spheres is often supported by such notions as image, shadow, and projection, which are, in fact, themselves analogical. The relation between the two spheres may be such that it brings about an inversion of certain structures. Maritain describes the destiny of Israel by an analogy with the destiny of the Church. Replying to an opponent who is shocked by this kind of inverted analogy, he states his position thus:

> We have said that it is a Church that has undergone precipitation and that its vocation, having, by its own fault, become ambivalent, continues the world's night; and we have warned that these things must be understood in an analogical way. ... Israel is not supernaturally apart from the world *in the same way* as the Church is. ... [117]

Furthermore, one may be obliged to invent the theme because, through inability to understand the terms of the discourse in their literal sense, one is impelled to give them a figurative meaning and so to discover the theme and reinvent an analogy which will give the discourse its real meaning:

> When the word of God, which is really true, is false literally, it is true spiritually. *Sede a dextris meis* [Psalm CIX]: this is false literally, therefore it is true spiritually.[118]

Since the discourse must be truthful, because of the nature of the person from whom it proceeds, the reader must discover the theme, in other words, the *spirit* of the phoros that will correspond to the author's intentions. This quest can give rise to new creations of an ethical, aesthetic, or religious nature.

It is to be observed that there is not necessarily a denial of physical or historical reality of the phoros when the literal interpretation is deemed inadequate. The assertion that God's resting on the seventh day can be interpreted as an analogy conveying the distance that separates

---

[117] Maritain, *Raison et raisons*, pp. 212-213.
[118] Pascal, *Pensées*, GBWW, vol. 33, p. 299.

the Creator from the universe, how he stands back from what he has done,[119] is without prejudice to the reality of the biblical account. We know indeed that the phoros of an analogy is often drawn from the sphere of reality and also that a work of fiction may—or may not—possess analogical significance. A poem of Chaucer, which is read by one man as a veiled confession of a personal experience of love, is read by others as an analogical creation with the death of a princess as its theme.[120]

The search for the analogical meaning, the deeper meaning, is sometimes due not to the fact that the literal meaning is false or uninteresting but to quite different reasons: conventions of style or of the period, or what one knows otherwise of the author's intentions.

A statement may more readily strike the reader as analogical because certain techniques have been used which tend to make it appear in this light. The use of multiple phoroi,[121] or of crude or oversimple phoroi,[122] may have this effect.

§ 85. *How Analogy Is Used*

Analogies are important in invention and argumentation fundamentally because they facilitate the development and extension of thought. With the phoros as starting point, they make it possible to give the theme a structure and to give it a conceptual setting. Thus, T. Swann Harding, who was actually mainly concerned with the role of language, writes:

> The scientists who first described electricity as a "current" forever shaped science in this field.[123]

The shape given to science in the field of electricity is due to the fact that the comparison of electrical and hydraulic phenomena occasioned developments which explain, complete, and extend the original analogy. But just how far can an analogy be extended?

In every field it is normal for an analogy to undergo development, which can extend as far as needs dictate, in the absence of opposition. As Richards has correctly observed, there is no whole to any analogy:

[119] Bevan, *Symbolism and Belief*, pp. 121-122.
[120] Stearns, "A Note on Chaucer's Attitude toward Love," *Speculum*, XVII (1942), 570-574.
[121] Whately, *Elements of Rhetoric* (Harper), p. 317. Appendix E to p. 74.
[122] Cf. Guitton, *Le temps et l'éternité chez Plotin et Saint Augustin*, pp. 154-155.
[123] Harding, "Science at the Tower of Babel," *Philosophy of Science*, 3 (1938), 347.

we are free to use as much of it as we need, but at the risk of seeing it break down if we take it too far.[124]

With the development of an analogy, a separation of its inventive and probative roles takes place. Where the inventive aspect is concerned, there is nothing to prevent extension of an analogy as far as possible, to see what it will yield. But, from the probative viewpoint, an analogy must be kept within certain limits if it is not to impair its function of strengthening conviction. Development of an analogy will sometimes confirm its validity, but it can also lay it open to attack by the interlocutor.

In some cases an analogy is developed without our being aware of the least break between the original analogy and its extensions. This analogy used by Kant to compare his philosophy with Hume's is an example:

> The latter [Hume] himself had absolutely no presentiment of the possibility of this formal knowledge, having brought his vessel, for its safety, to the shore (scepticism) where it could stay and rot; whereas I want to provide this vessel with a pilot who, observing the established principles of his art that are derived from knowledge of the globe and in possession of a complete chart and a compass, can sail it with confidence where he wills.[125]

Phoros and theme are here developed concurrently, and nothing separates the relationships that are successively evoked. The original analogy is, however, strengthened by the final phrases. The same thing happens to any extension of analogy which the author appears to have planned and on which he has relied.

Another type of argument by analogy is the one that exhibits two phases, with the second providing the main conclusion. It is illustrated by this passage from La Bruyère:

> The wheels, the springs, the movements are hidden; nothing of a watch appears but its hand, which insensibly moves round and finishes its circuit: the image of a courtier, all the more perfect as, after having covered enough ground, he often returns to the same point from which he set out.[126]

Here the expression to be noticed is "all the more perfect." It indicates that the analogy is better than the author had first imagined it to be. And often, as here, this development of the analogy has unexpected and even comical results.

Sometimes an argument exhibits stages, arising from the fact that advantage is taken of the apparent acceptance of an analogy to de-

---

[124] Richards, *The Philosophy of Rhetoric*, p. 133.
[125] Kant, *Prolégomènes à toute métaphysique future*, p. 15.
[126] La Bruyère, "Les caractères. De la cour," 65, *Œuvres complètes*, p. 257.

mand acceptance of its extension. In his treatise on genetic epistemology, Piaget, after showing that there is an analogy between the ideas held on evolution and those held about the theory of knowledge, goes on to say:

> If the correspondence, term for term, between the Lamarckian theses and the associationist or empiricist theses is exact, we must expect to find this correspondence between the objections raised to these two kinds of interpretation.[127]

And he expresses surprise that anti-Lamarckian biologists maintain a radical empiricism,

> as if the intelligence, contrary to the remainder of the organism, could possess no power of inner activity.[128]

It is the extension of the analogy which has argumentative value here, enabling an objection to the empiricist view to be formulated.

Instead of being extended by the author, an analogy may be extended by his critic, who will derive from it a means of refutation, all the more effective as the conceptual material has been taken from his opponent. Thus Berriat Saint-Prix, arguing against a jurist who, scorning any reference to Roman law and early jurisprudence, claimed in a work on the Civil Code, to describe "the veins, muscles, features, and soul of the law," expressed regret that the writer did not "follow his metaphor to the end," for "he would have soon perceived that every living being receives its organization from an earlier being from which it was begotten."[129]

This method of refutation assumes that one has always the right to extend an analogy beyond its original statement and that, if, as a result of being extended, it works against its author or becomes inadequate, it was already inadequate at the start.[130] As a matter of fact, this kind of refutation is nearly always possible, but what value does it have? The refutation is never compelling, as one may refuse to accept the extension. The main significance of the refutation is, however, that it emphasizes the fragility and arbitrary character of the analogy.

Sometimes an author will anticipate this and show in what respect an analogy is inadequate and develop his thesis as the counter to a possible analogy. This mode of argument uses what the writers of antiquity called *comparison by opposites*. This is not, as the author

---

[127] Piaget, *Introduction à l'épistémologie génétique*, vol. III, p. 102.

[128] *Ibid.*

[129] Berriat Saint-Prix, *Manuel de logique juridique*, p. 66, notes.

[130] Cf. Goldschmidt, *Le paradigme dans la dialectique platonicienne*, pp. 38-39, as to what Plato considered false paradigms.

of the *Rhetorica ad Herennium* says, mere ornamentation that could easily be dispensed with, as may be seen from an example taken from the same work:

> Indeed it is not like in an athletic contest, where the man who is handed the flaming torch is lighter of foot in the relay race than the man from whom he takes it. The new general, receiving an army, is not superior to his predecessor. For the tired runner is handing the torch to a runner who is quite fresh; but here an experienced general is handing over his army to a general without experience.[131]

One immediately occupies, in the military sense of the word, the hearer's mind, and he is shown the falseness of an idea that might arise spontaneously. It remains to be seen whether it was advisable to bring out this argument as yet unformulated by the interlocutor. It is undoubtedly a good idea, to the extent that the speaker manages to suggest that the sole basis for the disputed thesis is the argument by analogy that he is engaged in refuting.

One way that is sometimes used to refute an analogy is to amend it, by turning it round, so to speak, and describing what the phoros would be if the theme were properly conceived. This is not just a correction of the phoros designed to make it more suitable to the theme, even at the risk of removing it further from reality;[132] there is an amendment of the analogy as a whole. However, the part played by the terms of the phoros becomes very important, as the choice of these terms is no longer an open one, and they are what determine which relations are to be brought to the fore in amending the analogy. This technique can be seen in operation in Mill's *System of Logic*, where he deals with a passage in which Macaulay used the following analogy to deny the influence of great men:

> The sun illuminates the hills while it is still below the horizon, and truth is discovered by the highest minds a little before it becomes manifest to the multitude. This is the extent of their superiority. They are the first to catch and reflect a light which, without their assistance, must in a short time be visible to those who lie far beneath them.[133]

Mill dissents from Macaulay's view and, to make his own thought clearer, amends the analogy as follows:

> If this metaphor is to be carried out, it follows that if there had been no Newton the world would not only have had the Newtonian

---

[131] *Rhetorica ad Herennium*, IV, 59.

[132] Cf. § 84, supra: Effects of Analogy.

[133] Macaulay, "Essay on Dryden," in *Miscellaneous Writings*, I, 186, quoted in Mill, *A System of Logic*, bk VI, chap. XI, § 3, p. 612.

system, but would have had it equally soon, as the sun would have risen just as early to spectators in the plain if there had been no mountain at hand to catch still earlier rays. ... Eminent men do not merely see the coming light from the hilltop; they mount on the hilltop and evoke it; and, if no one had ever ascended thither, the light, in many cases, might never have risen upon the plain at all.[134]

The amended analogy gets its point from the total argumentative process of which it forms a part. Taken by itself, Mill's analogy would seem rather clumsy. The positive aspect of this analogy (men mounting the hilltop and evoking the light) is actually less important than the negative aspect (rays striking the plain without any screen). The advantage in this technique is that the user profits by such measure of adherence as was given to the analogy in its primitive form.

In philosophy an analogy sometimes acquires a special position whereby the progress of thought is measured by the successive amendments to which the analogy is subjected. Thus, Leibniz, in order to express his disagreement with the thought of Locke, who compared the mind to a block of marble, took up this analogy, and altered it to suit his own purposes:

> I have made use also of the comparison with a block of marble which has veins, rather than of a block of marble wholly even, or of blank tablets, that is, of what is called by philosophers a *tabula rasa*. For, if the soul resembled these blank tablets, truths would be in us as the figure of Hercules is in the marble, when the marble is wholly indifferent to the reception of this figure or of some other. But if there were veins in the block which should indicate the figure of Hercules rather than other figures, this block would be more determined thereto, and Hercules would be in it in a sense, although it would be needful to labor to discover these veins, to clear them by polishing and by cutting away what prevents them from appearing. Thus it is that ideas and truths are for us innate, as inclinations, dispositions, habits, or natural potentialities and not as actions; although these potentialities are always accompanied by some actions, often insensible, which correspond to them.[135]

The adaptation of an opponent's analogy to the needs of his own argument was an argumentative device to which Leibniz was very partial.[136] However, in some situations this technique proves inadequate, as where importance is attributed to some aspect of the theme that the phoros is incapable of illustrating, unless one is willing to turn the phoros into something fantastic. If analogical reasoning is to be

---

[134] Mill, *ibid.*, p. 612.
[135] Leibniz, *Die philosophischen Schriften*, vol. V, *Nouveaux essais sur l'entendement*, p. 45.
[136] Cf. Leibniz, *ibid.*, pp. 131-132.

pursued in such a case, the unsatisfactory phoros will have to be replaced by a more adequate one. Thus, because science gives an impression of completeness at each stage of its progress, Polanyi is not satisfied with the analogy used by Milton in his *Areopagitica*, where he compares the activity of scientists to that of a number of people, each of whom is independently engaged in the search for the scattered and hidden fragments of a statue, which he will later try to fit to those collected by others. Polanyi says that science should rather be compared to a growing organism.[137]

An analogy appears adequate when the phoros focuses attention on those features of the theme that are considered of prime importance. When a new analogy is substituted for it, the substitution more often than not consists of the replacement of one structure by another that emphasizes characteristics that are regarded as more essential. Acceptance of an analogy, therefore, is often equivalent to a judgment as to the importance of the characteristics that the analogy brings to the fore. Assertions that at first sight appear strange are explained by this circumstance. In his criticism of Wittgenstein's ideas, Moore takes exception to the analogy whereunder sentences are to facts as the grooves of a record are to sounds, in these terms:

> If a sentence did represent its fact as a line on a record records its sound, we probably should have to agree with Wittgenstein's contention.[138]

The acceptance or rejection of the analogy appears to be very decisive, as if a whole set of conclusions were necessarily bound up with it, and as if, summarizing what is essential in the theme, it imposed in a compelling fashion the manner of conceiving the theme.[139]

Different periods and philosophical tendencies show a preference for different phoroi. Classical thought favored spatial analogies, while modern thought prefers more dynamic phoroi. Bergsonian philosophy typically selects phoroi from the realm of the liquid, fluid and moving, while the thinking of its opponents is described by phoroi that feature what is solid and static. I. A. Richards has correctly observed that thought is governed as much by the metaphors that a philosophy

[137] Polanyi, *The Logic of Liberty*, pp. 87-89.

[138] Moore, "Structure in Sentence and in Fact," *Philosophy of Science*, 5 (1938), 87.

[139] Reasoning by analogy, when applied to the speech itself, assumes a great variety of forms. Here the relation between language and facts constitutes the theme, while the phoros is taken from the field of everyday experience. Often language itself is a phoros whose structure is intended to reveal the structure of the world. Often, too, the organization of the speech is the theme, which is illuminated by an analogy with a living organism. Cf. § 105, infra: Order and Method.

avoids as by those that it adopts[140]; thought can indeed be organized in terms of this rejection.

The passage of time is very commonly conveyed through spatial analogies, but much can be learnt from study of the particular form of the analogy. Sometimes the phoros used is the drawing of a line which extends indefinitely, sometimes it is a stream flowing, sometimes events are portrayed as moving past the spectator like a pageant, while sometimes they emerge from the darkness, like a row of houses lighted up one after another by a policeman's spotlight. Or time may be likened to the movement of a needle on a phonograph record or to a road, increasingly long stretches of which can be seen simultaneously as one draws away from it and gets a more unobstructed view. Each phoros emphasizes different aspects of the theme and paves the way for a different development.[141] This explains why our understanding of an analogy will very often be incomplete unless we take into consideration the earlier analogies which the new one amends or replaces. Then also, understanding of the phoros, particularly when it is taken from a social or spiritual sphere, presupposes adequate knowledge of the place it occupies in a given culture, as well as of the earlier, subjacent analogies in which the phoros in question was used, either as phoros for a different theme or as the theme for a different phoros.[142] The traditional connection between light and good makes the analogy of Scotus Erigena more plausible,[143] as it does those of Macaulay and Mill which were mentioned earlier. We are all familiar with the role played, since Plato's time, by the analogy which treats life as a play.[144] Mauriac's use of the hunt as phoros for the description of man as God's prey will be more accurately interpreted by one who knows that Mauriac uses the same phoros to describe woman as man's prey in the amorous pursuit.[145] Familiar, too, is the place given by Jung to this traditional analogical material in his study of archetypes.[146]

One special technique is to use several phoroi to explain a single theme. Such a procedure emphasizes the inadequacy of each phoros taken separately but impresses a general direction on the thought.

---

[140] Richards, *The Philosophy of Rhetoric*, p. 92.

[141] Cf. Bevan, *Symbolism and Belief*, pp. 85-94.

[142] Cf. reading and travel in Descartes, *Discourse on the Method*, GBWW, vol. 31, pp. 42-43; in Schopenhauer, *Sämtliche Werke* (Brockhaus), vol. 6: *Parerga und Paralipomena*, Zweiter Band, *Selbstdenken*, § 262, p. 525.

[143] Cf. § 83, supra: Relations Between the Terms of an Analogy.

[144] Cf. Goldschmidt, *Le système stoïcien* et *l'idée de temps*, §§ 89-91.

[145] Cf. Cormeau, *L'art de François Mauriac*, pp. 341-342.

[146] Jung, *Psychologie und Religion*, p. 93.

An example is the disconcerting variety of analogies used by Lecomte du Noüy to describe the relations he sees between the mechanisms of evolution itself.[147] The use of a number of phoroi is, however, a delicate matter. Since phoros and theme interact, a different phoros means a different theme. If the use of multiple phoroi yields a single theme, there is a danger of its being rather confused. So that the different phoroi may not interfere with one another, it will often be prudent to avoid—as does Lecomte du Noüy—putting them too close together. As each phoros contributes its structure to the theme, the juxtaposition of phoroi produces a comical effect, even when each of the structures is plausible and even when, from the standpoint of the value of the terms of the theme, they all yield the same conclusion. There are some good examples in Don Quixote:

> . . . for a knight errant without a lady is like a tree without leaves, a building without foundation, or a shadow without a body that causes it.[148]

Instead of being independent, multiple analogies can support each other. Thus, Locke, in his plea for tolerance, goes from the well-known analogy between the conditions of salvation and the paths leading to heaven to an analogy of remedies for disease, so that it is hard for the reader to know if it is the theme or the phoros of the first analogy which is the theme of the second. Locke writes as follows:

> There is only one of these which is the true way of eternal happiness: but in this great variety of ways that men follow it is still doubted which is the right one. Now neither the care of the commonwealth, nor the right enacting of laws, does discover this way more certainly to the magistrate than every private man's search and study discovers it unto himself. I have a weak body, sunk under a languishing disease, for which (I suppose) there is only one remedy, but that unknown. Does it therefore belong unto the magistrate to prescribe me a remedy because there is but one and because it is unknown.[149]

Analogies can also be grafted on one another in such a way that a part of the phoros is made the starting point of a new analogy. Vico resorts to this device to describe the effect the death of Angela Cimmino had on the Princess de la Roccella who had just lost her husband and

> whose recent bitter bereavement made her heart, great and courageous though it was, like a living vase of purest gold full of such

---

[147] Lecomte du Noüy, Human Destiny, pp. 64-69.

[148] Cervantes, El ingenioso hidalgo Don Quijote de la Mancha, vol. VI, pt. II, chap. xxxii, pp. 271-272.

[149] Locke, A Letter Concerning Toleration, GBWW, vol. 35, p. 9.

grief that nothing else could for any other reason or in any other way enter into it; nonetheless, so hard did sorrow for the death of our Marchioness strike it, that, like a hard body thrown into it, it made it ring with two sublime sonnets.[150]

There is nothing in the mechanism of analogy as we have described it which forbids use of these successive analogies. Yet many treatises on style speak contemptuously of "images that overlap." Were these to be proscribed, we should be surprised to find how many of our statements would have to be deleted. We shall return to these questions when we deal with metaphors.[151]

§ 86. The *Status of Analogy*

Analogy is an unstable means of argument. For the person who rejects the conclusions will tend to assert that "there is not even an analogy," and will minimize the value of the statement by reducing it to a vague comparison or merely verbal resemblance. On the other hand, the person invoking an analogy will almost invariably endeavor to assert that it is more than just a simple analogy. The analogy is thus stuck between two disavowals— disavowal by its opponents and disavowal by its supporters.

Sometimes an analogy will be outstripped before it is even recognized as an analogy. This is because the specific character of analogy lies in the confrontation of structures that are similar though they belong to different spheres. When these structures are not perceived, as happens in certain mental illnesses, any similarity between phoros and theme will tend to be explained by their possession of common characteristics— more particularly, by resemblances between their terms.[152]

Moreover, the distinction between spheres is not always easily made. It depends on the criteria used in establishing it. It is only in certain analogies of recognized type, such as allegories and fables, that the distinction between the two spheres appears beyond argument. This is also the case for certain philosophies where the analogical use of terms and structures results from the preliminary criteriology of being.

The outstripping of an analogy will sometimes be merely suggested. But often it will be explicit, even with reasons to justify it.

The first effort in outstripping the analogy and bringing phoros and theme closer together is directed to the establishment between them

---

[150] Vico, *Opere*, Ferrari ed, vol. 6: *Orazione in morte di Angiola Cimini*, p. 301.
[151] Cf. § 87, infra: Metaphor.
[152] Cf. Benary, "Studien zur Untersuchung der Intelligenz bei einem Fall von Seelenblindheit," *Psychologische Forschung*, 2(1922), 257-263, 268-272.

of a relationship of participation. The phoros is presented as a symbol, a figure, a myth, all of which are realities that derive their very existence from their participation in the theme to the better comprehension of which they are supposed to contribute. Thus Simone Weil, having discovered an analogy between certain supernatural hierarchies and certain aspects of energy, will write:

> And so it is not only mathematics but the whole of science that, without our thinking or noticing it, is a symbolized mirror of supernatural truths.[153]

Similarly, Buber writes:

> The relation with man is the real simile of the relation with God; in it true address receives true response.[154]

And Pascal defined in these terms the fundamental revelatory function of the concept of "figure," as developed by Christian tradition and used quite extensively by him:

> The figure has been made according to the truth, and the truth has been recognized according to the figure.[155]

Techniques of this kind which bring theme and phoros together but maintain their individuality tend nonetheless to unify the two spheres. The idea of figure assumes the reality of the phoros on the same footing as that of the theme.

Sometimes the outstripping of the analogy will be the result of showing that theme and phoros are both dependent on a common principle. Thus, after drawing certain analogies between physical inertia and force of habit, Schopenhauer goes on to say:

> All this is more than a simple analogy: it is the identification of the thing, that is, of the Will, with very different degrees of its objectivization, and, in conformity with these, the same law of motion presents itself differently.[156]

This common principle may be conceived as an essence, of which both theme and phoros are manifestations. When Eugenio d'Ors draws his brilliant analogies between architectural forms and the political system in which they develop, he does more than merely confront the two in such a way that they explain each other, while denying that he sees in one the cause of the other.[157]

153 Weil, *The Need for Roots*, p. 294.
154 Buber, *I and Thou*, 2d ed, p. 103.
155 Pascal, *L'œuvre, Pensées*, no 572, p. 1013 (no 673 ed. Brunschvicg).
156 Schopenhauer, *Sämtliche Werke* (Brockhaus), vol. 6: *Parerga und Paralipomena*, Zweiter Band, *Psychologische Bemerkungen*, § 307, p. 619.
157 Ors, *Coupole et monarchie*.

Often an indirect connection between theme and phoros will be established. So we have Fénelon writing that, if a speech full of antitheses and ornamentation is constructed like a Gothic church, it is because both are derived from the bad taste of the Arabs.[158]

It may even happen, as in the drawing of certain parallels between a person's feelings and his environment, that the analogy suggests some influence of the phoros on the theme. In such lines as

> Il pleure dans mon cœur
> Comme il pleut sur la ville[159]

the phoros can be regarded as a partial cause of the theme, and, in consequence, the writer has gone beyond mere analogy.

This outstripping will sometimes be expressed by the transference of a substantial element of the phoros to the theme. Thus, we find Leibniz writing:

> The late M. Van Helmont, the son, ... believed with some Rabbis in the passage of the soul of Adam into the Messiah as into the new Adam.[160]

In short, every kind of endeavor will be made to bring the sphere of the theme closer to that of the phoros. That this is a quite natural process is shown by the stress an author will often lay on efforts to guard against outstripping of the analogy. When Tarde points out the analogies between individual logic and social logic, he foresees the danger that exists of going beyond the analogy.[161] This danger is foreseen by Odier also when he draws analogies between Pavlov's reflexology and the psychology of the self.[162] The terms in which Odier expresses his apprehensions are significant:

> There is no neurotic symptom that cannot, in the long run, be described in physiological terms or be reduced to a collision between opposed energies. But let us never forget that what we have is a *reduction* and not an *explanation*. ... In the case of adult neurotics, only the psychology of the self can provide the elements of a real explanation.[163]

These authors emphasize the analogy because they deem it significant and capable of shedding light on certain phenomena. Going be-

---

[158] Fénelon, *Œuvres*, vol. XXI: *Dialogues sur l'éloquence*, p. 76.

[159] Verlaine, *Œuvres*, *Romances sans paroles*, III, p. 122.

[160] Leibniz, *Die philosophischen Schriften*, vol. V, *Nouveaux essais sur l'entendement*, p. 222.

[161] Tarde, *La logique sociale*, pp. 87 et seq.

[162] Odier, *L'homme esclave de son infériorité*, I: *Essai sur la genèse du moi*, pp. 93 et seq.

[163] *Ibid.*, p. 123.

yond the analogy could only have the effect of strengthening the proof contained in its structure. Yet they are afraid that this outstripping would be to the exclusive benefit of the phoros. Tarde, making use of a new analogy, goes on to say this:

> It is impossible, then, to abolish social logic by incorporating it in individual logic. Their duality is irreducible, like that of the curve and the asymptote, which go on approaching one another indefinitely.[164]

Actually, both Odier and Tarde themselves try to go beyond the analogy. The former stresses that the identity lies "in the consequences,"[165] while the latter speaks of "the mutual transactions" that will have to exist between the two fields.[166]

In the natural sciences, analogy—in our conception of the term—does nothing but provide a support for creative thought. It is here a question of going beyond analogy in order to infer a resemblance, with the possibility of applying the same concepts to both theme and phoros. By making the same methods applicable to them, the scientist tries to unite theme and phoros in a single field of investigation.

In chemistry, for instance, observation of analogical reactions will lead the researcher to classify the substances under examination in a single family. Cournot relates how Gay-Lussac and Thénard, struck by certain analogies, developed the hypothesis that the substance known as oxidized muriatic acid was an element, which they called chlorine; and how it was put in a natural family along with bromine and iodine. He goes on to say that because of these analogies they provided for the inclusion in the same family of fluorine which had not yet been discovered.[167] ·

As a link in the chain of inductive reasoning, analogy finds a place in science, where it serves rather as a means of invention than as a means of proof. If the analogy is a fruitful one, theme and phoros are transformed into examples or illustrations of a more general law, and by their relation to this law there is a unification of the fields of the theme and the phoros. This unification of fields leads to the inclusion of the relation uniting the terms of the phoros and of the relation uniting the terms of the theme in a single category, and, with respect to this category, the two relations become interchangeable. There is no longer any asymmetry between theme and phoros.

---

[164] Tarde, *La logique sociale*, p. 114.
[165] Odier, *L'homme esclave de son infériorité*, I: *Essai sur la genèse du moi*, p. 122.
[166] Tarde, *La logique sociale*, p. 113.
[167] Cournot, *Essai sur les fondements de nos connaissances*, II, pp. 237-238.

The precariousness of the status of analogy is thus largely due to the fact that the very success of an analogy can destroy it.

Analogy can be excluded also by the conditions governing reasoning. We have seen that, in law, reasoning by analogy has a much smaller place than one might think for the reason that, when it is a question of applying a rule to new cases, we are at once confined within a single field, as a basic requirement of law, for we cannot move out of the field which the rule imposes on us.

Broadly speaking, outstripping an analogy has the effect of making it appear as the result of a discovery, as an observation of what is, rather than as the product of an original effort at structuration. In some cases, the problem is reversed. There are philosophies which consider analogy as the result of a differentiation within a unitary whole; this is true of monistic philosophies which refuse to allow any distinction between fields. This refusal may be regarded as an extreme method of sanctioning the outstripping of the analogy by making it, as it were, preliminary to it. The analogy then merely makes explicit that which was included in the undifferentiated whole that preceded it. However, these philosophical considerations with respect to the status of analogy do not, in practice, disturb the normal possibilities of using analogy and its tendency to be outstripped.

The status of analogy is precarious on another score. Being a confrontation of structures, an analogy may, because of the interaction of its terms,[168] lead to associations concerning these terms. This resemblance between terms has almost always comical results, which shows that it is a misuse of argument by analogy. The person who in the classical analogy between the bishop and his congregation, on the one hand, and the shepherd and his flock, on the other, primarily sees a resemblance between sheep and church members and terms the praying church member a bleating sheep will easily attract attention, but at the expense of distorting the function of the analogy. However, the distinction between analogy and resemblance is not absolute. An element of resemblance between terms often seems to be the start of an analogy, even though it plays no essential role in its structure. Thus when Francis Ponge[169] in his poem on the lizard suggests—by means of a new phoros—an analogy between the movements of a lizard on a wall, his disappearance into a hole, and the stages of poetic creation, "a little string of gray thoughts moving about at full speed," and "gladly coming back into the tunnels of the mind," it is probable that the

---

[168] Cf. § 83, supra: Relations Between the Terms of an Analogy.
[169] Ponge, Le Lézard, in fine.

similarities between a wall and a sheet of writing paper (form, color) underlie the choice of terms.

On the other hand, an analogy, when successful, can result in an extension of the field of application of certain notions. Thus, N. Rotenstreich, after showing an analogy between the relation of the concrete subject to experience and the relation of man to language, goes on to say:

Language must be regarded as an extension of experience.[170]

This way of outstripping an analogy by its terms is all the easier, it would seem, when the terms are abstract in nature and can be felt to express structures. Such a procedure undoubtedly plays an important part in the development of concepts.

In certain cases, such as the one just discussed, the influence of the analogy is primarily manifested in the extension of concepts. But the analogy can also introduce confusion into them. Analogical argument can contribute to this confusion in many ways. When Pitt draws a lengthy analogy between the envied political situation of England and the situation of the temperate zone on the surface of the globe,[171] we can see quite clearly the structures of the theme as well as those of the phoros, but the interaction between theme and phoros inevitably makes the notions of happy mean and equilibrium more confused.

We have seen, moreover, that notions designating properties of the physical world, because of their analogical use in cultural circles, become impressed with a value which from then on forms part of their meaning.

It seems to us indisputable that analogy can modify concepts and increase their confusion. The reluctance of so many contemporary writers to allow analogy a role in the birth of certain notions[172] is undoubtedly explained by an extreme anti-associationism. The repugnance they feel would probably be lessened if a conception of analogy were held in which a greater place were given to the interaction between theme and phoros. It would also no doubt diminish the repugnance to consider metaphor as derived from analogy.[173]

§ 87. Metaphor

In the tradition of the masters of rhetoric, a *metaphor* is a trope, that is, "the artistic alteration of a word or phrase from its proper mean-

---

[170] Rotenstreich, "The Epistemological Status of the Concrete Subject," *Revue internationale de Philosphie*, 22 (1952), 414-415.

[171] Pitt, *Orations on the French War*, "Preparation for War, February 1, 1793", p. 4.

[172] Sartre, *Being and Nothingness*, pp. 604-605.

[173] Cf. Cohen, *A Preface to Logic*, p. 83.

ing to another."[174] It would even be the trope par excellence.[175] By the use of metaphor, according to Dumarsais, "we convert a noun's proper meaning to another meaning, which it can only bear by virtue of a comparison that resides in the mind."[176]

With good reason, Richards rejects the idea of comparison as misleading and inadequate. With vigor and insight he insists on the immense variety of the relations between concepts that a metaphor expresses in a single word. To him metaphor is much more a matter of interaction than of substitution,[177] a technique of research as much as one of embellishment.[178]

But no conception can be fully satisfactory which does not cast light on the importance of metaphor in argumentation. In our view, the role of metaphor will appear most clearly when seen in the context of the argumentative theory of analogy. Actually, in asserting the connection between metaphor and analogy, we are being faithful to an old tradition, to be found in the writings of philosophers and, more especially, logicians, from Aristotle to John Stuart Mill.[179] The existence of this connection will become acceptable once more, we believe, inasmuch as the theory of analogy is developed more deeply.

In the context of argumentation, at least, we cannot better describe a metaphor than by conceiving it as a condensed analogy, resulting from the fusion of an element from the phoros with an element from the theme.

Aristotle gives some examples of metaphors in which the analogical relation is made completely explicit. Thus, he writes:

> As old age is to life, so is evening to day. One will accordingly describe evening as the "old age of the day" and old age as the "evening of life."[180]

In examples such as this, phoros and theme are dealt with symmetrically, in textbook fashion, so to speak, outside the context which would show which is the theme and which the phoros. This is why they enable us to see clearly how a metaphorical expression can arise from an analogy. In the passage quoted, the analogy "*A* is to *B* as *C* is to *D*" yields the expression "*C* of *B*" to designate *A*. As we shall

---

[174] Quintilian, VIII, vi, 1; cf. Volkmann, *Rhetorik der Griechen und Römer*, p. 40.

[175] Dumarsais, *Des tropes*, pp. 167-168.

[176] *Ibid.*, p. 103.

[177] Richards, *The Philosophy of Rhetoric*, pp. 93 et seq.

[178] Richards, "A Symposium on Emotive Meaning," *The Philosophical Review*, 1948, p. 146.

[179] Aristotle, *Poetics*, XXI, 1457b; *Rhetoric*, III, 10, 7; Mill, *A System of Logic*, bk V, chap. v, § 7, p. 524.

[180] Aristotle, *Poetics*, XXI, 1457b.

see, this is by no means the only way of effecting a fusion between phoros and theme.

Through this fusion, the analogy is presented not as a suggestion but as a datum. In other words, metaphor can be used to enhance the standing of the analogy.

It is accordingly not surprising to find in arguments by analogy that the author not infrequently employs metaphors derived from the proposed analogy, so as to accustom the reader to see things as he depicts them. It is only quite rarely that theme and phoros will be stated independently of each other. Plotinus, after describing life as a play, goes on to speak of the soul in these terms:

> It sings its part, that it to say, it acts and gives forth in accordance with its own character.[181]

Here terms are taken from the sphere of the phoros, inserted into the sphere of the theme, and are at once made explicit in terms that belong to the latter.

The degree of contamination between phoros and theme can vary considerably. Fusion of the terms of the theme and phoros, bringing their respective spheres closer together, makes it easier to obtain argumentative effects. When an analogy is developed and the effort is made, with the phoros as starting point, to draw conclusions concerning the theme, the strength of the argument will be greater where, as a result of the fusion of theme and phoros, the phoros has previously been described at length in terms of the theme. This process is particularly well illustrated by Ronsard's famous ode "To Cassandra":

> Mignonne, allons voir si la rose
> Qui ce matin avait desclose
> Sa robe de pourpre au Soleil,
> A point perdu ceste vesprée
> Les plis de sa robe pourprée,
> Et son teint au vostre pareil. ... [182]

Before he speaks of Cassandra in terms taken from the domain of the phoros (*Tandis que vostre âge fleuronne En sa plus verte nouveauté*), the poet has already applied to the rose language applicable to a girl, describing the folds of its dress and its complexion and expressing indignation at the cruelty shown it by *marastre Nature*.

The richest and most significant metaphors are not, however, like those of Plotinus or Ronsard, which arise out of the expression of an analogy, but those that are from the outset presented as metaphors,

---

[181] Plotinus, *Enneads*, III, 2, § 17.
[182] Ronsard, *Œuvres complètes*, vol. I: *A sa maistresse*, Ode XVII, pp. 419-420.

generally by coupling the superior terms of the theme and phoros (*A* and *C*) and leaving unexpressed the inferior terms (*B* and *D*). These terms cannot be considered to be implied, for it must be granted that fusion, once it has occurred, yields an expression that is complete in itself. But close analysis would yield a wide variety of possible substitutes. Thus, the metaphor "an ocean of false learning"[183] suggests different viewpoints and attitudes according as terms *B* and *D* are considered to be represented by "a swimmer" and "a scientist" or as "a stream" and "the truth" or as "terra firma" and "the truth." All these analogies, simultaneously present to the mind, influence and enrich one another and suggest a number of different developments between which only the context allows one to choose. And even then the choice is rarely unambiguous and definite. Metaphor can also take the form of a bringing together of terms *B* and *C* of a three-term analogy,[184] as in the expression, "life is a dream." In this case, it is term *A* of the theme ("eternal life," for example) which will be inferred thanks to the metaphor, "life" being the term common to the two spheres.

The kind of merger brought about by metaphorical fusion is quite different from that produced by double hierarchy[185] or by going beyond analogy by establishing a symbolic connection between theme and phoros.[186] Metaphorical fusion does not involve closer relations between phoros and theme than exist in a simple analogy, but its effect is to consecrate the relation between them. If the analogy is admitted, acceptance of the metaphor follows as a matter of course. Writers have often advised paving the way for a metaphor in order to get it accepted[187] or softening it by suitable precautions.[188] Cicero and, later, Quintilian, suggested that bold metaphors should be introduced by such expressions as "so to speak," or "if I may say so." But, when one examines the examples they give and for which this procedure would be useful, one finds that the metaphors, far from being too bold, suffer from an excess of timidity. They confront spheres that are not far enough apart, and, in consequence, the metaphor is in danger of not being recognized; more exactly, the expression may be taken literally and become ludicrous:

[183] Berkeley, *Works*, vol. II: "Three Dialogues Between Hylas and Philonous," Third Dialogue, p. 259.

[184] Cf. § 83, supra: Relations Between the Terms of an Analogy.

[185] Cf. § 84, supra: Effects of Analogy.

[186] Cf. § 86, supra: The Status of Analogy.

[187] Baron, *De la Rhétorique*, p. 324.

[188] Cicero, *De Oratore*, III, 165; Quintilian, VIII, iii, 37; Dumarsais, *Des tropes*, p. 115.

If, in the past, they had said that Cato's death left the Senate "an orphan," the metaphor would have been somewhat forced; but to say "an orphan so to speak" would make it a little less stark.[189]

The fusion of the terms of the theme and phoros can occur in various ways: by simple determination ("the evening of life," or "an ocean of false learning"), by means of an adjective (a "hollow" or "luminous" account), through use of a verb ("she began to squeal"), or by a possessive ("our" Waterloo). Sometimes there will even be identification ("life is a dream," "man is a reed"); here the sole function of the copula is to indicate the position of homologues in an analogical relation. The metaphor can be strengthened by the device of speaking of the identification as something in the future. In this way, a traditional, recognized metaphor can serve as starting point for detailed development and argument, just like an unquestioned fact. This use of metaphor is seen in this passage from La Bruyère:

> The world will be the same a hundred years hence as it is now; there will be the same theater and decorations, though not the same actors.

And the conclusion, though it brings us back to the sphere of the theme, is again expressed in a metaphor:

> What reliance on a character in a comedy![190]

Sometimes, when the fusion of spheres leads to the creation of compound words, the language is enriched with very expressive abbreviations. An instance that comes to mind is the word *bateau-mouche*—literally "fly-boat"—which Estève has termed "a shameful metaphor."[191] It would seem not unlikely that such coined words as *genpillehommes*[192] (a play on *gentilhommes* and *piller*, "to rob"), and "banksters" are the result of metaphorical fusion.

Even when metaphorical fusion is associated with analogies of a picturesque character, the fusion does not confront us with a picture. Such expressions as "feather-flower," "bunch of wings,"[193] and "scaly vessel" do not evoke a real or fantastic concrete thing whose whole complex and clear features would represent a bird or a fish. To conceive metaphor as derived from analogy and analogy as a confrontation of relations seems to us the most effective way of combating

---

[189] Cicero, *ibid.*

[190] La Bruyère, "Les caractères. De la cour," 99, *Œuvres complètes*, p. 266.

[191] Estève, *Etudes philosophiques sur l'expression littéraire*, p. 268.

[192] Cf. Rolland, *Colas Breugnon*, p. 27; cf. Balzac's earlier use of "gens-pille-hommes," *La comédie humaine*, vol. VII, *Les Chouans*, p. 808.

[193] Calderón, *La vida es sueño*, I, 2.

at the theoretical level the error—justly stigmatized by Richards [194] — of regarding metaphor as imagery. At the practical level, the most effective defense is, first, to be on guard against metaphors that could be confused with a resemblance of terms, particularly where there is a fusion of terms A and C of an analogy and, secondly, to free ourselves of the limitations which some authorities would like to impose on the use of a series of apparently irreconcilable metaphors.[195]

Any analogy—unless, like allegory or parable, it is confined within a rigid form—turns into metaphor quite spontaneously. It is the very absence of fusion in an allegory or a parable that compels us to regard them as conventional forms which, by tradition, systematically decline to make a fusion. Far from being a metaphor,[196] an allegory would consist of a double chain unfolding with virtually no contact between the two parts. The very act of extending an analogy tends to bring about fusion. The action involved presupposes a development in time which a nondiscursive representation generally cannot convey. For this reason painting, because of its timeless nature, must either express exclusively the phoros of an allegory, which will always remain independent of the theme, or else must pass immediately to metaphor through the use of metaphorical fusion. This second alternative results in the creation of strange, fantastic beings. When he wishes to speak of the universe in human terms, the painter will show a man equipped with a head in the form of a globe. Satirical cartoonists often make use of this metaphorical fusion.

It lends itself admirably to comical effects of all kinds: the derisive effect of such expressions as "Carnival Caesar" and "Mudville Milton" arises from the very opposite values of the terms brought into apposition.

There is one use of metaphorical fusion which is not easily distinguishable from hyperbole.[197] When we say that a person running is doing ninety, are we using metaphor or hyperbole? Perhaps the expression represents the summation of both devices? Metaphor contributes a different sphere which adds to the hyperbolic unlimited development.

It is not surprising that metaphor, with its fusion of spheres and transcendence of traditional classifications, should be, par excellence,

[194] Richards, *The Philosophy of Rhetoric*, p. 16.
[195] Cf. the criticism of a poem of Lamartine's by Baron, *De la Rhétorique*, pp. 325-327.
[196] Quintilian, VIII, vi, 44.
[197] Cf. § 67, supra: Unlimited Development.

the tool of poetic and philosophic creation. Pascal's celebrated thought, "Man is but a reed, the most feeble thing in nature; but he is a thinking reed,"[198] achieves the fusion of theme and phoros in an immortal expression.

If one loses sight of the metaphorical aspect of such formulations, they can easily lead into the world of the fairy tale. A story describing the tribulations of a thinking reed would cause wonder, as it would be taking literally an expression that did no more than effect a fusion of spheres in the conceptual world.

Metaphors can also unintentionally produce comical effects, as in the anecdote of the customer who asked the salesman in the hardware store for "one of those iron curtains everyone is talking about."

Though we may seek in vain in nature for beings corresponding to the creations of metaphor, this does not prevent such creations from having an influence on the life of notions. The influence of a metaphor is not felt only in the argument for which it was created. It can also contribute to the confusion of concepts. Once use has been made of the notion of slave in such metaphors as "slave of the employer" and "slave of passions," the need is felt to investigate what are the elements common to the term "slave" in all its various uses which have a reaction on each other.

The masters of rhetoric saw in metaphor a means of overcoming the poverty of language.[199] That it can have this role is not to be doubted, though it would seem to be a very secondary role, and the notion of poverty, in this connection, is hard to define.

Be this as it may, the frequent use of a metaphor is bound to contribute to an assimilation of theme and phoros, and this explains why so many relations within a given cultural milieu seem to fit quite as naturally into the sphere of the theme as into that of the phoros. Are we to suppose that we have here a metaphorical use of notions originating in one of the spheres or on the contrary notions properly applicable, in their own right, to several spheres? The answer to this question will be decided, more often than not, by considerations of a philosophical order to which we have referred more than once.[200] If such words as "opaque" and "transparent" are taken as examples, we are inclined, when they are applied to the spiritual sphere, to feel that there is here a metaphorical use of a concept originating in a dif-

---

[198] Pascal, *Pensées*, GBWW, vol. 33, p. 233.

[199] Cicero, *De Oratore*, III, § 155; Quintilian, VIII, vi, 4; cf. Estève, *Études philosophiques sur l'expression littéraire*, pp. 227 et seq.

[200] Cf. § 76, supra: The Double Hierarchy Argument; § 86, supra: The Status of Analogy.

ferent sphere. For, whatever certain writers may say,[201] it would seem that the use of these terms is still felt to be metaphorical.

§ 88. *Dormant Metaphors or Expressions with a Metaphorical Meaning*

A danger to which metaphors are subject is erosion. The metaphor is no longer seen as a fusion, as a bringing together of terms taken from different spheres, but as the application of a vocable to that which it normally designates. From being active, the metaphor has become "dormant"—a qualification which, better than other adjectives (e. g., unrecognized, forgotten, faded), intimates that this state of inactivity may only be transitory and that the metaphor can be awakened and become active again.

The dormant metaphor, or expression with a metaphorical meaning, seemed to Whately, as it did to Stewart and Copleston before him, a tool far superior to the active metaphor, having lost its contact with the initial idea it denoted.[202] Stevenson, again, finds that the dormant metaphor, being interpreted in a single, fixed way, can give a *reason*, unlike the active metaphor, which is merely suggestive.[203]

Our own view in this matter is that the value of the dormant metaphor in argument is so great mainly on account of the great persuasive force it exerts when, with the help of an appropriate technique, it is reactivated. This strength is due to the fact that it obtains its effect by drawing on a stock of analogical material that gains ready acceptance because it is not merely known, but is integrated by language into the cultural tradition.

The most usual way of awakening a metaphor is to develop a fresh analogy, with the metaphor as its starting point. Thus, to awaken the dormant metaphor contained in the expression "carried away by his passions," Bossuet develops the phoros, which may be regarded as underlying the forgotten analogy:

> See this madman on the bank of a river, who, wishing to reach the other bank, waits until the river has flowed by and does not perceive that it flows without ceasing. We must pass over the river; we must advance against the current, resist the flow of our passions, and not wait to see an end to the flow of that which never flows by completely.[204]

---

[201] Marcel, *Le monde cassé. Position et approches concrètes du mystère ontologique*, p. 296; Bernanos, *La joie*, p. 119.

[202] Whately, *Elements of Rhetoric* (Harper), p. 317. (Appendix E, referring to p. 74).

[203] Stevenson, *Ethics and Language*, p. 143.

[204] Bossuet, *Sermons*, vol. II: *Sur l'ardeur de la pénitence*, p. 588.

In the same way, Kant develops the metaphorical expression "to shed light on the subject" in order to make it active again:

> He [Hume] shed no light on this kind [metaphysical] of knowledge, but he did nonetheless strike a spark from which one might well have got light, had the spark fallen on an ignitable wick, whose glow would have been carefully maintained and increased.[205]

As soon as the phoros of a metaphorical expression has been evoked by some detail, preferably by an extension of the analogy, even the most banal cliché can be brought to life again:

> The great and the humble have the same misfortunes, the same griefs, the same passions; but the one is at the top of the wheel, and the other near the centre and so less disturbed by the same revolutions.[206]

As this example shows, there need be no explicit statement of the metaphorical expression that is being awakened. "The wheel of fortune" is here but a cliché underlying the text.

The awakening is sometimes obtained merely by placing several metaphorical expressions side by side. When they can be fitted in as elements of a single analogy, they react on each other and bring about the awakening of the metaphors. Consider this passage from Demosthenes:

> You are grateful to them for giving you what is your own. As for them, after trapping you in the city, they give you the dogs' share and tame you for domestication.[207]

The words "trapping," "dogs' share," "tame," and "domestication," which separately might be taken to be metaphorical expressions, are perceived as active metaphors by being brought together.

Another way of reviving a metaphor is to use the same word twice, first in its metaphorical meaning and afterwards in its literal meaning, as in the following statement:

> We must all hang together or we shall all hang separately.

The same result can be obtained by setting the metaphorical expression in opposition to another derived from the domain of the phoros:

> Instead of being a dead end, as the earlier psychology proclaimed, abstraction is an intersection of avenues.[208]

Sometimes a metaphor is awakened by taking a metaphorical expression and grafting onto it a new metaphor which completes it:

---

[205] Kant, *Prolégomènes à toute métaphysique future*, p. 10.
[206] Pascal, *Pensées*, GBWW, vol. 33, p. 204.
[207] Demosthenes, *Third Olynthiac*, § 31.
[208] Bachelard, *Le rationalisme appliqué*, p. 22.

When the rocks grind their teeth on the tongue of sand.[209]

The distinction between the development of a metaphor and its complementation by another metaphor is a delicate one. But it seems to us to have value as a means of indicating the element of unexpectedness where one metaphorical expression is grafted on another. Bergson very frequently uses the device of complementation to bring expressions of extreme banality back to life:

> Modern science is the daughter of astronomy; it has come down from heaven to earth along the inclined plane of Galileo, for it is through Galileo that Newton and his successors are connected with Kepler.[210]

Care must be taken, however, to consider what effect will be produced by bringing two metaphorical expressions into close proximity. It can be disastrously comical, as in this description:

> That top banana who is the cream of society.

The awakening of a metaphor can be brought about also by a change in its usual context by using the metaphorical expression under circumstances that give it an unusual character and draw attention to the metaphor contained in it. Quite a mild distortion may suffice to restore analogical power to the expression. Thus, the metaphorical expression "to fade away," which goes unnoticed in the combination "to gently fade away," becomes active again in the phrase "to suddenly fade away." The new context may simply be the personality of the writer or speaker who uses the expression. A stereotyped metaphorical expression can come to life again in the mouth of certain speakers,[211] because it is presumed that, when they use it, it cannot have its usual banal meaning. Poets and philosophers are perhaps privileged in this respect.

Since metaphorical expressions vary from one language to another, and a metaphor in one language may be more or less "dormant" than the same metaphor in another language, translation will always somewhat alter the original text. More often than not, translation will cause a revival of the metaphors. Then again, if a reader reads a foreign work in its original language and he is not entirely familiar with this language, he will get from the work a particular pleasurable impression of life and movement, due to the circumstance that he will perceive what was perhaps only a dormant metaphor as an active one.

---

[209] Quoted by du Bouchet, "Envergure de Reverdy," *Critique* 47 (1951), 315.
[210] Bergson, *Creative Evolution* (Modern Library), p. 364.
[211] Cf. Reyes, *El Deslinde*, p. 204.

Sharing of the same cultural milieu is necessary to reduce metaphors to the dormant state. The linguistic expressions used in the professions and in slang seem to us to be metaphorical, but to the person using them they are the normal means of expression.[212] The frequent references to the abundance of metaphors in primitive speech, and in the speech of peasants and unlettered people,[213] are perhaps partially explained by the distance, culturally, between them and the observer.

An awakened metaphor can, of course, give rise to a variety of themes. The unspoken understanding between speaker and hearer is never more than partial; neither of them usually has a precise idea of how a metaphorical expression originates. The expression owes its force in part to the hearer's familiarity with it, in part to a somewhat vague awareness of the analogy at its source.

It is actually of little importance whether the expression really has a metaphorical origin. For the "awakening" is something that takes place in the present. For awakening to occur, it is necessary only that the expression should be perceived metaphorically, perhaps by analogy with other expressions. According to the writers of antiquity, *catachresis* is a figure defined as "the inexact use of a like and kindred word in place of the precise and proper one."[214] Some writers, such as Vico,[215] Dumarsais,[216] and Baron,[217] stress its relationship to metaphor, while others carefully distinguish it from metaphor.[218] "Sheet of paper" would be an example of this. Even if there is nothing metaphorical about the expression, and it has a quite different origin, being an extension or "projection" rather than a fusion, this does not prevent its becoming an active metaphor through use of the techniques of awakening that we have discussed.

These techniques can even be applied to quite normal expressions, in particular to certain adjectives. Only from the context can we tell that the writer intends that they should be read with a metaphorical meaning. Thus, when Kelsen writes:

---

[212] Cf. Estève, *Etudes philosophiques sur l'expression littéraire*, p. 206.

[213] Dumarsais, *Des tropes*, p. 2; Baron, *De la Rhétorique*, p. 308; Hayakawa, *Language in Thought and Action*, p. 121.

[214] *Rhetorica ad Herennium*, iv, 45.

[215] Vico, *Delle instituzioni oratorie*, p. 137.

[216] Dumarsais, *Des tropes*, pp. 32 et seq.

[217] Baron, *De la Rhétorique*, p. 349.

[218] Quintilian, VIII, vi, 34; Estève, *Etudes philosophiques sur l'expression littéraire*, pp. 244 et seq; cf. Ullmann, *Précis de sémantique française*, pp. 253 et seq.

The law of nations is still a primitive system of law. It is only at the beginning of a development already achieved by the law of each state.[219]

the context shows us that the writer intends the adjective "primitive" as a phoros indicating the possibilities for development possessed by primitive peoples. Similarly, when Bacon writes:

These times are the ancient times, when the world is ancient, and not those which we account ancient *ordine retrogardo*, by a computation backward from ourselves.[220]

the distinction which he makes turns "ancient times" into a metaphor whose phoros is human life, with its content of wisdom and experience. The persuasive force of such an argument resides in the analogy that is evoked.

In the preceding section we laid stress on the tendency there is to go beyond an analogy. The dormant metaphor is one form of this outstripping; but there is no awareness of the process, and it is accepted. The metaphorical term and the proper, literal, term may even be included in the same category.

But a metaphor may be awakened for the express purpose of showing that one is in the presence of a resemblance of relations and for the purpose of outstripping the analogy in a way that directly affects the analogy itself, as distinct from its terms. Thus Köhler writes:

Life has sometimes been compared to a flame. This is more than a poetical metaphor since, from the point of view of function and energetics, life and a flame have actually much in common.[221]

He goes on to develop their similitude of structure at some length and so shows that the analogy is better than it might have been thought and does not affect only certain aspects of the terms visible to everyone. Further on, he writes:

In a metaphorical fashion the springs of human action have often been called "forces." It appears that, if these springs have any counterparts, these counterparts can *be* forces only in the strict sense of the term. On the other hand, if they are actually forces, their behavior within contexts of neural events will resemble human motivation to such an extent that I doubt whether structurally and functionally any difference will be left.[222]

Here the purpose, in reactivating the metaphor, is to make it possible to go beyond the analogy in a new direction, while continuing to bene-

---

[219] Kelsen, *Reine Rechtslehre*, p. 131.
[220] Bacon, *Advancement of Learning*, GBWW, vol. 30, p. 15.
[221] Köhler, *The Place of Value in a World of Facts*, p. 320.
[222] *Ibid.*, p. 357.

fit from the acceptance of the earlier outstripping of the analogy which is assumed to be based on an intuition.   Language is taken as the basis, its pitfalls are stressed, but, notwithstanding these, use is made of the partial acquiescence expressed by the language in the theses being sustained.

Metaphor, an analogical fusion, fulfils all the functions of analogy itself.   In certain regards it works even better, because it strengthens the analogy; the condensed metaphor integrates it into the language. But it is only by awakening the metaphor that one can isolate its structure and, after this step has been taken, outstrip the analogy. Criticism, on the other hand, can use all the devices available for rejecting the analogy.   In addition, it can often also object to the obscurity of the metaphor.

The different possible attitudes toward a metaphor show that it can be considered in terms of the argumentation.   Its study from this viewpoint is in some respects easier than from that of individual psychology.   The difficulties of the latter approach have received sufficient attention elsewhere.[223]   It is concerned with the creator of the metaphor. But often the discussion will decide whether there is or is not a metaphor, whether one is or is not confronted with different categories. The very concept of "literal meaning" and "metaphorical meaning" may be a dissociation arising out of the discussion, and not a "primitive" datum.[224]

---

[223] Cf. Stutterheim, "Psychologische Interpretatie van Taal-Verschynselen," *Nieuwe Taalgids*, XXXI (1937), 265, and *Het Begrip Metaphoor*, pp. 188 et seq, pp. 525 et seq.

[224] Cf. § 93, infra: The Expression of Dissociations.

CHAPTER 4

The Dissociation of Concepts

§ 89. *Breaking of Connecting Links and Dissociation*

In the first three chapters we examined connecting links in argumentation that have the effect of making interdependent elements that could originally be considered independent. Opposition to the establishment of such an interdependence will be displayed by a refusal to recognize the existence of a connecting link. Objection will, in particular, take the form of showing that a link considered to have been accepted, or one that was assumed or hoped for, does not exist, because there are no grounds for stating or maintaining that certain phenomena under consideration exercise an influence on those which are under discussion and that it is consequently irrelevant to take the former into account:

> To be sure, if by leaving out all that is disagreeable to say, to avoid giving you offense, a speaker could thereby do away with events, one should only make speeches that are pleasing.[1]

Lack of connection may be proved by actual or mental experience, by changes in the conditions governing a situation, and, more particularly, in the sciences, by the examination of certain variables. Efforts will also be made to bring forward all the drawbacks of the connection.

The technique of breaking connecting links therefore consists in affirming that elements which should remain separate and independent have been improperly associated. Dissociation, on the other hand, assumes the original unity of elements comprised within a single con-

---

[1] Demosthenes, *First Philippic*, § 38.

ception and designated by a single notion. The dissociation of notions brings about a more or less profound change in the conceptual data that are used as the basis of argument. It is then no more a question of breaking the links that join independent elements, but of modifying the very structure of these elements.

At first glance, the difference between breaking connecting links and dissociation of concepts seems a profound and immediately discernible one, but actually this distinction, like the other so-called differences of nature, may be a matter of much controversy. Depending on whether the connecting links between elements are regarded as "natural" or "artificial," as "essential" or "accidental," one person will see a dissociation where another sees only the breaking of a connecting link.

In a well-known passage, Locke, maintaining that the Church is merely a voluntary association whose aim is the salvation of its members, rejects the connection established, in the period in which he lived, between State and religion:

> Neither the right nor the art of ruling does necessarily carry along with it the certain knowledge of other things, and least of all true religion. For if it were so, how could it come to pass that the lords of the earth should differ so vastly as they do in religious matters?[2]

To Locke the temporal is from the very beginning separate from the spiritual, he is opposed to their being joined, and shows the absurd results of such a union. To an opponent of Locke, the temporal implies the spiritual, and the endeavor to separate them is regarded as a dissociation of elements which are quite naturally united. Locke recognizes this union solely in the theocratic form of government, which no longer exists in modern states: in maintaining the union of the temporal and the spiritual, they are treating as a rule what is merely an exception, unrelated to the existing situation.[3] That which is merely accidental and proper to a particular political system cannot be an integral part of the concept of civil government: the union between the State and religion must therefore be rejected.

In final analysis, the factors that will show that we are in the presence of a dissociation of notions and not of a mere rejection of connecting links are the argumentative situation in its totality and, more particularly, the notions on which the argumentation rests, the changes to which it leads, and the techniques that make the changes possible.

[2] Locke, *A Letter Concerning Toleration*, GBWW, vol. 35, p. 9.
[3] Locke, *ibid.*, pp. 15 et seq.

What Rémy de Gourmont terms phenomena of association and dis-sociation[4] and Kenneth Burke terms identifications[5] are, in our view, simply connections and rejections of connections, for the associated and dissociated concepts appear, after the operation, to remain as they were in their original state, like bricks saved intact from a building that has been pulled down. The dissociation of concepts, as we understand it, involves a more profound change that is always prompted by the desire to remove an incompatibility arising out of the confrontation of one proposition with others, whether one is dealing with norms, facts, or truths. There are practical solutions enabling the difficulty to be resolved exclusively on the plane of action; they can prevent the incompatibility from occurring, or dilute it in time, or sacrifice one or even both of the conflicting values. At this practical level, the disso-ciation of notions amounts to a compromise, but, on the theoretical level, it leads to a solution that will also be valid for the future, be-cause, by remodeling our conception of reality, it prevents the reap-pearance of the same incompatibility. It preserves, at least partially, the incompatible elements. The operation, though bringing about the disappearance of the object, is nonetheless carried out at a minimum cost, because the thing that is valued is given its rightful place in the thought, and the latter is given a coherence that is beyond the range of difficulties of the same order. A typical example is the Kantian solution to the antinomy between universal determinism and man's freedom, which is to dissociate the concept of causality in' intelligible causality and perceptible causality.[6] This dissociation is itself made possible by the dissociation of the concept of reality into phenomenal reality and noumenal reality.

The new concepts resulting from the dissociation may acquire such a consistency, be so fully developed, and appear so indissolubly linked to the incompatibility whose removal they make possible, that the forceful presentation of the incompatibility may seem to be another way of stating the dissociation. The idea of original sin—which, by dissociating the concept of man into "man as created" and "fallen man" resolves certain incompatibilities between the goodness of God and the existence of evil and between man's free will and God's free will—is to Pascal a reason for insisting on the incompatibility between the greatness and the wretchedness of man:

The knot of our condition takes its twists and turns in this abyss,

---

[4] de Gourmont, *La culture des idées*, pp. 79 et seq.
[5] Burke, *A Rhetoric of Motives*, p. 150.
[6] Kant, *Critique de la raison pure*, pp. 457-460.

so that man is more inconceivable without this mystery than this mystery is inconceivable to man.[7]

The accepted solution sometimes seems so firmly based that failure to take it into consideration will be regarded as a logical error, as a fallacy. Thus, Candrasiṃha, the author of learned studies on logic, cites the assertion that an incompatibility exists between the Hindu rule of nonviolence and the Vedic custom of blood sacrifices as a good example of a fallacy. For, according to him, there is cruelty only when a rule has been broken and an unlawful act has been committed.[8] This definition of cruelty departs from the usual meaning of the word and is the result of a dissociation, but to Candrasiṃha it seems so unquestionable that he regards a return to the original meaning as an error of logic.

We shall show later that any new philosophy presupposes the working out of a conceptual apparatus, at least part of which, that which is fundamentally original, results from a dissociation of notions that enables the problems the philosopher has set himself to be solved. It is for this reason, among others, that we consider study of the technique of dissociation to be so significant.

Prominent jurists have observed before us that law is the favorite sphere of compromise, the technique for the resolution of incompatibilities. The aim of judicial endeavor, in Demogue's view, is not logical synthesis, but compromise. Legal progress consists of the development of techniques—which are always capable of improvement—that make it possible to reconcile conflicting claims.[9] Much the same idea is expressed by the great American jurist Cardozo:

> The reconciliation of the irreconcilable, the merger of antitheses, the synthesis of opposites, these are the problems of the law.[10]

This effort to resolve incompatibilities is carried on at every level of legal activity. It is pursued by the legislator, the legal theorist, and the judge. When a judge encounters a juridical antinomy in a case he is hearing, he cannot entirely neglect one of the two rules at the expense of the other. He must justify his course of action by delimiting the sphere of application of each rule through interpretations that restore coherence to the juridical system. He will introduce distinctions for the purpose of reconciling what, without them, would

---

[7] Pascal, *Pensées*, GBWW, vol. 33, p. 249.

[8] Annambhatta, *Le compendium des topiques*, pp. 146-147.

[9] Demogue, *Les notions fondamentales du droit privé*, particularly pp. 38, 75, 196, 198.

[10] Cardozo, *The Paradoxes of Legal Science*, p. 4.

be irreconcilable.[11] The same function is performed by the "distinguo" of scholastic theology.

When laws have not to be applied, when they have lost their compulsory character, it is possible to show their antinomic relationship in specific instances by rigidly fixing the juridical categories. But the jurist's endeavor is directed away from such rigidity. His task is to develop a system that makes the resolution of conflicts possible. When Napoleon, at the time he was already consul for life, exclaimed at a meeting of the Council of State: "How is the concept of a hereditary throne to be reconciled with the principle of the people's sovereignty?" he was not asking the jurists who were listening to him to note a contradiction but, rather, to produce a solution for an incompatibility.

It must not be forgotten, moreover, that a single incompatibility can yield several adjustments of concepts designed to resolve it. These rival solutions may themselves also appear as incompatible. This struggle between solutions is especially apparent in law, but it is also seen in theology. Particularly at the beginning of the Christian era, church quarrels often represented a confrontation of solutions arrived at for the settling of certain theological difficulties. These solutions in turn might give rise to new adjustments in order that they might be reconciled.

At the theoretical level, it is the compromise solution to incompatibilities which calls for the greatest effort and is most difficult to justify because it requires a new structuration of reality. On the other hand, once it is established, once the concepts have been dissociated and restructured, compromise tends to appear as the inescapable solution and to react on the aggregate of concepts into which it is inserted.

§ 90. *The "Appearance-Reality" Pair*

We think the reader will understand more clearly the dissociation of ideas and be able to form a better estimate of its results if we examine in greater detail the dissociation that yields the pair "appearance-reality." We consider this dissociation to be the prototype of all conceptual dissociation because of its widespread use and its basic importance in philosophy.

There is no doubt that the need to distinguish appearance from reality arises out of certain difficulties, certain incompatibilities between appearances; these could no longer all be regarded as expressing

---

[11] Berriat Saint-Prix, *Manuel de logique juridique*, p. 233.

reality, if one makes the hypothesis that all aspects of the real are mutually compatible. When a stick is partly immersed in water, it seems curved when one looks at it and straight when one touches it, but *in reality* it cannot be both curved and straight. While appearances can be opposed to each other, reality is coherent: the effect of determining reality is to dissociate those appearances that are deceptive from those that correspond to reality.

This first statement brings out immediately the ambiguous character and uncertain meaning and value of appearance: while appearance may correspond to and merge with reality, it may also lead us into error concerning it. As long as we have no reason to doubt it, appearance is simply the aspect under which reality is presented to us, and we mean by appearance the manifestation of the real. It is only when, because of their incompatibility, appearances cannot all be accepted together that the distinction between the deceptive and the nondeceptive ones brings about the dissociation yielding the pair "appearance-reality," the two terms of which are related in a manner that we must consider more closely.

In order that our conclusions may be of general application, it will be convenient to make "appearance" term I and "reality" term II of the couple. In order that the correlativity of the terms may be seen clearly, we shall from now on indicate a pair arising from a dissociation as follows:

$$\frac{\text{appearance}}{\text{reality}} \quad \text{or, in general,} \quad \frac{\text{term I}}{\text{term II}}.$$

Term I corresponds to the apparent, to what occurs in the first instance, to what is actual, immediate, and known directly. Term II, to the extent that it is distinguishable from it, can be understood only by comparison with term I: it results from a dissociation effected within term I with the purpose of getting rid of the incompatibilities that may appear between different aspects of term I. Term II provides a criterion, a norm which allows us to distinguish those aspects of term I which are of value from those which are not; it is not simply a datum, it is a *construction* which, during the dissociation of term I, establishes a rule that makes it possible to classify the multiple aspects of term I in a hierarchy. It enables those that do not correspond to the rule which *reality* provides to be termed illusory, erroneous, or apparent (in the depreciatory sense of this word). In relation to term I, term II is both normative and explanatory. After the dissociation has been made, term II makes it possible to retain or to disqualify the various aspects under which term I is presented. It makes it possible to distinguish, out of a number of appearances of doubtful status, those which are merely appearance and those which represent reality.[12]

This point seems to us essential because of its importance in argumentation. While the original status of what is presented as the starting point of the dissociation is unclear and undetermined, the dissociation into terms I and II will attach value to the aspects that correspond to term II and will lower the value of the aspects that are in opposition to it. Term I, appearance in the strict sense of the word, is merely illusion and error.

In actual fact, term II is not always accompanied by a precise criterion that makes separation of the various aspects of term I possible. The standard it provides can only be potential, and its principal effect is to order the terms resulting from the dissociation in a hierarchy. Kant, in order to solve the cosmological antinomies, dissociated reality and distinguished between phenomena and things in themselves. The term II he constructed in this way is not known, but this did not prevent the phenomenal world, conditioned by our power of knowledge, from being devalued as compared to the reality of things in themselves. Term II profits from its oneness, from its coherence, when set against the multiplicity and incompatibility of the aspects of term I, some of which will be disqualified and marked ultimately for disappearance.

In term II, then, reality and value are closely linked. This connection is specially pronounced in all the constructions of the metaphysicians. So we find the American philosopher Ducasse writing:

> When the adjectives *real* and *unreal* are used in the statement of a metaphysical position, they do not designate any characteristic that particular things possess independently of men's interest in them, but are, on the contrary, adjectives of human appreciation.[13]

This preference for what is real appears not only in philosophical discussions but is also expressed in everyday thinking in a wide variety of circumstances. The ordinary use of language testifies to the mutual conditioning of reality and value. When Pitt declares:

> I shall certainly endeavour, Sir, to confine what I have to say to the real point under consideration. ... [14]

this means, primarily, that he will confine himself to what he deems important. The metaphysicians' search for what is real is simply the

---

[12] Perelman, "Réflexions sur l'explication," *Revue de l'Institut de Sociologie*, 1939, no. 1, p. 59.

[13] Ducasse, *Philosophy as a Science*, p. 148.

[14] Pitt, *Orations on the French War*, p. 90. "On Wilberforce's Motion in Favour of a General Pacification," May 27, 1795.

systematized expression of the connection between reality and value that is charactertistic of term II. For this reason, we shall refer to pairs which, like

$$\frac{\text{appearance}}{\text{reality}},$$

result from a dissociation of concepts as "philosophical pairs."

Though the opposition between appearance and reality may be regarded as the prototype of a philosophical pair, this opposition does not warrant assigning all the advantages to reality at the expense of appearance. For, whereas appearance is given, reality is constructed, knowledge of it is indirect, sometimes even impossible, and rarely capable of communication in an exhaustive and unquestionable manner. To some it has the serious fault that it cannot be grasped. And, as Gracian says: "What is not seen is as if it were not."[15] What Pascal said about true justice could apply also to reality:

> Certainly, had he known it, he would not have established the maxim, the most general of all that obtain among men, that each should follow the custom of his own country. The glory of true equity would have brought all nations under subjection, and legislators would not have taken as their model the fancies and caprice of Persians and Germans instead of this unchanging justice.[16]

When the criterion or standard laid down by reality is not in fact challenged, or when the distinction it introduces is too indeterminate to give rise to controversy, reality doubtless gains in value in relation to appearance. Certain philosophies, however, reject this very dissociation between appearance and reality, affirming that conceptions of reality are in opposition to each other and denying any reason to choose between them. These philosophies—the antimetaphysical, positivistic, pragmatic, phenomenological, and existentialist philosophies— affirm that the sole reality is that of appearances.

This view finds clear expression in Sartre's attitude:

> Modern thought has realized considerable progress by reducing the existent to the series of appearances which manifest it. ... The appearances which manifest the existent are neither interior nor exterior; they are all equal, they all refer to other appearances, and none of them is privileged. ... The dualism of being and appearance is no longer entitled to any legal status within philosophy. The appearance refers to the total series of appearances and not to a hidden reality which would drain to itself all the *being* of the existent. ...

[15] Gracian, *L'homme de Cour*, p. 158.
[16] Pascal, *Pensées*, GBWW, vol. 33, p. 225.

To the extent that men had believed in noumenal realities, they have presented appearance as a pure negative. ... But if we once get away from what Nietzsche called "the illusion of worlds-behind-the-scene" and if we no longer believe in the being-behind-the-appearance, then the appearance becomes full positivity; its essence is an "appearing" which is no longer opposed to being but is on the contrary the measure of it. For the being of an existent is exactly what it *appears*. ... The essence of an existent ... is the manifest law which presides over the succession of its appearances, it is the principle of the series. ... But essence, as the principle of the series, is definitely only the concatenation of appearances. ... The phenomenal being manifests itself; it manifests its essence as well as its existence and it is nothing but the well-connected series of its manifestations.[17]

But opposition to the dissociation

$$\frac{appearance}{reality}$$

leaves entirely unresolved the problem that is raised by the incompatibility of appearances. The criterion for choosing from among the appearances will be provided by another pair corresponding, like the pair

$$\frac{appearance}{reality},$$

to a difference in nature. Or, failing that, a purely quantitative distinction will be drawn by according a preference to the whole over the part, to the infinite over the finite, to that which exhibits in a higher degree the property that serves as criterion. We find a characteristic expression of this mode of procedure in this passage by Merleau-Ponty:

I run through appearances and reach the real color or the real shape when my experience is at its maximum clarity. ...

I have visual objects because I have a visual field in which richness and clarity are in inverse proportion to each other and because these two demands, either of which taken separately might be carried to infinity, when brought together, produce a certain culmination and optimum balance in the perceptual process. In the same way, what I call experience of the thing or of reality—not merely of a reality-for-sight or for-touch, but of an absolute reality—is my full coexistence with the phenomenon, at the moment when it is in every way at its maximum articulation, and the "data of the different senses" are directed towards this one pole, as my "aims" as I look through a microscope vacillate about one predominant "target. I run through appearances and reach the real colour or the real shape when my experience is at its maximum of clarity...."[18]

---

[17] Sartre, *Being and Nothingness*, pp. XLIV-XLVI.
[18] Merleau-Ponty, *Phenomenology of Perception*, pt. II, chap. III, p. 318.

§ 91. *Philosophical Pairs and Their Justification*

As a prototype of the dissociation of notions, the pair

$$\frac{\text{appearance}}{\text{reality}}$$

was selected. The fact that the process can be reduced to a schematic form does not mean that the result is, on that account, purely formal or verbal. The dissociation expresses a vision of the world and establishes hierarchies for which it endeavors to provide the criteria. For the effort to be successful, other sectors of thought have to lend their assistance. It very often happens that a discussion involving term II will have to be founded on another pair whose terms I and II are not disputed.

These pairs all form the characteristic object of philosophical inquiry. In Table I are some examples, chosen from among those of most frequent occurrence in Western thought.

TABLE I

Pairs Characteristic of Philosophical Inquiry

means	consequence		act	accident
end	fact or principle		person	essence
occasion	relative	subjective	multiplicity	normal
cause	absolute	objective	unity	standard
individual	particular	theory	language	letter
universal	general	practice	thought	spirit

The fact that we are able to point to a large number of pairs and to assign each of their terms a specific place, without its being necessary, in order to do so, to insert them into a systematized thought sequence, is indicative of the influence of philosophical elaborations on ordinary thinking, in the shape of a series of pairs representing the residue of a dominant cultural tradition. (Actually, it would be impossible to insert all these pairs in a systematized thought sequence, as some of them are formed in diametrically opposite ways and represent different tendencies in philosophical thought.)

All systematic thinking tries to relate elements which, in an undeveloped thought, are just so many isolated pairs. This process of relating pairs is useful for avoiding the adoption of positions which result in qualifying the same phenomena by means of incompatible pairs. It is indispensable when, instead of being satisfied to pick up dissociations that are accepted in a cultural milieu, a thinker creates new dissociations or declines to admit certain of his predecessors' dissociations. Because of this rupture and to show its consequence on the other pairs, the philosopher will establish a *system* that will lead essentially to the relating of the various philosophical pairs with each other.

Thus in the *Phaedrus* Plato's philosophical thought can be expressed by the pairs shown in Table II. Spinoza's *Ethics* yields the pairs shown in Table III. In the following passage from Lefebvre we find a linking of the pairs (see Table IV) which are characteristic of Marxist thought:

TABLE II

Pairs Characteristic of Plato's *Phaedrus*[19]

appearance	opinion	sensible knowledge	
reality	knowledge	rational knowledge	
body	becoming	plurality	human
soul	immutability	unity	divine

TABLE III

Pairs Characteristic of Spinoza's *Ethics*

inadequate knowledge		image	imagination	universal
adequate knowledge		idea	understanding	individual
abstract	contingency		change	body
concrete	necessity		immutability	reason
passion	slavery	duration	joy	superstition
action	freedom	eternity	beatitude	religion

TABLE IV

Pairs in Lefebvre Characteristic of Marxist Thought

abstract	metaphysical	understanding	
concrete	dialectical	reason	
	immobility	form	
	movement	content	

---

[19] Plato, *Phaedrus*, 247e, 248b.

As we already know, intelligence or understanding can be defined as the power to separate certain objects from the world by ideal or real lines of cleavage and to immobilize, to determine, these objects. Intelligence is able to *abstract*, to *reduce*, the *concrete* to its simplest expression.

If an object is isolated by thought, it is immobilized in thought and becomes a "metaphysical abstraction." It loses its truth; in this sense, then, the object ceases to be. But if it is regarded as a momentary object, drawing its validity, not from its form and contours, but from its objective content, if it is regarded, not as a definitive result, but as a *means* or intermediate stage for penetrating reality, if intelligence is completed by reason, then the abstraction is justified. It is a step toward the rediscovered concrete, now analyzed and understood. It is concrete in a sense. ... The *truth of the abstract resides thus in the concrete.* For dialectical reasoning, *the true is the concrete;* and the abstract can be no more than a step in the penetration of the concrete—an instant of movement, a halting-place, a means for grasping, analyzing, determining the concrete. *The true is the rational; it is the real, the concrete.* Accordingly, geometric quantity and space are *true* only if their relationships with quality are rationally maintained and if the space is peopled with real objects.[20]

To philosophical pairs, which follow from a dissociation, we may oppose, on the one hand, pairs in which the second term is the opposite of the first, e. g., high/low, good/evil, just/unjust, and, on the other, classificatory pairs which, at first sight, serve no argumentative purpose and appear simply to be intended to subdivide a whole into separate parts (the past into periods, an area into regions, a genus into species).

These pairs are often introduced as data, not for discussion, as instruments that make it possible to structure the discourse in a manner that appears objective. But in systematized thought the pairs are related to, and influence, each other. Terms II of philosophical couples will normally, if possible, be related to that which has positive value in the antithetical pair, while terms I will be related to that which has negative value. There is thus a tendency to transform the antithetical pair into a philosophical pair. Dissociations of a philosophical nature also often play an essential part in the elaboration of pairs that appear to be classificatory.

L. Febvre has made a penetrating study of Michelet's creation of the concept of *Renaissance*.[21] Michelet felt the need to distinguish this

---

[20] Lefebvre, *A la lumière du matérialisme dialectique. I:Logique formelle, logique dialectique*, pp. 83-84 (author's italics).

[21] Febvre, "Comment Jules Michelet inventa la Renaissance," *Studi in onore di Gino Luzzatto*, 1950, vol. III, pp. 1-11.

period preceding modern times, but hesitated between two conceptions: the Renaissance as a revival of the original Middle Ages and the
Renaissance as replacing the Middle Ages. When he decided in favor
of the second solution, he struck out some admirable pages written
in terms of the first conception. Under the first alternative, the new
reality would have brought about purer and truer Middle Ages than
the earlier period, which was merely the *appearance* of the Middle
Ages. Under the second alternative, the earlier period forms the genuine Middle Ages and, instead of being the *appearance* of the Middle
Ages, is the *appearance* of civilization: the pair

$$\frac{\text{appearance}}{\text{reality}}$$

is thus applied to a different notion. But once the concepts have become stabilized independently of their origins, they come to seem
purely classificatory and have a role to play even in the work of the
historian who considers the centuries preceding the Renaissance a
peak of civilization.

The concepts resulting from a dissociation, once they have become
linguistic common property, seem thus to take on an independent
existence. Those notions which served as the basis of our study of
connecting links are all, without distinction, found in philosophical
pairs. With this as our starting point, we have embarked on a systematic study which is advanced enough for us to assert that it is capable
of being brought to a successful conclusion. It is not a question of
constructing a particular philosophy, but simply of observing what happens in the various systematizations of the mind and in the different
philosophies, irrespective of their tendency. The pairs

means	act	individual	act	symbol	particular
end	person	group	essence	thing	general

with their variants and connections, provide the terms of the most
common connecting links that form the basis of the interdependences
established in argument. Accordingly, one and the same pair of concepts
is at one moment presented as the result of a dissociation and at another
as two independent concepts between which there are characteristic
links and, so, an interaction, but also, as earlier chapters showed, pri-
macies of value that are not unrelated to their position as term I or
term II in a philosophical pair. Whenever the latter is emphasized,
it is an indication that the passage from one term to the other cannot
be made without restrictions. Though the act makes it possible to
judge the person and the end makes it possible to judge the means,

and conversely, evocation of the philosophical pair is a reminder that they must not be confused.

Very often there is no need for the connection between couples to be explicit. It may be established and, if needs be, justified by a great variety of means: direct connection based on the structure of reality between term I of one pair and term I of another; or between term II of one pair and term II of another; a pair considered as a particular instance of another; arguments presenting a quasi-logical aspect, and, more particularly, assertion of the identity of pairs; and, most commonly, analogical relations between pairs.

On these "horizontal" connections, which form chains of pairs, are superimposed relations of a different kind. For in argumentation, what one person terms appearance is generally what was reality to someone else, or was confused with reality or else it would not be given this new status. The argument will develop on different planes depending on the size, nature, and role of the audience supposed to have made the confusion. Sometimes the argument seems to concern the object under discussion, sometimes the idea that particular persons formed of the object, and sometimes the status that particular persons accorded or were supposed to have accorded it for the purposes of argument. These different planes are intermingled, supporting one another. Let us give an example. It has been pointed out that one of the devices used in ideological conflicts is

> ... to treat the statement of ideal as description of fact and to present reports of actual situations as if they were the ideal intended.[22]

In both these acts can be discerned the use of a pair

$$\frac{\text{normal}}{\text{standard}}$$

with respect to what concerns the speaker and the use of a pair

$$\frac{\text{standard}}{\text{normal}}$$

with respect to what concerns his opponent. But it is only the person exposing this device who makes a distinction between fact and ideal and effects a dissociation. This person, however, by using the dissociation has overcome a difficulty and made a choice; he moves, nevertheless, supposedly in the realm of the undifferentiated. And we might, with regard to him, establish the pair

$$\frac{\text{apparent impartiality}}{\text{real impartiality}}.$$

[22] McKeon, *Democracy in a World of Tensions*, p. 524, Appendix II.

Pairs established on one plane can thus give rise to a series of pairs set up on other planes. So, to avoid a difficulty on the plane of the object, a pair may be established on the plane of opinion. When the Belgian liberal leader Paul Janson demands the prohibition of work in the mines for children, he resorts to the concept of error and asserts that, if particular private interests, contrary to liberal doctrine, do not coincide with the public interest, they can be only apparent interests:

> ... It is undeniable that when private interests are mistaken and go astray, when they get into conflict with social and public interests, it is our duty to tell them so and to bring them back within the just limits beyond which they should not go.[23]

Generally speaking, the concept of error is used to assert that there is a rule, that the rule exists despite observations that appear to contradict it, and that what stands outside the rule either cannot be taken into consideration or, if taken into account, must be treated with reservation.

Often the effort to get a dissociation admitted will go to greater lengths. A speaker will try to explain why there is a conflict between terms I and II and, more especially, why the multiplicity, the partiality, of term I corresponds to the unicity of term II. Appeal will be made, for example, to the diversity of viewpoints regarding the object, or to the metamorphoses of term I, in justification of the multiplicity of appearances. The emergence of term I will be explained by locating it in a framework that makes it normal. In particular, the subject will be introduced with his passion, his helplessness, his ignorance, his state of sin. Gide puts these words in the Savior's lips:

> Do not wonder at being sad, and sad for my sake. The felicity that I hold out to you excludes forever what you took for happiness.

Happiness, in the initial sense of the word, becomes term I of the pair

$$\frac{\text{happiness}}{\text{joy}}:$$

> Joy, joy. ... I know, Lord, that the secret of your Gospel wholly abides in this divine word.[24]

Often the appearance will be explained by introducing a particular factor. Thus, to Schopenhauer, it is the cunning of the Intellect that

---

[23] Janson, *Discours parlementaires*, vol. I, pp. 35-36, Session of the Chamber of Representatives, Feb. 13, 1878.
[24] Gide, *Journal 1889-1939* (Gallimard), p. 600. *Numquid et tu ...*

explains our illusion of freedom[25]; the superego, according to the psychoanalysts, is the source of pseudomorality.[26] Sometimes term I will be depicted as fulfilling a natural function:

> So that, if intelligence was to be kept at the outset from sliding down a slope which was dangerous to the individual and society, it could be only by the statement of apparent facts, by the ghosts of facts: failing real experience, a counterfeit of experience had to be conjured up.[27]

These explanations are not given solely for the purpose of getting pairs accepted. In particular, the dissociation

$$\frac{\text{fable}}{\text{reality}}$$

is not involved. But the explanation helps to provide the criterion for term II and to insert the pair into a system of thought. It completes the work that was accomplished by the establishment of connections between pairs.

§ 92. The Role of Philosophical Pairs and Their Transformations

Although the use of some dissociations does not seem to introduce much that is new, since reliance is placed on notions that were developed a very long time ago, a modification of those notions is, nonetheless, brought about as the result of their application to a new sphere and of the adoption of new criteria for term II and through bringing the ideas into contact with new pairs.

Thus a pair as commonplace as that of

$$\frac{\text{appearance}}{\text{reality}}$$

will indirectly undergo constant modification. Such a dissociation as

$$\frac{\text{positive religion}}{\text{natural religion}}$$

will have repercussions on the pair

$$\frac{\text{appearance}}{\text{reality}}$$

if it happens to be brought into association with it.

---

[25] Schopenhauer, *Sämtliche Werke* (Brockhaus), vol. 6: *Parerga und Paralipomena*, Zweiter Band, Zur Ethik, § 118, pp. 249-250.

[26] Odier, *Les deux sources, consciente et inconsciente, de la vie morale*, ed. 2, pp. 42, 58, 59.

[27] Bergson, *The Two Sources of Morality and Religion*, p. 109.

The endeavor in argument will sometimes be to make good use of dissociations already admitted by the audience, sometimes to introduce dissociations created *ad hoc*, sometimes to present to an audience dissociations admitted by other audiences, sometimes to recall a dissociation that the audience is presumed to have forgotten. As for opposition to a dissociation, it will be directed toward the characteristics of its term I or term II or toward the very principle of the dissociation. If the latter course is pursued, one will claim that a global concept should have been retained. However, it is very difficult to repudiate terms when the mere mention of them, even for the purpose of attacking them, recalls their existence. Contemporary thought strives, in many fields, to abolish pairs. Much effort is required because the hearer will feel satisfied only if he can give a place in his mind to the old concepts. Often, in order to get a pair rejected, one will fall back on another pair. The easiest course is to claim that the dissociation was illusory, by relying on the couple

$$\frac{\text{verbal}}{\text{real}}.$$

Another technique consists in showing that the problem that the dissociation was meant to solve was factitious, using the pair

$$\frac{\text{factitious}}{\text{genuine}}$$

as a basis. Or else it may be shown that the problem will arise afresh under the same conditions without any contribution having been made to the coherence of thought by the provisional agreement on the dissociation.[28]

Very often the effort in argument will be directed not to the rejection of established pairs, but to their reversal. Only one or two pairs will be the object of this effort because the significance of such reversals arises precisely from the fact that they are inserted into an aggregate that is otherwise accepted.

Needless to say, the reversal of a pair is never complete, in the sense that a concept which becomes term I is no longer what it was when we knew it as term II—a term being conceivable only in its relation to the other term of the couple. Almost always a change of terminology will show the devaluation undergone by the idea that has become term I and the rise in value attached to the idea that becomes term II; it will show that the reversal fits in with a different view of the particular situation or of the world. Over against the pair

---

[28] Cf. for instance, Ryle, *The Concept of Mind*, pp. 25 et seq.

$$\frac{\text{interpretation}}{\text{letter}} \quad \text{stands the pair} \quad \frac{\text{letter}}{\text{spirit}}.$$

This reversal is readily postulated when a lawyer argues for a particular interpretation, and the interpretation that prevails becomes term II. Over against the pair

$$\frac{\text{theory}}{\text{fact}} \quad \text{we may have the pair} \quad \frac{\text{phenomenon}}{\text{principle}}.$$

Unwonted use of certain concepts as term II, even when made incidentally, shows originality of thought. The pair

$$\frac{\text{normal}}{\text{norm}} \quad \text{connected with the pair} \quad \frac{\text{example}}{\text{archetype}}$$

is very well known[29]; however, in Salacrou's play *Un homme comme les autres*, the central reality of the hero, that which defines him as an individual and, in the final analysis, gives him his value as a human being, is not the norm but the normal.[30]

Reversal, without changing any term, often has a provoking appearance, even if justified by a difference in field:

... the word which is the specter of a thought in a prose expression, in verse becomes the very substance of the expression in which, by an iridescence, the thought appears.[31]

When the reversal is shown by the position of the words, it can assume the aspect of a figure. Certain antitheses, particularly many *commutations* or, as some call them, *reversions*[32] consist of considering a single phenomenon first as term I and then as term II. Here are two examples:

One should eat to live, not live to eat.[33]

We should not judge rules and duties by morals and customs, but we should judge customs and morals by duties and rules.[34]

According to the author of the *Rhetorica ad Herennium*, these figures "give the impression that the second part is deduced from the first, although it contradicts it."[35] Actually, it is a question of setting the phenomenon in connection with the pairs

[29] Cf. Kant, *The Critique of Pure Reason*, GBWW, vol. 42, p. 173.
[30] Salacrou, *Théâtre III: Un homme comme les autres*, cf. Act I, p. 242; Act II, pp. 277, 298; Act III, pp. 310, 311, 325.
[31] Bousquet, in Aragon, *Les yeux d'Elsa*, p. 146.
[32] Baron, *De la Rhétorique*, p. 360.
[33] Quoted in *Rhetorica ad Herennium*, iv, § 39.
[34] Quoted by Baron, *De la Rhétorique*, p. 360, Bourdaloue.
[35] *Rhetorica ad Herennium*, iv, § 39.

$$\frac{\text{means}^{36}}{\text{end}} \qquad \frac{\text{normal}}{\text{norm}}$$

and of choosing its position in the pair.

Some of these commutations could be analyzed as inversions of metaphors:

A poem should be a speaking picture, and a picture a mute poem.[37]

The same thing is envisaged first as a phoros and then as a theme in the pair

$$\frac{\text{phoros}}{\text{theme}}$$

for it is possible to interpret any analogy as a dissociation with the theme as term II and the various possible phoroi as term I.

There are notions which, because of our habits of mind, cannot easily be used as term I. This is particularly true of the concept of reality; nevertheless, it occurs in the pair

$$\frac{\text{real}}{\text{ideal}}$$

Similarly the notions "fact" and "datum," which are commonly identified with the concept of reality, can occur as term I. The former occurs in the pair

$$\frac{\text{fact}}{\text{law}}$$

which is found in:

To members of the Catholic Party, freedom of conscience, freedom of worship, freedom of the press, freedom of association are not natural rights that are inalienable and indefeasible. They are facts, mere facts, which the Roman Church tolerates because it cannot prevent them.[38]

The second is found in the pair

$$\frac{\text{datum}}{\text{explanation}}$$

as it occurs in:

---

[36] Cf. § 64, supra: Ends and Means.

[37] *Rhetorica ad Herennium, ibid.*; cf. Vico, *Instituzioni oratorie*, p. 150.

[38] Janson, *Discours parlementaires*, vol. I, p. 53, Session of the Chamber of Representatives, May 17, 1878.

The datum, which nobody doubts, is regarded as appearance, whereas that which serves as explanation, although rarely as certain, is treated as being characteristic of true reality.[39]

Much of the interest attached to reversals, particularly in philosophy, is attributable to the retention by notions, as they are handed down, of their connections, of a portion of what they were when they had a place in pairs:

> What you call the empty forms and outside of things, seem to me the very things themselves. Nor are they empty or incomplete otherwise, than upon your supposition, that matter is an essential part of all corporeal things. We both therefore agree in this, that we perceive only sensible forms: but herein we differ, you will have them to be empty appearances, I real beings.[40]

The old term I is transformed into term II; yet what memories are evoked, more especially by the use of the word "matter," to indicate the primitive place of the concepts.

The keeping of some of the old traditional terms, after reversal is apparent in this passage from Bergson:

> ... Now, life is an evolution. We concentrate a period of this evolution in a stable view which we call a form. ... There is no form, since form is immobile, and the reality is movement. What is real is the *continual change* of form: *form is only a snapshot view of a transition.* ... When the successive images do not differ from each other too much, we consider them all as the waxing and waning of a single *mean* image or as the deformation of the image in different directions. And to this mean we really allude when we speak of the *essence* of a thing, or of the thing itself.[41]

Although Bergson's viewpoint is entirely new, we can see the advantage to him from the viewpoint of philosophy of stressing the reversal of the pair

$$\frac{\text{act}}{\text{essence}} \quad \text{in favor of the pair} \quad \frac{\text{essence}}{\text{becoming}} \quad \text{or} \quad \frac{\text{form}}{\text{becoming}}.$$

His original viewpoint has its foundation in a well-known pair, which he then proceeds to refute. Essence ceases to be the reality and becomes the appearance, as a theory, a form. Conversely, act becomes term II, as something living, concrete.

---

[39] Perelman, "Réflexions sur l'explication," *Revue de l'Institut de Sociologie* 1939, no. 1, p. 59.

[40] Berkeley, "Three Dialogues between Hylas and Philonous," Third Dialogue, in *The Works of George Berkeley*, vol. II, pp. 244-245.

[41] Bergson, *Creative Evolution* (Holt), p. 302.

The dissociation of a notion provides shelter from the incompatibility it resolves. But new difficulties arise concerning the terms established in this way. There is a noticeable tendency, in everyday thought as well as in philosophical thought, toward new subdivisions. These subdivisions sometimes affect term I and sometimes term II, and we get diagrams of the following type, which may be called "fan-type" dissociations:

$$\frac{\mathrm{I}}{\mathrm{II} \; < \; \dfrac{\mathrm{I}}{\mathrm{II}}} \quad \text{or} \quad \frac{\mathrm{I} \; < \; \dfrac{\mathrm{I}}{\mathrm{II}}}{\mathrm{II}}$$

Very good examples may be found in Schopenhauer's philosophy. A characteristic pair would be

$$\frac{\text{objectivity}}{\text{will}} \quad \left(\frac{\text{Objektität}}{\text{Wille}} \right)$$

as in the selection:

> There is only this thing in itself ... the will ... it does not know multiplicity, it is single. ... The multiplicity of things in space and time, which in their aggregate are its objectivity, does not touch it.[42]

But this objectivity, this representation, is split into the two terms

$$\frac{\text{things}}{\text{ideas}}$$

(in the Platonic sense), while the term "ideas" in turn yields the pair

$$\frac{\text{concept}}{\text{intuition}} \quad \left(\frac{\text{Begriff}}{\text{Anschauung}} \right), \text{ which is linked to the pair } \frac{\text{partial}}{\text{total}}$$

as in the following:

> Ideas in reality are something intuitive and hence ... inexhaustible. ... The simple concept, on the contrary, is something completely determinable, and exhaustible.[43]

These successive, more thorough analyses, which make it possible not to sacrifice the results already obtained, the agreements reached, the notions available, are found in all fields of thought. It may be asked whether they are not mostly characteristic of fields in which

---

[42] Schopenhauer, *Sämtliche Werke* (Brockhaus), vol. 2: *Die Welt als Wille und Vorstellung*, Erster Band, § 25, p. 152.

[43] Schopenhauer, *Sämtliche Werke* (Brockhaus), vol. 3: *Die Welt als Wille und Vorstellung*, Zweiter Band, Kap. 34, p. 466.

there is reluctance to effect reversal or pairs. Saint Thomas wishes to stick to the letter of the Scriptures and so to maintain the pair

$$\frac{\text{interpretation}}{\text{text}}.$$

But, to avoid incompatibilities with science, he gives a preference to the interpretation which, though "superficially less literal,"[44] is rationally more satisfying, and so introduces the pair

$$\frac{\text{apparent letter}}{\text{real letter}}.$$

The new, deep, dissociations are of course made in accordance with criteria that may be quite different from the criterion that governed the dissociation into which they are fitted. This is actually the reason why they are of interest. However, their effect, from the viewpoint of value, is to bring all the terms I closer together. Thus, Mauriac makes some harsh judgments by effecting a dissociation within a term II:

> There is a false saintliness—not in the sense of the gross imposture of Tartuffe—false despite or perhaps even because of the sincere and heroic effort of the man who applies himself to it.[45]

These few observations are sufficient to show the role played by dissociations in both philosophical and everyday thought. We shall confine ourselves here to a consideration of some lines of argument which relate the pair

$$\frac{\text{appearance}}{\text{reality}} \quad \text{to the pairs} \quad \frac{\text{means}}{\text{end}} \quad \text{and} \quad \frac{\text{consequence}}{\text{fact}}.$$

When there is hesitation as to which of several courses to adopt and the question arises of allotting them an order of priority, it is usual to set them in a whole which is systematized in relation to an end that one is endeavoring to achieve. The end becomes a criterion making it possible to evaluate the means and arrange them in a hierarchy; it becomes normative with respect to the means, which are multiple, whereas it is unique. In our activity the means is only an apparent end, whereas the end is the real object of our preoccupations. On the other hand, we can use the pair

$$\frac{\text{means}}{\text{end}} \quad \text{as a criterion for the pair} \quad \frac{\text{appearance}}{\text{reality}},$$

---

[44] Gilson, *Le thomisme*, p. 246.
[45] Mauriac, *Les maisons fugitives*, p. 19.

the reality being that which we wish to really know and the appearance being simply the means of reaching that reality by manifold and equivocal means. Thus Schopenhauer sees in the illusion of love simply a means whereby the will of the species is manifested, this will being the profound reality which alone is of consequence.[46] Consequently if a girl obstinately refuses to marry the rich old man her parents want her to marry because she loves some young man, she is only selfish in semblance and in reality is sacrificing herself for the good of the species.[47] The fact that, in the event, the girl's desire coincides with the good of the species is merely accidental; under other circumstances—if, for example, she refuses to have children— the two will be in opposition. Individual love is a manifestation of the will of the species which alone is essential. The manifestation itself is simply a means, an appearance, a purely contingent accident. The real end accordingly makes it possible to oppose the real to its apparent, contingent, and accidental manifestations.

To treat something as a means is to lower the value of that thing, to take away its absolute value—the value that is attributed to that which has value in itself, as an end, or as a principle. This is one of the criticisms the idealists make of the utilization of the pragmatic argument: if a fact is appraised in terms of its consequences, one seems to be regarding it as a means to those consequences and, by that very fact, to be devaluing it.[48]

We have seen also that a given phenomenon has not the same value when treated as a means to an end as it has when it is treated as a fact or principle producing a consequence.[49] For what was term II in the pair

$$\frac{\text{consequence}}{\text{fact or principle}} \quad \text{is turned into term I of the pair} \quad \frac{\text{means}}{\text{end}}.$$

If something is regarded as a means, it is equivalent to saying that our concern with it is only apparent. Praise is a consequence of virtue. If virtue is envisaged as a means to impressing people, then we accord it only a secondary value:

> Thus the eagerness he has for honor makes one think he does not love virtue, and next makes him appear unworthy of honor.[50]

---

[46] Schopenhauer, *Sämtliche Werke* (Brockhaus), vol. 3: *Die Welt als Wille und Vorstellung*, Zweiter Band, Kap. 44, p. 636.

[47] *Ibid.*, p. 640.

[48] Cf. § 62, supra: The Pragmatic Argument.

[49] Cf. § 63, supra: The Causal Link as the Relation of a Fact to Its Consequence or of a Means to Its End.

[50] Bossuet, *Sermons*, vol. II: *Sur l'honneur du monde*, p. 726.

We see, then, that certain results can be obtained only on condition that one does not strive after them, or, at least, that they present themselves as the consequence of facts independent of the will or as the consequence of behavior determined by other preoccupations. The reader will recall the passage from Proust which we quoted earlier.[51] A fact is devalued and ceases to have its normal consequences if it is perceived as a means for obtaining these consequences. The means—term I—will be pejoratively described as a *device*. We shall see later how techniques of argumentation are themselves liable to be so designated.

The device *par excellence* is the diplomatic illness in which one does not believe because it suits the purposes of the supposed patient too nicely, by enabling him to excuse his absence as something unintentional because it is simply the consequence of a factual situation.

The means, when put forward as the end, will be termed a *pretext*:

> Between ourselves, Henriette is an amusement,
> A cleverly devised screen, a pretext, brother,
> To hide another flame of which I know the mystery.[52]

What passed as the end can therefore become term I in the pair

$$\frac{\text{consequence}}{\text{fact}} \quad \text{or in the pair} \quad \frac{\text{pretext}}{\text{end}}.$$

The value attached to phenomena is closely dependent on their position in pairs. That which is only consequence, and is not fact or principle, has less importance. This explains why any study of the causes of criminality showing that the latter is only the consequence of a preexisting state of affairs is bound to lessen even the most legitimate moral indignation, whether this result is wished for or not. For the same reason, the transformation of phenomena of conscience into epiphenomena, the attempt to make man a product of his environment, is inescapably felt as a devaluation. Assessing Taine's views, which present cultural phenomena as a consequence, as term I of a pair in which social environment is term II, Chaignet spontaneously writes:

> Man is no longer the measure of things; he is their toy. Genius which up to now we had liked to consider a force, a cause, is merely a result; it is no longer a light, it is a reflection; it is no longer a voice, it is an echo.[53]

---

[51] Proust, *A la recherche du temps perdu*, vol. 12: *La prisonnière*, II, p. 210, in *Œuvres complètes*; cf. § 63, supra.

[52] Molière, *Femmes savantes*, Act II, scene 3; cf. Littré, *Dictionnaire de la langue française*, under the word *prétexte*.

[53] Chaignet, *La rhétorique et son histoire*, p. xv.

Man, even when inspired, is no longer the reality that counts: he is a reflection, an epiphénomenon, an appearance. The consequence is valued only in terms of the fact on which it depends, just as the means is valued only in terms of its end. A given phenomenon will thus have its value enhanced or diminished depending on whether the pair

$$\frac{means}{end} \quad or \ the \ pair \quad \frac{consequence}{fact}$$

is selected.

The existentialists' fundamental value is freedom. Yet, when it is a matter of depreciating the freedom enjoyed by Roman women in classical times, Simone de Beauvoir does not scruple to transform their freedom into a means and, what is more, a means toward an end that is without substance. She makes of it a freedom "for nothing."[54] Conversely, in order to enhance the value of courage, which is normally esteemed as a precious means in action, we find Jankélévitch writing:

... This virtue is at once formal and categorical; you must understand that it is always beautiful and always virtuous, whatever its subject, and it does not depend on the value of its end.[55]

To view knowledge as a consequence of reality, and action as the result of knowledge, is an affirmation of an ontological realism, of the primacy of the theoretical over the practical. Pragmatism, on the other hand, will evaluate in terms of action, which is the sole end and the sole criterion of knowledge as well as of the conception one has of reality. Thus Dupréel wants to see nothing but its end in ontologism itself:

... The philosopher approaches being and tells us what it is, to what end? That we may be acquainted with what is *precedent and inevitable*, with all that which, in the planning of our actions and in the formulation of our purposes, is imposed on us as an obstacle or is offered as a means. To come to know being brings the joy of discovery, but is also the principle of a resignation. In the philosopher we know it is an enthusiastic resignation, because as the first to resign himself he will appear to those he teaches as a guide and sometimes as a chief. After kneeling before the god, the priest turns round and commands.[56]

Recognition of an end does not make it an absolute end. A new dissociation may change it into a means toward an ulterior end, which will make it possible to discern in the original end—that has lost its value as term II— what is good and what is bad in it as means. In

[54] Beauvoir, *Le deuxième sexe*, vol. I, p. 153.
[55] Jankélévitch, *Traité des vertus*, p. 189.
[56] Dupréel, *Esquisse d'une philosophie des valeurs*, p. 24.

other words, the ulterior end will show what in the original end retains a certain value as term I.

Theoretically there is nothing to prevent an indefinite repetition of this operation of transforming ends into means through dissociation, with the ensuing loss of value. This process enables an opponent of rationalism, such as Buber, to stigmatize the outlook of those for whom everything is technique, relationship of means to end. To Buber, everything that derives from the useful belongs to the sphere of *It*:

> The development of the ability to experience and use comes about mostly through the decrease of man's power to enter into relation ... The unbelieving core in the self-willed man can perceive nothing but unbelief and self-will, establishing of a purpose and devising of a means. Without sacrifice and without grace, without meeting and without presentness, he has as his world a mediated world, cluttered with purposes. ...[57]

Buber's philosophic effort, with its insistence on the constant possibility of transforming term II of any pair

$$\frac{\text{means}}{\text{end}}$$

into a term I, disqualifies this pair in its entirety, together with the view of the world that is linked to it, in favor of a world in which the meeting and love of man and the meeting and love of God are of prime importance. He furnishes an interesting example showing how the technique of dissociating philosophical pairs can bring about rejection of both terms of the pair and repudiation of the viewpoint presupposed by resorting to the pair, on the behalf of another outlook and another criterion of reality.

§ 93. *The Expression of Dissociations*

To one who is familiar with the usages of a language, the presence of a philosophical pair is revealed by characteristic expressions which make it possible to distinguish term I from term II at a glance. Thus from the moment there is opposition of the terms

$$\frac{\text{appearance}}{\text{reality}} .$$

any idea can be dissociated by the addition of the adjectives "apparent" or "real," or of the adverbs "apparently" or "really." As a general rule, each time a dissociation is registered by a pair consisting of

---

[57] Buber, *I and Thou*, pp. 38-39, 60-61.

nouns, the adjectives and adverbs derived from them can indicate further dissociations. The pair

$$\frac{\text{name}}{\text{thing}}$$

makes it possible to oppose nominal wages to real wages, and the pair

$$\frac{\text{letter}}{\text{spirit}}$$

makes it possible to write that when the word of God is false literally, it is true spiritually.[58]

The use of the definite article (*the* solution) and the demonstrative (*this* world, *ille* homo) may show that one is in the presence of the true solution, world, or man which are alone of importance. Term II can be announced also by use of capital letters: *the* War is the real war; and Amphion will ask:

> Have I wounded, bruised,
> Charmed, perhaps,
> The secret Body of the world?
>
> * * *
>
> And touched the very Being hidden from us
> By the presence of all things?[59]

The expression "properly so-called" is generally applied to term II, while pinning to a noun such prefixes as *pseudo, quasi,* and *non* announces the presence of term I:

> The *pseudo-atheist,* when he denies God's existence, denies the existence of an imaginary being which he calls God, but which is not God. He denies God because he confuses God with that imaginary entity. ... The *real atheist,* when he denies God's existence, really denies the existence of that very God who is the authentic object of reason and faith—and of whom the atheist has a true idea— by an intellectual act which demands that he transform his whole table of values and descend into the depths of his being.[60]

Term II is that which is authentic, true, real; here, as often, term I designates an imaginary entity, an illusory construct, an inadequate theory.

---

[58] Cf. § 84, supra: Effects of Analogy. It is to be observed that the content of a dissociation may correspond to the theme and phoros of an analogy (cf. p. 429).

[59] Valéry, *Poésies. Amphion,* scene V, p. 283.

[60] Maritain, *Raison et raisons,* p. 161.

Sartre speaks of "quasi-multiplicity," which is, in point of fact, "a unity that multiplies itself."[61] Husserl disqualifies the sceptical philosophies by dubbing them "non-philosophies":

> The spiritual struggles properly so-called of European humanism as such develop in the form of *struggles between philosophies*, that is, struggles between the sceptical philosophies—though these are really "non-philosophies" [Unphilosophien] which have kept the name but not the mission—and the true and still living philosophies.[62]

In addition to disqualifying prefixes, there is a series of other expressions to indicate that a term I is involved, ranging from use of the word "claim" to setting a word between quotation marks.

Thus we find Lefebvre, apropos of the arguments of idealism, writing:

> Idealism finds arguments (if they can be termed such) only by overthrowing not merely the real process of knowledge. ... [63]

And the same author also writes:

> The paradox, to which modern idealism is driven, is a judge of the weight of its "criticism."[64]

This form of disqualification is very commonly used in communist polemics.[65]

These various designations of term I have reference to the pairs

$$\frac{\text{opinion}}{\text{truth}} \qquad \frac{\text{subjective}}{\text{objective}} \quad \text{and} \quad \frac{\text{verbal}}{\text{real}},$$

which distinguish what is claimed by others from what really is.

Such opinions are disqualified as naive[66] or as being errors, illusions, myths, reveries, prejudices, or fantasies. Their object is a false image, a phantasmagoria. They form a screen, a veil, a mask, an obstacle to knowledge of reality. For term I is apparent and visible, it is immediately given; to the extent that it does not reveal term II to us, it is in danger of concealing it from us. The Hindu philosophers ordinarily oppose reality to appearance in this way:

---

[61] Sartre, *Being and Nothingness*, p. 137.

[62] Husserl, "La crise des sciences européenes et la phénoménologie transcendentale," *Les études philosophiques*, 2(1949), 139.

[63] Lefebvre, *A la lumière du matérialisme dialectique, I: Logique formelle, logique dialectique*, p. 24.

[64] *Ibid.*

[65] Cf. Koestler in Crossman, *The God That Failed*, p. 56.

[66] Husserl, "La crise des sciences européenes et la phénoménologie transcendentale," *Les études philosophiques*, 2(1949), 140; cf. also the line of the Negro poet Césaire, who calls the whites "omniscient and naive conquerors." It is mentioned by J.-P. Sartre, *Situations*, III, p. 265.

The soul, the psychic being, is in direct contact with the divine truth, but in man the soul is screened off by the mental, by the vital being, and by physical nature.[67]

Similarly, in Levinas' phenomenology, the image is not the reproduction of the object but has a certain opacity which conceals reality from us.[68] In a beautiful philosophical poem by Girolamo Fracastoro, reality is presented as that which shows through in the night:

Do you not know that all things which this night covers
Are not true as they are, but are shades or
Specters, through which shows an Extraneous Shape?[69]

Mention of a substitution often signals the presence of a dissociation. The writer intends to show that the subject, by taking as term II what is only term I, manages to deceive himself:

The intellect always substitutes its own representations, constructions, and opinions for true knowledge.[70]

Hence the subject gives himself apparent reasons for acting which must be exorcised:

We must not make of submission to the Divine an excuse, a pretext, or an occasion for submitting to our own desires, to our inferior motions, to our ego, or to some force of ignorance or darkness which falsely gives itself the appearance of the Divine.[71]

To avoid this pitfall, it is necessary to get rid of all impurity which causes disturbance and error. Purification is a process which makes it possible to separate term II from that which merely has its appearance, from that which is only its more or less imperfect approximation. According to Odier, the task of the practising psychologist is "to reduce obstacles hampering the free sweep of the spirit. ... It is a work of purification."[72]

The apparent is the visible, that which is on the surface, which is superficial, and it is consequently only a small fragment of reality wanting to pass itself off as the whole:

... this little mental, this little vital, this little body that we call "us" is merely a superficial movement and not at all our true "I".

---

[67] Shrî Aurobindo, Œuvres complètes, III: Le guide du yoga, p. 187.

[68] Levinas, "La realité et son ombre," Les temps modernes, Nov. 1948, pp. 777, 780.

[69] Toffanin, Storia dell' umanesimo, p. 303. Fracastoro, Opera omnia: Carminum liber unus, Ad. M. Antonium Flaminium et Galeatium Florimontium, p. 206a.

[70] Shrî Aurobindo, Œuvres complètes, III: Le guide du yoga, p. 186.

[71] Ibid., p. 56.

[72] Odier, Les deux sources, consciente et inconsciente, de la vie morale, ed. 2, p. 31.

All this is only a purely external fragment of personality, put in the forefront during a brief existence for the play of ignorance.[73]

The same can be said of contradictory theses in a discussion which are outstripped in the synthesis:

> The opposing theses are then exposed as incomplete and super-ficial, as momentary appearances, as shreds of truth. ... "We give the name *dialectic* to the higher movement of reason in which these separate appearances pass into one another ... and are exceeded" [Hegel, Grande Logique, I, 108].[74]

The fragmentary, which is merely fugitive and accidental, is fated to disappear; on the contrary, that which is profound and durable, per-manent and essential, is real. It is normal for all the activities that aim at isolating term II in its full purity to be regarded as a liberation, as a struggle against the obstacles accumulated by term I. In order to succeed, everything that has to do with term I must be treated as something foreign and hostile:

> When one is living in true consciousness, one feels desires are outside oneself, coming from without. ... The first condition for rid-ding oneself of desire is therefore to acquire true consciousness, for it is then much easier to drive desire away than if one has to struggle against it as against a constituent part of one's being that will have to be cast far away from oneself. It is easier to get rid of an accretion than to amputate what one feels to be a portion of one-self.[75]

This passage is particularly interesting, because the rejection in a term I of the elements one wants to get rid of is openly advocated as being a more effective technique than that of mastering them by moral constraint involving the sacrifice of an actual part of oneself.

Term I will often be disqualified as being factitious or artificial, as being opposed to that which is authentic and natural. Tarde rebelled against this technique of disqualification widely practised by the Romanticists:

> People have the bad habit of applying the term *artificial* to the order established by the *uni-consciousness* in any category of social phenomena; they call artificial the durable codifications introduced in the field of languages by some famous grammarian like Vaugelas; artificial, the legislative codes and written constitutions; artificial, most of all, the theological *Summae*, those great encyclopaedic philosophies that have sprung from the head of an Aristotle, a Des-cartes, or a Kant and out of the myriad pieces of science make a

[73] Shrî Aurobindo, *Œuvres complètes*, III: *Le guide du yoga*, p. 189.

[74] Lefebvre, *A la lumière du matérialisme dialectique, I: Logique formelle, logique dialectique*, p. 148.

[75] Shrî Aurobindo, *Œuvres complètes*, III: *Le guide du yoga*, p. 99.

single rich raiment—or disguise—for the truth ... ; artificial, finally, according to the old-school economists, every industrial and economic regime which did not, so to speak, spring up on its own, any arrangement and ordering of the various productions and interests which, even though liberal, and, to some extent, individualistic, would be born with the original sin of having been consciously developed in a single head, using the labors of a thousand earlier minds.[76]

Instances of disqualification of views as being artificial are numerous. Thus, we find the opponents of metaphysics branding its assertions as being "fictitious," as opposed to "genuine"[77]; Pareto, the adversary of compromise, of persuasive reasoning, terms these "derivations" as compared with the "residues" which are the true social reality[78]; and the contemporary existentialists, in their efforts toward disqualification, use such adjectives as "inauthentic" and "mechanical."

Each doctrine elaborates its own philosophical pairs, term II of which indicates what serves as a criterion of value, whereas term I indicates that which does not satisfy this criterion. But, as we see, there are certain features that are particularly characteristic of term I. These are well brought out in this rather lengthy passage by Nelly Cormeau. Having detected in Mauriac's writing several themes which fit readily round a central pair

$$\frac{\text{social}}{\text{individual}},$$

she proceeds to apply to Mauriac himself the values that he accentuated:

> There is in Mauriac something audacious and *authentic*—we might aptly say *unpolluted*—a personal *integrity, a kernel of purity*, which do not let themselves be intimidated or *led astray* by the world and social life. ... But all that is purely social *superstructure*, to put it mildly, leaves him indifferent: we have seen with what virulence he cudgels "proprieties," compromises, and prejudices. ... He detests castes ... *factitious* groupings. ... The world *pollutes pure nature* formed by the Creator. ... His real frame is *free* nature. ... Need one remind the reader of all those people who in a drawing room or bar—in the *spurious* and *artificial* atmosphere of the "world"— suddenly feel themselves overwhelmed by an immense wave of despair? ... Mauriac is always for the *truth* against the *lie*, for the *spirit* against *tradition*, for the *genuineness* of direct person-to-person relations. ... And it is this *innate* nobility, this honest *purity*, this incorruptible *ingenuousness*, this fearless resolve to denounce every

[76] Tarde, *La logique sociale*, pp. 203-204.
[77] Ayer, *Language, Truth, and Logic*, pp. 37, 40, 43, 50.
[78] Pareto, *The Mind and Society*, § 1403, vol. III, pp. 890-891.

falsification which makes any work by Mauriac sound like a pressing appeal to what is most *sincere* and throbbingly alive deep within us. ... It is all this too—this *undisguised genuineness*, this bold, open absence of *mask* and *armor*— which brings Mauriac, with his great sense of equity and candor, into contact with unbelievers, despite his absolute Catholicism.[79]

The critic's pen has here gathered most of the expressions we have considered characteristic of term II (unpolluted, kernel, genuine, truth); those which characterize term I (impurity, superstructure, factitious, spurious, artificial, lie); the idea of mask, of disguise; the idea that term I is an obstacle (armor); finally the idea of error (lead astray).

Though we have been speaking about the terms of pairs, we must not forget that an expression commonly used to show a dissociation by no means always fulfils this function. Thus the adjective "eternal" often refers to a term II: to Germans opposed to the Third Reich, eternal Germany was the real Germany as opposed to apparent, transitory, Nazi Germany; but to Hitler, the use of the adjective "eternal" with the word "Germany" was merely a form of superlative.[80]

§ 94. *Statements Prompting Dissociation*

When we read or hear certain statements, we cannot avoid a dissociation of notions if we have regard, as is usual, to both the meaning and the coherence of the thought expressed. There are expressions which invite us to dissociate a notion without specifying in what manner the dissociation is to be effected. The context will show what is to be considered term I and what term II. Take, for instance, Schiller's couplet:

> What religion do I profess? None of all those
> That you mention. —And why none? —For
> religion's sake![81]

To understand these lines, the reader is compelled to recognize that the word "religion" is used in two ways, which correspond to an implied dissociation

---

[79] Cormeau, *L'art de François Mauriac*, pp. 183-184. The italics are those of the present authors.

[80] Klemperer, *L.T.I., Notizbuch eines Philologen*, pp. 202, 277.

[81] Welche Religion ich bekenne? Keine von allen
Die du mir nennst.—Und warum Keine?—Aus Religion!
Quoted by Erdmann, *Die Bedeutung des Wortes*, p. 61.

$$\frac{\text{apparent religion}}{\text{true religion}} \quad \text{or} \quad \frac{\text{positive religion}}{\text{natural religion}}.$$

The rejected religions correspond to term I, while the religion professed forms term II in the pair.

The same dissociative effort is required by the expression *Si duo faciunt idem, non est idem,* by Mirabeau's remark "a king, in this case, is no longer a king."[82]

Several of these expressions are what we termed quasi-logical figures: apparent tautology, negation of a term by itself, identity of contradictory propositions.[83] In such expressions as "business is business," "a penny is not a penny," the repeated word must be understood in two different ways. The way to resolve the difficulty is to make a dissociation into terms I and II.

This dissociation will be both the aim sought by the use of the expression and its justification. Thus Sartre uses the expression "being is what it is." In a lengthy argument, he contests its analytical character. The interpretation he puts forward amounts to a dissociation of being-in-itself from being-for-itself. His formulation, he says,

> ... designates a particular region of being, that of *being-in-itself.* We shall see that *being-for-itself* is defined, on the contrary, as being what it is not and not being what it is. ... The fact of being what one is ... is a contingent principle of being-in-itself.[84]

Dissociation may be required as the result of opposition between a word and what is ordinarily regarded as a synonym for it, as, for instance, in this statement by Panisse:

> I do not mind dying. But it grieves me to depart from life.[85]

Paradoxical expressions always call for an effort at dissociation. Every time an adjective or verb which seems incompatible is attached to a noun (learned ignorance, happy misfortune, bitter joy, thinking the unthinkable, expressing the unexpressible, the conditions of unconditional surrender),[86] only a dissociation makes it possible to understand the expression.

The same thing happens when an inadmissible relation is asserted between concepts, as in this definition of a poet by Orpheus:

> It is to write without being a writer.[87]

---

[82] Cf. Timon, *Livre des orateurs,* p. 193.

[83] Cf. § 51, supra: Analyticity, Analysis, and Tautology.

[84] Sartre, *Being and Nothingness,* p. LXV.

[85] Pagnol, *César,* p. 24.

[86] As to this final paradox, see *The Memoirs of Cordell Hull,* pp. 1570-1578.

[87] Cocteau, *Orphée* (film), in *Empreintes,* May-July, 1950, p. 163.

Another instance is in Cocteau's *Plain-Chant*:

> The ink I use is the blue blood of a swan,
> Who dies when he must in order to be more alive.[88]

Somewhat similar is the maxim "losing in order to win" which plays such an influential role in Japanese life. From its applications as described by Ruth Benedict, one can see that what is lost is merely term I in comparison with what is won.[89]

Determination of a given term by the identical term not only invites a dissociation, but suggests that this dissociation will deepen an original dissociation. An illustration of this is Jankélévitch's use of the expression "soul of the soul"[89a] which is superimposed on a dissociation in which "soul" was term II.

Turns of phrase like those we have just been describing form what has been called *paradoxism*, an antithesis formulated by uniting words that appear to be mutually exclusive[90] or the figure that Vico calls *oxymoron*, which is "to deny of something that it is what it is.[91] Such expressions are also very often found in *polyptoton* (repetition of the same word in several grammatical forms) and in *antimetathesis* or *antimetabole*[92] (repetition of the same words in transposed order in two successive phrases), which is sometimes confused with commutation.[93]

§ 95. *Dissociative Definitions*

Definition is an instrument of quasi-logical argumentation.[94] It is also an instrument of the dissociation of concepts, more especially whenever it claims to furnish the real, true meaning of the concept as opposed to its customary or apparent usage. So Shrî Aurobindo, after eliminating the more usual definitions of "work," gives us what he considers "the deeper truth of work":

> By "work" I mean action done for the Divine and increasingly in union with the Divine—for the Divine alone, and nothing else.[95]

---

[88] Cocteau, *Plain-Chant*, in *Empreintes*, May-July, 1950, p. 9.
[89] Benedict, *The Chrysanthemum and the Sword*, p. 266.
[89a] Jankélévitch, *Traité des vertus*, p. 58.
[90] Baron, *De la rhétorique*, p. 361.
[91] Vico, *Instituzioni oratorie*, p. 151.
[92] *Ibid.*, p. 150.
[93] Cf. § 92, supra: The Role of Philosophical Pairs and Their Transformations.
[94] Cf. § 50, supra: Identity and Definition in Argumentation.
[95] Shrî Aurobindo, *Œuvres complètes*, III: *Le guide du yoga*, pp. 207-208.

Adam Smith, rejecting existing criteria by which the value of commodities was "commonly estimated" as unreliable, though more easily
understood and more "natural and obvious," gave this definition:

> Labour ... is the real measure of the exchangeable value of all
> commodities.[96]

Spinoza, when he opposes the nature of things to the meaning of
words, warns, that his definitions are a departure from what is customary:

> I am aware that these names in common usage bear a different
> meaning. But my object is not to explain the meaning of words
> but the nature of things and to indicate them by words whose cus-
> tomary meaning shall not be altogether opposed to the meaning
> which I desire to bestow upon them. I consider it sufficient to have
> said this once for all.[97]

Rejection of the old conception, as not corresponding to reality, is
completely explicit in this passage of Berkeley dealing with the possibility of retaining the concept of matter, thanks to a new definition:

> ... There is no *matter*, if by that term be meant an unthinking
> substance existing without the mind: but if by *matter* is meant
> some sensible thing, whose existence consists in being perceived,
> then there is *matter*. ...[98]

Term II is never known directly, and so any attempt to communicate it discursively may be regarded as a definition of the term, that is,
an expression of the criteria that will enable us to determine it. Thus
the whole system may serve as a definition. But certain expressions
constitute pauses or turning points in the chain of thought because
they represent a relatively condensed formulation of that which characterizes a given term II.

This formulation can assume a great variety of forms, with the
statement of a condition as a particular feature:

> A religious thought is genuine when it is universal in its orienta-
> tion.[99]

Often the statement that something falls or does not fall within a
given concept amounts to the indirect introduction of a dissociative
definition, especially when the introduction of a new characteristic
becomes the criterion for the correct use of the concept. So we find

---

[96] A. Smith, *The Wealth of Nations*, GBWW, vol. 39, pp. 13-14.

[97] Spinoza, *Ethics*, pt III, Explanation, (The Affects, Definition 20), GBWW,
vol. 31, p. 418.

[98] Berkeley, "Three Dialogues between Hylas and Philonous," Third Dialogue
in *The Works of George Berkeley*, vol. II, p. 261.

[99] Weil, *The Need for Roots*, p. 93.

Isocrates, though he recognizes that the Spartans were overwhelmed at Thermopylae, declaring that

> ... one may not say that they were defeated, for none of them consented to flee.[100]

The extension of particular concepts sometimes represents a dissociative redefinition, as in this passage from Cicero:

> No, judges, the violence threatening our lives and persons is not the only kind of violence. There is that other, much more serious form, which by the threat of death fills our minds with terror and often turns them from their natural condition.[101]

The extension of the concept is combined with a playing down of what constituted the usual concept: if one is not careful, the most obvious violence, violence to the person, easily turns into term I.

A rather odd device is to give two definitions, which, instead of being treated as interchangeable,[102] correspond respectively to term I and term II of a pair. Lecomte du Noüy uses this technique in speaking of civilization:

> First, the static definition: Civilization is the descriptive inventory of all the modifications brought about in the moral, esthetic, and material conditions of the normal life of man in society, by the brain alone.
> Second, the dynamic definition: Civilization is the global outcome of the conflict between the memory of man's earlier evolution which persists in him and the moral and spiritual ideas which tend to make him forget it.[103]

From what he says, it is obvious that the author considers the dynamic definition primordial, the one that corresponds to what is real and profound. The static definition corresponds to what is transitory and mere appearance; thanks to it, room is made for what is *grosso modo* the customary definition of the term. The two definitions together stand in a relationship that corresponds to the pair

$$\frac{\text{static}}{\text{dynamic}}$$

encountered in the philosophy of Bergson.

In a discussion of ethical argumentation, Stevenson applies the term "persuasive definitions"[104] to definitions of the kind we have been

---

[100] Isocrates, *Panegyricus*, § 92.
[101] Cicero, *Pro Caecina*, xv, 42, quoted by Quintilian, VII, iii, 17.
[102] Cf. § 50, supra: Identity and Definition in Argumentation.
[103] Le comte du Noüy, *Human Destiny*, p. 106.
[104] Stevenson, *Ethics and Language*, p. 210; cf. also The Emotive Theory of

speaking of, because they preserve the emotive meaning of the concepts, the meaning that is to influence the interlocutor, while they modify their descriptive meaning. Undoubtedly in very many cases it is to the speaker merely a matter of a simple persuasive technique. But, apart from the fact that the distinction between the emotive aspect and the descriptive aspect of a concept is questionable,[105] the change brought about may be the result of an inner conviction which the speaker believes to conform to the reality of things and is ready to justify. We prefer to emphasize the way in which the definition dissociates a concept into terms I and II, regardless of the reason for this dissociation. Be it observed that, as was the case with Shrî Aurobindo's definition of "work," the purpose of the device may not be to transfer an accepted value over to a new meaning, but rather to enhance the value of a concept by conferring on it a prestige that it lacked in its former use.

Sometimes the dissociation will oppose a technical meaning to a more customary one. The adoption of a technical meaning, limited to a particular field, may be virtually without influence on the old concept and may be accepted as a mere linguistic convention. But it is rare for a discussion to be conducted wholly within the frame of an established science.[106] And when the technical concept and the customary concept are confronted, one of them—the one that counts for the audience being addressed— may assume the role of term II in relation to the other. Generally, it will be the technical term which enjoys this privilege. But, occasionaly, it may become term I, as in this argument by Demosthenes:

> So far from saying—as that individual slanderously stated just now—that I am not liable to submit accounts, I fully admit that all my life I have been accountable for everything I have done or advised in my public capacity.[107]

The "submission of accounts," in a technical, administrative sense, gives place to the more general and more essential moral concept, and the remainder of the argument will be largely based on this latter meaning, regarded as term II.

Many *antitheses* are applications of dissociative definition inasmuch as they oppose to the normal meaning, which might be thought to be

---

Ethics, A Symposium, *Aristotelian Society Supplementary Volume* XXII, 1948, communications of Robinson, pp. 89-92, and Paton, p. 112.

[105] Cf. § 35, supra, and Perelman and Olbrechts-Tyteca, "Les notions et l'argumentation," *Archivio di Filosofia*, vol. *Semantica*, p. 254.

[106] Cf. § 50, supra: Identity and Definition in Argumentation.

[107] Demosthenes, *On the Crown*, § 111.

unique, another meaning which will constitute a term II. Vico quotes from Cicero this example of the special form of antithesis known as *enantiosis*:

> There you have not written law, but natural law.[108]

A definition is always a matter of choice.[109] Anyone making such a choice, particularly if a dissociative definition is involved, will generally claim to have isolated the single, true meaning of the concept, or at least the only reasonable meaning or the only meaning corresponding to current usage. Thus, Simone Weil says:

> There is no other way of defining the word "nation" than as a territorial aggregate whose various parts recognize the authority of the same state.[110]

And Schopenhauer declares:

> The purpose of *art* is to promote knowledge of *Ideas* (in the Platonic sense which is the only one I allow to the word Idea) ... [111]

This claim is akin to the process of nonformal discourse. It is not unknown even among those who object to the improper role played by the definitions of some terms: Crawshay-Williams considers that discussions of the meaning of the word "good" are otiose because:

> Insofar as the word "good" has a reasonable objective meaning "in usage," it seems it must be identified with the happiness and well-being of *people* and of as many people as possible.[112]

In order to justify the definition, appeal is sometimes made to scientific or popular etymology. A usage of the notion will be advanced as being primitive, authentic, that is to say real, having been separated out from later falsifications. Jean Paulhan has devoted some thought to this matter of recourse to etymology and has made some pertinent observations.[113]

Very close to argumentation by means of etymology is argumentation based on syntax, exemplified by this passage from Sartre:

> The *self* cannot be a property of being-in-itself. By nature it is a *reflexive*, as syntax sufficiently indicates—in particular the logical rigor of Latin syntax with the strict distinctions imposed by grammar between the use of *ejus* and *sui*. ... It indicates a relation between the subject and himself, and this relation is precisely a dual-

---

[108] Vico, *Instituzioni oratorie*, p. 150. Cicero, *Pro Milone*.

[109] Cf. § 50, supra: Identity and Definition in Argumentation.

[110] Weil, *The Need for Roots*, p. 99.

[111] Schopenhauer, *Sämtliche Werke* (Brockhaus), vol. 3: *Die Welt als Wille und Vorstellung*, Zweiter Band, Kap. 34, p. 466.

[112] Crawshay-Williams, *The Comforts of Unreason*, p. 125.

[113] Paulhan, *La preuve par l'étymologie*.

ity, but a particular one since it requires particular verbal symbols.[114]

Also closely related is argumentation consisting in the harking back to primitive institutions and rudimentary practices for the purpose of giving present-day concepts their true meaning, as distinct from their ordinary one.[115]

The intemperate use of etymology by both French and German existentialists is well known. However, under certain circumstances, a writer who is fond of basing his argument on etymology will explicitly reject this connection between language and reality:

> The necessity of syntax has compelled us hitherto to speak of "nonpositional consciousness *of* self." But we can no longer use this expression in which the "of self" still evokes the idea of knowledge. (Henceforth we shall put the "of" inside parentheses to show that it merely satisfies a grammatical requirement.)[116]

In order to justify this rejection of the syntactical bond which he has elsewhere invoked, the writer will inevitably resort to a fresh dissociation

$$\frac{\text{grammar}}{\text{syntax}}$$

and will reject in grammar, here term I, that which does not correspond to philosophical reality as he conceives it.

Etymology is not resorted to only in order to find the "proper" meaning of a word and to dissociate it as term II by linking the use of etymology, in effect, with the idea of a world in process of degeneration. Sometimes the emphasis, as in this passage from a book by Alain, will be put on the passage from one term to another:

> There is no thought at all without culture, or without cult either, for it is the same word.[117]

Recognition of the relation between "cult" and "culture" is presented as the discovery of a truth. The semantic development is regarded as the forgotten achievement of a rational humanity, as a path hidden from us by the veil of ignorance and which must be rediscovered.

Either because it is technical or because it is advanced as being the only valid one or because it is inserted in an aggregate of connected philosophical pairs, the dissociation of notions tends to make their

---

[114] Sartre, *Being and Nothingness*, p. 76.
[115] See, for example, Bataille, "Le temps de la révolte" II *Critique* 56, p. 33, on the subject of amok and authentic sovereignty.
[116] Sartre, *Being and Nothingness*, p. LIV.
[117] Alain, *Histoire de mes pensées*, p. 217, mentioned by Paulhan, *La preuve par l'étymologie*, p. 17.

meaning more precise. But this effort toward precision is successful only in so far as one remains within a technical framework, completely dismisses all other meanings, or adheres to a system in its entirety. To one who does not keep within these limits, the dissociative definition more often than not opens up a fresh possibility for making use of the primitive notion, which is added to the earlier usages and by this very fact makes the notion more confused.

We should add that the dissociative definition of a concept may consist of an assertation that it is irremediably confused, that its univocal use is merely an illusion, a term I, a partial, momentary usage and that, for the resolution of the inconsistencies that inevitably arise from these aspects of term I, the only course open is to distinguish the latter carefully from a term II which will be the real, essential concept, not capable of being grasped directly in its plenitude and confusion.

§ 96. *Rhetoric as a Process*

Dissociations, besides operating on the notions used in presenting an argument, affect also the discourse itself. For the hearer—either of his own accord or because he is invited to—carries out with respect to the discourse dissociations that are of fundamental importance.

A process is a method of operating in order to obtain a given result, as where we speak of a manufacturing process—the technical means for manufacturing some product. That which is obviously a means or process is given its proper value in proportion to its effectiveness. But very often the term "process" is disqualifying, designating term I of a philosophical pair, and is synonymous with fallacious appearance. We find this criticism being directed at that which claims to be the natural consequence of certain circumstances but which is really pretence, artifice, a contrived means to an end: insincere tears, excessive compliments are but devices to arouse pity or to flatter.

Argument addressed to others and eloquence in all its forms has always been subject to this disqualification and is constantly exposed to it. The attack may be aimed at a particular argument, a particular speech, or even at the whole art of oratory. It is often sufficient to qualify what has been said as "rhetorical" to rob it of its effectiveness. Many statements are like those actions which have an effect only when they were not carried out to achieve this effect.[118]

---

[118] Cf. § 92, supra: The Role of Philosophical Pairs and Their Transformations.

When treated as oratorical or rhetorical devices, the means of persuasion are pronounced to be artificial, formal, and verbal—terms I characteristic of the pairs

artificial	form	verbal
natural	substance	real

This devaluation reaches the point where the spontaneous, unprepared speech, whatever its imperfections, is preferred to the considered, premeditated speech which the hearer considers as a device.

That which is the consequence of an irresistible urge cannot be a process. Thus the writer, poet, or orator will claim to be under the influence of a Muse who inspires him or of an indignation that inflames him: he becomes the spokesman for a dominating force which dictates his words. This romantic vision conveys through what is today a well-worn cliché a point emphasized by all the masters of style and the great orators from the time of pseudo-Longinus to Bossuet: the most effective eloquence is the eloquence which appears to be the normal consequence of a situation. Paraphrasing Saint Augustine, Bossuet declares:

> ... Eloquence, to be worthy of a place in the speeches of Christians, must not be pursued with too much zeal. It must come by itself, drawn out by the greatness of things and to serve as interpreter to Wisdom as she speaks.[119]

The speech which is felt not to arise from its object will strike the hearer as a process. When the hearers share the speaker's respect or admiration for values extolled in an epidictic speech, such a speech will rarely be felt to be a process. But this does not apply to others to whom these values do not appeal. "Those are just words" is the accusation we throw at others when they glorify things that we consider barren or futile because they are not our values.[120] Chaignet is unquestionably right when, repeating what so many have said before him, he declares:

> It is the natural which persuades, whereas artifice in composition or expression seems, when it is perceived, to be a snare set for the confidence of the hearer, who is indignant at this deceit and feels a dissatisfaction which does not aid persuasion.[121]

(Note the expressions "snare," "artifice," "deceit" characteristic of what has been changed into term I.) However, there is one reservation to be made: very often what has been said or written will be termed

---

[119] Bossuet, *Sermons*, vol. II: *Sur la parole de Dieu*, p. 151.
[120] Cf. Paulhan, *Les fleurs de Tarbes*, p. 84.
[121] Chaignet, *La rhétorique et son histoire*, p. 455.

a process as a result of a disagreement as to substance. It is because the hearer cannot conceive that anyone can be moved by the evocation of certain values that he regards the expression of the emotion as a pretence and a snare set for others.

Even when there is agreement on values, one may get the impression that a device is being used when the speaker seems to adopt rules or techniques which, because they are too uniform or too farfetched, do not seem to fit the object in an altogether natural manner. One cannot carp at an article in a Swiss propaganda journal which, in boasting of the trips available to tourists, describes a funicular railway as the longest or the most sensational,[122] but quite a comical suggestion of device is produced when the same journal contains in addition a score of advertisements, each headed by a different superlative. The typical device is the false window which does not satisfy reality because its sole purpose is symmetry:

> Those who make antitheses by forcing words are like those who make false windows for symmetry. Their rule is not to speak accurately, but to make apt figures of speech.[123]

Even if there is nothing mechanical, forced, or factitious in the means employed for persuasion, the mere presence of schemes of argument and techniques of persuasion that are theoretically transferable to other discourses may be enough to suggest the charge of device.

For the charge to be sustained, the argumentative technique castigated as a device must not be capable of being better interpreted as corresponding to the very nature of things. Owing to the ambiguity of argumentative situations, this is often a difficult question to resolve. When the ancient writers applied the term "color" to an interpretation of reality that favored the thesis being defended,[124] they assumed an objective reality of facts—a reality tailored and modified by the speaker. Here again the terminology recalls that characteristic of terms I.[125] But the existence of this objective reality, which seems not exactly to coincide with the interpretation put forward, is not proved. An easily exposed device is not only ineffective, but, like an obvious lie, it merely serves to discomfit its author. However, the price paid for the difficulty that arises from detecting a device is that every act with consequences favorable to the agent is liable to be considered a device. At

[122] *La Suisse*, Aug.-Sept., 1948.
[123] Pascal, *Pensées*, GBWW, vol. 33, p. 175.
[124] Cf. § 30, supra: The Interpretation of Data.
[125] Quintilian, IV, ii, 88, 97; Sénèque le rhéteur, *Controverses et Suasoires*, Editor's introduction, p. ix (Seneca the Rhetorician).

the limit, this means that all conscious behavior is suspect,[126] and it explains why, with each person believing he knows his own motives,

> ... people are generally better persuaded by the reasons which they have themselves discovered than by those which have come into the mind of others.[127]

Dissociation is therefore brought about only to remove an incompatibility. It implies that one possesses—at a level which may vary—a conception of reality, a criterion enabling one to penetrate the device ("real arguments," "reality of the speaker's sentiments," "reality of the facts stated"). A conception of reality implies a conception of the device, and vice versa, as in any dissociation there can be no term I without a term II. But we must not overlook that everything that promotes perception of a device—the mechanical, farfetched, abstract, codified, and formal aspects of a speech—will prompt the search for a reality that is dissociated from it.

How can one react against the branding of a discourse as a device, or, better still, how can one prevent it?

One may do so, as we have seen, by asserting that the speech is the consequence of a fact. But there are also available a series of techniques, some of which aim mostly at preventing the evocation of a dissociation, while others provide criteria to show that it is not justified.

Adoption of a style appropriate—in the hearer's estimation—to the object of the discourse avoids the dissociations of which there is most immediate danger:

> This aptness of language is one thing that makes people believe in the truth of your story: their minds draw the false conclusion that you are to be trusted from the fact that others behave as you do when things are as you describe them; and therefore they take your story to be true, whether it is so or not.[128]

Some speakers and writers, when they wish to emphasize the seriousness and sincerity of their attitude, will contrast it to what would be a device. So we find Mirabeau, in his speech on the *contribution du quart*, declaring:

> Ah, gentlemen, apropos of a ridiculous proposal of the Palais Royal and an absurd revolt ... you heard a short while ago these frenzied words: "Cataline is at the gates of Rome, and you are debating!" Around us there was, indeed, no Cataline, no dangers,

---

[126] Schopenhauer, *Sämtliche Werke* (Brockhaus), vol. 6: *Parerga und Paralipomena, Zweiter Band, Psychologische Bemerkungen*, § 340, p. 637.

[127] Pascal, *Pensées*, GBWW, vol. 33, p. 173.

[128] Aristotle, *Rhetoric*, III, 7, 1408a.

no factions, no Rome. ... But today there is bankruptcy, hideous bankruptcy. ... [129]

Similarly Simone Weil refers to the danger of having a form of expression taken as propaganda:

> To bring discredit on words like these [the spirituality of work] by launching them among the general public, without taking infinite precautions beforehand, would be to cause irreparable harm. ... They must not be made a slogan. ...
> The only difficulty lies in the painful mistrust—alas, only too well founded—of the masses, who look upon any slightly elevated proposition as a snare set to trap them.[130]

This technique, referring, as it does, to the existence of devices, is not without its dangers, particularly where the adequacy of the statement vis-à-vis reality is not strongly guaranteed independently. However, a speaker may often take considerable risks along this line. P. H. Spaak, for instance, by terming a tribute paid to America in the middle of a speech on behalf of Europe an "oratorical precaution," deliberately creates the dissociation

$$\frac{\text{device}}{\text{reality}};$$

while the warmth of the tribute prompts its acceptance as reality, the dissociation makes it possible to avoid the charge of pro-Americanism.

One of the pieces of advice most insistently given by the classical masters of rhetoric was to praise the oratorical skill of one's opponent while concealing or minimizing one's own.[131] Antony followed the advice when he said:

> I am no orator, as Brutus is.[132]

So did Bismarck, when he declared:

> Moreover, gentlemen, eloquence is not my field. ... I am not an orator [denials on all sides], an advantage I willingly concede to the speaker who preceded me.[133]

In addition to having words of praise for one's opponent's eloquence, it is a good thing never to refute his arguments in such a way that he seems a poor advocate.[134] If too great a reputation for eloquence is

---

[129] Mirabeau L'Aîné, *Collection complète des travaux à l'Assemblée nationale*, vol. 2: *Discours sur l'établissement de la contribution patriotique*, pp. 186-187.

[130] Weil, *The Need for Roots*, p. 98.

[131] Quintilian, IV, I, 8; XI, I, 15, 17, 19.

[132] Shakespeare, *Julius Caesar*, Act III, scene 2.

[133] Quoted by Wunderlich, *Die Kunst der Rede in ihren Hauptzügen an den Reden Bismarcks dargestellt*, p. 1.

[134] Cf. Quintilian, V, XIII, 37.

§ 96. Rhetoric as a Process

dangerous,[135] and still more a reputation for cleverness, they can be forestalled by showing that, since a loss of persuasion is inevitable because of such a reputation, this is a factor which must be taken into account:

> ... It is my actual speeches that Lysimachus has calumniated, in order that, if I shall seem eloquent, it may appear that I deserve the charges he has made about my cleverness while, if my speeches do not come up to what he has led you to expect, you may think that my actions are still worse.[136]

Everything that proclaims talent is to be scrupulously avoided if one wishes to avoid dissociation. No more elaborate defense can be found than that naturalness of which the ancient writers speak so highly. The Chevalier de Méré has some illuminating remarks on this question:

> The fine art of excellence in speaking is seen only in the guise of naturalness. This art likes only what is simple and unaffected, and, although it labors to make its delights visible, it thinks mainly of hiding itself. ... I consider the most perfect to be that which is least noticed, for, when things have the odor of study and art about them, people may conclude that those who utter them have little of either art or study or that they do not know how to use them.[137]

Elements which can be interpreted as indications of spontaneity are particularly efficacious for ensuring correspondence with reality and, accordingly, for aiding persuasion:

> A young woman unwittingly does little things which are very persuasive and deeply flattering to the one to whom they are addressed. Men almost never do anything unwittingly; their caresses are deliberate; they speak, act, show attentions, and are less persuasive.[138]

However, these indications can themselves be regarded as devices, and it is difficult, when examining a text, to determine its spontaneity: romantic outbursts in the moonlight rapidly become clichés difficult to take seriously.

J. Paulhan has given an excellent description of the terrorists and counterterrorists in literature.[139] He shows that there is no literature without rhetoric, by which term he means an art of expression. But

---

[135] Cf. Cicero, *De Oratore*, ii, 4, where he speaks of the ignorance paraded by Crassus and Antony; Whately, *Elements of Rhetoric* (Harper) pt. II, chap. III, pp. 154-156.

[136] Isocrates, *Antidosis*, § 16.

[137] Méré, *Œuvres complètes*, vol. I: *Les conversations*, no. 3, p. 47.

[138] La Bruyère, "Les caractères. Des femmes," 14, *Œuvres complètes*, p. 130.

[139] Paulhan, *Les fleurs de Tarbes*.

the means employed in this art lose some of their effectiveness as they are recognized as devices. Argumentation is subject to the same devaluation except to the extent that the speaker can suggest a picture of the facts and of himself that does not prompt the hearer to make the dissociation

$$\frac{\text{device}}{\text{reality}}.$$

Indications of clumsiness or of sincerity—the two are in many cases confused—are both useful for avoiding the dissociation

$$\frac{\text{device}}{\text{reality}}.$$

Sometimes they will be effective merely by their presence, while sometimes they will be emphasized by the speaker or by someone else. All the imperfections which, at first sight, harm the effectiveness of an argument may, from the angle we are discussing, help it. One of the advantages of improvisation is the spontaneous production of indications of clumsiness or sincerity.

These indications concern not only the formal expression but the very nature of the arguments. A choice of arguments that are irrelevant to the discussion, but that closely affect the feelings of the speaker, will in the same way as the tone of his voice serve as an indication of sincerity. The renunciation of certain techniques and the introduction of arguments that are not well suited to the audience can sometimes turn out to be effective, and it is not always the perfectly suited argument which turns out to be the best. Just as Montaigne recognizes the sincerity of Tacitus by the fact that his narratives "are not always applied to the conclusions of his judgments,"[140] Pascal finds proof of the sincerity of the Evangelists in what appear to be imperfections in Jesus:

> Why do they make Him weak in His agony [Luke 22:41-44]? Do they not know how to paint a resolute death? Yes, for the same Saint Luke paints the death of Saint Stephen as braver than that of Jesus Christ [Acts 7:59][141]

Indications of emotion can give rise to the figures of *hesitation*,[142] *hyperbaton*, or *inversion*, in which an order brought about by emotion is substituted for the natural order of the phrase. The absence of conjunctions and the mixing of figures were well described by Longinus

---

[140] Montaigne, *Essais*, bk. III, chap. VIII, p. 913.
[141] Pascal, *Pensées*, GBWW, vol. 33, p. 328.
[142] Quintilian, IX, II, 19.

as signs of emotion.[143] In a study of the degradations language undergoes as a result of emotion, a perceptive psychologist, A. Ombredane, has pointed out that:

All these degradations of language can be deliberately striven after as a literary device, and a number of them have a settled place in stylistics. We may mention repetition, strings of words, impoverishment of the vocabulary, hyperbole, suppression of the verb, substitution of juxtaposition for subordination, suppression of the copula, break in construction, etc.[144]

His list includes such features as parataxis and hyperbole which can be indications of sincerity, as well as having, as we have seen, a role in the argumentation itself.

Everything that furnishes an argument against the thesis being defended by the speaker, including objections to his own hypotheses,[145] becomes an indication of sincerity and straightforwardness and increases the hearers' confidence. Any painful declaration, particulary a confession, will be presumed to be sincere.[146] So will any statement that threatens to alienate the audience. Here again there are some characteristic figures: *license*[147] and *pseudo-license*,[148] sometimes called *asteism*.[149]

Since any technique which seems contrary to the end to be attained makes a big impression, one will not scruple to use such a technique as the ultimate device. Thus Gracian writes:

Human life is a struggle against the malice of man himself. The man who is shrewd arms himself in the struggle with the strategems of intention. ... And then, when his artifice is detected, he uses a more subtle dissimulation by utilizing the truth for purpose of deceit. He changes his weapons and tactics to try a different trickery. The stratagem is to have no strategem, and all his cunning is directed to passing from the dissimulation he was practising to candor. The penetrating observer, who knows his adversary's skill, will be on guard and will discover the darkness clothed in light. He ferrets out the device, all the more hidden as it is full of sincerity.[150]

Confession, in an ironic tone of voice, of a pretended passion for someone gives the hero a chance to be taken seriously. The novelist

---

[143] Longinus, *Treatise on the Sublime*, xix, xx.

[144] Ombredane, *L'aphasie et l'élaboration de la pensée explicite*, p. 268.

[145] Aristotle, *Topics*, viii, 1, 156b.

[146] Cf. Dupréel, *Essais pluralistes*, "La deuxième vertu du xixe siècle," p. 114.

[147] *Rhetorica ad Herennium*, iv, 48.

[148] *Ibid.*, 49.

[149] Cf. Baron, *De la rhétorique*, p. 365; Paulhan, "Les figures ou la rhétorique décryptée," *Cahiers du Sud*, 295 (1949), 371.

[150] Gracian, *L'homme de Cour*, p. 12.

explains it as modern sensibility,[151] but it is, first and foremost, a normal mechanism of persuasion.

When is behavior sincere? When is it merely a device in which there is just the appearance of sincerity? In the absence of a criterion that is beyond argument the dissociation

$$\frac{\text{device}}{\text{reality}}$$

can operate indefinitely and contradictorily. The use of this opposition seems to be a feature of that extremely ancient *techně* attributed to Corax,[152] of which the exhange of letters published some years ago in the *New York Herald Tribune*[153] provides a modern example. A correspondent had sent to the paper a letter with a pro-fascist bent and insulting the United States. Several readers commented on it, including one who saw in it a subtle form of communist propaganda. Then, other readers wondered whether it would not be a fascist who would write such a letter in the hope that it would be set down as communist propaganda, so as to stir up opinion against such propaganda. This game of interpretation, alternately attributing pro-communist and pro-fascist views to the writer of the letter could go on indefinitely.

Aristotle classifies this device among the apparent enthymemes and gives the following example:

> If the accused is not open to the charge—for instance if a weakling be tried for violent assault—the defence is that he was not likely to do such a thing. But if he *is* open to the charge—i. e., if he is a *strong* man—the defence is still that he was not likely to do such a thing, since he could be sure that people would think that he *was* likely to do it![154]

This device had already been developed, but much less clearly, in Plato's *Phaedrus*.[155]

Involved in this technique are arguments which oppose what Aristotle calls absolute probability to relative probability and which rely on a probability based on what we know as normal, these elements varying constantly as the argument proceeds. The person who performs an act, or argues, is supposed to know the criteria of reality that his audience will apply and to act accordingly.

---

[151] Curtis, *Chers corbeaux*, p. 96.

[152] Aristotle, *Rhetoric*, II, 24, 1402a. Cf. Navarre, *Essai sur la rhétorique grecque avant Aristote*, pp. 16 et seq.

[153] From April 24 to May 4, 1948, Paris edition.

[154] Aristotle, *Rhetoric*, II, 24, 1402a

[155] Plato, *Phaedrus*, 273b-c.

This device is often used in legal proceedings, as in this passage written by Antiphon:

> If the hate I bore the victim makes the accusations now made against me seem probable, is it not likewise probable that, foreseeing these suspicions, I would have taken good care not to commit the crime? ...
> And what about those who hated the victim as much as I—for there were quite a few—is it not probable that it was they, rather than I, who murdered him? For they had no doubt that suspicion would fall on me, while I knew very well that it would be I and not they who would be incriminated.[156]

The *corax* is simply an application of the dissociation

$$\frac{\text{device}}{\text{reality}}$$

to the field of conjecture. It incites one to perform an act precisely because it is improbable and, for converse reasons, diminishes the chances that probable acts will be committed.[157] Quintilian advised taking precautions before a friendly judge because

> there are judges without a conscience who will sometimes commit an injustice in order to avoid the appearance of so doing.[158]

Can the batting back and forth in the *corax* be continued indefinitely? It can. But the time will come when it will lose almost all its persuasive force and become merely comical, because it implies an excessive capacity for foresight. Nor must it be overlooked that often, where court proceedings are concerned, it does not suffice to develop the *corax* vis-à-vis only one of the parties. The anticipations of one party will have to be matched by contrary anticipations attributed to the other party.

Since the *corax* involves the knowledge that the person acting could have of what will be deemed probable, a possible countermove is to allege ignorance of the criteria serving as a basis for this determination and thus rule out the interpretation of the situation in terms of a device. But this is often a difficult thing to do. The mere fact of being unable to foresee that there would be a dispute or that a problem of conjecture would arise, may, however, be sufficient to avert suspicion.

The *corax* is a typically rhetorical device in argument because it is based on the possibility of a wide variety of interpretations. It is characteristic of nonformal discourse and can be imagined only in an ambiguous situation.

---

[156] Antiphon, *Première tétralogie*, 2, 3: 2, 6. Quoted by Navarre, *Essai sur la rhétorique grecque avant Aristote*, p. 139.

[157] Cf. Aristotle, *Rhetoric*, I, 12, 1372a.

[158] Quintilian, IV, ɪ, 18.

CHAPTER 5

The Interaction of Arguments

§ 97. *Interaction and Strength of Arguments*

At the outset of our analytical study of arguments, we drew attention to its schematic and arbitrary character.[1] In reality, the elements isolated for purposes of study form a whole. They are in constant interaction at more than one level: interaction between various arguments put forward, interaction between the arguments and the overall argumentative situation, between the arguments and their conclusion, and, finally, between the arguments occurring in the discourse and those that are about the discourse.

The limits for the play of the elements involved are imprecise on all sides.

The description of the arguments that may be regarded as interacting can always be extended in two directions: first, by a more thorough, closer, or differently conducted analysis of the statements made and, second, by giving consideration to an increasing number of spontaneous arguments having the discourse as their subject.

Then, too, the body of accepted opinions that determines the argumentative situation always lacks clear definition. It is capable of extension, depending on the fields taken into consideration; it shifts each moment as argumentation proceeds; and it may be divided up in various ways depending on how it is sectioned.

As to the discourse itself, it may have a relatively well-defined unity in a lawyer's pleading or in a preacher's sermon, but in parliamentary

---

[1] Cf. § 44, supra: General Remarks.

debates or family discussions it may spread over several days and involve the participation of quite a few people. And that is not all. It
may happen that the thesis under discussion is not conceived in the
same way by the opposing sides: what for one side is the end of the
debate is for the other merely a step toward a later conclusion. Since
the reality the argument is dealing with is split up differently, an
opinion or decision in one direction is not the exact counterpart of the
opinion or decision in the opposite direction. Accordingly, one of the
basic considerations in a legal controversy is the determination of the
point to be discussed. This involves an attempt to isolate the issue
and to insert it into a framework set up by law or convention.

However indefinite the conditions governing the development of the
phenomena of interaction, it is they which largely determine the choice
of arguments, and the amplitude and order of the argumentation.

As a guide in his argumentative effort, the speaker uses a confused,
but apparently essential, concept, that of *strength of the arguments.*

This notion is certainly connected both with the intensity of the
hearer's adherence to the premises (including the connecting links used)
and with the relevance of the arguments in the particular discussion.
But intensity of adherence as well as relevance are at the mercy of argumentation directed against them. Thus the strength of an argument
shows itself as much by the difficulty there is in refuting it as by its
inherent qualities.

The strength of arguments varies therefore with the audience and
the object of the argumentation. Aristotle observed that "argument by
'example' is highly suitable for deliberative oratory; argument by
'enthymeme' is more suited for judicial debates."[2] Whately's advice
was that one should argue from cause to effect if addressing minds
desiring instruction or use examples if addressing opponents whose
criticisms have to be refuted.[3] These two pieces of advice amount to
advocacy of the example, that is, of what is capable of establishing
new connections, in situations where one has few premises available.

The central principle, in this connection, is always adaptation to
the audience and to the propositions it admits, with due regard to the
intensity of its adherence to these propositions. It is not sufficient to
choose premises on which to rely. Since the strength of an argument
depends in large measure on its capacity for resisting objections, regard must be had to all that is admitted by the audience, even if it is

---

[2] Aristotle, *Rhetoric*, III, 17, 5, 1418a; cf. Volkmann, *Rhetorik der Griechen und
Römer*, p. 33.

[3] Whately, *Elements of Rhetoric* (Harper), pt. I, chap. 3, § 1.

something one has no intention of using but which could stand in the way of the argument.[4]

The same conditions apply to refutation, with the additional requirement that one's choice should be guided by the argument one is opposing.

In the course of our study, we have often indicated the refutations to which a particular mode of argumentation is subject: the connecting link to refusal of the link,[5] the example to the invalidating example,[6] analogy to prolongation of the analogy,[7] and dissociation to reversal of the pair.[8] These methods of refutation have the advantage that they can easily claim relevance, but all the other methods can be used. However, the objection will generally remain within the framework adopted by the speaker: thus a quantitative *locus* will be met by a qualitative *locus*, a *locus* relating to order by one of those relating to the existent[9] and a custom by the custom of another group to which one also belongs. Thus, of all the reasons that might be given for not going into mourning for a relative, the most usual will be that "in my family it is not customary to wear mourning."[10] If the speaker relies on the value of utility, his opponent will ground himself on the value of justice.

In view of the complexity of the factors to be taken into consideration even just to judge whether an argument has any strength at all, it is curious that the writers of treatises on rhetoric should so glibly state, almost incidentally, that the strength of arguments is common knowledge and that they should base their advice regarding the order of discourse and the sequence of replies, on the degree of conviction that the arguments must have produced, which "it is not hard for us to know, because we know what ordinarily brings this about."[11] One may consider this an illusion, in the light of what we have just said. Pascal, it will be recalled, confessed himself unequal to the task of making a study of the various ways of pleasing.[12]

Knowledge of individual reactions by itself, and the most thoroughgoing investigations of differential psychology, are insufficient to

---

[4] Cf. § 29, supra: Selection of Data and Presence.

[5] Cf. § 89, supra: Breaking of Connecting Links and Dissociation.

[6] Cf. § 78, supra: Argumentation by Example.

[7] Cf. § 85, supra: How Analogy Is Used.

[8] Cf. § 92, supra: The Role of Philosophical Pairs and Their Transformations.

[9] Cf. § 25, supra: Use and Systematization of *Loci*.

[10] Smets, "Carnet sociologique, note 50," *Revue de l'Institut de Sociologie* 1(1950), 148-149.

[11] *Rhetorica ad Herennium*, I, 10.

[12] Pascal, *On Geometrical Demonstration*, GBWW, vol. 33, pp. 441 et seq.

measure this strength, for it includes a normative factor that may be regarded as one of the premises of argumentation or is at least inseparable from the concept of strength. Is a strong argument an *effective* argument which gains the adherence of the audience, or is it a *valid* argument, which ought to gain it? Is the strength of an argument a descriptive or a normative quality? Does its study come under the head of individual and social psychology, or rather under that of logic?

This distinction between two different viewpoints, based on the dissociation

$$\frac{\text{normal}}{\text{norm}}$$

cannot be an absolute one, for the normal, as well as the norm, is definable only in relation to an audience whose reactions provide the measure of normality and whose adherence is the foundation of standards of value. However, the distinction is valuable where the reactions of a particular audience determine what is normal and the conceptions of a different audience provide the criteria for the standard. The superiority of the norm over the normal is correlative to the superiority of one audience over another, and, as we have seen, it is to this classification of audiences in a hierarchy that the distinction between persuading and convincing corresponds.[13] By dissociating the effectiveness of an argument from its validity, one makes the argument suspect and lessens its effectiveness even in the eyes of one who recognizes this effectiveness because the argument persuaded him. This is apparent in the following passage from a play by Sartre:

> HUGO: What do you want me to think? I told you he was shrewd.
> JESSICA: Hugo! He was right.
> HUGO: My poor Jessica, what could you know about it?
> JESSICA: And you, what do you know about it? You didn't look so big in front of him.
> HUGO: Oh, for heaven's sake! With me, he had it lucky. ...
>
> * * *
>
> JESSICA: Hugo! You don't mean what you're saying. I watched you while you were arguing with Hoederer; he convinced you.
> HUGO: He didn't convince me. No one can convince me that one should lie to one's comrades. But if he had convinced me, that would be one more reason to kill him, because that would prove that he's capable of convincing others. ...[14]

A conclusion to which the hearer does not want to yield casts doubts on the validity of the arguments whose effectiveness he has himself experienced.

---

[13] Cf. § 6, supra: Persuading and Convincing.
[14] Sartre, *Dirty Hands*, Act V, in *Three Plays*, pp. 124-125.

The interaction between the normal and the standard acts both ways. Although, under some circumstances, what is effective provides the criterion for what is valid, one's idea of what is valid is not without some influence on the effectiveness of the techniques aiming at persuasion and conviction.

What guarantees this validity? What provides the criterion for it? More often than not it is a theory of knowledge, which consists in the adoption of techniques that have proved their effectiveness in various fields of learning or in the transfer of techniques that were successful in a specialized field and may provide a model for other fields. Hence arises the well-known conflict between the recognition of a number of different methodologies, each of which is effective in a limited field, and the conception of the unity of science, based on an ideal methodology that is derived from a kind of superscience and could be applied to any science worthy of the name. Under the latter alternative, the criterion of rational or sensible self-evidence does away with the dissociation between normal and norm. That which is self-evident is simultaneously effective and valid and convinces because it bears conviction in it. The self-evident, as the criterion of validity, is the authority for totally discrediting *all argumentation*, on the grounds that it is effective though it does not provide real proof and can therefore be rooted only in psychology, and not in logic, even in the broad sense of the term.[15]

Whatever may be the importance of this philosophical position-taking and whatever the effect, on the evaluation of the strength of arguments, of its double aspect, both descriptive and normative, that is, of the concepts of effectiveness or of validity, and however complex the factors involved, there can be no doubt that a practical distinction is made between strong arguments and weak ones.

Our hypothesis is that this strength is appraised by application of the rule of justice: that which was capable of convincing in a specific situation will appear to be convincing in a similar or analogous situation. The comparison of situations will be the subject of constant study and refinement in each particular discipline. Initiation into a rationally systematized field will not merely furnish knowledge of the facts, truths, and special terminology of the branch of learning involved and of the method of using the available tools, it will also provide instruction in assessing the strength of the arguments used in these connections.

---

[15] Perelman and Olbrechts-Tyteca, *Rhétorique et philosophie*, De la preuve en philosophie, p. 121.

The strength of arguments therefore depends considerably on a traditional context. Sometimes the speaker can take up any subject and use any kind of argument. But there are times when his argumentation is limited by custom, by law, or by the methods and techniques peculiar to the discipline within which his argument is developed. The discipline often determines also the level at which the argumentation must be presented, laying down what is beyond dispute, and what must be regarded as irrelevant to the debate.

Naturally, the different philosophies influence any argumentative scheme by their determination of the structure of reality and the justifications they give of it, by their criteria for valid knowledge and proofs and by the hierarchy in which they place audiences. The philosophical context gives added force to certain kinds of arguments: essential realism will encourage all forms of argument relying on essences, whether it is a matter of argument by division or by the dissociation

$$\frac{act}{essence} \; ;$$

an outlook admitting the existence of a hierarchy of degrees of reality will encourage argument by analogy; empiricism, arguments based on facts put forward as indisputable; rationalism, argument on the basis of principles; and nominalism, resort to the particular case. But we must not forget that a philosopher, like the rest of us, will use a great variety of arguments, even though in his system— and if he had to adopt a position on them— he may assign them a subordinate role, or even ignore them completely.[16]

§ 98. *Assessment of the Strength*
of Arguments as a Factor in Argumentation

The strength of arguments can itself be used—either explicitly or implicitly—by the speaker or his hearers as an argumentative factor. The rich complexity of interactions to be taken into consideration is thus further increased.

Deliberate overestimation, by the speaker, of the strength of the arguments he advances generally tends to increase their strength. For him to put forward a conclusion as more certain than he himself considers it to be is to engage his person and use the prestige attached to it, thus adding an extra argument to those already advanced. Bentham considered this procedure to be "a middle state between that

[16] Cf. Gouhier, "La résistance au vrai et le problème cartésien d'une philosophie sans rhétorique," in *Retorica e Barocco*, pp. 85-97.

of evil consciousness and that of pure temerity."[17] It is, of course possible for a speaker to be convinced by reasons other than those he puts forward in his argumentation, and his motives may be honorable. But sooner or later he will have to justify his attitude.

Another way of overvaluing the strength of an argument is for the speaker to extend specific agreements reached in the course of discussion without his interlocutor's having given his explicit adherence. Schopenhauer regards it as in the nature of a trick to treat adherence to examples as involving agreement on the generalization drawn from them[18] or to consider a debatable conclusion as one that is fully established.[19]

Actually there is overestimation of the strength of arguments in any discourse that does not explicitly describe itself as being rhetorical. This occurs particularly in quasi-logical argumentation that purports to be demonstrative, when in reality it is only such by virtue of premises that can be disputed. The trick denounced by Schopenhauer, consisting in drawing a conclusion without obtaining adherence to all the premises,[20] is nothing but a crude form of an unavoidable process.

An opposite technique, which is very effective, is to restrict the scope of the debate and to advance a conclusion that falls short of what might be anticipated from the writer or speaker. Thus, Reinach, after arguing at length in favor of the genuineness of the so-called tiara of Saïtaphernes, concludes by calling for a withholding of judgment:

> At the present moment, I do not think any archeologist has the right to be absolutely affirmative with regard to the tiara. He must weigh the pros and cons, investigate,... and wait.[21]

The reader, given a feeling of confidence by this excessive moderation, of his own accord goes further in his conclusions than he would if the writer had endeavored to lead him to them forcibly.

All the techniques of restraint[22] give a favorable impression of sincerity and balanced judgment and help to dispel the idea that argumentation is a device, a trick.[23]

---

[17] Bentham, *Works*, vol. II: *The Book of Fallacies*, p. 485.

[18] Schopenhauer, *Sämtliche Werke* (Piper), vol. 6: *Eristische Dialektik*, p. 413, Kunstgriff 11.

[19] *Ibid.*, p. 414, Kunstgriff 14.

[20] *Ibid.*, p. 416, Kunstgriff 20.

[21] Vayson de Pradenne, *Les fraudes en archéologie préhistorique*, p. 545.

[22] Whately, *Elements of Rhetoric* (Harper), pt. II, chap. II, § 5.

[23] Cf. § 96, supra: Rhetoric as a Process.

Certain figures, such as those of *insinuation*,[24] *reticence*,[25] *litotes*,[26] *reduction*, [27] and *euphemism*, are a part of the techniques of restraint insofar as the speaker expects that they will be interpreted as the expression of a desire for moderation. From this standpoint, all these figures have a common function, whereas in other circumstances they may differ widely in their roles and they probably originate in quite different sectors of thought and behavior.

The claims made in argumentation can be toned down also by use of hypotheses. Thus, an analogy is often put forward as a hypothesis. This seems moderate at the time, but its consequences lead compellingly to the conclusion.[28]

Utopias also appear as a hypothesis from which, nevertheless, consequences flow in a perfectly rational manner.

Just as the strength of arguments can be increased by acting as if it were superior to what one has grounds for believing it to be, or by moderating the claims, so one can, by converse techniques, diminish the force of arguments, particularly those of one's opponent. The speaker himself often runs this risk: exaggerated emotion, out of proportion with the object, the purpose aimed at, or the nature of the arguments, suggests pretensions that will make the whole argumentation seem weak.

Either in advance, or after delivery, the effect of some arguments can be played down by attributing their effect to factors inherent in the person of the speaker, instead of to their own value. Everything granted to the person will be subtracted from some of his manifestations.

This technique operates at various levels.

At the level of opinion, the impact of a harsh appraisal may be lessened by pointing out that the person making it is usually severe in his judgments. He will then cease to be regarded as an objective judge, but will be seen as one whose coefficient of severity should be discounted. The same line of reasoning obviously entitles one to attribute more importance to the least sign of praise or approbation emanating from such a person.

At the level of the discourse, emphasis may be put on such qualities of the speaker as his wit, humor, talent, prestige, and power of suggestion. In this way a dissociation will be effected between the real in-

---

[24] Quintilian, IX, ii, 65 et seq.
[25] *Rhetorica ad Herennium*, iv, 67.
[26] Cf. § 67, supra: Unlimited Development.
[27] *Rhetorica ad Herennium*, iv, 50.
[28] Cf. § 85, supra: How Analogy Is Used.

trinsic force of the arguments and their apparent strength, a compound of what properly belongs to them and other elements. This dissociation corresponds to other dissociations having the same end in view, notably the dissociation between the universal audience, which is untouched by the prestige attaching to the speaker, and particular audiences which are subject to it, and the dissociation of validity and effectiveness. The reader will recall the dialogue between Hugo and Jessica in Sartre's *Dirty Hands*,[29] which illustrates the three dissociations just mentioned.

At the level of the theory of argumentation, one will sometimes deny any strength at all to the arguments themselves, attributing their effect to wholly irrational factors or to the form of the discourse alone.[30]

Another way of lessening the strength of arguments is to emphasize their routine, easily foreseeable character, making them old stuff to the hearer.

All the masters of rhetoric have insisted on the advantage possessed by argumentation which is "appropriate to the case" and not a mere commonplace that can be met by some other commonplace. Quintilian suggests this reply as being appropriate to the case, where a priest taken in adultery relies on a law permitting him to pardon a guilty person and proposes to apply it to himself:

> "You would save more than one guilty person, since, if you were discharged, it would not be lawful to put the adulteress to death." For such an argument follows from the law forbidding the execution of the adulteress apart from the adulterer.[31]

Unlike more general arguments which might have been hit upon spontaneously by anyone, without the help of the speaker, it is characteristic of an argument particular to the matter at issue that it generally contributes something either to our stock of information or to our habits of thought. We should add that this will often merely be an added argument developing out of a stock of general arguments not explicitly brought out, but one that avoids the devaluation associated with anything that, because it is familiar to everyone and applicable to every situation, can readily be regarded as a device.[32]

An anticipated argument is a banal argument. It is also an argument which, though he was aware of it, did not prevent the person defending

[29] Cf. § 97, supra: Interaction and Strength of Arguments.
[30] Cf. Pareto's theory of the opposition of derivations to residues.
[31] Quintilian, V, x, 104.
[32] Cf. § 96, supra: Rhetoric as a Process.

a certain decision from making it.[33] One therefore presumes that the strength of the argument was not very great. The anticipation of an argument is, in addition, a sign of competence. The effect of a speaker's foreseeing an argument is that, when it is put forward by his opponent, the argument will not diminish the confidence felt for the speaker. He will not be put out by it, and his opinions will not require revision. In short, an anticipated argument, however effectively it may be advanced, has lost its critical power. Let us add that the reasons that make it possible to foresee an argument often contribute also to its loss of value: it is very likely trite and banal, and it may be regarded as a device, but the reason may perhaps also have to do with the personality of the opponent, with his well-known prejudices, with what is known of his character. The damage caused by anticipation of an argument extends to discourse of the kind in which the conclusion is known in advance and so no freedom is left to the speaker. Special difficulties thus attend sermons and epidictic discourse in general.[34]

An argument can lose its force also, not by having been anticipated in its concrete singularity, but if it can be shown, by labeling it with a technical term, that it belongs to the category of arguments that the theoreticians have picked out and classified as overbold.[35] The audience thus enlightened and enabled to recognize the banality of the argument and to appreciate that it is a device, will retroactively modify its appraisal of its strength. Conversely, the one attacking it will have given useful evidence of his competence.

The acknowledged advantages of argument that is particular to the matter at issue, of unanticipated argument, doubtless explain a good deal of the strength attached to the taking up of one's opponent's argument and drawing from it a conclusion different from, or even opposite to, the conclusion he drew from it. Thus Bossuet, in his sermon on almsgiving, shows at length that the fact that a donor has a great number of children, far from being an obstacle to the exercise of charity as might be maintained, should, on the contrary, help it. In this passage, he takes up an exhortation of Saint Cyprian and makes a new application of it:

> "But you have several children, and a large family. ...": This imposes on you the obligation to exercise a more abundant charity, for you have more persons for whose sake you ought to placate God. ...

---

[33] Cf. § 9, supra: Self-Deliberating.

[34] Cf. Estève, *Études philosophiques sur l'expression littéraire*, pp. 62-63.

[35] Cf. Schopenhauer, *Sämtliche Werke* (Brockhaus), vol. 2: *Die Welt als Wille und Vorstellung*, Erster Band, § 9, p. 55; vol. 3: *Zweiter Band*, p. 113; *Sämtliche Werke* (Piper), vol. 6: "Eristische Dialektik," note, p. 409.

> If then you love your children, if you would open to their necessities the source of a truly fatherly gentleness and love, commend them to God by your good works. ...
>
> You who give your children an example of storing up an inheritance on earth rather than in heaven, you are doubly guilty—guilty because you do not get for your children the protection of such a Father, and guilty because you also teach them to love their inheritance more than Jesus Christ himself.[36]

Any refutation—whether it be of an accepted proposition, of one's opponent's argument, of an unexpressed argument, or of an objection to an argument—implies an attribution to what is refuted of a certain force deserving attention and effort. To make the refutation of consequence and deserving of consideration, one has to make a sufficiently high estimate of what one is attacking: This is necessary not only for purposes of prestige, but in order to better gain the attention of the audience and secure certain strength for the future for the arguments one uses. And one has to make a sufficiently low estimate of what one is attacking, so that the refutation is strong enough.

This evaluation of the strength of what one is attacking may be more or less explicitly stated, or it may be inferred from the manner in which one deals with it, even from the way one reproduces the opponent's argument. Sometimes a speaker will make his evaluation of statements by his opponent in terms of the latter's behavior, of his assurance or the lack of assurance.

The opponent's behavior may also be used for inferring the strength of the speaker's own arguments: the anger of an opponent who finds himself cornered in debate, the opponent's resort to diversions, or the fact that he asks questions instead of replying.[37] Allusion to these reactions is a way of emphasizing and so of increasing the strength of the arguments which occasioned them.

These reactions also convey information to the speaker that will enable him to pursue the discussion in a direction where his opponent has given evidence of being on shaky ground, and this even when the speaker does not know exactly what affected his interlocutor so deeply. For the effectiveness of his own discourse may come as a surprise to the speaker and influence his subsequent argumentation. Montaigne laid emphasis on pleasant surprise and encouragement that the reaction of the audience can bring to a speaker:

> I have sometimes, in the necessity and heat of combat, employed sudden whisks, that have gone through and through, beyond my

[36] Bossuet, *Sermons*, vol. II, pp. 690-691.

[37] Cf. Schopenhauer, *Sämtliche Werke* (Piper), vol. 6: "Eristische Dialektik," p. 424, Kunstgriff 34.

expectation and design: I only gave them in number; they were received in weight.[38]

In the opposite direction, Pascal points out the means for making a speaker doubtful of the worth of his own arguments:

> ... our not having for what he says the esteem it deserves: we shall find more often than not that he will disavow it on the spot and that, led away from a thought whose worth he does not know, he will fall into another thoroughly common and ridiculous.[39]

§ 99. *Interaction by Convergence*

Under the theory of probability very precise techniques have been developed for determining the probability of a conclusion based on several premises whose relations and probability are known, and, conversely, for working out the probability of the premises from an observed conclusion. However, the interaction between arguments can only very rarely be dealth with in this way for, unless the arguments are inserted in a system, they never present the necessary exactness and univocity. Nonetheless everyone recognizes that arguments do interact. One of the most important interactions is due to what we shall broadly call *convergence*.

If several distinct arguments lead to a single conclusion, be it general or partial, final or provisional, the value attributed to the conclusion and to each separate argument will be augmented, for the likelihood that several entirely erroneous arguments would reach the same result is very small. This interaction between separate but convergent arguments can arise either from their mere enumeration, from their systematic exposition, or from an explicitly stated "convergence argument."

The strength of such an argument is in fact almost always recognized. There may, of course, be theoretical discussions on the question of knowing to what extent convergence of itself suffices to bring about persuasion[40] and how far a minimum initial probability is requisite for an increase of likelihood, but these are matters connected with the substructure of the convergence argument and not with its use in debate.

However, in a nonformal system, an affirmation of convergence is one that can always be challenged, as it depends on the interpretation given to the arguments. The identity of their conclusions is never absolute, because the conclusions are an integral part of the argu-

---

[38] Montaigne, *Essais*, bk. III, chap. VIII, p. 908.
[39] Pascal, *On Geometrical Demonstration*, GBWW, vol. 33, p. 444.
[40] Pareto, *The Mind and Society*, vol. I, §§ 563 et seq, p. 340.

ments and derive their meaning from the way in which they were reached.[41]

Sometimes, however, convergence can be verified and then we have what Whewell calls *consilience*, which he regards as the most secure foundation for inductive reasoning. The most noteworthy example of consilience is the determination, by different methods, of Avogadro's number.

An experimental basis also underlies the idea of *congruence*, which is often contrasted with simple coherence: when four card players at the beginning of a game are dealt in turn the ace, king, queen, and jack of hearts, the probability that the pack was never shuffled, or that it was rearranged before being dealt, is low as regards each player, but increases when their observations are brought together.[42] Similarly, if witnesses which are untrustworthy individually testify to the same effect, without the possibility of a previous agreement between them, the value of each testimony is increased. In the same way, the concordance of the opinions of a large number of people can strengthen individual opinions.

The convergence between arguments may cease to carry weight if the result arrived at by the reasoning shows up elsewhere some incompatibility which makes it unacceptable. This brings us to another type of convergence, that which may be established between a known aggregate, such as a religious belief or scientific or philosophical system, and an argument that confirms it. Thus, a new fact may arise which corroborates a scientific system, or there may be an interpretation of a particular text which corroborates a legal principle, a conception of values.

The assertion of such a convergence does not necessarily promote adherence to the system or help the new arguments being advanced. Sometimes the convergence will be considered irrelevant because the hearer does not attach the same importance to the system as does the speaker, or because the convergence is regarded as without significance. To a person who rejects the connection between science and ideology, it is of no moment that Lysenko's scientific theories are more or less in line with dialectical materialism.[43] The problem of the significance of the convergence will arise every time there is an effort made to relate fields that are regarded as separate from one another, with barriers to be broken down before the convergence can be taken into account. In final analysis, argumentation will try to converge to the total body

---

[41] Cf. § 34, supra: Clarification and Obscuration of Notions.

[42] Lewis, *An Analysis of Knowledge and Valuation*, pp. 338 et seq.

[43] Huxley, *Soviet Genetics and World Science*, p. 33.

of knowledge and beliefs, but this is a very diffuse convergence, incapable of being explicitly stated. This enlarged concept of convergence merges into the general rule we formulated earlier, that it is advisable to take everything admitted by the audience into account in order to give full strength to an argument.

Convergence can also cause mistrust: it may be feared that the new elements were arranged specifically in order to bring about the convergence. Plebiscites and elections yielding results too favorable to the propositions or candidates of the government side have rarely been regarded as a sincere expression of the voters' opinions. In another sphere, little serious attention was paid to the argumentation of Chasles in favor of the genuineness of the autographed documents he presented to the Paris Academy of Sciences, his argument being to show that one item supported the other.[44] It was too easy to answer that both the old and the new items under discussion had been manufactured to form a coherent whole. It may also happen that the convergence between arguments, like that between arguments and a doctrine, is perceived only when each element has taken its place in a complex: discourses which aroused no mistrust while they were separate will arouse it as soon as they are fitted into an overly coherent aggregate. This phenomenon is clearly seen in the public reaction to certain forms of political propaganda.

Because of the distrust felt for excessive coherence, a certain measure of incoherence is taken as a sign of sincerity and seriousness. M.-L. Silberer, who asked a number of persons, in a questionnaire, which were the greatest virtue and the greatest vice, noted with satisfaction that the two replies were rarely opposites and considered this proof that the questions had been taken seriously.[45]

The persuasive force of a convergence may accordingly be modified as a result of a reflection about this very convergence. It is then no longer a matter of interaction between arguments located on the same plane, but between arguments closely dependent on each other, the first ones being the subject of the second ones. Reflection is directed, for instance, to the relations between the conclusion and the arguments; one wonders to what extent the latter were influenced by the former.

We have seen that most people accept more readily propositions that are pleasing to them.[46] But this tendency of the human mind toward "wishful thinking" can be taken into account, and there will according-

---

[44] Vayson de Pradenne, *Les fraudes en archéologie préhistorique*, pp. 391-395.
[45] Silberer, "Autour d'un questionnaire," in *Le diagnostic du caractère*, p. 197.
[46] Cf. § 14, supra: Argumentation and Commitment.

ly be a reduction of the strength of arguments that culminate in theories or forecasts corresponding too closely with desires. One may go further and show that the expression of an opinion as to what will happen tends to modify events: in wartime, the defeatist is not only the man who foresees defeat because defeat is not sufficiently repugnant to him, but the man who contributes to the defeat by giving expression to this fear. The charge of defeatism is intended to force the defeatist to recognize the dubious sources of his judgment as well as the possible consequences of it.

§ 100. *Amplitude of the Argumentation*

Where two demonstrations, both of them compelling, start from the same premises and reach the same conclusions, the shorter of the two will almost seem the more elegant. Since it has the same consequences, leads to the same degree of conviction, and is just as complete and satisfactory, its brevity is pure advantage. The same is not true of argumentation: the role played by amplitude in argumentation vividly emphasizes the difference between demonstration and argumentation.

Except where argumentation develops within a previously established frame, the premises can always be advantageously buttressed by integrating them with other accepted theses. Similarly, unless the point at issue is very definite, conclusions can be bound up with certain of their consequences, which makes it possible to prolong the argumentation by changing the subject of the discussion.

In argumentation, neither the starting point nor the result is narrowly circumscribed, and the intermediate links are still more indefinite. In a rigorous demonstration, only the links essential to the development of the proof need be shown, but none of these can be omitted. In argumentation, on the other hand, there is no absolute limit to the accumulation of arguments, and it is also permissible not to state all the premises essential to an argument.

The advantages offered by the accumulation of arguments fall into two groups: those that have to do with the relations between arguments and those that are referable to the diversity of audiences.

We have seen that different arguments reaching the same conclusion reinforce each other.[47] The quest for convergence between arguments will lead a speaker to range farther afield in arguing. The same is true of any effort to integrate arguments in a more complete system, with

---

[47] Cf. § 99, supra: Interaction by Convergence.

more varied connections, and one that is more detailed and less exposed to possible objections. This extension of the argumentative process is simply a new form of the endeavor to get premises that are more solid.

One instance of extension deserves special mention: that of arguments introduced as complements to earlier arguments of which they are therefore closely dependent. As we have seen, any dissociation of the type

$$\frac{\text{appearance}}{\text{reality}}$$

can advantageously be complemented by explaining the difference between term I and term II.[48] The role attributed to *idols* by Francis Bacon may be conceived as the complement of a preceding dissociation and of the criteria advanced for knowledge of reality. The same complementary function is detectable in the role attributed to the imagination and the passions in rationalistic philosophy, to prejudices in the philosophy of the enlightenment, and to habits and repressions in modern psychology. These disturbing factors are not used simply to explain the possibility of error, but efforts are made to combat them. Fénelon has the use of these complementary arguments in mind when he describes the technique of a clever and experienced speaker:

> Either he goes back to the principles on which depend the truths that he would persuade his hearers of, or he attempts to cure the passions which prevent the truths from making an impression.[49]

Since positive argument is not compelling, negative argument, which bares and brushes aside the obstacles to the effectiveness of the positive argument, will be found extremely useful. We should point out that the passions as obstacles must not be confused with the passions which provide a support for positive argument. The latter will generally be designated by a less pejorative term, such as *value*, for instance.

Complementary argumentation, explaining the attraction of appearance, evil or error, can give rise, in conjunction with a positive argument, to a convergence argument. Pascal makes use of an argument of this kind in his apologia on Christianity:

> ... what advantage can they obtain, when, in the negligence with which they make profession of being in search of the truth, they cry out that nothing reveals it to them; and since that darkness in which they are, and with which they upbraid the Church, estab-

---

[48] Cf. § 91, supra: Philosophical Pairs and Their Justification.

[49] Fénelon, *Œuvres*, vol. XXI: *Dialogues sur l'éloquence*, p. 65.

lishes only one of the things which she affirms, without touching the other and, very far from destroying, proves her doctrine.[50]

Being in darkness can only strengthen adherence to the doctrine of the Church, as she makes room for this condition and expressly foresees it.

Negative argument, tending to show why the audience did not react as it should have to a speech or events, will often take the line of stating, in order to fight them, explicit or implicit arguments deemed to have had an influence on the audience.[51] A speaker will sometimes show that the hearer is governed by motives he is himself unaware of, or does not dare admit. This leads to a new aspect of the amplitude of argumentation: instead of being content to combat imagination and passions as such, a speaker will develop the arguments capable of exercising an attraction, and held responsible for the attitude taken. The question then is to know what arguments can profitably be brought into the limelight—arguments that the audience will recognize as its own, but which the speaker can easily counteract once they have been laid on the table.

Very often a consequence depends on a certain number of conditions, and these can be examined one by one to see whether or not they were present. In logic, proof of the falseness of one premise makes it unnecessary to examine the others; but in argumentation this proof is never compelling, and critical examination of the other conditions is rarely superfluous. It is only when one has an argument that seems hard to refute that it will be advantageous to keep it concise, in order to ensure its prominence.

A notable example of successive criticism is the defense in a court case in terms of law as well as in terms of fact.[52] Similar instances can be found quite frequently in argumentation in other fields. Berkeley has Philonous say:

> That innovations in government and religion are dangerous, and ought to be discountenanced, I freely own. But, is there the like reason why they should be discouraged in philosophy?

A little later on he continues:

> But it is none of my business to plead for novelties and paradoxes. ... It is against these and the like innovations I endeavour to vindicate Common Sense.[53]

---

[50] Pascal, *Pensées*, GBWW, vol. 33, p. 206.

[51] Cf. Wisdom, "Gods," in Flew, *Essays on Logic and Language*, pp. 199-200.

[52] Cf. Quintilian, IV, v, 13.

[53] Berkeley, "Three Dialogues between Hylas and Philonous," Third Dialogue, pp. 109-110.

Is there not a double defense here, one dealing with the rule (law), the other with its application (fact)?

The two arguments are not only alternative arguments for use on recalcitrant audiences: they interact, in the sense that each will be more easily accepted because the speaker, being under no absolute necessity to use them, will be thought to ascribe real value to them.

The varied make-up of audiences is nonetheless sufficient to justify the accumulation of arguments, independently of all interaction between the arguments. And this principle applies even when only one hearer is involved.[54]

> If one had to appear before only one judge, perhaps only one kind of argument would be necessary. The diversity of minds requires proofs of several kinds. "I at once take my opponent by the throat," says an orator in Pliny [Regulus, in *Letters of Pliny*, I, 20], and Pliny replies, "As for me, who do not know where his throat is, I attack every part in order to hit it."[55]

All this sufficiently explains why in discourses one finds arguments that appear inconsistent, but are not really so because they apply to different situations or different audiences. Thus, in his criticism of the quantitative theory of money, Nogaro writes in consecutive sentences that the deductive theoreticians prefer to ignore the facts which would invalidate their theories, and

> it is very rare for them not to find in their theory itself the arguments necessary to get rid of the contradiction which it is claimed the facts introduce.[56]

In his sermon on evangelical preaching, Bossuet presents the Gospel as both command and counsel:

> The preachers of the Gospel proclaim the law of God in the pulpits in two august capacities: in the capacity of a commandment, insofar as it is necessary and indispensable; and in the capacity of counsel, insofar as it is profitable and beneficial.[57]

The strange effects that the accumulation of arguments can produce are made use of in this comic kind of argument:

> Do not quarrel with an angry person, but give him a soft answer. It is commanded by the Holy Writ and, furthermore, it makes him madder than anything else you could say.[58]

---

[54] Cf. § 4, supra: The Audience as a Construction of the Speaker.

[55] Gibert, *Jugemens des savans sur les auteurs qui ont traité de la Rhétorique*, III, p. 147. Cf. Pliny, *Letters*, I, 20.

[56] Nogaro, *La valeur logique des théories économiques*, p. 37.

[57] Bossuet, *Sermons*, vol. II: *Sur la prédication évangélique*, p. 53.

[58] *Fun Fare*, p. 64.

The different arguments adduced may not seem inconsistent, but simply redundant, because the fact of accepting one of them makes the others unnecessary. Thus the two consecutive arguments used by Winston Churchill when speaking in Parliament, in 1939, during a debate on the military budget of Great Britain:

> It is much better for parties or politicians to be turned out of office than to imperil the life of the nation. Moreover, there is no record in our history of any Government asking Parliament and the people for the necessary measures of defence and being refused.[59]

The redundant character of an argument will be both more pronounced and less surprising when the arguments are simply a repetition of one another. Amplitude in argument may be due, not to the use of different arguments which support and complete each other and are addressed to different audiences, but simply to the more or less exact reproduction of the same arguments. The purpose of this insistence is to make the arguments more present. In this connection, we encounter again such figures as *repetition* and *amplification*.[60]

Apart from the fact that redundancy is fully justified in argumentation, it must be pointed out that it is generally noticed only when arguments are analyzed in a certain way. For distinction between arguments is not a datum. In certain cases, it may be fixed by tradition, as in the distinction between defense in law and defense in fact. It can emerge also from the way the discourse is presented. Thus, the division of the arguments, in the sense of their enunciation, can, by emphasizing the plan of the argument, emphazise that there is a plurality of arguments. Conversely, the plurality will be much less noticeable if the speaker does not separate his reasons from each other. Sometimes the reasons will even tend to merge in a single *a fortiori* line of argument as in the following passage:

> You will judge, then, whether at such a period it becomes us as statesmen to announce our own weakness and inability to continue the contest and so declare our readiness immediately to negotiate, without so much as knowing who are to receive the declaration.[61]

The various factors operating to prolong argumentation indefinitely are nevertheless held in check, both in writing and speaking, by certain social and psychological considerations. Limits—in space or time—are imposed by rules of procedure which are often very strict[62] or good

---

[59] Churchill, *The Second World War: The Gathering Storm*, p. 112.

[60] Cf. § 42, supra: Figures of Choice, Presence, and Communion.

[61] Pitt, *Orations on the French War*, Pitt versus Fox, Oct. 29, 1795, p. 107.

[62] Cf. Rome, "La vitesse de parole des orateurs attiques," *Bulletin de la Classe des Lettres de l'Académie Royale de Belgique*, series 5 (1952), 12.

manners and, most of all, by the attention that the audience is able and willing to give to the speaker.

The amplitude of a speech depends also on the number of speakers taking part in the discussion, on the distribution of tasks that may be made among them, and on the opportunity each speaker has to speak again, either to introduce fresh arguments, or to restate or further develop arguments already enunciated.

Amplitude will depend also on the kind of speech and on the role assigned to the audience. Is it considered part of the universal audience, and does the speaker renounce all arguments that would be without effect on it? Does the speaker wish to persuade the members of a particular audience, and does he rely on its particularities? Is the speaker going to put forward all the arguments he deems relevant to the discussion, because they may have some effect on its outcome, or does he propose to develop only what is favorable to a particular viewpoint, while criticizing that which is opposed to it? The amplitude of argument will vary also depending on whether the deliberation is public or private and whether the speech is pleading a case or of the epidictic kind.

It is understandable, with such a vast number of factors to take into consideration, that Prodicus should have dismissed the protagonists of both the long speech and the short speech and should have proclaimed that the only valid rule is that a speech should be of "a proper length."[63] It is important that a speech should be of a proper length so as not to exasperate the audience, but also because there are disadvantages attached to the use of certain arguments either separately or in conjunction with others. "Proper length" may sometimes even consist of saying nothing at all.

§ 101. *The Dangers of Amplitude*

For a proper estimate of the dangers of amplitude, it is desirable to consider separately the argument that furnishes the reasons for believing in what we already admit and the argument that aims at securing our adherence. In other words, it is desirable to distinguish that which concerns premises and schemes of argument from that which concerns a thesis which serves as conclusion.

As regards the first category, it must be remembered that all argumentation is indicative of a doubt, for it assumes the advisability of strengthening, or of making more explicit, agreement on a given opinion,

---

[63] Plato, *Phaedrus*, 267b.

which would not be sufficiently clear or compelling. The weaker the arguments seem to be, the greater will be the doubt raised by the mere fact of arguing in favor of a thesis, for the thesis will appear to depend on these arguments. The danger lies both in the mere adjunction of proofs and in the quality of the proofs. Except in the case of a recognized scientific or professional technique, indication of the source of a piece of information casts a certain doubt on that item, either because it implies that the speaker does not accept responsibility for it, or simply because it awakens the critical faculty. On the other hand, if a piece of news is presented as a fact, without more ado, it gives the impression that there is not the least doubt regarding it and that it does not even occur to the speaker to justify it. Moreover, indicating the source will be all the more dangerous as the prestige attached to the source is small. Similarly, the man who thinks he enjoys an indisputable authority is loath to give reasons for what he decrees. And greater confidence in divine perfection is shown where it is maintained that everything that God does is good, than where proofs of his goodness are furnished. Just as a proof of compelling force makes further proof unnecessary, so a self-evident truth makes any proof superfluous.

Napoleon was afraid that long preambles to laws would weaken their authority. Bentham had already observed that the assignment of a reason to a proposal can result in the rejection of the proposal and that those opposed to a motion are free to attack what they deem an inacceptable reason for it as well as the terms of the motion itself. He describes at length how a proposed tax on soap was rejected because the reasons given for it met with disapproval, and shows the effect that a particular motive would have on a proposal for the repeal of the penal laws relating to blasphemy:

> "Considering that there is no God, all penal laws relative to the divinity are abolished."
> Even should all the members of the assembly be unanimous in favour of the abolition of these penal laws, there might not perhaps be found a single one who would not be shocked by this declaration of atheism, and who would not rather choose to reject the measure altogether, than to obtain it at this price.[64]

When argumentation proves indispensable because, since the question is debatable, none of the propositions at hand enjoys a sufficient measure of agreement, one might think that any argument, with even the least value, might advantageously be introduced into the discussion. But this is far from being the case. As many have found to their

---

[64] Bentham, *An Essay on Political Tactics*, chap. X, in *The Works of Jeremy Bentham*, vol. II, p. 357.

cost, the use of certain arguments is dangerous on account, essentially, of the interaction between all the arguments involved.

The arguments that are used contribute to the opinion one has of the speaker and, through the intermediacy of this idea, may have an effect on the speech as a whole. If a weak, easily refutable argument is put forward, it harms the prestige of the person who commits himself thus to defending it against possible objections.

On the other hand, any argument, by its presence, draws the attention of the audience to certain facts and makes it give consideration to matters that it may not have previously thought about. By this indirect path, an argument may raise objections to ground the speaker had already perhaps gained:

> To argue about a thing with a person, in terms whether favourable or unfavourable, may arouse in him an inclination—if he hasn't it already—to interest himself in that thing; if he already has the inclination, it may whet it.[65]

The same mechanism of presence operates when a speaker refers to a statement of his opponent for the purpose of refuting it. As a result, most speakers prefer to ignore an objection which they could counter only by a weak refutation. In experiments on the change of attitude brought about by oral or written dicourse, it was found that the opinion of the hearers or readers was in fact considerably changed, but sometimes unfortunately, in a direction opposed to that desired.[66] The probable explanation is that the discourse had brought to the hearers' attention elements they had completely ignored up to that time. Moreover, each argument invites an appraisal of its strength, and these repeated attempts at mental refutation, even if only occasionally successful, may degenerate into a systematic negativism which one cannot afford to overlook, even in private, inner deliberation.

Finally, the new arguments introduced into a discussion may seem incompatible, either with what the speaker has asserted, or with the propositions already accepted by the audience. The former incompatibility makes the speaker seem ridiculous or casts doubts on his sincerity, while the latter puts the audience in the awkward situation of having itself to seek an accommodation with the incompatibility if it finds some substance in the new arguments.

---

[65] Pareto, *The Mind and Society*, § 1749, vol. III, p. 1205.

[66] Cf. Bird, *Social Psychology*, pp. 215 et seq, referring to Knower, "Experimental Studies of Changes in Attitudes," *Journal of Social Psychology*, 6 (1935), 315-347; *Journal of Abnormal and Social Psychology*, 30 (1936), 522-532; *Journal of Applied Psychology*, 20 (1936), 114-127. Cf. also Hovland, Lumsdaine, and Sheffield, *Experiments on Mass Communication*, pp. 46-50, 215-216.

This drawback exists also where the arguments are put forward only as hypotheses. At first sight, there would seem to be no objection to putting forward a number of different hypotheses to explain an occurrence, even if they are incompatible, for one might imagine that their accumulation would merely make the occurrence seem more convincing. However, one can often downgrade the opponent by suggesting that the new hypotheses prove that he did not place great confidence in his earlier arguments. Thus, the student Huber, defending the genuineness of the Würzburg "iconoliths," derides one of his critics who

> passes from the hypothesis of a caprice of Nature to the hypothesis of vestiges of paganism, and from the latter to the idea of an imposture. ... [67]

The more essential the points are on which the incompatibility turns, the greater the danger will be. Seen in a very wide perspective, closely related hypotheses may merge into a single argument. Thence arises the opportunity for fresh debate directed to establishing whether several arguments are or are not to be envisaged as a single argument presented in slightly varied forms.

The incompatibility will be particularly apparent if statements of fact are involved. There is no dearth of amusing anecdotes at the expense of the speaker who is inconsistent in the use of facts. There is, for instance, the comic argument used by the housewife defending herself against the charge that she did not return a dish. "First of all, I never saw the dish, and, next, I didn't borrow it; in any case, I have already returned it, and, what's more, it was already cracked." We can see here quite clearly the damage caused by accumulation of arguments for, taken in pairs, several of these arguments are not irreconcilable.

Will the hearer view the incompatibilities within the narrow frame of the particular point being discussed, or will he view them in a wider frame? A judge, for instance, may have to decide if the standpoint adopted by a jurist in a doctrinal work can be imputed to him when in his capacity as an advocate he develops arguments inconsistent with it.

Does the danger extend to the use of different aspects of a concept in a single work? Thus, we find Lefebvre making reference to "primitives," at one moment in an attack on idealism in which are found traces of primitive thought and, at another moment, in an effort to

---

[67] Memorandum by Huber in Vayson de Pradenne, *Les fraudes en archéologie préhistorique*, p. 41.

run down the theories of Comte by showing that primitive thought comprises elements that are superior to those found in later thought.[68] Each argument has its claims to validity. It is up to the reader to decide if he will accept each argument as it stands by itself, if he will himself adjust the incompatibility, or if he will hold it against the author.

It is the danger arising from the use of redundant and, still more, incompatible arguments, which often accounts for certain arguments being abandoned. Arguments may be given up on account of other elements of the discourse, but also because of opinions professed by the audience—be this the particular audience being addressed or an audience which includes the speaker. The defenders of Rutilius would have renounced— to his disadvantage—the use of arguments that did not meet the approval of the Stoics.[69] One of the most famous instances of renunciation is Socrates' refusal to ask for the indulgence of his judges.

In general, a speaker or writer who desires to win the adherence of the universal audience will give up arguments that this audience— as he conceives it—would find inadmissible, even when he is addressing a particular audience. He will deem it almost immoral to resort to an argument which is not, in his own eyes, a rational one.

On the other hand, it is often impolitic to attack directly, or merely to shock, a particular audience. In addressing a Christian audience it is best not to cite consecutively, as has been done, the Prophets, Jesus, Spinoza, and Marx as illustrating the universalist tendency of the Jewish people. Cicero listed some of the things it was prudent to avoid: they included excessive praising which causes envy, inveighing against a person esteemed by the judges, taunting someone with failings present in the judges, and appearing to plead for oneself when one is pleading for a client.[70]

Quite apart from any question of their mutual incompatibility, or of their incompatibility with opinions held by the audience, making use of a whole bunch of arguments creates the impression that one lacks sufficient confidence in any one of them. The deployment of arguments is often even more dangerous in refutation, as it suggests that what may have been a casual remark by one's opponent had ample justification since no stone is left unturned in combating it.[71]

[68] Lefebvre, *A la lumière du matérialisme dialectique, I: Logique formelle, logique dialectique*, pp. 20, 40.

[69] Cicero, *De Oratore*, I, LIII, § 230.

[70] Cicero, *De Oratore*, II, LXXV, §§ 304, 305.

[71] Cf. Baird, *Argumentation, Discussion, and Debate*, pp. 330-331.

There is a further consideration. Since a speaker is supposed to be aware of the dangers of weak arguments capable of harming his prestige, making use of them raises the serious presumption that he has no better arguments available, or even that there are no others.[72] Without realizing it, a speaker who advances weak arguments may destroy other stronger arguments which might have spontaneously entered the hearer's mind. Silence can have the same effect as a weak argument and make people think there are no good arguments. An unfortunately chosen argument and silence can thus both have the same disastrous effect. It is to be noted, in all this, that the hearer assumes that the speaker is familiar with the techniques of argumentation and that he is making deliberate use of them. It is in fact usual, even in the presence of someone one does not consider to be particularly clever, to make use of the kind of knowledge we have been discussing: thus, *B* will often claim that *A* did not, at the beginning of a controversy, hold the interpretation of a text which would have been decisive in his favor, or else *A* would not have advanced the weak arguments he did use in support of his thesis.

There is also danger in any argument that is open to a ready rejoinder: it will end up by being to the advantage of the party who did not introduce it into the discussion.[73] There is danger, again, in arguments on which the hearer can place an unfavorable interpretation. Thus, the pamphlet which, in arguing in favor of a new vaccine, lays stress on the difficulties attending its discovery, and the disappointments and setbacks experienced earlier, may suggest the idea that, on this occasion too, confidence would be misplaced.

There are some arguments that can obviously be used by all sides. A classical instance of such an argument is the affirmation:

> It is because my cause is just that I have made such a short speech.[74]

The danger in such an argument is not so much that one's opponent will pick it up and use it for his own benefit—he will generally take care not to—but that it will be called a device.[75]

A problem connected with the dangers of amplitude and deserving special mention is that of diversion or the shifting of the discussion over to another subject that is considered irrelevant.[76] This would be a

---

[72] Cf. Demosthenes, *On the Embassy*, § 213.

[73] Cf. § 98, supra: Assessment of the Strength of Arguments as a Factor in Argumentation.

[74] Cicero, *De Inventione*, I, XLVIII, § 90.

[75] Cf. § 96, supra: Rhetoric as a Process.

[76] Cf. Aristotle, *Topics*, II, 5, 112a; Schopenhauer, *Sämtliche Werke* (Brockhaus),

dangerous device, subject to all the drawbacks of a weak argument, if there were always agreement as to the irrelevancy. But there seldom is. The charge of diversion and the charge of fallacy are alike in that they both assume that the introduction of the irrelevant or fallacious argument was deliberate. Now the charge can be sustained only in cases where there is a substantial departure from what is usual. It is indeed theoretically possible to deny that such parts of a discourse as the exordium and peroration have any argumentative value, and to treat them as diversions. It is the application of the rule of justice that enables one to arrive at an opinion in this matter.

What is called diversion often consists in turning the discussion onto secondary points which can easily be defended with success. A more characteristic example of diversion is the introduction into the discussion of elements and distinctions that will not be used later. Raised perhaps as a precaution, such distinctions are dangerous because, from the failure to make use of them, one's opponent can easily extract an implicit avowal of their irrelevant nature.

When the time available is limited, the sole purpose of a diversion may be to call attention away from delicate points. The clever student who is short on knowledge is apt to practice this technique in examinations. In a discussion the purpose of such a diversion is really to prevent the discussion: diversion is then tantamount to sabotage of the preconditions of discussion. At the limit, we find the filibuster, in which no effort is made to disguise the intention of bringing in extraneous matters. The danger in introducing a number of overdeveloped arguments is that it suggests the filibuster.

Diversion lends itself to caricature. A good many anecdotes exploit the comic aspect of diversion:

> A husband returns home in the early hours and is greeted by his wife with a golf club in her hand. "What?" he asks her. "Are you going off to play golf at this time of day?"

The husband's remark is not unrelated to the situation, but results from a reinterpretation of it. A diversion of this kind carries the discussion over into a new sphere; it confers a certain prestige on the user and gives him a breathing space. In short, it provides, in a comic context, all the services usually sought from diversion.

---

vol. 6: *Parerga und Paralipomena*, Zweiter Band, *Zur Logik und Dialektik*, § 26, p. 31, Neuntes Stratagem; *Sämtliche Werke* (Piper), vol. 6: "Eristische Dialektik," p. 416, Kunstgriff 18; p. 419, Kunstgriff 29.

§ 102. *Offsetting the Dangers of Amplitude*

The dangers we have mentioned can be offset by use of all the various procedures calculated to avoid refutation, or to make it more difficult.

If the problem is to protect the person of the speaker from the bad effects of certain arguments he has used, he will declare that they were suggested to, or even imposed on, him. So we have Demosthenes, in one of his speeches, showing that circumstances or his opponent's attitude compel him to engage in self-praise,[77] to get away from the subject,[78] or to use a kind of argument he dislikes.[79]

When a speaker realizes that a group of arguments that might be used to support his thesis harbor inconsistencies which would lay him open to the charge of incoherence if he advanced them one after the other, he will normally make a choice between them. But if he is unwilling to adopt this course, he will use various methods to secure coherence: One approach—used in dialogues, plays, and novels—is to put the arguments in the mouths of different characters. Another is to publish the different opinions under different names; the pseudonyms under which Kierkegaard wrote represent the furthest degree of dissociation to which the desire to advance every possible alternative can lead, without any renunciation of incompatible arguments.[80]

As a rule, a speaker who wishes to avoid the harm that comes from the use of incompatible arguments will have to introduce a complementary line of argument which will underscore the apparent inconsistencies between his various arguments, or between his arguments and the beliefs of the audience, and seek to forestall their harmful effects. He will explain the changes of viewpoint, present hypotheses as alternative, and define the field of application of norms so that they are not mutually exclusive.

The danger of a weak argument may be obviated by saying that it was introduced in a subsidiary capacity only. If one fears that the interlocutor will underestimate an argument that possesses a certain strength, one will try to make it the central issue of the discussion and so compel the opponents to take it seriously. We have here something akin to the technique that consists in indicating in advance one's agreement as to certain proofs.[81]

---

[77] Demosthenes, *On the Crown*, § 3.

[78] *Ibid.*, § 9.

[79] *Ibid.*, § 123.

[80] Cf. Holmer, "Kierkegaard and Ethical Theory," *Ethics*, LXIII (1953), 159.

[81] Cf. § 27, supra: Agreements Particular to Each Discussion.

A final precaution against the charge of practising diversion, or against the consequences of using it, is to stress the relevancy of every argument advanced.

If a speaker wishes to avoid having to use certain arguments, he will see to it that his opponent does not make the necessity arise. If one party forgoes examining a particular witness, he may hope that the other party will do likewise.

The specific remedy open to a speaker who is afraid to use a particular argument is to hint at it.[82] Too explicit use of some arguments is contrary to good taste, dangerous, or even prohibited. There are arguments that can be referred to only by insinuation or allusion, or by a threat to use them. The threat may actually be one of these forbidden arguments.

This semi-renunciation of arguments gives rise to figures of renunciation which do something more than express the speaker's moderation.[83] Thus, *reticence* makes it possible to evoke an idea, while leaving its development to the hearer: this development may be suggested by the use of such forms of expression as rhythm and alliteration. *Preterition* is the pretended sacrifice of an argument. The argument is briefly outlined while the speaker is announcing that he will not use it. Here is a rather commonplace example taken from the *Ad Herennium*:

> Of your childhood, prostituted to all comers, I would speak if I thought the moment were ripe. But I am keeping silent intentionally.[84]

The sacrifice of the argument satisfies the proprieties, while it suggests also that the other arguments are sufficiently strong to make this one unnecessary. This passage in which Demosthenes seems to feel a repugnance to singing his own praises can be related to preterition:

> Philip was sounding us all out. How? He sent word to each of us with the offer, men of Athens, of a really large sum of money. Having failed in a certain person's case—let the facts and the record show who it was, it is not for me to name myself—he had the idea that all would find no difficulty in accepting a gift offered to the whole group; thus those who had sold themselves individually would be shielded if we were all to share, even to a small extent, in the common gift.[85]

---

[82] Quintilian, IX, II, 73.
[83] Cf. § 98, supra: Assessment of the Strength of Arguments as a Factor in Argumentation.
[84] *Rhetorica ad Herennium*, IV, 37.
[85] Demosthenes, *On the Embassy*, § 167.

Is this an instance of the use of an argumentative figure? Its insertion in the text seems so normal that not everyone would agree that it is. Demosthenes is, at all events, using a palliative.

Sometimes semirenunciation is expressed still more indirectly. A significant silence, or even the ostentatious use of weak and irrelevant arguments, can serve to show that there are others.

All renunciations and semirenunciations may be regarded as concessions. However, concessions are concerned not as much with the range of the arguments used as with the extent of the speaker's claim and with the dynamism of the agreements.

Concession is above all the antidote to lack of moderation; it expresses the fact that one gives a favorable reception to some of the opponent's real or presumed arguments. By restricting his claims, by giving up certain theses or arguments, a speaker can strengthen his position and make it easier to defend, while at the same time he exhibits his sense of fair play and his objectivity. Seen from this angle, the effects of concession are similar to those which come from not systematically eliminating every unfavorable circumstance from a statement.[86] However, concession will be disastrous if it brings about a break in a whole all the parts of which are considered to be interdependent. But the consequences can only be favorable if the elements affected by the concession are secondary. Accordingly, a speaker should not be annoyed by irrelevant questions, but should, on the contrary, regard them as a good opportunity for making concessions:

> ... As a rule, it increases the confusion of questioners if, after all propositions of this kind have been granted them, they can then draw no conclusion.[87]

Concession sometimes gives rise to the figure called *epitrope*, whereby, according to Vico:

> Out of a superabundance of fairness, we concede things to our opponent even though they are iniquitous, false, inept or dubious.[88]

Very often one of the interlocutors in an argument appears to call on the other either to recognize the merit of a position ("Admit I am right on this point") or to admit he has certain inclinations which explain his attitude ("Admit that you are fond of paradox") or to recognize that he supports certain ideas ("Admit you are a reactionary," the liberal may say to his conservative interlocutor). Only in the first instance is an effort made to snatch an agreement that may directly

---

[86] Cf. Bentham, *Works*, vol. II: *The Book of Fallacies*; *Œuvres*, vol. I, p. 473.
[87] Aristotle, *Topics*, II, 5, 112a.
[88] Vico, *Instituzioni oratorie*, p. 148.

serve to forward the discussion. In the second instance, an attempt is made to minimize the opponent's arguments by reducing their seriousness and significance. In the last instance, the speaker insinuates that if his opponent will admit he is a reactionary, discussion will be facilitated; by the establishment of a position more in accord with the facts, the discussion may take a new turn. In every case, the admission sought is regarded as a concession which must to some extent benefit the person from which it is asked, or the speaker would not dare to request it.[89]

Each time a speaker follows the interlocutor onto his own ground he makes a concession to him, but one which may be full of traps.

One of these is to recognize that the opponent's position cannot be invalidated, and to give up opposing it at a certain level, while pointing out at the same time the little importance of that level. This is the familiar attitude of the neopositivists with respect to metaphysical statements.

Another form is to make a concession, only to immediately go one better: the speaker admits the erroneousness of the opinion attributed to him, or even denies having expressed it, and then turns round to formulate a still more disagreeable one:

> Me reproach you with Alexander's hospitality? ... I am not so mad, unless one is to call harvesters and others working for a wage the friends and guests of those who pay them.[90]

The following anecdote, related by Quintilian, shows the comic aspect of a disclaimer:

> Domitia complained that, by way of accusing her of meanness, Junius Bassus had alleged that she even sold her old shoes. "No," he replied, "I never said anything of the sort. I said you bought old shoes."[91]

Generally, denial has much the same role as concession. The speaker renounces an assertion that he himself might have supported, or that has the support of third parties, but he retains just enough of it to let it be seen how well informed and perspicacious he was to have recognized the lack of value in a proposition.

This aspect of negation is used with comic effect in this passage in *Tristram Shandy*:

> In a word, my work is digressive, and it is progressive too, at the same time. This, Sir, is a very different story from that of the earth's moving round her axis. ...[92]

---

[89] Cf. Paulhan, *Entretien sur des faits divers*, pp. 135-138.

[90] Demosthenes, *On the Crown*, § 51.

[91] Quintilian, VI, III, 74.

[92] Sterne, *Tristram Shandy*, p. 63.

Because of this argumentative significance of the negative, it is rare, in argumentation, for a double negative to be the equivalent of an affirmative. Such a remark as "I am glad I did not have not to be there" points to complex relationships and suggests reasons behind reasons. The double negative can sometimes sum up the whole of an underlying argument in a condensed form.

The problems connected with the dangers of amplitude and with the offsetting of these dangers depend on the pretensions of those engaged in argument. A speaker may be content to adopt a passive attitude, and simply give a clear expression of his disagreement, when refusing— with supporting reasons—to adhere to the view of his interlocutor. He may, on the other hand, wish to modify his interlocutor's viewpoint and to influence his beliefs. With the former attitude, he can use certain arguments that would be dangerous with the latter; he can indicate every point of disagreement; but if he adopts the second approach, he must proceed with prudence, and make careful, successive moves. The problems connected with amplitude of argument accordingly require further examination in terms of each different argumentative situation.

§ 103. *Order and Persuasion*

In what order should subjects and arguments be presented? This question has been a constant preoccupation of the theorists of dialectic and mostly of rhetoric, under such rubrics as *exposition, arrangement,* and *method.*

This fact is not surprising as the problems connected with order arise essentially in argumentation rather than in demonstration.

In a formal demonstration we begin with axioms and end with theorems. There is, then, an order. But it is of limited importance as the variants in a demonstration are strictly equivalent. The order in which the axioms are presented, and the successive steps of the demonstration, are actually of little importance, provided each step is warranted under the application of the adopted rules of inference.

It is only if the adherence of minds is taken into account, if one goes from a formal to a psychological, argumentative, viewpoint, that order assumes importance in demonstration. Order matters where, instead of considering the axioms as arbitrary, the self-evidence or acceptability of the axioms is a preoccupation, and where, in the choice of steps, one is preoccupied with the relative intelligibility of particular orders of demonstration. In some interesting experiments, Wertheimer has shown that comprehension of certain mathematical demonstrations is affected by the appearance of the figure illustrating the demonstrations. In such cases, the variants are no longer equivalent, as there is a departure from the purely formal conditions of the demonstration in order to examine the persuasive force of the proofs.[93]

In argumentation, in any case, order is bound to be important, as adherence depends on the audience. Now, as the argument unfolds, it changes the situation of the audience, and this no matter what its reception of the arguments. As we have seen, the conditioning of the audience can be brought about by a variety of auxiliary factors, such as perfume, music, and crowd effects. But it is also brought about by the discourse. A speech does not leave the hearer the same as he was at the beginning. On the other hand, it does not change his beliefs irresistibly, as would the steps in a demonstration. If it did, order would not be of such importance. The order adopted is crucial precisely because the changes in the audience are both effective and contingent.

This is as true of the different incarnations of the universal audience as it is of particular audiences. At first sight, order does not matter to the universal audience. But the universal audience is no less than other audiences a concrete audience, which changes with time, along with the speaker's conception of it.

In inner deliberation, order seems again to be without importance, but this is probably not true. The most that can be said is that it is easier to take up the argumentation again, in a new order. This may even constitute the new argumentation with which the original argumentation will be confronted.

If argumentation is essentially adaptation to the audience,[94] in choosing the order in which arguments are to be presented in persuasive discourse, account should be taken of all the factors capable of furthering acceptance of the arguments by the hearers. There are at least three basic points of view that can be adopted in the choice of order for the purpose of persuasion. One is the argumentative situation itself, by which is meant the influence of the earlier stages of the discussion on the argumentative possibilities open to the speaker. The second is the conditioning of the audience, which comprises changes of attitude brought about by the speech. The third viewpoint is that of the reactions occasioned in the audience by its perception of the order or arrangement adopted in the speech.

[93] Wertheimer, *Productive Thinking*, chap. I: "The Area of the Parallelogram."
[94] Cf. § 4, supra: The Audience as a Construction of the Speaker.

In all three cases it is a question of effects on the audience. What distinguishes the three viewpoints is that, under the first, attention is mainly focused on the premises the audience is progressively led to admit, while under the second—to be discussed in the next section—the speaker is principally concerned with the successive impressions made on the audience; the third viewpoint—dealt with in the final section of the book—pays attention to order or arrangement as a matter for reflection.

In a demonstration everything is given, whether one is dealing with a hypothetico-deductive system or whether the axioms are provided by rational or sensible intuition. In argumentation, on the other hand, the premises are labile. They can be enriched as argument proceeds, but they always remain precarious, and they are adhered to with a shifting intensity. The order of the arguments will accordingly be dictated in large measure by the desire to bring forward new premises, to confer presence on certain elements, and to extract certain agreements from the interlocutor.[95]

The order in which these agreements are obtained is not without its importance. It will be recalled that in the interminable postwar meetings between representatives of the United States, France, Great Britain and the Soviet Union, there was endless discussion on the drawing up of the agenda for the negotiations. Normally "negotiation" does not involve discussing and persuading, but is a matter of making mutual concessions, and the order in which the problems should be discussed would not have preoccupied them so much if they had regarded the problems as connected, and had negotiated with the wish to reach a solution. But owing to the lack of spirit of mutual understanding, the situation resembled a discussion rather than a negotiation. Hence the high importance attributed to the question of order, for adoption of a definite position on a matter was a commitment without any reciprocal engagement.

The part played by such agreements is most clearly seen when the discussion is in question and answer form. The modification of the situation, as argument proceeds, is always considerable, whether in a continuous speech or in a discussion. But in the first case only the speaker states his position, while in the second, one moves toward a conclusion by proceeding from a succession of *points d'appui* that result from explicit commitments of the hearer.

It is an indubitable advantage to the person arguing to be able to put the questions of his choice, and to choose the order in which they are to be put. The efficaciousness of the Socratic method depends on the skillful use of this privilege.

Often the questions aim at making one choose between several possibilities. In such a case they merely provide information regarding the interlocutor's opinions, but the answer is also a commitment and often an adherence to what the speaker has asserted. Now, it must not be overlooked that, in final analysis, the aim of discussion is to modify an opinion, that it therefore presupposes basic disagreement between the parties. Accordingly, the order of questions is often designed to conceal for as long as possible the relation between the partial agreements secured and the basic disagreement: questions put in no apparent order,[96] questions whose importance is not grasped,[97] even questions that are quite purposeless.[98]

In most discussions, both interlocutors enjoy the privilege of putting questions and of choosing to some extent the order of their arguments. They also enjoy the possibility of conferring presence on certain elements of their material.

A recent study[99] showed that if guided discussion makes it possible, in a concrete problem—a production problem, actually—to reach a solution satisfactory to the group, but which it had not reached without such guidance, the chief reason for the success was the order introduced into the discussion by someone who knew what would be a desirable solution towards which to work. For order is also one of the conditions that determine amplitude; it is the selection of the matters that will be taken into consideration by the participants. Attention to order ensures not only that individual reflection shall not stray into wrong paths, but also—and this is the most interesting point—that fruitful paths shall not be prematurely abandoned. In other words, order ensures that particular premises are given sufficient presence for them to serve as starting points for reflection.

This concern to channel thought into directions that appear fruitful before proceeding any further is probably the basis of such figures as *suspension* (*sustentation*).[100] The speaker asks a question, to which he gives an immediate answer, but this answer is simply a hypothesis which, more often than not, he will himself reject.

---

[96] Cf. Aristotle, *Topics*, VIII, 1, 156a; *On Sophistical Refutations*, 15, 174a; Schopenhauer, *Sämtliche Werke* (Piper), vol. 6: "Eristische Dialektik," p. 413, Kunstgriff 9.

[97] *Ibid.*, p. 412, Kunstgriff 7.

[98] Aristotle, *Topics*, VIII, 1, 157a; cf. § 101, supra: The Dangers of Amplitude.

[99] Maier, "The Quality of Group Decisions as Influenced by the Discussion Leader," *Human Relations*, III (1950), 162-163.

[100] Quintilian, IX, ii, 22.

Some arguments can only be understood and accepted if other arguments have already been stated. Order is then a necessity. Sometimes it can even be said that arguments actually consist of this order, as in the arguments of direction, gradation, and amplification. But cannot the same be said of any argument? There is hardly ever a change in order which is not also a change in the argument, or, better, the creation of a new argument. Even in a formal demonstration, in which the order variants are equivalent, there is not only a change in the sequence of the steps in the demonstration, but the operations carried out can also be different. In argumentation, a change in order is hardly ever a simple permutation. This is even true of what might be considered the elements of the argumentation. Since, as a general rule, the laying of firm premises is a prime consideration in argumentation, it will not be disputed that the statement of the facts will be advantageously placed at the beginning of a discourse, since facts command the largest measure of agreement. Most scientific reports, as well as most political and legal writings, proceed in this manner. But it must not be forgotten that though facts may play an important role as elements of agreement, they are often only admitted because their interpretation remains open. This is well brought out in this passage from Quintilian:

> "You committed the murder, for your clothes were stained with blood." This argument is not so strong if the accused admits that his clothes were bloodstained as if the fact is proved against his denial. For if he admits it, there are a number of ways in which the blood could have got on to his clothes.[101]

The same facts, if they were preceded by their interpretation, would not command unanimous adherence but would give rise to dissociations between appearance and reality. In other words, the place allotted to the elements alters their significance.

To a certain extent, however, arguments can be regarded as distinct statements which, though they interact, can be arranged with a fair degree of freedom. Thus, praise of a person may, in different cases, precede or follow the statement that he is being put forward as a model. Similarly, convergent arguments can be grouped together or can be dispersed, without such dispersal destroying the effect of convergence. The method chosen will nonetheless affect the argumentation. In particular, the grouping together of the arguments will accentuate the effect of convergence, while their separation will diminish it. Thus, in prosecution, the person of the accused can advantageously be made a center on which all the arrows converge in concentrated fashion, whereas in defense, the lawyer will try to make the whole set of argu-

---

[101] Quintilian, V, xii, 3.

ments he is refuting look like a mosaic of separate pieces whose connections are as tenuous as possible.[102] In the same way, examples may be advantageously grouped together to strengthen a generalization, and the arguments of one's opponent can be advantageously grouped together to show an incompatibility between them. As a rule, in a discussion, the reasons that lead one side to adopt a certain order should normally tend to make the other side adopt a different order. However, other considerations will often prevent such a reversal.[103]

§ 104. *The Order of the Speech and Conditioning of the Audience*

An exposition cast in the form of a demonstration, as in a treatise on geometry, is reducible to a statement of the proposition, followed by its demonstration. An argumentative speech will nearly always be more complex. This has been recognized from the earliest times. Plato lists, with a readiness aimed at ridiculing them, the divisions of speech taught by the sophists.[104] Aristotle is almost as critical of this artificial division.[105] Nonetheless, most of the writers of antiquity admit that normally a legal speech has these minimum divisions: exordium, narration, proof, refutation, conclusion, and epilogue. In a deliberative speech, introduction and narration are not as essential.[106]

It is noteworthy that all the writers have dwelt on that part of a speech which at first sight seems the least necessary of all: the exordium. Aristotle, Cicero and Quintilian all dealt with it at length,[107] while the author of the *Rhetorica ad Herennium* claimed to have been the first to recognize some of its modalities.[108] The interest of the introduction to us is that it is the part of the discourse which is most specifically designed to influence the disposition of the audience.

The purpose of the exordium is to make the audience well disposed toward the speaker and to secure its goodwill, attention, and interest.[109] It also provides certain elements that will give rise to spontaneous arguments dealing with the speech and the speaker.

---

[102] Cf. Quintilian, V, xiii, 15.

[103] Cf. § 105, infra: Order and Method.

[104] Plato, *Phaedrus*, 266d-267a.

[105] Aristotle, *Rhetoric*, III, 13, 1414a-1414b.

[106] Volkmann, *Rhetorik der Griechen und Römer*, p. 33.

[107] Aristotle, *Rhetoric*, III, 14, 1414b-1416a; Cicero, *De Inventione*, I, §§ 20 et seq; Quintilian, IV, i.

[108] *Rhetorica ad Herennium*, I, 16.

[109] Cicero, *De Oratore*, II, § 323; Quintilian, IV, i, 5.

Aristotle compares the introduction to the prologue and the prelude, thus making it an independent preliminary with a mainly esthetic significance.[110] But in many cases the introduction is indispensable to the persuasive effect of the discourse. It assures the preconditions for argument.[111] Although it can be cut down or even eliminated when these preliminary conditions are completely assured, it becomes a necessity where one or other of the preconditions is lacking and must be supplied, more especially with respect to the quality of the speaker, his relations with the audience, and the subject or occasion of the speech.

In his introduction, the speaker will seek to establish his competence, impartiality, and good character, "for it is to persons of good character that the hearer is most apt to pay attention."[112]

If the speech is one that sets out to convince the universal audience, an introduction is not on that account excluded: the speaker will show, in particular, his respect for facts, his objectivity.

Valuable prestige can sometimes be conferred on a speaker through a few simple preliminary observations. When Robert Browning makes Bishop Blougram open his apology with some slighting references to the architectural style of his church, the author's intention is doubtless to convey to the reader's mind the setting of the discourse and the characters, but the opening remarks also have the role—and this is what completely justifies their inclusion—of an introduction which confers on the Bishop, in his interlocutor's eyes, the attributes of a man of refinement and good taste.[113]

The speaker will make a special effort to play up qualities the absence of which would harm his prestige, and his possession of which may be in doubt. Thus, the man who is commonly accused of excessive cleverness will try to gain the confidence of the public, while one who because of his social position, interests, and past record is deemed to be haughty, and remote from or hostile to his audience, will begin by dispelling such suspicions and will emphasize his community of feeling with the audience.[114] An allusion to the friendship between two peoples or to a common culture, or the use of a well-chosen quotation, will suffice to create a feeling of confidence, by showing that the speaker and his audience have common values.

The exordium will always be adapted to the circumstances of the speech, to the speaker and to the audience, to the matter being dealt with, and to possible opponents.

---

[110] Chaignet, *La rhétorique et son histoire*, pp. 359-360.
[111] Cf. Part I: The Framework of Argumentation.
[112] Aristotle, *Rhetoric*, III, 14, 1415a.
[113] Browning, *Complete Poetical Works*, Cambridge ed., p. 349.
[114] Carnegie, *Public Speaking*, pp. 295-297.

There is no better illustration of this requirement than the preliminary declaration, "I am no speaker," and other apologetic remarks of the same kind. Such statements, though often advisable, are strongly criticized by Dale Carnegie.[115] Though they may save the speaker from the accusation of using oratorical devices,[116] or from having some of the strength of an argument ascribed to his personal talent,[117] they are of no help to a person of no particular reputation who takes it upon himself to address an audience or put pen to paper. The main problem here is to get a sufficiently large audience, and so an introduction which makes out that the speaker is unskilled or incompetent is of little help. Cato made game of the writer who began with excuses for writing in Greek, though nothing compelled him to use that language.[118]

Under some circumstances, so far from playing down his oratorical skill, a speaker with a sufficient reputation may even avail himself of his skill. Thus Isocrates, at the beginning of the *Panegyricus*, and in order to use this again in the peroration, points out that great though his talents may be, the task is beyond him.[119]

An introduction that refers to the audience will try to develop its self-esteem by references to its abilities, common sense, and goodwill. The preacher who publicly calls on God to ask that hearts may be opened puts his audience in a favorable frame of mind by making such an invocation, as he recognizes thereby that his argument will not be a demonstration with compelling force.

An introduction referring to the subject of the speech will emphasize that the subject is a significant one, because it is important, strange or paradoxical, or because it is one that is "neglected, misunderstood, or misrepresented."[120] The speaker may also explain why the speech is opportune, showing why it is the moment to speak, and how the circumstances make it necessary to take a stand. The exordium will vary according as the matter is "noble, confused, paradoxical, or shameful."[121]

---

[115] *Ibid.*, p. 268.

[116] Cf. § 96, supra: Rhetoric as a Process.

[117] Cf. § 98, supra: Assessment of the Strength of Arguments as a Factor in Argumentation.

[118] Quoted by Gwynn, *Roman Education from Cicero to Quintilian*, p. 45, from Polybius, XXXIX, 1 (Büttner-Wobst ed.).

[119] Isocrates, *Panegyricus*, §§ 13, 187.

[120] Cf. Whately, *Elements of Rhetoric* (Harper), pt. I chap. iv: "Of Introductions," pp. 131 et seq.

[121] "Principia Rhetorices," in Appendix to Saint Augustine, *Patrologie latine*, vol. XXXII, col. 1447 and 1448; cf. Cicero, *De Inventione*, I, § 20 (honorable, astonishing, low, doubtful, obscure); *Rhetorica ad Herennium*, I, 5 (honorable, discreditable, doubtful, petty).

Sometimes the exordium is unnecessary, or can be replaced by other techniques. Thus, the introduction of the speaker by the chairman of a meeting has no other purpose than to make it unnecessary for the speaker to sing his own praises.[122] Moreover when an exordium is recognized as a device to palliate deficiencies in the preconditions of argument, it may draw the attention of the audience to this weakness. On account of this correlation between amplitude of the exordium and deficiencies for which it is designed to make up, many speakers devote most of their introduction to saying that no introduction is necessary. This tactic assumes, of course, that the audience is aware of the usual considerations that warrant an introduction. Once again we note that argumentation often presupposes that the audience possesses knowledge, at least intuitively, of the rules of argumentation.

Sometimes a speaker will insert another particularly appropriate introduction at the beginning of an important division of his speech. Goldschmidt has correctly observed that, in the dialogues of Plato,

> these solemn invocations to the gods are not just literary or dramatic embellishments, but, in many instances, lend emphasis to the philosophical importance of the passages.[123]

With the audience prepared to listen to the substance of the speech should the speaker begin by announcing the proposition he is going to defend, or should he only state his conclusion after he has expounded his reasons? In his *Partitiones Oratoriae*, Cicero advises different approaches for different kinds of argumentation:

> But there are two kinds of argumentation, one of which aims directly at convincing, whereas the other is less direct and is aimed mostly at the feelings. It is direct when after stating what it proposes to prove, it gives the reasons on which it depends and when these have been established, it comes back to its original proposition, and concludes. But the other kind of argumentation, proceeding as it were backwards and in an inverse way, first of all presents the reasons it has chosen and establishes them solidly and then, having excited the minds of the hearers, it finally lets out that which it should have described to begin with.[124]

A proposition that contains nothing out of the way or shocking, and so requires no special preparation of the audience, should be stated at the outset.[125] The proposition gives a direction to the speech, but also involves the assumption of a definite position that is binding on

---

[122] Cf. § 72, supra: The Speech as an Act of the Speaker.

[123] Goldschmidt, *Le paradigme dans la dialectique platonicienne*, note, p. 16.

[124] Cicero, *Partitiones Oratoriae*, § 46.

[125] Whately, *Elements of Rhetoric* (Harper), pt. I, chap. III, § 4, pp. 104-108.

the speaker. The advantage in the immediate statement of the proposition is that it brings enlightenment to the audience; it takes possession of the ground. However, an alternative technique is for the speaker to avoid committing himself so soon, and to formulate his proposition in the light of the development of the discussion. This enables him to take objections into account, and to come forward with a proposition that is very likely to win acceptance.[126] The relative advantage of speaking first or last must be assessed in the light of the foregoing considerations. These will determine, in part, the order in which arguments are presented in the discourse.

To the extent that the order of the arguments is within the control of the speaker, one factor for him to take into account is the strength of each of the available arguments. When the strength of an argument is irresistible, argumentation can be compressed, and the speaker can content himself with the argument he is sure will bring conviction. But he is not often in this fortunate position.[127] When a speaker has a number of arguments to support his proposition, in what order should he arrange them?

Three possible orders have been considered: the order of decreasing strength; the order of increasing strength; and the Homeric or Nestorian order, (so called because it is related in the *Iliad* that Nestor placed his least dependable troops in the middle),[128] by which the speaker uses the strongest arguments at the beginning and the end.[129]

The disadvantage of the order of increasing strength is that the mediocre arguments may antagonize the hearer and make him restive. The drawback of the order of decreasing strength is that the final impression left with the hearers— and often the only one that remains present to their minds—is unfavorable. It is to avoid these two pitfalls that the Nestorian order is advocated, as it strains the most solidly based arguments by presenting them at the beginning and at the end, and puts all the other arguments in the middle of the argumentation.

These considerations assume that the strength of the arguments remains constant whatever their position in the speech. In fact, an argument will often appear strong only because preceding arguments have

[126] Cf. Kotarbinski, *Traktat o dobrej robocie (Treatise on Good Work)*, chap. XIII.
[127] Cf. § 100, supra: Amplitude of the Argumentation.
[128] Cf. Homer, *Iliad*, bk. iv, lines 297 et seq.
[129] Cicero, *De Oratore*, II, 313; *Rhetorica ad Herennium*, III, 18; Quintilian, V, XII, 14; VII, I, 10; Volkmann, *Hermagoras oder Elemente der Rhetorik*, p. 197; cf. Libanios' argument and the anonymous argument preceding Demosthenes' speech in *Demosthenes and Aeschines on the Crown*, pp. 133-135.

laid the ground for it. Thus, in Shakespeare's *Julius Caesar*, it is only at the end of his speech that Antony discloses the really clinching argument, Caesar's will in favor of the people, after he has created the necessary context to ensure that the will will receive the interpretation he desires.[130]

Arguments, then, must be advanced in the order which gives them the greatest strength, and this means that ordinarily one will begin with that argument whose strength is independent of the strength of the others. In a twofold defense, based on both fact and law, order is not without importance: the strongest defense will always be put forward first, in the hope that the conviction brought by this first point will help to win acceptance for the other.[131] As a general rule, arguments must be presented in an order such that they seem plausible in the light of the elements of the discussion that are already known. In his apologia on Christianity Pascal recommends an order in which the proof of the truth is given only when the framework that will make it more readily accepted has already been provided:

> We must begin by showing that religion is not contrary to reason:
> that it is venerable, to inspire respect for it; then we must make it
> loveable, to make good men hope it is true; finally we must prove
> it is true.[132]

If a serious objection will burden the whole course of a speech it is no good advancing arguments that will all be interpreted in terms of this objection. The objection must first be disposed of so as to leave the field open to more favorable interpretations.[133] For the same reason, Quintilian's advice was to begin with the refutation of an accusation that raised a continuing doubt as to the moral integrity of the defendant, unless minor arguments against him were obviously false, in which case they should be refuted first, in order to discredit the prosecution by demonstrating their falsity.[134]

In certain cases, the defense will not wait for the accusation to be formulated, but will refute it in advance. However, this procedure has its drawbacks. It demands that the accusation be stated, and thus attributes to the opposite side ideas it might not have, or would not have dared to express. Anticipatory refutation carries the implication that the accusation was in the normal course of things, and that consequently it must be taken into account. As this anecdote related by

---

[130] Shakespeare, *Julius Caesar*, Act III, scene ii.
[131] Cf. § 100, supra: Amplitude of the Argumentation.
[132] Pascal, *Pensées*, GBWW, vol. 33, p. 205.
[133] Cf. Whately, *Elements of Rhetoric* (Harper), pt. I, chap. iii, § 6, p. 112.
[134] Quintilian, VII, i, 11, 12.

Quintilian shows, anticipatory refutation if incautiously used, can produce some comic effects:

> Fulvius Propinquus, when asked by the representative of the emperor whether the documents he produced were signed, replied, "Yes, Sir, and the signature is genuine."[135]

When anticipatory refutation takes the form of an objection to the speaker's own argument, it can give rise to *prolepsis*, a figure which has a definite argumentative connotation.[136]

Anticipatory refutation can also occur in the form of a concession. We have already seen the advantages of the latter.[137] A concession made subsequent to a point made by the opponent constitutes a compromise. But if made first, particularly at the beginning of a speech, it is an advance defense against the charge of having overlooked value or fact of importance. It has both the advantages and the disadvantages of anticipatory refutation. It can also follow the statement of weak arguments, in which case it testifies to the speaker's good faith. According to Quintilian, this is why a speaker may decide to begin with weak arguments which he will abandon forthwith.[138] We see here a very close connection between the arrangement of the arguments and the role they are given in the conditioning of the audience.

If disparagement of one's opponent is called for, it will be made at the end of one's speech if one is the accuser, and at the beginning if one is replying.[139] In legal proceedings, the ancient orators used to end their speech with an attack on the person accused so as to rob, in advance, his defense of all value, thus making it necessary for the accused to regain in his exordium the goodwill of his hearers and judges, by trying to get rid of the unfavorable state of mind created by his adversary's peroration. In this case, as in many others, the order to be followed in the speech is dictated by adaptation to the audience and the argumentative situation, and any rules that may be formulated in this matter are functional. Any more definite precepts are simply a codification of what is normally found to give good results, but what is normal in this connection is itself a shifting entity.

The tactic to be used will vary with the nature of the audience. Aristotle pointed out that some listeners evince a more critical spirit

---

[135] Quintilian, VI, III, 100.
[136] Cf. § 41, supra: Rhetorical Figures and Argumentation.
[137] Cf. § 102, supra: Offsetting the Dangers of Amplitude.
[138] Quintilian, VII, I, 16.
[139] Cf. Aristotle, *Rhetoric*, III, 14, 1414b; cf. Whately, *Elements of Rhetoric* (Harper), pt. II, chap. III, § 5, p. 177.

at the end of a discussion than at its beginning[140]; of other listeners, the reverse is true. The reactions one hopes for may be of an emotional nature. A speaker may even gradually induce anger in his audience.[141] The more the tactic followed gambles on weaknesses in the interlocutor that are not necessarily those of everybody, namely, of the universal audience, the less will be the esteem in which the success of the tactic will be held by others. There is, however, no clear-cut dividing line between techniques of order designed for the universal audience and techniques that only have validity for some particular listener. For certain features of the universal audience will always coincide with the real concrete person: the universal audience will only differ from a particular audience in the measure that the conception held of the universal audience transcends given particular audiences.

Then, too, the reactions of a given audience, even if they are capable of interpretation in psychological, or even political terms, are nevertheless very often capable of being explained and justified on grounds that could be accepted by the universal audience, and which make those reactions to some extent rational.

§ 105. *Order and Method*

Order involves a choice whose sole governing rule is the most perfect adaptation possible to the successive states of the audience as these are conceived by the speaker, who may even claim as a right the liberty of "every litigant to dispose and arrange his topics of defense according to his own discretion and judgment."[142] However, Demosthenes, after making this demand for complete freedom, goes on in the same speech to declare:

> ... I will take the charges one by one in the same order as the prosecutor, without any intentional omission.[143]

Is this just a courtesy to the hearer to make his task easier? Is this a matter of custom?

This brings us to a very important point, which is that the order adopted can itself be a matter for the hearer to reflect upon, and can, in this way, directly affect the result of the argumentation. We have often had occasion to mention those spontaneous arguments with the

---

[140] Cf. Aristotle, *Topics*, VIII, 1, 156b.

[141] Schopenhauer, *Sämtliche Werke* (Piper), vol. 6: "Eristische Dialektik," p. 413, Kunstgriff 8. Aristotle, *On Sophistical Refutations*, 15, 174a.

[142] Demosthenes, *On the Crown*, § 2.

[143] *Ibid.*, § 56.

speech as their subject, which have effects that are superimposed on those of the presented arguments.[144] The question of the order of the arguments is very much a case in point.

For order to be the subject of reflection, the hearer must first be conscious that there is an order. This condition is satisfied whenever the order of statements is correlated with an order external to the speech, and this external order is either known to, or can be quickly grasped by, the hearers. The observance of chronological order in the relation of facts is the most characteristic example of an order external to the speech. It would seem to be the simplest form of that "natural order" which has so much preoccupied the theorists.[145]

But the chronological order is by no means the only one available to the hearer as a scheme of reference. Oratorical custom can also provide schemes which constitute *patterns*, and so seem to be external to any particular speech. Particularly in continuous discourse, we find it difficult to distinguish what part is attributable to habit or custom when the speech strikes us as corresponding to a normal order.

The order adopted by the opponent is no less capable of being used as a scheme of reference. So too can a given part of the speech already delivered by the speaker himself, which can be used by him as the scheme of argument for a later portion of his exposition. What is more, it is likely that certain arguments are grasped as a function of the rhythm they have suggested. One wonders whether the Chinese sorites does not derive a part of its efficacity from the scheme originating from it: the first links cause the later ones to be apprehended as the successive elements of one and the same process. The same is true of certain analogies and double hierarchies.

External order, in the shape of chronological order and customary order, as well as the order arising out of the argumentation, are examples of *good forms* developing in time, and possessing all the characteristics that Gestalt psychology attributes to that term. In other words, these forms are easily grasped, satisfy the understanding, and, what is more, have the capacity of bringing back to themselves slightly divergent perceptions and also of enabling certain elements to find their place in a series. As a consequence, it is possible that certain implied arguments will be understood because of the place they occupy in such an ordered sequence.

---

[144] Cf. § 72, supra: The Speech as an Act of the Speaker; § 96, supra: Rhetoric as a Process.

[145] Cf. Agricola, *De Inventione Dialectica*, bk. III, pp. 167 et seq; Vives, *Obras completas*, vol. II: *Arte de hablar*, bk. III, chap. iii, p. 783.

Good form, by the very fact that it develops in time, is often characterized by a growing intensity, a summation. This is the case, for instance, with *gradation* (climax), which is a figure relating to order. The verbal linking of clauses by means of a repetition of terms suggests an increase of intensity. Repetition gives a feeling of presence,[146] but it does more than this. As Quintilian says, "Before proceeding to the next step, one stops on those below."[147] This passage from Demosthenes is often cited as an example:

> And it is untrue that I spoke without making a formal proposal to that effect; that I made a formal proposal without undertaking the embassy; that I undertook the embassy without persuading the Thebans.[148]

Are we confronted here with a series of actions that require increasing determination? Is it not just as much a matter of diminishing gaps in the action? Doubtless the viewpoint differs from one hearer to another. If anticlimax is hardly ever spoken of as a figure, the reason is that perception of an order is almost always envisaged as a progression.

When a speech and a series external to it are joined by a connection of reality, their relationship will sometimes take the form of a clearly marked double hierarchy argument.[149] Thus we find certain authors advising that the most natural order for arguments is that of increasing strength because

> It seems that one is led to this order by a law of nature which warms, excites, and transports the imagination and the reason, as it does the voice of the speaker as his speech proceeds.[150]

This advice is naive if it merely means that arguments should be arranged with their strength, for we have seen that this very strength largely depends on position, but it is an interesting observation if it is to point out the role played by double hierarchies in reflections on order. Where the features of arguments enable them readily to be recognized as fitting within a double hierarchy, the very fact that they figure in such a hierarchy justifies their order. Their arrangement will not seem a device, as it becomes the result of a fact.[151]

Any indication touching on the question of order helps to secure its ready recognition as such. A mere allusion, such as allusion to the

---

[146] Cf. § 42, supra: Figures of Choice, Presence, and Communion.
[147] Quintilian, IX, III, 55.
[148] Demosthenes, *On the Crown*, § 179.
[149] Cf. § 76, supra: The Double Hierarchy Argument.
[150] Chaignet, *La rhétorique et son histoire*, p. 401.
[151] Cf. § 96, supra: Rhetoric as a Process.

customary order, may suffice. Another method is the well-known technique of division in which the parts of the speech are announced. Or the division may rather be into points for discussion, or into proofs to be adduced. The disadvantages of division, particularly in this last case, have been pointed out by several writers. Thus Quintilian says that division robs a speech of spontaneity, gives an advance view of arguments that are unlikely to be readily accepted, and deprives the speaker of the advantage of producing arguments in a body.[152] However, division has the advantage of creating, as soon as it is proposed, and even though it may not correspond to any order external to the speech, a scheme of reference. The proof of this is that any departure from the division announced will seem to be a breach of an accepted order, and will require justification.

This justification will be that which is required by any change.[153] In fact there is a danger that deviation from an expected order, whatever it may be, will be taken as a sign or indication: desire to confuse the hearers, desire to bring into the foreground an argument which the speaker considers to be strong, or desire to ignore certain questions.

The importance attached to the expected arrangement of a speech is such that it will often be followed in preference to one that is just as satisfactory from other viewpoints. The danger of postponing arguments is that the hearer's expectations are disappointed, and the arguments lose their strength through not being advanced at the proper time.[154] Doubtless there can be a deliberate departure from any anticipated order for the purpose of arousing curiosity or of appearing original, but there is the danger that the deviation, instead of giving an impression of naturalness and sincerity, will provoke the dissociation

$$\frac{\text{device}}{\text{reality}}$$

As we have seen, when a speech follows a scheme that is perceived as external to itself, the order adopted immediately appears to be a natural order, be it the chronological order or one corresponding to the increasing exaltation of the speaker. But reflection on what may be deemed the natural order has been carried much further than this. When Agricola[155] and Ramus[156] try to make a sharp separation between dia-

---

[152] Quintilian, IV, v, 4-8; cf. Fénelon, Œuvres, vol. XXI: Dialogues sur l'éloquence, pp. 68-71.

[153] Cf. § 27, supra: Agreements Particular to Each Discussion.

[154] Cf. Quintilian, IV, v, 18; V, xiii, 51; VII, i, 11.

[155] Agricola, De Inventione Dialectica Libri Tres, bk. II, pp. 132 et seq.

[156] Ramus, Dialecticae Libri Duo, 1560 ed., bk. I, note, p. 10; 1566 ed., bk. I, note, p. 156, fuller treatment.

lectic and rhetoric by reducing the latter to the study of pleasing and ornate means of expression, they transfer to dialectic the problems of order, arrangement and method that were traditionally dealt with in works on rhetoric. It seems that this is where rhetoric merges with dialectic, despite the effort to separate them.[157] The problems, however, are changing. The inquiry is increasingly directed to the question whether there is not a single necessary order— that of the nature of things—which rational discourse should follow. To the method of prudence, which relates to opinion, is opposed the method of doctrine or nature "under which that which is naturally more obvious should come first."[158] To the classical thinkers the method of nature is the chain of reasoning appropriate to a natural, objective order that is inherent in the world, and, for that matter, in thought, for the method is supposed to represent the workings of a mind that is adapted to reality. The model for this universal method is generally taken from science. The whole of Descartes' endeavor was to give this natural order the constructive appearance of mathematics.

By its uniqueness, this rational order is sharply differentiated both from an argumentative order and from a purely formal order, as this is understood by modern logic. Formal demonstration and the rational method are both rigorous; but the latter also claims objectivity; it is connected with such notions as clarity, simplicity, and self-evidence, which guarantee the premises, the lines of argument, and the conclusions.

This unique order, enjoying such a privileged position, is a preoccupation of most of the theorists who, though they may depart from classical thought, retain its aspirations. Whately is content with the assertion that the natural order is that in which what is most *obvious* is placed first.[159] Tarde considers that errors, as well as truths, have a rational order:

> ... Among all the ways of stating the dogmas of the most extravagant religion or the myths of the most fantastic mythology, is there not a combination more appropriate than any other for conveying the *raison d'être* of any particular dogma or myth?[160]

This mode of presentation would not reflect an order of appearances, but a natural internal relationship that effectively unites the elements in the construction.

---

[157] Cf. Morpurgo Tagliabue, "La retorica aristotelica e il barocco," *Retorica e Barocco*, p. 124.

[158] Ramus, *Dialecticae Libri Duo*, 1560 ed., bk. II, p. 208.

[159] Whately, *Elements of Rhetoric* (Harper), I, chap. iii, § 7, p. 131.

[160] Tarde, *La logique sociale*, p. 180.

The natural or rational order is not independent of every audience but is adapted to the universal audience and the rationality attributed to this audience. If this rational order is regarded as unique, it is because the universal audience is envisaged as an abstract entity, outside time, and not as a concrete audience, that is, one that varies according to the image formed of it.[161] One overlooks the fact that such notions as clarity and simplicity which form the basis of the rational order were developed psychologically, and, later, made absolute. In fact, rational argument is simply a particular instance of argumentation *ad hominem*—the one we have termed argumentation *ad humanitatem*. However, the idea of a natural order, that is objective in character, resulted in having discourse be reduced to a more or less poor makeshift, inasmuch as it was something other than the application of a method in conformity with this order. It is only if entrance to the "true way" is closed to him that the dialectician

> will devise another way by force of intellect and prudence, and will seek on all sides for every aid that custom and usage can give.[162]

Ramus is still concerned with this activity, for it is to him, at least partially, that of the philosopher as well as of the poet or orator. But it ceases to be of interest to Descartes.

The quest for a single, objective, natural method is almost always found to go hand in hand with a conception that regards rhetoric as a mere technique of ornamentation. For the natural method leaves the form of the discourse undecided; all the variable elements, that is, all those elements not imposed by the natural order, appear as external; in this area no attempt is made to justify the form by the substance.

The protagonists of a universal, natural dialectic method conforming to the nature of things may look on a discourse as a work of art or entity in itself. And when they draw an analogy between a discourse and an organism, terming it, for instance, "a living creature having its body and head and feet,"[163] this is a way of separating the form of the speech from its content, while still giving the form a structured order which is characteristic of it. The analogy is limited to an assertion of a relationship between parts, and does not define the nature of the relations. It envisages the speech as something isolated and sufficient in itself. Similarly with analogies between a speech and other forms of works of art. Just as Gillo Dorfles can draw an analogy between the theater and music, in terms of limited instrumentation, se-

---

[161] Cf. § 7, supra: The Universal Audience.
[162] Waddington, *Ramus, sa vie, ses écrits et ses opinions*, p. 372.
[163] Cf. Plato, *Phaedrus*, 264c.

quence of rhythmic movements, the entrance of persons or instruments, retrograde actions, repetitions and transpositions,[164] so can one compare discourse with either of these arts, and, among other things, see in indirect speech a perspective within a perspective. These are analogies that will enter certain hearers' minds, and may increase their goodwill through the medium of esthetic satisfaction. They do not enlighten the theorist of argumentation.

Our own view is that a theory of argumentation should neither seek a method that conforms to the nature of things, nor envisage a speech as an opus whose structure is to be found within itself. Either one of these complementary conceptions separates form and substance, and overlooks that argumentation is a totality intended for some definite audience. Under these two conceptions a problem of communication is turned into a matter of ontology and esthetics, whereas in reality the ontological order and the organic order constitute two deviations from an adaptative order. The guiding consideration in the study of order in a speech should be the needs of adaptation to the audience. This adaptation will operate either directly or through reflections of the hearer on the question of order. What the hearer envisages as the natural order, and the analogies he may see with an organism or a work of art are no more than arguments among others. The speaker will have to take them into account on the same footing as all the factors that are capable of conditioning the audience. Method and form can each assume more or less importance according as the audience is a particular one, a technical one, or universal. But a theory of argumentation which fails to give consideration to all these elements in conjunction will never succeed in its object. The dissociation between form and substance, which has resulted in the dehumanization of the very notion of method, has also had the consequence of accentuating the irrational aspect of rhetoric. It is safe to say that the argumentative viewpoint will yield, in questions which are usually regarded as pertaining exclusively to expression, insights that reveal their hidden rationality.

[164] Dorfles, *Discorso tecnico delle arti*, pp. 180-181.

CONCLUSION

It is not without difficulty that we have kept our treatise on argumentation to its present dimensions. Far from exhausting the subject we have barely scratched its surface and, at times, have done no more than point to its richness. Schematic treatments, some of them old and almost forgotten, others quite recent, have illuminated each other and have been integrated into an ancient discipline that has, however, been distorted for centuries and is neglected today. Problems generally approached from a purely literary viewpoint, together with others that are the concern of the most abstract speculation (derived either from the existentialist wave or from English analytical philosophy), are set in a dynamic context which brings out their significance and permits the vivid apprehension of the dialectical relationship between thought and action.

Each one of the points, which we have done no more than sketch, deserves more thorough study. The various kinds of discourse, their variation in the different disciplines and with different audiences, the way in which ideas undergo modification and organization, the history of these transformations, the methods and systems that have originated from the adaptation of notional complexes to problems of knowledge—these and many other questions just touched on here provide the study of argumentation with a field of research of incomparable wealth.

Up to now all these questions have either been entirely neglected or have been studied by a method and in a spirit that are foreign to the rhetorical point of view. The effect of restricting logic to the examination of the proofs termed "analytical" by Aristotle, together with the reduction of dialectical proofs—when anyone felt they were worth analyzing—to analytical proofs, was to remove from the study of reasoning all reference to argumentation. We hope that our treatise may provoke a salutary reaction and that the mere fact of its being written may for the future prevent the reduction of all the techniques of proof to formal logic and the habit of seeing nothing in reason except the faculty to calculate.

If a narrow conception of proof and logic has led to a constricted view of reason, the broadening of the concept of proof and the resulting enrichment of logic must likewise react on the way in which our reasoning faculty is conceived. For this reason we wish to conclude with some considerations that are too general to fall within a theory of argumentation, but provide it with a framework that emphasizes its philosophical significance. Just as the *Discourse on the Method*, though not a work on mathematics, secures to the "geometrical" method its widest sphere of application (though there is nothing to prevent one from being a geometrician without being a follower of Descartes), so the views we shall advance—though the theory and practice of argumentation are not necessarily bound up with them— accord argumentation a place and importance they in no wise possess in a more dogmatic vision of the universe.

We combat uncompromising and irreducible philosophical oppositions presented by all kinds of absolutism: dualisms of reason and imagination, of knowledge and opinion, of irrefutable self-evidence and deceptive will, of a universally accepted objectivity and an incommunicable subjectivity, of a reality binding on everybody and values that are purely individual.

We do not believe in definitive, unalterable revelations, whatever their nature or their origin. And we exclude from our philosophic arsenal all immediate, absolute data, be they termed sensations, rational self-evidence, or mystical intuitions. This rejection does not, of course, imply that we deny the effect of experience or reasoning on our opinions, but we will stay clear of that exorbitant pretension which would enthrone certain elements of knowledge as definitively clear and solid data, and would hold these elements to be identical in all normally constituted minds, independently of social and historical contingencies, the foundation of necessary and eternal truths.

The purpose of this dissociation of certain irrefutable elements from the sum total of our opinions (the imperfect and perfectible character of which nobody has yet contested), and of making them independent of the conditions of perception and linguistic expression, is to withdraw them beyond the realm of discussion and argumentation. To conceive of all progress in knowledge exclusively as an extension of the sphere occupied by these clear, distinct elements, to the point even of imagining that ultimately, with a perfect thought imitating divine thought, one could eliminate from knowledge everything that does not conform to this ideal of clarity and distinction—this means progressively reducing resort to argumentation up until the moment when its use becomes entirely superfluous. Pending the arrival of this moment, making use of it would stigmatize the branches of knowledge resorting to it as imperfectly constituted fields still in search of their method, and unworthy of the name of *science*. It is not surprising that such an attitude has turned logicians and philosophers away from the study of argumentation as something unworthy of their attention, leaving it in the hands of public-relations and propaganda experts who are generally suspected of lack of scruple and of constant opposition to any sincere search for the truth.

Our own position is quite different. Instead of basing our philosophy on definitive, unquestionable truths, our starting point is that men and groups of men adhere to opinions of all sorts with a variable intensity, which we can only know by putting it to the test. These beliefs are not always self-evident, and they rarely deal with clear and distinct ideas. The most generally accepted beliefs remain implicit and unformulated for a long time, for more often than not it is only on the occasion of a disagreement as to the consequences resulting from them that the problem of their formulation or more precise definition arises.

Common sense regularly opposes facts to theories, truths to opinions, and that which is objective to that which is not. By this opposition it indicates what opinions are to be preferred to others, whether or not the preference be based on generally accepted criteria. John Stuart Mill and André Lalande are hardly saying anything new when they ask that we bring our beliefs face to face with the facts or with true statements, and though it may not be difficult to follow their advice when the facts and truths are not subjected to challenge, this is unfortunately not always the case. Everyone is disposed to recognize that facts and truths play a normative role in relation to opinion, but the person who challenges a fact or doubts a truth will be reluctant to accord it this favored status, and will qualify the statement he declines to accept quite differently. Similarly, most people are normally disposed to act in accordance with what seems to them logical or reasonable, but will refuse to apply these epithets to solutions they do not recognize as well founded.

Those who hold facts and truths to be the sole norms for guiding opinions will endeavor to attach their convictions to some form of evidence that is indubitable and beyond discussion. There can be no question, with this outlook, of providing in turn a foundation for these self-evident things, for in their absence the very notion of foundation would appear incomprehensible. With these self-evident things as starting point, proof will take the form of a calculation or of resort to experiment.

The increased confidence thus brought about in the procedures and results of the mathematical and natural sciences went hand in hand with the casting aside of all the other means of proof, which were considered devoid of scientific value. Now this attitude was quite justifiable as long as there was the hope of finding a scientifically defensible solution to all actual human problems through an increasingly wide application of the calculus of probabilities. But if essential problems involving questions of a moral, social, political, philosophical, or religious order by their very nature elude the methods of the mathematical and natural sciences, it does not seem reasonable to scorn and reject all the techniques of reasoning characteristic of deliberation and discussion—in a word, of argumentation. It is too easy to disqualify all reasoning that does not conform to the requirements of the proof which Pareto called "logico-experimental" as being "sophistical." If all argumentation of this kind must be considered a misleading form of reasoning, then the lack of "logico-experimental" proofs would leave the field wide open, in all the essential spheres of life, to suggestion and violence. The assertion that whatever is not objectively and indisputably valid belongs to the realm of the arbitrary and subjective creates an unbridgeable gulf between theoretical knowledge, which alone is rational, and action, for which motivations would be wholly irrational. Practice ceases to be reasonable in such a perspective, for critical argumentation becomes entirely incomprehensible, and it is no longer even possible to take seriously philosophical reflection itself. For it is only those fields from which all controversy has been eliminated that can thenceforth lay claim to a certain rationality. As soon as a controversy arises, and the agreement of minds cannot be reestablished by "logico-experimental" methods, one would be in the sphere of the irrational—which would be the sphere of deliberation, discussion, and argumentation.

The distinction, so common in twentieth-century philosophy, between judgments of reality and value judgments characterizes an effort—though in this form we feel it is a hopeless one—by those who recognize that scientific investigation enjoys a special, preeminent status, but wish to save the norms of human action from arbitrariness and irrationality. But this distinction, stemming from an absolutist epistemology which tends to sharply separate two sides of human activity, has not given the results for which one hoped. There are two reasons for this. One is the lack of success in developing a logic of value judgments, the other is the difficulty of satisfactorily defining value judgments and judgments of reality.

If it is possible to discern in argumentative practice, as we have done, some statements that relate to facts, and others that relate to values, the distinction between these two forms of statement can never be clear cut: it is the consequence of precarious agreements of varying intensity, agreements which may not be explicitly stated. In order to be able to distinguish clearly between two kinds of judgments criteria enabling them to be identified would have to be put forward and these criteria would themselves have to be beyond discussion. And, more particularly, there would have to be an agreement about the linguistic elements without which no judgment can be formulated.

If judgments of reality are to provide an indisputable object of common understanding, the terms they contain must be free of all ambiguity, either because it is possible to know their true meaning, or because a unanimously accepted convention does away with all controversy on this subject. These two possibilities, which are respectively the approaches of realism and nominalism in the linguistic field, are both untenable, as they regard language either as a reflection of reality or as an arbitrary creation of an individual, and forget an essential element, the social aspect of language, which is an instrument of communication and influence on others.

All language is the language of a community, be this a community bound by biological ties, or by the practice of a common discipline or technique. The terms used, their meaning, their definition, can only be understood in the context of the habits, ways of thought, methods, external circumstances, and traditions known to the users of those terms. A deviation from usage requires justification, and, in this connection, realism and nominalism are simply two diametrically opposed attempts at justification, both linked to philosophies of language that are equally inadequate.

Adherence to particular linguistic usages normally expresses the explicit or implicit adoption of certain definite positions which are neither the reflection of an objective reality nor the manifestation of individual arbitrariness. Language is part of the traditions of a community, and, like the others, it only undergoes revolutionary modification where there is a radical failure to adapt to a new situation; otherwise its transformation is slow and imperceptible. But an agreement on the use of terms, no less than an agreement about the conception of reality and the vision of the world, even though it may not be disputed, is not indisputable; it is linked to a social and historical situation which fundamentally conditions any distinction that one might wish to draw between judgments of reality and value judgments.

The transcendence of these social and historical conditions of knowledge, with the transformation of certain *de facto* agreements into agreements *de jure*, is only possible through the adoption of a philosophical position which, if it is rational, is only conceivable as the consequence of a preceding argumentaton.[165] The theory and practice of argumentation are, in our view, correlative with a critical rationalism that transcends the duality "judgments of reality-value judgments," and makes both judgments of reality and value judgments dependent on the personality of the scientist or philosopher, who is responsible for his decisions in the field of knowledge as well as in the field of action.[166]

Only the existence of an argumentation that is neither compelling nor arbitrary can give meaning to human freedom, a state in which a reasonable choice can be exercised. If freedom was no more than necessary adherence to a previously given natural order, it would exclude all possibility of choice; and if the exercise of freedom were not based on reasons, every choice would be irrational and would be reduced to an arbitrary decision operating in an intellectual void.[167] It is because of the possibility of argumentation which provides reasons, but not compelling reasons, that it is possible to escape the dilemma: adherence to an objectively and universally valid truth, or recourse to suggestion and violence to secure acceptance for our opinions and decisions. The theory of argumentation will help to develop what a logic of value judgments has tried in vain to provide, namely the justification of the possibility of a human community in the sphere of action when this justification cannot be based on a reality or objective truth. And its starting point, in making this contribution, is an analysis of those forms of reasoning which, though they are indispensable in practice, have from the time of Descartes been neglected by logicians and theoreticians of knowledge.

---

[165] Cf. Perelman, "Philosophies premières et philosophie régressive," *Rhétorique et philosophie*, pp. 99-100, 105, and "Réflexions sur la justice," *Revue de l'Institut de Sociologie*, 1951, 280-281.

[166] Cf. Perelman, "La quête du rationnel," *Rhétorique et philosophie*, pp. 110-120, and "The Role of Decision in the Theory of Knowledge," *The Idea of Justice and the Problem of Argument*, pp. 79-87.

[167] Cf. Perelman, "Liberté et raisonnement," *Rhétorique et philosophie*, pp. 44-48; "Le problème du bon choix," *ibid.*, p. 160.

BIBLIOGRAPHY

Abbagnano, Bobbio, Buzano, Codegone, Frola, Geymonat, Nuvoli, De
   Finetti, *Saggi di critica delle scienze*, series Maestri e compagni, Biblio-
   teca di studi critici e morali, 17, Centro de Studi metodologici di
   Torino (Turin, Italy, De Silva) 1950.
Ad C. Herrennium de ratione dicendi, see *Rhetorica ad Herennium*.
Agricola (Rodolphus), *Rodolphi agricolae phrisii de inventione dialectica
   libri tres* (Argentina, Joannem Knoblouchum) 1521.
Alain, *Histoire de mes pensées*, Les Essais (Paris, Gallimard) ed. 8,
   1936.
Aleichem, Sholom, *see* Sholom.
Amy (René), "Hommes et bêtes, action réciproque," *Revue de l'Institut
   de Sociologie* (Belgium) 1953, no. 4, pp. 520-598; 1954, no. 1, pp.
   105-216.
Angyal (Andras), *Foundations for a Science of Personality* (New York,
   The Commonwealth Fund; London, Oxford University Press) 1946,
   first edition, 1941.
Annales parlementaires de Belgique. Chambre des Représentants (Brus-
   sels, Belgium, Imprimerie du Moniteur belge).
Annambhatta, *Le Compendium des Topiques* (*Tarka-Samgraha*) with
   extracts from three Indian commentaries. Text, translation, and
   commentary by A. Foucher (Paris, Maisonneuve) 1949.
Anselm (Saint), "Dialogus de Libero Arbitrio," *Patrologie latine de Migne*,
   vol. CLVIII, columns 489-506.
Aragon, *Les yeux d'Elsa* (Brussels, Belgium, Ed. Cosmopolis) 1945.
Aristotle, *Aristotle*, Great Books of the Western World (GBWW), vol. 8
   (Chicago, Illinois, Encyclopaedia Britannica, Inc.) 1952.
Aron (Raymond), *Introduction à la philosophie de l'histoire*, Essai sur les
   limites de l'objectivité historique, Bibliothèque des Idées (Paris,
   Gallimard) 1948.
Asch (S.E.), "The Doctrine of Suggestion, Prestige and Imitation in
   Social Psychology," *Psychological Review*, vol. 55, 1948, pp. 250-276.
Asch (S. E.), *Social Psychology* (Englewood Cliffs, New Jersey, Prentice-
   Hall, Inc.) 1952.
Aubry and Rau, *Cours de droit civil français*, reviewed and interpreted
   for legislative and judicial matters by Etienne Bartin, vol. XII
   (Paris, Godde) ed. 5, 1922.

Auerbach (Erich), *Mimesis, Dargestellte Wirklichkeit in der abendlän-dischen Literatur* (Bern, Switzerland, A. Francke) 1946.

Augustine (Saint), "Principia Rhetorices," *Patrologie latine de Migne*, in the appendix to the works of Saint Augustine, columns 1439-1448, vol. XXXII (Paris) 1865.

Aurobindo (Shrî), "Le guide du Yoga," *Œuvres complètes*, 3, in the collection Spiritualités vivantes, published under the direction of P. Masson-Oursel and Jean Herbert (Paris, Éditions Albin Michel) 1951.

Ayer (Alfred Jules), *Language, Truth and Logic* (London, Victor Gollancz) 1947, with the introduction to ed. 2, 1946; first edition, 1936.

Aymé (Marcel), *La tête des autres*, play in 4 acts, (Paris, Grasset) 1952.

Bachelard (G.), *Le rationalisme appliqué* (Paris, Presses Universitaires de France) 1949.

Back (Kurt W.), "Influence through Social Communication," *Journal of Abnormal and Social Psychology*, vol. 46, 1951, pp. 9-23.

Bacon (Francis), *Francis Bacon*, Great Books of the Western World, (GBWW) vol. 30 (Chicago, Illinois, Encyclopaedia Britannica, Inc.) 1952.

Baird (A. Craig), *Argumentation, Discussion, and Debate*, McGraw-Hill, Series in Speech, Clarence T. Simon, consulting editor (New York McGraw-Hill Book Company) 1950.

Balzac (Honoré de), *La comédie humaine*, text prepared and prefaced by Marcel Bouteron, Bibliothèque de la Pléiade, 10 vol. (Paris, Gallimard) 1935-1937, N.R.F.

Barnes (Winston H.F.) "Ethics without Propositions," address in *Logical Positivism and Ethics*, symposia read at the joint session of the Aristotelian Society and the Mind Association at Durham, July 9-11, 1948. Aristotelian Society Supplementary Volume XXII, 1948.

Baroja (Pío), *La taverna del humorismo* (Madrid, Spain, Rafael Caro Raggio) 1920.

Baron (A.), *De la Rhétorique ou de la composition oratoire et littéraire*, (Brussels and Liège, Belgium, Librairies polytechniques de Decq) ed. 4, 1879, first edition 1849.

Baruk (H.), "Le psychiatre dans la société," *La Semaine des Hôpitaux de Paris*, 25th year, no. 74, Oct. 6, 1949, pp. 3041-3048.

Bataille (Georges), "Le temps de la révolte," I, *Critique*, *55*, 1951, pp. 1019-1027; II, *Critique*, *56*, 1952, pp. 29-41.

Beauvoir (Simone de), *Le deuxième sexe*, 2 vol. (Paris, Gallimard) 1949.

Beckett (Samuel), *Molloy*, translated by Patrick Bowles in collaboration with the author (New York, Grove Press, Inc.)

Beckett (Samuel), *Molloy* (Paris, Éditions de Minuit) 1953.

Belaval (Yvon), *Les philosophes et leur langage*, Les Essais L, (Paris, Gallimard) 1952.

Bellak (Léopold), "The Nature of Slogans," *Journal of Abnormal and Social Psychology* vol. 37, 1942, pp. 496-510.

Benary (Wilhelm), "Studien zur Untersuchung der Intelligenz bei einem Fall von Seelenblindheit," VIII, contribution to the "Psychologischen Analysen hirnpathologischer Fälle auf Grund von Untersuchungen Hirnverletzer," edited by Gelb and Goldstein, *Psychologische Forschung*, vol. 2, no. 3-4, 1922, pp. 209-327.

Benda (Julien), *La trahison des clercs* (Paris, Grasset) 1928.

Benda (Julien), *Du style d'idées, réflexions sur la pensée, sa nature, ses réalisations, sa valeur morale* (Paris, Gallimard) 1948, N.R.F.

Benedict (Ruth), *The Chrysanthemum and the Sword, Patterns of Japanese Culture* (Boston, Massachusetts, Houghton Mifflin Company) 1946.

Benjamin (A. Cornelius), "Science and Vagueness," *Philosophy of Science*, vol. 6, no. 21, Apr. 1939, pp. 422-431.

Bentham (Jeremy), *The Works of Jeremy Bentham*, 11 vol. (Edinburgh, Tait; London, Simpkin, Marshall and Co.) 1843.

Bentham (Jeremy), *The Theory of Legislation* edited by C. K. Ogden (London, Routledge & Kegan Paul) 1931.

Bentham (Jeremy) *Œuvres*, following the French edition of E. Dumont, 3 vol, Société belge de Librairie (Brussels, Belgium, Hauman & Cie) ed. 3, 1840.

Berelson (Bernard), "Content Analysis," *Handbook of Social Psychology*, vol. I, pp. 488-522. *See* Lindzey.

Bergson (Henri), *Creative Evolution*, translated by Arthur Mitchell, (New York, Modern Library, Inc.) 1944.

Bergson (Henri), *The Two Sources of Morality and Religion*, translated by R. Ashely Audra and Cloudesley Brereton, Anchor Books (Garden City, New York, Doubleday & Company, Inc.) 1954.

Bergson (Henri), *L'évolution créatrice* (Paris, Alcan) ed. 39, 1932.

Bergson (Henri), *Les deux sources de la morale et de la religion* (Paris, Alcan) ed. 3, 1932.

Berkeley (George), "Three Dialogues between Hylas and Philonous," in *The Works of George Berkeley* (London and New York, Nelson) 1949.

Berl (Emmanuel), *Sylvia* (Paris, Gallimard) 1952, N.R.F.

Bernanos (Georges), *La joie* in the collection La Palatine (Paris, Plon) 1929.

Bernanos (Georges), *Scandale de la vérité*, (Paris, Gallimard) 1939, N.R.F.

Berriat Saint-Prix (F.), *Manuel de logique juridique* (Paris, Cotillon) ed. 2, no date.

Bevan (Edwyn), *Symbolism and Belief*, Gifford Lectures (London, Allen and Unwin) 1938.

Bidez (J.), *La vie de l'empereur Julien*, Collection d'études anciennes, under the patronage of the Association Guillaume Budé (Paris, Les Belles-Lettres) 1930.

Bird (Charles), *Social Psychology*, The Century Psychology Series, editor Richard M. Elliott (New York, Appleton-Century) 1940.

Black (Max), "Vagueness, an Exercise in Logical Analysis," *Philosophy of Science*, vol. 4, 1937, pp. 427-455.

Black (Max) editor *Philosophical Analysis*, a collection of essays (Ithaca, New York, Cornell University Press) 1950.

Blass (Friedrich), *Die attische Beredsamkeit*, 4 vol, (Leipzig, Germany, Teubner) ed. 2, 1887-1898.

Bobbio (Norberto), *L'analogia nella logica del diritto*, Memorie dell' istituto giuridico, series II, memoria XXXVI, (Turin, Italy, Istituto giuridico della R. Università) 1938.

Bobbio (Norberto), "Libertà dell'arte e politica culturale," *Nuovi Argomenti*, no. 2, 1953, pp. 245-259. Reprinted in *Politica e cultura*.

Bobbio (Norberto) *Politica e cultura* (Turin, Italy, Einaudi) 1955.

Bobbio (Norberto), "Scienza del diritto e analisi del linguaggio," *Saggi di critica delle scienze*, pp. 23-66. *See* Abbagnano.

Boileau-Despréaux (Nicolas), *Œuvres, avec éclaircissemens historiques donnez par lui-même,* 4 vol (Amsterdam, François Changuion) 1729.

Bossuet (Jacques-Bénigne), *Sermons,* 4 vol. (Paris, Garnier).

Bossuet (Jacques-Bénigne), *Oraisons funèbres, Panégyriques,* text established and annotated by Bernard Velat, Bibliothèque de la Pléiade (Paris, Gallimard) 1936, N.R.F.

Boulanger (André), *Aelius Aristide et la sophistique dans la province d'Asie au IIe siècle de notre ère,* Bibliothèque des Écoles françaises d'Athènes et de Rome (Paris, E. de Boccard) 1923.

Bowles (Chester), *Ambassador's Report* (New York, Harper & Brothers *now* Harper and Row, Publishers) 1954.

Britton (Karl), *Communication, A Philosophical Study of Language,* International Library of Psychology, Philosophy and Scientific Method (London, Kegan Paul, Trench, Trubner and Co. *now* Routledge & Kegan Paul, Ltd.) 1939.

Bross (Irwin D. J) *Design for Decision* (New York, The Macmillan Company) 1953.

Browning (Robert), *Complete Poetical Works,* Cambridge Edition, (Boston, Massachusetts, Houghton Mifflin Co.) 1895.

Browning (Robert), *The Ring and the Book,* Oxford edition (London, Oxford University Press) 1912.

Browning (Robert), *Poems,* Oxford Edition, (London, Oxford University Press) 1919.

Bruner (Katherine Frost), "Of Psychological Writing, Being Some Valedictory Remarks on Style," *Journal of Abnormal and Social Psychology,* vol. 37, 1942, pp. 52-70.

Brunot (Ferdinand), *La pensée et la langue, Méthode, principes et plan d'une théorie nouvelle du langage appliquée au français* (Paris, Masson) 1922.

Buber (Martin), *I and Thou* (New York, Charles Scribner's Sons) ed. 2, 1958.

Burke (Kenneth), *A Grammar of Motives* (New York, George Braziller, Inc.) 1955.

Burke (Kenneth), *A Rhetoric of Motives* (Englewood Cliffs, New Jersey, Prentice-Hall, Inc.) 1950.

Burnet (J.), *Early Greek Philosophy* (London, Black) 1920.

Caillois (Roger), *Poétique de St-John Perse* (Paris, Gallimard) 1954, N.R.F.

Calderón de la Barca (Pedro), *La vida es sueño, Comedia en tres jornadas,* Biblioteca Universal (Madrid, Spain; Perlado, Páez y Compañía) 1922.

Calogero (Guido), "Vérité et liberté," *Actes du Xe Congrès international de Philosophie, Amsterdam* 1948 (Amsterdam, North-Holland Publishing Co.) 1949, pp. 96-98.

Calogero (Guido), *Logo e Dialogo, Saggio Sullo spirito critico e sulla libertà di coscienza.* Contains in Italian as Appendix I, pp. 193-198, "Verità e Libertà," a paper presented at the Tenth International Congress of Philosophy in Amsterdam, August, 1948, and published in French in the Acts of the Congress. (Milan, Italy, Edizione di Comunità) 1950.

Calogero (Guido), "Why Do We Ask Why? Some Observations on the Ethics of Dialogue: The Will to Understand as the Absolute Foundation of Liberalism and Morals," *Actes du XIe Congrès international de Philosophie, Bruxelles,* 20-26 *août 1953,* vol. XIV, pp. 260-265, (Amsterdam, North-Holland Publishing Co; Louvain, Belgium, E. Nauwelaerts).

Calvin (John), *Institutes of the Christian Religion,* translated by F. L. Battles, Library of Christian Classics, vol. XX (Philadelphia, Pennsylvania, Westminster Press; London S.C.M. Press, Ltd.) 1960.

Calvin (John), *Institution de la religion chrétienne,* based on the French edition of 1560, revised and corrected by Frank Baumgartner. Preceded by the *Lettre au Roy de France très chrétien François premier de ce nom.* (Geneva, Switzerland, Beroud & Cie.) 1888.

Camus (Albert), *Actuelles, Chroniques 1944-1948.* (Paris, Gallimard) 1950, N.R.F.

Cardozo (Benjamin N.), *The Paradoxes of Legal Science,* Columbia University Lectures, James Carpentier Foundation (New York, Columbia University Press) 1928.

Carnegie (Dale), *Public Speaking. A Practical Course for Business Men* (New York, Association Press) 1928.

Carnegie (Dale), *L'Art de parler en public et de persuader dans les affaires,* translated from the American by Maurice Beerblock and Marie Delcourt (Liège, Belgium, Desoer) 1950.

Carroll (Lewis), *Alice's Adventures in Wonderland; Through the Looking-Glass; The Hunting of the Snark,* introduction by Alexander Woollcott (New York, Modern Library, Inc.)

Casey (Ralph), *see* Lasswell.

Cassirer (E.), "Le langage et la construction du monde des objets," *Journal de Psychologie,* vol. XXX, 1933, pp. 18-44.

Cassirer (E.), *The Philosophy of Symbolic Forms,* translated by Ralph Manheim, preface and introduction by Charles W. Hendel (New Haven, Connecticut, Yale University Press; London, Oxford University Press) vol. I, *Language,* 1953; vol. II, *Mythical Thought,* 1955.

Castelli (E.), editor, *Atti Congresso internazionale di studi umanistici Venezia, 1954: Retorica & Barocco* (Rome, Italy, Fratelli Bocca) 1955.

Catherine de Gênes (Sainte), *Les œuvres,* preceded by her life by the Vicomte Marie-Théodore de Bussierre (Paris, A. Tralin) 1926.

Ceccato (Silvio), "Divagazioni di animal semioticum," *Sigma,* 4-5 (Rome, Italy, Partenia) 1947, pp. 294-302.

Cervantes, *Don Quixote,* (London, Dent; New York, Dutton) 1943.

Cervantes, *El ingenioso hidalgo Don Quijote de la Mancha,* with notes by Francisco Rodríguez Marín, Clássicos Castellanos, 8 vol. (Madrid, La Lectura) 1913.

Chaignet (A. E.) *La rhétorique et son histoire* (Paris, E. Bouillon & E. Vieweg) 1888.

Chassé (Charles), "La clé de Mallarmé est chez Littré," *Quo Vadis,* Mar-Apr-May 1950.

Chassé (Charles), *Les clés de Mallarmé,* L'histoire littéraire (Paris, Aubier) 1954.

Chesneau (César), *see* Dumarsais.

Chlepner (B.S.) "Réflexions sur le problème des nationalisations," *Revue de l'Institut de Sociologie* (Brussels, Belgium) no. 2, Apr-June 1949, pp. 207-232.

Churchill (Winston), *The Second World War: The Gathering Storm* (Boston, Massachusetts, U.S.A., Houghton Mifflin Co.) 1948.

Cicero, *De l'Invention* (*De Inventione*), text revised and translated into French with an introduction and notes by Henri Bornecque (Paris, Garnier) 1932.

Cicero, *De l'orateur* (*De Oratore ad Quintum Fratrem Libri Tres*) vol. I, text established and translated into French by Edmond Courbaud, 1938; vol. II, ibid., 1927; vol. III, text established by Henri Bornecque and translated into French by Edmond Courbaud and Henri Bornecque, Collection des Universités de France under the patronage of the Association Guillaume Budé (Paris, Les Belles-Lettres) 1930.

Cicero, *Divisions de l'art oratoire* (*Partitiones Oratoriae*) and *Topiques* (*Topica*), text established and translated into French by Henri Bornecque, Collection des Universités de France under the patronage of the Association Guillaume Budé (Paris, Les Belles-Lettres) 1924.

Cicero, *L'orateur* (*Orator*) and *Du meilleur genre d'orateurs* (*De Optimo Genere Oratorium*), text established and translated into French by Henri Bornecque, Collection des Universités de France under the patronage of the Association Guillaume Budé (Paris, Les Belles-Lettres) 1921.

Cicero, *De officiis*, with an English translation by Walter Miller, The Loeb Classical Library (London, Heinemann; New York, G. P. Putnam's Sons) 1928; first printed, 1913.

Cicero, *Paradoxa Stoicorum*, with an English translation by H. Rackham, The Loeb Classical Library (London, Heinemann; New York, G. P. Putnam's Sons) 1948; first printed, 1942.

Claparède (E.), "La genèse de l'hypothèse," extract from the *Archives de Psychologie*, vol. XXIV, (Geneva, Switzerland, Kundig) 1934.

Cocteau (Jean), *Plain-chant* (Paris, Stock) 1923.

Cocteau (Jean), "Orphée" (film), extracts in *Empreintes* (Brussels, Belgium) May-July 1950, number on Jean Cocteau.

Cocteau (Jean), *La difficulté d'être* (Monaco, Editions du Rocher) 1953.

Cohen (Morris R.), *A Preface to Logic* (New York, Henry Holt and Company *now* Holt, Rinehart, and Winston) 1946, fourth printing.

Colette, *Le fanal bleu* (Paris, Ferenczi) 1949.

Confucius, *see* Legge, Pauthier.

Coombe-Tennant (A.H.S.), "Mr Wisdom on Philosophical Analysis," *Mind*, vol. XLV, no. 180, Oct 1936, pp. 432-449.

Copilowish (Irving M.), "Border-Line Cases, Vagueness and Ambiguity," *Philosophy of Science*, vol. 6, no. 2, Apr. 1939, pp. 118-195.

Cormeau (Nelly), *L'art de François Mauriac* (Paris, Grasset) 1951.

Corneille (Pierre), *Œuvres complètes* with notes by all the commentators, 2 vol. (Paris, Firmin-Didot) 1880.

Cossio (C.), "Phenomenology of the Decision," *Latin-American Legal Philosophy* (Cambridge, Massachusetts, U.S.A., Harvard University Press) 1948.

Cournot (A.-A.), Essai sur les fondements de nos connaissances et sur les caractères de la critique philosophique, 2 vol. (Paris, Hachette) 1851.

Crawshay-Williams (Rupert), *The Comforts of Unreason, a Study of the*

Motives behind Irrational Thought (London, Kegan Paul, Trench, Trubner and Company) 1947.

Crossman (Richard), *Palestine Mission, a Personal Record, with Speech Delivered in the House of Commons, 1st July 1946* (London, Hamish Hamilton) 1947.

Crossman (Richard) editor, *The God that Failed*, six studies in communism by Arthur Koestler, Ignazio Silone, André Gide, presented by Enid Starkie, Richard Wright, Louis Fischer, Stephen Spender, with an introduction by Richard Crossman (London, Hamish Hamilton) 1950.

Crossman (Richard) editor, *The God that Failed* (New York, Bantam Books, Inc.) 1952.

Curtis (Jean-Louis), *Chers corbeaux* (Paris, Julliard) 1951.

De Coster (S.), "L'idéalisme des jeunes," *Morale et enseignement*, bulletin published by the Institut de Philosophie of the University of Brussels, Belgium, 1951-1952, no. 2, pp. 3-7; no. 3, pp. 5-16.

Demogue (René), *Les notions fondamentales du droit privé, essai critique* (Paris, Arthur Rousseau) 1911.

Demosthenes, *Demosthenes and Aeschines on the Crown* (Oxford, U.K., Clarendon Press) 1872.

Demosthenes, *Olynthiacs, Philippics, Minor Public Speeches, Speech against Leptinos*, translated by J. H. Vince, Loeb Classical Library (New York, Putnam; London, Heinemann) 1930.

Demosthenes, *Harangues et plaidoyers politiques*, Collection des Universités de France under the patronage of the Association Guillaume Budé: vol. I, *Harangues*, text established and translated into French by Maurice Croiset, 1924; vol. II, ibid, 1925; vol. III, *Plaidoyers politiques*, text established and translated into French by G. Mathieu, 1945; vol. IV, ibid, 1947.

Descamps (Edouard), *Etudes d'art oratoire et de législation* (Louvain, Belgium, Peeters) 1889.

Descartes (René), *Descartes, Spinoza*, translated by E. S. Haldane et al., Great Books of the Western World, (GBWW), vol. 31 (Chicago, Illinois, U.S.A., Encyclopaedia Britannica, Inc.) 1952.

Descartes (René), *Règles pour la direction de l'esprit (Regulae)*, translated into French by V. Cousin in *Œuvres* (Paris) 1826.

Descartes (René), *Méditations métaphysiques (Meditationes de Prima Philosophia)* Latin text with a translation into French by the Duc de Luynes, introduction and notes by Geneviève Lewis (Paris, Vrin) 1945.

Descartes (René), *Discours de la Méthode*, with introduction and notes by E. Gilson (Paris, Vrin) 1946.

De Vivier (Marie), *Le mal que je t'ai fait* (Paris, Debresse) 1955.

Dorfles (Gillo), *Discorso tecnico delle arti*, introductory note by Francesco Flora (Pisa, Italy, Nistri-Lischi) 1952.

Dorolle (Maurice), *Le raisonnement par analogie*, Bibliothèque de Philosophie contemporaine (Paris, Presses Universitaires de France) 1949.

Driencourt (Jacques), *La propagande, nouvelle force politique* (Paris, A. Colin) 1950.

Drilsma (R. L.), *De woorden der Wet of de Wil van de Wetgever, proeve ener Bydrage tot de leer der rechtsuitlegging uitgaande van de beschouwingen van Raymond Saleilles en François Geny*, Academisch proefschrift (Amsterdam, Noord-Hollandsche uitg. maats.) 1948.

Du Bouchet (André), "Envergure de Reverdy," *Critique 47*, Apr. 1951, pp. 308-320.

Ducasse (C. J.), *Philosophy as a Science, Its Matter and Its Method* (New York, Oskar Piest) 1941.

Dumarsais (César Chesneau, sieur du Marsais), *Des tropes ou des différents sens dans lesquels on peut prendre un même mot dans une même langue* (Paris, Mme. Vve. Dabo at the Librairie stéréotype) 1824; first edition in 1730.

Dumas (G.), *Traité de psychologie*, vol. II (Paris, Alcan) 1924.

Dupréel (Eugène), "Sur les rapports de la logique et de la sociologie ou théorie des idées confuses, *Revue de métaphysique et de morale*, July 1911, pp. 517-522.

Dupréel (Eugène), *Le rapport social, essai sur l'objet et la méthode de la sociologie* (Paris, Alcan) 1912.

Dupréel (Eugène), "La logique et les sociologues," *Revue de l'Institut de Sociologie* (Brussels, Belgium) 1924, no. 1 and 2, pp. 71-116 and 215-238.

Dupréel (Eugène), "De la nécessité," *Archives de la Société belge de Philosophie*, no. I, 1928, reprinted in *Essais pluralistes*.

Dupréel (Eugène), "Le problème sociologique du rire," *Revue philosophique*, vol. CVI, 1928, reprinted in *Essais pluralistes*.

Dupréel (Eugène), "La deuxième vertu du XIXe siècle," discourse given at the opening convocation of the Institut des Hautes Études (Brussels, Belgium, Imprimerie médicale et scientifique); reprinted in *Essais pluralistes*.

Dupréel (Eugène), "La pensée confuse," *Annales des Hautes Études de Gand*, vol. III, *Études philosophiques*, pp. 17-26, 1939; reprinted in *Essais pluralistes*.

Dupréel (Eugène), *Esquisse d'une philosophie des valeurs*, Bibliothèque de Philosophie contemporaine (Paris, Alcan) 1939.

Dupréel (Eugène), *Sociologie générale*, Travaux de la Faculté de Philosophie et Lettres, Université Libre de Bruxelles (Paris, Presses Universitaires de France) 1948.

Dupréel (Eugène), *Les Sophistes: Protagoras, Gorgias, Prodicus, Hippias*, Bibliothèque scientifique 14, (Neuchâtel, Switzerland, Ed. du Griffon) 1948.

Dupréel (Eugène) *Essais pluralistes* (Paris, Presses Universitaires de France) 1950.

Dupréel (Eugène), "Fragments pour la théorie de la connaissance de M. E. Dupréel," collected by C. Perelman, *Dialectica 4, 5*, 1947.

Dürr (Karl), "Die Entwicklung der Dialektik von Platon bis Hegel," *Dialectica 1*, 1947.

Eliasberg (W. G.), "Speaking and Thinking," in the symposium *Thinking and speaking*, pp. 93-110, *see* Révész.

Empson (William), *Seven Types of Ambiguity* (London, Chatto & Windus Ltd.; Ontario, Canada, Oxford University Press) ed. 2, revised and reset, 1947; first published 1930.

Epictetus, translated by P. E. Matheson in *The Stoic and Epicurean Philosophers* (New York, Random House, Inc.) 1940.

Epictetus, *Entretiens* (Paris, Les Belles-Lettres), Collection des Universités de France under the patronage of the Association Guillaume

Budé, text established and translated by Joseph Souilhé, 2 vol.; vol. I, 1943, vol. II, 1949.

Epictetus, *Les entretiens* collected by Arrien and translated by V. Courdaveaux (Paris, Didier) 1862.

Erdmann (Karl Otto), *Die Bedeutung des Wortes; Aufsätze aus dem Grenzgebiet der Sprach-psychologie und Logik* (Leipzig, Germany, Haessel) ed. 4, 1925; ed. 1, 1904.

Erigena (Jean Scotus) *see* Scotus Erigena.

Estève (Claude-Louis), *Études philosophiques sur l'expression littéraire*, foreword by M. Gueroult (Paris, Vrin) 1938.

Febvre (Lucien), "Comment Jules Michelet inventa la Renaissance," *Studi in onore di Gino Luzzatto*, vol. III, pp. 1-11 (Milan, Italy, Giuffré) 1950.

Fénelon, *Œuvres* (Paris, Lebel) 1824, vol. XXI, *Dialogues sur l'éloquence en général et sur celle de la chaire en particulier.*

Feigl (Herbert), "De Principiis Non Disputandum ... ?" *Philosophical Analysis*, pp. 119-156, *see* Black (Max).

Festinger (Léon), "Informal Social Communication," from the Research Center for Group Dynamics of the University of Michigan, *Psychological Review*, vol. 57, no. 5, Sept. 1950, pp. 271-282.

Festinger (Léon) and Thibaut (John), "Interpersonal Communication in Small Groups," *Journal of Abnormal and Social Psychology*, no. 46, 1951, pp. 92-99.

Findlay (J. N.), "Morality by Convention," *Mind*, vol. LIII, new series, 1944, pp. 142-169.

Fléchier (abbé de S. Severin), *Oraison funèbre de tres-haut et tres-puissant prince Henri de La Tour d'Auvergne, Vicomte de Turenne*, delivered in the Église de Saint Eustache on January 10, 1676 (Paris) 1676.

Flew (A.), *Essays on Logic and Language* (Oxford, Blackwell Scientific Publications, Ltd.) 1951.

Fracastoro (Girolamo), *Hieronymi Fracastorii Veronensis Opera Omnia*, in unum proxime post illius mortem collecta, accessit index locupletissimus, (Venice, Italy, Juntas) ed. 2, 1574.

Fracastoro (Girolamo) *Sifilide ossia del mal francese, libri III*, translation, introduction, and notes by Fabrizio Winspeare with the Latin text of the poem separately printed, Biblioteca della Rivista di storia delle scienze mediche et naturali, vol.VI. (Florence, Italy, Leo S. Olschki) 1955.

France (A.), *La rôtisserie de la reine Pédauque* (Paris, Calmann-Lévy) ed. 58, without date.

Fun Fare, A Treasury of Reader's Digest *Wit and Humor* (New York, Simon and Schuster) 1949.

Gandon (Yves), *Le démon du style* (Paris, Plon) 1938.

Garin (Eugenio), *L'umanesimo italiano, Filosofia e vita civile nel rinascimento*, Biblioteca di cultura moderna (Bari, Italy, Laterza e Figli) 1952. This had appeared in German: *Der italienische Humanismus* (Bern, Switzerland, Francke) 1947.

Garlan (Edwin N.), *Legal Realism and Justice* (New York, Columbia University Press) 1941.

Gellner (Ernest), "Maxims," *Mind*, vol. LX, new series, no. 239, July 1951, pp. 383-393.

Gheorghiu (C. Virgil), *La vingt-cinquième heure*, translated from the Rumanian by Monique Saint-Côme, preface by Gabriel Marcel, in the collection Feux Croisés (Paris, Plon) 1949.

Gibert (Balthasar), *Jugemens des savans sur les auteurs qui ont traité de la Rhétorique, avec un précis de la doctrine de ces auteurs* (Paris, Estienne) 3 vol., 1713, 1716, 1719.

Gibson (Ch.) *see* Richards.

Gide (André), *The Journals of André Gide*, translated by Justin O'Brien (New York, Alfred A. Knopf, Inc., now a subsidiary of Random House, Inc.) 1951.

Gide (André), *Journal, 1889-1939* Bibliothèque de la Pléiade (Paris, Gallimard) 1940, N.R.F.

Gide (André), *Journal, 1939-1942* (Paris, Gallimard) 1946, N.R.F.

Gide (André), *Prétextes* (Paris, Mercure de France) 1947.

Gilson (Etienne), *The Christian Philosophy of Saint Thomas Aquinas*, translated by L. K. Shook (New York, Random House, Inc.) 1956.

Gilson (Etienne), *L'esprit de la philosophie médiévale* (Paris, Vrin) ed. 2, 1944.

Gilson (Etienne), *Le thomisme* (Paris, Vrin) ed. 5, 1945.

Giraudoux (Jean), *Lectures pour une ombre* (Paris, Emile-Paul) 1930.

Giraudoux (Jean), *La Française et la France* (Paris, Gallimard) 1951, N.R.F.

Goblot (Edmond), *La logique des jugements de valeur* (Paris, Colin) 1927.

Goblot (Edmond), *Traité de logique* (Paris, Colin) ed. 6, 1937.

Goldschmidt (Victor), *Le paradigme dans la dialectique platonicienne*, Bibliothèque de philosophie contemporaine (Paris, Presses Universitaires de France) 1947.

Goldschmidt (Victor), *Le système stoïcien et l'idée de temps*, Collège philosophique (Paris, Vrin) 1953.

Gonseth (F.), "L'idée de dialectique aux Entretiens de Zurich, "*Dialectica 1*, 1947, pp. 21-37.

Gonseth (F.) "La notion du normal," *Dialectica 3*, 1947, pp. 243-252.

Gonseth (F.), "Interventions dans les deuxièmes Entretiens de Zurich, sur l'idée de dialectique," *Dialectica 6*, 1948, pp. 89-303.

Gonseth (F.), "Réponse au R. P. Isaye," *Dialectica 21*, 1952, pp. 53-66.

Gonseth (F.), "Interventions dans les troisièmes Entretiens de Zurich, Le principe de dualité," *Dialectica 22-25*, 1952-1953.

Good (I. J.), *Probability and the Weighing of Evidence* (London, Charles Griffin and Co.) 1950.

Gouhier (Henri), "La résistance au vrai et le problème cartésien d'une philosophie sans rhétorique," in *Retorica e Barocco* (Rome, Italy, Fratelli Bocca) 1955. *See* Castelli.

Gourmont (Rémy de), *La culture des idées* (Paris, Mercure de France) 1900.

Gracian (Baltasar), *L'homme de Cour (Oráculo manual y arte de prudencia)*, French translation and commentary by the Sieur Amelot de La Houssaie, an Epître au Roi and a Preface, "J'ai moissonné le Discreto, ainsi que le Héros pour enrichir ma traduction de tout ce qu'il y a de plus beau ..." (Augsburg, Germany, Paul Kühtze) 1710.

Grenet (Paul), *Les origines de l'analogie philosophique dans les Dialogues de Platon* (Paris, Boivin) 1948.

Guigues (le Chartreux), "Quinti meditaciones," *Patrologie latine de Migne*, vol. CLIII (Paris) 1880.

Guillaume (Paul), *Manuel de psychologie* (Paris, Presses Universitaires de France) 1948, new revised and augmented edition.

Guitton (Jean), *Le temps et l'éternité chez Plotin et saint Augustin* (Paris, Boivin) 1933.

Gurwitsch (Aron), "Sur une racine perceptive de l'abstraction," *Actes du XIᵉ Congrès international de Philosophie, Bruxelles, août 1953* (Amsterdam, The Netherlands, North-Holland Publishing Co.; Louvain, Belgium, E. Nauwelaerts) vol. II, pp. 43-47.

Gwynn (Aubrey), *Roman Education from Cicero to Quintilian* (Oxford, U. K, The Clarendon Press) 1926.

Halkin (L.-E.), *Initiation à la critique historique*, Cahiers des Annales, 6 (Paris, Colin) ed. 2, 1953.

Harding (T. Swann), "Science at the Tower of Babel," *Philosophy of Science*, vol. 5, no. 3, July 1938, pp. 338-353.

Hayakawa (S. I.), in consultation with Basil H. Pillard, *Language in Thought and Action* (New York, Harcourt, Brace and Co., *now* Harcourt, Brace & World, Inc.) 1949, which is the revised edition of *Language in Action*, 1941.

Hayakawa (S.I.) *Language, Meaning and Maturity*, selections from ETC, a Review of General Semantics, 1943-1953 (New York, Harper and Brothers, *now* Harper and Row, Publishers) 1954.

Hebb (D. O.), *The Organization of Behavior* (New York, John Wiley & Sons, Inc.) 1949.

Hebb (D. O.) and Thompson W. R.), "The Social Significance of Animal Studies," *Handbook of Social Psychology*, vol. I, pp. 532-561. *See* Lindzey.

Helson (Harry), "Adaptation Level as a Basis for a Quantitative Theory of Frames of Reference," *The Psychological Review*, vol. 55, no. 6, Nov. 1948, pp. 297-313.

Hempel (Carl G.), "Vagueness and Logic," *Philosophy of Science*, vol. 6, no. 2, Apr. 1939, pp. 163-180.

Hempel (Carl G.), *Fundamentals of Concept Formation in Empirical Science*, International Encyclopedia of Unified Science, vol. I and II: Foundations of the Unity of Science, vol. II, no. 7 (Chicago, Illinois, The University of Chicago Press) 1955, first published in 1952.

Hempel (Carl G.) and Oppenheim (Paul), *Der Typusbegriff im Lichte der neuen Logik* (Leiden, The Netherlands, Sythoff) 1936.

Hollingworth (H. L.), *The Psychology of the Audience* (New York, American Book Company) 1935.

Holmer (Paul L.) "Kierkegaard and Ethical Theory," *Ethics*, vol. LXIII, no 3, part I, Apr. 1953, pp. 157-170.

Homer, *Iliade*, text established and translated into French by P. Mazon in the Collection des Universités de France, 4 vol. (Paris, Les Belles-Lettres) vol. I, 1937.

Hovland (Carl I.), "Effects of the Mass Media of Communication," *Handbook of Social Psychology*, vol. II, pp. 1062-1103. *See* Lindzey.

Hovland (Carl I.), Lumsdaine (Arthur A.), Sheffield (Fred D.), *Experiments on Mass Communication*, Studies in Social Psychology in World War

II, vol. III (Princeton, New Jersey, Princeton University Press) 1949.

Hovland (Carl I.) and Weiss (W.), "The Influence of Source Credibility on Communication Effectiveness," *Public Opinion Quarterly*, vol. 15, 1952, pp. 635-650.

Hovland (Carl I.), *see also* Kelman.

Hoyle (Fred), *The Nature of the Universe, a Series of Broadcast Lectures* (Oxford, U. K, Basil Blackwell) 1951, impression 10.

Hsiao King, see Legge.

Hull (Cordell), *The Memoirs of Cordell Hull*, vol. I, 1871-1941; vol. 2, 1941-1945 (New York, The Macmillan Company) 1948.

Hume (David), *A Treatise on Human Nature* (Oxford, U. K., Clarendon Press) 1951.

Husserl (Edmund), *Gesammelte Werke*, vol. 6, edited by Walter Biemel, *Die Krisis der europäischen Wissenschaften und die Transzendentale Phänomenologie* (Den Haag, The Netherlands, Nyhoff) 1954.

Husserl (Edmund), "La crise des sciences européennes et la phénoménologie transcendantale," translated into French by E. Gerrer, *Études philosophiques*, 4th year, 1949, no. 2, pp. 127-159.

Huxley (Julian), *Soviet Genetics and World Science; Lysenko and the Meaning of Heredity* (London, Chatto and Windus) 1949.

Isaye (Gaston), "La justification critique par rétorsion," *Revue philosophique de Louvain*, vol. 52, series 3, no. 34, May 1954, pp. 205-233.

Isocrates, *Isocrates*, translated by Larne van Hook (Cambridge, Massachusetts, U.S.A., Harvard University Press; London, Heinemann) 1954.

Isocrates, *Discours*, Collection des Universités de France under the patronage of the Association Guillaume Budé, vol. I, text established and translated into French by Georges Mathieu and Emile Brémond, 1928; vol. II, idem, 1942; vol. III, text established and translated into French by G. Mathieu, 1942. (Paris, Les Belles-Lettres).

Jamati (G.), "Le langage poétique," *Formes de l'art, formes de l'esprit* (Paris, Presses Universitaires de France) 1951, pp. 261-279.

James (W.), *Essays in Pragmatism*, first essay "The Sentiment of Rationality," edited with an introduction by Albury Castell (New York, Hafner Publishing Company) 1948, 1960.

Jankélévitch (V.), *Traité des vertus* (Paris, Bordas) 1949.

Janson (Paul), *Discours parlementaires*, 2 vol. (Brussels, Belgium, Vve Monnom) 1905.

Jaspers (K.), *Psychopathologie générale*, translated into French from the third German edition by A. Kastler and J. Mendousse, Bibliothèque de Philosophie contemporaine (Paris, Alcan) 1927; first German edition published in 1913.

Jerome (Saint), "Epistolae," *Patrologie latine de Migne*, vol. XXII (Paris) 1845.

Jouhandeau (Marcel), *Essai sur moi-même* (Lausanne, Switzerland, Marguerat) 1946.

Jouhandeau (Marcel), *Un monde* (Paris, Gallimard) 1950, N.R.F.

Jouhandeau (Marcel), *De la grandeur* (Paris, Grasset) 1952.

Jouhandeau (Marcel), *Les Ana de Madame Apremont* (*Asperimontisana*) (Paris, Gallimard) 1954, N.R.F.

Jung (C. G.), *Psychology and Religion* (New Haven, Connecticut, Yale University Press; and London, U.K., Oxford University Press) 1938.

Jung (C. G.), *Psychologie und Religion* (Zürich, Switzerland, Rascher) 1940.

Kant (Emmanuel), *Kant*, translated by T. K. Abbott et al., Great Books of the Western World (GBWW), vol. 42, *Kant* (Chicago, Illinois, Encyclopaediae Britannica, Inc.) 1952.

Kant (Emmanuel), *Prolégomènes à toute métaphysique future*, translation by J. Gibelin (Paris, Vrin) 1930.

Kaufmann (Felix), *Methodology of the Social Sciences* (New York, Oxford University Press) 1949; first printed in 1944.

Kelman (Herbert C.) and Hovland (Carl I.), "'Reinstatement' of the Communicator in Delayed Measurement of Opinion Change," *The Journal of Abnormal and Social Psychology*, vol. 48, no. 3, July 1953, pp. 327-335.

Kelsen (Hans), *Reine Rechtslehre* (Leipzig, Germany and Vienna, Austria, Deuticke) 1934.

Keynes (John Maynard), *A Treatise on Probability* (London, Macmillan & Company) 1921.

Keynes (John Maynard), *A Treatise on Money*, 2 vol. (London, Macmillan & Company) 1930.

Keynes (John Maynard) *The General Theory of Employment, Interest and Money* (London, Macmillan & Company) 1936.

Klages (Ludwig), "Notions fondamentales de la caractérologie," *Le diagnostic du caractère*, Bibliothèque scientifique internationale (Paris, Presses Universitaires de France) 1949, pp. 4-20.

Klein (Viola), *The Feminine Character, History of an Ideology* edited with a foreword by Karl Mannheim, The International Library of Sociology and Social Reconstruction (London, Kegan Paul, Trench, Trubner and Co.) 1946.

Klemperer (Victor), *L.T.I., Notizbuch eines Philologen* (Berlin, Germany, Aufbau Verlag) 1947.

Kneebone (G. T.), "Induction and Probability," *Proceedings of the Aristotelian Society*, new series, vol. L, 1950, pp. 27-42.

Knower (F. H.), "Experimental Studies of Changes in Attitudes: I. A Study of the Effect of Oral Argument on Changes of Attitude," *Journal of Social Psychology*, vol. 6, 1935, pp. 315-347. "II. A study of the Effect of Printed Argument on Changes in Attitudes," *Journal of Abnormal and Social Psychology*, vol. 30, 1936, pp. 522-532. "III. Some Evidence of Attitude Changes," *Journal of Applied Psychology*, vol. 20, 1936, pp. 114-127.

Koestler (Arthur), *see* Crossman, *The God That Failed*.

Köhler (Wolfgang), *The Place of Value in a World of Facts* (New York, Liveright Publishing Corporation) 1938.

Kotarbinski (T.), *Traktat o dobrej robocie* (A treatise on good work) (Lodz, Poland, Societas scientiarum Lodziensis) 1955.

Kou Hong Ming and Borrey (Francis), *Le Catéchisme de Confucius, Contribution à l'étude de la sociologie chinoise* (Paris, Marcel Rivière) 1927.

La Bruyère (Jean de) *Œuvres complètes*, text established and annotated by Julien Benda, Bibliothèque de la Pléiade (Paris, Gallimard) 1941, N.R.F.

Lalande (André), *La raison et les normes*, collection "A la recherche de la vérité" (Paris, Hachette) 1948.

Lalo (Charles), *Esthétique du rire*, Bibliothèque de Philosophie scientifique (Paris, Flammarion) 1949.

Lasswell (Harold D.), Casey (Ralph D.), and Smith (Bruce Lannes), *Propaganda and Promotional Activities, an Annotated Bibliography* (Minneapolis, Minnesota, University of Minnesota Press; London, Oxford University Press) 1935. Prepared under the direction of the advisory committee on pressure groups and propaganda of the Social Science Research Council. Lead article by Lasswell, "The Study and Practice of Propaganda." For the next volume, *see* Smith (Bruce Lannes).

Lasswell (Harold D.), Leites (Nathan), and Associates, *Language of Politics, Studies in Quantitative Semantics* (New York, Stewart) 1949.

Lecomte du Noüy (Pierre), *Human Destiny*, Mentor Books (New York, New American Library, Inc.) 1956.

Lecomte du Noüy (Pierre), *L'homme et sa destinée*, Éditions du Vieux Colombier (Paris, La Colombe) 1948.

Lefebve (M.-J.), *Jean Paulhan, une philosophie et une pratique de l'expression et de la réflexion* (Paris, Gallimard) 1949, N.R.F. Les Essais XXXIII.

Lefebvre (H.), *A la lumière du matérialisme dialectique: I. Logique formelle, logique dialectique* (Paris, Éditions Sociales) 1947.

Legge (James), *The Sacred Books of the East*, translated by various scholars and edited by F. Max Müller (London, Henry Frowde, Oxford University Press, Oxford, Clarendon Press) vol. III, *The Texts of Confucianism*, part I, *The Shû King* ..., *the Hsiâo King or Classic of Filial Piety*, translated by James Legge, 1879; vol. XXVIII, *The Texts of Confucianism*, part IV, *The Lî Kî*, book XXXIX, *Tâ Hsio or the Great Learning*, translated by James Legge, 1885.

Legge (James), *The Chinese Classics*, with a translation, critical, and exegetical notes, prolegomena and copious indexes, 7 vol. (London, Henry Frowde; New York, The Macmillan Company; Oxford, U.K., Clarendon Press) 1893, ed. 2.

Leibniz (Gottfried Wilhelm), *Discourse on Metaphysics* (Chicago, Illinois, and London, Open Court Publishing Company) 1927.

Leibniz (Gottfried Wilhelm), *Die philosophischen Schriften*, edited by C. J. Gerhardt, vol. 4, *Discourse on Metaphysics*, in French (Berlin, Germany, Weidmann) 1880; vol. 5, *New Essays on Human Understanding*, in French (Berlin, Germany, Weidmann), 1882; vol. 6, *Essays on Theodicy*, in French (Leipzig, Germany, A. Lorenz) 1932.

Leites (Nathan), "Interaction, The Third International on its Changes of Policy," revised from Document 25, Experimental Division for the Study of Wartime Communications, Library of Congress, May 1, 1942, in *Language of Politics*, pp. 293-333. *See* Lasswell.

Lenoble (Robert), "Histoire et Physique, à propos des conseils de Mersenne aux historiens et de l'intervention de Jean de Launoy dans la querelle gassendiste," *Revue d'histoire des sciences et de leurs applications* (Paris, Presses Universitaires de France) 1953, pp. 112-135.

Levinas (Emmanuel), "La réalité et son ombre," *Les temps modernes*, Nov. 1948, pp. 771-789.

Lewis (Clarence Irving), *An Analysis of Knowledge and Valuation* (La Salle, Illinois, The Open Court Publishing Company) 1946.

Lindzey (Gardner) editor, *Handbook of Social Psychology*, 2 vol. (Reading, Massachusetts, Addison-Wesley Publishing Company) 1954.

Lippitt (Ronald), Polansky (Norman), and Rosen (Sidney), "The Dynamics of Power, a Field Study of Social Influence in Groups of Children," *Human Relations*, vol. V, no. 1, 1952, pp. 37-64.

Lippmann (Walter), "The Election: Taft, Dewey and Vandenberg," *New York Herald Tribune*, Paris edition, March 12, 1948.

Locke (John), *Locke et al.*, Great Books of the Western World (GBWW), vol. 35 (Chicago, Encyclopaedia Britannica, Inc.) 1952.

Locke (John), *An Essay concerning Human Understanding* (London, Routledge) 1894.

Locke (John), *The Second Treatise of Civil Government* and *A Letter concerning Toleration*, edited by J. W. Gough (Oxford, U.K., Blackwell) 1948.

Longinus, *On the Sublime*, translated by W. R. Roberts (Cambridge, U.K., Cambridge University Press) 1907.

Longinus, "Traité du sublime ou du merveilleux dans le discours," translated from Greek into French by Nicolas Boileau-Despréaux, his *Œuvres*, vol. III (Amsterdam, The Netherlands, François Changuion) 1729.

Lumsdaine (Arthur A.), *see* Hovland.

Lund (Frederick Hansen), "The Psychology of Belief," *Journal of Abnormal and Social Psychology*, vol. XX, 1925, pp. 13-21, 63-81, 174-196.

Mach (E.), *Erkenntnis und Irrtum, Skizzen zur Psychologie der Forschung* (Leipzig, Germany, Barth) 1905.

McKeon (Richard) editor, with the assistance of Stein Rokkan, *Democracy in a World of Tensions*, a symposium prepared by UNESCO (Chicago, Illinois, University of Chicago Press) 1951.

McKeon (Richard), "Dialectic and Political Thought and Action," *Ethics*, vol. LXV, no. 1, Oct. 1954, pp. 1-33.

Madariaga (Salvador de), *Englishmen, Frenchmen, Spaniards* (London, Oxford University Press) 1949.

Madariaga (Salvador de), *Anglais, Français, Espagnols*, preceded by a note by André Maurois (Paris, Gallimard) 1930, N.R.F.

Maier (Norman R.F.) "The Quality of Group Decisions as Influenced by the Discussion Leader," *Human Relations*, vol. III, no. 2, 1950, pp. 155-174.

Malraux (André), *Saturne, Essai sur Goya*, La Galerie de la Pléiade (Paris, Gallimard) 1950, N.R.F.

Mannoury (G.), *Handboek der analytische signifika* (Bussum, the Netherlands, F. G. Kroonder). Vol. I, *Geschiedenis der begripskritiek*, 1947; vol. II, *Hoofdbegrippen en methoden der signifika, ontogenese en fylogenese van het verstandhoudingsapparaat*, 1948.

Marangoni (Matteo), *Apprendre à voir (Saper vedere)*, translated into French from the 9th Italian edition by Denise Lombard (Neuchâtel, Switzerland, Ed. du Griffon) 1947.

Marcel (Gabriel), *Un homme de Dieu*, 4 acts, Les Cahiers verts, 51 (Paris, Grasset) 1925.

Marcel (Gabriel), *Le monde cassé*, 4 acts, followed by *Position et approches concrètes du mystère ontologique* (Paris, Desclée de Brouwer) 1933.

Marcel (Gabriel), *Le chemin de crête*, 4 acts (Paris, Grasset) 1936.

Marcel (Gabriel), *Rome n'est plus dans Rome*, 5 acts (Paris) *Théâtre*, no. 56, Jan. 1952.

Maritain (Jacques), Introduction to *Human Rights*, a collection made by UNESCO (London and New York, Wingate) 1950, p. 10.

Maritain (Jacques), *Raison et raisons, essais détachés* (Paris, L.U.F.; Fribourg, Switzerland, Egloff) 1947.

Maritain (Jacques), "Introduction," *Autour de la nouvelle déclaration universelle des droits de l'homme*, texts collected by UNESCO (Paris, Sagittaire) 1949, pp. 11-18.

Marouzeau (J.), *Précis de stylistique française* (Paris, Masson) 1950.

Marrou (H. I.), *Histoire de l'éducation dans l'Antiquité*, collection "Esprit" (Paris, Éditions du Seuil) 1948.

Massillon (Jean-Baptiste), *Œuvres complètes*, edited by the Abbé Migne, vol. 42 and 43 in the *Collection intégrale et universelle des orateurs sacrés* (Paris) 1854.

Mauriac (François), *Génitrix*, Les cahiers verts, 30 (Paris, Grasset) 1923.

Mauriac (François), *Le mystère Frontenac* (Paris, Grasset) 1933.

Mauriac (François), *Les maisons fugitives*, illustrated with 100 photographs by Jean-Marie Marcel (Paris, Grasset) 1939.

Meng-Tseu, *see* Pauthier.

Méré (Antoine Gombaud, chevalier de), *Œuvres complètes*, 3 vol., Collection des Universités de France (Paris, Les Belles-Lettres) 1930.

Meredith-Jones (C.), "The Conventional Saracen of the Songs of Geste, *Speculum*, vol. XVII, no. 2, Apr. 1942.

Merleau-Ponty (Maurice), *Phenomenology of Perception* (New York, Humanities Press) 1962.

Merleau-Ponty (Maurice), *Phénoménologie de la perception*, Bibliothèque des Idées (Paris, Gallimard) 1945, N.R.F.

Mill (John Stuart), *American State Papers, The Federalist, J.S. Mill*, Great Books of the Western World (GBWW), vol. 43 (Chicago, Illinois, Encyclopaedia Britannica, Inc.) 1952.

Mill (John Stuart), *A System of Logic* (London, Longmans, Green) 1959.

Mill (John Stuart), *L'utilitarisme*, ed. 2, translated into French by P.-L. Le Monnier (Paris, Alcan) 1889.

Millioud (Maurice), "La propagation des idées," *Revue philosophique*, 1910, vol. 69, pp. 580-600; vol. 70, pp. 168-191.

Minkowski (Eugène) "Le langage et le vécu," *Archivio di Filosofia*, vol. *Semantica* (Rome, Fratelli Bocca) 1955, pp. 351-372.

Mirabeau l'Aîné, *Collection complète des travaux de Mirabeau l'Aîné à l'Assemblée nationale*, edited by M. Etienne Méjan, 5 vol. (Paris, vol. I and II, Lejay, 1791; vol. III through V, Devaux, 1792).

Molière (Jean-Baptiste Poquelin, called), *Œuvres complètes*, text established and annotated by Maurice Rat, Bibliothèque de la Pléiade, 2 vol. (Paris, Gallimard) 1932.

Montaigne (Michel de), *Essais*, text established and annotated by Albert Thibaudet, Bibliothèque de la Pléiade (Paris, Gallimard) 1946, N.R.F.

Montesquieu (Charles de Secondat, baron de), *Œuvres complètes* with notes by Dupin, Crevier, Voltaire, Mably, Servan, La Harpe, etc. (Paris, Firmin Didot) 1843.

Moore (Willis), "Structure in Sentence and in Fact," *Philosophy of Science*, vol. 5, no. 1, Jan 1938.

Morpurgo Tagliabue (Guido), "La retorica aristotelica e il barocco," *Retorica e Barocco*, pp. 119-195. *See* E. Castelli.

Morris (Charles), *Signs, Language and Behavior* (Englewood Cliffs, New Jersey, Prentice-Hall, Inc.) 1946.

Mullahy (Patrick) editor, *The Contributions of Harry Stack Sullivan, A Symposium on Interpersonal Theory in Psychiatry and Social Science*, Meetings of the William Alanson White Association, Oct. 13-14, 1951 (New York, Hermitage House) 1953, second printing.

Naess (Arne), *Interpretation and Preciseness, A Contribution to the Theory of Communication* (Oslo, Norway, Dybwad) 1953.

Navarre (Octave), *Essai sur la rhétorique grecque avant Aristote* (Paris, Hachette) 1900.

Nève (Joseph), *Antoine de La Salle, Sa vie et ses ouvrages*, also included is the *Réconfort de Mme Du Fresne*, based on the only manuscript of the Bibliothèque Royale of Belgium (Paris, Champion, and Brussels, Belgium, Falk) 1903.

Newman (Cardinal John Henry), *Grammaire de l'assentiment*, translated from the 1870 English edition into French by Mme Gaston Paris, Études de philosophie et de Critique religieuse (Paris, Bloud) 1907.

Nogaro (Bertrand), *La valeur logique des théories économiques*, Bibliothèque de Philosohie contemporaine (Paris, Presses Universitaires de France) 1947.

Noulet (E.), *Le premier visage de Rimbaud, Huit poèmes de jeunesse, Choix et commentaire* (Brussels, Belgium, Académie royale de Langue et Littérature françaises de Belgique) 1953.

Odier (Dr. Charles), *Les deux sources, consciente et inconsciente, de la vie morale*, Être et Penser Collection, Cahiers de philosophie, 4-5 (Neuchâtel, Switzerland, Éditions de la Baconnière) ed. 2, 1947.

Odier (Dr. Charles), *Le rôle des fonctions du moi dans l'évolution psychique*, Actualités pédagogiques et psychologiques de l'Institut J.-J. Rousseau, Geneva, Switzerland. Part I, *L'angoisse et la pensée magique, Essai d'analyse psychogénétique appliqué à la phobie et à la névrose d'abandon*, 1948; part II, *L'homme esclave de son infériorité*, vol. I, *Essai sur la genèse du moi*, 1950.

Ogden (C. K.) and Richards (I. A.), *The Meaning of Meaning, a Study of the Influence of Language upon Thought and of the Science of Symbolism* (London, Kegan Paul, Trench, Trubner and Co.) ed. 4, 1936; first edition appeared in 1923.

Olbrechts-Tyteca (L.), *see* Perelman, Ch.

Ombredane (Dr. André) *L'aphasie et l'élaboration de la pensée explicite* (Paris, Presses Universitaires de France) 1950.

Ors (Eugenio D') *Coupole et monarchie*, followed by other studies on the morphology of culture, translated into French by Andrée de Stoutz, Les Cahiers d'Occident, vol. 6, series 2. (Paris, Librairie de France) 1929, pp. 1-112.

Ossowska (Marie), *Podstawy Nauki o Moralności*, (The Foundations of a Science of Morality) (Warsaw, Poland, Czytelnik) 1947.

Paechter (Heinz) in association with Hellman (Bertha), Paechter (Hedwig), and Paetel (Karl O.), *Nazi-Deutsch, A Glossary of Contemporary German Usage* (New York, Frederik Ungar Publishing Co.) 1944.

Pagnol (Marcel), *César* (Lausanne, Switzerland, Henri Kaeser) 1949.

Parain (Brice), *Recherches sur la nature et les fonctions du langage*, Bibliothèque des Idées (Paris, Gallimard) 1942, N.R.F.

Pareto (Vilfredo), *The Mind and Society* (New York, Harcourt, Brace and Co., now Harcourt, Brace and World) 1935.

Pareto (Vilfredo), *Traité de sociologie générale*, French edition by Pierre Boven under the direction of the author, 2 vol. (Paris, Payot) 1917-1919.

Pascal (Blaise), *Pascal*, translated by W. F. Trotter et al., Great Books of the Western World (GBWW) vol. 33 (Chicago, Illinois, Encyclopaedia Britannica, Inc.) 1952.

Pascal (Blaise), *L'œuvre*, text established and annotated by Jacques Chevalier, Bibliothèque de la Pléiade (Paris, Gallimard) 1950, N.R.F.

Paton (H. J.), "The Emotive Theory of Ethics," symposia read at the Joint Session of the Aristotelian Society and the Mind Association at Durham, July 1948, in *Logical Positivism and Ethics*, Aristotelian Society Supplement, vol. XXII (London, Harrison and Sons) 1948, pp. 107-126.

Paulhan (Jean), *Le guerrier appliqué* (Paris, Gallimard) 1930, N.R.F.

Paulhan (Jean), *Les hain-tenys* (Paris, Gallimard) 1938, N.R.F. Published in 1914 by Genthner.

Paulhan (Jean), *Les fleurs de Tarbes ou la terreur dans les lettres* (Paris, Gallimard) 1941, N.R.F.

Paulhan (Jean), *Entretien sur des faits divers*, illustrated by André Lhote (Paris, Gallimard) 1945.

Paulhan (Jean), "Les figures ou la rhétorique décryptée," *Cahiers du Sud*, year 36, no. 295, 1949, pp. 361-395. (*Questions rhétoriques*, an investigation directed by Francis Ponge.)

Paulhan (Jean), *La preuve par l'étymologie*, Métrique collection (Paris, Les Éditions de Minuit) 1953.

Pauthier (G.), *Les Sse Chou, ou les quatre livres de philosophie morale et politique de la Chine*: I. *Le Tá-Hio ou la grande étude*, by Khoung-Fou-Tseu and his disciple Theng-Tseu, translated into French with a Latin version and the Chinese text facing, accompanied by the complete commentary by Tchoû-Hî (Paris, Firmin-Didot) 1837.

Pauthier (G.), *Confucius et Mencius, Les quatre livres de Philosophie morale et politique de la Chine* (Paris, Charpentier) 1852.

Pegis, (A. C.) editor, *Basic Writings of Saint Thomas Aquinas* (New York, Random House, Inc.)

Perelman (Ch.), *The Idea of Justice and the Problem of Argument* (London, Routledge and Kegan Paul) 1963.

Perelman (Ch.), "Réflexions sur l'explication, note sociologique," *Revue de l'Institut de Sociologie* (Brussels, Belgium) 19th year, no. 1, Jan.-Mar. 1939.

Perelman (Ch.), *De la Justice*, Actualités sociales, new series, Université Libre de Bruxelles, Institut de Sociologie Solvay (Brussels, Belgium, Office de Publicité) 1945.

Perelman (Ch.), "Philosophies premières et philosophie régressive," *Dialectica 11*, 1949. Reprinted in *Rhétorique et philosophie*.

Perelman (Ch.), "La quête du rationnel," *Études de philosophie des sciences, en hommage à F. Gonseth* (Neuchâtel, Switzerland, Éditions du Griffon) 1950. Reprinted in *Rhétorique et philosophie*.

Perelman (Ch.), "Réflexions sur la justice," *Revue de l'Institut de Sociologie*, no. 2, 1951, pp. 255-281.

Perelman (Ch.), "De la preuve en philosophie," *Mélanges G. Smets* (Brussels, Belgium, Librairie encyclopédique) 1952. Reprinted in *Rhétorique et philosophie*.

Perelman (Ch.), "Raison éternelle, raison historique," *L'homme et l'histoire, Actes du VIᵉ Congrès des Sociétés de Philosophie de Langue française* (Paris, Presses Universitaires de France) 1952. Reprinted in *Justice et raison*.

Perelman (Ch.), "Education et Rhétorique," *Revue belge de psychologie et de pédagogie*, vol. XIV, no. 60, Dec. 1952, pp. 129-138. Reprinted in *Justice et raison*.

Perelman (Ch.), "La vulgarisation scientifique, problème philosophique," *Revue des Alumni* (Brussels, Belgium) Mar. 1953, pp. 321-323. Reprinted in *Justice et raison*.

Perelman (Ch.), "Le rôle de la décision dans la théorie de la connaissance," *Actes du IIᵉ Congrès international de l'Union internationale de Philosophie des Sciences, Zurich*, 1954, (Neuchâtel, Switzerland, Éditions du Griffon) 1955, vol. I, pp. 150-159. Reprinted in *Justice et raison*.

Perelman (Ch.), "La méthode dialectique et le rôle de l'interlocuteur dans le dialogue," communication to the Entretiens d'Athènes of the Institut international de Philosophie on the theme "Dialogue et Dialectique," Apr. 1955, *Revue de métaphysique et de morale* Jan.-June 1955, pp. 26-31. Reprinted in English in *The Idea of Justice and the Problem of Argument*.

Perelman (Ch.), "Problèmes de logique juridique," Communication IV in "Essais de logique juridique, à propos de l'usufruit d'une créance," *Journal des Trbunaux*, 71st year, no. 4104, Apr. 22, 1956, pp. 272-274.

Perelman (Ch.), *Justice et raison* (Brussels, Belgium, Presses Universitaires de Bruxelles) 1963.

Perelman (Ch.) and Olbrechts-Tyteca (L.), "Logique et rhétorique, *Revue philosophique*, Jan.-Mar. 1950. Reprinted in *Rhétorique et philosophie*. See infra.

Perelman (Ch.) and Olbrechts-Tyteca (L.), "Acte et personne dans l'argumentation," English version in *Ethics*, July 1951. Reprinted in *Rhétorique et philosophie*. See infra.

Perelman (Ch.) and Olbrechts-Tyteca (L.), *Rhétorique et philosophie, Pour une théorie de l'argumentation en philosophie*, with a preface by Emile Bréhier, Bibliothèque de Philosophie contemporaine (Paris, Presses Universitaires de France) 1952.

Perelman (Ch.) and Olbrechts-Tyteca (L.), "Les notions et l'argumentation," *Archivio di Filosofia*, vol. *Semantica* (Rome) 1955, pp. 249-269.

Perelman (Sophie), "Introduction aux relations diplomatiques entre la Belgique et les États-Unis, Sept. 1830-Jan. 1832," *Bulletin de la Commission royale d'histoire*, vol. CXIV (Brussels, Belgium, Académie royale de Belgique) 1949, pp. 189-226.

Petronius (Arbiter Titus), *Le Satiricon*, text established and translated into French by Alfred Ernout, Collection des Universités de France, under the patronage of the Association Guillaume Budé (Paris, Les Belles-Lettres) 1931.

Piaget (Jean), *Le jugement et le raisonnement chez l'enfant* (Neuchâtel and Paris, Delachaux & Niestlé) 1924.

Piaget (Jean), *La causalité physique chez l'enfant* (Paris, Alcan) 1927.

Piaget (Jean), *Traité de logique* (Paris, Colin) 1949.

Piaget (Jean), *Introduction à l'épistémologie génétique* 3 vol. (Paris, Presses Universitaires de France) 1950.

Pichon (E.), *Le développement psychique de l'enfant et de l'adolescent, Evolution normale-pathologie-traitement* (Paris, Masson) 1936.

Pitt (William), *Orations on the French War to the Peace of Amiens*, Everyman's Library (London, J. M. Dent; New York, E. P. Dutton) 1917.

Plato, *Plato*, translated by Benjamin Jowett, Great Books of the Western World (GBWW), vol. 7 (Chicago, Illinois, Encyclopaedia Britannica, Inc.) 1952.

Plautus, "The Threepenny Day (Trinummus)," *The Complete Roman Drama* (New York, Random House, Inc.) 1942.

Plautus, *Comédies VII, Trinummus*, Collection des Universités de France, under the patronage of the Association Guillaume Budé, text established and translated into French by Alfred Ernoult (Paris, Les Belles-Lettres) 1940.

Pliny the Younger, *Lettres*, Collection des Universités de France, under the patronage of the Association Guillaume Budé, 4 vol., the texts of volumes 1-3 were established and translated into French by Anne-Marie Guillemin (Paris, Les Belles-Lettres) 1927-1928.

Plotinus, *Ennéades*, Collection des Universités de France under the patronage of the Association Guillaume Budé, text translated into French by Emile Bréhier, 6 parts in 7 volumes (Paris, Les Belles Lettres) 1924-1938.

Plotinus, *Plotinus*, translated by S. MacKenna and P. S. Porge, Great Books of the Western World (GBWW), vol. 17 (Chicago, Illinois, Encyclopaedia Britannica, Inc.) 1952.

Plutarch, *Plutarch's Moralia*, translation by Frank Cole Rabbitt, Loeb Classical Library (New York, G. P. Putnam's Sons; London, Heinemann) 1927-1936.

Poe (Edgar Allan), "The Fall of the House of Usher" (1838) in *Tales of Mystery and Imagination*, Everyman's Library (London, J. M. Dent; New York, E. P. Dutton) 1908.

Poincaré (Henri), *La valeur de la science*, with an introduction by Louis Rougier, Editions du Cheval Ailé, Classiques français du xxe siècle (Geneva, Switzerland, Constant Bourquin) 1946.

Polak (Dr. Fred. L.), *Kennen en keuren in de sociale wetenschappen* (Leiden, the Netherlands, Stenfert Kroese) 1948.

Polansky (Norman), *see* Lippitt.

Polanyi (Michael), *The Logic of Liberty*, International Library of Sociology and Social Reconstruction (London, Routledge and Kegan Paul) 1951.

Ponge (Francis), *Le Lézard* (Paris, Galerie Jeanne Bucher) 1953.

Popper (Karl), *Logik der Forschung* (Vienna, Austria, Springer Verlag) 1935.

Porzig (Walter), *Das Wunder der Sprache, Probleme, Methoden und Ergebnisse der modernen Sprachwissenschaft* (Bern, Switzerland, Francke) 1950.

Pradines (Maurice), *Traité de psychologie générale*, Logos, Introduction aux études philosophiques, 2 vol. (Paris, Presses Universitaires de France) 1946.

Principia Rhetorices, see Augustine (Saint).

Prior (Arthur N.), *Logic and the Basis of Ethics* (Oxford, U.K., Clarendon Press) 1949.

Proust (Marcel), *The Guermantes Way* (New York, Modern Library, Inc.) 1952.

Proust (Marcel), *Œuvres complètes; A la recherche du temps perdu,* 15 vol. (Paris, Gallimard) 1946-1947.

Puget (Claude-André), *La peine capitale,* drama in 3 acts (Paris, Stock) 1948.

Quetelet (Adolphe), *Physique sociale,* 2 vol., (Brussels, Belgium, C. Mucquardt) ed. 2, 1869.

Quintilian, *The Institutio Oratoria of Quintilian,* translated by H. E. Butler, Loeb Classical Library (New York, G. P. Putnam's Sons; London, Heinemann) 1921-1933.

Racine (Jean), *Œuvres complètes,* vol. 1, *Théâtre,* text established by R. Groos, E. Pilon, and R. Picard; presentation, notes, and commentaries by Raymond Picard, Bibliothèque de la Pléiade (Paris, Gallimard) 1951, N.R.F.

Ramus (P.), *Dialecticae Libri Duo, Audomari Talaei Praelectionibus Illustrati* (Paris, Wechelum) 1560.

Ramus (P.), *Dialecticae Libri Duo, Audomari Talaei Praelectionibus Illustrati* (Paris, Andream Wechelum) 1566. This edition differs from the preceding one.

Réau (L.), "L'influence de la forme sur l'iconographie médiévale," *Formes de l'art, formes de l'esprit* (Paris, Presses Universitaires de France) 1951, pp. 85-105.

Révész (G.), editor, *Thinking and Speaking,* a symposium (Amsterdam, The Netherlands, North-Holland Publishing Company) 1954.

Reyes (Alfonso), *El Deslinde, Prolegomenos a la teoría literaria* Centro de estudios literarios del Colegio de Mexico, vol. I (Mexico City, Mexico, El Colegio de Mexico) 1944.

Rhetorica ad Herennium, Loeb Classical Library (New York, G. P. Putnam's Sons; London, Heinemann).

Richards (Ivor Armstrong), *Principles of Literary Criticism* (New York, Harcourt, Brace and World) 1924.

Richards (Ivor Armstrong), *Principles of Literary Criticism* (London, Routledge and Kegan Paul) 1952, 13 impression. First published in 1924; second edition with two new appendices 1926.

Richards (Ivor Armstrong), *The Philosophy of Rhetoric,* the Mary Flexner Lectures at Bryn Mawr (New York and London, Oxford University Press) 1936.

Richards (Ivor Armstrong), *Interpretation in Teaching* (London, Routledge and Kegan Paul) 1949, impression 2; first published 1938. Also (New York, Harcourt, Brace and World) 1938.

Richards (Ivor Armstrong), "Interventions in a symposium on Emotive Meaning," *The Philosophical Review,* 1948, pp. 145-157.

Richards (I. A.) and Gibson (Christine), *Learning Basic English, a Practical Handbook for English Speaking People* (New York, W.W. Norton and Co.) 1945.

Richards (I. A.) *see also* Ogden.

Riezler (Kurt), "Political Decisions in Modern Society," *Ethics*, vol. LXIV, no. 2, part II, Jan. 1954, pp. 1-55.

Rignano (Eugenio), *Psychologie du raisonnement*, Bibliothèque de Philosophie contemporaine (Paris, Alcan) 1920.

Rimbaud (Arthur), *Œuvres complètes*, text established and annotated by Rolland de Renéville and Jules Mouquet, Bibliothèque de la Pléiade (Paris, Gallimard) 1951, N.R.F.

Rivadeneira (Padre Pedro de), *Vida del bienaventurado padre Ignacio de Loyola, Fundador de la religión de la compañía de Jesus* (Madrid, Spain, Administración del apostolado de la prensa) 1920.

Rivière (Jacques), *Aimée* (Paris, Gallimard) 1922, N.R.F.

Robinson (Richard), "The Emotive Theory of Ethics," Symposia read at the Joint Session of the Aristotelian Society and the Mind Association at Durham, July 1948, in *Logical Positivism and Ethics*, Aristotelian Society Supp. vol. XXII (London, Harrison and Son's) 1948, pp. 79-106.

Rogge (Eberhard), *Axiomatik alles möglichen Philosophierens, Das grundsätzliche Sprechen der Logistik, der Sprachkritik und der Lebens-Metaphysik* (Meisenheim, Hain) 1950, posthumous work.

Rolland (Romain), *Colas Breugnon*, Le Livre de poche (Paris, Albin Michel).

Romains (Jules), *Les hommes de bonne volonté*, 27 vol.; vol. XII, *Les créateurs* (Paris, Flammarion) 1936.

Romains (Jules), *Psyché*, 3 vol,; vol. III, *Quand le navire ...* (Paris, Gallimard) 1929, N.R.F.

Rome (Canon A.), "La vitesse de parole des orateurs attiques," *Bulletin Classe des Lettres de l'Académie Royale de Belgique*, series 5, 1952, 12.

Ronsard, *Œuvres complètes*, text established and annotated by Gustave Cohen, Bibliothèque de la Pléiade, 2 vol (Paris, Gallimard) 1938, N.R.F.

Rosen (Sidney), *see* Lippitt.

Rostand (François), *Grammaire et affectivité* (Paris, J. Vrin) 1951.

Rotenstreich (Nathan), "The Epistemological Status of the Concrete Subject," *Revue internationale de Philosophie 22*, year 6, no. 4, 1952, pp. 409-427.

Rousseau (Jean-Jacques), *Émile* (London, Dent; New York, E. P. Dutton & Company, Inc.) 1950.

Rousseau (Jean-Jacques), *Émile ou De l'Éducation* (Paris, Firmin-Didot) 1898.

Russell (Bertrand), *Political Ideals* (New York, Century, *now* Appleton-Century) 1917.

Ruyer (Raymond), *L'utopie et les utopies* (Paris, Presses Universitaires de France) 1950.

Ryle (Gilbert), *The Concept of Mind* (London, Hutchinson) 1950, first published in 1949.

Ryle (Gilbert), *Dilemmas*, The Tarner Lectures, 1953 (London, Cambridge University Press) 1954.

Saint-Aubin, *Guide pour la classe de rhétorique, Philosophie, éloquence et didactique* (Namur and Brussels, Belgium, La Procure; Gembloux, Belgium, Duculot) 1945.

Saint-Évremond (Charles de), *Œuvres*, 12 vol (publisher and place of publication not given) 1753.

Saint-Exupéry (Antoine de), *Night Flight*, translated into English by S. Gilbert (New York and London, Century Co. now Appleton-Century-Cropts) 1932.

Saint-Exupéry (Antoine de) *Vol de nuit*, preface by André Gide (Paris, Gallimard) 1931, N.R.F.

Salacrou (Armand), *Théâtre*, III, *Un homme comme les autres* (Paris, Gallimard) 1942, N.R.F.

Sartre (J.-P.), *Being and Nothingness*, translated by Hazel E. Barnes (New York, Philosophical Library, Inc.) 1956.

Sartre (J.-P.), *Dirty Hands* in *Three Plays* (New York, Alfred A. Knopf Inc.) 1949.

Sartre (J.-P.), *La nausée* (Paris, Gallimard) ed. 12, 1938, N.R.F.

Sartre (J.-P), *L'être et le néant, Essai d'ontologie phénoménologique*, Bibliothèque des Idées (Paris, Gallimard) 1943, N.R.F.

Sartre (J.-P.), *Les mains sales*, play in 7 scenes (Paris, Gallimard) 1948, N.R.F.

Sartre (J.-P.), *Situations* (Paris, Gallimard) vol. I, 1947; vol. II, 1948; vol. III, 1949, N.R.F.

Saulnier (Verdun L.), "L'oraison funèbre au xvie siècle," *Bibliothèque d'Humanisme et Renaissance*, studies and documents, vol. X, 1948 (Geneva, Switzerland, Droz).

Schaerer (René), "Le mécanisme de l'Ironie dans ses rapports avec la Dialectique," *Revue de métaphysique et de morale*, year 48, July 1941, pp. 181-209.

Scheler (Max), *Der Formalismus in der Ethik und die materiale Wertethik, Neues Versuch der Grundlegung eines ethischen Personalismus. Sonderdruck aus Jahrbuch für Philosophie und phänomenologische Forschung*, vol. I and II, edited by E. Husserl, Freiburg i. B. (Halle a.d. S., Germany, M. Niemeyer) ed. 3, 1927; ed. 1 published in 1916.

Schopenhauer (Arthur), *Sämtliche Werke*, based on the first complete edition under the direction of Julius Frauenstadt, newly revised and edited by Arthur Hubscher, 6 vol. (Leipzig, Germany, Brockhaus) 1937-1939.

Schopenhauer (Arthur), "Eristische Dialektik," *Sämtliche Werke*, edited by Dr. Paul Deussen, the 6th volume containing "Eristische Dialektik" edited by Franz Mockrauer (Munich, Germany, Piper und Co.) 1932, pp. 393-428.

Schuhl (Pierre-Maxime), *Le merveilleux, la pensée et l'action* (Paris, Flammarion) 1952.

Scott (Walter Dill), *Influencing Men in Business, The Psychology of Argument and Suggestion* (New York, The Ronald Press Company) 1920; ed. 1, 1911; ed. 2, revised and augmented, 1916.

Scotus Erigena (Jean), "Joannis Scoti liber de praedestinatione," *Patrologie latine de Migne*, vol. CXXII (Paris) 1853.

Sechehaye (M.-A.), *Journal d'une schizophrène, Auto-observation d'une schizophrène pendant le traitement psychothérapique*, Bibliothèque de Psychanalyse et de Psychologie clinique (Paris, Presses Universitaires de France) 1950.

Seneca the Rhetorician, *Controverses et suasoires (Controversiarum liber I-X; Suasoriarum liber)*, new revised and corrected edition by Henri Bornecque, 2 vol. (Paris, Garnier) 1932.

Shakespeare (William), *Works*, 1 vol. (London, Ward Lock and Co.)

Sheffield (Fred D.), *see* Hovland.

Sholom Aleichem (Shalom Rabinowitz), *Tevye's Daughters* (New York, Crown Publishers, Inc.) 1949.

Shri Aurobindo, *see* Aurobindo.

Silberer (M.-L.), "Autour d'un questionnaire," *Le diagnostic du caractère*, Bibliothèque scientifique internationale (Paris, Presses Universitaires de France) 1949, pp. 187-201.

Smets (Georges), "Carnet sociologique, note 50," *Revue de l'Institut de Sociologie* (Brussels, Belgium) no. 1, 1940, pp. 148-149.

Smith (Adam), *Adam Smith*, Great Books of the Western World (GBWW) vol. 39 (Chicago, Illinois, Encyclopaedia Britannica, Inc.) 1952.

Smith (Adam), *An Inquiry into the Nature and Causes of the Wealth of Nations*, The Modern Library, edited by Edwin Cannan with a new introduction by Max Lerner (New York, Random House, Inc.) 1937.

Smith (Bruce Lannes), Lasswell (Harold D.), and Casey (D.), *Propaganda, Communication, and Public Opinion, a Comprehensive Reference Guide* (Princeton, New Jersey, Princeton University Press; London, Oxford University Press) 1946. *See also* Lasswell.

Solages (Mgr. Bruno de), *Dialogue sur l'analogie à la société toulousaine de philosophie* (Paris, Aubier) 1946.

Sophocles, "Antigone," *The Theban Plays*, translated by E. F. Watling (Hardmondsworth, Middlesex, U.K., and Baltimore, Maryland, U.S.A., The Penguin Books).

Spender (Stephen), *see* Crossmann, *The God that Failed.*

Spinoza (Baruch), *Ethics*, Great Books of the Western World (GBWW), vol. 31 (Chicago, Illinois, Encyclopaedia Britannica, Inc.) 1952.

Stanton (Alfred H.), "Sullivan's Conceptions," *The Contributions of Harry Stack Sullivan*, pp. 61-100, *see* Mullahy.

Stearns (Marshall W.), "A Note on Chaucer's Attitude toward Love," *Speculum*, vol. XVII, 1942, pp. 570-574.

Stebbing (L. S.), "The Method of Analysis in Metaphysics," *Proceedings of the Aristotelian Society*, new series, vol. XXXIII, 1932-1933, pp. 65-94.

Sterne (Laurence), *The Life and Opinions of Tristram Shandy* (New York, Modern Library, Inc.)

Stevenson (Charles L.), *Ethics and Language* (New Haven, Connecticut, Yale University Press; London, Oxford University Press) 1947, first edition published in 1945.

Stevenson (Charles L.), "Meaning: Descriptive and Emotive," in a symposium on emotive meaning, *The Philosophical Review*, 1948, pp. 111-157.

Stokvis (Dr. Berthold), *Psychologie der suggetie en autosuggestie met een inleiding over significa en moderne begripscritiek* door Prof. G. Mannoury (Lochem, the Netherlands, De Tijdstroom) 1947.

Stroux (Johannes), *Römische Rechtswissenschaft und Rhetorik* (Potsdam, Germany, Eduard Stichnote) 1949.

Stutterheim (C.F.P., Jr.), "Psychologische Interpretatie van Taal-Verschijnselen (Een immanente Critiek)," *De Nieuwe Taalgids*, vol. XXXI, 1937, pp. 259-271.

Stutterheim (C.F.P., Jr.), *Het Begrip Metaphoor, Een taalkundig en wysgeerig Onderzoek* (Amsterdam, The Netherlands, H. J. Paris) 1941.

Sullivan (Harry Stack), *The Interpersonal Theory of Psychiatry* (posthumous work) edited by Helen Swick Perry and Mary Ladd Gawel with an introduction by Mabel Blake Cohen, The William Alanson White Psychiatric Foundation Committee on publication of Sullivan's writings (New York, W.W. Norton & Company, Inc.) 1953. *See also* Mullahy.

Süss (Dr. Wilhelm), *Ethos, Studien zur älteren griechischen Rhetoric* (Leipzig, Germany, Teubner) 1910.

Tá Hio, see Legge, Pauthier.

Talon, (Omer), *Audomari Talaei Rhetoricae Libri Duo P. Rami Praelectionibus Illustrati* (Coloniae Agrippinae) 1572.

Tarde (G.), *Les lois de l'imitation, Étude sociologique*, Bibliothèque de Philosophie contemporaine (Paris, Alcan) 1895, ed. 2, revised and enlarged.

Tarde (G.), *La logique sociale*, Bibliothèque de Philosophie contemporaine (Paris, Alcan) 1895.

Tchoung-Young, see Pauthier.

Teresa de Jesús (Saint), *Vida*, published by the Sociedad Foto-tipográfico-católica in accordance with the original (Madrid, Spain, D.E. Aguado) 1873.

Thibaut (Jones), *see* Festinger.

Thomas Aquinas (Saint), *Somme théologique*, text and French translation by the Société Saint-Jean l'Évangéliste (Paris, Tournai, Rome, Desclée et Cie) 1925-1945.

Thomas Aquinas (Saint), *Opera Omnia*, Secundum impressionem Petri Fiaccadori Parmae 1852-1873 photolithographice reimpressa, Introduction by Vernon J. Bourke, 25 vol. (New York, Musurgia) 1948-1950.

Thompson (W. R.), *see* Hebb.

Thouless (Robert H.), *How to Think Straight* (New York, Simon and Schuster) 1948.

Timon (Cormenin), *Livre des orateurs*, Société belge de Librairie (Brussels, Belgium, Hauman & Cie.) ed. 12, 1843.

Toffanin (Giuseppe), *Storia dell'umanesimo dal XIII al XVI secolo* (Naples, Italy, Francesco Perrella), preface dated 1933.

Trier (Jost), *Der deutsche Wortschatz im Sinnbezirk des Verstandes*, vol. I, *Von den Anfängen bis zum Beginn des 13. Jahrhunderts*, Germanische Bibliothek, II, 31 (Heidelberg, Germany, Winters) 1931.

Trier (Jost), "Sprachliche Felder," *Zeitschrift für deutsche Bildung*, vol. 8, no. 1, Jan. 1932, pp. 417-427.

Trier (Jost), "Das sprachliche Feld, Eine Auseinandersetzung," *Neue Jahrbücher für Wissenschaft und Jugendbildung*, vol. 10, no. 5, 1934, pp. 428-480.

Ullmann (S.), *Précis de sémantique française* (Bern, Switzerland, A. Francke) 1952.

Valéry (Paul), *Poésies* (Paris, Gallimard) 1942, ed. 11, N.R.F.

Van Danzig (D.), *Blaise Pascal en de betekenis der wiskundige denkwyze voor de studie van de menselijke samenleving.* Rede uitgesproken op 4 Oct. 1948 (Groningen-Batavia, The Netherlands, P. Noordhoff) 1949.

Van Danzig (D.), *Democracy in a World of Tensions*, pp. 46-61. *See* McKeon.

Vayson de Pradenne, *Les fraudes en archéologie préhistorique avec quelques exemples de comparaison en archéologie générale et sciences naturelles* (Paris, Emile Nourry) 1932.

Verlaine (P.), *Œuvres poétiques complètes*, text established and annotated by Y. G. Le Dantec, Bibliothèque de la Pléiade (Paris, Gallimard) 1951, N.R.F.

Vico (G.-B.) *Opere*, arranged and illustrated with the historical analysis from the thought of Vico in relation to the science of civilization, by Giuseppi Ferrari, (Milan, Italy, Soc. Tipogr. de' classici italiani) 1837, 6 vol. (vol. 2-6, Genoa, 1835-1836).

Vico (G.-B.), *Delle instituzioni oratorie*, unedited work translated into Italian from the Latin by Padre Don Luigi Parchetti C. R. Somasco, Novi, Moretti, 1844. Not published in the Ferrari 1837 edition. On the subject of the Latin text see:

Vico (G.-B.), *Opere, VIII: Versi d'occasione e scritti di scuola con appendice e bibliografia generale delle opere*, edited by Fausto Nicolini, Scrittori d'Italia, 183 (Bari, Italy, Laterza & Figli) 1941, and see also:

Vico (G.-B.), *Opere*, edited by Fausto Nicolini, La letteratura italiana, vol. 43 (Milan and Naples, Italy, Ricardo Ricciardi) 1953.

Viehweg (Theodor), *Topik und Jurisprudenz* (Munich, Germany, Beck), 1953.

Villiers de L'Isle-Adam, "L'intersigne," in *Contes cruels* (Paris, Calmann-Lévy) 1889, pp. 238-262.

Vives (Juan Luis), *Obras completas*, 2 vol., first complete and direct translation into Castilian by Lorenzo Riber (Madrid, Spain, Aguilar) 1947-1948.

Volkelt (Johannes), *Gewissheit und Wahrheit, Untersuchung der Geltungsfragen als Grundlegung der Erkenntnis theorie* (Munich, Germany, Beck) ed. 2, 1930; ed. 1, 1918.

Volkmann (Richard), *Hermagoras oder Elemente der Rhetorik* (Stettin, in Polish Szczecin, Poland, von der Nahmer) 1865.

Volkmann (Richard), *Rhetorik der Griechen und Römer*, third edition by Caspar Hammer, *Handbuch der klassischen Altertumswissenschaften* edited by Dr. Iwan von Müller, vol. 2, part 3 (Munich, Germany, Beck) 1901, pp. 1-61.

Waddington (Charles), *Ramus (Pierre de la Ramée), Sa vie, ses écrits et ses opinions* (Paris, Meyrueis) 1855.

Wahl (Jean), *A Short History of Existentialism*, translated by F. Williams and S. Maron (New York, Philosophical Library, Inc.) 1949.

Wahl (Jean), "Sur les philosophies de l'existence," *Glanes*, Cahiers de l'amitié franco-néerlandaise vol. 15-16, 3d year, Nov. 1950-Feb. 1951 (Amsterdam, The Netherlands) pp. 10-32.

Waismann (F.), "Verifiability," *Essays on Logic and Language*, pp. 17-144. *See* Flew.

Weaver (Richard M.), *The Ethics of Rhetoric* (Chicago, Illinois, Henry Regnery Company) 1953.

Weil (Eric), *Logique de la philosophie* (Paris, Vrin) 1950.

Weil (Simone), *The Need for Roots*, translated by Arthur Wills (New York, G. P. Putnam's Sons) 1952.

Weil (Simone), *L'enracinement, Prélude à une déclaration des devoirs envers l'être humain*, in the collection Espoir, edited by Albert Camus (Paris, Gallimard) 1949.

Weiler (Jean), *Problèmes d'économie internationale.* Vol. I, *Les échanges du capitalisme libéral,* 1946; vol. II, *Une nouvelle expérience, l'organisation internationale des échanges,* 1950, Centre national d'Information économique (Paris, Presses Universitaires de France).

Weiss (Walter), "A 'Sleeper' Effect in Opinion Change," *Journal of Abnormal and Social Psychology,* vol. 48, no. 2, Apr. 1953, pp. 173-180.

Weiss (Walter), *see also* Hovland.

Wertheimer (Max), *Productive Thinking,* posthumous work edited by S. E. Asch, W. Köhler, and C. W. Mayer (New York and London, Harper and Brothers, *now* Harper and Row, Publishers) 1945.

Whately (Richard D.D.), *Elements of Rhetoric* (New York, Harper and Brothers, *now* Harper and Row, Publishers) 1893.

Whately (Richard D.D.), *Elements of Rhetoric,* comprising the substance of the article in the *Encyclopaedia Metropolitana* with additions, etc., (London, John Murray; Oxford, J. Parker) 1828.

White (Mary J.), "Sullivan and Treatment," *see* P. Mullahy.

White (Walter), "Deux races se rencontrent en moi," *Écho,* June 1948, pp. 415-420, based on material in *The Saturday Review of Literature* (New York).

Whorf (Benjamin Lee), "The Relation of Habitual Thought and Behavior to Language," *Language, Meaning and Maturity,* pp. 225-251. *See* S. I. Hayakawa.

Wilder (R. L.), "The Origin and Growth of Mathematical Concepts, "*Bulletin of the American Mathematical Society,* vol. 59, no. 5, Sept. 1953, pp. 423-448.

Wisdom (John), "Gods," in *Essays on Logic and Language,* pp. 187-206. *See* Flew.

Wisdom (John), "Logical Constructions," *Mind,* vol. XL, 1931, pp. 188-216; vol. XL, 1931, pp. 460-475; vol. XLI, 1932, pp. 441-464; vol. XLII, 1933, pp. 43-46; vol. XLII, 1933, pp. 186-202.

Wittgenstein (Ludwig), *Philosophische Untersuchungen; Philosophical Investigations,* German and English versions, English translation by G.E.M. Anscombe (Oxford, U.K., Blackwell Scientific Publications) 1953.

Wood (Ledger), *The Analysis of Knowledge* (London, Allen and Unwin) 1940.

Wunderlich (Hermann), *Die Kunst der Rede in ihren Hauptzügen an den Reden Bismarcks Dargestellt* (Leipzig, Germany, S. Hirzel) 1898.

Zobel (Joseph), *La rue Cases-Nègres* (Paris, Jean Froissart) 1950.

INDEX OF NAMES

n—name found in note at foot of page
nn—name found in two or more notes
an or ann—name found in text as well as in note or notes

Achilles, 343
Adam, 224, 332, 379, 395
Adonis, 242, 292
Aeschines, 108, 110, 146, 223, 238, 499n
Afer, Domitius, 223
Agricola, Rodolphus, 503n, 505an
Ajax, 343
Alain (Émile-Auguste Chartier), 353, 449an
Alcibiades, 125
Alexander, The Great, 365, 489
Amadeus, Duke of Savoy, 378
Amy, René, 273n
Angyal, Andras, 293n
Annambhatta, 266n, 352n, 414n
Anselm, Saint, 338an
Antigone, 340an
Antiphon, 113, 114, 459an
Antonius, Marcus, 455n
Antony, Marc, the Triumvir, 117, 147, 183, 330, 361, 454, 500
Aragon, Louis, 145an, 428n
Aristides, 358
Aristippus, 16
Aristophon, 340
Aristotle, 2, 3, 5an, 6, 7n, 9an, 16, 17n, 20an, 21n, 25n, 47, 48an, 49, 53an, 56an, 57n, 79an, 83ann, 84an, 85an, 86nn, 87ann, 91ann, 95an, 108n, 112an, 117, 126n, 143, 144an, 151n, 166ann, 172, 203n, 204, 209n, 221an, 225nn, 226an, 230an, 234ann, 235, 253an, 264an, 269an, 299, 318an, 319, 339an, 340ann, 341n, 342n, 343n, 352n, 354n, 357, 358an, 360an, 362n, 363an, 373an, 399ann, 440, 453n, 457n, 458ann, 459n, 461an, 484n, 488n, 493nn, 495ann, 496an, 501an, 502nn, 506n, 509
Aron, Raymond, 120n, 265an, 296an
Arvers, Felix, 280
Asch, Salomon Elliott, 317n
Aubry, Charles-Antoine, 102n, 103nn
Audiberti, Jacques, 291
Auerbach, Erich, 43n, 157ann, 208n, 255an, 333an
Augustine, Saint, 307, 316, 385n, 451, 497n
Augustus, 181, 271
Aurobindo, Shrî, 341n, 439nn, 440nn, 444an, 447
Ayer, Alfred Jules, 441n
Aymé, Marcel, 351n

Bachelard, Gaston, 406n
Back, Kurt W., 57n
Bacon, Francis, 16n, 117ann, 236, 358an, 409an, 475
Baird, A. Craig, 37n, 483n
Balzac, Honoré de, 332, 333, 402n
Barnes, Winston H. F., 274n
Baroja, Pío, 208an
Baron, Auguste, 91n, 93n, 172, 173n, 177an, 217an, 336n, 401n, 403n, 408ann, 428nn, 444n, 475n
Bartin, Étienne, 103nn.
Baruk, Henri, 284an
Bataille, Georges, 449n
Beauvoir, Simone de, 127an, 128an, 277n, 361n, 435an
Beckett, Samuel, 94an
Belaval, Yvon, 25n
Bellak, Léopold, 167n
Benary, Wilhelm, 393n
Benda, Julien, 26an, 82an
Benedict, Ruth, 96an, 199n, 203an, 314n, 444an
Benjamin, A. Cornelius, 130an
Bentham, Jeremy, 40an, 107an, 114an, 118, 129, 202an, 205an, 257an, 266an, 283an, 309an, 313, 326n, 328an, 465, 466n, 480an, 488n
Berelson, Bernard, 82n
Bergson, Henri, 3, 86an, 155an, 170–71, 236an, 346, 347n, 407an, 426n, 430an, 446
Berkeley, George, 285n, 353, 354an, 355, 401n, 430n, 445an, 476an
Berl, Emmanuel, 295n
Bernanos, Georges, 254n, 326an, 405n
Berriat Saint-Prix, Félix, 278n, 306n, 387an
Bevan, Edwyn, 385n, 391n
Bidez, Joseph, 157n
Bird, Charles, 61an, 309n, 481n
Bismarck, Otto von, 326an, 454an
Black, Max, 130an, 204n, 215an, 267n
Blass, Friedrich, 113an, 114
Bobbio, Norberto, 131an, 183an, 374n
Boccaccio, Giovanni, 208n
Boileau-Despréaux, Nicolas, 208n
Borrey, Francis, 77n.
Bossuet, Jacques-Bénigne, 24an, 50an, 128an, 153an, 191an, 244an, 249an, 251an, 253an, 261an, 262an, 274an, 279an, 290an, 308n, 311n, 316an, 328an,

543

ineffective act, 316
inertia, 105–7, 138, 350, 352, 363, 394
  and rule of justice, 218–19
infinity, 259, 419
initiation, 54, 99–100, 321, 335, 464
injunctive modality, 158
innovation, 107
  See also change, new
inspiration, 451
institutions, 18, 38, 56, 57–59, 110, 322
intention, 38, 149, 180, 278, 301–3, 314,
    317, 328, 385
  of legislator, 106
interaction:
  between act and person, 296–316, 423–
    24
  in analogy, 378–83, 397, 399, 404
  in comparison, 243–44, 257, 366
  in discourse, 187, 190, 460–61, 465, 471–
    74, 481, 494–95
  between examples, 354–57
  between group and members, 321–27,
    423
  in language, 214
  between means and ends, 247, 273–78
  between model and imitation, 366
  in sacrifice, 250, 255, 257
  between speaker and speech, 316–21
interpretation(s), 120–26, 134, 140–41,
    204, 333, 428, 432, 452
  choice between, 121, 172
  of discourse, 123–26, 165, 278
  of formal system, 14, 133, 212
  incompatible, 121
  of legal and religious texts, 101, 106,
    122, 134, 135–36, 241, 278, 384, 414,
    428, 472
  levels of, 121–22, 228
interrogative modality, 158, 159–60, 168
  See also questions
intuition, 2, 3, 33, 44, 130, 431, 492, 510
invention, *see* analogy
irony, 207–9, 271, 292, 330, 361
irrational, 3, 29, 42, 47, 61, 159, 306, 318,
    335, 347, 468, 508, 512, 514
  See also loci
irrelevant, *see* relevant

Japan, 96, 198, 203, 314, 414
Jesuits, 224, 259, 276, 364
judge, 102, 104, 106, 108, 119, 131, 134,
    136, 198, 225, 316, 319, 414, 459, 482,
    483
judicial:
  competence, 310
  debates, 38, 109–10, 316, 461, 500, 501;
    see also discussion
  decision, 42–43, 107, 131, 241, 357; *see
    also* decision
  institutions, 18, 56, 58

  See also oratorical genres, procedure,
    proceedings, proof, trial
juridical:
  antinomies, 196, 414–15; *see also* com-
    promise, incompatibilities
  argumentation, 75, 99–104, 105, 131,
    230, 241
  framework, 285
  notion of civil death, 334
  notion of negligence, 73
  system, 107, 115, 131, 133, 197, 357, 414
  See also law, legal
jurist, 102, 197, 230, 257, 306, 357, 364,
    414, 428, 482
justice, 77, 79, 87, 95, 98, 132, 134, 306,
    462
  denial of, 131, 310
  divine, 311, 377
  formal, 219
  rule of, 218–20, 363, 464, 485
  rule of—and symmetry, 221–22
  true, 418

knowledge, 100, 421, 510

language, 8, 15, 355–56, 390, 398, 510, 513
  agreements underlying, 126, 153, 356,
    405, 410; *see also* grammar, syntax
  artificial, 13, 130
  formalized, 99, 214; *see also* formal
  functions of, 130, 132, 133, 140, 217
  hearer's considerations about, 189
  interpretation of, 123
  ordinary, 130, 149, 153, 195, 212–14, 215
  poverty of, 404
  professional, 408
  restricted, 163–64
  scientific, 130
  segregative role of, 163
  and social types, 164
  technical, 99
  versus thought, 420
law, 10, 59, 99, 102, 107, 108, 131, 295,
    314, 325, 351, 354, 356, 357, 415, 461
  See also analogy, fact, judge, juridical,
    jurist, legal
laws of nature, 356
legal:
  argumentation, 72–73, 101, 298
  logic, 306
  presumptions, 103, 356
  principle, 351
  texts, 101–2, 196–97, 241
  See also law, judicial, juridical
letter:
  apparent, 432
  Versus spirit, 123, 124, 420, 428, 437;
    see also literal
liberty, 134, 165
lie, 199–200, 346, 442, 452
likelihood, 70